Contemporary

Business Statistics

with **Canadian** Applications, Third Edition

S. A. Hummelbrunner

L. J. Rak

Peter Fortura

Patrick Taylor

PEARSON
Prentice Hall

Toronto

National Library of Canada Cataloguing in Publication

Contemporary business statistics with Canadian applications, 3/C/e/
S.A. Hummelbrunner . . . [et al.].– 3rd ed.

Includes index
Previous ed. By S.A. Hummelbrunner, L.J.Rak and John Gray
ISBN 0-13-121581-7

1. Commercial statistics. I. Hummelbrunner, S.A. (Siegfried August)

HA29.H84 2003 519.5 C2003-901424-X

ISBN 0-13-121581-7

Vice President, Editorial Director: Michael J. Young
Acquisitions Editor: Gary Bennett
Marketing Manager: Deb Meredith
Associate Editor: Angela Kurmey
Production Editor: Emmet Mellow
Copy Editor: Bonnie DiMalta
Production Coordinator: Deborah Starks
Page Layout: Pronk&Associates
Art Director: Mary Opper
Interior/Cover Design: David Chung
Cover Image: Getty Images

3 4 5 08 07 06 05 04

PEARSON
Prentice Hall

Contents

Preface *ix*

Introduction *1*

CHAPTER 1 **Organizing and Presenting Data** *6*

1.1 Looking at Data 7
1.2 Presenting Data — Graphs and Charts 8
1.3 *XY* Graphs (Scatter Diagrams) 9
1.4 Line Graphs 11
USING EXCEL 1.1 11
1.5 Bar and Area Charts 14
1.6 Stacked Bar and Area Charts, Pie (Circle) Charts 17
USING EXCEL 1.2 22
1.7 Specialty Charts 25
1.8 A Summary of Chart Types and Their Uses 29
Review Exercise 30
Self-Test 35
Key Terms 36

CHAPTER 2 **Frequency Distributions and Their Graphs** *39*

2.1 Frequency Distributions 40
USING EXCEL 2.1 45
2.2 Graphs of Frequency Distributions 52
2.3 Percentiles 60
Review Exercise 72

Self-Test 79
Key Terms 80
Summary of Formulas 81

CHAPTER 3 **Measures of Central Tendency** ***82***
3.1 Central Values 83
3.2 The Mean — Arithmetic Average 83
3.3 The Median 88
3.4 The Mode 92
3.5 Relationships among Mean, Median, and Mode 95
USING EXCEL 3.1 99
Review Exercise 101
Self-Test 106
Key Terms 107
Summary of Formulas 108

CHAPTER 4 **Measures of the Variability of Data** ***109***
4.1 The Range and the Interquartile Range 110
4.2 The Average Deviation from the Mean 116
4.3 The Variance and Standard Deviation 119
USING EXCEL 4.1 120
Review Exercise 130
Self-Test 138
Key Terms 139
Summary of Formulas 139

CHAPTER 5 **Index Numbers** ***141***
5.1 Nature of Index Numbers 142
5.2 Construction and Interpreting Simple Indexes 143
5.3 Aggregate Indexes 146
USING EXCEL 5.1 148
5.4 Special-Purpose (Composite) Indexes 151
5.5 The Consumer Price Index and Its Uses 152
5.6 Shifting the Base and Splicing 155
Review Exercise 158
Self-Test 168
Key Terms 170
Summary of Formulas 170

CHAPTER 6 **Time-Series Analysis** ***172***
6.1 Components of a Time Series 173
6.2 Secular Trend Analysis 174
6.3 Percent of Trend 180
6.4 Cyclical Analysis — The Moving Average Method 182
USING EXCEL 6.1 185
6.5 Seasonal Analysis 189
6.6 Irregular Movements 199
Review Exercise 200
Self-Test 207
Appendix 6: The Coded Least Squares Method 208
Key Terms 213
Summary of Formulas 214

CHAPTER 7 **An Introduction to Probability** ***215***
7.1 Approaches to Probability 216
7.2 Tree Diagrams 221
7.3 Counting Rules 223
USING EXCEL 7.1 228
USING EXCEL 7.2 232
7.4 Venn Diagrams 234
7.5 The Basic Rules of Probability 241
Review Exercise 253
Self-Test 258
Key Terms 260
Summary of Formulas 260

CHAPTER 8 **A First Look at Probability Distributions** ***261***
8.1 Continuous versus Discrete Probability Distributions 262
8.2 The Expected Value (Mean), Variance, and Standard Deviation of a Discrete Probability Distribution 263
8.3 The Binomial Distribution 270
USING EXCEL 8.1 276
Review Exercise 281
Self-Test 285
Key Terms 286
Summary of Formulas 286

CHAPTER 9 The Normal Distribution *288*

9.1 Characteristics of the Normal Distribution 289

9.2 Areas under the Normal Curve 290

9.3 The Standardized Normal Curve 294

USING EXCEL 9.1 301

9.4 Applications of the Normal Curve 308

9.5 Using the Normal Distribution to Approximate the Binomial Distribution 314

Review Exercise 320

Self-Test 324

Key Terms 325

Summary of Formulas 325

CHAPTER 10 Sampling Distributions *326*

10.1 Sampling Considerations 327

10.2 The Sampling Distribution of the Means 329

10.3 Properties of the Sampling Distribution of the Means 333

10.4 The Sampling Distribution of Proportions 338

Review Exercise 343

Self-Test 347

Key Terms 348

Summary of Formulas 349

CHAPTER 11 Interval Estimation *350*

11.1 Estimating Concepts 351

11.2 Interval Estimation around the Mean When σ Is Known 354

11.3 Interval Estimation around the Mean for Large Samples ($n > 30$) when σ Is Unknown 359

USING EXCEL 11.1 363

11.4 Interval Estimation of Proportions for Large Samples ($n > 30$) when π Is Unknown 366

11.5 Determination of Sample Size 368

11.6 Interval Estimation around the Mean for Small Samples ($n \geq 30$) when σ Is Unknown 373

Review Exercise 382

Self-Test 388

Key Terms 390

Summary of Formulas 390

CHAPTER 12 Hypothesis Testing of a Mean or a Proportion ***393***

12.1 The Hypothesis Testing Procedure 394

12.2 Basic Concepts 394

12.3 Hypothesis Testing of a Mean 402

USING EXCEL 12.1 412

12.4 Hypothesis Testing of a Population Proportion for Large Samples ($n > 30$) 414

12.5 Type I and Type II Errors, p Values 417

Review Exercise 421

Self-Test 427

Key Terms 429

Summary of Formulas 430

CHAPTER 13 Simple Linear Regression and Correlation Analyses ***431***

13.1 Simple Linear Regression Analysis 432

13.2 The Least Squares Method 433

USING EXCEL 13.1 438

13.3 Measuring Variability about the Regression Line 444

13.4 Constructing Confidence Intervals 445

13.5 Correlation Analysis 452

USING EXCEL 13.2 458

Review Exercise 465

Self-Test 473

Key Terms 475

Summary of Formulas 475

Answers to Selected Problems, Review Exercises, and Self-Tests ***477***

Index ***487***

Preface

Contemporary Business Statistics with Canadian Applications is intended for use as a textbook in introductory statistics courses in Canadian college business programs. It also provides a comprehensive base for those who wish to review and extend their understanding of statistics.

Contemporary Business Statistics is essentially a teaching text using the learning outcomes approach. The systematic and sequential development of the material is supported by carefully selected and worked-out examples. The detailed, step-by-step solutions are particularly helpful in allowing students, in either the classroom setting or independent studies, to carefully monitor their own progress.

ORGANIZATION OF THE BOOK

The book is designed to introduce statistical concepts through the solution of practical business problems. An emphasis has been placed on selecting topics that college graduates will find useful as decision-making tools.

Statistics courses are organized in a variety of ways with emphasis on different concepts. We have developed this book based on experience in the classroom, where we have found the use of graphing along with descriptive measurements to be an effective lead into inferential statistics. The book contains enough material to permit a good deal of latitude in the order and selection of topics.

Each chapter is organized into several parts:

Introduction Every chapter begins with a discussion of how the ideas and techniques presented in the chapter fit into the big picture. A student with little or no work experience will find the introduction provides useful direction in an unfamiliar area.

Learning Outcomes Each chapter contains a statement of the main learning outcomes of the chapter. The outcomes act as a target and checklist of skills and concepts the student should possess after completing the chapter. As with any new or unfamiliar subject, the study of statistics requires a good understanding of the material already covered before proceeding on to new topics.

Sections Every chapter contains from three to eight sections, with each section covering a major topic or concept. The length of the sections varies, depending on complexity and depth of coverage. A topic is first discussed and then developed through examples with complete step-by-step solutions. Some broader topics require several subsections as well as several examples with their solutions worked out. Our experience teaching statistics shows that students learn more effectively by following through problems and their answers than by being presented with only abstract concepts.

Exercises The text contains over 750 problems of varying difficulty. Most of the problems are based on Canadian business situations covering a wide range of topics.

At the end of most sections there is a set of exercise problems for the student to practise and develop the skills covered in the section. In addition, review exercises are given at the end of each chapter and are designed to assist in the integration of all the material studied. Numerical answers to the odd-numbered exercises are listed at the back of the text.

CGA examination questions are also included in the end-of-chapter problems. In some cases, these problems have been modified to suit a particular chapter.

Formulas Key formulas are numbered and highlighted in boxes to facilitate references by students and teachers. A summary of the key formulas is provided at the end of each chapter.

Self-Test Each chapter includes a self-test that enables students to evaluate their progress. The test usually takes one to two hours to complete. Students can check all their numerical solutions against the answers in the back of the text.

Key Terms At the end of each chapter is a list of key terms with page references to their definitions in the chapter. This summary is useful to students when reviewing chapter material.

CHANGES IN THE THIRD EDITION

Subsequent editions of any successful book combine approaches that have worked well in previous editions and new ideas passed along to improve the students' learning. There are four significant improvements in this edition:

- The most significant change in the third edition is the integration of Microsoft EXCEL into the fabric of the text. The use of computer software is now an integral part of learning statistics. Using built-in statistical functions and the Data Analysis Tool of Microsoft EXCEL, the student is able to perform statistical analysis for most of the topics covered in the text. Throughout the text, EXCEL examples are provided where most appropriate. Each EXCEL example provides easy-to-follow instructions and screen captures that allow even a novice user of EXCEL to see the power of EXCEL, and to quickly become comfortable with its use. This approach will reduce the emphasis on doing computations, and allow more focus on analyzing data and on interpreting the output from EXCEL. However, because of the limitations of computer access faced by professors and students in the classroom and particularly in examination situations, the textbook continues to provide detailed step-by-step solutions for all examples.

- A Companion Website, at **www.pearsoned.ca/hummelbrunner**, will provide real-world data sets and corresponding problems that the student can use for practise in problem solving on the computer.
- Over 100 new problems have been added, providing professors with new material for homework, assignments, and exams.
- Examples and exercise problems have been updated where appropriate. Up-to-date Canadian data are incorporated into many examples and exercises.

SUPPLEMENTS

The *Instructor's Resource Disk* (ISBN 0-13-122919-2) includes the following items:

Instructor's Solution Manual with Transparency Masters. This manual provides complete solutions to all of the exercises, review exercises, and self-tests in the textbook. It also includes transparency masters for all of the figures in the textbook.

Pearson TestGen. The Pearson TestGen is a special computerized version of the Test Item File that enables instructors to view and edit the existing questions, add new questions, and generate custom tests. It contains approximately 750 questions.

The *Companion Website* (**www.pearsoned.ca/hummelbrunner**) provides students with an online study guide, complete with self-tests, learning objectives, a glossary, and data sets with additional exercises.

ACKNOWLEDGEMENTS

We are grateful to the following professors for reviewing the second edition and providing useful suggestions for this revision: Ross Bryant, Conestoga College; Ken Chung, Camosun College; Aruna Sarkar, Algonquin College; Marie Scragg, School of Business; Sin Phing Strube, Fanshawe College; and Tom Sutton, Mohawk College.

We would especially like to thank Paul Balog of George Brown College who contributed over 100 new questions to the textbook.

The authors would also like to thank Statistics Canada, the Bank of Canada, CGA, and the Investment Funds Institute of Canada for their assistance in the preparation of this edition. All questions from the Certified General Accountants' Association of Canada are denoted with the abbreviation CGA in parenthesis before the question at the beginning.

Finally, the authors owe an enormous debt to the editorial team at Pearson Education Canada for their effort that brought this edition from the early revision stages to its completion: Gary Bennett, Acquisitions Editor, who provided the opportunity for two new authors to be involved with this successful textbook; Angela Kurmey, Developmental Editor, who provided key experience and insights to the entire project; Emmet Mellow, Production Editor, who brought the project to completion under a very tight production schedule; and Bonnie Di Malta, Copy Editor, who helped create the final product.

S. A. HUMMELBRUNNER
L. J. RAK
PETER FORTURA
PATRICK TAYLOR

2003

The Pearson Education Canada **COMPANION WEBSITE**

A Great Way to Learn and Instruct Online

The Pearson Education Canada Companion Website is easy to navigate and is organized to correspond to the chapters in this textbook. Whether you are a student in the classroom or a distance learner you will discover helpful resources for in-depth study and research that empower you in your quest for greater knowledge and maximize your potential for success in the course.

Companion Website

[www.pearsoned.ca/hummelbrunner]

Enter

PEARSON Prentice Hall

Jump to... http://www.pearsoned.ca/hummelbrunner

Home | Search | Help | Profile

Companion Website

Home >

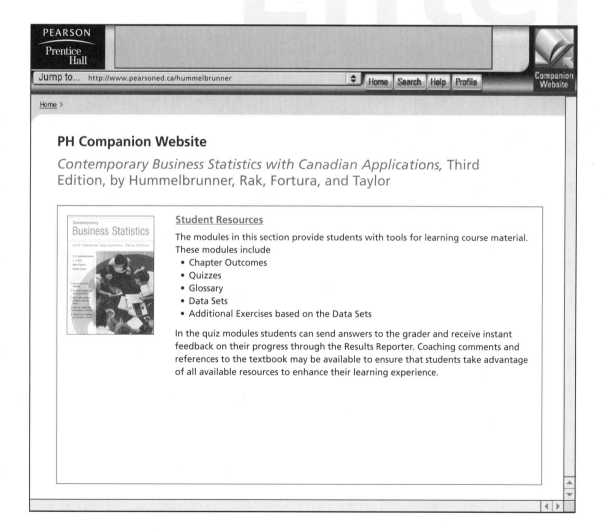

PH Companion Website

Contemporary Business Statistics with Canadian Applications, Third Edition, by Hummelbrunner, Rak, Fortura, and Taylor

Student Resources

The modules in this section provide students with tools for learning course material. These modules include

- Chapter Outcomes
- Quizzes
- Glossary
- Data Sets
- Additional Exercises based on the Data Sets

In the quiz modules students can send answers to the grader and receive instant feedback on their progress through the Results Reporter. Coaching comments and references to the textbook may be available to ensure that students take advantage of all available resources to enhance their learning experience.

Introduction

The word "statistics" brings to mind many different things. Some people think of baseball batting averages when they hear the word, while others think of the unemployment rate. In fact both are right. Statistics is a science with many different applications. In this text we introduce you to this science and to its applications in the business world.

Statistics has two major branches: (1) descriptive statistics and (2) inferential statistics. **Descriptive statistics** deals with collecting, organizing, summarizing, and presenting data in a numerical or graphic form. For most people, statistics means descriptive statistics. Most of the statistical information in newspapers, magazines, reports, and other publications is descriptive statistics, which is why this branch of the science is so well known.

Although the first step in any statistical study is the collection of the data, we will assume in this book that the data have already been collected for us. The first half of this book, which examines descriptive statistics, looks at the various methods and tools that can be used to organize, summarize, and present large data sets.

Inferential statistics goes beyond the graphic or numerical description of a particular set of data. Taking the descriptive statistics further by analyzing and interpreting them relies on inferential statistics. Frequently, this involves working with a subset (a **sample**) selected from the total set of data being studied (the **population**) whose characteristics we wish to estimate. The inferences or conclusions made about the larger data set (or population) by analyzing the smaller data set (or sample) are useful in making important decisions.

Time, cost, and other practical considerations lead business people to analyze samples instead of whole data sets. For example, a manufacturer of photographic film may have wanted information about the quality of *all* film produced on a particular day. Since it would have been too expensive and too time consuming to test the quality of every roll of film produced that day, a sample of 30 rolls of film was used to draw an inference (or conclusion). Another consideration for the manufacturer is that once a roll of film is tested for quality it cannot be reused.

Inference, or making educated guesses about larger sets of data, is the primary role of statistics. But making an inference is only part of the work. We also need to know how good the educated guess is. The second half of this book, on inferential statistics, looks at the various methods and tools that can be used to analyze and interpret data and to test our inferences.

Having introduced the two major branches of statistics, descriptive statistics and inferential statistics, we can now give a complete answer to the question "What is statistics?" Statistics is the science concerned with the (1) collection, (2) organization, (3) summation, (4) presentation, (5) analysis, and (6) interpretation of data. Although it uses mathematics, statistics is a science distinct from mathematics.

Application — The Consumer Price Index (CPI)

Canadian consumers are obviously interested in the prices charged by retailers for goods and services. An increase in the general level of prices paid by consumers is reported as *inflation*. If the general level of prices decreases (which rarely happens), the situation is referred to as *deflation*. In order to estimate the change in prices over time, Statistics Canada, an agency of the federal government, developed the consumer price index (CPI) to measure the cost of a "basket" of goods and services bought by a typical household. To determine the CPI for each month, survey takers in 64 cities across Canada record the prices of nearly 600 goods and services in the "basket." Statistical procedures are used to compute the CPI (a descriptive statistic) from the sample price data. By comparing the value of the CPI at different points in time, it is possible to estimate (make an inference about) the rate of inflation or deflation over some period of time.

Reasons for Studying Statistics

As Canada's firms face increasing global competition, the need for good business decisions becomes critical. Every person in a business organization makes several decisions every day. The quality of a decision depends on the quality and quantity of information available at the time the decision is made. Advances in information technology and telecommunications make more and more data available to the decision-maker. This may sound like a good thing, but piles of data actually complicate the making of informed and intelligent decisions. What is needed is not more data but good information.

The two words *data* and *information* are often used interchangeably, but there is a big difference between them. **Data** are the facts and figures that are collected to make a decision. By themselves they are nothing but numbers and letters. To get information we must organize, summarize, analyze, and interpret the data. In other words, the data must be changed using statistical methods so that information emerges. Statistics makes sense out of the data.

Employers expect a business graduate to make decisions and solve problems. Working effectively in our increasingly complex business environment will require better and timely information in the presence of considerable uncertainty. For anyone who wants to succeed in a business career the study of statistics and its methods is essential.

Application — Data versus Information

The image presented below could be considered a graphic piece of data. Like so much data available it is not very useful for solving a problem like "What has this picture got to do with everyday life?" Look at the image. Can you solve our problem?

What we really need is information about the image. To get it we could collect more data. It is (a) a close-up, (b) part of a larger image, (c) associated with restrictions in public places. Now if you analyze the image along with the additional data the no-smoking symbol (information) may emerge.

If we use the information we now have available, the answer to our problem is simple. The no-smoking symbol is recognized around the world.

Where Is Statistics Used?

Statistical methods and information are widely used in business and government. All functions or areas in an organization apply statistical techniques in decision-making situations. In addition, virtually all fields of study use statistics, including science, technology, education, and the social sciences.

Marketing This group of professionals includes sales, promotion, advertising, marketing research, and all the other positions associated with bringing buyer and seller together. Each area uses statistics in a variety of ways. Students often think that only marketing research uses statistics. That certainly is not the case. Sales people use statistical analysis for forecasting. Promotions and advertising personnel use statistics to measure the impact of their programs on the customer. Marketing researchers use statistics to measure attitudes toward new or improved products or services to see if they are likely to prove successful. There are many hot topics in marketing where statistics are being used to make decisions. For example, companies are being required to substantiate product performance claims such as "makes your laundry outdoor-fresh" or "leaves glass streak-free." In either claim a representative sample of consumers is used to collect data about the products. Then the data are analyzed and interpreted to come up with information that is used to determine whether or not the product's claim is valid.

Accounting The work done by accountants varies from firm to firm. One thing all accountants are responsible for is the accuracy of financial documents. Checking documents for accuracy is called auditing. Since it is impractical to check every document, statistical methods can be applied. For example, going through a year's worth of invoices in a company with a large customer base is not a worthwhile task. Instead, a sample of invoices from different times of the year can be checked and the results used to say something about the accuracy of all the invoices.

Finance Most finance professionals work for investment dealers, insurance companies, banks, trust companies, fund management firms, or in the finance departments of large corporations. Statistics is widely applied in finance, from evaluating the risk of making a loan to setting a price for car insurance for a first-time driver. Many people associate the buying and selling of stocks, bonds, and commodities with statistics. For example, financial analysts use statistical information to look for stocks that are likely to increase in value. An analyst would look at some of the leading companies in the industry, forecast future profits, and analyze the stock's past performance to evaluate investment opportunities.

Quality Control Quality is no longer only an attribute applied to parts coming out of the plant. Quality requirements have moved from the plant floor into every office of a company. When we speak of quality, we could be referring to how quickly a customer is served, the response time to customer complaints, or the production of a product without defects. Statistical quality control, statistical process control, and total quality management are different names for the evaluations done in all areas of a company using statistically based methods. For example, when a bolt is manufactured for a car company its diameter could be bigger or smaller than the customer wanted. The machine making the bolt has many moving parts that change the accuracy of the machine as they wear out. The machine operator must check that the bolts are a size acceptable to the customer. Rather than measuring every one, the operator measures a handful of bolts. Using statistical methods the machine operator can determine whether the machine must be adjusted.

Economics Statistics Canada is the largest collector of statistics in Canada. The information is used to project economic trends, measure the effects of government policy, and guide the creation of new government initiatives. "Statscan" makes much of its data available (for a price) to anyone who wishes to use them. There is a wide selection of useful data. For example, take a company thinking of opening a new retail outlet. The company could buy information about the people living in the area from Statistics Canada, classified by postal code district. The company could then determine if a store in that location would be successful.

For an online glossary, go to **www.pearsoned.ca/hummelbrunner**.

Key Terms

Data 2
Descriptive statistics 1
Inferential statistics 1
Population 1
Sample 1

CHAPTER 1

Organizing and Presenting Data

Introduction

Statistical analysis is concerned with procedures by which data are collected, organized, summarized, presented, analyzed, and interpreted. Raw data collected for the purpose of analysis must first be organized. Tables, graphs, and charts are widely used to display statistical data.

The purpose of a graph or chart is to allow the reader to see the relationships in the data without intensive study. To obtain the desired impact, care must be taken to select the appropriate type of graph or chart and to present it in a clear, readable manner.

Learning Outcomes

Upon completion of this chapter you will be able to

1. construct *XY* graphs (scatter diagrams) from given sets of paired data;
2. construct single line graphs and multiple line graphs;
3. construct simple bar charts, simple area charts, and clustered bar charts;
4. construct stacked area charts and stacked bar charts;
5. construct pie (circle) charts;
6. construct bi- (two-) directional bar charts;
7. construct high-low-close charts.

SECTION 1.1

Looking at Data

Statistics is concerned with *collecting*, *organizing*, *summarizing*, *analyzing*, and *presenting* data to assist in decision making.

Data collected in tabular form can be presented graphically in their entirety or in part by various methods to provide a pictorial indication of relationships without requiring intensive study of the data. In fact, a graphical illustration of data may be more revealing than the statistical measures that are commonly used to describe data.

To demonstrate this point let us look at a collection of four sets of data referred to as *Anscombe's Quartet* and presented in Table 1.1.

TABLE 1.1 Anscombe's Quartet

Set 1		Set 2		Set 3		Set 4	
x	y	x	y	x	y	x	y
12.0	10.84	12.0	9.13	12.0	8.15	8.0	5.56
4.0	4.26	4.0	3.10	4.0	5.39	19.0	12.50
9.0	8.81	9.0	8.77	9.0	7.11	8.0	8.84
7.0	4.82	7.0	7.26	7.0	6.42	8.0	7.91
14.0	9.96	14.0	8.10	14.0	8.84	8.0	7.04
6.0	7.24	6.0	6.13	6.0	6.08	8.0	5.25
10.0	8.04	10.0	9.14	10.0	7.46	8.0	6.58
11.0	8.33	11.0	9.26	11.0	7.81	8.0	8.47
8.0	6.95	8.0	8.14	8.0	6.77	8.0	5.76
13.0	7.58	13.0	8.74	13.0	12.74	8.0	7.71
5.0	5.68	5.0	4.74	5.0	5.73	8.0	6.89

Source: F.J. Anscombe, "Graphs in Statistical Analysis," *American Statistician* 27 (February 1973). Reprinted with permission from *The American Statistician*.

○ EXAMPLE 1.1a

Review the four sets of data in Table 1.1 and identify similarities, oddities, and relationships that you see in the data.

● SOLUTION

When looking at the table you may have noticed that the x values for Sets 1, 2, and 3 are the same and take the whole number values 4, 5, . . ., 14, while ten of the x values for Set 4 are the whole number 8. Otherwise, presentation of the data in the form of a table reveals very little about the data.

The graphical representation of the four sets of data clearly indicates the differences and patterns in the data.

FIGURE 1.1 **Graphical Representation of Set 1**

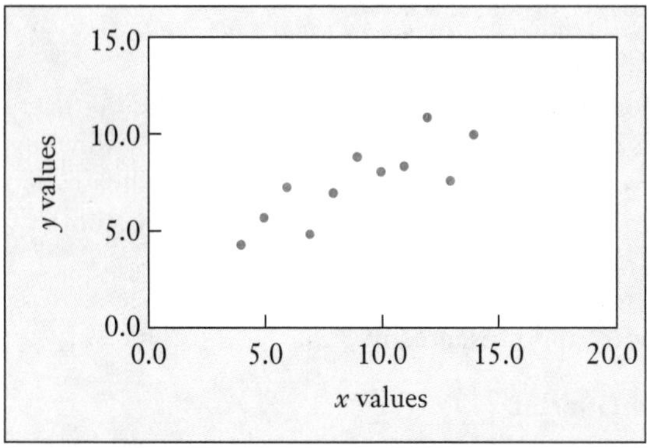

FIGURE 1.2 **Graphical Representation of Set 2**

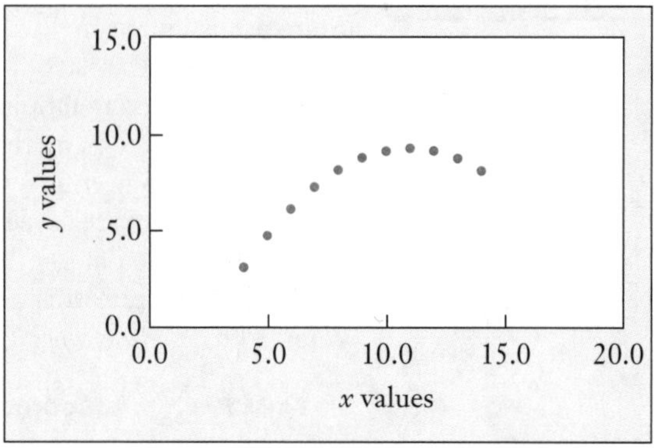

FIGURE 1.3 **Graphical Representation of Set 3**

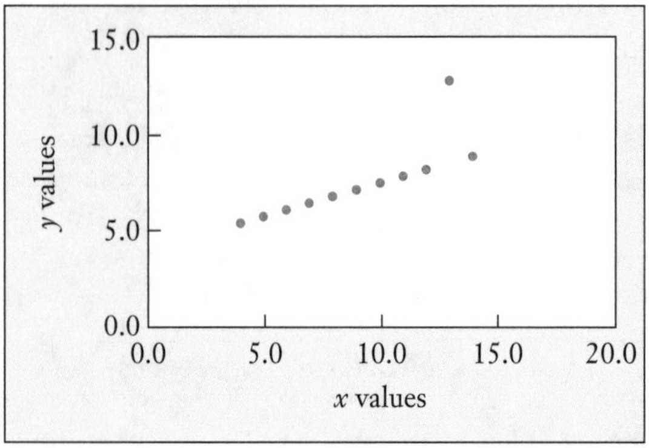

FIGURE 1.4 **Graphical Representation of Set 4**

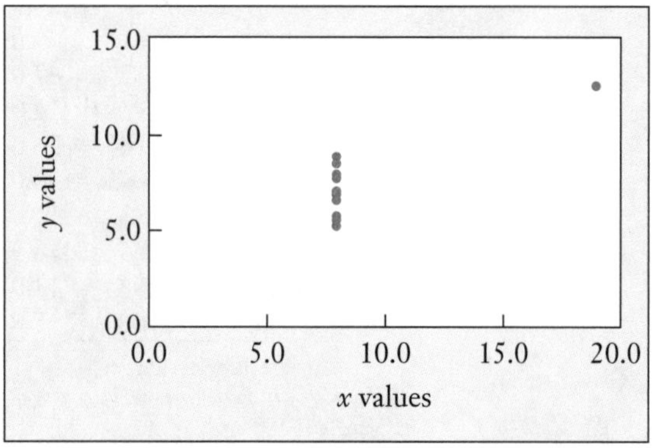

SECTION 1.2

Presenting Data—Graphs and Charts

The types of graphs and charts most commonly used in business are *XY* graphs (scatter diagrams), single and multiple line graphs, bar and area charts, and specialty graphs such as stacked bar and area charts, pie charts, bi- (two-) directional graphs and high-low-close graphs.

Table 1.2 is a collection of data presenting information about assets held by Canadian mutual funds for the period 1997 to 2002. Data from this table are used to demonstrate the construction of most of the common types of graphs and charts referred to in the previous paragraph.

TABLE 1.2 Total Assets Held by Canadian Mutual Funds (in $ Billions)

	Balanced funds	Equity funds		Bond funds		Fixed income funds		Money market funds		
Year	Balanced	Cdn.	Foreign	Cdn.	Foreign	Dividend	Mortgage	Cdn.	Foreign	Total
1997	44.4	81.1	69.2	21.1	2.5	14.5	12.1	31.8	1.3	278.0
1998	55.1	83.5	89.3	30.1	3.6	19.4	8.9	34.9	1.8	326.6
1999	60.9	87.9	133.7	30.4	5.1	18.7	7.7	43.3	2.0	389.7
2000	66.7	100.9	151.0	27.1	4.1	19.5	5.8	41.5	2.2	418.8
2001	67.1	97.8	137.4	29.4	3.8	21.9	5.9	59.3	3.8	426.4
2002	65.2	85.9	110.1	31.7	4.5	27.2	6.3	57.0	3.4	391.3

Source: The Investment Funds Institute of Canada.

SECTION 1.3

XY Graphs (Scatter Diagrams)

The diagrams presented for the four sets of data in Example 1.1a are referred to as ***XY* graphs**. This type of graphing may be used either when only one value of the variable y (called the *dependent variable*) is associated with each value of the variable x (called the *independent variable*) or when more than one value of the y-variable is associated with each value of the x-variable. Such graphs, particularly those of the second type, are also called **scatter diagrams**.

XY graphs or scatter diagrams can be, and most often are, used to present a picture of the *shape* of the relationship between two variables.

To construct a scatter diagram, draw a set of rectangular axes. Use the horizontal axis (x-axis) for one set of values and the vertical axis (y-axis) for the second set, and plot pairs of values. Although it is not absolutely necessary to do so, it is advisable to use graph paper to obtain neat and accurate graphs.

EXAMPLE 1.3a

Construct an *XY* graph (scatter diagram) for the following data:

Year	1997	1998	1999	2000	2001	2002
Bank rate (average %)	3.5	5.1	4.9	5.8	4.3	2.7
Total assets in Canadian bond funds ($ billions)	21.1	30.1	30.4	27.1	29.4	31.7

Source: ©Bank of Canada and the Investment Funds Institute of Canada.

SOLUTION

FIGURE 1.5 Total Assets in Canadian Bond Funds in Relation to the Bank Rate (%)

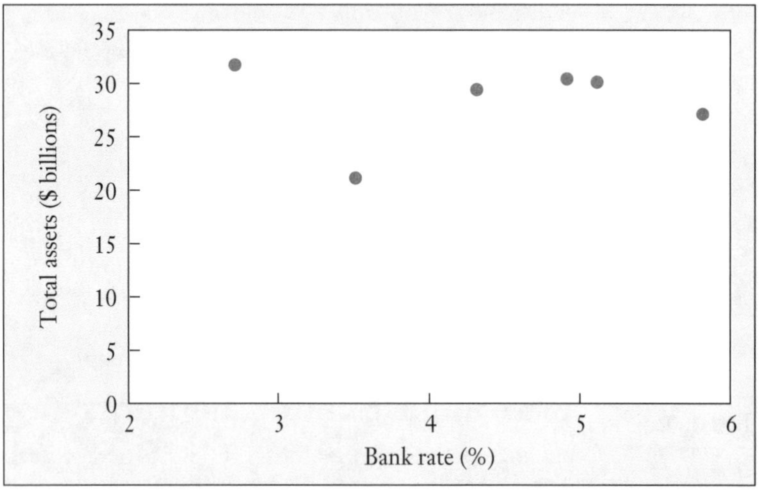

Use the bank rate figures as x-values to create the horizontal scale and the assets as y-values to create the vertical scale. Start the x-axis at 2 and take it to 6 by intervals of 1 to accommodate the bank rate values. Start the y-axis at 0 and take it to 35 by intervals of 5 to accommodate the asset values. Now plot each pair of values given in the data set. For the pair of values (3.5, 21.1) move to 3.5 on the x-axis and move up vertically to the point opposite the value 21.1 on the y-axis, and place a mark (dot, cross, or other symbol) at this point. Plot the remaining pairs of points in the same manner. The graph should look like Figure 1.5.

EXERCISE 1.3

1. Plot the following set of numbers on an *XY* graph (scatter diagram):

y	16	8	14	6	16	20	20	14	10
x	4	18	10	18	5	2	4	5	14

2. Plot an *XY* graph (scatter diagram) using the horizontal axis for consumption (litres) and the vertical axis for the associated total cost ($).

Total cost ($)	18	18	5	24	12	12	30	18
Consumption (litres)	20	40	12	30	20	5	40	24

SECTION 1.4

Line Graphs

Line graphs are *XY* graphs (of the type with only one *y* value associated with each *x* value) in which the data points are joined by a line. The line starts at the first point and ends at the last.

If one set of data is presented, a **single line graph** results. If two or more sets of data are presented, a **multiple line graph** can be constructed. In such cases, each line needs to be distinctly identified with the data set it represents.

Line graphs are used primarily to present *changes in data* over a period of time.

○ EXAMPLE 1.4a

Use the data in Table 1.2 to construct a multiple line graph of total assets in Canadian equity and foreign equity funds for the period 1997 to 2002.

● SOLUTION

These calculations can be completed using EXCEL, as demonstrated in USING EXCEL 1.1.

USING EXCEL 1.1

Use the data in Table 1.2 to construct a multiple line graph of total assets in Canadian equity and foreign equity funds for the period 1997 to 2002.

SOLUTION

Using EXCEL,

1. Type the column heading **Equity Funds** into cell B1.
2. Type the column headings **Year**, **Cdn.**, and **Foreign** into cells A2, B2, and C2.
3. Enter the years **1997** to **2002** into cells A3–A8.
4. Enter the corresponding data found in Table 1.2 into cells B3–C8.
5. On the toolbar, click on the **Chart Wizard** button (or on the **Insert** menu, click **Chart...**).
6. The **Chart Wizard** dialog box appears. Click on the **Standard Types** tab and from the **Chart type** list, select **Line** and in the **Chart sub-type** section select the chart that corresponds to the **Line with markers displayed at each data value** image; then click the **Next >** button.
7. Click on the **Data Range** tab and click on beside the **Data range** input box to temporarily minimize the chart wizard; select cells B3–C8 on the worksheet; then click on or press the **Enter** key; select **Columns** from the **Series in** options.
8. Click on the **Series** tab. From the **Series** list, select **Series1** and in the **Name** input box type **Cdn.** (or click on the beside the **Name** input box to return to the worksheet; select cell B2 on the worksheet; then click on or press the **Enter** key). Repeat this again for **Series2** found in the **Series** list to represent the **Foreign** equity funds (cell C2). Click on beside the **Category (X) axis labels** input box; select cells A3–A8; click on or press the **Enter** key; then click on the **Next >** button.
9. Click on the **Titles** tab. In the **Category (X) axis** labels input box, type **Year**. In the **Value (Y) axis** input box, type **$ billions**. In the **Chart title** input box you may want to give the graph a title, such as **Total Assets in Canadian Equity and Foreign Funds, 1997–2002**.

10. Click on any of the other remaining tabs found in the dialog box to select or deselect options to customize the display of your graph. When you are finished with your selections, click on the **Next >** button.
11. From the **Place chart** options, select the **As object in** option and then click on the **Finish** button.

By clicking on your chart and selecting the **Chart Area**, you can resize your chart or move your chart to different locations on your worksheet. Additionally, you can format the look of your chart by selecting the various components of your chart and then clicking on the **Format** menu to change the format of the selected chart item.

OUTPUT

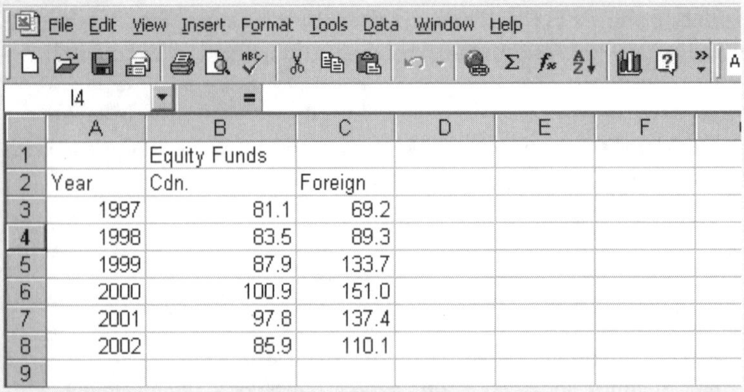

	A	B	C	D	E	F
1		Equity Funds				
2	Year	Cdn.	Foreign			
3	1997	81.1	69.2			
4	1998	83.5	89.3			
5	1999	87.9	133.7			
6	2000	100.9	151.0			
7	2001	97.8	137.4			
8	2002	85.9	110.1			
9						

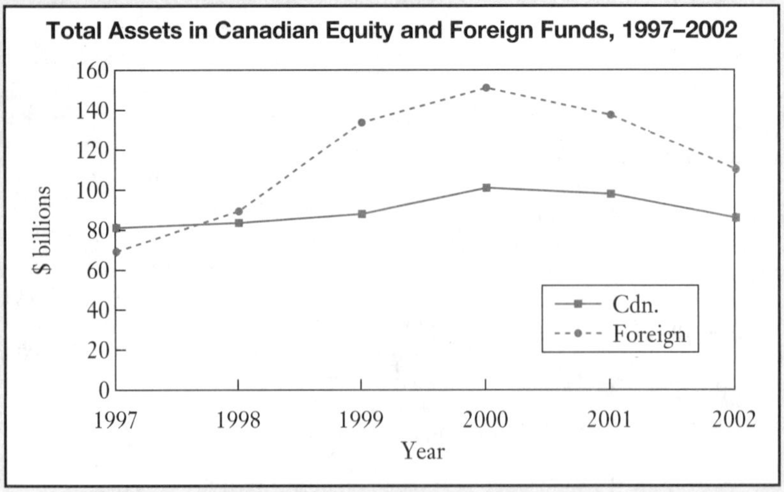

EXERCISE 1.4

1. The following data represent the average values of the U.S. dollar in Canadian cents for the period 1992 to 2002, reported on a yearly basis by the Bank of Canada. Construct a single line graph to present the data.

Year	1992	1993	1994	1995	1996	1997
U.S. dollar (in Cdn. cents)	120.8	127.0	136.6	137.2	136.3	138.4

Year	1998	1999	2000	2001	2002
U.S. dollar (in Cdn. cents)	148.3	148.5	148.5	154.9	157.0

Source: ©Bank of Canada.

2. Cellular Text Inc. has predicted the sales of its wireless text devices to be as follows:

Year	2004	2005	2006	2007	2008	2009
Shipments (millions of units)	0.266	0.373	0.474	0.962	2.360	4.835

Construct a single line graph to represent the data.

3. The operating results (in $000) for the Jenning Company for 2002 were as follows:

Quarter	First	Second	Third	Fourth
Revenue	76	93	85	88
Cost of sales	35	45	40	45
Net income	20	22	18	15

Construct a multiple line graph to represent the data.

4. Promotional expenditures and net profit for Ace Inc. for the last six months of 2002 (in $ millions) were as follows:

Month	July	August	September	October	November	December
Promotion	1.0	5.0	5.0	8.0	10.0	12.0
Net profit	7.2	8.2	10.0	15.6	18.0	15.0

Draw a multiple line graph to represent the data.

SECTION 1.5

Bar and Area Charts

A. Simple Bar Charts

A **simple bar chart** displays the relationship among a set of numerical values by means of either *vertical* or *horizontal* bars. Vertical bar charts are generally used when *time* is the independent variable, while horizontal bars are used for sets of data in which time is *not* a factor.

In bar charts the numerical scale should start at zero and should be devised to accommodate the magnitude of the numbers involved.

Bar charts are used for *comparing* the values of several categories of a variable.

EXAMPLE 1.5a

Use the data in Table 1.2 to compare the total assets held by Canadian mutual funds in 2002 by category by means of a simple bar chart.

SOLUTION

First calculate the value (in $billions) of the total assets (Canadian + foreign) in each category:

Balanced funds	Equity funds	Bond funds	Fixed income funds	Money market funds
65.2	196.0	36.2	33.5	60.4

Since time is *not* a factor, a horizontal bar chart is appropriate in this case.

FIGURE 1.7 **Total Assets in Canadian Mutual Funds by Category, 2002**

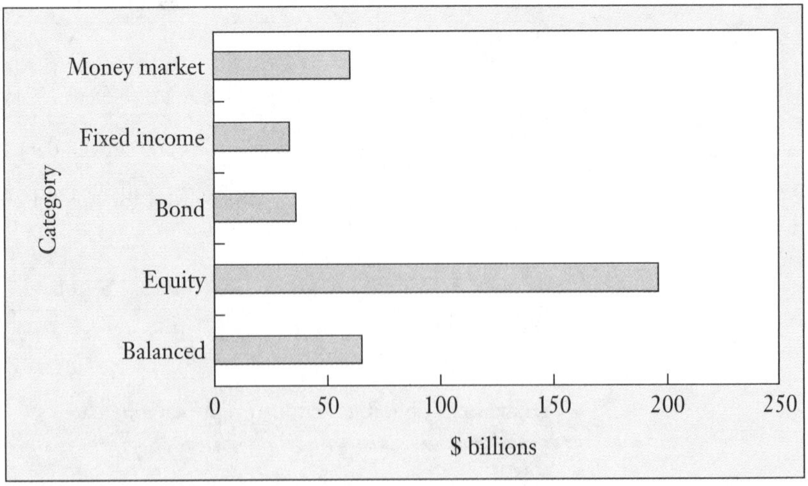

○ **EXAMPLE 1.5b**

Use the data in Table 1.2 to construct a bar chart of the balanced fund assets for the time period 1997 to 2002.

● **SOLUTION**

No calculations are necessary. Since time *is* a factor in this case, a vertical bar chart is used.

FIGURE 1.8 **Assets Held by Canadian Mutual Funds in Balanced Fund Assets, 1997–2002**

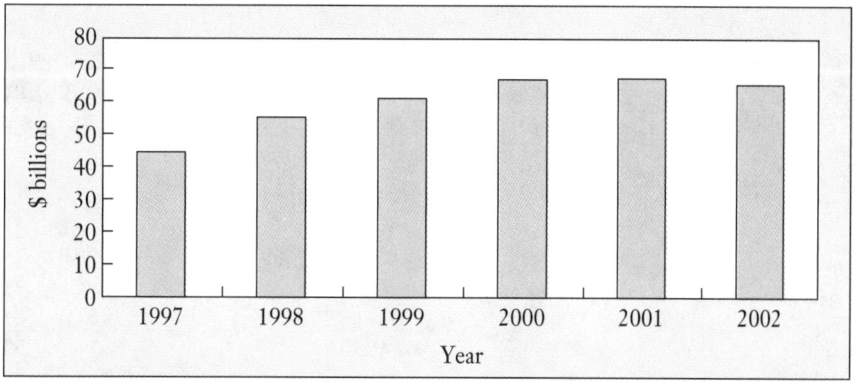

B. Simple Area Charts

A **simple area chart** is a simple line chart with the space under the line filled in with some appropriate pattern. Such charts are most often used to emphasize changes in a variable over time.

○ **EXAMPLE 1.5c**

Use the same data as for Example 1.5b to construct a simple area chart.

● **SOLUTION**

FIGURE 1.9 **Assets Held by Canadian Mutual Funds in Balanced Fund Assets, 1997–2002**

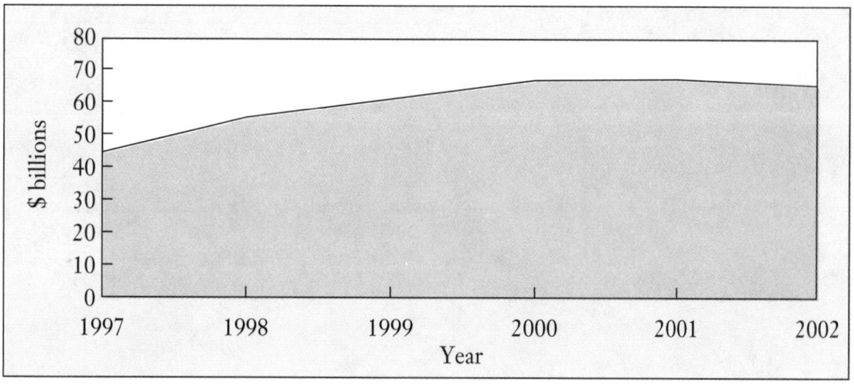

C. *Clustered Bar Charts*

Clustered bar charts are used to compare two or more sets of data that share a common variable. As with simple bar charts, vertical bars are used when the common variable is *time* and horizontal bars are used when it is not.

EXAMPLE 1.5d

Use the data in Table 1.2 to construct a clustered bar chart of total assets held by Canadian mutual funds in equity and bond funds for the period 1997 to 2002.

SOLUTION

First calculate the total assets (Canadian + foreign) in the equity and bond funds for the period required:

Year	Equity funds	Bond funds
1997	150.3	23.6
1998	172.8	33.7
1999	221.6	35.5
2000	251.9	31.2
2001	235.2	33.2
2002	196.0	36.2

Since time *is* a factor in this case, a vertical clustered bar chart is appropriate. (Note that the same data could also be presented as a multiple line graph.)

FIGURE 1.10 Total Assets in Equity and Bond Funds, 1997–2002

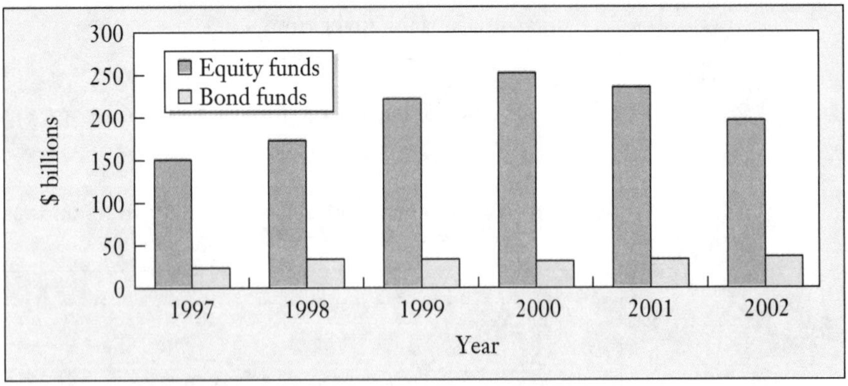

EXERCISE 1.5

1. The Quip Company had the following number of employees in its various departments at the end of May:

Cutting	Machining	Folding	Shipping
30	45	24	12

Represent the data on a bar chart.

2. Net sales for Dreamers Inc. (in $000) for the period January to August were as follows:

January	February	March	April	May	June	July	August
150	180	160	190	150	170	190	200

Represent the data on a bar chart.

3. Exports (in $ millions) for Company A and Company B from 1996 to 2002 were as follows:

Year	1996	1997	1998	1999	2000	2001	2002
Company A	20	16	12	15	10	7	8
Company B	2	5	8	10	13	17	19

Draw a clustered bar chart to represent the data.

4. Attendance figures for the Lake Winnipeg Festival were as follows:

	Saturday	Sunday
Rubber ducky race	120	255
Concert	380	520
Dog show	174	153
Wagon races	215	228
Surprise event	357	263

Draw a clustered bar chart to represent the data.

SECTION 1.6

Stacked Bar and Area Charts, Pie (Circle) Charts

Stacked bar and area charts are used to show relationships among the parts of a total. These charts may present the categories that make up the total either in their original values or, in the case of 100% stacked charts, as percents of the total.

Pie charts are always presented as 100% charts. Each "slice" of the pie represents the percentage of the total represented by a particular category.

A. Stacked Bar Charts

Five types of funds are tracked in the assets data of Table 1.2: balanced, equity, bond, fixed income, and money market funds. The value of the assets in each category can be thought of as part of a whole — the combined assets of various funds for a particular year. To emphasize this fact they can be displayed in a **stacked bar chart**. The height of a bar shows the *total* asset value for the year, while patterned segments show the *individual* asset contribution of each type of fund.

To show how the percentage contribution of each type of asset changes from year to year, ignoring how the total asset value changes, a 100% stacked bar chart is used. In this type of stacked bar chart the total asset value for each year is equated to 100% and the patterned segments of each bar show the percentage contribution of each type of fund to the total.

○ **EXAMPLE 1.6a**

Use the data in Table 1.2 to construct

a) a stacked bar chart of the total assets in Canadian mutual funds by type for the years 2000 and 2002;

b) a 100% stacked bar chart of the same data.

● **SOLUTION**

First calculate and tabulate the required data:

Type of fund	2000				2002			
	Total assets	Cum. total	% of total	Cum. %	Total assets	Cum. total	% of total	Cum. %
Balanced	66.7	66.7	15.93	15.93	65.2	65.2	16.66	16.66
Equity	251.9	318.6	60.15	76.08	196.0	261.2	50.09	66.75
Bond	31.2	349.8	7.45	83.53	36.2	297.4	9.25	76.00
Fixed income	25.3	375.1	6.04	89.57	33.5	330.9	8.56	84.56
Money market	43.7	418.8	10.43	100.00	60.4	391.3	15.44	100.00
Totals	418.8		100.00		391.3		100.00	

The cumulative totals are required for constructing the stacked bar charts by hand. When using software packages it is not necessary to calculate these cumulative values — the software does it automatically.

a) **FIGURE 1.11 Total Assets by Type in Canadian Mutual Funds, 2000 and 2002**

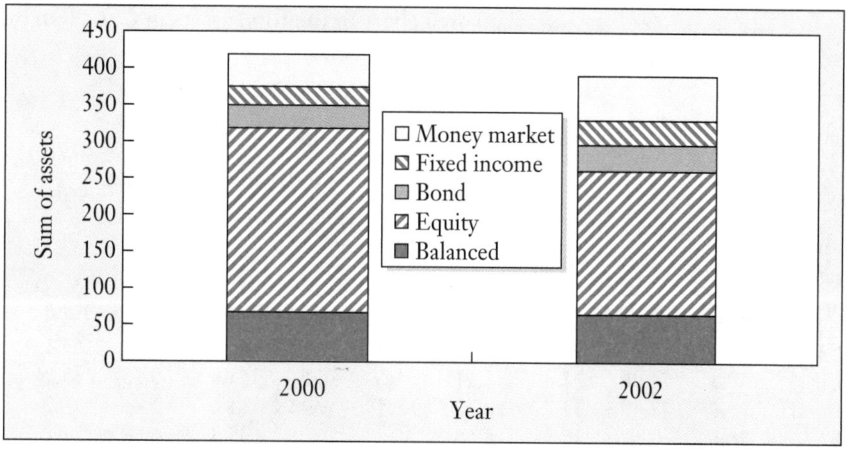

b) **FIGURE 1.12 Total Assets by Type in Canadian Mutual Funds, 2000 and 2002 (as a Percent of Total Assets)**

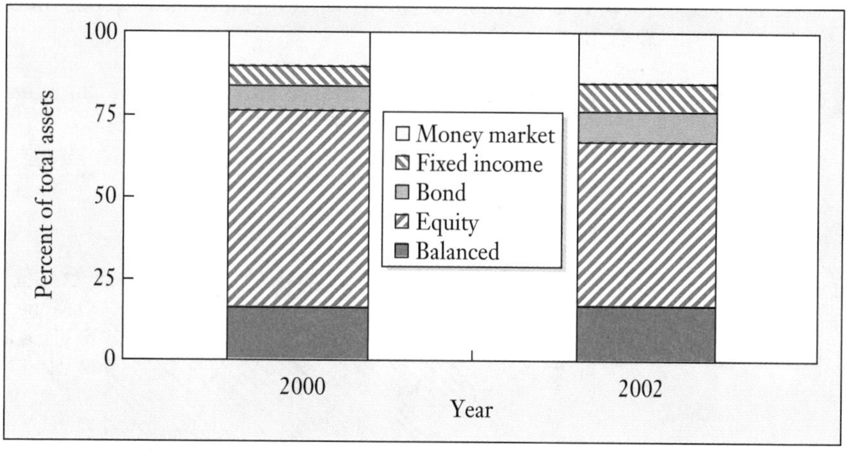

B. Stacked Area Charts

Stacked area charts are similar in many ways to stacked bar charts but are more useful for emphasizing the sequential nature of the changes in data over several time periods. As with the stacked bar chart, two types of stacked area chart can be produced, using either raw values or percentages.

○ **EXAMPLE 1.6b**

Use the data in Table 1.2 to construct

a) a stacked area chart of the total assets in Canadian mutual funds by type for the period 1997 to 2002;

b) a 100% stacked bar chart of the same data.

● **SOLUTION**

First calculate and tabulate the necessary data:

Fund type	1997		1998		1999		2000		2001		2002	
	Total	%	Total	%	Total	%	Total	%	Total	%	Total	%
Bal.	44.4	15.97	55.1	16.87	60.9	15.63	66.7	15.93	67.1	15.74	65.2	16.66
Eqty.	150.3	54.06	172.8	52.91	221.6	56.86	251.9	60.15	235.2	55.16	196.0	50.09
Bond	23.6	8.49	33.7	10.32	35.5	9.11	31.2	7.45	33.2	7.78	36.2	9.25
FI	26.6	9.57	28.3	8.66	26.4	6.78	25.3	6.04	27.8	6.52	33.5	8.56
MM	33.1	11.91	36.7	11.24	45.3	11.62	43.7	10.43	63.1	14.80	60.4	15.44
Totals	278.0	100.00	326.6	100.00	389.7	100.00	418.8	100.00	426.4	100.00	391.3	100.00

To construct the chart by hand, cumulative totals for each year would have to be calculated.

a) **FIGURE 1.13 Total Assets by Type in Canadian Mutual Funds, 1997–2002**

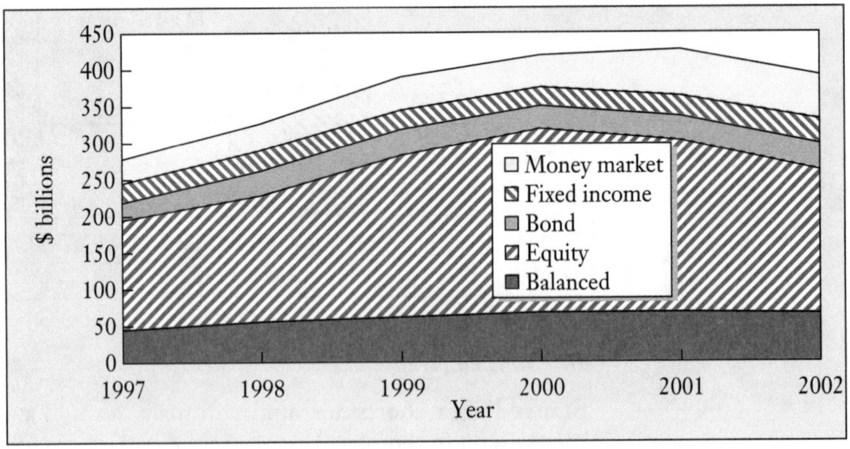

b) **FIGURE 1.14 Total Assets by Type in Canadian Mutual Funds, 1997–2002 (as a Percent of Total Assets)**

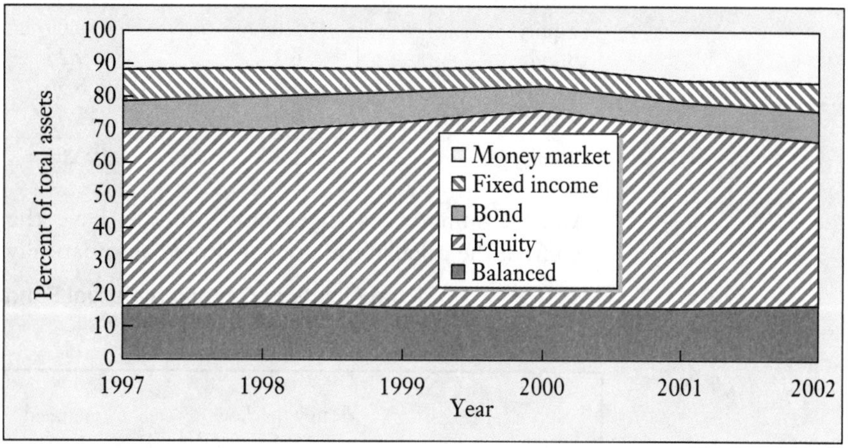

C. Pie Charts

Pie charts serve the same purpose as 100% stacked bar and area charts but are more limited in the sense that each chart can present only one data set at a time. Two pie charts would be required to present the data contained in the single 100% bar chart of Example 1.6a, and six would be needed to present the information contained in the 100% stacked area chart of Example 1.6b.

The plot of a pie chart is a circle (the plots are sometimes called circle graphs) that represents the total of all values in the data set. The circle is divided into wedges, one for each value. The size of a wedge represents the percent contribution that each value makes to the total of 100%.

To construct a pie chart by hand, change the data into percentage form and then multiply each percent by 360 to determine the number of degrees required for each component. A protractor is required to construct an accurate pie chart by hand.

EXAMPLE 1.6c

Use the data in Table 1.2 to construct a pie chart of total assets of Canadian mutual funds by type for 2002.

SOLUTION

First calculate the total assets in each type of fund for 2002, convert each to a percent of the grand total and then multiply each by 360. Setting up the data in tabular form simplifies the procedure:

Fund type	Total assets	% of grand total	Degrees
Balanced	65.2	16.66	60.0
Equity	196.0	50.09	180.3
Bond	36.2	9.25	33.3
Fixed income	33.5	8.56	30.8
Money market	60.4	15.44	55.6
Totals	391.3	100.00	360.0

Note Computer packages only need to have the categories and values entered; the calculations are performed automatically.

FIGURE 1.15 Total Assets in Canadian Mutual Funds by Type, 2002 (as a Percent of Total Assets)

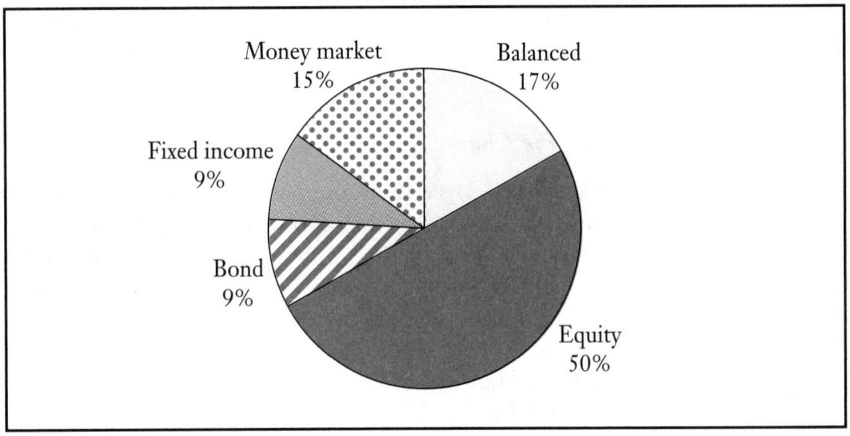

These calculations can be completed using EXCEL, as demonstrated in USING EXCEL 1.2.

USING EXCEL 1.2

Use the data in Table 1.2 to construct a pie chart of total assets of Canadian mutual funds by type for 2002.

SOLUTION

Using EXCEL,

1. Type **Year 2002** into cell A1.
2. Type the column headings **Type of Fund** and **Total Assets** into cells A3 and B3.
3. Type the column heading **Balanced**, **Equity**, **Bond**, **Fixed income**, and **Money market** into cells A4–A8.
4. Enter the corresponding 2002 data (65.2, 196.0, 36.2, 33.5, 60.4) found and derived from Table 1.2 into cells B4–C8.
5. On the toolbar, click on the **Chart Wizard** button (or on the **Insert** menu, click **Chart...**).
6. The **Chart Wizard** dialog box appears. Click on the **Standard Types** tab and from the **Chart type** list, select **Pie** and in the **Chart sub-type** section select the chart that corresponds to the **Pie – Displays the contribution of each value to a total** image; then click the **Next >** button.

7. Click on the **Data Range** tab and click on beside the **Data range** input box to temporarily minimize the chart wizard; select cells B4–C8 on the worksheet; then click on or press the **Enter** key; select **Columns** from the **Series in** options. Click on the **Next >** button.
8. Click on the **Titles** tab. In the **Chart title** input box you may want to give the graph a title, such as **Total Assets in Canadian Mutual Funds by Type, 2002.**
9. Click on any of the other remaining tabs found in the dialog box to select or deselect options to customize the display of your graph. When you are finished with your selections, click on the **Next >** button.
10. From the **Place chart** options, select the **As object in** option and then click on the **Finish** button.

By clicking on your chart and selecting the **Chart Area**, you can resize your chart or move your chart to different locations on your worksheet. Additionally, you can format the look of your chart by selecting the various components of your chart and then clicking on the **Format** menu to change the format of the selected chart item.

OUTPUT

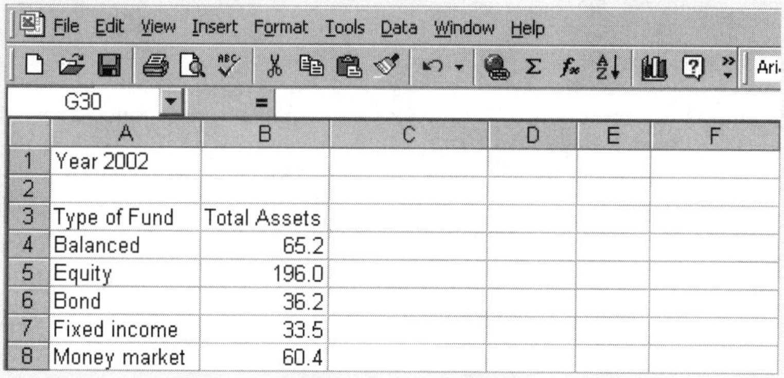
File Edit View Insert Format Tools Data Window Help

G30 =

	A	B	C	D	E	F
1	Year 2002					
2						
3	Type of Fund	Total Assets				
4	Balanced	65.2				
5	Equity	196.0				
6	Bond	36.2				
7	Fixed income	33.5				
8	Money market	60.4				

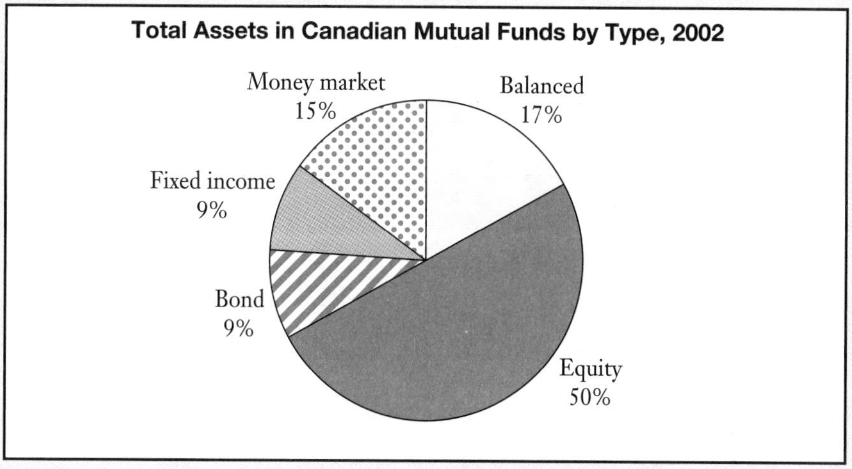

EXERCISE 1.6

1. A survey of inventory levels for manufacturers in three cities yielded the following information:

	Percent of total respondents		
Inventory	Montreal	Toronto	Vancouver
High	24	10	18
Adequate	65	55	62
Low	11	35	20

Show the inventory levels for the three cities by means of a stacked bar chart.

2. Revenues for Ontario Media Corporation for 2000 to 2002 (in $ millions) were as follows:

Revenues	2000	2001	2002
Newspaper	43	50	58
Book publishing	32	35	40
Catalogue marketing	12	10	8

Represent the data by means of a stacked bar chart.

3. Operating expenses (in $000) for the Corner Boutique were as follows:

Operating expenses	2000	2001	2002
Salaries	24	28	36
Rent	6	6	8
Utilities	4	5	6
Other	5	8	10

Represent the data by means of a stacked area chart.

4. Component sales for HSI Inc. (in $ millions) are as follows:

Component	1996	1998	2000	2002
Radios	16	14	12	13
TV sets	18	20	24	27
Stereos	12	14	16	16
Parts	9	12	12	14

Construct a stacked area chart to represent the data.

5. Appliance World sold the following number of major appliances in 2002:

Ranges	Refrigerators	Freezers	Washers	Dryers
380	300	90	210	120

Represent the data by means of a pie chart.

6. The government of Canada's revenue comes from the following sources (2001–2002):

Income taxes	62.4%
Consumption taxes	21.0%
Contribution to social insurance plans	9.7%
Other revenue	6.9%

Source: Statistics Canada.

Represent the data by means of a pie chart.

SECTION 1.7

Specialty Charts

A. Bi- (Two-) Directional Bar Charts

Bi-directional bar charts are used to show the percent changes in value of a variable over time.

If only two time periods are being considered, a *vertical* line is used to represent the origin or base line. Increases in value of the variable are represented by bars to the right of this line, and decreases by bars to its left.

If more than two time periods are being considered, a *horizontal* line is used to represent the origin. Increases in value of the variable are represented by bars above the base line, and decreases by bars "hanging" from the base line. Such charts are known as **hanging bar charts.**

○ **EXAMPLE 1.7a**

Use the data in Table 1.2 to construct a bi-directional bar chart showing the changes of total assets in Canadian mutual funds by type between 2001 and 2002.

a) Use a vertical line as base line.
b) Use a horizontal line as base line.

● **SOLUTION**

First calculate the percent change for the five types of funds between 2001 and 2002.

Fund type	2001	2002	Increase (decrease)	Percent change
Balanced	67.1	65.2	(1.9)	$\frac{-1.9}{67.1} = -2.83$
Equity	235.2	196.0	(39.2)	$\frac{-39.2}{235.2} = -16.67$
Bond	33.2	36.2	3.0	$\frac{3.0}{33.2} = 9.04$
Fixed income	27.8	33.5	5.7	$\frac{5.7}{27.8} = 20.50$
Money market	63.1	60.4	(2.7)	$\frac{-2.7}{63.1} = -4.28$

a) **FIGURE 1.16 Percent Change in Total Assets in Canadian Mutual Funds by type, 2001–2002**

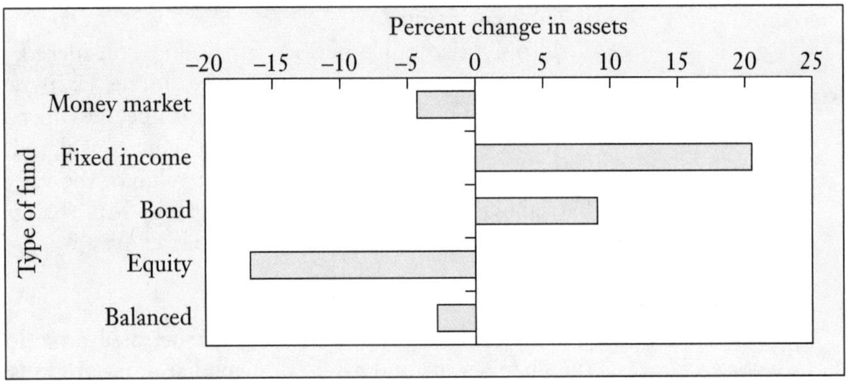

b) **FIGURE 1.17 Percent Change in Total Assets in Canadian Mutual Funds by type, 2001–2002**

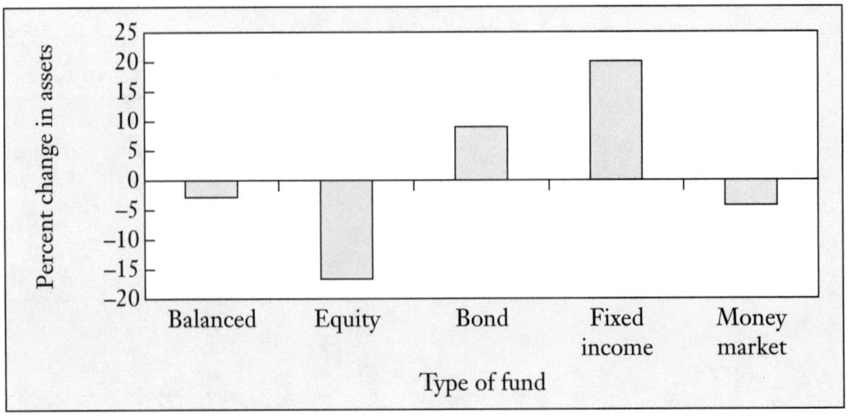

B. High-Low-Close Charts

The **high-low-close chart,** commonly found in the financial section of daily newspapers and in other financial publications, serves the special purpose of showing the periodic (daily, weekly, monthly, or yearly) fluctuations in values of stock exchange indexes and share prices. In some cases the *opening price* — as well as the high, low, and closing prices — is recorded. Such charts are known as **HLCO charts.**

The high and low values for each time period are represented by a vertical line on the chart. The top end of the line represents the highest value reached during the time period, and the bottom end of the line represents the lowest value. The closing value for the time period is represented by a tick mark on the line. In open-high-low-close charts the opening and closing values are represented by tick marks pointing in opposite directions.

Although most commonly used for financial data, high-low-close charts can be used to illustrate other variables that fluctuate in a periodic manner — for example, daily temperature readings at a particular location, high and low tides, currency fluctuations, etc.

EXAMPLE 1.7b

The following are the yearly highs, lows, and closes (without decimals) of the S&P/TSX Composite Index for the period 1998 to 2002.

Year	High	Low	Close
1998	731	504	613
1999	866	595	852
2000	1091	818	1018
2001	1066	812	971
2002	996	685	802

Source: Adapted from www.finance.yahoo.com.

Construct a high-low-close chart.

SOLUTION

FIGURE 1.18 S&P/TSX Composite Index, 1998–2002

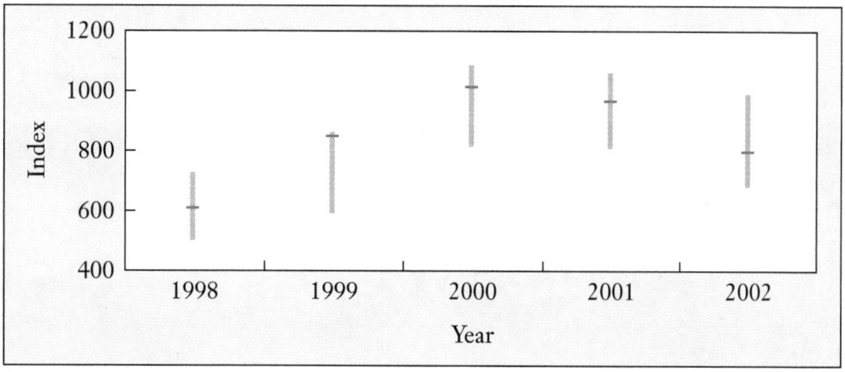

EXERCISE 1.7

1. Draw a bi-directional bar chart to portray the percent change for the following information:

Department	A	B	C	D	E	F
Sales 2001	60	80	70	25	20	25
Sales 2002	66	72	56	35	18	20

2. Represent the percent change in the following sales figures by means of a bi-directional bar chart.

Company	1	2	3	4	5	6
2002	40	50	20	45	20	25
1997	44	60	15	36	30	35

3. The monthly high, low, and close values for the Barrick Gold Corporation stock for the period January to December 2002 are as follows:

Month	High	Low	Close
January	28.08	25.35	27.30
February	31.20	27.30	28.80
March	30.20	26.80	29.15
April	32.15	27.30	31.65
May	36.05	30.70	33.32
June	35.16	28.75	28.83
July	29.70	21.30	24.43
August	25.79	22.52	25.25
September	28.92	23.50	24.75
October	25.09	21.85	23.45
November	26.09	22.19	22.43
December	26.00	22.30	24.35

Source: Data provided by CSI, Copyright CSI, Boca Raton, FL.

Construct a high-low-close chart.

4. Listed below are the high, low, and close values for Royal Bank of Canada shares on the Toronto Stock Exchange for the period January to December 2002. Construct a high-low-close chart to represent the data.

Month	High	Low	Close
January	52.19	48.90	50.00
February	51.25	46.36	50.71
March	54.05	50.80	53.20
April	57.07	52.55	54.97
May	58.74	53.35	58.60
June	58.89	50.60	52.50
July	53.98	45.05	53.45
August	56.10	52.30	56.00
September	55.48	49.50	52.70
October	57.55	48.80	54.41
November	59.56	53.91	58.55
December	59.86	56.40	57.85

Source: Data provided by CSI, Copyright CSI, Boca Raton, FL.

SECTION 1.8

A Summary of Chart Types and Their Uses

To illustrate a particular set of data there are often several different types of chart to choose from. The following table categorizes the different chart types according to the objective being sought:

To illustrate	Use
Relationships between variables	*XY* graphs; scatter diagrams
Ranges of data	Bar charts; high-low-close charts
Data obtained at a *specific* point in time	Bar charts; stacked bar charts
Data covering *several time periods*	Line graphs; multiple line graphs; high-low-close charts; bar charts; stacked bar charts; area charts; stacked area charts
Data expressed as a percent of a total:	
a) at a *specific* point in time	Pie charts; 100% stacked bar charts
b) over *several time periods*	100% stacked bar charts; 100% stacked area charts

REVIEW EXERCISE

1. A person who is thinking of moving should consider the movers' vehicle volume used each month as a percent of available capacity.

Month	Jan	Feb	Mar	Apr	May	Jun
Volume	29	27	30	43	49	68
Month	Jul	Aug	Sep	Oct	Nov	Dec
Volume	90	98	60	30	30	28

a) Draw a horizontal line graph to represent the data.
b) When would you advise a person not to move? Explain.

2. The following data represent the average daily electricity consumption (in kWh) for a family in Oakville, Ontario for the year 2001.

Month	Jan	Feb	Mar	Apr	May	Jun
Consumption	29	35	36	30	32	36
Month	Jul	Aug	Sep	Oct	Nov	Dec
Consumption	38	54	42	30	36	37

a) Draw a horizontal line graph to represent the data.
b) Give a possible reason for the high value in August.

3. Draw a multiple line graph to represent the following data:

	Number of Employed Persons (000s)					
Province	1996	1997	1998	1999	2000	2001
Ontario	5180	5313	5490	5688	5872	5962
Quebec	3145	3195	3281	3357	3437	3474

Source: Statistics Canada.

4. Draw a multiple line graph to represent the following data:

	Births and Deaths in Canada				
	1996	1997	1998	1999	2000
Births	372 453	357 313	345 123	339 562	336 373
Deaths	209 746	217 220	217 688	219 782	221 236

Source: Statistics Canada, Table 051-0004 – Components of population growth, Canada, provinces and territories, computed annual total.

5. A marketing research company has recently surveyed senior citizens on their ownership of certain household appliances. Draw a clustered bar chart to represent the following data:

	Proportion of senior households with appliance				
Year	VCR	Microwave oven	Colour TV	Home computer	Video camera
1995	58.8	63.4	96.2	11.6	16.3
2002	79.2	81.5	98.2	40.8	25.0

6. Draw a clustered bar chart to represent the following data:

	Production of new motor car vehicles			
Month	Chrysler	Ford	General Motors	Honda
January 2002	11 323	22 076	33 073	33 211
February 2002	20 044	20 293	48 287	30 792

Source: Statistics Canada, Table 303-0018 – Production of new motor vehicles, monthly (units).

7. The following is a listing of the number of people employed in Canada in 2001 in various industries:

Industry	Number of employees (000s)
Goods-producing industries:	
Agriculture	328
Natural Resources	293
Manufacturing	2274
Construction	843
Utilities	123
Service industries:	
Transportation	773
Trade	2383
Finance, insurance and real estate	874
Other	7184

Source: Statistics Canada.

a) Draw a vertical bar chart to represent the goods-producing industries.
b) Draw a horizontal bar chart to represent the service industries.
c) What can be done to either chart to make it more readable?

8. The following is a listing of the number of trips taken in Ontario in 1996 for various activities:

Category	Number of trips (000s)
Indoor:	
Visiting museum, art gallery	1208
Shopping	10 532
Going to bar/nightclub	2030
Going to casino	444
Outdoor:	
Golfing	1027
Fishing	2676
Downhill skiing	546
Walking, hiking	5083
Cycling	779

Source: Statistics Canada, Table 426-0006 – Canadian travel survey, activity participation, by province of destination, annual (Person-trips × 1000).

a) Draw a vertical bar chart to represent the indoor activities.
b) Draw a horizontal bar chart to represent the outdoor activities.

9. The International Fabrics Institute has determined that the following are responsible for various dry-cleaning problems:

Responsibility	Problems	Percent of problems
Manufacturer	Colour loss, shrinkage	43.3
Consumer	Stains, damage by bleach	34.7
Dry cleaner	Colour loss, shrinkage	15.4
Unknown	Mechanical and chemical damage	6.6

Construct a stacked bar chart of dry-cleaning problems by responsibility.

10. The household expenses of one family related to telephone use are listed below:

Company	Service	Expenses
Bell	Local Phone Service	27.48
Microcell	Cell Phone Service	20.61
Primus	Long-Distance Phone Service	34.35
AOL	Internet Service	17.56

Construct a stacked bar chart of telephone expenses by type of service.

11. The local board of education, concerned about drop-out rates, surveyed high school students. The following data compare the drop-out rate by sex to the amount of part time work:

	School drop-out rate (%)	
Hours of work per week	Males	Females
No job	25	22
Less than 20	16	7
20 or more	33	18
Total	25	16

Draw a clustered bar chart to represent the data.

12. Students at a major Canadian college are failing a first semester technical mathematics course at an increasing rate.

	Failure Rate (%)				
Year	1997	1998	1999	2000	2001
Male	25	21	33	38	40
Female	20	24	26	30	37

Draw a clustered bar chart to represent the data.

13. The levels of education obtained by employees of a large Canadian corporation are as follows:

Level of education	Male	Female
0 to 8 years	536	322
Some secondary	1375	922
High-school diploma	1520	1426
Some post-secondary	688	605
College diploma	2243	2000
University degree	1351	2222

a) Construct a 100% stacked bar chart to represent the data.
b) Use a pie chart to represent the male labour force.
c) Use a pie chart to represent the female labour force.

14. The time in which 1995 college graduates started their first job is as follows:

Time	Men	Women
5 or more years before graduation	5	6
1 to 4 years before graduation	11	13
less than 1 year before graduation	9	9
less than 1 year after graduation	53	52
between 1 and 2 years after graduation	14	11

Source: Statistics Canada, *Search for success: Finding work after graduation*, catalogue No. 11-088.

a) Use a pie chart to represent the male graduates.
b) Use a pie chart to represent the female graduates.
c) Construct a 100% stacked bar chart to represent the data.

15. Average hourly earnings, including overtime, in January 2000 were as follows:

Province	Salaried employees	Hourly-paid employees
Newfoundland	$19.08	$14.00
Prince Edward Island	19.12	12.16
Nova Scotia	19.13	13.97
New Brunswick	20.16	13.91
Quebec	20.55	14.59
Ontario	22.85	16.59
Manitoba	19.92	14.28
Saskatchewan	20.03	14.67
Alberta	22.14	16.24
British Columbia	22.32	16.27
Canada	21.77	15.73

Source: Statistics Canada.

a) Compare salary earnings and hourly wages by means of a multiple line graph.
b) Use a bi-directional bar chart to compare provincial averages with the national average for salaried employees.

16. Average undergraduate tuition fees for 2001/02 and 2002/03 were as follows:

Province	2001/02	2002/03
Newfoundland	$3036	$2729
Prince Edward Island	3710	3891
Nova Scotia	4855	5214
New Brunswick	3863	4186
Quebec	1842	1851
Ontario	4492	4634
Manitoba	3243	3248
Saskatchewan	4142	4106
Alberta	4030	4165
British Columbia	2527	3165
Canada	3585	3733

Source: E-Stat-*The Daily*, Wednesday, August 21, 2002, University tuition fees.

a) Compare tuition for each year by means of a multiple line graph.
b) Use a bi-directional bar chart to compare the 2002/03 tuition fees with the national average for that year.

17. A large retailer is analyzing departmental sales year over year and compiles the following data:

	Sales ($ millions)	
Department	May 2001	May 2002
Toys	1.2	1.14
Men's clothing	2.7	2.97
Women's clothing	8.8	10.12
Hardware	3.6	3.78
Furniture	13.5	11.88

Construct a bi-directional bar chart showing the change in departmental sales from 2001 to 2002.

18. From 1995 to the present, the average spending on cigarettes, alcohol, and lotteries have increased by 20%, 40%, and 70% respectively, while the average donations to charities have decreased by 10%.

a) Construct a bi-directional bar chart showing the change in spending.

b) If the average spending for alcohol was $300 per year in 1995, what would be the average spending today?

19. Shown below is a reproduction of a product information card for a new DVD player and the data compiled from returned cards.

Model Number ____________ Date Purchased ____________

Name ____________ Address ____________

City ____________ Province ________ Postal Code ________

Name of Store ____________

1. Is this your first DVD player?
☐ YES ☐ NO

2. Purchaser's sex
☐ FEMALE
☐ MALE

3. Do you own a car?
☐ YES ☐ NO

4. Purchaser's age
☐ UNDER 20 ☐ 31 – 40
☐ 20 – 24 ☐ OVER 40
☐ 25 – 30

5. If a gift, what was the occasion?
☐ BIRTHDAY ☐ GRADUATION
☐ CHRISTMAS ☐ OTHER

6. What was the most important factor that influenced your purchase?
☐ PRICE
☐ SALESPERSON
☐ RECOMMENDED
☐ BRAND NAME
☐ ADVERTISING
☐ FEATURES

The following data were compiled from the returned cards:

Question no.	Survey results	
1	Yes (490)	No (50)
2	Male (308)	Female (182)
3	Yes (242)	No (198)
4	Under 20 (66)	20–24 (110)
	25–30 (92)	31–40 (42)
	Over 40 (130)	
5	Birthday (32)	Christmas (41)
	Graduation (28)	Other (12)
6	Price (102)	Salesperson (20)
	Recommended (80)	Advertising (32)
	Brand name (120)	Features (86)

a) What are the two main pieces of information the survey is designed to supply to the researcher?
b) Draw a vertical bar chart showing the factors influencing the decision to buy.
c) Draw a horizontal bar chart showing the reasons for purchasing a DVD player.
d) Construct a pie chart summarizing the age distribution of the purchasers.

20. Draw a high-low-close chart to represent the following data:

	Canadian dollar per U.S. dollar (nearest cent)		
Year	High	Low	Close
1994	$1.41	$1.31	$1.40
1995	1.43	1.33	1.36
1996	1.39	1.33	1.37
1997	1.44	1.33	1.43
1998	1.58	1.40	1.53
1999	1.55	1.44	1.44
2000	1.56	1.43	1.50
2001	1.61	1.49	1.59
2002	1.62	1.50	1.58

Source: © Bank of Canada.

21. Draw a high-low-close chart to represent the following.

	Hi-tech Company		
Year	High	Low	Close
1998	$ 60	$40	$ 55
1999	90	40	80
2000	135	80	132
2001	22	4	6

22. The following table shows the monthly stock prices for Unexpected Technologies Inc. for February through September 2002. Construct a high-low-close chart to represent the data.

	Unexpected Technologies Inc.		
Month	High	Low	Close
February	$27.50	$26.13	$27.00
March	29.50	27.00	28.50
April	34.50	32.13	33.75
May	36.00	33.50	35.00
June	35.00	33.50	33.50
July	35.00	33.75	34.50
August	52.00	34.50	40.00
September	43.00	41.50	42.00

SELF-TEST

1. Investors who put $10 000 into an equity fund or a bond fund on January 1, 1998, came out about the same at the end of 2002. Use the given information to graph their rather different paths on a multiple line graph.

Date	98-01-01	98-12-31	99-12-31	00-12-31	01-12-31	02-12-31
Equity fund	10 000	11 800	13 920	12 980	14 430	16 100
Bond fund	10 000	12 380	12 000	11 650	13 650	16 120

2. After the introduction of the GST in Canada, prices for some goods and services went up, while others went down. Below are a few selected examples for analysis:

Item	Price before GST	Price after GST
Fast food	$ 3.30	$ 3.50
Luggage	80.00	78.27
Telephone	11.50	12.15
Cable TV	20.00	19.13
Taxi fare	8.50	8.91
Long-distance charges	55.00	52.61

a) Draw a clustered bar chart to represent the data.

b) Compare the prices of the items before and after GST by means of a horizontal bi-directional bar chart.

3. The Cousins family compiled a record of their yearly expenditures as follows:

Expenditure	1999	2000	2001	2002
Housing	$15 000	$15 000	$16 800	$15 500
Transportation	1 200	2 800	5 600	5 700
Food	6 200	6 500	5 900	7 800
Clothing	7 400	6 100	10 000	8 900
Entertainment	5 300	2 200	7 300	12 300

a) Construct a stacked area chart for the Cousins family expenditures for the period 1999 to 2002.
b) Construct a stacked bar chart for the 2001 expenditures.
c) Construct a pie chart for the 2002 expenditures.

4. The following table shows the high, low, and closing values for Fly-by-Chance Airlines shares for the period May 8 to May 12, 2002. Construct a high-low-close chart.

Date	High	Low	Close
Monday, May 8	50	45	48
Tuesday, May 9	46	43	46
Wednesday, May 10	59	50	51
Thursday, May 11	38	36	36
Friday, May 12	42	30	36

For an online glossary, go to **www.pearsoned.ca/hummelbrunner**.

Key Terms

Bi-directional bar chart 25
Clustered bar chart 16
Hanging bar chart 25
High-low-close chart 27
HLCO chart 27
Line graph 11
Multiple line graph 11
Pie chart 21
Scatter diagram 9
Simple area chart 15
Simple bar chart 14
Single line graph 11
Stacked area chart 19
Stacked bar chart 18
***XY* graph** 9

CHAPTER 2

Frequency Distributions and Their Graphs

Introduction

Before we can analyze statistical data, they must first be organized. A simple way of doing this is to arrange the data in order of magnitude from lowest to highest value, or vice versa. Such an arrangement is called an array.

Sets of data often contain many values. In such cases arranging data in an array is very time-consuming. A more useful procedure is to group the data into classes. The resulting arrangement is called a frequency distribution.

For a visual picture of the characteristics of a frequency distribution, graphs of the distribution can be constructed. The three types of graphs used are the histogram, the frequency polygon, and the cumulative frequency diagrams.

The relative position of values in a frequency distribution is often of interest. These positional measures, called percentiles, can be determined graphically or by formula.

Learning Outcomes

Upon completion of this chapter you will be able to

1. arrange a small set of unorganized data into an array and use the array to determine the mean, the median, and the mode of the data set;
2. arrange larger sets of unorganized data into frequency distributions;
3. convert a frequency distribution into a relative frequency distribution;
4. calculate, from a frequency distribution, the less-than and more-than cumulative frequency distributions and convert them into cumulative percent distributions;
5. construct the histogram and the frequency polygon of a frequency distribution;
6. construct the two types of cumulative frequency diagrams for a frequency distribution;

7. graphically determine the values of specific percentiles from a less-than cumulative frequency diagram;
8. use formulas to determine the values of specific percentiles for grouped and ungrouped data;
9. compute the percentile rank of a given value in a frequency distribution.

SECTION 2.1

Frequency Distributions

A. Arranging Data in an Array

Table 2.1 is an example of unorganized data.

TABLE 2.1 Number of Units Produced

180	195	194	197	188	176	205	178
200	214	227	162	221	190	198	174
185	200	204	195	216	195	181	188
195	209	198	210	202	215	172	186

A simple way of organizing raw data is to arrange the values in *ascending* or *descending* order of magnitude. Such an arrangement is called an **array**.

○ EXAMPLE 2.1a

Arrange the data in Table 2.1 in the form of an array.

● SOLUTION

To arrange the numbers in ascending order, first rearrange the numbers in each column in order:

180	195	194	162	188	176	172	174
185	200	198	195	202	190	181	178
195	209	204	197	216	195	198	186
200	214	227	210	221	215	205	188

Now list the numbers in their final order by selecting the smallest number across the top of each column (cross the numbers off as you use them):

162	178	186	194	195	200	205	215
172	180	188	195	197	200	209	216
174	181	188	195	198	202	210	221
176	185	190	195	198	204	214	227

B. Advantages of an Array

Apart from the ease with which they can be set up, arrays have other advantages:

1. We can immediately read out the *lowest* value (162) and the *highest* value (227). By computing the *difference* between the two extreme (lowest and highest) values we obtain a statistical measure referred to as the **range** (65).

2. We can easily identify values that appear more than once and thus determine the *most frequently occurring* value. This value represents another statistical measure called the **mode**. Since the value 195 appears four times, the mode of the set of data is 195.
3. We can readily group the data into sections. Since the data set contains 32 values, the lower half ranges from 162 to 195, while the upper half ranges from 195 to 227. The halfway point, called the **median**, is therefore 195.

C. Arranging Data in a Frequency Distribution

While an array of values is useful, arranging large data sets into arrays is tedious and time-consuming. In addition, it is difficult for most humans to recognize underlying relationships in a large, unorganized mass of data. A more useful procedure is to group the data into *classes*. Such an arrangement is called a **frequency distribution**.

○ **EXAMPLE 2.1b**

Construct a frequency distribution for the data set shown in Table 2.1.

● **SOLUTION**

Step 1 Determine the class width and the number of class intervals.

The first thing to consider in constructing a frequency distribution is the number of classes we wish to use and the width of the class interval. The number of **class intervals** is influenced by the number of observations that make up the data set. The larger the number of observations, the larger the number of classes that can be justified. However, it is recommended that the number of classes be no fewer than 6 and no more than 15.

To determine the number of classes and the width of the class intervals we first need to compute the range of values. As previously indicated, the range is the difference between the highest value and the lowest value, that is, $227 - 162 = 65$.

Because of the small number of observations (32 items), the number of classes should be kept low.

For 6 classes, the width of the class intervals would be $65 \div 6 = 10.8$; for 15 classes, the width of the class intervals would be $65 \div 15 = 4.3$.

The **class width** selected needs to be between 4.3 and 10.8. The width selected should be a convenient number such as 5 or 10. Because of the small number of observations in this example, a class width of 10 is a reasonable choice.

We can now obtain the number of class intervals by dividing the range by the class width ($65 \div 10 = 6.5$); this means 7 classes will have to be set up.

Step 2 Set up the classes.
To set up the classes it is now necessary to select the **lower limit** of the first class. While it is preferable to centre class intervals on or near frequently occurring values, it is usually acceptable to select a convenient value less than the smallest observed value as the lowest class limit.

Since the lowest observed value in the data set is 162, a convenient lowest class limit is 160. The lower limits of all classes can now be established by repeatedly adding the width of the class intervals until the highest value in the data set is reached. Accordingly, the lower class limits are 160, 170, 180, 190, 200, 210, 220, and the classes can now be set up as shown in Table 2.2.

Step 3 Determine the class frequencies.
The **class frequencies** are the number of observations that fall into the given classes. Each observation must be assigned to a class, but no observation can appear in more than one class.

The process of assigning the observations in the data set to the classes is referred to as *taking a tally*. This is done by checking off the observations and making a mark for each observation beside the class interval to which the observed value belongs.

For ease of counting, tally marks are usually arranged in groups of five (~~////~~), as shown in Table 2.2.

The class frequencies are now obtained by counting the tallies assigned to each class and then listing the count.

TABLE 2.2 Frequency Distribution

Class interval	Tally	Class frequencies
160 to under 170	/	1
170 to under 180	////	4
180 to under 190	~~////~~ /	6
190 to under 200	~~////~~ ////	9
200 to under 210	~~////~~ /	6
210 to under 220	////	4
220 to under 230	//	2

Note The frequency distribution in Table 2.2 is an example of a *closed-ended* frequency distribution. If the first class (160 to under 170) read "under 170" and/or the last class (220 to under 230) read "220 and over," the distribution would be an *open-ended* frequency distribution.

D. Relative Frequency Distributions

The total number of observations in a data set influences the number of observations in each class. For purposes of comparison the class frequencies can be expressed as a fraction of the total number of observations. These fractions, presented in either fractional, decimal, or percent form, constitute a **relative frequency distribution**.

○ **EXAMPLE 2.1c**

Construct a relative frequency distribution for the frequency distribution shown in Table 2.2.

● **SOLUTION**

The relative frequencies are obtained by dividing the class frequencies by the total number of observations and can be shown in the form of a common fraction, decimal, or percent as shown in Table 2.3.

TABLE 2.3 Relative Frequency Distribution

Class intervals	Class frequencies	Relative frequencies: Fraction	Decimal	Percent
160 to under 170	1	$\frac{1}{32}$	0.031 25	3.125
170 to under 180	4	$\frac{4}{32}$	0.125 00	12.500
180 to under 190	6	$\frac{6}{32}$	0.187 50	18.750
190 to under 200	9	$\frac{9}{32}$	0.281 25	28.125
200 to under 210	6	$\frac{6}{32}$	0.187 50	18.750
210 to under 220	4	$\frac{4}{32}$	0.125 00	12.500
220 to under 230	2	$\frac{2}{32}$	0.062 50	6.250
Totals	32	$\frac{32}{32}$	1.000 00	100.000

Note The sum of the relative frequencies is always 1 (i.e., 100%).

E. Cumulative Frequency Distributions

A **cumulative frequency distribution** shows a running total of the frequencies in the distribution. It can be used to determine how many observations are below or above certain values.

A **cumulative *relative* frequency distribution** is obtained by keeping a running total of the *relative* frequencies. The resulting values are fractions of the total observations in the data set and can be used to determine what percent of the observations are below or above specified values.

○ EXAMPLE 2.1d

Construct a cumulative frequency distribution and a cumulative relative frequency distribution for the class frequencies given in Table 2.3.

● SOLUTION

Compute and record the running totals for the class frequencies and obtain the cumulative relative frequencies by dividing the numbers in the running totals by the total class frequency as shown in Table 2.4.

TABLE 2.4 Cumulative Frequency Distribution and Cumulative Relative Frequency Distribution

Class intervals	Class frequencies	Cumulative frequencies	Cumulative relative frequencies
160 to under 170	1	1	$\frac{1}{32} = 3.125\%$
170 to under 180	4	(1 + 4) = 5	$\frac{5}{32} = 15.625\%$
180 to under 190	6	(5 + 6) = 11	$\frac{11}{32} = 34.375\%$
190 to under 200	9	(11 + 9) = 20	$\frac{20}{32} = 62.500\%$
200 to under 210	6	(20 + 6) = 26	$\frac{26}{32} = 81.250\%$
210 to under 220	4	(26 + 4) = 30	$\frac{30}{32} = 93.750\%$
220 to under 230	2	(30 + 2) = 32	$\frac{32}{32} = 100.000\%$
Total	32		

These calculations can be completed using EXCEL, as demonstrated in USING EXCEL 2.1.

USING EXCEL 2.1

Arrange the data found in Table 2.1 in ascending order. Use EXCEL's built-in statistical functions to determine the largest value, the smallest value, the range, the mode, and the median of the data set. Construct a frequency distribution using EXCEL's Analysis ToolPak, then construct the relative frequency distribution and cumulative frequency distribution of the data.

SOLUTION

Using EXCEL to sort the data,

1. Type the column heading **Number of Units Produced** into cell A1.
2. Enter the data found in Table 2.1 into cells A2–A33 and then select one of the cells in this list.
3. On **Data** menu, click **Sort....**
4. The **Sort** dialog box appears. From the **Sort by** drop-down list, select **Number of Units Produced**; select the **Ascending** option; from the **My list has** options, select the **Header row** option; then click on the **OK** button.

Using EXCEL to determine the largest value, the smallest value, the range, the mode, and the median,

5. Type the notes **is the largest, is the smallest, is the range, is the mode**, and **is the median** into cells D2–D6.
6. Select cell C2.
7. On the toolbar, click on the **Paste Function** button (or on the **Insert** menu, click **Function...**).
8. The **Paste Function** dialog box appears. From the **Function category** list, select **Statistical**; from the **Function name** list, select the **MAX** function; and then click the **OK** button.
9. The input dialog box appears. In the **Number1** input box, type **A2:A33** (or click on beside the **Number1** input box to temporarily hide the input dialog box; select cells A2–A33 on the worksheet; then click on or press the **Enter** key); then click the **OK** button.
10. Select cell C3.
11. Repeat steps 7–9; however in the **Paste Function** dialog box, from the **Function name** list, select the **MIN** function.
12. Select cell C4, and type **=C2-C3** in the formula bar and enter.
13. Select cell C5.
14. Repeat steps 7–9; however in the **Paste Function** dialog box, from the **Function name** list, select the **MODE** function.
15. Select cell C6.
16. Repeat steps 7–9; however in the **Paste Function** dialog box, from the **Function name** list, select the **MEDIAN** function.

Using EXCEL to construct the frequency distribution,

17. Type the column headings **Class Interval** and **Bin** into cells C8 and D8.
18. Using the class intervals determined in Example 2.1b (Table 2.2), type the class interval notes into cells C9–C15.
19. Type the values **169**, **179**, **189**, **199**, **209**, **219**, and **229** into cells D9–D15.To EXCEL, these represent the upper limit of each class interval.
20. On the Tools menu, click **Data Analysis...** (You may need to install the **Analysis ToolPak** add-in on your computer and then load it into EXCEL with the **Add-Ins** dialog box accessed on the **Tools** menu. If you try to load the **Analysis ToolPak** add-in and EXCEL does not install it, you can either install it with the **Add/Remove Programs** feature found in Windows' **Control Panel** or from Microsoft's Office 2000 CD-ROM).
21. The **Data Analysis** dialog box appears. From the **Analysis Tools** list, select **Histogram** and click the **OK** button.
22. The **Histogram** dialog box appears. In the **Input Range** input box, type **$A$2:$A$33** (or click on to select cells A2–A33; then

click on or press the **Enter** key). In the **Bin Range** input box, type **$D$9:$D$15** (or select the cells D9–D15 and return to the input dialog box). Ensure the **Labels** checkbox is deselected (unchecked). From the **Output options**, select the **Output Range** option and type **$C$17** in its input box (or select cell C17 and return to the input dialog box). Ensure that the **Pareto**, **Cumulative Percentage**, and **Chart Output** checkboxes are deselected (unchecked). Click the **OK** button when finished. Delete the contents of cells C25–D25.

Using EXCEL to construct the relative frequency distribution,

23. Select cell C25 and type in the note **Total.**
24. Select cell D25, and type **=SUM(D18:D24)** in the formula bar and enter.
25. Select cell E17 and type the note **Relative Frequencies %.**
26. Select cell E18, and type **=D18/D$25** in the formula bar and enter. **Copy** and **Paste** cell E18 into cells E19–E25. Select cells E18–E25; click on the **Format** menu and select **Cells....** On the **Format Cells** dialog box, click on the **Number** tab and from the **Category** list, select **Percentage** and set the **Decimal places** to 3. Click the **OK** button when finished.

Using EXCEL to construct the cumulative relative frequency distribution,

27. Select cell C27.
28. Repeat steps 20–22, however, from the **Output options** ensure that the **Output Range** option has a cell location of **$C$27** in its input box and that the **Cumulative Percentage** option is selected (checked). Click the **OK** button when finished.
29. Select cells E27–E34 and move them to cells F17–F24. Reformat cells F18–F24 to reflect 3 decimal places (see step 26) and then reformat cells C17–F25 and adjust column widths to make a clear and readable table. Clear the contents and formatting of cells C27–E35 (select cells C27–E35; on the **Edit** menu, click **Clear** and then select **All**).

Some of the steps outlined above can be combined or even eliminated by using other EXCEL methods such as using the **Descriptive Statistics** analysis tool found in the **Analysis ToolPak.**

OUTPUT

File Edit View Insert Format Tools Data Window Help

H1 =

	A	B	C	D	E	F
1	Number of Units Produced					
2	162		227	is the largest value.		
3	172		162	is the smallest value.		
4	174		65	is the range.		
5	176		195	is the mode.		
6	178		195	is the median.		
7	180					
8	181		Class Interval	Bin		
9	185		160 to under 170	169		
10	186		170 to under 180	179		
11	188		180 to under 190	189		
12	188		190 to under 200	199		
13	190		200 to under 210	209		
14	194		210 to under 220	219		
15	195		220 to under 230	229		
16	195					
17	195		*Bin*	*Frequency*	*Relative Frequencies %*	*Cumulative %*
18	195		169	1	3.125%	3.125%
19	197		179	4	12.500%	15.625%
20	198		189	6	18.750%	34.375%
21	198		199	9	28.125%	62.500%
22	200		209	6	18.750%	81.250%
23	200		219	4	12.500%	93.750%
24	202		229	2	6.250%	100.000%
25	204		Total	32	100.000%	
26	205					
27	209					
28	210					
29	214					
30	215					
31	216					
32	221					
33	227					

Two types of cumulative frequency distribution are used:

1. the *less-than* cumulative frequency distribution, which shows the number and/or percentage of the observations that have a value *less than* the **upper limit** of each class;
2. the *more-than* cumulative frequency distribution, which shows the number and/or percentage of the observations that have a value *more than* the **lower limit** of each class.

EXAMPLE 2.1e

For the frequency distribution given in Table 2.5, compute

a) the less-than cumulative frequencies and percents;

b) the more-than cumulative frequencies and percents.

TABLE 2.5 Frequency Distribution

Class interval	Frequency
0 to under 10	4
10 to under 20	8
20 to under 30	7
30 to under 40	3
40 to under 50	2
50 to under 60	1

SOLUTION

a) To construct a less-than cumulative frequency distribution, accumulate the frequencies, starting with the lowest class, and continue through the highest class as shown in Table 2.6.

TABLE 2.6 Less-Than Cumulative Frequency Distribution

Class interval	Class frequency	Upper class limit	Cumulative frequencies	Cumulative percents
0 to under 10	4	10	4	$\frac{4}{25} = 16$
10 to under 20	8	20	$4 + 8 = 12$	$\frac{12}{25} = 48$
20 to under 30	7	30	$12 + 7 = 19$	$\frac{19}{25} = 76$
30 to under 40	3	40	$19 + 3 = 22$	$\frac{22}{25} = 88$
40 to under 50	2	50	$22 + 2 = 24$	$\frac{24}{25} = 96$
50 to under 60	1	60	$24 + 1 = 25$	$\frac{25}{25} = 100$

Notes

1. In a less-than cumulative frequency table, the cumulative frequencies column indicates the number of observations that have a value less than the upper limit of each class; that is,

   4 observations have a value less than 10;
   12 observations have a value less than 20;
   19 observations have a value less than 30;
   22 observations have a value less than 40;
   24 observations have a value less than 50;
   25 (all) observations have a value less than 60.

2. In a similar way the cumulative percents column shows the percent of observations that have a value less than the upper limit of each class; that is,

   16% of the observations have a value less than 10;
   48% of the observations have a value less than 20;
   76% of the observations have a value less than 30;
   88% of the observations have a value less than 40;
   96% of the observations have a value less than 50;
   100% of the observations have a value less than 60.

b) To construct a more-than cumulative frequency distribution, accumulate the frequencies, starting with the highest class, and continue through the lowest class as shown in Table 2.7.

TABLE 2.7 More-Than Cumulative Frequency Distribution

Class interval	Class frequency	Lower class limit	Cumulative frequencies	Cumulative percents
0 to under 10	4	0	$21+4=25$	$\frac{25}{25}=100$
10 to under 20	8	10	$13+8=21$	$\frac{21}{25}=84$
20 to under 30	7	20	$6+7=13$	$\frac{13}{25}=52$
30 to under 40	3	30	$3+3=6$	$\frac{6}{25}=24$
40 to under 50	2	40	$1+2=3$	$\frac{3}{25}=12$
50 to under 60	1	50	1	$\frac{1}{25}=4$

Notes

3. In a more-than cumulative frequency distribution the cumulative frequencies column indicates the number of observations that have a value equal to or more than the lower limit of each class; that is,
   25 out of 25 observations have a value of 0 or more;
   21 out of 25 observations have a value of 10 or more;
   13 out of 25 observations have a value of 20 or more;
   6 out of 25 observations have a value of 30 or more;
   3 out of 25 observations have a value of 40 or more;
   1 out of 25 observations has a value of 50 or more.
4. In a similar way, the cumulative percents column shows the percent of observations that have a value equal to or more than the lower limit of each class; that is,
   100% of the observations have a value of 0 or more;
   84% of the observations have a value of 10 or more;
   52% of the observations have a value of 20 or more;
   24% of the observations have a value of 30 or more;
   12% of the observations have a value of 40 or more;
   4% of the observations have a value of 50 or more.

EXERCISE 2.1

1. Last week's production for a plant of 24 employees was as follows:

213	240	260	203	234	245	245	247
267	256	219	227	266	251	245	239
238	245	250	225	253	242	248	271

a) Arrange the data in the form of an array.
b) From the array in **(a)** determine
  i) the range;
  ii) the mode;
  iii) the median.
c) Arrange the data in the form of a frequency distribution, using equal class intervals of size 10 starting with 200.
d) Compute the less-than cumulative frequencies and percents.
e) Compute the more-than cumulative frequencies and percents.

2. The following data represent the daily earnings ($) of the employees in an assembly plant:

120	60	132	96	116	92	116	116
92	100	160	166	196	176	108	126
68	192	144	128	152	128	144	130
100	116	140	96	168	126	98	144
116	72	180	66	176	88	164	120

a) Arrange the data in the form of an array.
b) From the array in (a) determine
   i) the range;
   ii) the mode;
   iii) the median.
c) Arrange the data in the form of a frequency distribution using equal class intervals of size 20 with 60 as the lowest class limit.
d) Compute the less-than cumulative frequencies and percents.
e) Compute the more-than cumulative frequencies and percents.

3. Consider the following frequency distribution:

Class interval	Frequency
0 to under 10	4
10 to under 20	6
20 to under 30	10
30 to under 40	8
40 to under 50	6
50 to under 60	4
60 to under 70	2

a) Construct the less-than and more-than cumulative frequency and percent distributions.
b) How many of the observations in the given frequency distribution have
   i) a value less than 40?
   ii) a value of 20 or more?
c) What percent of the observations in the given frequency distribution have
   i) a value less than 50?
   ii) a value of 40 or more?

4. Consider the following information about the wages of a group of employees:

Weekly wages ($)	Frequency
360 to under 400	24
400 to under 440	40
440 to under 480	55
480 to under 520	36
520 to under 560	25
560 to under 600	12
600 to under 640	3

a) Construct the less-than and more-than cumulative frequency and percent distributions.
b) How many employees earn weekly wages of
   i) $440 or more?
   ii) less than $560?

c) What percent of the employees earn weekly wages of
   i) $520 or more?
   ii) less than $600?

SECTION 2.2

Graphs of Frequency Distributions

A. The Histogram of a Frequency Distribution

The **histogram** of a frequency distribution is a vertical bar graph of the class frequencies. The horizontal axis is used for the class limits and the vertical axis for the class frequencies.

EXAMPLE 2.2a

Construct a histogram for the frequency distribution in the following table:

TABLE 2.8

Test score	Number of students
40 to under 50	1
50 to under 60	3
60 to under 70	9
70 to under 80	14
80 to under 90	11
90 to under 100	2

SOLUTION

The lowest class limit (40) in the distribution is arbitrarily marked as the starting point for the horizontal scale. The remaining class limits are then marked at equal intervals.

The vertical scale starts at zero and must accommodate the largest class frequency (14).

Vertical bars are then drawn over each class interval to represent the number of observed values in that class. In our example a bar of height "1" is drawn over the line segment "40 to 50"; a bar of height "3" is drawn over the line segment "50 to 60"; and so on.

For ease of construction it is best to draw the first bar over the interval showing the highest frequency. In our case, a bar of height "14" over the line segment "70 to 80" should be the first bar drawn. The remaining bars can then be drawn easily to the left and right of the highest bar.

Note that, unlike simple bar graphs, there is no space between the bars in a histogram.

FIGURE 2.1 Histogram

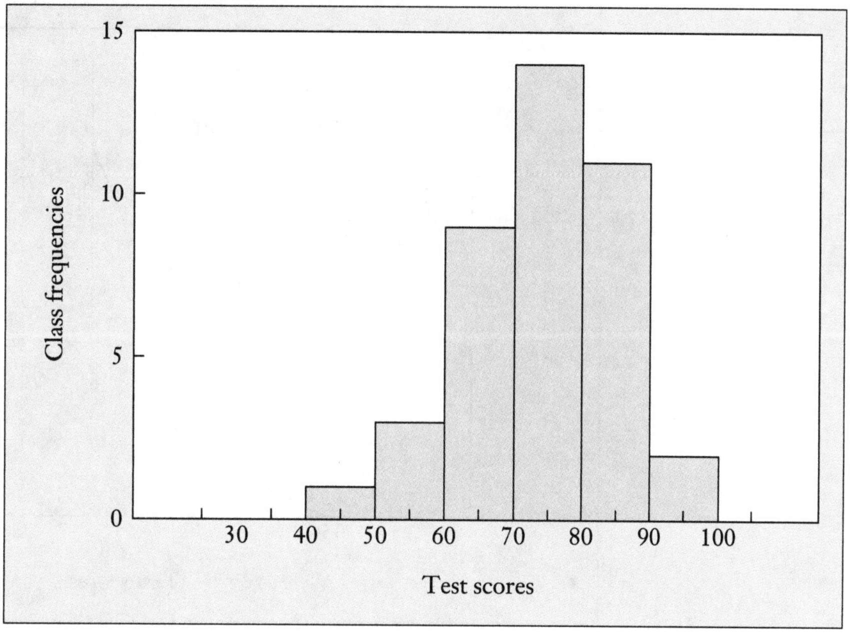

B. The Frequency Polygon of a Frequency Distribution

The **frequency polygon** of a frequency distribution is a simple line graph joining the *midpoints* of the bars of a histogram.

○ EXAMPLE 2.2b

Construct the frequency polygon for the frequency distribution given in Example 2.2a (Table 2.8).

● SOLUTION

Mark the class midpoint (45) of the lowest class (40 to under 50) on the horizontal scale. Mark the remaining class midpoints (55, 65, 75, 85, 95) at equal intervals. Mark one additional point at each end of the scale (35 and 105).

Use the vertical axis for the class frequencies. The scale used starts at zero and must accommodate the greatest class frequency. Now plot the frequency in each class as a dot above the class midpoint. Join the dots by straight line segments. Complete the polygon by connecting the points representing the frequencies in the lowest and highest class respectively to the extra midpoints on the horizontal axis.

FIGURE 2.2 Frequency Polygon

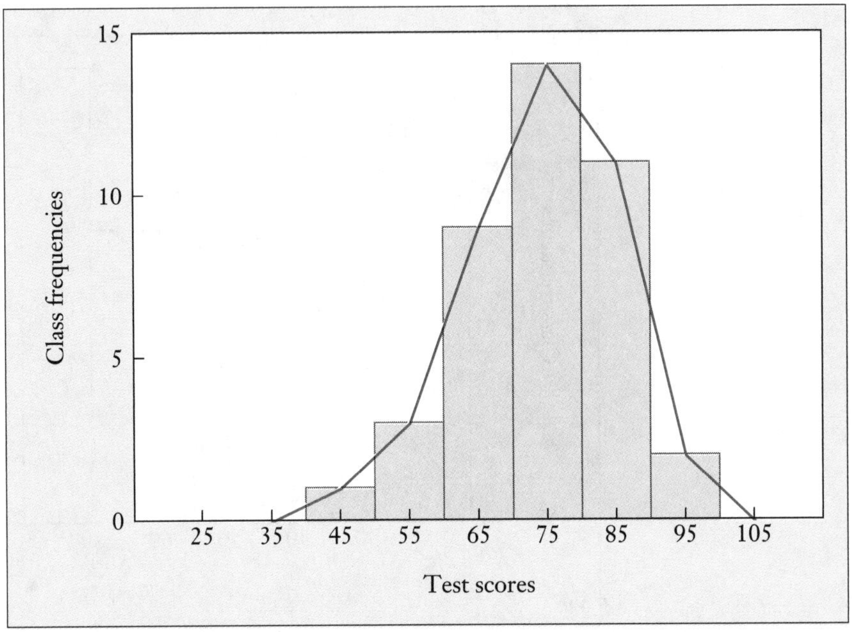

C. Cumulative Frequency Diagrams

Cumulative frequency diagrams are constructed by plotting the cumulative frequencies. Depending on the type of cumulative frequency distribution (as introduced in Section 2.1), we distinguish between two cumulative frequency diagrams:

1. the *less-than cumulative frequency diagram*, obtained by plotting the less-than cumulative frequencies against the upper class limits;
2. the *more-than cumulative frequency diagram*, obtained by plotting the more-than cumulative frequencies against the lower class limits.

○ **EXAMPLE 2.2c**

For the frequency distribution used in Example 2.2a (Table 2.8),

a) construct the less-than cumulative frequency diagram;
b) determine how many students scored less than 65 on the test.

● **SOLUTION**

a) First obtain the less-than cumulative frequencies and the less-than cumulative percents shown as follows:

Test score	Number of students	Less-than cumulative frequency	Less-than cumulative percents
40 to under 50	1	1	2.50
50 to under 60	3	4	10.00
60 to under 70	9	13	32.50
70 to under 80	14	27	67.50
80 to under 90	11	38	95.00
90 to under 100	2	40	100.00
Total	40		

The horizontal axis of the diagram is used to mark the class limits, while the vertical axis is used for the cumulative frequencies or the cumulative relative frequencies (percents).

Since the cumulative relative frequencies range from 0% to 100% for any frequency distribution, the cumulative percents are preferred for the vertical scale.

Now plot the less-than cumulative percents against the upper limits of the corresponding class. For example, plot

2.5% against the upper limit (test score) 50;
10.0% against the upper limit (test score) 60;
32.5% against the upper limit (test score) 70;
67.5% against the upper limit (test score) 80;
95.0% against the upper limit (test score) 90;
100.0% against the upper limit (test score) 100.

By now, a point is plotted against every class limit except the lowest limit of 40.

Since no observation in the frequency distribution has a value less than the lowest limit, zero is plotted against the lowest limit of 40. The points can now be joined to obtain the less-than cumulative frequency curve.

b) The less-than frequency diagram indicates the number of observations in the frequency distribution that have a value less than a chosen value.

To determine how many students scored less than 65, draw a perpendicular line from the point marked 65 on the horizontal axis to the less-than cumulative frequency line.

The point of intersection indicates the percent of students who scored less than 65 on the test.

To read the percent on the vertical scale, draw a line at right angles to the vertical scale from the point of intersection. The indication is that approximately 20% of the number of students in the class, that is 8 students, scored less than 65 on the test.

FIGURE 2.3 Less-than Cumulative Frequency Diagram

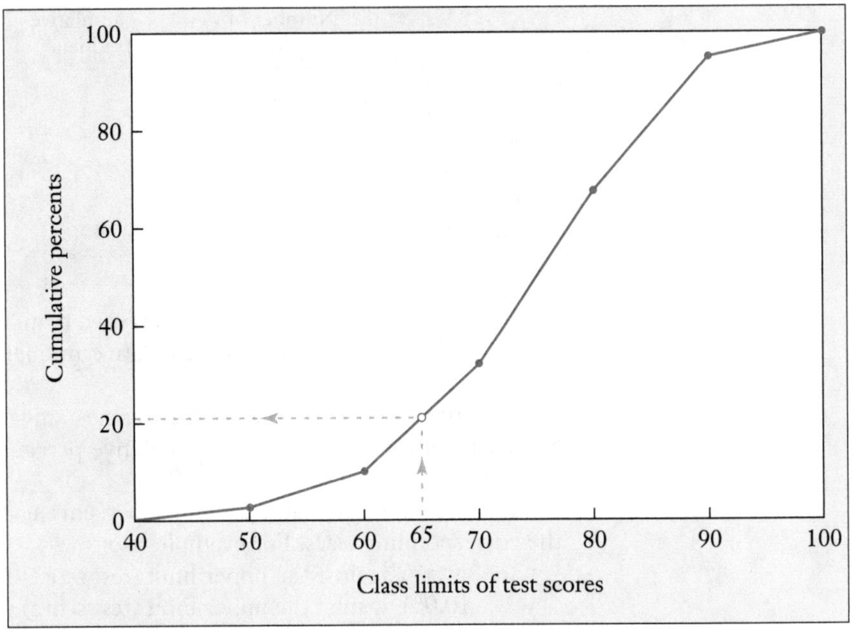

○ **EXAMPLE 2.2d**

For the frequency distribution used in Example 2.2a (Table 2.8),

a) construct the more-than cumulative frequency diagram;

b) determine how many students scored 85 or more on the test.

● **SOLUTION**

a) First determine the more-than cumulative frequencies and the more-than cumulative percents as shown:

Test score	Number of students	More-than cumulative frequency	More-than cumulative percents
40 to under 50	1	40	100.00
50 to under 60	3	39	97.50
60 to under 70	9	36	90.00
70 to under 80	14	27	67.50
80 to under 90	11	13	32.50
90 to under 100	2	2	5.00
Total	40		

The axes are used in the same way as for the less-than cumulative frequency diagram, and the scales are identical. However, the more-than cumulative percents are plotted against the lower limits of the corresponding class. For example, plot

100.0% against the lower limit (test score) 40;
97.5% against the lower limit (test score) 50;
90.0% against the lower limit (test score) 60;
67.5% against the lower limit (test score) 70;
32.5% against the lower limit (test score) 80;
5.0% against the lower limit (test score) 90.

By now, a point is plotted against every class limit except the highest limit, 100.

Since no observation in a frequency distribution has a value more than the highest limit, zero is plotted against the highest class limit 100. The points can now be joined to graph the more-than cumulative frequency curve.

b) The more-than frequency diagram indicates the number of observations in the frequency distribution that have a value more than or equal to a chosen value.

To determine how many students scored 85 or more, draw a perpendicular from the point marked 85 on the horizontal axis to the more-than cumulative frequency curve. The point of intersection represents the number of students who scored 85 or more on the test.

Draw a line from that point at right angles to the vertical axis. The line indicates that approximately 20% of the number of students, that is, 8 students, scored 85 or more on the test.

FIGURE 2.4 More-than Cumulative Frequency Diagram

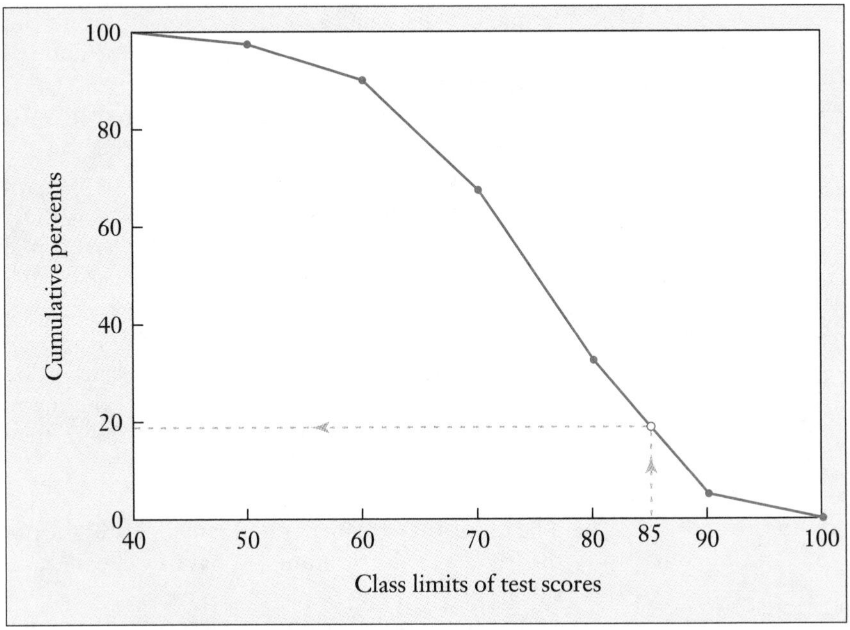

EXERCISE 2.2

1. For the following frequency distribution (refer to Exercise 2.1, Question **3**),
   a) construct the histogram;
   b) construct the frequency polygon;
   c) construct the less-than cumulative frequency diagram;
   d) construct the more-than cumulative frequency diagram;
   e) graphically determine the number of observations that have
      i) a value less than 45, and
      ii) a value of 25 or more.

Class interval	Frequency
0 to under 10	4
10 to under 20	6
20 to under 30	10
30 to under 40	8
40 to under 50	6
50 to under 60	4
60 to under 70	2

2. For the following frequency distribution (refer to Exercise 2.1, Question **4**),
   a) construct the histogram;
   b) construct the frequency polygon;
   c) construct the less-than cumulative frequency diagram;

d) construct the more-than cumulative frequency diagram;
e) graphically determine the number of employees who earned weekly wages
  i) of $450 or more, and
  ii) less than $515.

Weekly wages (in dollars)	Frequency
360 to under 400	24
400 to under 440	40
440 to under 480	55
480 to under 520	36
520 to under 560	25
560 to under 600	12
600 to under 640	3

3. For the following frequency distribution,
a) construct the histogram;
b) construct the frequency polygon;
c) construct the less-than cumulative frequency diagram;
d) construct the more-than cumulative frequency diagram;
e) determine the number of observations having
  i) a value less than 190, and
  ii) a value of 150 or more.

Class interval	Frequency
100 to under 120	4
120 to under 140	18
140 to under 160	44
160 to under 180	92
180 to under 200	54
200 to under 220	26
220 to under 240	2

4. For the following frequency distribution,
a) construct the histogram;
b) construct the frequency polygon;
c) construct the less-than cumulative frequency diagram;
d) construct the more-than cumulative frequency diagram;
e) determine the number of observations that have
i) a value of 10 or more, and
ii) a value less than 16.

Class interval	Frequency
0 to under 4	42
4 to under 8	76
8 to under 12	135
12 to under 16	140
16 to under 20	127
20 to under 24	56
24 to under 28	24

SECTION 2.3

Percentiles

A. Meaning of the Term Percentile

Percentiles divide a set of data into 100 equal parts. They are used as *positional* measures to indicate what percent of the observations in the data set have a value less than a specified value. Percentiles are numbered from 1 to 100. The position number or rank of a desired percentile is selected from the set of whole numbers defined by $x = \{1, 2, 3, 4, \ldots, 98, 99, 100\}$.

The value of a particular percentile is represented by the symbol P_x. Thus the symbol P_{20} refers to the value of an observation that lies at the 20th percentile. In Example 2.2c we determined that 20% of the number of students in the class scored less than 65; that is, $P_{20} = 65$.

B. Graphical Determination of Percentiles

The value of a desired percentile as well as the rank number of a given value in a data set can be obtained graphically from the less-than cumulative frequency diagram.

EXAMPLE 2.3a

The frequency distribution that follows represents the hourly earnings of a group of employees.

a) Determine the hourly earnings of an employee at the 90th percentile.
b) Determine the percentile rank of an employee who earns \$7.20/h.

Hourly earnings (in dollars)	Number of employees
6.00 to under 6.50	3
6.50 to under 7.00	28
7.00 to under 7.50	64
7.50 to under 8.00	56
8.00 to under 8.50	42
8.50 to under 9.00	22
9.00 to under 9.50	2
9.50 to under 10.00	3

SOLUTION

First compute the less-than cumulative frequencies and percents as shown below:

Hourly earnings (in dollars)	Number of employees	Cumulative frequencies	Cumulative percents
6.00 to under 6.50	3	3	1.4
6.50 to under 7.00	28	31	14.1
7.00 to under 7.50	64	95	43.2
7.50 to under 8.00	56	151	68.6
8.00 to under 8.50	42	193	87.7
8.50 to under 9.00	22	215	97.7
9.00 to under 9.50	2	217	98.6
9.50 to under 10.00	3	220	100.0

Now construct the less-than cumulative frequency diagram (see Figure 2.5).

a) To determine the hourly earnings at the 90th percentile, draw a line parallel to the horizontal axis from the 90% mark to the less-than cumulative frequency diagram. From the point of intersection draw a line parallel to the vertical axis to the horizontal axis and read the value at the horizontal scale. This indicates that hourly earnings of \$8.60 lie at the 90th percentile.

FIGURE 2.5 Less-than Cumulative Frequency Diagram

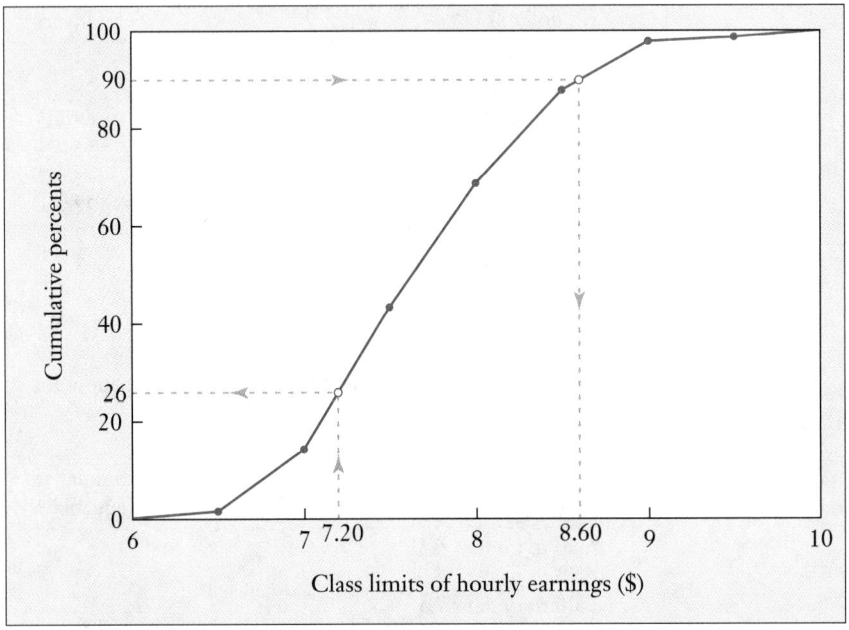

b) To determine the percentile rank for hourly earnings of \$7.20, reverse the process used in (a). Locate the position of \$7.20 on the horizontal scale. Draw a line parallel to the vertical axis to the less-than cumulative frequency line. From the point of intersection draw a line parallel to the horizontal axis to the vertical axis and read off the percent on the vertical scale. This indicates that hourly earnings of \$7.20 lie at the 26th percentile.

C. *Special Cases*

Some of the more frequently used percentiles have specific names, as follows:

1. The **median** is the value that occupies the *halfway* position:

$$\text{MEDIAN} = P_{50}$$

2. The **quartiles** are the values that occupy the *quarter* positions:

$$\text{FIRST QUARTILE}, \quad Q_1 = P_{25}$$
$$\text{THIRD QUARTILE}, \quad Q_3 = P_{75}$$

3. The **deciles** are the values that occupy the positions evenly divisible by 10:

$$D_1 = P_{10}; \qquad D_2 = P_{20}; \qquad D_3 = P_{30}; \qquad \text{etc.}$$

○ EXAMPLE 2.3b

For the frequency distribution in Example 2.3a, graphically determine the value of

a) the median;
b) Q_1 and Q_3;
c) D_6.

● SOLUTION

Use the less-than cumulative frequency diagram constructed in Example 2.3a and reproduced as follows. From the percentile positions marked on the vertical scale, draw lines parallel to the horizontal axis to the less-than cumulative frequency line. From the points of intersection, draw lines parallel to the vertical axis to intersect the horizontal axis.

Read off the hourly earnings on the horizontal scale.

a) The value of the median (P_{50}) = 7.64.
b) The value of Q_1 (P_{25}) = 7.19; the value of Q_3 (P_{75}) = 8.16.
c) The value of D_6 (P_{60}) = 7.83.

FIGURE 2.6 Less-than Cumulative Frequency Diagram

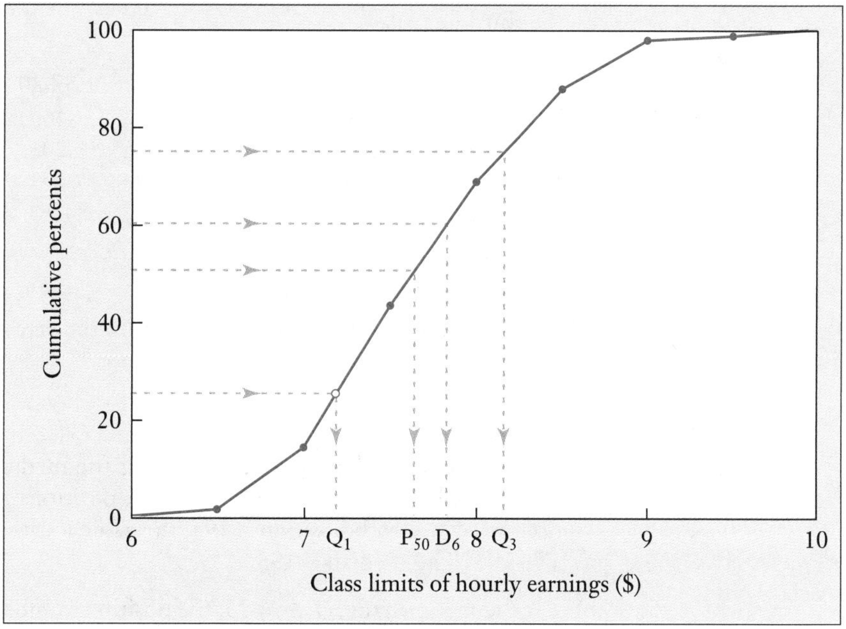

D. Computing Percentiles by Formula — Ungrouped Data

Provided the data are first arranged in an *ascending* array, the position number of the percentiles within the array can be computed by using the formula

$$\text{Position number of } P_x \text{ within the array} = \frac{N+1}{100}(x)$$ ←*Formula* 2.1

where P_x = the value at the xth percentile;
x = the number of the desired percentile;
N = the total number of observations in the data set.

This formula can also be used to determine the position number of percentiles for arrays that have been grouped by value. In this case N is the sum of the frequencies in the groups of values.

EXAMPLE 2.3c

For the following data (arranged into an array in Example 2.1a), determine
a) the median;
b) the first quartile;
c) the third quartile.

162	178	186	194	195	200	205	215
172	180	188	195	197	200	209	216
174	181	188	195	198	202	210	221
176	185	190	195	198	204	214	227

SOLUTION

a) The number of observations in the array, $N = 32$; for the median, $x = 50$; the position number of the median within the array

$$= \frac{(N+1)}{100}(x) = \frac{(32+1)}{100}(50) = \frac{33}{2} = 16.50.$$

The position number 16.5 indicates that the median lies halfway between the values located at the 16th and 17th positions in the array. The value occupying the 16th position is 195; the value located at the 17th position is also 195. The median is 195.

b) For the first quartile, $Q_1, x = 25$; the position number of Q_1 within the array

$$= \frac{(32+1)}{100}(25) = \frac{33}{4} = 8.25.$$

This means Q_1 lies one-quarter of the distance between the values located at the 8th and 9th position in the array. The value occupying the 8th position is 185; the value at the 9th position is 186.

$$Q_1 = 185 + 0.25(186 - 185) = 185 + 0.25 = 185.25$$

c) For the third quartile, Q_3, $x = 75$; the position number of Q_3 within the array

$$= \frac{(32+1)}{100}(75) = \frac{33}{4}(3) = 24.75.$$

Q_3 lies three-quarters of the distance between the values located at the 24th and 25th position in the array. The value located at the 24th position is 204; the value at the 25th position is 205.

$$Q_3 = 204 + 0.75(205 - 204) = 204 + 0.75 = 204.75$$

E. Computing Percentiles by Formula — Grouped Data

For frequency distributions the *value* at a given percentile can be obtained by using the formula

$$P_x = L_x + (i)\left(\frac{\frac{Nx}{100} - \sum f_c}{f_x}\right)$$ ←*Formula 2.2*

where P_x = the value at the xth percentile;
x = the number of the desired percentile;
N = total number of observations;
i = the size of the class interval;
L_x = the *lower* limit of the class containing the xth percentile;
f_x = the number of observations in the class containing the xth percentile;
$\sum f_c$ = the *cumulative* frequencies below the class containing the xth percentile.

Note The symbol $\sum$, read "sigma," is the Greek capital letter "S" and denotes the summation of values.

EXAMPLE 2.3d

For the frequency distribution given below (see Example 2.3a), compute (a)P_{85}; (b) D_6; (c) Q_1; (d) Q_3; (e) the median.

Hourly earnings (in dollars)	Number of employees
6.00 to under 6.50	3
6.50 to under 7.00	28
7.00 to under 7.50	64
7.50 to under 8.00	56
8.00 to under 8.50	42
8.50 to under 9.00	22
9.00 to under 9.50	2
9.50 to under 10.00	3

SOLUTION

First compute the less-than cumulative frequencies and percents as shown here:

Hourly earnings (in dollars)	Number of employees	Cumulative frequencies	Cumulative percents
6.00 to under 6.50	3	3	1.4
6.50 to under 7.00	28	31	14.1
7.00 to under 7.50	64	95	43.2
7.50 to under 8.00	56	151	68.6
8.00 to under 8.50	42	193	87.7
8.50 to under 9.00	22	215	97.7
9.00 to under 9.50	2	217	98.6
9.50 to under 10.00	3	220	100.0

a) The values of the variables appearing in the formula are now determined as follows:

$x = 85$ This is the rank number of the desired percentile.

$N = 220$ This is the total number of observations in the frequency distribution; it is the final number in the cumulative frequencies column.

$i = 0.50$ This is the width of the class intervals; it is determined by computing the difference between two successive class limits (e.g., $6.50 - 6.00 = 0.50$).

$L_x = 8.00$ This is the *lower* limit of the class containing the desired percentile. To determine this value, locate the cumulative percent that is closest to but greater than the rank number of the desired percentile. For the 85th percentile, the cumulative percent closest to 85 but greater than 85 is 87.7. Now read off the lower limit of the class in the column listing the class limits.

$f_x = 42$ This is the frequency in the class containing the desired percentile. This number is located in the frequency column next to the class.

$\sum f_c = 151$ This is the cumulative frequency below the class containing the desired percentile. The number is located in the cumulative frequencies column just before the class containing the desired percentile.

Now substitute in Formula 2.2 and compute P_{85}:

$$P_{85} = 8.00 + (0.50)\left(\frac{\frac{(220)(85)}{100} - 151}{42}\right)$$

$$= 8.00 + (0.50)\left(\frac{187 - 151}{42}\right)$$

$$= 8.00 + (0.50)\frac{36}{42}$$

$$= 8.00 + 0.43$$

$$= 8.43$$

The value at the 85th percentile is \$8.43; that is, 85 percent of the employees earn hourly wages of less than \$8.43.

b) $D_6 = P_{60}$; $x = 60$; $N = 220$; $i = 0.50$; $L_x = 7.50$; $f_x = 56$; $\sum f_c = 95$
Use the following pattern to locate L_x, f_x, and $\sum f_c$ in the frequency distribution table:

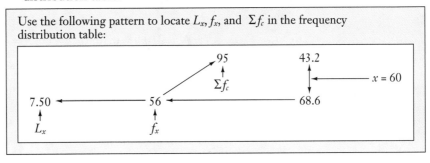

Use the following pattern to locate L_x, f_x, and Σf_c in the frequency distribution table:

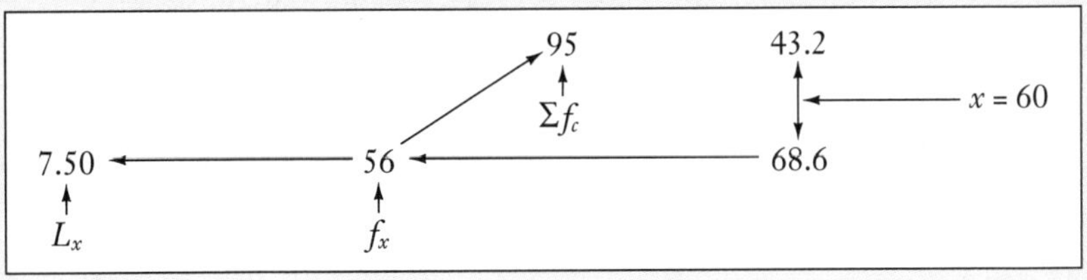

$$D_6 = P_{60} = 7.50 + (0.50)\left(\frac{\frac{(220)(60)}{100} - 95}{56}\right)$$

$$= 7.50 + (0.50)\left(\frac{132 - 95}{56}\right)$$

$$= 7.50 + (0.50)\frac{37}{56}$$

$$= 7.50 + 0.33$$

$$= 7.83$$

The 6th decile is \$7.83; that is, 60 percent of the employees earn less than \$7.83 per hour.

c) $Q_1 = P_{25}$; $x = 25$; $N = 220$; $i = 0.50$; $L_x = 7.00$; $f_x = 64$; $\sum f_c = 31$

$$Q_1 = 7.00 + (0.50)\left(\frac{\frac{(220)(25)}{100} - 31}{64}\right)$$

$$= 7.00 + (0.50)\frac{24}{64}$$

$$= 7.00 + 0.19$$

$$= 7.19$$

The first quartile is \$7.19; that is, 25 percent of the employees earn less than \$7.19.

d) $Q_3 = P_{75}$; $x = 75$; $N = 220$; $i = 0.50$; $L_x = 8.00$; $f_x = 42$; $\sum f_c = 151$

$$Q_3 = 8.00 + (0.50)\left(\frac{\frac{(220)(75)}{100} - 151}{42}\right)$$

$$= 8.00 + (0.50)\frac{14}{42}$$

$$= 8.00 + 0.17$$

$$= 8.17$$

The third quartile is 8.17; that is, 75 percent of the employees earn less than \$8.17.

e) Median = P_{50}; $x = 50$; $N = 220$; $i = 0.50$; $L_x = 7.50$; $f_x = 56$; $\sum f_c = 95$

$$\text{Median} = 7.50 + (0.50)\left(\frac{\frac{(220)(50)}{100} - 95}{56}\right)$$

$$= 7.50 + (0.50)\frac{15}{56}$$

$$= 7.50 + 0.13$$

$$= 7.63$$

The median is 7.63; that is, 50 percent of the employees earn less than \$7.63.

F. *Computing the Percentile Rank of a Given Value*

The percentile rank of any given value in a frequency distribution can be found using the percentile formula. The difference in this type of problem is that the value of P_x is known, while x has to be determined.

This can be done by determining N, i, L_x, f_x, and $\sum f_c$, and then substituting in the formula and solving the resulting equation for x.

○ **EXAMPLE 2.3e**

For the frequency distribution given in Example 2.3a, determine the percentile rank of hourly earnings of (a) \$8.90; (b) \$6.45.

● **SOLUTION**

a) $P_x = 8.90$; $N = 220$; $i = 0.50$; $L_x = 8.50$ (since 8.90 is located between 8.50 and 9.00); $f_x = 22$; $\sum f_c = 193$.

$$8.90 = 8.50 + (0.50)\left(\frac{\frac{220x}{100} - 193}{22}\right)$$

$$8.90 = 8.50 + (0.50)\frac{2.20x - 193}{22}$$

$$8.90 - 8.50 = (0.50)\frac{2.20x - 193}{22}$$

$$(0.40)(22) = (0.50)(2.20x - 193)$$

$$8.80 = 1.10x - 96.50$$

$$105.30 = 1.10x$$

$$x = 95.7$$

Hourly earnings of \$8.90 lie at the 96th percentile.

b) $P_x = 6.45$; $N = 220$; $i = 0.50$; $L_x = 6.00$; $f_x = 3$; $\sum f_c = 0$ (the cumulative frequency below 6.00 is zero)

$$6.45 = 6.00 + (0.50)\left(\frac{\frac{220x}{100} - 0}{3}\right)$$

$$0.45 = (0.50)\frac{2.20x - 0}{3}$$

$$3(0.45) = (0.50)(2.20x - 0)$$

$$1.35 = 1.10x$$

$$x = 1.23$$

Hourly earnings of \$6.45 lie at the 2nd percentile.

EXERCISE 2.3

1. For the following frequency distribution (refer to Exercise 2.1, Question **3**), determine graphically the value of
a) the 65th percentile;
b) the 4th decile;
c) the first quartile;
d) the median;
e) the percentile rank of a value of 15.

Class interval	Frequency
0 to under 10	4
10 to under 20	6
20 to under 30	10
30 to under 40	8
40 to under 50	6
50 to under 60	4
60 to under 70	2

2. For the following frequency distribution (refer to Exercise 2.1, Question **4**), determine graphically the value of
a) the 35th percentile;
b) the 9th decile;
c) the third quartile;
d) the median;
e) the percentile rank of weekly wages of \$550.

Weekly wages (in dollars)	Frequency
360 to under 400	24
400 to under 440	40
440 to under 480	55
480 to under 520	36
520 to under 560	25
560 to under 600	12
600 to under 640	3

3. Use the percentile formula to verify your solutions to Question **1**.

4. Use the percentile formula to verify your solutions to Question **2**.

5. For the following frequency distribution (refer to Exercise 2.2, Question **3**),
a) determine graphically the value of
i) Q_1,
ii) Q_3,
iii) the median,
iv) the percentile rank of the value 190;
b) verify your answers in **(a)** by using the percentile formula.

Class interval	Frequency
100 to under 120	4
120 to under 140	18
140 to under 160	44
160 to under 180	92
180 to under 200	54
200 to under 220	26
220 to under 240	2

6. For the following frequency distribution (refer to Exercise 2.2, Question **4**),
a) determine graphically the value of
i) Q_1,
ii) Q_3,
iii) the median,
iv) the percentile rank of the value 16;
b) verify your answers in **(a)** by using the percentile formula.

Class interval	Frequency
0 to under 4	42
4 to under 8	76
8 to under 12	135
12 to under 16	140
16 to under 20	127
20 to under 24	56
24 to under 28	24

7. The frequency distribution of soccer players in Canada is as follows:

Age of players	Number of players
10 to under 15	196 500
15 to under 20	107 400
20 to under 35	32 900

Using the percentile formula, determine the value of

a) the median;
b) the third quartile;
c) the 95th percentile;
d) the percentile rank of a 21-year-old player.

8. A major Canadian commercial real estate developer's office buildings have the following age distribution:

Building age (years)	Number of buildings
1 to under 10	18
10 to under 20	37
20 to under 30	44
30 to under 40	134
40 to under 50	107

Using the percentile formula, determine the value of

a) the first decile;
b) the first quartile;
c) the median;
c) the 80th percentile;
d) the percentile rank of a 7-year-old building.

REVIEW EXERCISE

1. A provincial government's education survey has determined that, on average, 100 high school students will achieve the following levels of education:

Grade	9	10	11	12
Number of students	8	27	26	39

a) Construct the less-than and more-than cumulative frequency and percent distributions.
b) What percent of students
  i) do not graduate from high school?
  ii) have less than Grade 11 education?

2. Final marks earned by 1000 college students in an introductory statistics course were as follows:

Marks	A	B	C	D	F
Number of Students	100	300	500	50	50

a) Construct the less-than and more-than cumulative frequency and percent distribution.
b) What percent of students
  i) do not get a grade of C or better?
  ii) have a grade of lower than B?

3. The following open-ended distribution of share prices was recorded by the Toronto Stock Exchange at the close of trading on Friday:

Share price	Number of stocks
Penny stocks (under $5.00)	492
$5.00 to under $10.00	264
$10.00 to under $15.00	168
$15.00 to under $20.00	96
$20.00 to under $25.00	60
$25.00 and over	120

a) Construct the less-than and more-than cumulative frequencies and the percent distributions.
b) How many of the stocks were not penny stocks?
c) What percent of the stocks were
  i) $15.00 or more?
  ii) $25.00 or more?
  iii) less than $20.00?
  iv) under $10.00?
d) Compute the share price for a stock at
  i) the 60th percentile;
  ii) the first quartile.
e) Compute the percentile rank for a stock trading at $12.00.

4. Family incomes reported from a survey taken at a recent boat show were as follows:

Incomes	Number of Respondents
$0 to under $20 000	5
$20 000 to under $40 000	30
$40 000 to under $60 000	41
$60 000 to under $80 000	20
$80 000 and over	4

a) Construct the less-than and more-than cumulative frequency and percent distribution.
b) What percent of incomes were $40 000 or more?
c) Compute the income for the 80th percentile.

5. An industry survey has determined that the average hourly earnings of construction employees in each province are as follows:

BC	Alta	Sask	Man	Ont
$19.91	$19.19	$17.62	$17.48	$20.82

Que	NB	NS	PEI	Nfld
$18.67	$17.60	$17.55	$16.35	$17.75

a) Organize the data in an ascending array.
b) Which province appears to be
  i) the poorest?
  ii) the richest?
c) Determine
  i) the range;
  ii) the mode;
  iii) the median.

6. The following are IQ scores for 10 university students who were tested at the Student Counselling Services:

Student IQ Scores				
98	132	125	118	115
118	122	120	134	109

a) Organize the data in an ascending array.
b) Determine
  i) the range;
  ii) the mode;
  iii) the median.

7. The manager of a college pub recorded the number of beverages each student consumed on a Friday night and organized the data as follows:

Number of beverages	1	2	3	4	5	6 or more
Number of students	28	48	43	11	8	2

a) Construct the less-than and the more-than cumulative frequency and percent distributions.
b) How many students consumed
  i) 3 beverages or more?
  ii) less than 5 beverages?
c) What percent of the students had
  i) more than 5 beverages?
  ii) 2 beverages or less?

8. The supervisor of a postal station has recorded the number of sick days taken by his employees in a year and organized the data as follows:

Number of sick days	1	2	3	4	5 or more
Number of employees	100	150	500	200	50

a) Construct the less-than and the more-than cumulative frequency and percent distribution.
b) How many employees took 3 or more sick days?
c) What percent of employees had less than 2 sick days?

9. The data below lists the test marks, out of 100, for a night-school statistics class:

74	45	53	84	63	72	88	92	56	74	79	63
97	49	67	73	78	80	51	66	61	80	68	64
58	66	70	78	64	69	42	85	73	65	68	62
55	63	71	79	87	62	67	72	77	71	61	51

a) Arrange the data in the form of an array.
b) Determine
 i) the range;
 ii) the mode;
 iii) the median.
c) Organize the data into a frequency distribution with a lowest class limit of 40 and class intervals of 10.
d) Compute the less-than cumulative frequencies and percents.
e) Compute the more-than cumulative frequencies and percents.
f) Compute the test score that lies at
 i) the 4th decile;
 ii) the third quartile.
g) Compute the percentile rank for a test score of 81.
h) Construct the histogram and the frequency polygon.
i) Construct the less-than and more-than cumulative frequency diagrams.

10. The following data lists the sales per day that a telemarketer had during his first 20 days of work:

Day	1	2	3	4	5	6	7	8	9	10
Number of Sales	2	2	1	5	6	6	7	10	10	9

Day	11	12	13	14	15	16	17	18	19	20
Number of Sales	15	14	12	12	8	6	6	6	9	10

a) Arrange the data in the form of an array.
b) Determine
 i) the range;
 ii) the mode;
 iii) the median.
c) Compute the 3rd decile.

11. A survey of firms produced the following average starting salaries for college graduates by academic area:

Nursing	$38 742	Marketing	$28 684
Engineering	36 614	Accounting	27 551
Computer science	35 849	Business admin.	26 650
Social Work	32 852	Hotel management	25 447
Legal Assistant	29 538	Early Childhood Education	24 779
Chemistry	28 814	Graphic Design	23 719

a) Determine the range for average starting salaries.
b) What is the median starting salary?
c) List the academic areas whose average starting salaries fall within the middle 50% of the data.

12. Ten bids submitted to a community college for the design and construction of a new technology building are listed below:

Bids (in $millions)										
Bid	1	2	3	4	5	6	7	8	9	10
Amount	1.9	1.6	1.2	1.8	2.1	2.1	2.5	4.0	2.4	2.5

a) Determine the range for these bids.
b) Determine the median bid.

13. For the following set of data,
a) draw the histogram and the frequency polygon;
b) construct the less-than and more-than cumulative frequency diagrams.

Driver's age	Probability of having an accident
Under 25	42%
25 to under 35	30%
35 to under 45	18%
45 to under 55	11%
55 to under 65	26%
65 and over	41%

14. For the following data, construct the less-than and more-than cumulative frequency diagrams.

Employee's age	Under 25	25–35	36–45	46–55	56–65	66–75
Probability of promotion	5%	45%	30%	15%	4%	1%

15. For the given distribution of hourly earnings,
a) construct the histogram and the frequency polygon;
b) construct the less-than and more-than cumulative frequency diagrams;
c) compute
i) the median,
ii) the 9th decile,
iii) $Q_3 - Q_1$.

Hourly earnings (in dollars)	Number of employees
5.00 to under 10.00	6
10.00 to under 15.00	16
15.00 to under 20.00	9
20.00 to under 25.00	7
25.00 to under 30.00	4

16. For the given distribution of college student study hours,
a) construct the less-than and more-than cumulative frequency diagrams;
b) compute the 70th percentile.

Hours Studied	Number of Students
0 to under 10	20
10 to under 20	30
20 to under 30	45
30 to under 40	5

17. A recent survey of expenditures per consumer for vacations showed the following results:

Amount spent for vacations (in dollars)	Number of respondents
0 to under 500	179
500 to under 1000	187
1000 to under 1500	82
1500 to under 2000	49
2000 to under 2500	53

a) Construct the less-than and more-than cumulative frequency diagrams for the given data.
b) What is the name of the point of intersection of the two curves?
c) Compute the value of the median.
d) Compute $Q_3 - Q_1$.
e) Determine the percent of the respondents who spent
i) less than $1500;
ii) more than $500.
f) Given that a particular respondent spent $2200,
i) compute the percentile rank for that respondent;
ii) determine how many respondents spent more than $2200.
g) Compute how many respondents spent less than $400.

18. A survey of 100 people showed how far people travel to go on vacation.

Distance travelled	Number of people surveyed
0 to under 1000 km	80
1000 to under 2000 km	14
2000 to under 3000 km	3
3000 to under 4000 km	2
4000 to under 5000 km	1

a) Construct the less-than and more-than cumulative frequency diagrams.
b) Calculate the median and where this is on the frequency diagrams.
c) What percent of respondents travelled more than 2000 km?

19. A recent survey has shown that the distribution of drivers by age group in Alberta was as follows:

Driver's age	Frequency (%)
16 to under 25	6
25 to under 35	25
35 to under 45	27
45 to under 55	18
55 to under 65	17
65 and over	7

a) Construct the following
  i) the histogram;
  ii) the frequency polygon;
  iii) the less-than cumulative frequency diagram;
  iv) the more-than cumulative frequency diagram.
b) Use the cumulative relative frequencies to determine the percent of drivers in the following age groups:
  i) under 55;
  ii) between 25 and 45;
  iii) 35 and over;
  iv) under 25 and 65 or over.
c) Compute the following:
  i) the first quartile;
  ii) the median;
  iii) the 85th percentile;
  iv) the percentile rank of a 37-year-old driver.

20. The distributon of commuters who use public transit was as follows:

Commuter's Age	Percent (%)
16 to under 25	20
25 to under 35	10
35 to under 45	15
45 to under 55	24
55 and over	31

a) Construct the less-than and more-than cumulative frequency and percent distribution.
b) What percent of commuters are under 45?

SELF-TEST

1. The owner of a small business has kept track of the number of customers for each of the last 24 business days:

67	57	43	59	80	25	48	51	62	53	65	44
78	23	34	84	60	74	38	75	26	88	33	41

a) Organize the data in the form of a descending array.
b) Determine
  i) the range;
  ii) the median.
c) Organize the data into a frequency distribution with equal class intervals of size 10.

2. The coordinator of a business administration program gave a short test to a group of first-year students during the first week of classes. The results of the test were as follows:

Correct answers	6	5	4	3	2	1	0
Number of students	42	72	65	18	12	5	2

a) Construct a histogram for the data.
b) Construct the more-than and less-than cumulative frequency diagrams.
c) What percent of the students had three or more correct answers?
d) What percent of the students had fewer than four correct answers?

3. The hourly wages paid by Heavy Metal Inc. to its labour force are summarized below:

Hourly rate of pay	Number of employees
\$10.00 to under \$15.00	9
\$15.00 to under \$20.00	22
\$20.00 to under \$25.00	14
\$25.00 to under \$30.00	10
\$30.00 to under \$35.00	5

Compute

a) the first quartile;
b) the median;
c) the 4th decile;
d) the 80th percentile;
e) the percentile rank of an employee earning \$28.00;
f) the percentile rank of an employee earning \$12.00.

For an online glossary, go to **www.pearsoned.ca/hummelbrunner**.

Key Terms

Array 40
Class frequency 42
Class interval 41
Class width 41
Cumulative frequency diagram 54
Cumulative frequency distribution 43
Cumulative relative frequency distribution 43
Decile 62
Frequency distribution 41
Frequency polygon 53
Histogram 52
Lower limit 42, 48
Median 41, 62
Mode 41
Percentile 60
Quartile 62
Range 40
Relative frequency distribution 42
Upper limit 48

Summary of Formulas

1. Percentiles

a) Ungrouped data:

$$\text{Position number of } P_x \text{ within array} = \frac{N+1}{100}(x)$$ ←*Formula* 2.1

b) Grouped data:

$$P_x = L_x + (i)\left(\frac{\frac{Nx}{100} - \sum f_c}{f_x}\right)$$ ←*Formula* 2.2

CHAPTER 3

Measures of Central Tendency

Introduction

Percentiles provide useful information about the relative position of observations in an array or in frequency distributions. However, much additional information can be obtained by computing *central values*. These values, referred to as *measures of central tendency*, are the values that are most representative of the array or the frequency distribution, since they are the central values around which the data tend to cluster.

Learning Outcomes

Upon completion of this chapter you will be able to

1. differentiate between the mean, the median, and the mode of data;
2. determine the value of the mean, the median, and the mode of ungrouped data;
3. determine the value of the mean, the median, and the mode of grouped data;
4. identify the relationships among the three measures of central tendency for symmetrical and skewed distributions;
5. state the advantages and disadvantages of the three measures.

SECTION 3.1

Central Values

Presenting statistical data by means of tables and graphs is a first step toward analyzing data. Additional insights can be obtained by using values that are representative of a set of data.

The most common types of central values are the *mean*, the *median*, and the *mode*. These three measures are referred to as **measures of central tendency** since they are indicators of typical middle values in the data set.

The **mean** is the arithmetic average of all values in the data set; the **median** indicates the halfway point; the **mode** is the most frequently occurring value.

SECTION 3.2

The Mean—Arithmetic Average

A. The Mean of Ungrouped Data

The mean (arithmetic average) of a set of observations is determined by adding the values and dividing by the number of values.

○ EXAMPLE 3.2a

The scores for a group of students on a test were 73, 86, 52, 6, 93, 74, 81, 70, 68. Determine the mean test score.

● SOLUTION

To determine the mean, add the values and divide by the number of values:
The sum of the values = 73 + 86 + 52 + 6 + 93 + 74 + 81 + 70 + 68 = 603;
the number of values = 9;

$$\text{the mean} = \frac{\text{the sum of the values}}{\text{the number of values}} = \frac{603}{9} = 67.$$

B. Formula for Computing the Mean

The computations performed in Example 3.2a can be described by the following notation:

μ (pronounced "mu") = the mean of the data set;
N = the number of observations in the data set;
x = the individual values of the N observations;
$\sum x$ = the sum of the individual values.

$$\mu = \frac{\sum x}{N}$$

←*Formula* 3.1

Note The symbol $\sum$, pronounced "sigma," is the summation symbol indicating that values are to be added.

$$\mu = \frac{\sum x}{N} = \frac{73 + 86 + 52 + 6 + 93 + 74 + 81 + 70 + 68}{9} = \frac{603}{9} = 67$$

C. *The Mean of Data Grouped by Value (Weighted Mean)*

Weighted mean calculations occur when specific values appear more than once in the data set. The frequency with which each value occurs is used as a weighting factor. The resulting products are added up and divided by the total frequency. The mean of data grouped by value is also commonly referred to as a weighted average.

EXAMPLE 3.2b

The following data summarize the test scores received by a group of students:

Test score	4	5	6	7	8	9	10
Number of students	3	17	24	45	21	9	1

Determine the mean test score for the group of students.

SOLUTION

Test score x	Frequency f	Weighted test score fx
4	3	(4)(3) = 12
5	17	(5)(17) = 85
6	24	(6)(24) = 144
7	45	(7)(45) = 315
8	21	(8)(21) = 168
9	9	(9)(9) = 81
10	1	(10)(1) = 10
Total	$N = \sum f = 120$	$\sum fx = 815$

The test scores are represented by x; the number of students (frequency) achieving a particular test score is represented by f; and the resulting products are represented by fx.

The mean value μ is now obtained by dividing the sum of the products fx by the number of observations N:

$$\mu = \frac{\sum fx}{N} = \frac{815}{120} = 6.79$$

From the above, the weighted mean formula is

$$\mu = \frac{\sum fx}{N}$$

←*Formula* 3.2

where μ = the mean of the data set;
x = the observed values;
f = the number of times each value occurs;
$N = \sum f$ = the number of observations in the data set;
fx = the weighted values of the observed values;
$\sum fx$ = the sum of the weighted values.

D. *The Mean of Grouped Data*

Computing the mean of grouped data involves a weighted mean calculation. The formula used is the same as that used for calculating a weighted mean. However, there is an important difference in the meaning of the symbol x.

For grouped data the individual values included in a class are no longer known. *The class midpoint is assumed to be the central value* for the individual values in the class, and the symbol x is used to represent the class midpoints. As a consequence, the calculation results in an *estimate* of the mean value for the frequency distribution.

The formula for finding the mean of data grouped into classes is Formula 3.2

$$\mu = \frac{\sum fx}{N}$$

where μ = the mean of the data set;
x = the individual class midpoints;
f = the number of observations in each class;
$N = \sum f$ = the total number of observations in the data set;
$\sum fx$ = the sum of the weighted values of the class midpoints.

○ **EXAMPLE 3.2c**

The following is a summary of the weekly wages of high school and college students employed in the summer by a municipal Parks and Recreation Department.

Weekly wages (in dollars)	Number of employees
360 to under 400	24
400 to under 440	40
440 to under 480	55
480 to under 520	36
520 to under 560	25
560 to under 600	12
600 to under 640	3

Determine the average weekly wage.

● **SOLUTION**

The given data and the required calculations are shown in Table 3.1:

TABLE 3.1 Calculation for Grouped Mean

Column 1	Column 2	Column 3	Column 4
Weekly wages (in dollars)	Number of employees f	Class midpoint x	Weighted class midpoint fx
360 to under 400	24	380	(24)(380) = 9 120
400 to under 440	40	420	(40)(420) = 16 800
440 to under 480	55	460	(55)(460) = 25 300
480 to under 520	36	500	(36)(500) = 18 000
520 to under 560	25	540	(25)(540) = 13 500
560 to under 600	12	580	(12)(580) = 6 960
600 to under 640	3	620	(3)(620) = 1 860
Totals	$N = \sum f = 195$		$\sum fx = 91\ 540$

Explanation of numbers in Table 3.1

1. The given class intervals of weekly wages are listed in Column 1.
2. The number of employees in each class (represented by f) is listed in Column 2.
3. The numbers in Column 2 are added to obtain $N = \sum f = 195$.
4. The class midpoints, represented by x, are listed in Column 3. The class midpoints are found by adding successive class limits and dividing by 2, e.g., $\frac{360 + 400}{2} = 380$. This repetitive calculation can be simplified by computing the class midpoint of the lowest class by the method described above and obtaining the remaining class midpoints by adding the width of the class interval. In Table 3.1 the midpoint of the lowest class is 380, and the width of the class intervals is 40. The successive remaining class midpoints are obtained by adding 40 — for example, 380 + 40 = 420; 420 + 40 = 460; and so on.
5. The weighted class midpoints fx, listed in Column 4, are obtained by multiplying the numbers in Column 2 and Column 3 in order.
6. The numbers in Column 4 are added to obtain $\sum fx = 91\ 540$. Now use Formula 3.2 and substitute:

$$\mu = \frac{\sum fx}{N} = \frac{91\ 540}{195} = \$469.44$$

EXERCISE 3.2

1. The results of a test for a statistics class were as follows:

   35, 63, 83, 74, 47, 63, 63, 88, 97, 78, 82, 55, 71

   Determine the mean test score.

2. The number of units produced by a group of workers were

   84, 76, 68, 64, 71, 77, 62, 87, 64, 64, 75, 66.

   Determine the average production per worker.

3. The weekly hours for a group of employees were as follows:

Weekly hours	36	37	38	39	40	41	42	43	44
No. of employees	4	9	12	12	14	22	26	19	2

Compute the mean weekly hours worked per employee.

4. Determine the mean test score for a group of job applicants from the following set of data:

Test score	45	50	55	60	65	70	75	80	85
Frequency	7	12	36	73	66	47	35	16	8

5. Compute the mean of the following frequency distribution:

Class interval	Frequency
0 to under 10	7
10 to under 20	20
20 to under 30	30
30 to under 40	27
40 to under 50	15
50 to under 60	10
60 to under 70	5
70 to under 80	5
80 to under 90	3

6. Determine the average lunch price from the given set of data:

Lunch prices (in dollars)	No. of orders (frequency)
5.00 to under 5.50	5
5.50 to under 6.00	22
6.00 to under 6.50	49
6.50 to under 7.00	63
7.00 to under 7.50	45
7.50 to under 8.00	25
8.00 to under 8.50	5
8.50 to under 9.00	4
9.00 to under 9.50	2

SECTION 3.3

The Median

A. The Median of Ungrouped Data

The median is the value that occupies the halfway point in a set of data.

To determine the median of ungrouped data, arrange the values in the form of an array. The position of the median can then be determined by Formula 2.1, $\frac{N+1}{100}(x)$, introduced in Section 2.3.

Since, for the median, $x = 50$ (i.e., the 50th percentile), Formula 2.1 simplifies to

$$\text{Position number of median in an array} = \frac{N+1}{2}$$ ←*Formula* 3.3

This means that the position of the median in an array can be quickly determined by adding 1 to the number of observations in the data set and dividing by 2.

EXAMPLE 3.3a

The test scores for the group of students in Example 3.2a were 73, 86, 52, 6, 93, 74, 81, 70, 68. Determine the median.

SOLUTION

First arrange the test scores in order of magnitude:

Position number	1	2	3	4	5	6	7	8	9
Test score	6	52	68	70	73	74	81	86	93

The number of values (test scores), $N = 9$;
the position number of the median $= \frac{N+1}{2} = \frac{9+1}{2} = 5$;
the fifth position in the array is occupied by the test score 73;
the median test score is 73.

EXAMPLE 3.3b

The hourly wages for a group of employees are

$9.00, $6.60, $7.00, $20.00, $8.40, $4.40, $9.60, $7.80.

Determine the median hourly pay.

SOLUTION

First arrange the hourly rates of pay in order of magnitude:

Position number	1	2	3	4	5	6	7	8
Hourly rate ($)	4.40	6.60	7.00	7.80	8.40	9.00	9.60	20.00

The number of values, $N = 8$;

the position number of the median $= \dfrac{N+1}{2} = \dfrac{8+1}{2} = 4.5$.

The fractional value 4.5 indicates that the median is located between the fourth and the fifth position.

The fourth position shows a value of $7.80;

the fifth position shows a value of $8.40.

The median is assumed to be the average value of the two middle positions $= \dfrac{7.80 + 8.40}{2} = \$8.10$.

Notes

1. If the number of observations in an array is an *odd* number, the computed middle position is always a *whole* number. The array has a single middle position, and the median is the value occupying that position.
2. If the number of observations in an array is an *even* number, the computed middle position is always a *fraction*. The array has two middle positions and the median is the average of the two values occupying the two middle positions.

B. The Median of Data Grouped by Value

○ **EXAMPLE 3.3c**

Determine the median for the test scores in Example 3.2b (see data below).

● **SOLUTION**

Test scores	4	5	6	7	8	9	10
No. of students	3	17	24	45	21	9	1
Cumulative no.	3	20	44	89	110	119	120

The test scores are arranged in order of magnitude and cumulative numbers are obtained by listing the running totals.

The total number of test scores, $N = 120$;

the median position $= \dfrac{120+1}{2} = 60.5$.

The middle positions are the 60th and 61st positions.

The cumulative totals indicate the positions occupied by the various test scores. Test score "4" occurs three times; the lowest 3 positions are occupied by a test score of "4." The next 17 positions (positions 4 to 20) are occupied by a test score of "5"; positions 21 to 44 are occupied by a test score of "6"; positions 45 to 89 are occupied by a test score of "7." Therefore, positions 60 and 61 are occupied by a test score of "7." The median is 7.

C. The Median of Grouped Data

For data arranged in class intervals, the median is the 50th percentile and can be found by using the percentile formula introduced in Section 2.3:

$$P_x = L_x + (i)\left(\frac{\frac{Nx}{100} - \sum f_c}{f_x}\right)$$ ←*Formula 2.2*

EXAMPLE 3.3d

Determine the median weekly wages for the group of employees in Example 3.2c (see data in the solution below).

SOLUTION

To determine a percentile, proceed as explained in Section 2.3.

Compute the cumulative frequencies and cumulative percents, determine the values needed and substitute in the formula.

Weekly wages (in dollars)	Number of employees	Cumulative frequencies	Cumulative percents
360 to under 400	24	24	12.3
400 to under 440	40	64	32.8
440 to under 480	55	119	61.0
480 to under 520	36	155	79.5
520 to under 560	25	180	92.3
560 to under 600	12	192	98.5
600 to under 640	3	195	100.0

$x = 50;\quad N = 195;\quad i = 40;\quad L_x = 440;\quad f_x = 55;\quad \sum f_c = 64$

$$P_{50} = 440 + (40)\left(\frac{\frac{(195)(50)}{100} - 64}{55}\right)$$

$$= 440 + (40)\left(\frac{97.50 - 64}{55}\right)$$

$$= 440 + (40)\frac{33.50}{55}$$

$$= 440 + 24.36$$

$$= 464.36$$

The median weekly wage is \$464.36.

EXERCISE 3.3

1. Compute the median test score for a statistics class whose results were as follows (refer to Exercise 3.2, Question 1):

   35, 63, 83, 74, 47, 63, 63, 88, 97, 78, 82, 55, 71

2. Compute the median number of units produced per worker for the following productivity results (refer to Exercise 3.2, Question 2):

   84, 76, 68, 64, 71, 77, 62, 87, 64, 64, 75, 66

3. The weekly hours for a group of employees were as follows (refer to Exercise 3.2, Question 3):

Weekly hours	36	37	38	39	40	41	42	43	44
No. of employees	4	9	12	12	14	22	26	19	2

   Determine the median weekly hours worked per employee.

4. The test scores for a group of job applicants were as follows (refer to Exercise 3.2, Question 4):

Test score	45	50	55	60	65	70	75	80	85
Frequency	7	12	36	73	66	47	35	16	8

   Determine the median test score for the job applicants.

5. Compute the median of the following frequency distribution (refer to Exercise 3.2, Question 5):

Class interval	Frequency
0 to under 10	7
10 to under 20	20
20 to under 30	30
30 to under 40	27
40 to under 50	15
50 to under 60	10
60 to under 70	5
70 to under 80	5
80 to under 90	3

6. Determine the median lunch price for the following frequency distribution (refer to Exercise 3.2, Question 6):

Lunch prices (in dollars)	No. of orders (frequency)
5.00 to under 5.50	5
5.50 to under 6.00	22
6.00 to under 6.50	49
6.50 to under 7.00	63
7.00 to under 7.50	45
7.50 to under 8.00	25
8.00 to under 8.50	5
8.50 to under 9.00	4
9.00 to under 9.50	2

SECTION 3.4

The Mode

The mode is the most frequently occurring value in a set of data.

A. The Mode of Ungrouped Data

The mode of ungrouped data is readily determined by arranging the data in the form of an array and locating the most frequently occurring value. If no value is repeated, the data have no mode.

EXAMPLE 3.4a

Test scores for a group of students were 12, 9, 16, 9, 14, 17, 12, 17, 14, 14, 19, 14. Determine the mode.

SOLUTION

First arrange the test scores in an array:

9, 9, 12, 12, 14, 14, 14, 14, 16, 17, 17, 19

The most frequent test score, 14, is the mode.

B. The Mode of Grouped Data

For data arranged in a frequency distribution, the mode is assumed to be located in the class having the highest frequency. The mode can be determined either graphically from the histogram of the distribution or by the formula

$$\text{MODE} = L_{MO} + (i)\left(\frac{d_1}{d_1 + d_2}\right)$$ ←*Formula* 3.4

where L_{MO} = the lower limit of the modal class (the class having the highest frequency);
i = the width of the modal class;
d_1 = the frequency in the modal class minus the frequency in the class below the modal class;
d_2 = the frequency in the modal class minus the frequency in the class above the modal class.

○ **EXAMPLE 3.4b**

Determine the mode for the data used in Example 3.2c (reproduced below) (a) graphically; (b) by formula.

● **SOLUTION**

Weekly wages (in dollars)	Number of employees	For formula use
360 to under 400	24	
400 to under 440	40 ←	$d_1 = 55 - 40 = 15$
440 to under 480	55 ←	Modal class
480 to under 520	36 ←	$d_2 = 55 - 36 = 19$
520 to under 560	25	
560 to under 600	12	
600 to under 640	3	

a) *Graphical solution.* First construct the histogram and locate the *modal class* represented by the highest bar. Mark the endpoints of the bar A and B as shown. Mark the top right corner of the bar representing the class below the modal class as C. Mark the top left corner of the bar representing the class above the modal class as D.

Join BC and AD and mark the point of intersection of the two line segments E. Draw a line from E perpendicular to the horizontal axis at F. Read the value for F from the horizontal scale as the value of the mode = 458 (approximately).

FIGURE 3.1 Histogram for Determining a Mode

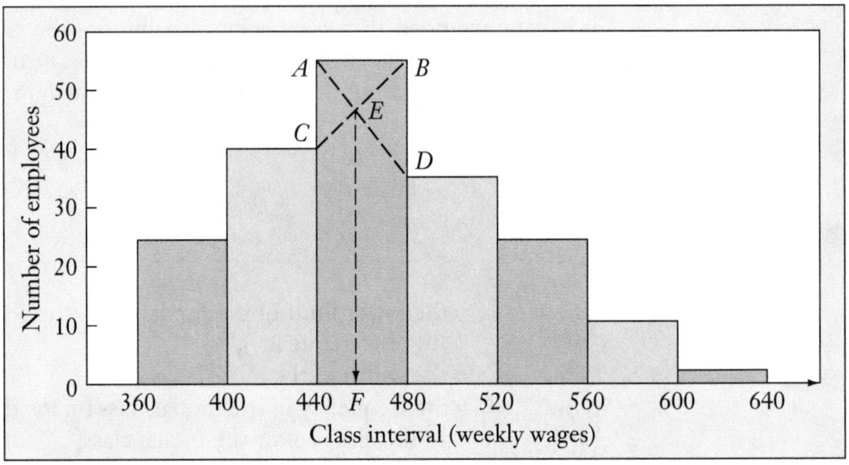

b) *Solution by formula.*
$L_{MO} = 440$ (lower limit of modal class)
$i = 40$ (width of modal class);
the frequency in the modal class = 55;
the frequency in the class below = 40;
the frequency in the class above = 36;
$d_1 = 55 - 40 = 15$; $d_2 = 55 - 36 = 19$.

$$\text{MODE} = 440 + (40)\frac{15}{15 + 19} = 440 + (40)\frac{15}{34} = 440 + 17.65 = \$457.65$$

EXERCISE 3.4

1. Compute the mode test score for a statistics class whose results were as follows (refer to Exercise 3.2, Question 1):
   35, 63, 83, 74, 47, 63, 63, 88, 97, 78, 82, 55, 71

2. Compute the mode number of units produced per worker for the following productivity results (refer to Exercise 3.2, Question 2):
   84, 76, 68, 64, 71, 77, 62, 87, 64, 64, 75, 66

3. Graphically determine the mode of the following frequency distribution (refer to Exercise 3.2, Question 5), and verify your answer using Formula 3.4:

Class interval	Frequency
0 to under 10	7
10 to under 20	20
20 to under 30	30
30 to under 40	27
40 to under 50	15
50 to under 60	10
60 to under 70	5
70 to under 80	5
80 to under 90	3

4. Graphically determine the mode lunch price for the following frequency distribution (refer to Exercise 3.2, Question 6), and verify your answer using Formula 3.4:

Lunch prices (in dollars)	No. of orders (frequency)
5.00 to under 5.50	5
5.50 to under 6.00	22
6.00 to under 6.50	49
6.50 to under 7.00	63
7.00 to under 7.50	45
7.50 to under 8.00	25
8.00 to under 8.50	5
8.50 to under 9.00	4
9.00 to under 9.50	2

SECTION 3.5

Relationships among Mean, Median, and Mode

A. Location of Central Values for Symmetrical Distributions

In a *symmetrical* (bell-shaped) distribution, the mean, the median, and the mode *coincide*. Their value is located under the highest point on the graph representing the distribution, as indicated in Figure 3.2.

FIGURE 3.2 A Symmetrical Distribution

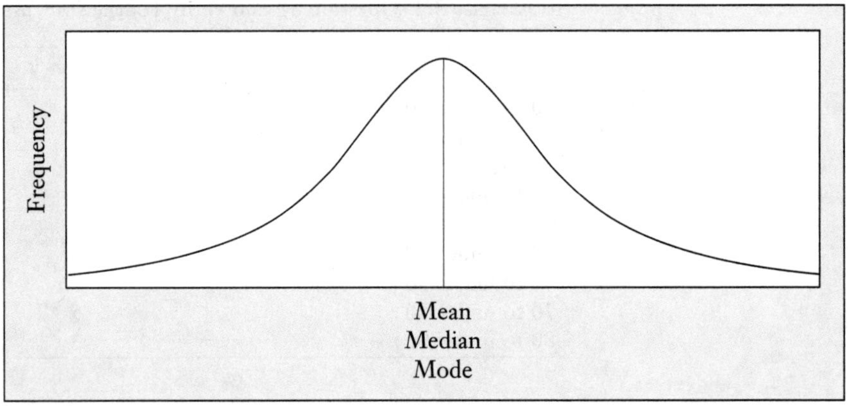

B. Location of Central Values for Skewed Distributions

Distributions that are not symmetrical are referred to as **skewed distributions**. For skewed distributions, only the mode is located under the highest point.

A distribution is *positively skewed* if more of the extreme values lie to the *right* of the highest point. The mode is least influenced by extreme values and lies under the highest point on the graph. The median is somewhat affected by extreme values and is located to the right of the mode. The mean is most affected and lies farther to the right, as shown in Figure 3.3.

FIGURE 3.3 A Positively Skewed Distribution

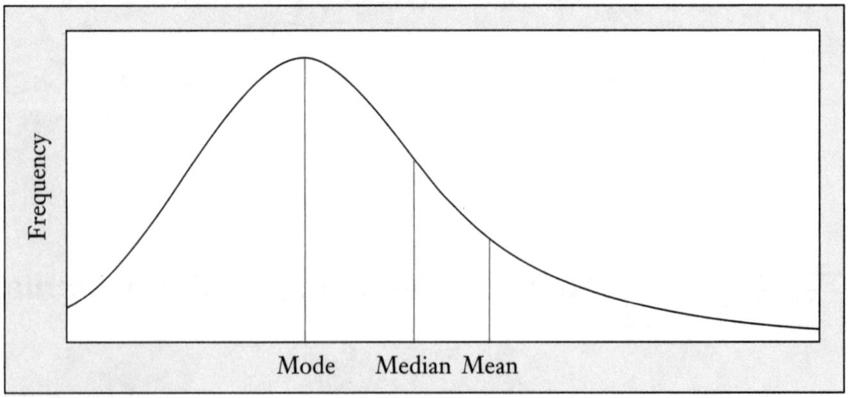

A distribution is *negatively skewed* if more of the extreme values lie to the *left* of the highest point on the graph. The mode is located under the highest point and the median and mean are located to the left of the mode, as indicated in Figure 3.4.

FIGURE 3.4 A Negatively Skewed Distribution

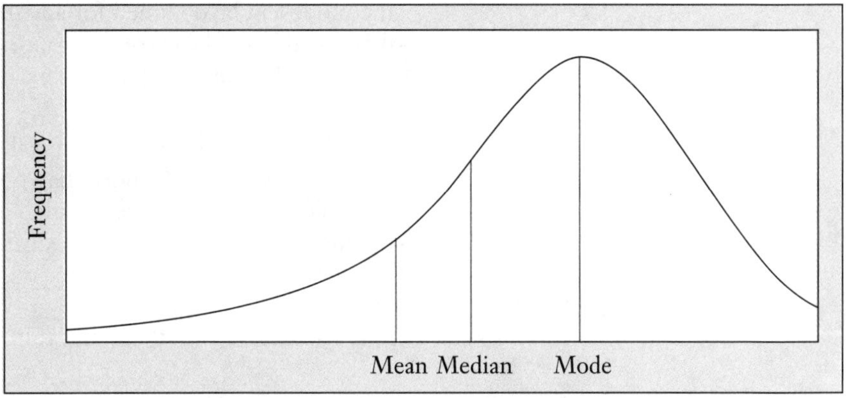

Note that for skewed distributions the median is located between the mean and the mode. If any two of the three central values are known, an estimate of the third central value can be obtained by using the relationship

$$\text{MEAN} - \text{MODE} = 3(\text{MEAN} - \text{MEDIAN}) \quad \leftarrow \textit{Formula } 3.5$$

This indicates that the difference between the mean and the mode is approximately three times the difference between the mean and the median.

C. *Advantages and Disadvantages of the Three Measures of Central Tendency*

1. **The Mean** –*Advantages*
   - –the mean reflects all values;
   - –the basic calculation is readily understood;
   - –the mean has mathematical properties that are useful in many statistical procedures.

   –*Disadvantages*
   - –the mean is unduly influenced by extreme values;
   - –it cannot be computed for open-ended distributions.

2. **The Median**–*Advantages*
   - –the concept is easy to understand;
   - –the median can be determined for any distribution, including open-ended distributions;
   - –it is not unduly influenced by extreme values.

   –*Disadvantages*
   - –arranging data in an array is time-consuming;
   - –the median lacks the useful mathematical properties that make the mean the preferred statistical measure of central tendency.

3. **The Mode** –*Advantages*
- –the mode can be obtained for any distribution;
- –it is not affected by extreme values;
- –it can be obtained for qualitative data.

–*Disadvantages*
- –not all sets of data have a modal value;
- –some sets of data have more than one modal value;
- –multiple modal values are usually difficult to interpret;
- –the mode lacks useful mathematical properties.

○ **EXAMPLE 3.5a**

The following were the scores on a mathematics test:

14	11	13	18	18	16	10
18	17	20	19	11	14	18
15	8	17	8	13	18	9
15	16	13	11			

a) Determine the median and the mode.
b) Estimate the mean using Formula 3.5

$$\text{MEAN} - \text{MODE} = 3(\text{MEAN} - \text{MEDIAN})$$

c) Compute the actual mean.
d) Comment on the nature of the distribution.

● **SOLUTION**

a) First arrange the test scores in an array:

8	8	9	10	11	11	11
13	13	13	14	14	15	15
16	16	17	17	18	18	18
18	18	19	20			

The data contain 25 test scores, $N = 25$;
the median position $= \dfrac{N+1}{2} = \dfrac{25+1}{2} = 13$;
the 13th position is occupied by a test score of 15;
the median is 15.
The most frequent score is 18, occurring 5 times;
the mode is 18.

b)
$$\text{MEAN} - \text{MODE} = 3(\text{MEAN} - \text{MEDIAN})$$
$$\mu - 18 = 3(\mu - 15)$$
$$\mu - 18 = 3\mu - 45$$
$$27 = 2\mu$$
$$\mu = 13.5$$

The estimated mean is 13.5.

c) $$\mu = \frac{\sum x}{N} = \frac{360}{25} = 14.4$$

The actual mean is 14.4.

d) Since the mode is the highest value (18), followed by the median (15) and the mean (14.4), the distribution is negatively skewed.

These calculations can be completed using EXCEL, as demonstrated in USING EXCEL 3.1.

USING EXCEL 3.1

Use the mathematics test scores given in Example 3.5a to calculate the mean, median, and mode of the data.

1. Type the column heading **Test Scores** into cell A1.
2. Enter the scores of the mathematics test into cells A2–A26.
3. On the **Tools** menu, click **Data Analysis...** (You may need to install the **Analysis ToolPak** add-in on your computer and then load it into EXCEL with the **Add-Ins** dialog box accessed on the **Tools** menu. If you try to load the **Analysis ToolPak** add-in and EXCEL does not install it, you can either install it with the **Add/Remove Programs** feature found in Windows' **Control Panel** or from Microsoft's Office 2000 CD-ROM).
4. The **Data Analysis** dialog box appears. From the **Analysis Tools** list, select **Descriptive Statistics** and click the **OK** button.
5. The **Descriptive Statistics** dialog box appears. In the **Input Range** input box, type **$A$2:$A$26** (or click on the button to select cells A2–A26; then click on the button or press the **Enter** key). From the **Group By** options, select **Columns**. Ensure that the **Labels in First Row** checkbox is deselected (unchecked). From the **Output options**, select the **Output Range** option and type **$C$2** in its input box (or select cell C2 and return to the input dialog box). Ensure that the **Summary Statistics** checkbox is selected (checked) and the **Confidence Level for Mean, Kth Largest** and **Kth Smallest** checkboxes are deselected (unchecked). Click the **OK** button when finished.
6. Resize column C to better view the output generated by the **Descriptive Statistics Analysis Tool.**

Notice that EXCEL calculated the mean as being 14.4, the median as 15, and the mode as 18. A measure for **Skewness** was calculated as well. The negative value calculated by EXCEL indicates that more of the extreme values lie to the left of the mode.

OUTPUT

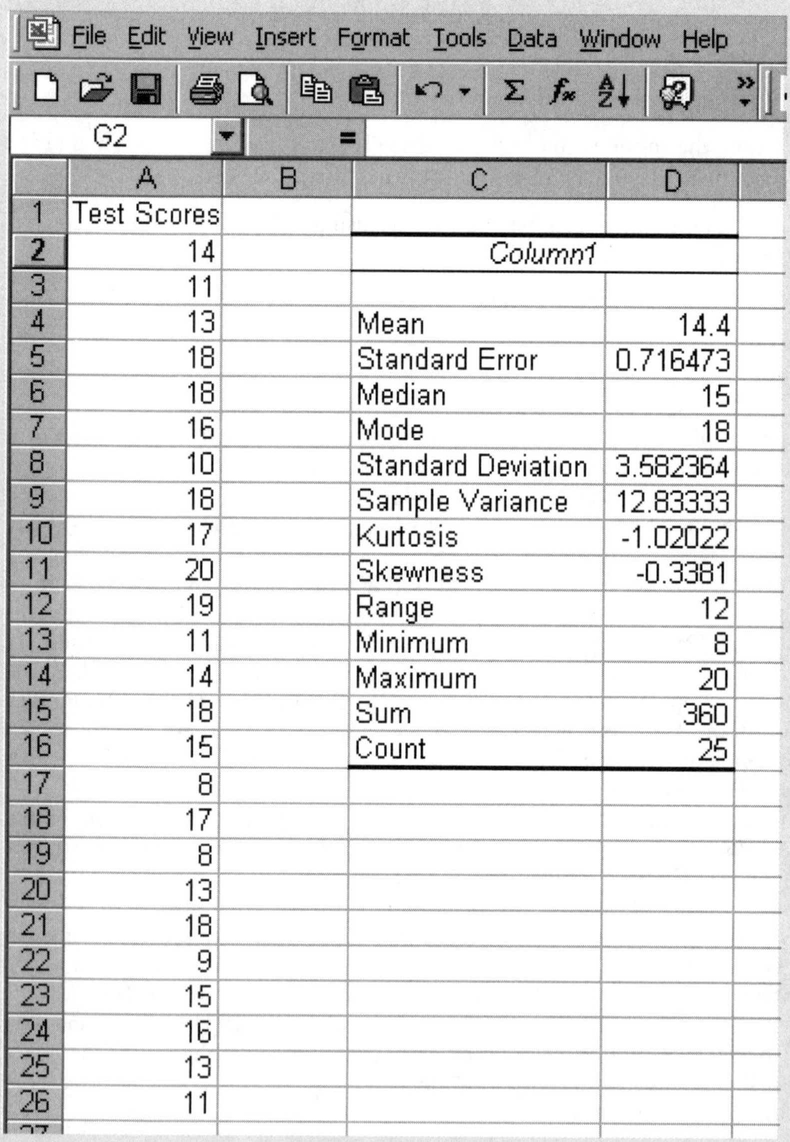

	A	B	C	D
1	Test Scores			
2	14		*Column1*	
3	11			
4	13		Mean	14.4
5	18		Standard Error	0.716473
6	18		Median	15
7	16		Mode	18
8	10		Standard Deviation	3.582364
9	18		Sample Variance	12.83333
10	17		Kurtosis	-1.02022
11	20		Skewness	-0.3381
12	19		Range	12
13	11		Minimum	8
14	14		Maximum	20
15	18		Sum	360
16	15		Count	25
17	8			
18	17			
19	8			
20	13			
21	18			
22	9			
23	15			
24	16			
25	13			
26	11			

EXERCISE 3.5

1. The following are measures of the time (in seconds) taken to look at a glossy ad insert by the members of a focus group:

5	11	4	18	8	15	17
20	14	7	16	13	8	16
20	11	8	8	12	8	14
10	15	5	8	15	9	14

a) Determine the median and the mode.
b) Compute the true mean.
c) Use the formula MEAN − MODE = 3(MEAN − MEDIAN) to estimate the mean.
d) Comment on the nature of the distribution.

2. For a particular set of observations the mode was determined to be 840 and the median was 810. Assuming a moderately skewed distribution,
a) sketch the distribution and label the positions of the mean, median, and mode;
b) calculate the approximate value of the mean.

3. In a frequency distribution the mean is 38 and the mode is 33. Determine whether the distribution is symmetrical, positively skewed, or negatively skewed.

4. Given that the difference between the mean and the median of a frequency distribution is 8, estimate the difference between the median and the mode.

REVIEW EXERCISE

1. Sales (in \$ millions) for Yummy Foods Inc. from 1997 to 2002 were as follows:

Year	1997	1998	1999	2000	2001	2002
Sales	19.7	18.5	19.3	18.3	21.8	24.9

For the time period, determine
a) the company's average sales;
b) the median sales.

2. The advertised prices (\$) for ten 1998–1999 used car vehicles as listed in the local newspaper are as follows:

10 495	15 886	10 900	19 500	9 950
13 000	15 900	16 000	14 800	13 500

Determine
a) the average used car price for 1998–1999;
b) the median car price for 1998–1999.

3. The number of automated banking machines (ABMs) across Canada from 1997–2001 were as follows:

Year	1997	1998	1999	2000	2001
ABMs	14 484	15 325	16 626	17 174	16 806

Source: Canadian Bankers Association

Compute the mean and median number of ABMs.

4. Sales (in $ billions) of Canada's largest companies have been summarized below:

Sales	4 to under 8	8 to under 12	12 to under 16	16 to under 20
Number of companies	19	7	1	2

a) Calculate the average sales for the group of companies.
b) Determine the median value of their sales.

5. The trustee for a bankrupt hardware store compiled the following inventory list by unit price. Compute the average price per item.

Cost per item ($)	2	3	5	10	20	30	50
Number of items	251	182	87	93	41	6	18

6. An auctioneer recently sold 500 lots of restaurant equipment listed as follows:

Number of lots	200	150	60	50	40
Price per lot ($)	20	22	28	30	50

Compute the average price per lot.

7. An ergonomic study found that a customer-service representative spent an average of 48 s on the phone helping a customer. After checking the accuracy of the results, management discovered that one of the 10 phone calls used to calculate the mean should have read 22 s instead of 72 s. Compute the average duration of the phone calls, using the corrected data.

8. If the arithmetic mean of 22 observations is 553, what will be the mean if one of the values is changed from 959 to 453?

9. If 12 students weigh an average 67 kg each, what will be the mean weight per student if another student whose weight is 106 kg is included in the calculation?

10. An elevator has a weight restriction of 1000 kg or 10 people. Ten students have the following weights (in kg):

100	110	40	50	200
100	105	70	100	140

Determine if

a) all ten students will be allowed on the elevator;

b) the average weight is above or below 100 kg and by how much.

11. Preliminary records showed that Bruce averaged 26 points per game in the college intramural basketball league. On rechecking, it was discovered that he had played a tenth game in which he had scored 36 points. What was Bruce's point average per game?

12. A sales associate is paid a commission of 5% if sales are over one million dollars and 3% if sales do not reach the million-dollar level. John had averaged \$90 000/month in sales last year. Calculate his commission for the year. How much will John's commission be changed if his sales for one month were overstated by \$85 000?

13. Anne and Randy calculated that their average hydro bill for the first six months of the year was \$98.23. Randy wanted to know how much they had paid each month but could only locate the following hydro bills:

January	February	March	April	May	June
\$135.29	\$128.73	\$?	\$67.22	\$50.98	\$77.21

What was the amount of the hydro bill for March?

14. The mean of 10 numbers is 177. Nine of the numbers are as follows:

58 82 47 23 15 79 36 61 25

a) Determine the size of the missing number.

b) Considering the magnitude of the missing number, is the mean a representative measure for the group of numbers? Explain.

15. An auditor just finished checking the books of a small company and found a missing entry. The average sales per month (\$) were \$50 000. Sales data for the first eleven months are as follows:

40 000	35 000	30 000	38 000	39 000	30 000
31 000	32 000	20 000	25 000	30 000	

a) Determine the sales for December.

b) Calculate the median.

c) Discuss the difference between the mean and median.

16. Joan Condie likes to "play the stock market." She recently purchased the following shares:

Company	Number of shares	Price per share
IBM	100	$110
Canadian Tire	500	24
BCE Inc.	200	42

Calculate the average price per share paid by Joan.

17. Dollar cost averaging is a technique recommended by many financial planners. The following represent 5 buy transactions:

Number of shares bought	Price per share
1000	10.00
300	8.00
500	6.50
150	7.00
50	3.00

Calculate the
a) average price per share;
b) price per share to receive a 10% return on the investment.

18. Nicola Rak owns some homes, which she rents to students at the following monthly rates per room:

Monthly rent	$250	$300	$350	$400
Number of rooms	6	5	3	2

Determine the average rent per room received by Nicola.

19. The ages of video renters at Blockbuster Video last Saturday were as follows:

21	15	19	29	16	19	23	23	12	39
22	15	19	37	49	46	19	22	15	10

a) Determine the median and the mode.
b) Estimate the value of the mean, using Formula 3.5.
c) Compute the actual mean.
d) Identify the type of skewness of the data.

20. The height, in metres, of a group of stores located consecutively along Yonge Street is as follows:

5	28	30	28	13	21	26	28
12	13	21	26	28	11	8	30

a) Determine the mean and the median.
b) Estimate the value of the mode using the values obtained in **(a)**.
c) Determine the value of the actual mode.
d) Comment on the nature of the distribution.

21. The following is data of donations ($) made while canvassing in your neighbourhood:

5	10	10	25	50	5	5	10	10	50
100	100	20	20	10	5	5	15	15	15

a) Determine the mean and median of the above data.
b) Determine the mode of this data.
c) Discuss the differences in the values obtained in (a) and (b).

22. For the following frequency distribution,
a) calculate the mean, the median, and the mode;
b) identify the type of distribution by skewness;
c) graphically determine the value of the mode.

Profit ($ millions)	Number of firms
0 to under 10	8
10 to under 20	11
20 to under 30	15
30 to under 40	5
40 to under 50	1

23. Given the following data,
a) graphically determine the value of the mode;
b) identify the nature of the skewness in the distribution;
c) compute the mean, the median, and the mode.

Class	0 to under 20	20 to under 40	40 to under 60	60 to under 80	80 to under 100
Frequency	2	4	24	15	5

24. The median unit cost and the mode unit cost of a company's inventory are $5.50 and $5.10 respectively.
a) Estimate the mean unit cost of the inventory by formula.
b) Identify the nature of skewness of the data.

25. A dollar store sells all items for $1.00 or less. Their median sales were $0.70 and mode sales were $0.80. Estimate the mean sales by formula and discuss the nature of skewness of the data.

26. Given that the mean and the mode for a set of test scores are 65 and 71 respectively,
a) estimate the median test score by formula;
b) comment on the nature of the distribution.

27. Your mean and mode sales for the year were $100 000 and $80 000 respectively. Estimate the median sales by formula and discuss which measure would be most beneficial in filling out government tax forms.

28. Given the three measures of central tendency, state whether each of the following distributions is symmetrical, positively skewed, or negatively skewed.

	Mean	Median	Mode
a)	92	93	95
b)	0.65	0.52	0.49
c)	10.0	10.0	10.0

29. Utilize the value of the three given measures to sketch each of the following distributions and indicate the nature of symmetry or skewness.

	Mean	Median	Mode
a)	111	1111	11111
b)	0.009	0.008	0.001
c)	349	359	364
d)	15 990	15 990	15 990

30. In the following table, determine the value(s) of the mode for the indicated nature of skewness.

	Mean	Median	Mode	Nature of Symmetry
a)	10	15	???	negatively skewed
b)	0.001	0.0009	???	positively skewed
c)	23.0	23.0	???	symmetrical

SELF-TEST

A. Questions **1** through **4** are based on the following data:

Linden Life Insurance Company
Seniority of Employees (in Months)
with Less Than Five Years' Service with the Company

51	2	24	20	11	43	42	22	24	59	12	38
33	25	24	8	18	31	47	24	3	35	17	45
28	55	51	13	8	30	7	34	42	17	27	24

1. Determine the median and the mode.

2. Estimate the mean, using the values obtained for the median and the mode in Question **1**.

3. Compute the true mean.

4. Identify the nature of skewness in the data.

B. Questions **5** through **8** are based on the following information:

Linden Life Insurance Company Seniority of Employees (in Years)	
Seniority	Number of employees
0 to under 5	36
5 to under 10	39
10 to under 15	28
15 to under 20	13
20 to under 25	15
25 to under 30	11
30 to under 35	7
35 to under 40	2

5. Compute Q_1 and Q_3.

6. Compute the mean, the median, and the mode.

7. Comment on the skewness of the distribution.

8. Graphically determine the value of the mode.

C. Answer the following question.

9. Marty was talking to Lise about his flight from Vancouver to Toronto, a distance of 4537 km. The plane left at 9:00 a.m. and arrived in Toronto at 4:00 p.m. Based on that information, Marty calculated the plane's speed to be 648.1 km/h. Lise pointed out to him that his calculation was incorrect because of the three-hour difference in time zones. What was the plane's true average speed per hour?

For an online glossary, go to **www.pearsoned.ca/hummelbrunner**.

Key Terms

Mean 83
Measures of central tendency 83
Median 83
Mode 83
Skewed distributions 96
Weighted mean 84

Summary of Formulas

1. Arithmetic mean

a) Ungrouped data:

$$\mu = \frac{\sum x}{N}$$ ←*Formula* 3.1

b) Grouped data:

$$\mu = \frac{\sum fx}{N}$$ ←*Formula* 3.2

2. Median

a) Ungrouped data:

$$\text{Position number of median in array} = \frac{N+1}{2}$$ ←*Formula* 3.3

b) Grouped data:

$$P_x = L_x + (i)\left(\frac{\frac{Nx}{100} - \sum f_c}{f_x}\right) \quad \text{where } x = 50$$ ←*Formula* 2.2

3. Mode

Grouped data:

$$\text{MODE} = L_{\text{MO}} + (i)\left(\frac{d_1}{d_1 + d_2}\right)$$ ←*Formula* 3.4

4. Empirical relationship

$$\text{MEAN} - \text{MODE} = 3(\text{MEAN} - \text{MEDIAN})$$ ←*Formula* 3.5

CHAPTER 4

Measures of the Variability of Data

Introduction

The measures of central tendency considered in Chapter 3 are useful because data tend to cluster around central values. However, as the individual values in a distribution of data differ from each other, central values provide only an incomplete picture of the features of the distribution.

For example, a mean of 6.79, a median of 7, and a mode of 7 (the three central values in Example 3.2b) indicate a fairly symmetrical distribution but provide no clue as to the spread of the data. Similarly, a mean of \$469.44, a median of \$464.40, and a mode of \$457.65 (the three central values for the grouped data in Example 3.2c) indicate a positively skewed distribution but again provide no information about the dispersion of the data.

To obtain a more complete picture of the nature of the distribution, the *variability* (or *dispersion* or *spread*) of the data needs to be measured.

The **measures of variability** considered in this chapter include the *range*, the *interquartile range*, the *average deviation from the mean*, the *variance*, the *standard deviation*, and the *coefficient of variation*.

Learning Outcomes

Upon completion of this chapter you will be able to

1. determine the range and interquartile range of grouped and ungrouped data;
2. determine the average deviation from the mean for ungrouped data;
3. compute the variance and the standard deviation for grouped and ungrouped data;
4. compute the coefficient of variation of different data sets and interpret the results.

SECTION 4.1 The Range and the Interquartile Range

A. The Range

The **range** is the difference between the *highest* and the *lowest* value in a set of data. For grouped frequency distributions, the highest value in the data set is assumed to be the upper limit of the class containing the greatest values. The lowest value is the lower limit of the class containing the smallest values.

RANGE = HIGHEST VALUE − LOWEST VALUE ←*Formula* 4.1

EXAMPLE 4.1a

Determine the range in test scores for the following data (see Example 3.2b):

Test score	4	5	6	7	8	9	10
Number of students	3	17	24	45	21	9	1

SOLUTION

The highest test score is 10;
the lowest test score is 4.
The range = HIGHEST VALUE − LOWEST VALUE = 10 − 4 = 6.

EXAMPLE 4.1b

Determine the range in weekly wages for the following data (see Example 3.2c).

Weekly wages (in dollars)	Number of employees
360 to under 400	24
400 to under 440	40
440 to under 480	55
480 to under 520	36
520 to under 560	25
560 to under 600	12
600 to under 640	3

SOLUTION

The upper limit of the highest class is \$640; the lower limit of the lowest class is \$360. The range = 640 − 360 = \$280.

Note The range is easily computed and its meaning is readily understood. However, it is at best a very rough indicator of dispersion since the calculation does not allow for the distribution of the data between the two extreme values.

B. The Interpercentile Range

The **interpercentile range** is the difference between two percentiles. For example, the interpercentile range may be calculated to measure the spread between the 10th percentile and the 90th percentile.

○ EXAMPLE 4.1c

Determine the spread between the 15th and 85th percentiles for the data used in Example 4.1a.

● SOLUTION

Test score	4	5	6	7	8	9	10
Number of students	3	17	24	45	21	9	1
Cumulative number	3	20	44	89	110	119	120

$N = 120.$

For the 15th percentile $x = 15$; its position in the array

$$= \frac{N+1}{100}(x) = \frac{120+1}{100}(15) = \frac{121}{100}(15) = 1.21(15) = 18.15.$$

This means the 15th percentile lies between the test scores obtained by the two students occupying positions 18 and 19. Since both students had a test score of 5, the 15th percentile = 5.

For the 85th percentile $x = 85$; its position in the array

$$= \frac{120+1}{100}(85) = \frac{121}{100}(85) = 1.21(85) = 102.85.$$

This means the 85th percentile lies between the test scores obtained by the two students occupying positions 102 and 103. Since both students had a test score of 8, the 85th percentile = 8.

The interpercentile range between P_{85} and $P_{15} = 8 - 5 = 3$.

EXAMPLE 4.1d

Determine the interpercentile range in weekly wages between the 10th and 90th percentile for Example 4.1b.

SOLUTION

Weekly wages (in dollars)	Number of employees	Cumulative total	Cumulative percents
360 to under 400	24	24	12.3
400 to under 440	40	64	32.8
440 to under 480	55	119	61.0
480 to under 520	36	155	79.5
520 to under 560	25	180	92.3
560 to under 600	12	192	98.5
600 to under 640	3	195	100.0

For the grouped data, use Formula 2.2, the percentile formula:

$$P_x = L_x + (i)\left(\frac{\frac{Nx}{100} - \sum f_c}{f_x}\right)$$

For P_{10},
$x = 10; \quad N = 195; \quad i = 40; \quad L_x = 360; \quad \sum f_c = 0; \quad f_x = 24.$

$$P_{10} = 360 + (40)\left(\frac{\frac{(195)(10)}{100} - 0}{24}\right)$$

$$= 360 + (40)\left(\frac{19.50}{24}\right)$$

$$= 360 + 32.50 = 392.50$$

For P_{90},
$x = 90; \quad N = 195; \quad i = 40; \quad L_x = 520; \quad \sum f_c = 155; \quad f_x = 25.$

$$P_{90} = 520 + (40)\left(\frac{\frac{(195)(90)}{100} - 155}{25}\right)$$

$$= 520 + (40)\left(\frac{175.50 - 155}{25}\right)$$

$$= 520 + (40)\left(\frac{20.50}{25}\right)$$

$$= 520 + 32.80 = 552.80$$

The interpercentile range, P_{10} to $P_{90} = 552.80 - 392.50 = \$160.30$.

C. *A Special Case — The Interquartile Range*

The **interquartile range** is the difference between the *first* and *third quartiles* in a set of data. This means it measures the spread of the *middle 50%* of the observed values. Measuring the spread of the middle 50% of the values is useful for distributions that have extremely high or low values.

$$\text{INTERQUARTILE RANGE} = Q_3 - Q_1$$ ←*Formula* 4.2

○ EXAMPLE 4.1e

Determine the interquartile range for the data used in Example 4.1a.

● SOLUTION

Test score	4	5	6	7	8	9	10
Number of students	3	17	24	45	21	9	1
Cumulative number	3	20	44	89	110	119	120

$N = 120$.

The position of the first quartile Q_1 in the array

$$= \frac{N+1}{100}(x) = \frac{120+1}{100}(25) = \frac{121}{4} = 30.25.$$

This means Q_1 lies one-quarter of the distance between the test scores obtained by the two students occupying positions 30 and 31. Since both students had a test score of 6, $Q_1 = 6$.

The position number of the third quartile (Q_3)

$$= \frac{120+1}{100}(75) = \frac{121}{4}(3) = 90.75.$$

This means Q_3 lies three-quarters of the distance between the test scores obtained by the two students occupying positions 90 and 91. Since both students had a test score of 8, $Q_3 = 8$.

The interquartile range $= Q_3 - Q_1 = 8 - 6 = 2$.

○ EXAMPLE 4.1f

Determine the interquartile range in weekly wages for Example 4.1b.

● SOLUTION

For grouped data, Formula 2.2, the percentile formula

$$P_x = L_x + (i)\left(\frac{\frac{Nx}{100} - \sum f_c}{f_x}\right)$$

can be used to compute the values of Q_3 and Q_1.

Weekly wages (in dollars)	Number of employees	Cumulative total	Cumulative percents
360 to under 400	24	24	12.3
400 to under 440	40	64	32.8
440 to under 480	55	119	61.0
480 to under 520	36	155	79.5
520 to under 560	25	180	92.3
560 to under 600	12	192	98.5
600 to under 640	3	195	100.0

For Q_1,

$x = 25$; $N = 195$; $i = 40$; $L_x = 400$; $\sum f_c = 24$; $f_x = 40$.

$$Q_1 = P_{25} = 400 + (40)\left(\frac{\frac{(195)(25)}{100} - 24}{40}\right)$$

$$= 400 + (40)\left(\frac{48.75 - 24}{40}\right)$$

$$= 400 + (40)\frac{24.75}{40}$$

$$= 400 + 24.75 = 424.75$$

For Q_3,

$x = 75; \quad N = 195; \quad i = 40; \quad L_x = 480; \quad \sum f_c = 119; \quad f_x = 36.$

$$Q_3 = P_{75} = 480 + (40)\left(\frac{\frac{(195)(75)}{100} - 119}{36}\right)$$

$$= 480 + (40)\left(\frac{146.25 - 119}{36}\right)$$

$$= 480 + (40)\frac{27.25}{36}$$

$$= 480 + 30.28 = 510.28$$

The interquartile range = 510.28 – 424.75 = \$85.53.

EXERCISE 4.1

1. A survey of firms produced the following average starting salaries for college graduates by academic area:

Social Work	\$32 852	Chemistry	\$28 814
Graphic Design	23 719	Accounting	27 551
Legal Assistant	29 538	Hotel management	25 447
Engineering	36 614	Nursing	38 742
Computer science	35 849	Early Childhood Educ.	24 779
Marketing	28 684	Business admin.	26 650

   a) Determine the range of starting salaries.
   b) What academic areas make up the interquartile range?
   c) What minimum starting salary is required to put you into the top quartile?
   d) Below what amount will your starting salary put you into the bottom quartile?

2. The numbers in the chart below were compiled from a survey.

66	50	59	26	46	49	51	62
48	68	20	37	40	23	67	20
18	54	5	49	44	71	31	29
50	64	35	44	53	50	37	15
59	37	13	36	53	64	55	44

   a) Determine the range and the interquartile range for the ungrouped data.
   b) Group the data in a frequency distribution using equal intervals of size 10 with a lowest class limit of 0.
   c) Determine the range and the interquartile range for the frequency distribution.
   d) Compare the answers to parts **(a)** and **(c)**. What is gained and what is lost by grouping data?

3. The data in the frequency distribution below represent the hourly wages paid to a group of employees.

Class interval (in dollars)	Frequency
14.00 to under 15.00	11
15.00 to under 16.00	39
16.00 to under 17.00	53
17.00 to under 18.00	35
18.00 to under 19.00	15
19.00 to under 20.00	5
20.00 to under 21.00	2

Determine **(a)** the range; **(b)** the interquartile range; **(c)** the interpercentile range P_{10} to P_{90}.

4. For the following frequency distribution determine **(a)** the range; **(b)** the interquartile range; **(c)** the interpercentile range P_{40} to P_{60}.

Class interval	Frequency
10 to under 30	14
30 to under 50	28
50 to under 70	40
70 to under 90	28
90 to under 110	16
110 to under 130	9
130 to under 150	2

SECTION 4.2

The Average Deviation from the Mean

A. Deviation from the Mean Defined

The term **deviation** refers to the *difference* between the value of an individual observation in a data set and the mean of the data set. Since the mean is a central value, some of the deviations will be positive and some will be negative.

EXAMPLE 4.2a

For the set of test scores 17, 11, 13, 15, 9, 16, 12, 11, compute the deviations of the test scores and the sum of the deviations from the mean.

SOLUTION

First determine the mean of the test scores

$$N = 8;$$
$$\sum x = 17 + 11 + 13 + 15 + 9 + 16 + 12 + 11 = 104;$$
$$\mu = \frac{\sum x}{N} = \frac{104}{8} = 13.$$

Now compute the deviations $(x-\mu)$ as shown below and add the deviations.

Test scores x	Deviation from mean $(x-\mu)$
17	$17 - 13 = 4$
11	$11 - 13 = -2$
13	$13 - 13 = 0$
15	$15 - 13 = 2$
9	$9 - 13 = -4$
16	$16 - 13 = 3$
12	$12 - 13 = -1$
11	$11 - 13 = -2$
$\sum x = 104$	$\sum(x-\mu) = 0$

Note The sum of the deviations from the mean is always zero.

B. Average Deviation from the Mean — Ungrouped Data

The **average deviation from the mean** is a measure of the average magnitude (absolute value — numerical value without + or – sign) of the deviations from the mean.

The average deviation from the mean can be determined by using the formula

$$\text{AVERAGE DEVIATION FROM THE MEAN} = \frac{\sum |x-\mu|}{N}$$ ←*Formula* 4.3

where x = the value of an observation in the data set;

μ = the mean of the data set = $\frac{\sum x}{N}$;

N = the number of observations in the data set;

$|x-\mu|$ = the absolute value of the deviation of an observation from the mean;

$\sum |x-\mu|$ = the sum of the absolute values of the deviations from the mean.

○ **EXAMPLE 4.2b**

For the set of test scores used in Example 4.2a, compute the average deviation from the mean.

● **SOLUTION**

Test scores x	Deviations from mean $(x - \mu)$	Absolute deviations $\lvert x - \mu \rvert$
17	$17 - 13 = 4$	4
11	$11 - 13 = -2$	2
13	$13 - 13 = 0$	0
15	$15 - 13 = 2$	2
9	$9 - 13 = -4$	4
16	$16 - 13 = 3$	3
12	$12 - 13 = -1$	1
11	$11 - 13 = -2$	2
$\sum x = 104$	$\sum(x - \mu) = 0$	$\sum \lvert x - \mu \rvert = 18$

$$\text{AVERAGE DEVIATION FROM THE MEAN} = \frac{\sum \lvert x - \mu \rvert}{N} = \frac{18}{8} = 2.25$$

This means that, on average, the test scores deviate from the mean by 2.25.

Note The meaning of the average deviation is easily understood and is a better measure of dispersion than the range or interquartile range since it takes into account all observations in the data set.

EXERCISE 4.2

1. The weekly incomes for a group of eight employees are \$581, \$570, \$625, \$660, \$630, and \$492. Compute the average deviation from the mean.

2. The following are the index numbers of production in an industry for the last 10-year period:

   100 122 120 112 114 90 89 101 109 113

   Determine the average deviation from the mean.

3. After a company's annual golf tournament, the best seven rounds were published as follows:

   71 73 78 81 82 82 86

   Compute the average deviation of the rounds from the mean.

4. A random selection of homeowners produced the following annual gas bills:

   \$785 \$1218 \$826 \$988 \$803

   Calculate the average deviation of the gas bills from the mean.

SECTION 4.3

The Variance and Standard Deviation

A. Computation for Ungrouped Data

The variance and the standard deviation are the most widely used measures of variability. The **variance** is the *average squared deviation* from the mean. It is similar to the average deviation from the mean in that it is based on the deviation of the individual values from the mean. It differs from the average deviation because the deviations are squared before summing.

The **standard deviation** is readily obtained from the variance as the *square root of the variance*. The symbol used for the standard deviation is the small Greek letter σ (pronounced "sigma"). Because of the relationship between the variance and the standard deviation, the variance is usually designated by the symbol σ^2.

The basic computational process is similar to that used for finding the average deviation from the mean and is summarized in the basic formulas for computing the variance and the standard deviation.

$$\text{VARIANCE,} \quad \sigma^2 = \frac{\sum(x-\mu)^2}{N}$$ ←*Formula* 4.4

$$\text{STANDARD DEVIATION,} \quad \sigma = \sqrt{\sigma^2}$$ ←*Formula* 4.5

where N = the number of observations in the data set;
x = the value of an observation;
μ = the mean = $\dfrac{\sum x}{N}$;
$x - \mu$ = the deviation of an observation from the mean;
$(x-\mu)^2$ = the square of a deviation from the mean;
$\sum(x-\mu)^2$ = the sum of the squared deviations.

○ EXAMPLE 4.3a

Compute the variance and the standard deviation for the data set used in Example 4.2a.

SOLUTION

Test scores x	Deviations from mean $(x-\mu)$	Squared deviations $(x-\mu)^2$
17	4	16
11	−2	4
13	0	0
15	2	4
9	−4	16
16	3	9
12	−1	1
11	−2	4
$\sum x = 104$	$\sum(x-\mu) = 0$	$\sum(x-\mu)^2 = 54$

$$\text{MEAN,}\quad \mu = \frac{\sum x}{N} = \frac{104}{8} = 13$$

$$\text{VARIANCE,}\quad \sigma^2 = \frac{\sum(x-\mu)^2}{N} = \frac{54}{8} = 6.75$$

$$\text{STANDARD DEVIATION,}\quad \sigma = \sqrt{\sigma^2} = \sqrt{6.75} = 2.5981$$

These calculations can be completed by using EXCEL, as demonstrated in EXCEL EXAMPLE 4.1.

USING EXCEL 4.1

Compute the mean, variance, and the standard deviation for the data set used in Example 4.2a.

1. Type the column heading **Test Scores** into cell A1.
2. Enter the test score data into cells A2–A9.
3. Type the notes **is the mean score, is the variance of the scores**, and **is the standard deviation of the scores** into cells B11, B12, and B13.
4. Select cell A11.
5. On the toolbar, click on the **Paste Function** button (or on the **Insert** menu, click **Function...**).
6. The **Paste Function** dialog box appears. From the **Function category** list, select **Statistical**; from the **Function name** list, select the **AVERAGE** function; and then click the **OK** button.
7. The input dialog box appears. In the **Number1** input box, type **A2:A9** (or click on beside the **Number1** input box to select cells A2–A9 on the worksheet; then click on or press the **Enter** key); then click the **OK** button.
8. Select cell A12.
9. Repeat steps 6–8, however in the **Paste Function** dialog box, from the **Function name** list, select the **VARP** function.
10. Select cell A13.
11. Repeat steps 6–8, however in the **Paste Function** dialog box, from the **Function name** list, select the **STDEVP** function.

Alternatively, the functions (**=AVERAGE(A2:A9)**, **=VARP(A2:A9)** and **=STDEVP(A2:A9)**) could have been used and typed directly into the cells A11, A12 and A13 to achieve the same results.

OUTPUT

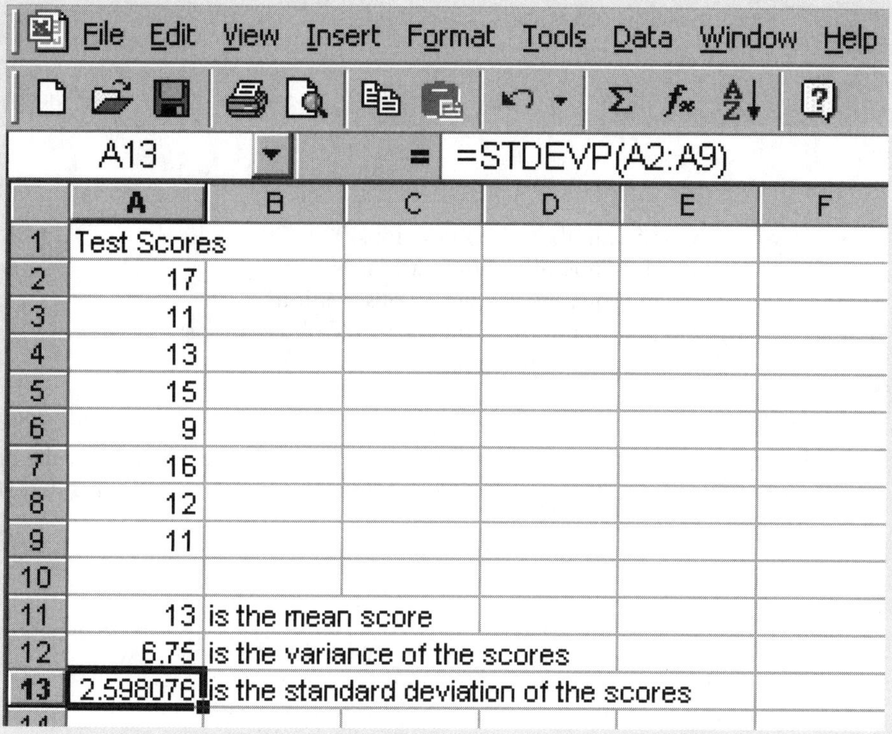

B. *Short-Cut Formula for Computing the Variance for Ungrouped Data*

The basic formula for computing the variance, $\sigma^2 = \frac{\sum(x-\mu)^2}{N}$, is normally used only for a set of data that contains few observations. For larger sets of data, the calculation of the deviation and the squared deviation for each observation is avoided by using an alternative formula derived by mathematical manipulation of the basic formula.

This alternative formula is

$$\sigma^2 = \frac{\sum x^2}{N} - \left(\frac{\sum x}{N}\right)^2 \quad \text{or} \quad \sigma^2 = \frac{\sum x^2}{N} - \mu^2$$

←*Formula* 4.6

where N = the number of observations;
x = the value of an observation;
x^2 = the squared value of an observation;
$\sum x$ = the sum of the values of the N observations;
$\sum x^2$ = the sum of the squared values.

○ **EXAMPLE 4.3b**

Use Formula 4.6, the short-cut formula, to compute the variance for the data set used in Example 4.2a. Then use Formula 4.5 to compute the standard deviation.

● **SOLUTION**

Test scores x	Squared scores x^2
17	$17^2 = 289$
11	$11^2 = 121$
13	$13^2 = 169$
15	$15^2 = 225$
9	$9^2 = 81$
16	$16^2 = 256$
12	$12^2 = 144$
11	$11^2 = 121$
$\sum x = 104$	$\sum x^2 = 1406$

$$\text{VARIANCE,} \quad \sigma^2 = \frac{\sum x^2}{N} - \left(\frac{\sum x}{N}\right)^2 = \frac{1406}{8} - \left(\frac{104}{8}\right)^2$$

$$= 175.75 - 13^2 = 175.75 - 169 = 6.75$$

$$\text{STANDARD DEVIATION,} \quad \sigma = \sqrt{\sigma^2} = \sqrt{6.75} = 2.5981$$

Notes

1. The results in Examples 4.3a and 4.3b are, of course, the same.
2. The value $\frac{\sum x}{N}$ in the short-cut formula equals μ and leads to the alternative version of the short-cut formula, $\sigma^2 = \frac{\sum x^2}{N} - \mu^2$. This form of the short-cut formula can be used to advantage when the mean has to be determined.

○ **EXAMPLE 4.3c**

Compute the variance for the following hourly wages of a group of workers, using (a) the basic formula, 4.4; (b) the short-cut formula, 4.6.

\$14.60	\$15.40	\$14.00	\$14.40	\$15.80
\$15.60	\$16.40	\$18.60	\$19.20	\$21.00

● **SOLUTION**

a)

Hourly wages x	Deviations from mean $(x - \mu)$	Squared deviations $(x - \mu)^2$
14.60	14.60 − 16.50 = −1.90	3.61
15.40	15.40 − 16.50 = −1.10	1.21
14.00	14.00 − 16.50 = −2.50	6.25
14.40	14.40 − 16.50 = −2.10	4.41
15.80	15.80 − 16.50 = −0.70	0.49
15.60	15.60 − 16.50 = −0.90	0.81
16.40	16.40 − 16.50 = −0.10	0.01
18.60	18.60 − 16.50 = 2.10	4.41
19.20	19.20 − 16.50 = 2.70	7.29
21.00	21.00 − 16.50 = 4.50	20.25
165.00	0.00	48.74

b)

Hourly wages x	Squared hourly wages x^2
14.60	213.16
15.40	237.16
14.00	196.00
14.40	207.36
15.80	249.64
15.60	243.36
16.40	268.96
18.60	345.96
19.20	368.64
21.00	441.00
165.00	2771.24

a) $\sum x = 165.00$

$$\mu = \frac{\sum x}{N} = \frac{165.00}{10} = 16.50$$

$$\sigma^2 = \frac{\sum (x-\mu)^2}{N} = \frac{48.74}{10} = 4.874$$

b) $\sum x = 165.00$

$$\sigma^2 = \frac{\sum x^2}{N} - \mu^2$$

$$= \frac{2771.24}{10} - (16.50)^2$$

$$= 277.124 - 272.25$$

$$= 4.874$$

C. *Variance and Standard Deviation for Grouped Data*

For grouped data the short-cut formula is modified to allow for the weighting of the class midpoints by the frequencies:

$$\sigma^2 = \frac{\sum fx^2}{N} - \left(\frac{\sum fx}{N}\right)^2 \quad \text{or} \quad \sigma^2 = \frac{\sum fx^2}{N} - \mu^2$$ ←*Formula* 4.7

where N = the number of observations;
x = the midpoint of a class;
x^2 = the square of a class midpoint;
f = the frequency in a class;
fx = the weighted value of a class midpoint;
$\sum fx$ = the sum of the weighted values of the class midpoints;
fx^2 = the weighted value of a squared class midpoint;
$\sum fx^2$ = the sum of the weighted values of the squared class midpoints.

EXAMPLE 4.3d

The frequency distribution of the test scores obtained by a group of students is shown in the following table in columns 1 and 2. Compute

a) the mean;
b) the variance;
c) the standard deviation.

SOLUTION

Column 1	Column 2	Column 3	Column 4
Class (test scores)	Class frequency f	Class midpoint x	Squared midpoint x^2
0 to under 10	2	5	25
10 to under 20	4	15	225
20 to under 30	12	25	625
30 to under 40	28	35	1225
40 to under 50	44	45	2025
50 to under 60	43	55	3025
60 to under 70	23	65	4225
70 to under 80	7	75	5625
80 to under 90	5	85	7225
90 to under 100	2	95	9025
Totals	$N = \sum f = 170$		

Column 1	Column 5	Column 6
Class (test scores)	Weighted midpoint fx	Weighted squared midpoint fx^2
0 to under 10	(2)(5) = 10	(2)(25) = 50
10 to under 20	(4)(15) = 60	(4)(225) = 900
20 to under 30	(12)(25) = 300	(12)(625) = 7 500
30 to under 40	(28)(35) = 980	(28)(1225) = 34 300
40 to under 50	(44)(45) = 1980	(44)(2025) = 89 100
50 to under 60	(43)(55) = 2365	(43)(3025) = 130 075
60 to under 70	(23)(65) = 1495	(23)(4225) = 97 175
70 to under 80	(7)(75) = 525	(7)(5625) = 39 375
80 to under 90	(5)(85) = 425	(5)(7225) = 36 125
90 to under 100	(2)(95) = 190	(2)(9025) = 18 050
Totals	$\sum fx = 8330$	$\sum fx^2 = 452\,650$

Step 1 Determine N by adding the frequencies in Column 1, $N = \sum f = 170$.

Step 2 Determine the class midpoints x (see Column 3).

Step 3 Determine the value of the squared midpoints x^2 (see Column 4).

Step 4 Determine the value of the weighted midpoints fx by multiplying the values in Column 2 and Column 3, and add the values to obtain $\sum fx$ (see Column 5).

Step 5 Determine the values of the weighted squared midpoints fx^2 by multiplying the values in Column 2 and Column 4, and add the values to obtain $\sum fx^2$ (see Column 6). The values in Column 6 can also be obtained by multiplying the values in Column 3 and Column 5: $fx(x) = fx^2$.

a) The mean, $\mu = \dfrac{\sum fx}{N} = \dfrac{8330}{170} = 49$

b) The variance, $\sigma^2 = \dfrac{\sum fx^2}{N} - \mu^2 = \dfrac{452\,650}{170} - 49^2$

$= 2662.6471 - 2401 = 261.6471$

c) The standard deviation, $\sigma = \sqrt{\sigma^2} = \sqrt{261.6471} = 16.1755$

D. *The Coefficient of Variation*

The **coefficient of variation** is a measure of the *relative* magnitudes of the standard deviation and mean of a data set. It is used to compare the relative variability of two or more data sets.

$$\text{COEFFICIENT OF VARIATION, CV} = \frac{\sigma}{\mu}$$ ←*Formula* 4.8

where σ = the standard deviation of the data set;
μ = the mean of the data set.

EXAMPLE 4.3e

The daily closing prices of the common shares of two companies for a two-week trading period are listed below:

Company A	\$8.00	\$8.40	\$7.80	\$8.30	\$8.60
	\$9.00	\$8.70	\$8.30	\$7.70	\$7.40
Company B	\$150.00	\$154.00	\$148.00	\$151.00	\$157.00
	\$157.00	\$160.00	\$152.00	\$148.00	\$153.00

Compare the variation in the prices of the two stocks over the two-week period.

SOLUTION

To compare the variability in the two sets of data, determine the mean, the standard deviation, and the coefficient of variation for both sets.

Company A		Company B	
Price x	x^2	Price x	x^2
8.00	64.00	150	22 500
8.40	70.56	154	23 716
7.80	60.84	148	21 904
8.30	68.89	151	22 801
8.60	73.96	157	24 649
9.00	81.00	157	24 649
8.70	75.69	160	25 600
8.30	68.89	152	23 104
7.70	59.29	148	21 904
7.40	54.76	153	23 409
$\sum x = 82.20$	$\sum x^2 = 677.88$	$\sum x = 1530$	$\sum x^2 = 234\ 236$

For Company A,

$$\mu = \frac{82.20}{10} = 8.22$$

$$\sigma^2 = \frac{677.88}{10} - 8.22^2$$
$$= 67.788 - 67.5684$$
$$= 0.2196$$

$$\sigma = \sqrt{0.2196} = 0.468\,615$$

$$CV = \frac{\sigma}{\mu} = \frac{0.468\,615}{8.22}$$
$$= 0.0570 = 5.70\%$$

For Company B,

$$\mu = \frac{1530}{10} = 153.00$$

$$\sigma^2 = \frac{234\,236}{10} - 153^2$$
$$= 23\,423.60 - 23\,409$$
$$= 14.60$$

$$\sigma = \sqrt{14.60} = 3.8210$$

$$CV = \frac{\sigma}{\mu} = \frac{3.8210}{153.00}$$
$$= 0.024\,974 = 2.50\%$$

Conclusion Based on absolute magnitudes, the variability of the share price of Company A with a standard deviation of \$0.47 is decidedly smaller than that of the share price for Company B showing a standard deviation of \$3.82. However, in terms of the price level, the price of the shares of Company A is more than twice as variable as the price of the shares of Company B.

EXERCISE 4.3

1. During the first quarter, the number of rejected units produced per week by a group of workers was as follows:

Worker	A	B	C	D	E	F
No. rejected	84	76	68	64	71	77

Worker	G	H	I	J	K	L
No. rejected	62	80	64	64	75	66

For the given data, compute
a) the mean;
b) the variance;
c) the standard deviation.

2. For the following set of class marks, compute
a) the mean;
b) the variance;
c) the standard deviation.

91	79	87	87	63	69	62	69	41	60	84	87
89	45	48	94	92	87	79	71	84	62	80	67

3. For the set of test scores given, determine
a) the mean;
b) the variance;
c) the standard deviation.

Test score	1	2	3	4	5	6	7	8	9	10
No. of students	2	4	12	28	44	48	28	7	5	2

4. The following information was compiled about the absences of a group of employees:

No. of days absent	2	4	6	8	10	12	14	16	18
No. of employees	4	13	21	36	38	27	15	4	2

Compute
a) the average number of days absent;
b) the variance;
c) the standard deviation.

5. For the frequency distribution below compute
a) the mean;
b) the variance;
c) the standard deviation.

Class	Frequency
0 to under 10	44
10 to under 20	62
20 to under 30	77
30 to under 40	52
40 to under 50	32
50 to under 60	20
60 to under 70	12
70 to under 80	6
80 to under 90	4
90 to under 100	1

6. Compute **(a)** the mean; **(b)** the variance; **(c)** the standard deviation for the following frequency distribution.

Class interval	Number in class
100 to under 150	28
150 to under 200	56
200 to under 250	85
250 to under 300	65
300 to under 350	32
350 to under 400	18
400 to under 450	10
450 to under 500	6

7. Determine the coefficient of variation of the following two sets of class marks and comment on their variability.

Class A	12	4	18	15	9	11	3	7
Class B	84	56	73	62	78	48	93	80
Class A	17	20	13	8	14	12	6	
Class B	66	75	73	88	56	64	83	

8. Compare the variability in the data contained in the following two frequency distributions:

Hourly wages (in dollars)	Number
10.00 to under 12.00	12
12.00 to under 14.00	25
14.00 to under 16.00	49
16.00 to under 18.00	46
18.00 to under 20.00	38
20.00 to under 22.00	18
22.00 to under 24.00	9
24.00 to under 26.00	3

Weekly salary (in dollars)	Number
300.00 to under 400.00	10
400.00 to under 500.00	19
500.00 to under 600.00	20
600.00 to under 700.00	18
700.00 to under 800.00	10
800.00 to under 900.00	6
900.00 to under 1000.00	4
1000.00 to under 1100.00	2
1100.00 to under 1200.00	1

REVIEW EXERCISE

1. For the following test scores, calculate
   a) the mean;
   b) the median;
   c) the range;
   d) the interquartile range;
   e) the average deviation from the mean;
   f) the variance;
   g) the standard deviation.

55	59	87	59	91	77	68	86
58	87	73	83	84	94	89	82

2. Starting salaries for ten recent community college graduates are as follows:

30 000	40 000	20 000	29 000	35 000
39 000	60 000	40 000	31 000	30 000

   Calculate
   a) the mean;
   b) the median;
   c) the range;
   d) the 35th percentile;
   e) the average deviation from the mean;
   f) the variance;
   g) the standard deviation.

3. For the years of seniority listed below, calculate
   a) the mean;
   b) the median;
   c) the range;
   d) the interquartile range;
   e) the average deviation from the mean;
   f) the variance;
   g) the standard deviation.

15	12	6	15	12	7	16	13	7	16
13	8	17	13	10	17	14	10	19	20

4. In a recent Canada-wide marketing research study of 1200 homes, the following data were collected:

After-tax family income (in dollars)	Number of families
10 000 to under 20 000	46
20 000 to under 30 000	152
30 000 to under 40 000	271
40 000 to under 50 000	282
50 000 to under 60 000	254
60 000 to under 70 000	101
70 000 to under 80 000	71
80 000 to under 90 000	14
90 000 to under 100 000	5
100 000 to under 110 000	3
110 000 to under 120 000	1

Calculate

a) the mean; **b)** the median;
c) the range; **d)** the interquartile range;
e) the 6th percentile; **f)** the 90th percentile;
g) the variance; **h)** the standard deviation.

5. In a recent survey of used car prices, the following data were taken:

Used car prices (in dollars)	Number of cars
0 to under 5 000	100
5 000 to under 10 000	121
10 000 to under 15 000	200
15 000 to under 20 000	300
20 000 to under 25 000	150
25 000 to under 30 000	100
30 000 to under 35 000	40
35 000 to under 40 000	50

Calculate

a) the mean; **b)** the median;
c) the range; **d)** the interquartile range;
e) the 16th percentile; **f)** the 80th percentile;
g) the variance; **h)** the standard deviation.

6. A recent review of a compact disc distributor's product line is summarized as follows:

Selling price (in dollars)	Number of titles
0 to under 5	51
5 to under 10	184
10 to under 15	241
15 to under 20	1468
20 to under 25	1339
25 to under 30	255
30 to under 35	98
35 to under 40	14

Determine

a) the mean; **b)** the median;
c) the range; **d)** the interquartile range;
e) the third decile; **f)** the 85th percentile;
g) the variance; **h)** the standard deviation.

7. One number is missing from the following data.

55	95	78	95	19	77	86	78
68	85	?	37	38	48	49	28

a) Given that the mean is 66.5, determine the missing number.
b) Determine
  i) the median;
  ii) the interquartile range;
  iii) the average deviation from the mean.

8. Your statistics instructor has told you that your final grade in this course is 63. You have misplaced one of your eight test marks. The other test scores are 50, 54, 60, 65, 90, 90, and 75.
a) Calculate the missing mark.
b) Calculate the average deviation from the mean.

9. The following 20 observations have been written in ascending order. The value of three data points is missing, but their position in the array is known and indicated by "xx."

xx	50	xx	56	57	63	68	72	73	73
75	79	81	82	85	87	87	88	xx	99

a) Determine
  (i) the median; **(ii)** the interquartile range.
b) Why can the interquartile range be determined but not the range or the mean?

10. Cadillacs have become classic show cars commanding high selling prices. Cars in excellent condition were recently selling for the following amounts:

Model year	1953	1954	1955	1956	1957	1958	1959
Amount ($)	91 437	51 939	61 045	45 530	52 026	40 890	39 585

For the given selling prices, determine the average deviation from the mean.

11. Sales of the top-selling vehicles in Canada for 2001 are listed below (in 000s):

84 79 66 66 59 49 46 41 39 42

Determine the average deviation from the mean sales.

12. A courier company tracks shipments of parcels. Data for the last six years were:

Year	1997	1998	1999	2000	2001	2002
Shipments	124 441	95 268	88 145	92 404	85 577	88 728

For the given data, determine the average deviation from the mean.

13. For the given data, determine
a) the average deviation from the mean;
b) the variance and the standard deviation.

Class	1 to 3	4 to 6	7 to 9	10 to 12	13 to 15	16 to 18
Frequency	2	9	29	58	37	12

14. Weekly sales at a discount shoe store are listed as follows:

Sales range ($)	0–19	20–39	40–59	60–79	80–99
Number of Sales	30	100	150	60	40

For the given data, determine
a) the average deviation from the mean sales;
b) the variance and the standard deviation.

15. Frequency distributions are sometimes reported by class midpoint instead of class intervals, as shown for the following data.

Class midpoint	0.5	1.5	2.5	3.5	4.5
Frequency	28	42	47	36	15

Compute
a) the average deviation from the mean;
b) the variance and the standard deviation.

16. Cream and Jelly Donuts keeps track of the number of customers per month in each of its Ottawa locations. The data for October 2002 were as follows:

Store location	Customers
Downtown	8836
Byward Market	8725
Nepean	8523
Kanata	8147
Orleans	8079
Airport	7637
Glebe	6907

Compute
(a) the mean; **(b)** the variance; **(c)** the standard deviation.

17. The following are the weights of cows (in kilograms) shipped from Tim Rak's cattle farm to the slaughterhouse:

841 820 910 885 945 905 875

For the shipment, compute
(a) the mean; **(b)** the variance; **(c)** the standard deviation.

18. During the holiday season, 10 parcels were sent to relatives. The weights (in kilograms) of these parcels are as follows:

20	10	30	35	10
15	20	15	25	25

Compute **(a)** the mean; **(b)** the variance; **(c)** the standard deviation of these parcels.

19. The Canadian wine industry keeps track of export shipments of wine to the following countries:

Country	Number of cases
United States	37 787
United Kingdom	12 824
France	12 574
Italy	11 765
Australia	10 118
New Zealand	7 604
Germany	7 155
Poland	6 757

Compute
(a) the mean; **(b)** the average deviation from the mean;
(c) the variance; **(d)** the standard deviation.

20. A survey of salaries of chief executive officers showed compensation packages as follows (in thousands of dollars):

3377	3000	2742	2248	1900
1364	1350	1280	1200	1179

Compute
(a) the mean; **(b)** the average deviation from the mean;
(c) the variance; **(d)** the standard deviation.

21. The most active stocks on the TSE (by volume) at the end of the first week in January of 2003 are listed below:

		Volume traded ($ millions)		
28.8	26.5	23.1	7.7	5.8
4.1	3.7	3.2	3.1	2.6

Calculate the **(a)** the mean; **(b)** the average deviation from the mean; **(c)** the variance; **(d)** the standard deviation.

22. A typical college telecommuncations call centre handles more calls in September than at any other time of the year. A tracking system is used to keep a record of the elapsed time before the calls are answered. The system produced the following data for a typical day in September:

Elapsed time (s)	0 to 3	4 to 7	8 to 11	12 to 15	16 to 19
Number of phone calls	48	923	1721	1387	69

Calculate
(a) the mean; **(b)** the median;
(c) the variance; **(d)** the standard deviation.

23. A survey was taken at a local bank to determine the queue wait time to see a teller. The bank has said that a customer waits no longer than 5 min on average. The data for the survey are below:

Wait time (in min)	0–2	3–5	6–8	9–11
Number of customers	60	28	10	2

Do you believe the manager?
Calculate **(a)** the mean; **(b)** the variance; **(c)** the standard deviation.

24. For the following data, compute
(a) the mean; **(b)** the median; **(c)** the variance; **(d)** the standard deviation.

Size (m)	0 to under 2	2 to under 4	4 to under 6	6 to under 8	8 to under 10
Frequency	1426	2292	2202	1332	465

25. A city councillor living near Abbotsford School requested a population analysis of the neighbourhood served by the school to determine if a request for a playground should be granted. The following data were provided:

Number of children per household	0	1	2	3	4	5	6
Number of households	15	89	71	46	28	7	4

Determine the mean and the standard deviation for the number of children per household.

26. Calculate the mean and the standard deviation for the following values of orders received by Ace Distributors:

Value of order ($)	2	4	6	8	10	12	14	16	18
Frequency	4	13	21	36	38	27	15	4	2

27. Enrollment at a community college is limited by the number of seats in each classroom. The following table lists the classroom size and number of classes held in each.

Classroom size	20	40	60	80	100
Number of classes	5	40	15	20	20

a) Calculate the average class size.
b) Calculate the standard deviation.

28. Because of the large registration for a charity golf tournament, the field was split into a morning group and an afternoon group. The morning group had 60 participants, with an average score of 82 and a variance of 6.25. The afternoon group had 80 participants, with an average score of 76 and a variance of 9.0.
a) Compare the variability of the scores for the two groups.
b) Determine the mean score for all participants.

29. Truck A delivered 84 boxes having an average weight of 4.2 kg with a variance of 0.81 kg. Truck B delivered 180 boxes with an average weight of 4.0 kg and a variance of 0.64 kg.
a) Comment on the variability in the weight of the boxes delivered by the two trucks.
b) Compute the mean for the combined shipments.

30. A collection of 35 blood samples had an average protein proportion of 6.3% and a standard deviation of 0.4%. If one of the blood samples with a protein proportion of 13.1% was found to be contaminated, determine the mean protein proportion for the 34 good blood samples.

31. A teacher with a class size of 40 students computes the class average for a test to be 61 with a standard deviation of 12. Shortly afterwards, John Doe, whose test score was 22, withdrew from the class. Recalculate the class mean on the test for the remaining students.

32. You are a manager of a 20-person department. The performance rating of your department last year was 6.5 (based on a scale of 1–10) with a standard deviation of 1.1. Your immediate supervisor has discussed with you that your rating should be at least 7.0. If your least-performing employee had a performance rating of 1.0, how much does he need to improve to meet the new standard?

33. Three companies produced the following sales data:

	Company A	Company B	Company C
Average yearly sales	\$2 500 000 000	\$125 000 000	\$5 750 000
Standard deviation	\$25 000 000	\$1 875 000	\$287 500

a) Determine the coefficient of variation for each company's sales.
b) If you were looking at long-term job prospects based on stability, which company should you choose to work for? Explain.

34. You are trying to make a decision on which stock to add to your portfolio. The two choices are listed below:

	Stock A	Stock B
Average share price last year (\$)	30	80
Standard deviation	3	20

a) Determine the coefficient of variation for each stock.
b) If you are a conservative investor, which stock would you invest in and why?

35. Ashley and Riley both sell for an electronics equipment distributor. Their monthly sales for the last six months are summarized below.

	July	Aug	Sept	Oct	Nov	Dec
Ashley	11 500	9 000	16 500	11 500	11 000	12 500
Riley	32 500	25 000	40 000	32 500	29 000	33 000

a) Compute the average monthly sales for each salesperson.
b) Compute the standard deviation for each.
c) Determine the coefficient of variation for each.
d) Compare the variation in monthly sales between the two.

SELF-TEST

A. Questions **1** through **5** are based on the following frequency distribution of stocks in a pension fund:

Stock price (in dollars)	Number of stocks
0.00 to under 5.00	4
5.00 to under 10.00	65
10.00 to under 15.00	80
15.00 to under 20.00	120
20.00 to under 25.00	135
25.00 to under 30.00	40
30.00 to under 35.00	11
35.00 to under 40.00	5

1. What is the range of prices in the portfolio?

2. Compute the interquartile range.

3. Compute the median stock price.

4. Compute the mean stock price.

5. Calculate the variance and the standard deviation.

B. Questions **6** through **11** are based on the following set of prices for a standard two-storey home in 2001 and 2002 (in $000):

2001	350	360	240	265	315	380	250	415
2002	270	300	205	210	300	295	225	320

6. What was the range of prices in 2001?

7. Determine the interquartile range for 2001.

8. Determine the mean and the median for both 2001 and 2002.

9. Calculate the average deviation from the mean for 2001.

10. Determine the standard deviation for both 2001 and 2002.

11. Determine the coefficient of variation for each year.

For an online glossary, go to **www.pearsoned.ca/hummelbrunner**.

Key Terms

Average deviation from the mean 117
Coefficient of variation 126
Deviation 116
Interpercentile range 111
Interquartile range 113
Measures of variability 109
Range 110
Standard deviation 119
Variance 119

Summary of Formulas

1. Range

$$\text{RANGE} = \text{HIGHEST VALUE} - \text{LOWEST VALUE}$$ ←*Formula* 4.1

2. Interquartile range

$$\text{INTERQUARTILE RANGE} = Q_3 - Q_1$$ ←*Formula* 4.2

3. Average deviation form the mean

$$\text{AVERAGE DEVIATION FROM THE MEAN} = \frac{\sum |x - \mu|}{N}$$ ←*Formula* 4.3

4. Variance

a) Ungrouped data:

$$\text{VARIANCE,} \quad \sigma^2 = \frac{\sum (x - \mu)^2}{N}$$ ←*Formula* 4.4

5. Standard deviation

$$\text{STANDARD DEVIATION,} \quad \sigma = \sqrt{\sigma^2}$$ ←*Formula* 4.5

or

$$\sigma^2 = \frac{\sum x^2}{N} - \left(\frac{\sum x}{N}\right)^2 \quad \text{or} \quad \sigma^2 = \frac{\sum x^2}{N} - \mu^2$$ ←*Formula* 4.6

b) Grouped data:

$$\sigma^2 = \frac{\sum fx^2}{N} - \left(\frac{\sum fx}{N}\right)^2 \quad \text{or} \quad \sigma^2 = \frac{\sum fx^2}{N} - \mu^2$$ ←*Formula* 4.7

6. Coefficient of variation

$$\text{COEFFICIENT OF VARIATION, CV} = \frac{\sigma}{\mu}$$ ←*Formula* 4.8

Index Numbers

Introduction

The use of index numbers in business has grown steadily since they were first introduced at the turn of the century. Indexes provide an easy way of expressing changes that occur in daily business. Converting data to indexes makes working with very large or small numbers easier and provides a basis for many types of analysis.

Learning Outcomes

Upon completion of this chapter you will be able to

1. construct simple price, quantity, and value indexes;
2. construct weighted price, quantity, and value indexes;
3. construct special-purpose (composite) indexes;
4. interpret indexes to identify trends in a data set;
5. use the consumer price index to determine the purchasing power of the dollar and to compute real income;
6. shift the base to make two series comparable;
7. splice an old series with a new series of index numbers.

SECTION 5.1

Nature of Index Numbers

An **index number** results from the comparison of two values measured at different points in time. The comparison of the two values is stated in the form of a ratio, changed into the form of a percent; when the percent symbol is dropped, the result is called an index number.

EXAMPLE 5.1a

The price of an article was \$12.00 in 1992 and \$18.00 in 2002. Compare the two prices to create an index number.

SOLUTION

The change in price over the time period 1992 to 2002 can be measured in relative terms by writing the ratio

$$\frac{\text{Price in 2002}}{\text{Price in 1992}} = \frac{18.00}{12.00} = 1.50 = 150\%.$$

The desired price index number = 150.

Note 1 The construction of the index number requires the selection of one of the two numbers as the denominator of the ratio. The point in time at which the selected number was measured is referred to as the **base period**—in our example 1992 has been selected as the base period. Usually the *chronologically earliest* year is chosen as the base period.

Note 2 The index for the base period is always 100. The difference between an index number and 100 indicates the change that has taken place. The index number 150 indicates that the price in 2002 was 50% higher than the price in 1992.

A wide variety of index numbers can be constructed. They are used in comparing and analyzing economic data and have become a widely accepted tool for measuring changes in business activity.

The most important index numbers are

1. *price indexes*, measuring relative change in price;
2. *quantity indexes*, measuring relative change in quantity;
3. *value indexes*, measuring relative change in value.

Price indexes, quantity indexes, and value indexes can be **simple index numbers** or **aggregate index numbers**. Indexes that compare individual items over time are called simple indexes, while indexes that involve a group of commodities are referred to as aggregate indexes.

SECTION 5.2

Constructing and Interpreting Simple Indexes

A. Simple Price Indexes

A **simple price index** can be constructed by means of the formula

$$P = \frac{P_n}{P_0}(100)$$

←*Formula* 5.1

where P_0 = the price in the chosen base period;
P_n = the price in any other given period.

EXAMPLE 5.2a

Construct index numbers for the prices listed below for the period 1990 to 2002 and interpret their meaning using 1990 as the base year.

Year	1990	1993	1996	1999	2002
Price	\$20	\$22	\$25	\$20	\$18

SOLUTION

The price in the chosen base year 1990, $P_0 = 20$.

a) For 1993, $P_n = 22$.

$$P = \frac{P_n}{P_0}(100) = \frac{22}{20}(100) = 1.1(100) = 110$$

Interpretation The price of the article in 1993 was 10% higher than the price in 1990.

b) For 1996, $P_n = 25$.

$$P = \frac{P_n}{P_0}(100) = \frac{25}{20}(100) = 1.25(100) = 125$$

The price in 1996 was 25% higher than the price in 1990.

c) For 1999, $P_n = 20$.

$$P = \frac{P_n}{P_0}(100) = \frac{20}{20}(100) = 1.00(100) = 100$$

The price in 1999 was the same as in 1990.

d) For 2002, $P_n = 18$.

$$P = \frac{P_n}{P_0}(100) = \frac{18}{20}(100) = 0.90(100) = 90$$

The price in 2002 was 10% lower than the price in 1990.

B. *Simple Quantity Indexes*

The formula for constructing a **simple quantity index** is

$$Q = \frac{Q_n}{Q_0}(100)$$

←*Formula 5.2*

where Q_0 = the quantity in the base period;
Q_n = the quantity in any other given period.

EXAMPLE 5.2b

Assume that the number of articles sold at the prices given in Example 5.2a were as follows:

Year	1990	1993	1996	1999	2002
Quantity	200	220	180	300	420

Construct index numbers for the quantities based on 1990 and interpret.

SOLUTION

The quantity in the chosen base period 1990, $Q_0 = 200$.

a) For 1993, $Q_n = 220$.

$$Q = \frac{Q_n}{Q_0}(100) = \frac{220}{200}(100) = 1.10(100) = 110$$

The quantity sold in 1993 was 10% higher than in 1990.

b) For 1996, $Q_n = 180$.

$$Q = \frac{Q_n}{Q_0}(100) = \frac{180}{200}(100) = 0.90(100) = 90$$

The quantity sold in 1996 was 10% lower than in 1990.

c) For 1999, $Q_n = 300$.

$$Q = \frac{Q_n}{Q_0}(100) = \frac{300}{200}(150) = 1.50(100) = 150$$

The quantity sold in 1999 was 50% higher than in 1990.

d) For 2002, $Q_n = 420$.

$$Q = \frac{Q_n}{Q_0}(100) = \frac{420}{200}(100) = 2.10(100) = 210$$

The quantity sold in 2002 was 110% higher than in 1990.

C. *Simple Value Indexes*

The formula for constructing a **simple value index** is

$$V = \frac{V_n}{V_0}(100) = \frac{P_nQ_n}{P_0Q_0}(100)$$ ←*Formula* 5.3

where $V_0 = P_0Q_0$ is the value in the chosen base period;
$V_n = P_nQ_n$ is the value in any other given period.

○ EXAMPLE 5.2c

Construct value indexes for the prices and quantities given in examples 5.2a and 5.2b respectively and interpret.

● SOLUTION

The value in the chosen base period 1990,

$$V_0 = (P_0)(Q_0) = (20)(200) = 4000$$

a) For 1993, $V_n = (P_n)(Q_n) = (22)(220) = 4840$.

$$V = \frac{V_n}{V_0}(100) = \frac{4840}{4000}(100) = 1.21(100) = 121$$

The value in 1993 was 21% higher than in 1990.

b) For 1996, $V_n = (P_n)(Q_n) = (25)(180) = 4500$.

$$V = \frac{V_n}{V_0}(100) = \frac{4500}{4000}(100) = 1.125(100) = 112.5$$

The value in 1996 was 12.5% higher than in 1990.

c) For 1999, $V_n = (P_n)(Q_n) = (20)(300) = 6000$.

$$V = \frac{V_n}{V_0}(100) = \frac{6000}{4000}(100) = 1.50(100) = 150$$

The value in 1999 was 50% higher than in 1990.

d) For 2002, $V_n = (P_n)(Q_n) = (18)(420) = 7560$.

$$V = \frac{V_n}{V_0}(100) = \frac{7560}{4000}(100) = 1.89(100) = 189$$

The value in 2002 was 89% higher than in 1990.

SECTION 5.3

Aggregate Indexes

A. Unweighted Aggregate Indexes

An **unweighted aggregate price index** is obtained by summing the prices of a number of commodities and comparing the sums over time.

$$\text{UNWEIGHTED AGGREGATE PRICE INDEX, } P = \frac{\sum P_n}{\sum P_0}(100)$$ ←*Formula* 5.4

○ **EXAMPLE 5.3a**

Use the following information to compute the aggregate commodity price index for 2002 with base period 1991.

Commodity	Price 1991	Price 2002
Loaf of bread	$0.80	$1.60
Beef (kg)	$10.00	$30.00
Car	$8000.00	$10 000.00

● **SOLUTION**

$$\sum P_0 = 0.80 + 10.00 + 8000.00 = 8010.80$$

$$\sum P_n = 1.60 + 30.00 + 10\,000.00 = 10\,031.60$$

$$P = \frac{\sum P_n}{\sum P_0}(100) = \frac{10\,031.60}{8010.80}(100) = 1.252\,26(100) = 125.2$$

Note Unweighted aggregate price indexes tend to be misleading, since all commodities in the group are given the same weight. A more appropriate approach to the construction of aggregate price indexes takes quantities into account.

B. Weighted Aggregate Indexes (Laspeyres Method)

Weighted aggregate indexes are obtained by allowing for quantities as well as prices. While there are several methods of constructing weighted aggregate indexes, the most frequently used method is referred to as the *Laspeyres method*.

In this method, an aggregate price index is obtained by using the base-year quantities to measure the relative change in prices.

$$P = \frac{\sum P_n Q_0}{\sum P_0 Q_0}(100)$$ ←*Formula* 5.5

A weighted aggregate quantity index is similarly obtained by using base-year prices to measure relative change in quantities.

$$Q = \frac{\sum P_0 Q_n}{\sum P_0 Q_0}(100) \qquad \leftarrow \textit{Formula 5.6}$$

A weighted aggregate value index to measure relative change in value can be constructed by using the formula

$$V = \frac{\sum P_n Q_n}{\sum P_0 Q_0}(100) \qquad \leftarrow \textit{Formula 5.7}$$

Note In all three formulas the *denominator* is $\sum P_0 Q_0$.

EXAMPLE 5.3b

Use the following information to compute weighted aggregate price, quantity, and value indexes for 2002 using 1991 as base year.

	1991		2002	
Commodity	Price P_0	Quantity Q_0	Price P_n	Quantity Q_n
Bread (loaves)	$0.80	400	$1.60	600
Beef (kg)	$10.00	100	$30.00	80
Car	$8000.00	1	$10 000.00	1

SOLUTION

The formulas require the calculation of the products

$$P_0 Q_0, \quad P_n Q_0, \quad P_0 Q_n, \quad P_n Q_n$$

as shown in the chart below.

$P_0 Q_0$	$P_n Q_0$	$P_0 Q_n$	$P_n Q_n$
0.80(400) = 320	1.60(400) = 640	0.80(600) = 480	1.60(600) = 960
10.00(100) = 1000	30.00(100) = 3 000	10.00(80) = 800	30.00(80) = 2 400
8000.00(1) = 8000	10 000.00(1) = 10 000	8000.00(1) = 8000	10 000.00(1) = 10 000
$\sum P_0 Q_0 = 9320$	$\sum P_n Q_0 = 13\,640$	$\sum P_0 Q_n = 9280$	$\sum P_n Q_n = 13\,360$

Now compute the index numbers by substituting the sum of the products determined above in the appropriate formula.

$$P = \frac{\sum P_n Q_0}{\sum P_0 Q_0}(100) = \frac{13\ 640}{9320}(100) = 146.4$$

Prices in 2002 were 46.4% higher than in 1991.

$$Q = \frac{\sum P_0 Q_n}{\sum P_0 Q_0}(100) = \frac{9280}{9320}(100) = 99.6$$

Quantities in 2002 were 0.4% lower than in 1991.

$$V = \frac{\sum P_n Q_n}{\sum P_0 Q_0}(100) = \frac{13\ 360}{9\ 320}(100) = 143.3$$

The value in 2002 was 43.3% more than in 1991.

These calculations can be completed using EXCEL, as demonstrated in USING EXCEL 5.1.

USING EXCEL 5.1

Use the information from the chart in Example 5.3b to calculate the weighted aggregate price, quantity, and value indexes.

1. Type the row labels **Commodity**, **Bread (loaves)**, **Beef (kg)** and **Car** into cells A2–A5.
2. Type column headings **1991** into cells B1 and C1, **2002** into cells D1 and E1.
3. Type column headings **Price (Po)**, **Quantity (Qo)**, **Price (Pn)** and **Quantity (Qn)** into the respective cells B2–E2.
4. Enter the price and quantity data of the commodities from the problem into cells B3–E5.
5. Type column headings **PoQo**, **PnQo**, **PoQn** and **PnQn** into the respective cells B9–E9.
6. Select cell B10 and type **=B3*C3** into the formula bar and enter. **Copy** and **Paste** cell B10 into cells B11 and B12.
7. Select cell C10 and type **=D3*C3** into the formula bar and enter. **Copy** and **Paste** cell C10 into cells C11 and C12.
8. Select cell D10 and type **=B3*E3** into the formula bar and enter. **Copy** and **Paste** cell D10 into cells D11 and D12.
9. Select cell E10 and type **=D3*E3** into the formula bar and enter. **Copy** and **Paste** cell B10 into cells E11 and E12.
10. Type the row label **Totals** into cell A13; select cells B13–E13 and from the toolbar click on the **AutoSum** button Σ (or select cell B13; type **=SUM(B10:B12)** into the formula bar and enter; and then **Copy** and **Paste** cell B13 into cells C13–E13).
11. Type in the notes **Price Index**, **Quantity Index** and **Value Index** into cells A18–A20.
12. To simulate the mathematical formula for the Price Index, $P = \frac{\Sigma P_n Q_0}{\Sigma P_0 Q_0}(100)$, select cell B18 and type **=(C13/B13)*100** into the formula bar and enter.
13. To simulate the mathematical formula for the Quantity Index, $Q = \frac{\Sigma P_0 Q_n}{\Sigma P_0 Q_0}(100)$, select cell B19 and type **=(D13/B13)*100** into the formula bar and enter.
14. To simulate the mathematical formula for the Value Index, $V = \frac{\Sigma P_n Q_n}{\Sigma P_0 Q_0}(100)$, select cell B20 and type **=(E13/B13)*100** into the formula bar and enter.

15. Type the note **(Prices in 2002 were 46.4% higher than in 1991.)** into cell C18.
16. Type the note **(Quantities in 2002 were 0.4% lower than in 1991.)** into cell C19.
17. Type the note **(The value in 2002 was 43.3% higher than in 1991.)** into cell C20.

Format the tables (changing column widths, altering font sizes and styles, creating borders, changing cell background patterns, etc.) to make it clear and readable.

OUTPUT

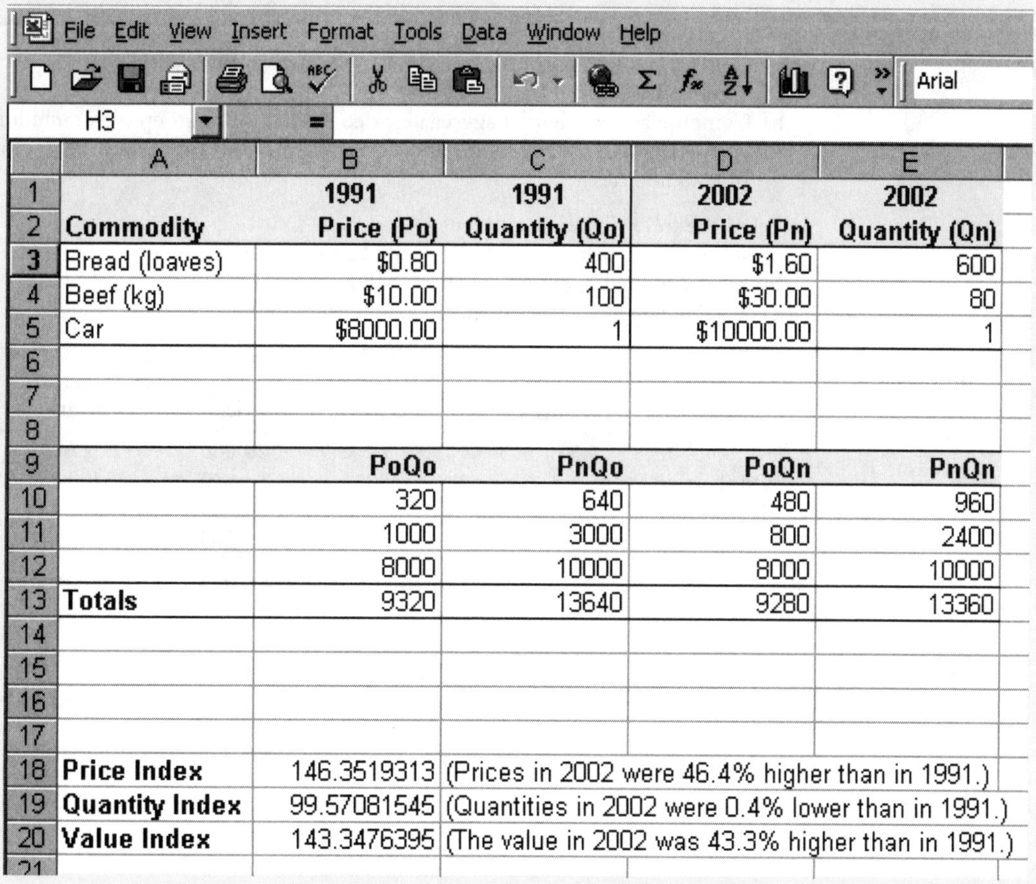

	A	B	C	D	E
1		1991	1991	2002	2002
2	Commodity	Price (Po)	Quantity (Qo)	Price (Pn)	Quantity (Qn)
3	Bread (loaves)	$0.80	400	$1.60	600
4	Beef (kg)	$10.00	100	$30.00	80
5	Car	$8000.00	1	$10000.00	1
6					
7					
8					
9		PoQo	PnQo	PoQn	PnQn
10		320	640	480	960
11		1000	3000	800	2400
12		8000	10000	8000	10000
13	Totals	9320	13640	9280	13360
14					
15					
16					
17					
18	Price Index	146.3519313	(Prices in 2002 were 46.4% higher than in 1991.)		
19	Quantity Index	99.57081545	(Quantities in 2002 were 0.4% lower than in 1991.)		
20	Value Index	143.3476395	(The value in 2002 was 43.3% higher than in 1991.)		
21					

EXERCISE 5.3

Note Unless otherwise specified, the base period is the chronologically earliest time period.

1. The following information has been compiled about a group of commodities:

	1990		2002	
Commodity	Price	Quantity	Price	Quantity
Bread (loaf)	$0.80	2000	$1.40	3600
Milk (litre)	$0.90	600	$1.20	800
Butter (kg)	$3.60	400	$4.80	300

   a) Compute simple price, quantity, and value indexes for each of the commodities listed.
   b) Compute an unweighted aggregate price index for the group of commodities.
   c) Compute weighted aggregate price, quantity, and value indexes for the group of commodities.

2. From the following data, compute
   a) simple price, quantity, and value indexes for each item;
   b) an unweighted aggregate price index for the items;
   c) weighted aggregate price, quantity, and value indexes.

	1986		2002	
Commodity	Price	Quantity	Price	Quantity
Automobile	$12 000	20	$20 000	25
Oil (barrel)	$15	1200	$20	2400
Transformers	$750	60	$600	80
Tires	$80	300	$200	200

SECTION 5.4

Special-Purpose (Composite) Indexes

Special-purpose (composite) indexes are created by a combination of business and/or economic indicators selected to measure trends in specific areas of concern.

○ EXAMPLE 5.4a

An index of general business activity is to be constructed from the following data (base 1992):

Indicator	1992	2002	Weight
Sales ($ millions)	60	126	40%
Index of employment	120	150	25%
Units of output (000)	100	120	15%
Unemployment (000)	60	45	20%

● SOLUTION

First compute the simple index for each indicator; then multiply the resulting index by the percent weight and add the weighted values.

Indicator	Simple index	Weighted value
Sales	$I = \frac{126}{60}(100) = 210$	$210(0.40) = 84.00$
Employment	$I = \frac{150}{120}(100) = 125$	$125(0.25) = 31.25$
Output	$I = \frac{120}{100}(100) = 120$	$120(0.15) = 18.00$
Unemployment	$I = \frac{45}{60}(100) = 75$	$75(0.20) = 15.00$
		General business index = 148.25

General business activity in 2002 was 48.3% higher than in 1992.

EXERCISE 5.4

1. Construct a special cost-of-living index from the following data, using 1992 as the base:

	Index		
Item	1992	2002	Weight
Food	$120	$180	35%
Rent	110	135	10%
Clothing	112	95	17%
Utilities	130	170	8%
Miscellaneous	104	120	30%

2. Construct an index of business progress from the following information (base 1992):

Indicator	1992	2002	Weight
Assets ($000)	3400	20 400	40%
Number of members	1774	5 140	25%
Capital ($000)	9	238	15%
Reserves ($000)	12	737	20%

SECTION 5.5

The Consumer Price Index and Its Uses

A. *The Consumer Price Index (CPI)*

The **consumer price index** (CPI) is the most widely used indicator of changes in the overall price level of goods and services. The Canadian consumer price index is currently based on 1992 price levels and is published monthly by Statistics Canada.

For example, a consumer price index of 110.5 in 1999 indicates that the price level has increased 10.5% relative to the base year (1992) price level.

The main uses of the CPI include the determination of the *purchasing power* of the Canadian dollar and the computation of *real income*.

B. *Purchasing Power of the Dollar*

The **purchasing power of the dollar** is the *reciprocal* of the consumer price index; that is,

$$\text{PURCHASING POWER OF DOLLAR} = \frac{\$1}{\text{CPI}}(100)$$ ←*Formula 5.8*

EXAMPLE 5.5a

Determine the purchasing power of the dollar for a CPI of 200, and interpret.

SOLUTION

$$\text{PURCHASING POWER OF DOLLAR} = \frac{\$1}{\text{CPI}}(100) = \frac{\$1}{200}(100) = \$0.50$$

This means that the current dollar is worth half of the base-year (1992) dollar. Assuming, for example, that the change in the price level of bread corresponds to the change in the CPI and that $10.00 would buy 10 loaves in 1992, you would be able to buy only 5 loaves when the CPI is 200.

EXAMPLE 5.5b

Compute the purchasing power of the Canadian dollar from 1992 to 2001.

SOLUTION

The Canadian consumer price indexes for the selected years according to Statistics Canada sources were as follows:

Year	1992	1995	1998	2001
CPI	100.0	104.2	108.6	116.4

Source: Statistics Canada

The calculations by means of the formula are shown below.

Year	CPI	Computation $\frac{\$1}{\text{CPI}}(100)$	Purchasing power of dollar
1992	100.0	$\frac{\$1}{100.0}(100) =$	$1.00
1995	104.2	$\frac{\$1}{104.2}(100) =$	$0.96
1998	108.6	$\frac{\$1}{108.6}(100) =$	$0.92
2001	116.4	$\frac{\$1}{116.4}(100) =$	$0.86

C. *Computing Real Income*

The CPI can be used to correct the effect of inflation on income by adjusting nominal income (income stated in current dollars) to **real income** (income stated in base-period dollars).

$$\text{REAL INCOME} = \frac{\text{INCOME IN CURRENT DOLLARS}}{\text{CPI}}(100)$$ ←*Formula* 5.9

EXAMPLE 5.5c

Anne's salary increased from \$28 600 in 1992 to \$38 581 in 1999 and \$39 811 in 2001. Given 1992 as the base year for the Canadian CPI and an index of 110.5 in 1999 and 116.4 in 2001,

a) determine Anne's real income in 1999 and 2001;
b) comment on the changes in stated income compared with the changes in real income.

SOLUTION

a) Real income in 1999 = $\frac{38\ 581}{110.5}(100) = \$34\ 915$

Real income in 2001 = $\frac{39\ 811}{116.4}(100) = \$34\ 202$

b) To compare nominal income with real income it is useful to determine income changes in absolute and relative terms:

Year	1992	1999	2001
Nominal income	\$28 600	\$38 581	\$39 811
Simple price index	100.0	134.9	139.2
\$ increase		\$9 981	\$11 211
Percent increase		34.9%	39.2%
Real income	\$28 600	\$34 915	\$34 202
Simple price index	100.0	122.1	119.6
\$ increase		\$6315	\$5602
Percent increase		22.1%	19.6%

While Anne's income in 1999 increased 34.9% over her 1992 income, her purchasing power, reflected by her real 1999 income, increased 22.1% over the seven-year period. Over the next two years her nominal income increased 39.2% over her 1992 income. Her real income, however, increased 19.6%, indicating that her real income actually declined from 1999 to 2001.

EXERCISE 5.5

1. Given the information below,
   a) determine the purchasing power of the dollar for 1996;
   b) determine Jack's real income for 2000;
   c) comment on Jack's purchasing power in 2000 relative to 1996.

Year	CPI	Jack's annual income
1992	100.0	\$40 000
1996	105.9	\$49 442
2000	113.5	\$54 155

2. Jane's monthly income from her part-time job was \$1200 in 1992 and \$2286 in 2000. Given that the CPI for 1992 was 100.0 and 113.5 for 2000,
   a) determine the purchasing power of the dollar for 2000;
   b) determine Jane's real income for 2000;
   c) comment on Jane's purchasing power in 2000 relative to 1992.

SECTION 5.6

Shifting the Base and Splicing

A. Shifting the Base (Rebasing)

The base of an existing index number series can be shifted to a more current year to bring the series up to date or to make it comparable with other series of index numbers.

The process of **shifting the base** is accomplished by dividing each index number in the old series by the index of the newly designated base year starting with the new base year.

This process was used by Statistics Canada to update the Canadian CPI for the years 1992 to 1996, with 1992 as the new base (see Example 5.6a).

EXAMPLE 5.6a

Given the Canadian consumer price indexes for 1992 to 1996 with base year 1986 (see Column 2 in the following chart), obtain the updated CPI numbers by shifting the base to 1992.

SOLUTION

Year	Old CPI with base year 1986	Computation to shift base	New CPI with base year 1992
1992	128.0	$\frac{128.0}{128.0}(100) =$	100.0
1993	130.3	$\frac{130.3}{128.0}(100) =$	101.8
1994	130.6	$\frac{130.6}{128.0}(100) =$	102.0
1995	133.4	$\frac{133.4}{128.0}(100) =$	104.2
1996	135.6	$\frac{135.6}{128.0}(100) =$	105.9

B. Splicing

Splicing is a procedure used to create a continuous series of index numbers from two separate series. For this, the two series of numbers must have an overlap for one year. Normally, the year of overlap is the base year for the spliced series.

EXAMPLE 5.6b

The following table contains two aggregate index number series for a group of commodities. The first series covers the time period 1993 to 1998 with base year 1993; the second series is a revised series for the time period 1998 to 2002 with base year 1998. Splice the two series with 1998 as base year.

Year	1993	1994	1995	1996	1997	1998	1999	2000	2001	2002
Old series	100.0	106.4	115.9	121.4	126.3	137.8				
Revised series						100.0	105.3	112.8	119.3	130.0

SOLUTION

To splice the two series compute the so-called index quotient for the overlap year.

$$\text{INDEX QUOTIENT} = \frac{\text{INDEX NUMBER OF REVISED SERIES FOR NEW BASE YEAR}}{\text{INDEX NUMBER OF OLD SERIES FOR NEW BASE YEAR}}$$

$$= \frac{100.0}{137.8} = 0.725\ 69$$

Now multiply each index number in the old series by the index quotient to obtain the spliced series index numbers for the years 1993 to 1997:

Year	Computation	Spliced values
1993	100.0(0.72569) =	72.6
1994	106.4(0.72569) =	77.2
1995	115.9(0.72569) =	84.1
1996	121.4(0.72569) =	88.1
1997	126.3(0.72569) =	91.7

Spliced series:

Year	1993	1994	1995	1996	1997	1998	1999	2000	2001	2002
Index numbers	72.6	77.2	84.1	88.1	91.7	100.0	105.3	112.8	119.3	130.0

EXERCISE 5.6

1. The following data represent index series of the average prices of common shares of two companies for the time period 1997 to 2002:

Year	1997	1998	1999	2000	2001	2002
Company A	154.3	167.9	184.7	200.9	204.3	195.3
Company B	129.3	134.6	144.8	167.8	179.6	184.3

Shift the base of both series to 1997 to make the two series comparable.

2. The assets (in millions of dollars) of Consolidated Municipal Credit Union for the 10-year period 1991 to 2000 were as follows:

1991	1992	1993	1994	1995	1996	1997	1998	1999	2000
4.4	5.2	6.8	7.9	9.5	11.1	13.0	15.0	18.1	20.4

a) Show the growth in assets in relative terms by creating an index number series with base year 1991.
b) Create a new series for the period 1991 to 2000 by shifting the base to 1996.

3. The following series is an index of reserves for the period 1992 to 1996 for Consolidated Municipal Credit Union:

1992	1993	1994	1995	1996
115.0	357.8	1865.6	3603.4	4983.3

Splice the above series with the corresponding series for the period 1996 to 2000:

1996	1997	1998	1999	2000
100.0	121.0	164.1	249.3	372.3

4. The Canadian consumer price indexes for the 13-year period 1988 to 2000 with base years 1986 and 1992 as applicable are listed below. Splice the two series using 1992 as base year.

Year	1988	1989	1990	1991	1992	1993	1994
Old	108.6	114.0	119.5	126.1	128.0		
New					100.0	101.8	102.0

Year	1995	1996	1997	1998	1999	2000
Old						
New	104.2	105.9	107.6	108.6	110.5	113.5

REVIEW EXERCISE

1. Grand Furniture has reported sales statistics for the deluxe five-piece dining room set as follows:

June 1, 2000–May 31, 2001		June 1, 2001–May 31, 2002	
Base price	Quantity	Base price	Quantity
$14 500	20	$17 500	30

a) Determine the simple price index, quantity index and value index for the dining room set sales.
b) Interpret the meaning of the indexes in part **(a)**.

2. Zafuto Groceries, a small family-owned grocery store, reported that they sold 1500-dozen eggs at a base price of $1.50/dozen in 2001. In 2002, 1600-dozen eggs were sold at a base price of $1.95/dozen.
a) Determine the simple price index, quantity index, and value index for the egg sales.
b) Interpret the meaning of part **(a)**.

3. The following data show crude oil production in Canada for the years 2000 and 2002:

	2000		2002	
Commodity	Price	Quantity (millions)	Price	Quantity (millions)
Crude oil production (m^3)	$209.96	60.020	$142.01	55.257

a) Compute the simple price, quantity, and value indexes for crude oil production for 2002 based on 2000.
b) Interpret the indexes computed in part **(a)**.

4. For the following data, compute the following for 2002 based on 2000:
   a) simple price, quantity, and value indexes for each item;
   b) an unweighted aggregate price index for the group of items;
   c) weighted aggregate price, quantity, and value indexes.

	2000		2002	
Item	Price	Quantity	Price	Quantity
Movie pass	$7.50	50	$9.00	42
Large popcorn	$1.75	70	$2.50	60
Bus ticket	$1.05	40	$1.25	30

5. For the data below, compute the following for 2002 based on 2000:
   a) simple price, quantity, and value indexes for each item;
   b) an unweighted aggregate price index for the group of items;
   c) weighted aggregate price, quantity, and value indexes.

	2000		2002	
Item	Price	Quantity	Price	Quantity
Tank of gas	$ 20.00	50	$ 32.00	40
Train pass	$140.00	8	$160.00	10
Subway token	$ 2.00	400	$ 2.25	500

6. For the following data, determine
   a) simple price, quantity, and value indexes for each commodity;
   b) unweighted aggregate price indexes for the group of commodities;
   c) price, quantity, and value indexes by the Laspeyres method.

	Commodity A		Commodity B		Commodity C	
Month	Price	Quantity	Price	Quantity	Price	Quantity
April	$0.54	240	$3.99	4	$2.30	50
May	$0.49	260	$3.49	7	$3.10	38

7. The data for the cost and consumption of natural gas, electricity, and water for a consumer in Ontario is listed.

	Gas		Electricity		Water	
	Price	Quantity	Price	Quantity	Price	Quantity
2001	$0.181/m^3	2700 m^3	$0.040/kWh	2300 kWh	$0.39/m^3	250 m^3
2002	$0.196/m^3	3000 m^3	$0.043/kWh	2400 kWh	$0.40/m^3	300 m^3

Determine
   a) simple price, quantity, and value indexes for each commodity;
   b) unweighted aggregate price indexes for the group of commodities;
   c) price, quantity, value indexes by the Laspeyres method.

8. Using 2000 as base for the data below, compute
a) the weighted aggregate price index for 2001;
b) the weighted aggregate quantity index for 2002;
c) value indexes for 2001 and 2002 by the Laspeyres method.

	Imports					
	2002		2001		2000	
Commodity	Price	Quantity (000)	Price	Quantity (000)	Price	Quantity (000)
Diamonds (carats)	$703.88	231.6	$610.51	181.8	$663.69	194.9
Gold (g)	$ 11.85	35 152.5	$ 12.46	53 690.8	$ 11.02	43 394.6
Silver (g)	$ 0.24	118 285.3	$ 0.15	214 131.1	$ 0.09	49 290.5

9. For the following data, determine
a) the Laspeyres price index for 2001 (base year 2000);
b) the 2001 quantity index by the Laspeyres method (base year 2000);
c) the weighted aggregate value index for 2001 (base year 2000).

	Exports (L)			
	2000		2001	
Commodity	Price (per litre)	Quantity (thousands)	Price (per litre)	Quantity (thousands)
Beer	$0.71	251 849.2	$0.70	303 609.5
Wine	$3.62	75.9	$2.72	73.9
Whiskey	$6.04	77 693.2	$6.72	74 497.2

10. For the following information,
a) use 2001 as the base period to compute the weighted aggregate price, quantity, and value indexes for 2002;
b) interpret the indexes computed in **(a)**.

	Building Permits Issued			
	Average permit price		Quantity	
Type	2001	2002	2001	2002
Industrial	$114.37	$152.05	1 018 000	1 123 000
Commercial	$ 70.21	$ 90.83	3 595 000	3 950 000

11. Use the following data to

a) compute weighted aggregate price, quantity, and value indexes for April 15, 2002 (April 15, 2001 = 100);

b) interpret the price index computed in **(a)**.

	Price of stock		Volume traded	
Company	01–04–15	02–04–15	01–04–15	02–04–15
A	\$34.50	\$39.00	10 000	15 000
B	\$17.00	\$11.25	40 000	30 000
C	\$7.00	\$7.25	20 000	10 000

12. Construct an index series (1996 = 100) for the following data:

Year	1996	1997	1998	1999	2000	2001	2002
Number of passengers (000)	3859	3968	3988	4126	4550	4642	4766

13. Construct an index series (year 1 = 100) for the following data:

	Year 1	Year 2	Year 3	Year 4	Year 5
Number of cellphone Users (\$ millions)	2	4	9	13	15

14. Construct an index series (1997 = 100) for the following data:

	Canadian Gross Domestic Product				
Year	1997	1998	1999	2000	2001
GDP (\$ billions)	882.7	914.9	980.5	1 064.9	1 092.2

Source: Statistics Canada

15. A shoe store compiled the following information about its sales for 2001 and 2002:

	Average price (per pair)		Total sales	
Shoe group	2001	2002	2001	2002
Women's	\$130	\$144	\$162 240	\$182 592
Men's	\$96	\$110	\$89 856	\$99 660
Children's	\$48	\$56	\$29 952	\$37 184

a) Determine the number of pairs of shoes sold for each year by shoe group.

b) Calculate the price, quantity, and value indexes for 2002 by the Laspeyres method (2001 = 100).

16. An electronics store had sales of DVD players and RF modulators as listed.

	Average Price (per unit)		Total Sales (in $000s)	
Product	2001	2002	2001	2002
DVD Player	200	120	1000	2000
RF Modulator	50	35	400	1300

a) Determine the number of DVDs and modulators sold each year.
b) Calculate the price, quantity, and value indexes for 2002 by the Laspeyres method (2001 = 100).

17. The purchasing records of Northern Grey Building Supplies for 1999 and 2002 showed the following:

	Number of units purchased		Total cost	
Item	1999	2002	1999	2002
Hammers	210	140	$1 785	$1 113
Screwdrivers	1200	860	$2 700	$1 677
Wrenches	3800	4020	$17 670	$18 291

a) Determine the average cost per item for each year.
b) Compute the weighted aggregate price, quantity, and value indexes for 2002 based on 1999.
c) Interpret the results in **(b).**

18. Construct a special-purpose index for 2002 based on 2001 to measure interest rate movements in the Canadian economy from the following data. Interpret your results.

	Bank rate	Prime business loan rate	Consumer loan rate	Residential mortgage (5 year) rate
2001	4.31%	5.81%	10.06%	7.40%
2002	2.71%	4.21%	9.36%	7.02%
Weight	25%	10%	30%	35%

Source: Statistics Canada

19. Compute an index of savings for 2001, based on 1996, from the following data:

	Savings Rate		
	Household	Corporate	Government
1996	9.5%	1.6%	1.5%
2001	10.9%	1.4%	0.9%
Weight	30%	20%	50%

20. For the following data of a small-business plastics manufacturer construct a special-purpose index for 2002 (1999 = 100) and interpret the meaning of the index.

	Production (units)	Average Wage	Revenue
1999	3984	$45 965	$235 669
2002	5154	$63 371	$295 345
Weight	30%	60%	10%

21. For the following data construct a special-purpose index for 2002 (1992 = 100) and interpret the meaning of the index.

Indicator	1992	2002	Weight
Sales of goods ($ millions)	10	40	60%
Cost of goods ($ millions)	6	10	30%
Overhead ($ millions)	1	9	10%

22. For the following data construct a leading indicator (special-purpose index) of economic activity for 2002, based on 2001, and interpret your results.

	Department store sales ($ millions)	Unemployment rate	Chartered bank loans ($ millions)
2001	13 914	7.5%	112 920
2002	14 184	8.1%	129 527
Weight	45%	20%	35%

23. Calculate a price index for 2002 given the following sub-group indexes (1992 = 100):

	Durable goods	Semi-durable goods	Non-durable goods	Services
2002 index	120.7	131.6	124.6	138.2
Weight	14.32%	8.09%	30.00%	47.58%

24. The simple indexes for goods and services for the year **200X** are given as follows. Calculate the CPI for year **200X** (1996 = 100).

	Durable goods	Semi-durable goods	Non-durable goods	Services
200X index	110.1	115.3	105.1	141.3
Weight	12%	8%	35%	45%

25. Calculate a price index for 2003, based on 1992, given the indexes for the following sub-groups:

	Durable goods	Semi-durable goods	Non-durable goods	Services
1992	100.0	100.0	100.0	100.0
2003	113.6	118.3	122.2	125.5
Weight	14.32%	8.09%	30.00%	47.58%

26. The Canadian consumer price indexes for 2000 and 2001 are 113.5 and 116.4 respectively, based on 1992. Calculate the purchasing power of the dollar for the two years relative to 1992.

27. The CPIs for 1998 and 1999 were 108.6 and 110.5 respectively, based on 1992. Compute the purchasing power of the dollar for the two years relative to 1992.

28. If the purchasing power of a consumer in 2002 is $0.82 based on 1996 dollars, calculate the CPI for the year 2002.

29. Sales of new houses in the local real estate market during 2000 and 2001 were as follows:

	Sales ($000)	CPI (1992 = 100)
2000	177 817	113.5
2001	196 153	116.4

Restate the sales in real terms using 1992 as the base period.

30. During salary negotiations, the following background information was available to the negotiating teams:

Year	Maximum salary	CPI (1992 = 100)
2000	$58 710	113.5
2001	$63 097	116.4
2002	$66 259	119.3

a) Express the salaries for the three years in real 1992 terms.
b) Comment on the results.

31. Statistics for Extreme Sports' snowboard sales are shown below.

Year	1997	1998	1999	2000	2001
Revenue ($ thousands)	6103.2	6623.6	7654.7	7862.8	8066.2
CPI (1992 = 100)	107.6	108.6	110.5	113.5	116.4

Determine Extreme Sports' revenue, in real terms, from 1997 to 2001 (Use 1992 dollars).

32. The average selling prices for townhouses and two-storey houses as recorded by the local real estate board for 2000 were

Townhouses	\$132 000
Two-storey houses	\$191 000

Using the consumer price index of 113.5 for 2000, adjust the selling prices to 1992 dollars.

33. For the following three items, shift the base to 2000:

Raw Material Price Indexes (1992 = 100)			
Year	Animal products	Mineral fuels	Non-ferrous metals
2000	101.1	98.2	127.6
2001	105.7	117.6	114.7

34. For the following data, shift the base to 1999:

Construction Price Indexes (1992 = 100)			
Year	New housing	Wages	Land prices
1999	140.7	112.9	157.5
2000	146.7	114.0	169.6
2001	130.3	119.8	157.3

35. Canadian wheat shipments for the period 1996 to 2001 were as follows:

Year	1996	1997	1998	1999	2000	2001
Value (\$ millions)	8401	8689	8186	8337	9091	9447

a) Show the industry growth by creating an index series, using 1996 as the base year.

b) Create a new series for the period 1996 to 2001 by shifting the base to 1998.

36. Revenue from long-distance calls originating in Canada for the period 1997 to 2001 was as follows:

Year	1997	1998	1999	2000	2001
Revenue (\$ millions)	5817	6055	6312	6791	7143

a) Show the growth in revenue in relative terms by creating an index number series with base year 1997.

b) Create a new series beginning with 1999 as base.

37. For the following data, show each country's capacity in relative terms by indexing both series to 1990:

Newsprint Paper Capacity by Country (in 000s tonnes)					
Year	1990	1993	1996	1999	2002
Canada	2030	2270	2320	2390	2509
U.S.	1640	1705	1730	1730	1735

38. The following data are index series of revenue for a Canadian manufacturer, by type of product, for the period 1997 to 2002.

Year	1997	1998	1999	2000	2001	2002
Consumer Goods	144.7	110.6	104.4	116.0	131.1	147.1
Industrial Goods	131.8	121.3	76.7	72.9	78.5	84.4

Shift the base for both companies to 1997 to compare their revenues.

39. The following data are index series of sales for two of British Columbia's lumber companies:

Year	1997	1998	1999	2000	2001	2002
Company A	80.3	90.1	100.1	105.1	110.5	115.6
Company B	60.8	70.5	82.3	100.1	105.3	108.5

Shift both companies to 2000 and compare their sales before and after 2000.

40. Splice the following two price index series using 1998 as base year.

1992	1993	1994	1995	1996	1997	1998	1999	2000	2001
92.0	95.8	100.0	104.0	109.2	114.5	116.0			
						126.2	128.1	130.4	130.7

41. A company changed ownership in 1999. The following represents two index number series for sales. The first series covers the time period from 1996 to 2000 with 1996 as the base year; the second series is a revised series from the time period 1999 to 2002. Splice the two series with 1999 as the base year.

1996	1997	1998	1999	2000	2001	2002
100	102	102.5	105			
			100	110	115	119.3

42. Given an index quotient of 0.85 and using 2000 as the new base year, calculate the missing value.

1996	1997	1998	1999	2000	2001	2002
100	105.3	109.2	111.4	XXX		
				100	101.2	105.1

43. The following is an index series of wage levels for a wholesaler for the period 1994 to 1998:

1994	1995	1996	1997	1998
103.1	109.9	116.2	124.5	133.3

Splice the foregoing series with the corresponding series for the period 1998 to 2002:

1998	1999	2000	2001	2002
116.9	122.0	127.7	134.0	138.5

44. (CGA) The following historical data describe monthly purchases by an average farm family:

	1970		1980	
Commodity	Price	Quantity	Price	Quantity
Milk (L)	0.30	30	0.40	30
Butter (kg)	1.00	3	1.75	2
Eggs (dozen)	0.60	8	1.00	4
Sugar (kg)	0.70	14	1.40	10

a) Compute the Laspeyres price index, using 1970 as the base year.

b) Assume that your index, calculated in **(a)**, applied in general for all foods. Suppose a certain family spent \$1500 in 1970 and \$2500 in 1980. In which of the two years would the family have had more to eat for their money?

45. (CGA) Consider a basic basket of foods with prices and quantities for 1982 and 1992 given below:

	Quantity		Prices ($)	
Item	1982	1992	1982	1992
Milk (L)	35	30	0.50	0.90
Bread (loaf)	25	20	0.60	0.89
Margarine (kg)	10	15	1.20	1.65
Eggs (dozen)	10	5	1.45	1.55
Margarine (kg)	20	18	0.40	0.45

a) Using 1982 as the base year, determine the Laspeyres price index for 1992.
b) Assume that your Laspeyres index, calculated in **(a)**, applied in general for all foods. Suppose a certain family spent $4000 on food in 1982 and $7000 in 1992. In which of the two years did the family have more food for its money? Explain.

SELF-TEST

1. The following data represent retail prices of 2-L ice cream containers for the period 1997 to 2002:

Year	1997	1998	1999	2000	2001	2002
Price	$4.75	$4.99	$5.25	$5.50	$5.99	$6.25

a) Construct a simple price index using 1998 as the base year.
b) Compute the percent change in price from 1998 to 2002.
c) Compute the percent change in price from 2000 to 2002.
d) Explain why indexes can make analysis easier and faster.

Questions **2** through **7** are based on the following data:

Year	Annual locker rental	Consumer price index	Annual wages of Mr. Key
1992	$17.50	100.0	$32 000
1995	21.25	104.2	35 900
1998	25.00	108.6	40 902
2001	26.55	116.4	42 484

2. Calculate the price index of a locker rental for 2001 based on 1992.

3. Determine Mr. Key's real income for 1998 based on 1992.

4. Can Mr. Key purchase more or fewer goods and services in 1998 compared with 1992? Explain.

5. Compute the purchasing power of the consumer dollar for 2001 compared with 1992.

6. Compare the price index of a locker rental for 2001 with the consumer price index for the same year and comment on the relative changes.

7. Price indexes for Country A for the years 1992, 1995, 1998 and 2001 are 131.0, 150.2, 163.4, and 169.6 respectively. Is the rate of inflation higher in Canada or in country A?

8. a) Construct weighted aggregate price, quantity, and value indexes by the Laspeyres method for 2002 based on 1997.

b) Briefly interpret the three indexes computed in **(a)**.

	1997		2002	
Item	Price per unit	Number of units	Price per unit	Number of units
W	$3000	20	$4000	25
X	6	1200	8	800
Y	150	60	200	80
Z	3	1500	5	2000

9. A special-purpose index is to be constructed for the financial sector of the Canadian economy. Four key series have been selected, and the base is to be 2000.

Item	Weight	2000	2001
Stock Index	20%	2380.8	2295.1
Money supply ($ billions)	10%	228	204
Consumer credit ($ billions)	30%	110	98
Money turnover index	40%	98.0	90.8

a) Compute the special-purpose index for 2001.

b) Interpret the index and comment on how it might be used.

10. The following data represent index series of net income of two companies for the time period 1997 to 2002:

Year	1997	1998	1999	2000	2001	2002
Company A – old	166.9	183.7	199.1			
– new			100.0	108.8	110.6	105.7
Company B	118.0	123.2	129.9	137.4	147.8	149.6

a) Splice the two series for Company A (1999 = 100).

b) Shift the base to 1997 to make the two series comparable.

c) Comment on the net income performance of Company A relative to Company B.

For an online glossary, go to **www.pearsoned.ca/hummelbrunner.**

Key Terms

Aggregate index number 142
Base period 142
Composite index 151
Consumer price index 152
Index number 142
Purchasing power of the dollar 152
Real income 154
Shifting the base 155
Simple index number 142
Simple price index 143
Simple quantity index 144
Simple value index 145
Special-purpose index 151
Splicing 156
Unweighted aggregate index 146
Weighted aggregate index 146

Summary of Formulas

1. Simple indexes

a) Price:

$$\text{PRICE INDEX, } P = \frac{P_n}{P_0}(100)$$ ←*Formula* 5.1

b) Quantity:

$$\text{QUANTITY INDEX, } Q = \frac{Q_n}{Q_0}(100)$$ ←*Formula* 5.2

c) Value:

$$\text{VALUE INDEX, } V = \frac{V_n}{V_0}(100) = \frac{P_nQ_n}{P_0Q_0}(100)$$ ←*Formula* 5.3

2. Unweighted aggregate price index

$$\text{UNWEIGHTED AGGREGATE PRICE INDEX, } P = \frac{\sum P_n}{\sum P_0}(100)$$ ←*Formula* 5.4

3. Weighted aggregate indexes (Laspeyres method)

a) Price:

$$\text{WEIGHTED AGGREGATE PRICE INDEX, } P = \frac{\sum P_n Q_0}{\sum P_0 Q_0}(100)$$ ←*Formula* 5.5

b) Quantity:

$$\text{WEIGHTED AGGREGATE QUANTITY INDEX} = \frac{\sum P_0 Q_n}{\sum P_0 Q_0}(100)$$ ←*Formula* 5.6

c) Value:

$$\text{WEIGHTED AGGREGATE VALUE INDEX, } V = \frac{\sum P_n Q_n}{\sum P_0 Q_0}(100)$$ ←*Formula* 5.7

4. Purchasing power

$$\text{PURCHASING POWER OF THE DOLLAR} = \frac{\$1}{\text{CPI}}(100)$$ ←*Formula* 5.8

5. Real income

$$\text{REAL INCOME} = \frac{\text{INCOME IN CURRENT DOLLARS}}{\text{CPI}}(100)$$ ←*Formula* 5.9

CHAPTER 6

Time-Series Analysis

Introduction

Forecasting or making predictions about the future is an integral part of the business planning process. A first step to looking at the future is to analyze the past. Business data collected over a number of time periods (days, months, quarters, years) provide the basis for such analysis. Time-series analysis provides the basic methods for detecting trends and patterns in the data and may lead to a better understanding of events.

Learning Outcomes

Upon completion of this chapter you will be able to, given an appropriate time series,

1. compute the linear trend equation using the least squares method;
2. construct the least squares trend line (line of best fit);
3. predict the value associated with a particular future time period;
4. determine and graph the percent of trend (cyclical relative);
5. compute and graph moving averages;
6. graph and interpret seasonal indexes;
7. deseasonalize data.

SECTION 6.1

Components of a Time Series

A time series is a set of values observed over a period of time such as the following sales data compiled for a number of years:

Year	1996	1997	1998	1999	2000	2001	2002
Sales ($ millions)	8	10	11	14	18	20	19

The analysis of such historical data is useful in identifying past and current trends and as an aid in forecasting.

The basic time-series model identifies four time-related components:

1. **Secular trend** — the long-term tendency of economic and business data to increase or decrease.
2. **Cyclical variation** — the up-and-down fluctuations associated with the business cycle.

FIGURE 6.1 The Four Components of a Time Series

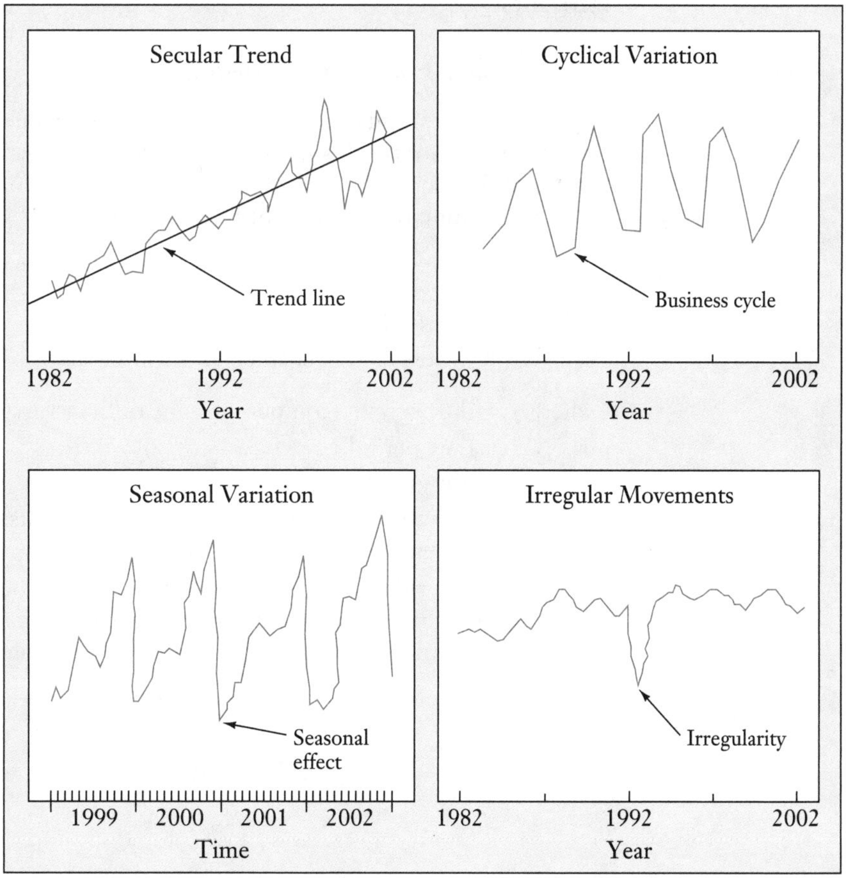

3. **Seasonal variation** — the annually recurring seasonal patterns present in monthly or quarterly data.
4. **Irregular movements** — the unpredictable changes resulting from unexpected events such as political upheaval, labour problems, catastrophic events.

SECTION 6.2

Secular Trend Analysis

A. Introduction

Secular trend is the most often analyzed component of a time series. Secular trend analysis is concerned with describing historical patterns and is useful in projecting persistent trends. Depending on the data, straight-line or curvilinear models are available to perform the analysis. This chapter will examine only the linear model known as the least squares method of fitting a straight line.

B. The Basic Least Squares Method

The long-term trend of many business data approximates a straight line. The **least squares method** is used to determine the equation of the straight line that best fits such data.

The equation of that straight line is of the form

$$y_p = a + bx$$

←*Formula* 6.1

where y_p = the *projected* (computed) value of the y variable for a selected time period x;

a = the value of y_p when $x = 0$;

b = the *slope* of the straight line and represents the average increase (when $b > 0$) or decrease (when $b < 0$) in y_p for one time unit;

x = the value assigned to a selected time period.

For a given time series, the specific straight-line equation can be determined by computing the values of a and b from the following:

$$b = \frac{n(\sum xy) - (\sum x)(\sum y)}{n(\sum x^2) - (\sum x)^2}$$

$$a = \frac{\sum y}{n} - b\left(\frac{\sum x}{n}\right)$$

←*Formula* 6.2

○ EXAMPLE 6.2a

Use the least squares method to fit the trend line for the following time series:

Year	1996	1997	1998	1999	2000	2001	2002
Sales ($ millions)	8	10	11	14	18	20	19

● SOLUTION

Step 1 Draw a scatter diagram.

A **scatter diagram** (see Figure 6.2) is a visual representation of the time series and indicates whether the use of the straight-line method is appropriate for the given time series. Furthermore, the diagram is useful for graphically fitting the straight line to the data.

To draw the diagram, use the *horizontal* axis (x-axis) for the *time* periods and the *vertical* axis (y-axis) for the *quantitative* values associated with the time periods.

FIGURE 6.2 Scatter Diagram of Sales (1996–2002)

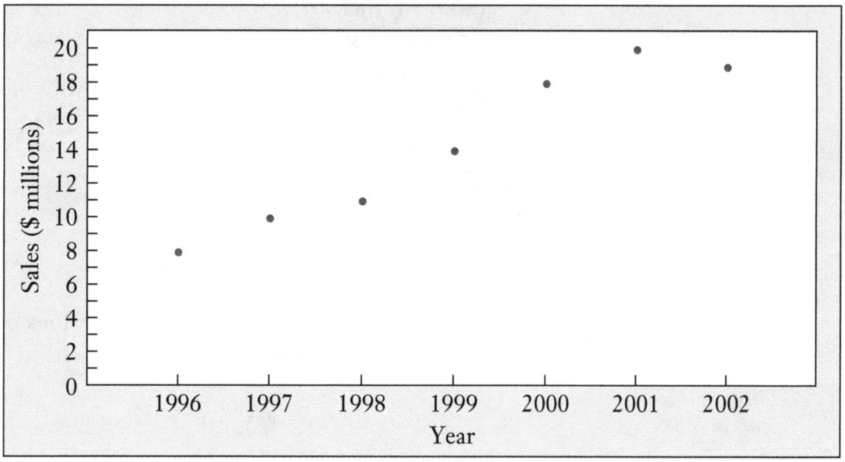

Step 2 Determine the values $\sum x$, $\sum y$, $\sum xy$, $\sum x^2$.

To compute the numerical values of a and b, we must first determine the values $\sum x$, $\sum y$, $\sum xy$ and $\sum x^2$.

In a time series the x values are assigned to the time periods, while the y values are the quantitative values associated with the time periods. However, rather than use the numerals identifying the years (1996, 1997, 1998, etc), assign to the first year (1996) the x value 1; 1997 becomes 2, 1998 becomes 3 and so on, as shown in Table 6.1. The values in the y column are the sales figures associated with each of the years. The values in the xy column are obtained by multiplication and the values in the x^2 column are found by squaring the respective x values.

TABLE 6.1 Determination of $\sum x, \sum y, \sum xy, \sum x^2$

Year	x	y	xy	x^2
1996	1	8	(1)(8) = 8	(1)(1) = 1
1997	2	10	(2)(10) = 20	(2)(2) = 4
1998	3	11	(3)(11) = 33	(3)(3) = 9
1999	4	14	(4)(14) = 56	(4)(4) = 16
2000	5	18	(5)(18) = 90	(5)(5) = 25
2001	6	20	(6)(20) = 120	(6)(6) = 36
2002	7	19	(7)(19) = 133	(7)(7) = 49
$n = 7$	$\sum x = 28$	$\sum y = 100$	$\sum xy = 460$	$\sum x^2 = 140$

$\sum x, \sum y, \sum xy, \sum x^2$ are obtained by adding the values in the respective columns; n represents the number of observed values.

Step 3 Substitute the values obtained in Table 6.1 in the formulas for a and b contained in Formula 6.2:

$$b = \frac{n(\sum xy) - (\sum x)(\sum y)}{n(\sum x^2) - (\sum x)^2} \qquad a = \frac{\sum y}{n} - b\left(\frac{\sum x}{n}\right)$$

$$= \frac{7(460) - (28)(100)}{7(140) - 28^2} \qquad = \frac{100}{7} - (2.142\,857\,1)\left(\frac{28}{7}\right)$$

$$= \frac{3220 - 2800}{980 - 784} \qquad = 14.285\,714 - 8.571\,428\,4$$

$$= \frac{420}{196} \qquad = 5.714\,285\,6$$

$$= 2.142\,857\,1$$

Step 4 Substitute the computed numerical values of a and b in the general equation $y_p = a + bx$ to obtain the trend line equation

$$y_p = 5.714 + 2.143x.$$

Step 5 Plot the trend line equation on the scatter diagram drawn in Step 1. To plot the line, substitute values for x in the trend line equation $y_p = 5.714 + 2.143x$ and compute the corresponding values of y_p; for example:

for $x = 1, y_p = 5.714 + 2.143(1) = 5.714 + 2.143 = 7.857$
for $x = 4, y_p = 5.714 + 2.143(4) = 5.714 + 8.572 = 14.286$
for $x = 7, y_p = 5.714 + 2.143(7) = 5.714 + 15.001 = 20.715$

Now plot the three points (1, 7.86), (4, 14.29), and (7, 20.72) and join the three points to draw the graph of the trend line equation, as shown in Figure 6.3.

FIGURE 6.3 Scatter Diagram with Trend Line and Trend Line Projection

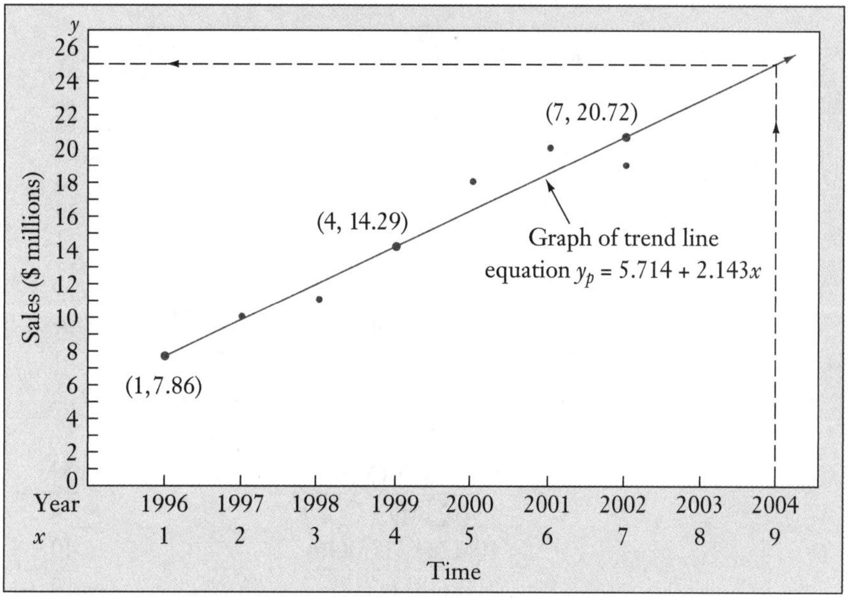

Step 6 Forecast future values.

The graph of the trend line equation or the equation itself can be used to project sales into the future.

For 2004 the projected sales are obtained graphically by drawing a vertical line from the x-axis to the graph of the trend line. From there draw a horizontal line to intersect the y-axis at approximately 25.

The exact value can be calculated by substituting $x = 9$ in the trend line equation:

$$y_p = 5.714 + 2.143(9) = 5.714 + 19.287 = 25.001$$

○ **EXAMPLE 6.2b**

For the following time series,

a) determine the trend line equation;
b) draw a scatter diagram and plot the trend line equation.

Year	1993	1994	1995	1996	1997	1998	1999	2000	2001	2002
Units	7	8	6	5	6	4	5	3	2	3

SOLUTION

a) Determining the trend line equation by the basic method:

Year	x	y	xy	x^2
1993	1	7	7	1
1994	2	8	16	4
1995	3	6	18	9
1996	4	5	20	16
1997	5	6	30	25
1998	6	4	24	36
1999	7	5	35	49
2000	8	3	24	64
2001	9	2	18	81
2002	10	3	30	100
$n = 10$	$\sum x = 55$	$\sum y = 49$	$\sum xy = 222$	$\sum x^2 = 385$

$$\begin{aligned} b &= \frac{n(\sum xy) - (\sum x)(\sum y)}{n(\sum x^2) - (\sum x)^2} \\ &= \frac{10(222) - (55)(49)}{10(385) - 55^2} \\ &= \frac{2220 - 2695}{3850 - 3025} \\ &= \frac{-475}{825} \\ &= -0.575\,757\,6 \end{aligned}$$

$$\begin{aligned} a &= \frac{\sum y}{n} - b\left(\frac{\sum x}{n}\right) \\ &= \frac{49}{10} - (-0.575\,757\,6)\left(\frac{55}{10}\right) \\ &= 4.9 + 3.166\,666\,8 \\ &= 8.066\,666\,8 \end{aligned}$$

The trend equation is $y_p = 8.0667 - 0.5758x$.

b) Scatter diagram, see Figure 6.4.

To plot the trend line, substitute values for x in the trend line equation $y_p = 8.0667 - 0.5758x$ and compute the corresponding values of y_p; for example

for 1993 when $x = 1$,

$$\begin{aligned} y_p &= 8.0667 - 0.5758(1) \\ &= 7.4909 \end{aligned}$$

for 2001 when $x = 9$,

$$\begin{aligned} y_p &= 8.0667 - 0.5758(9) \\ &= 8.0667 - 5.1822 \\ &= 2.8845 \end{aligned}$$

for 1997 when $x = 5$,

$$\begin{aligned} y_p &= 8.0667 - 0.5758(5) \\ &= 5.1877 \end{aligned}$$

FIGURE 6.4 Scatter Diagram with Trend Line

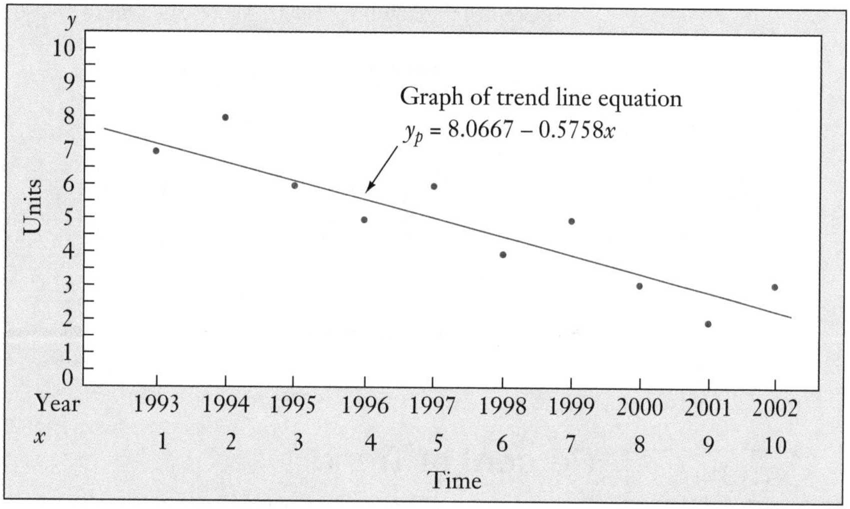

EXERCISE 6.2

1. For the following time series,

a) draw a scatter diagram;

b) use the least squares method to obtain the trend line equation and plot the graph of the trend equation;

c) predict sales for **(i)** 2003 and **(ii)** 2005.

Year	1996	1997	1998	1999	2000	2001	2002
Sales	10	11	12	14	12	13	15

2. For the following time series,

a) draw a scatter diagram;

b) obtain the trend line equation by the least squares method;

c) plot the graph of the trend equation;

d) predict production for **(i)** 2004 and **(ii)** 2006.

Year	1997	1998	1999	2000	2001	2002
Production	86	80	72	60	54	48

3. For the following time series,

Year	1996	1997	1998	1999	2000	2001	2002	2003
Debt	21	19	16	17	15	11	12	9

a) draw a scatter diagram;

b) determine the trend line equation;

c) plot the trend line;
d) predict the amount of debt for (i) 2005 and (ii) 2007.

4. For the following time series,
a) draw a scatter diagram;
b) determine the trend line equation;
c) plot the trend line;
d) predict the volume for (i) 2003 and (ii) 2006.

Year	1995	1996	1997	1998	1999	2000	2001
Volume	60	85	113	135	152	180	205

SECTION 6.3

Percent of Trend

The **percent of trend**, also referrred to as the **cyclical relative**, is used to describe the deviation of the observed values from the computed trend line as a percent. It has two important uses in business applications:

1. It permits us to see the relative size of the deviations of the individual values in the time series.
2. It can be used to determine the length of the business cycle that is used in computing moving averages (see Section 6.4).

The percent of trend (cyclical relative) is computed by means of the formula

$$\text{PERCENT TREND (or CYCLICAL RELATIVE)} = \frac{y}{y_p}(100)$$ ←*Formula* 6.3

○ **EXAMPLE 6.3a**

For the time series in Example 6.2a, the trend equation was determined to be $y_p = 5.714 + 2.143x$. Compute the percent of trend and graph the percent of trend.

● **SOLUTION**

First compute y_p for each value of x by substituting in the trend equation as shown in Table 6.2. Then divide each observed value y by the corresponding value y_p and multiply by 100 to obtain the percent of trend values.

Note The following observations can be made about the percent of trend:

1. When $y > y_p$, the percent of trend > 100.
2. When $y = y_p$, the percent of trend = 100.
3. When $y < y_p$, the percent of trend < 100.

TABLE 6.2 Computation of Percent of Trend

Year	x	Observed values y	Computed trend values $y_p = 5.714 + 2.143x$	Computation of the percent of trend $\frac{y}{y_p}(100)$
1996	1	8	$5.714 + 2.143(1) = 7.857$	$\frac{8}{7.857}(100) = 101.8$
1997	2	10	$5.714 + 2.143(2) = 10.000$	$\frac{10}{10.000}(100) = 100.0$
1998	3	11	$5.714 + 2.143(3) = 12.143$	$\frac{11}{12.143}(100) = 90.6$
1999	4	14	$5.714 + 2.143(4) = 14.286$	$\frac{14}{14.286}(100) = 98.0$
2000	5	18	$5.714 + 2.143(5) = 16.429$	$\frac{18}{16.429}(100) = 109.6$
2001	6	20	$5.714 + 2.143(6) = 18.572$	$\frac{20}{18.572}(100) = 107.7$
2002	7	19	$5.714 + 2.143(7) = 20.715$	$\frac{19}{20.715}(100) = 91.7$

To represent the observations over time in terms of their variation from the trend, a graph can be constructed by plotting the percent of trend against the time periods with the trend line set at 100% (see Figure 6.5).

FIGURE 6.5 Graph of Percent of Trend

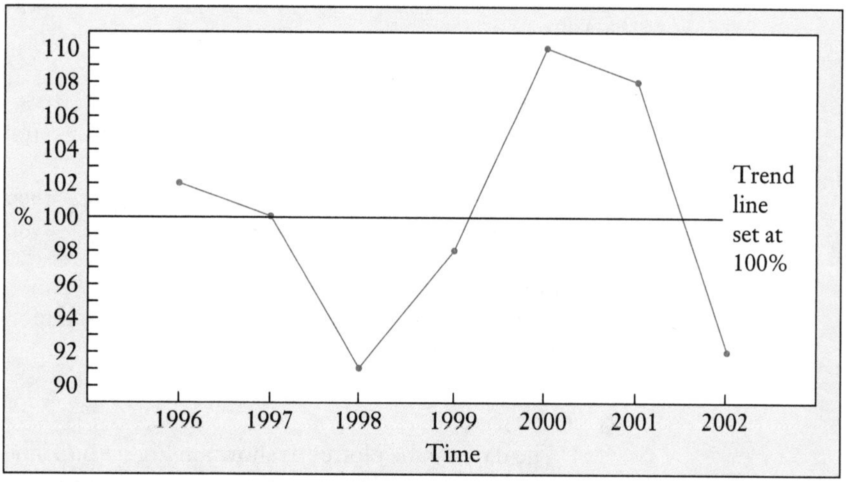

The graph points out the ups and downs associated with the cyclical component of the time series much better than Figure 6.3, which shows the actual time series and the trend line. The *relative* variation over time can be observed by noting the extent to which the plotted line deviates from the trend line set at 100%.

EXERCISE 6.3

1. Compute and graph the percent of trend for Question **3** in Exercise 6.2.
2. Compute and graph the cyclical relative for Question **4** in Exercise 6.2.

SECTION 6.4

Cyclical Analysis—The Moving Average Method

The **moving average method** can be used to smooth cyclical fluctuations in order to provide a better picture of the overall long-term trend in a time series. The results of the smoothing procedure are affected by the time period selected for computing the averages.

While the selection of the time period is somewhat arbitrary, the period chosen should be a whole number that approximates the average length of a cycle in the time series or is a multiple of the length of the cycle. A rough indicator of the length of a cycle can be obtained from the data by counting the number of time periods from one peak to another peak.

EXAMPLE 6.4a

The annual sales (in $ millions) of a product line are given for the time period 1981 to 2002.

1981	1982	1983	1984	1985	1986	1987	1988	1989	1990	1991
6	5	6	7	10	9	8	12	13	11	14

1992	1993	1994	1995	1996	1997	1998	1999	2000	2001	2002
12	12	13	16	17	15	18	19	18	17	20

a) Plot the data.
b) Fit a seven-year moving average to the data and plot the results on the graph produced in part (a).

SOLUTION

a) The data can be plotted as shown in Figure 6.6. The graph shows that there are peaks every three to seven years, indicating a business cycle of three to seven years in length.

FIGURE 6.6 Annual Sales Chart with Seven-Year Moving Average

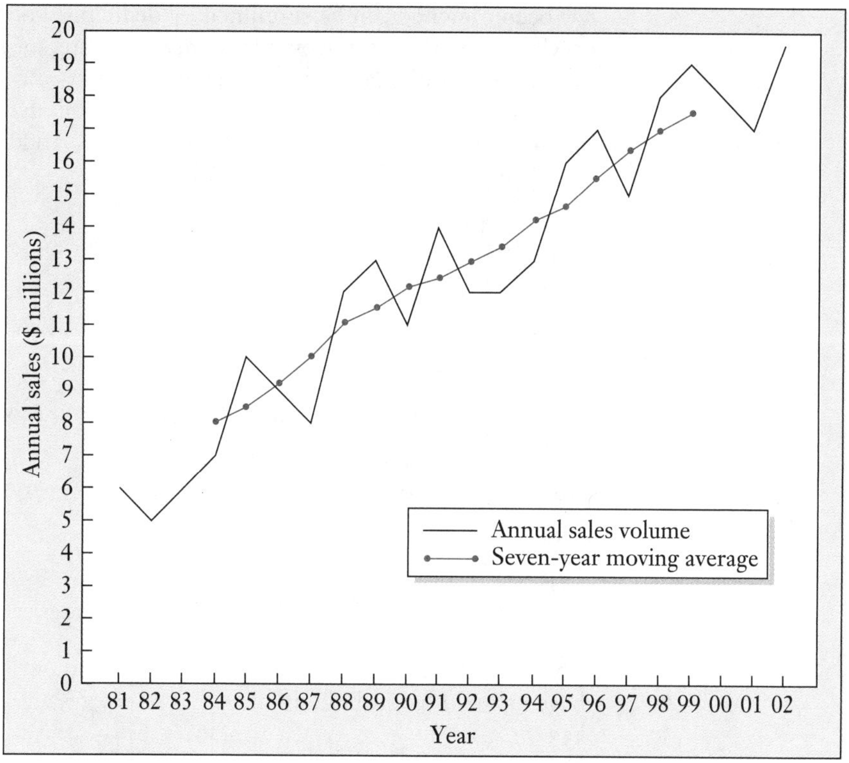

b) Computation of a seven-year moving average.
   Details of the computations are shown in Table 6.3. A step-by-step explanation of the computation follows.

Step 1 Determine the seven-year moving totals.
The first such total is obtained by adding the annual sales figures for the first seven years, 1981 to 1987 inclusive (6 + 5 + 6 + 7 + 10 + 9 + 8 = 51). The total (51) is then written opposite the *middle* year 1984, as shown in Table 6.3.

The next total can be obtained by adding the next group of seven years, 1982 to 1988 inclusive (5 + 6 + 7 + 10 + 9 + 8 + 12 = 57). This total is located against the new middle year 1985.

Successive totals can be obtained in a similar manner, e.g.,

1983 to 1989, 6 + 7 + 10 + 9 + 8 + 12 + 13 = 65;
1984 to 1990, 7 + 10 + 9 + 8 + 12 + 13 + 11 = 70;
1985 to 1991, 10 + 9 + 8 + 12 + 13 + 11 + 14 = 77;

and so on, until the last possible seven-year total for the group of seven years from 1996 to 2002 (17 + 15 + 18 + 19 + 18 + 17 + 20 = 124) is obtained and located against the middle year 1999.

The computation of the successive seven-year totals after the first such total has been obtained can be simplified by deducting the first sales figure in the previous group of seven from that total and adding the sales figure for the year following the last year in that group.

For example, to obtain the 1982 to 1988 total, deduct the sales figure for the dropped year 1981 (6) from the total (51) and add the sales figure for the added year 1988 (12); that is, 51 – 6 + 12 = 57.

For 1983 to 1988, 57 – 5 + 13 = 65;
for 1984 to 1990, 65 – 6 + 11 = 70;
for 1985 to 1991, 70 – 7 + 14 = 77;

and so on, until the last possible grouping 1996 to 2002, 120 – 16 + 20 = 124, is reached.

TABLE 6.3 Computation of the Seven-Year Moving Average

Year	Annual sales	Seven-year moving totals	Seven-year moving averages
1981	6		
1982	5		
1983	6		
1984	7	6 + 5 + 6 + 7 + 10 + 9 + 8 = 51	51 ÷ 7 = 7.29
1985	10	51 – 6 + 12 = 57	57 ÷ 7 = 8.14
1986	9	57 – 5 + 13 = 65	65 ÷ 7 = 9.29
1987	8	65 – 6 + 11 = 70	70 ÷ 7 = 10.00
1988	12	70 – 7 + 14 = 77	77 ÷ 7 = 11.00
1989	13	etc. 79	etc. 11.29
1990	11	82	11.71
1991	14	87	12.43
1992	12	91	13.00
1993	12	95	13.57
1994	13	99	14.14
1995	16	103	14.71
1996	17	110	15.71
1997	15	116	16.57
1998	18	120	17.14
1999	19	124	17.71
2000	18		
2001	17		
2002	20		

Step 2 Compute the seven-year moving averages.
The seven-year moving averages are determined by dividing the successive seven-year moving totals by the number of sales figures in each total (that is, divide by 7) as shown in Table 6.3.

Step 3 Plot the seven-year moving averages.
Each average can now be plotted against the middle year. The average 7.29 is plotted against 1984; 8.14 against 1985; and so on, until the last average 17.71 is plotted against 1999.

When the points are joined, a graphical picture of the smoothing effect of this method is obtained (see Figure 6.6).

These calculations can be completed using EXCEL, as demonstrated in USING EXCEL 6.1.

USING EXCEL 6.1

Use the annual sales (in $ millions), of a product line for the time period 1981 to 2002 given in Example 6.4a. Plot the data, fit a seven-year moving average to the data and plot the results on the graph produced in part (a).

SOLUTION

Using EXCEL,

1. Type the column heading **Year**, **Annual Sales (in $ millions)**, and **Seven-Year Moving Average** into cells A1–C1.
2. Enter the years **1981** to **2002** into cells A2–A23.
3. Enter the corresponding annual sales data into cells B2–B23.
4. On the **Tools** menu, click **Data Analysis...** (You may need to install the **Analysis ToolPak** add-in on your computer and then load it into EXCEL with the **Add-Ins** dialog box accessed on the **Tools** menu. If you try to load the **Analysis ToolPak** add-in and EXCEL does not install it, you can either install it with the **Add/Remove Programs** feature found in Windows' **Control Panel** or from Microsoft's Office 2000 CD-ROM).
5. The **Data Analysis** dialog box appears. From the **Analysis Tools** list, select **Moving Average** and click the **OK** button.
6. The **Moving Average** dialog box appears. In the **Input** section, select the **Input Range** option and type **$B$2:$B$23** into its input box (or click on to select cells B2:B23; then click on or press the **Enter** key). Ensure that the **Labels in First Row** checkbox is deselected (unchecked). In the **Interval** input box, enter 7 (representing the moving average time period). From the **Output options**, select the **Output Range** option and type **$C$2** into its input box (or select cell C2 and return to the input dialog box). Ensure that the **Chart Output** checkbox is selected (checked) and the **Standard Errors** checkbox is deselected (unchecked). Click the **OK** button when finished.
7. Resize columns A, B, and C to better view the contents of your table.
8. Notice that EXCEL places the beginning of the 7-year moving average time series at the end of our time period (cell C8 representing 1987) rather than in the middle. Therefore, we need to move the moving average time series such that it begins in the middle of the time period (cell C5 representing 1984). Select cells C8–C23; from the **Edit** menu, click **Cut**; select cell C5; from the **Edit** menu and click **Paste**. Select cells C2–C4 and clear their contents.
9. Notice that the **AVERAGE** function is used in cells C5–C20 to calculate the moving average time series.

By clicking on the chart that was generated and selecting the **Chart Area**, you can resize your chart or move your chart to different locations on your worksheet. Additionally, you can format the look of your chart by selecting the various components of your chart (vertical axis, horizontal axis, axis titles, time serie(s), chart area, plot area, legend) and then clicking on the **Format** menu to change their attributes.

OUTPUT

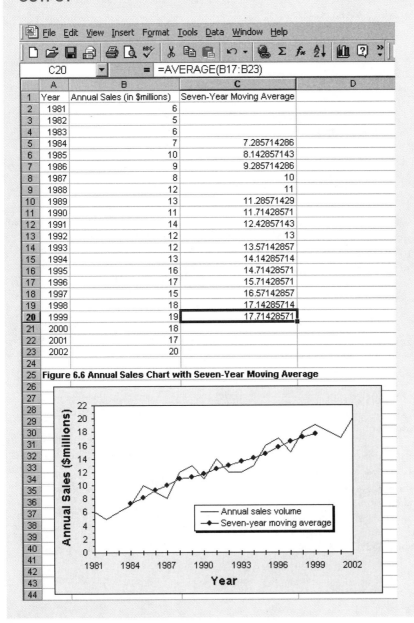

File Edit View Insert Format Tools Data Window Help

C20 = =AVERAGE(B17:B23)

	A	B	C	D
1	Year	Annual Sales (in $millions)	Seven-Year Moving Average	
2	1981	6		
3	1982	5		
4	1983	6		
5	1984	7	7.285714286	
6	1985	10	8.142857143	
7	1986	9	9.285714286	
8	1987	8	10	
9	1988	12	11	
10	1989	13	11.28571429	
11	1990	11	11.71428571	
12	1991	14	12.42857143	
13	1992	12	13	
14	1993	12	13.57142857	
15	1994	13	14.14285714	
16	1995	16	14.71428571	
17	1996	17	15.71428571	
18	1997	15	16.57142857	
19	1998	18	17.14285714	
20	1999	19	17.71428571	
21	2000	18		
22	2001	17		
23	2002	20		

Figure 6.6 Annual Sales Chart with Seven-Year Moving Average

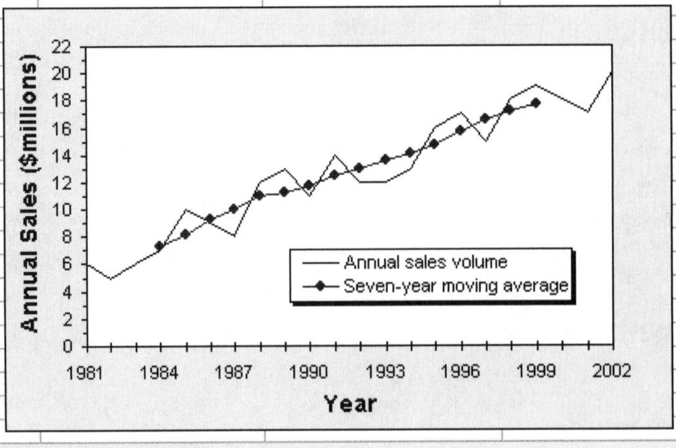

○ EXAMPLE 6.4b

For the data used in Example 6.4a, fit a six-year moving average and plot the results.

● SOLUTION

The computation of six-year moving averages is similar to the computation of seven-year averages except that six sales figures are included in each total. The average values are then obtained by dividing by 6.

Care must be taken in locating the totals and the averages. Since there is *no single* middle year for an even number of years, the totals and averages are located halfway between the two middle years in each group of six, as shown in Table 6.4.

The same approach is taken when plotting the averages in the sales chart. Each average is plotted as a point located between the respective middle years, as shown in Figure 6.7.

TABLE 6.4 Computation of the Six-Year Moving Averages

Year	Annual sales ($ millions)	Six-year moving totals	Six-year moving averages
1981	6		
1982	5		
1983	6		
	←	$6+5+6+7+10+9=43$	$43 \div 6 =$ 7.17
1984	7		
	←	$43-6+8=45$	$45 \div 6 =$ 7.50
1985	10		
	←	$45-5+12=52$	$52 \div 6 =$ 8.67
1986	9		
		59	9.83
1987	8		
		63	10.50
1988	12		
		67	11.17
1989	13		
		70	11.67
1990	11		
		74	12.33
1991	14		
		75	12.50
1992	12		
		78	13.00
1993	12		
		84	14.00
1994	13		
		85	14.17
1995	16		
		91	15.17
1996	17		
		98	16.33
1997	15		
		103	17.17
1998	18		
		104	17.33
1999	19		
		107	17.83
2000	18		
2001	17		
2002	20		

FIGURE 6.7 Annual Sales Chart with Six-Year Moving Average

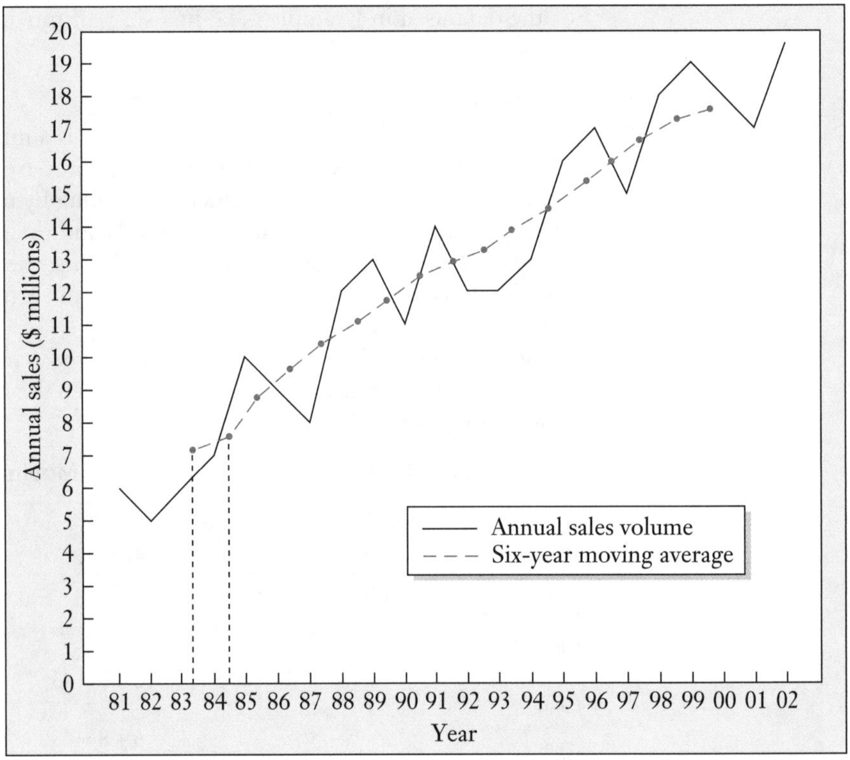

EXERCISE 6.4

1. Plot the following data, compute a five-year moving average, and plot the results:

1990	1991	1992	1993	1994	1995	1996	1997	1998	1999	2000	2001
10	8	9	10	14	12	12	13	16	19	9	9

2. The following tabulation summarizes the yearly average cost per unit to produce a steel frame. Graph the data, compute a seven-year moving average, and graph the results.

Year	1983	1984	1985	1986	1987	1988	1989	1990	1991	1992
$ Unit cost	281	280	337	406	402	452	432	582	598	618

Year	1993	1994	1995	1996	1997	1998	1999	2000	2001	2002
$ Unit cost	577	602	629	602	657	775	878	893	905	898

3. Plot the following data, compute a four-year moving average, and plot the results.

1989	1990	1991	1992	1993	1994	1995
7	10	8	9	10	14	12

1996	1997	1998	1999	2000	2001
12	14	16	17	14	11

4. Graph the following data, compute a six-year moving average, and graph the results.

1988	1989	1990	1991	1992	1993	1994	1995
97	109	76	84	102	113	76	83

1996	1997	1998	1999	2000	2001	2002
105	117	75	86	102	106	77

SECTION 6.5

Seasonal Analysis

A. Introduction

Business activity in many industries is subject to identifiable seasonal variation or seasonal cycles. These regular patterns occur in a time series where the time interval of cycle is one year or less. Different industries have different seasonal patterns; these are generally due to climate (e.g., fluctuations in housing construction) or custom (e.g., the Christmas shopping rush).

Examination of such seasonal patterns is referred to as **seasonal analysis.** It is an important short-range planning tool in both the private and public sector.

There are various methods available by which seasonal variation can be measured, but they all begin with the examination of a time series with quarterly or monthly data. The aim of any method is to produce **seasonal indexes.** As for any index, the base is 100.

The following sub-sections will show how a seasonal index can be used to remove the seasonal variation from data.

B. Quarterly Indexes

Analysis of quarterly data produces four seasonal indexes. Each **quarterly index** indicates the seasonal importance of a particular quarter of the year. The arithmetic mean of the four quarterly indexes is 100. For example, if the seasonal sales index of a retail store's fourth quarter is 125, it means that sales for October through December are on average 25% higher than the average sales for the year as a whole.

Seasonal indexes can be used to **deseasonalize data**. This technique removes fluctuations from data and allows us to determine what the values would be without the effect of seasonal variation. It is used to make quarterly forecasts or to simplify comparisons between quarters because of seasonal variation.

The resulting numbers are referred to as **seasonally adjusted values** and are computed by the formula

$$\text{SEASONALLY ADJUSTED VALUE} = \frac{\text{ACTUAL VALUE}}{\text{SEASONAL INDEX}}(100)$$

←*Formula* 6.4

EXAMPLE 6.5a

For the following series of quarterly sales (in $ millions),
a) plot the quarterly data in the form of a line graph;
b) deseasonalize the data;
c) plot the deseasonalized data on the graph in part (a).

Year	Quarter I	Quarter II	Quarter III	Quarter IV
1998	4	17	18	7
1999	8	21	24	10
2000	9	26	27	13
2001	12	33	36	15
2002	11	32	34	14
Seasonal index	51.9	138.0	148.9	61.2

SOLUTION

a) Plot the quarterly data.

FIGURE 6.8 Quarterly Sales, 1998–2002

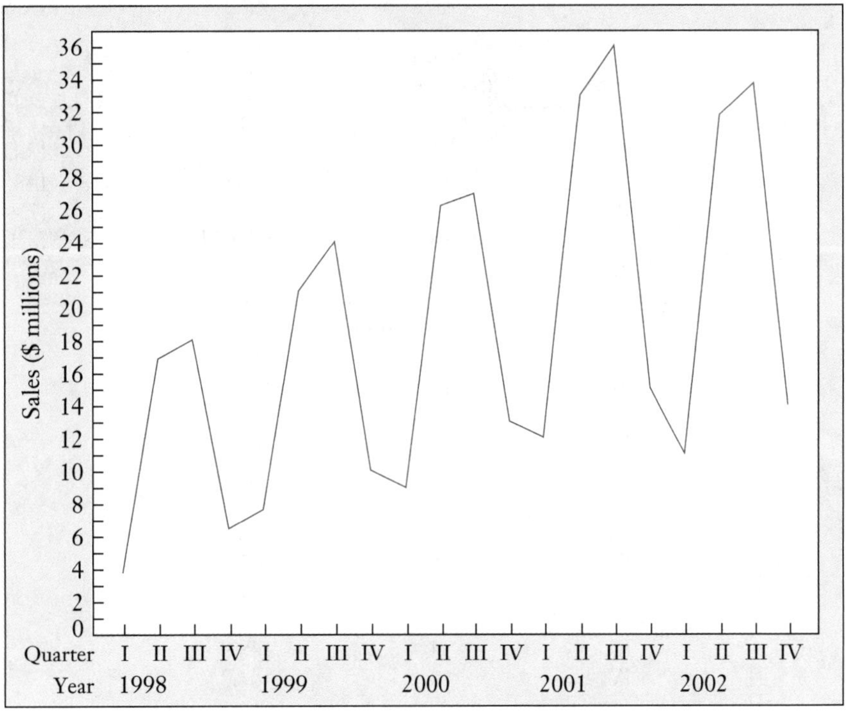

b) The seasonally adjusted values are calculated as shown in Table 6.5:

TABLE 6.5 Seasonally Adjusted Quarterly Sales, 1998–2002

Year	Quarter	Sales ($ millions)	Seasonal indexes	Seasonally adjusted quarterly sales ($ millions)
1998	I	4	51.9	(4 ÷ 51.9)(100) = 7.71
	II	17	138.0	(17 ÷ 138.0)(100) = 12.32
	III	18	148.9	(18 ÷ 148.9)(100) = 12.09
	IV	7	61.2	(7 ÷ 0.612) = 11.44
1999	I	8	51.9	(8 ÷ 0.519) = 15.41
	II	21	138.0	15.22
	III	24	148.9	16.12
	IV	10	61.2	16.34
2000	I	9	51.9	(9 ÷ 0.519) = 17.34
	II	26	138.0	18.84
	III	27	148.9	18.13
	IV	13	61.2	21.24
2001	I	12	51.9	23.12
	II	33	138.0	23.91
	III	36	148.9	24.18
	IV	15	61.2	24.51
2002	I	11	51.9	21.19
	II	32	138.0	23.19
	III	34	148.9	22.83
	IV	14	61.2	22.88

Notes

1. The purpose of adjusting for seasonal variation is to compare values of a time series at different points in time. Seasonally adjusted values permit us to determine whether differences in the original data can be explained by the regular seasonal fluctuations.

   To illustrate, for 2002 the drop in third-quarter sales of $34 million to $14 million in the fourth quarter looks quite significant (Table 6.5). However, the corresponding seasonally adjusted values (what sales would have been without seasonal effects) of $22.83 million for the third quarter and $22.88 million for the fourth quarter indicate that there was very little change.
2. Displaying data in columns as in Table 6.5 makes certain comparisons difficult. Showing actual data with deseasonalized data together as done in Table 6.6 makes it easier to compare data by year and by quarter.

TABLE 6.6 Actual Data and Seasonally Adjusted Values

	Quarter I		Quarter II		Quarter III		Quarter IV	
Year	Sales ($ millions)	Seasonally adjusted quarterly sales ($ millions)	Sales ($ millions)	Seasonally adjusted quarterly sales ($ millions)	Sales ($ millions)	Seasonally adjusted quarterly sales ($ millions)	Sales ($ millions)	Seasonally adjusted quarterly sales ($ millions)
1998	4	7.71	17	12.32	18	12.09	7	11.44
1999	8	15.41	21	15.22	24	16.11	10	16.34
2000	9	17.34	26	18.84	27	18.12	13	21.24
2001	12	23.12	33	23.91	36	24.16	15	24.51
2002	11	21.19	32	23.19	34	22.83	14	22.88

c)

FIGURE 6.9 Actual Quarterly Sales versus Deseasonalized Sales, 1998–2002

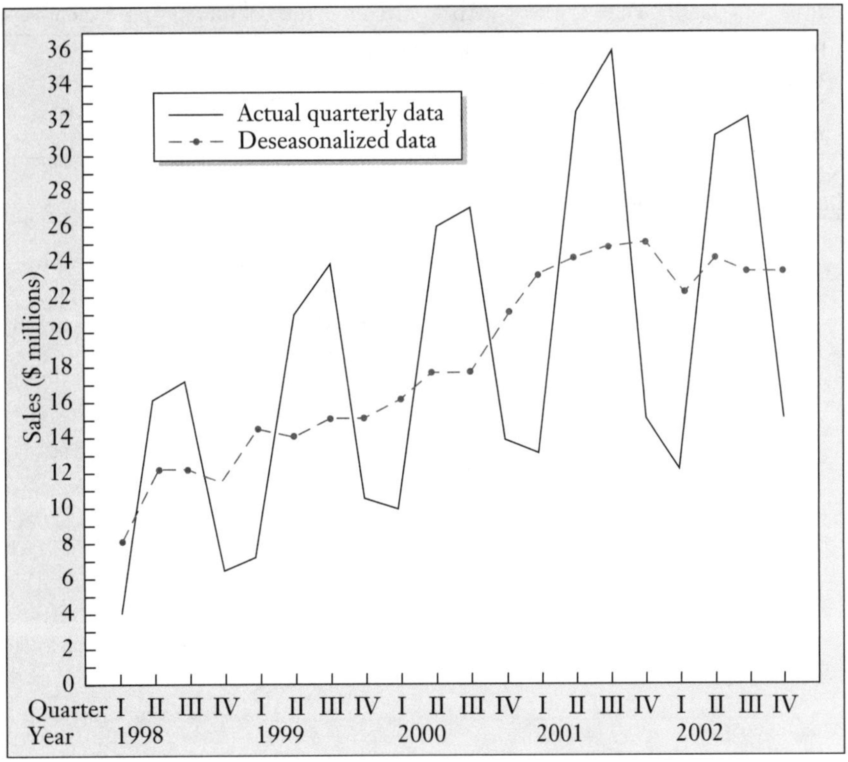

C. Monthly Indexes

Analysis of monthly data produces 12 seasonal indexes. Each **monthly index** indicates the seasonal importance of a particular month of the year. The arithmetic mean of the 12 monthly indexes is 100. For example, if the seasonal sales index for the month of March is 115, it means that March sales are on average 15% higher than the average sales for the year as a whole.

The series of 12 seasonal indexes shows the extent of the seasonal variation in each month. These seasonal fluctuations affect production and sales. As in the case of quarterly data, these fluctuations can be eliminated by computing a series of seasonally adjusted values using Formula 6.4,

$$\text{SEASONALLY ADJUSTED VALUE} = \frac{\text{ACTUAL VALUE}}{\text{SEASONAL INDEX}}(100).$$

○ EXAMPLE 6.5b

The monthly sales (in $ millions) of Custom Golf Inc. for the time period 1999 to 2002 are listed.

Year	Jan	Feb	Mar	Apr	May	Jun	Jul	Aug	Sept	Oct	Nov	Dec
1999	1	1	2	4	6	7	6	5	7	3	1	3
2000	2	3	3	5	7	9	8	7	9	4	2	4
2001	3	2	4	6	9	11	9	8	10	5	3	5
2002	4	3	5	8	11	14	12	10	13	7	4	4
Seasonal index	51.7	40.0	64.8	99.2	136.6	173.9	151.0	132.1	169.5	74.3	36.4	70.5

a) Plot the monthly data in the form of a line graph.
b) Deseasonalize the data.
c) Plot the deseasonalized data on the graph in part (a).

SOLUTION

a) A graph of the data is useful as a visual aid in identifying the existing seasonal pattern, as illustrated in Figure 6.10.

FIGURE 6.10 Monthly Sales of Custom Golf Inc., 1999–2002

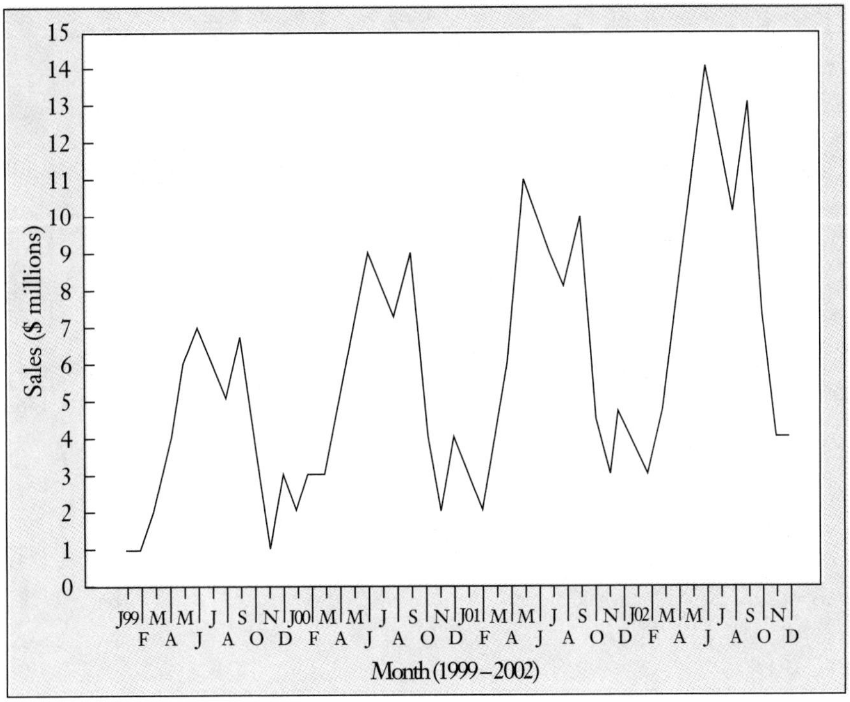

b) The seasonally adjusted values are calculated as shown in Table 6.7 using the sales data and seasonal indexes given for Example 6.5b.

TABLE 6.7 Seasonally Adjusted Monthly Sales Calculations

Data for Example 6.5b				Seasonally adjusted monthly sales ($ millions)
Year	Month	Sales ($ millions)	Seasonal indexes	
1999	Jan	1	51.7	$\left(\frac{1}{51.7}\right)(100) = 1.93$
	Feb	1	40.0	$\left(\frac{1}{40.0}\right)(100) = 2.50$
	Mar	2	64.8	$\left(\frac{2}{64.8}\right)(100) = 3.09$
	Apr	4	99.2	$\left(\frac{4}{99.2}\right)(100) = 4.03$
	May	6	136.6	$\left(\frac{6}{136.6}\right)(100) = 4.39$
	Jun	7	173.9	$\left(\frac{7}{173.9}\right)(100) = 4.03$
	Jul	6	151.0	$\left(\frac{6}{151.0}\right)(100) = 3.97$
	Aug	5	132.1	$\left(\frac{5}{132.1}\right)(100) = 3.79$
	Sept	7	169.5	$\left(\frac{7}{169.5}\right)(100) = 4.13$
	Oct	3	74.3	$\left(\frac{3}{74.3}\right)(100) = 4.04$
	Nov	1	36.4	$\left(\frac{1}{36.4}\right)(100) = 2.75$
	Dec	3	70.5	$\left(\frac{3}{70.5}\right)(100) = 4.26$
2000	Jan	2	51.7	$\left(\frac{2}{51.7}\right)(100) = 3.87$
	Feb	3	40.0	$\left(\frac{3}{40.0}\right)(100) = 7.50$
	Mar	3	64.8	$\left(\frac{3}{64.8}\right)(100) = 4.63$
	Apr	5	99.2	$\left(\frac{5}{99.2}\right)(100) = 5.04$
	May	7	136.6	$\left(\frac{7}{136.6}\right)(100) = 5.12$
⋮	⋮	⋮	⋮	⋮

The deseasonalized data for all four years are shown in Table 6.8 along with the actual sales history.

TABLE 6.8 Actual Monthly Sales (Act) versus Seasonally Adjusted Monthly Sales (Adj) ($ Millions)

	1999		2000		2001		2002	
Month	Act	Adj	Act	Adj	Act	Adj	Act	Adj
Jan	1	1.93	2	3.87	3	5.80	4	7.74
Feb	1	2.50	3	7.50	2	5.00	3	7.50
Mar	2	3.09	3	4.63	4	6.17	5	7.72
Apr	4	4.03	5	5.04	6	6.05	8	8.06
May	6	4.39	7	5.12	9	6.59	11	8.05
Jun	7	4.03	9	5.18	11	6.33	14	8.05
Jul	6	3.97	8	5.30	9	5.96	12	7.95
Aug	5	3.79	7	5.30	8	6.06	10	7.57
Sept	7	4.13	9	5.31	10	5.90	13	7.67
Oct	3	4.04	4	5.38	5	6.73	7	9.42
Nov	1	2.75	2	5.49	3	8.24	4	10.99
Dec	3	4.26	4	5.67	5	7.09	4	5.67

FIGURE 6.11 Monthly Sales of Custom Golf Inc., 1999–2002

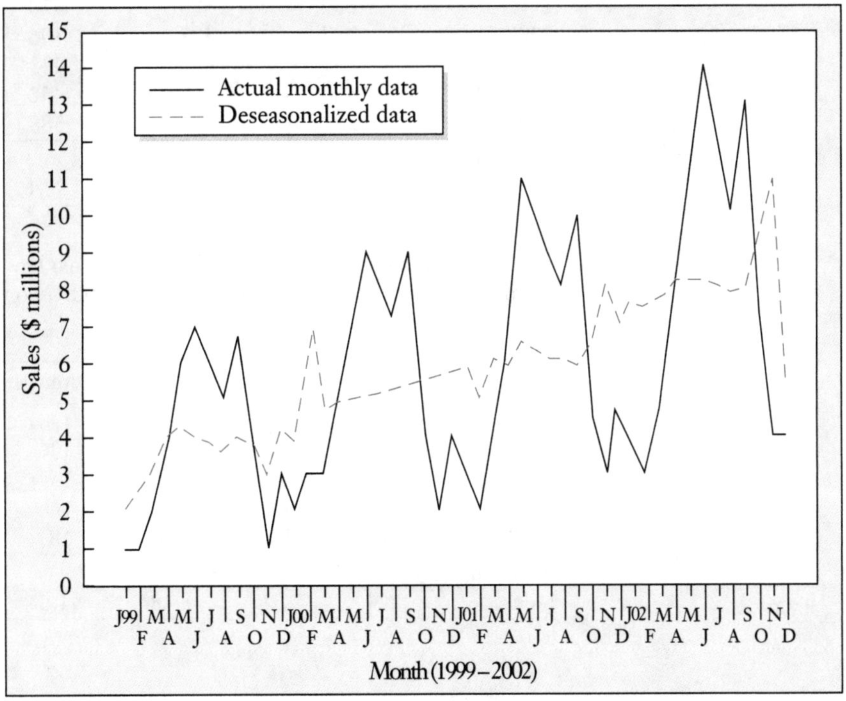

EXERCISE 6.5

1. The following table shows sales for the Outlet Retail Store (in $000) for the period July 1, 1998, to June 30, 2003. Compute the seasonally adjusted values.

Year	Quarter			
	I	II	III	IV
1998	–	–	4	8
1999	3	6	5	10
2000	4	8	6	13
2001	6	10	7	16
2002	5	9	4	12
2003	4	9	–	–
Seasonal index	57.5	108.0	74.2	160.3

2. The following table shows quarterly shoe sales (in $000) for Shoes R Us for the period October 1, 1998, to September 30, 2003. Compute the seasonally adjusted quarterly shoe sales.

Year	I	II	III	IV
1998				360
1999	269	380	370	471
2000	287	405	396	507
2001	299	439	423	520
2002	386	510	452	556
2003	281	423	388	
Seasonal index	73.0	105.0	98.1	123.9

3. The following monthly sales figures (in $ millions) have been compiled for a chain of restaurants for the period 1998 to 2002. Compute the seasonally adjusted sales figures.

Year	Jan	Feb	Mar	Apr	May	Jun
1998	12	10	12	14	13	13
1999	12	11	15	13	14	14
2000	14	12	14	15	15	15
2001	15	13	15	16	17	18
2002	16	14	16	18	18	19
Seasonal index	86.4	76.2	86.8	91.6	93.8	94.9

Year	Jul	Aug	Sep	Oct	Nov	Dec
1998	11	12	12	15	17	27
1999	12	11	11	16	20	32
2000	13	15	14	16	19	31
2001	16	19	17	20	23	36
2002	17	21	18	21	26	40
Seasonal index	80.5	89.7	85.9	105.4	120.3	188.7

4. The following table shows the monthly average employment of an auto-parts manufacturer for the period 1999 to 2002. Compute the seasonally adjusted values.

Year	Jan	Feb	Mar	Apr	May	Jun
1999	123.2	130.8	123.1	124.9	147.6	135.3
2000	158.5	160.0	154.6	144.2	137.7	136.9
2001	153.2	141.7	142.7	123.0	118.5	126.3
2002	86.0	84.8	83.2	97.2	104.5	108.6
Seasonal index	110.6	105.1	106.4	97.4	95.1	105.2

Year	Jul	Aug	Sep	Oct	Nov	Dec
1999	137.7	125.3	133.4	124.5	130.4	143.2
2000	146.0	154.8	142.3	136.1	137.8	143.8
2001	107.7	105.3	100.4	105.2	91.2	78.2
2002	114.4	108.1	122.0	111.7	115.6	106.5
Seasonal index	99.2	96.5	96.3	94.9	92.2	101.1

SECTION 6.6

Irregular Movements

In business, the practice of forecasting or predicting is based on past events and anticipated future events. As with any prediction, the best-laid plans do not always work out as a result of unanticipated events.

Unpredictable changes can result from events such as

1. political events (dissolution of the USSR, reunification of East and West Germany);
2. labour problems (Canadian postal strikes);
3. catastrophic events (tornado in Edmonton, *Exxon Valdez* oil spill).

In spite of the difficulties inherent in the forecasting process, business cannot afford *not* to devote time, energy, and resources to predicting the future.

REVIEW EXERCISE

1. Sales of a popular college-level marketing textbook in Canada are shown:

Year	1995	1996	1997	1998	1999	2000	2001	2002
Number of textbooks	3784	3859	3968	3988	4126	4550	4642	4719

a) Plot the data on a scatter diagram.
b) Compute the trend line equation using the basic least squares method, and plot the line.
c) Estimate the number of textbooks sold for **(i)** 2003 and **(ii)** 2005.

2. Improved global competitiveness was a factor in increasing exports of Canadian resource-based products during the period 1998 to 2002, as shown:

Year	1998	1999	2000	2001	2002
Exports ($ billions)	104.9	105.3	156.1	188.0	216.1

a) Draw a scatter diagram.
b) Obtain the least squares equation and plot the trend line.
c) Estimate Canadian resource-based exports for **(i)** 2004 and **(ii)** 2006.
d) What was the average annual change in exports?

3. Share prices for a company listed on the Toronto Stock Exchange have eroded, as summarized below:

Year	1996	1997	1998	1999	2000	2001	2002
Share price	$9.75	$7.00	$5.50	$4.56	$4.00	$3.60	$3.32

a) Draw a scatter diagram.
b) Calculate the least squares equation and plot the trend line.
c) Predict the share price for 2003.

4. Property taxes for an Ontario resident over the last six years are listed.

Year	1997	1998	1999	2000	2001	2002
Taxes	$2900	3000	3150	3300	3400	3600

a) Draw a scatter diagram.
b) Calculate the least square equation and plot the trend line.
c) Predict the property tax for the year 2010. Do you feel this is a realistic estimate?

5. Electrical power production has increased over the period shown:

Year	1997	1998	1999	2000	2001	2002
Electricity Production (millions of MWh)	472.8	465.7	471.5	476.5	483.8	490.8

a) Construct a scatter diagram.
b) Determine the trend line equation and plot the trend line.
c) Predict the level of energy production for (i) 2004 and (ii) 2006.

6. Warranty repairs for J.R. Electronics Canada were as follows:

1995	1996	1997	1998	1999	2000	2001	2002
2929	2633	2418	2163	1916	1711	1549	1434

a) Construct a scatter diagram.
b) Determine the trend line equation and plot the line.
c) Forecast warranty repairs for (i) 2004 and (ii) 2006.

7. The number of student complaints about food service at a major Ontario college from 1998 to 2002 were as follows:

Year	1998	1999	2000	2001	2002
Complaints	1200	1100	1000	700	500

a) Construct a scatter diagram.
b) Determine the trend line equation and plot the line.
c) Predict dissatisfaction with the food service in the year 2005.

8. Flook Transport's records indicate that damage to items shipped has increased over the period shown:

1995	1996	1997	1998	1999	2000	2001	2002
62	69	79	90	102	116	136	153

a) Represent the data on a scatter diagram.
b) Obtain the least squares equation and plot the trend line.
c) Predict the number of items damaged for (i) 2004 and (ii) 2006.

9. Defective parts (per thousand) due to a manufacturing process have decreased over the last five years as shown:

Year 1	Year 2	Year 3	Year 4	Year 5
105	90	65	40	20

a) Represent the data on a scatter diagram.
b) Obtain the least squares equation and plot.
c) Predict the number of defective parts in year 7 if 1 000 000 were manufactured.

10. From the trend line equation $y_p = 520 + 30x$, where y represents annual unit sales and 1998 is the first year ($x = 1$), determine
a) the expected sales for 2001;
b) the average annual change in unit sales;
c) the estimated sales for 2004.

11. The trend line equation $y_p = 1080 + 500x$ represents the cost of tuition at an Ontario college. Using 1999 as the first year ($x = 0$) and y is the annual tuition, determine
a) the expected tuition for 2003;
b) the average change in tuition;
c) the estimated tuition for 2008.

12. Using the least squares equation $y_p = 60 - 3x$, with 1999 as the first year ($x = 1$), determine
a) the trend value for 2004;
b) the average annual change.

13. The use of photocopying paper in your company is decreasing each year. Using the least squares equation $y_p = 100\ 000 - 5000x$, with 2000 as the first year ($x = 1$), determine
a) the trend value for the year 2004;
b) in which year you can expect your company not to use any more paper.

14. Investment spending for the years 1998 to 2002 in billions of dollars, was 66, 73, 78, 87, and 99 respectively. The least squares equation best describing the data is $y_p = 56.6 + 8x$, with 1998 as the first year ($x = 1$).
a) Plot the observed values on a line graph.
b) Plot the trend line on the graph in part (a).
c) Compute the trend values for the years 1998 to 2002.
d) Compute the percent of trend for the time period.
e) Construct a graph depicting the percent of trend.

15. The equation $y_p = 9.8 - 1.4x$, first year 1998 ($x = 1$), is the least squares equation for the following time series:

Year	1998	1999	2000	2001	2002
y	9	7	4	5	3

a) Plot the observed values, y.
b) Plot the trend line.
c) Compute the trend value for each year.
d) Calculate the cyclical relatives.
e) Construct a graph of the cyclical relatives.

16. The equation $y_p = 2.29 + 1.08x$ represents the least squares equation for the following data:

Year	1997	1998	1999	2000	2001	2002
Cell phone use (in millions)	3.0	4.1	6.2	7.1	7.9	8.1

Let 1997 be $x = 1$.

a) Plot the observed values of y and join the points.
b) Plot the trend line.
c) Compute the trend value for each year.
d) Calculate the cyclical relatives.
e) Construct a graph of the cyclical relatives.

17. Total revenue of Mini Italia Restaurant for the period 1998 to 2002 is shown:

Year	1998	1999	2000	2001	2002
Total revenue ($ 000)	318.0	321.9	346.3	332.2	350.3

a) Determine the trend line equation.
b) Construct a scatter diagram and plot the trend line.
c) Estimate the restaurant's total revenue for 2005.
d) Compute the percent of trend and graph the percent of trend.

18. Employment in the fishing industry in a Newfoundland community has declined over the period 1997 to 2001.

Year	1997	1998	1999	2000	2001
Number of Employees	5154	2582	2202	1603	1618

a) Construct a scatter diagram.
b) Determine the trend line equation and plot the line.
c) Predict the number of employees for 2004.
d) Calculate and graph the cyclical relatives.

19. The number of people losing their jobs in the financial sector has increased from 1998 to 2002.

Year	1998	1999	2000	2001	2002
Lost jobs (000s)	4	5	8	12	13

a) Construct a scatter diagram.
b) Determine the trend line equation and plot the line.
c) Predict the number of people who will be losing their jobs in 2006.
d) Calculate and graph the cyclical relations.

20. The number of corporate tax returns processed by a tax accountant for the period 1987 to 2002 is listed below:

1987	1988	1989	1990	1991	1992	1993	1994
65	51	65	70	60	97	69	50

1995	1996	1997	1998	1999	2000	2001	2002
42	46	41	37	24	22	36	40

a) Compute the five-year moving averages.
b) Plot the time series and the moving averages.

21. For the following data,
a) calculate six-year moving averages;
b) plot the time series and the moving averages.

1992	1993	1994	1995	1996	1997	1998	1999	2000	2001
170	180	205	205	180	195	210	230	245	215

22. At a local convenience store, the following data is collected for milk sales (000s of litres):

1993	1994	1995	1996	1997	1998	1999	2000	2001	2002
30	35	35	40	45	50	45	60	55	65

a) Calculate the 5-year moving average.
b) Plot the time series and moving averages.

23. The number of sick days taken at a manufacturing plant are listed:

1995	1996	1997	1998	1999	2000	2001	2002
155	160	145	140	140	125	135	130

a) Calculate the four-year moving average.
b) Plot the time series and moving averages.

24. Over the years, sales of a special pump used in hospital operating rooms have increased, as shown in the following data:

1980	1981	1982	1983	1984	1985	1986	1987
123	143	153	157	152	187	196	199

1988	1989	1990	1991	1992	1993	1994	1995
190	226	244	248	222	257	262	274

1996	1997	1998	1999	2000	2001	2002
280	288	324	309	305	327	362

a) Determine the computed trend and the percent of trend.
b) Construct a graph of the percent of trend and estimate from it the length of the business cycle for the pump.
c) Fit a moving average to the data based on your results in **(b)**.
d) Plot the sales data and the moving averages on a separate graph.

25. Annual sales ($000) for Connex Variety Stores are given below:

1984	1985	1986	1987	1988	1989	1990	1991	1992	1993
52.8	88.6	78.7	72.1	88.0	96.9	85.1	87.8	108.1	130.8

1994	1995	1996	1997	1998	1999	2000	2001	2002
79.4	61.5	70.3	71.4	50.8	48.2	54.7	62.3	48.3

a) Compute a four-year moving average.
b) Plot the sales data and the four-year moving averages.

26. Monthly restaurant sales in the clubhouse of a local vacation resort offering golfing and skiing were as follows. Determine the 12-month moving average.

Month	1999	2000	2001	2002
January	31 800	32 100	34 500	37 800
February	40 200	40 500	42 900	47 400
March	29 100	28 800	26 700	27 900
April	19 500	16 500	19 500	22 800
May	16 200	19 200	21 900	24 300
June	21 900	22 200	20 700	24 300
July	27 900	30 300	33 900	23 700
August	31 500	31 800	34 200	31 600
September	25 500	22 500	25 500	
October	15 300	14 400	19 500	
November	8 100	8 700	10 500	
December	10 200	8 400	11 700	

27. Sales (in $000) of the Play-With-Me Toy Store for the three-year period 2000 to 2002 are listed. Compute the monthly moving average.

Month	2000	2001	2002
January	500	400	600
February	600	700	500
March	700	800	700
April	1000	1100	1000
May	900	900	900
June	600	800	700
July	700	800	900
August	500	400	400
September	800	700	900
October	1000	1000	1100
November	1200	1300	1300
December	1500	1700	1600

28. Coffee sales (000s of cups) at the neighbourhood coffee shop from 2001–2002 are listed. Compute the monthly moving average.

Year	Jan	Feb	Mar	Apr	May	Jun
2001	3000	3200	3300	3400	3100	3000
2002	3100	3100	3400	3500	3150	2900

Year	Jul	Aug	Sep	Oct	Nov	Dec
2001	2900	2500	2800	2800	2900	3000
2002	2900	2550	2700	2900	3000	3100

29. The following data summarize the number of units of production of telecommunications equipment by an Ontario high-technology firm over a four-year period:

	Quarter			
Year	I	II	III	IV
1	717	693	693	543
2	651	502	495	565
3	616	497	411	546
4	554	477	532	636
Seasonal index	113.7	91.4	90.4	104.2

a) Compute the quarterly moving average.
b) Construct a graph of the time series.
c) Deseasonalize the data.
d) Plot the seasonally adjusted values on the graph in **(b)**.

30. The following data summarize the overnight guests at a bed and breakfast operation from 1999–2002:

	Quarter			
Year	I	II	III	IV
1999	180	190	270	250
2000	190	210	285	250
2001	210	220	300	260
2002	200	190	250	250
Seasonal index	80	85	120	115

a) Compute the quarterly moving average.
b) Construct a graph of the time series.
c) Deseasonalize the data.
d) Plot the seasonally adjusted values on the graph in **(b)**.

31. Unemployment rates (in percents) in Canada for a four-year period are shown below:

	Quarter			
Year	I	II	III	IV
1	5.3	3.2	1.7	2.4
2	5.6	3.8	2.9	5.0
3	9.4	6.6	4.5	6.0
4	9.3	5.7	3.7	5.5
Seasonal index	153.6	95.8	60.9	89.7

a) Adjust the data for seasonal fluctuation.
b) Construct a graph showing the original data and the deseasonalized values.

SELF-TEST

1. A historical study of the hourly earnings at Clarkson Manufacturing Company yielded the following data:

1994	1995	1996	1997	1998	1999	2000	2001	2002
11.36	12.34	13.40	14.54	15.98	16.98	17.66	19.46	19.38

a) Determine the trend line equation.
b) Construct a scatter diagram and plot the trend line.
c) Predict the hourly earnings for **(i)** 2004 and **(ii)** 2006.

2. Sales for the B & B Audio Entertainment Centre have declined over a period of years due to the intense competition from large, national-chain electronics stores.

Year	1996	1997	1998	1999	2000	2001
Sales ($000)	560	552	538	522	517	497

a) Compute the equation of the least squares trend line.
b) Determine the average change in sales of records over the time period 1996 to 2001.
c) Forecast sales for 2004.
d) Compute the cyclical relatives.
e) Construct a graph of the percent of trend.

3. The growth of revenue for the firm Niagara Accounting Associates can be described by the following trend model:

$$y_p = 1\ 600\ 000 + 110\ 000x$$

where y_p is the annual dollar value of revenue;
x represents the year under consideration (for 1998, $x = 1$).
a) What is the average expected annual change in revenue?
b) What was the trend value for 2002?
c) Predict the firm's revenue for 2006.

4. The following number of building starts were recorded over the last 12-year period:

Year	1	2	3	4	5	6
Starts	32 064	14 473	45 727	43 237	23 875	8410

Year	7	8	9	10	11	12
Starts	40 437	39 678	33 815	17 788	55 413	48 856

a) Compute the four-year moving average.
b) Construct a graph showing the original data and the moving average.

5. Spending by Canadians on imported consumer goods (in $ millions) is shown in the table. Compute the seasonally adjusted values.

Year	Quarter I	Quarter II	Quarter III	Quarter IV
1998	8 672	8 628	8 792	9 220
1999	9 152	9 504	9 724	10 148
2000	10 072	10 632	10 948	11 212
2001	11 480	11 792	12 216	12 356
Seasonal index	98.7	100.0	99.8	101.5

APPENDIX 6 The Coded Least Squares Method

A. Formulas for Computing a and b

When using the least squares method, simplification is possible by coding the time periods in such a way that $\sum x = 0$.

When $\sum x = 0$,

the equation $a = \frac{\sum y}{n} - b\frac{\sum x}{n}$ simplifies to

$$a = \frac{\sum y}{n}$$

and the equation $b = \frac{n(\sum xy) - (\sum x)(\sum y)}{n(\sum x^2) - (\sum x)^2}$ simplifies to

$$b = \frac{\sum xy}{\sum x^2}$$

The use of the coded method centres around the condition that $\sum x = 0$. In creating this condition, two cases must be considered:

1. when the number of observations n is an odd number;
2. when the number of observations n is an even number.

B. Using the Coded Method When n Is an Odd Number

To make $\sum x = 0$ when n is an odd number, assign to the *middle* year the value $x = 0$. The years after the middle years are numbered $x = 1, 2, 3$, etc., while the years before the middle year are numbered $x = -1, -2, -3$, etc., as shown in Example 6.A1 below.

○ EXAMPLE 6.A1

For the time series used in Example 6.2a, determine the trend line equation by the coded method.

Year	1996	1997	1998	1999	2000	2001	2002
Sales ($ million)	8	10	11	14	18	20	19

● SOLUTION

Step 1 Construct the scatter diagram (as done for Example 6.2a).

FIGURE 6.A1 Scatter Diagram of Sales, 1996–2002

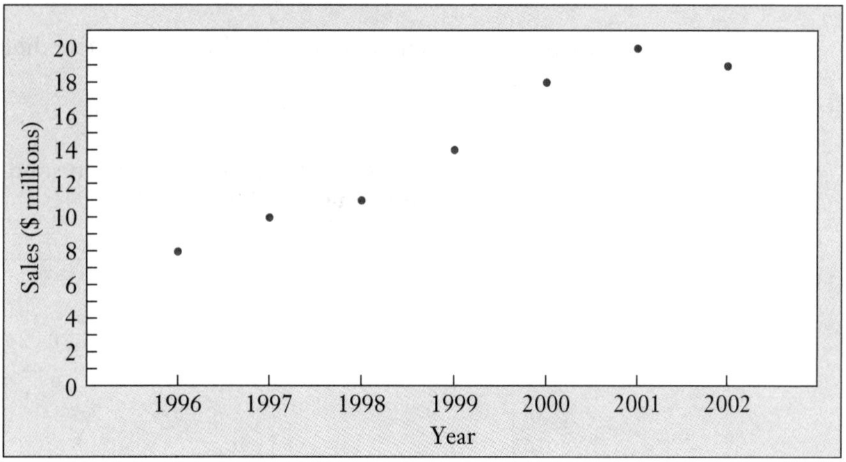

Step 2 Assign the value $x = 0$ to the middle year 1999. The year 2000 becomes $x = 1$, 2001 becomes $x = 2$, 2002 becomes $x = 3$, 1998 becomes $x = -1$, 1997 becomes $x = -2$ and 1996 becomes $x = -3$. See Figure 6.A2.

Step 3 Determine the values $\sum x$, $\sum y$, $\sum xy$, $\sum x^2$, as shown in Table 6.A1.

TABLE 6.A1 **Computation of the Values $\sum x, \sum y, \sum xy, \sum x^2$ (When n Is an Odd Number)**

Year	x	y	xy	x^2
1996	−3	8	(−3)(8) = −24	(−3)(−3) = 9
1997	−2	10	(−2)(10) = −20	(−2)(−2) = 4
1998	−1	11	(−1)(11) = −11	(−1)(−1) = 1
1999	0	14	(0)(14) = 0	(0)(0) = 0
2000	1	18	(1)(18) = 18	(1)(1) = 1
2001	2	20	(2)(20) = 40	(2)(2) = 4
2002	3	19	(3)(19) = 57	(3)(3) = 9
$n = 7$	$\sum x = 0$	$\sum y = 100$	$\sum xy = 60$	$\sum x^2 = 28$

Step 4 Use the formulas to compute a and b.

$$a = \frac{\sum y}{n} = \frac{100}{7} = 14.285\ 71$$

$$b = \frac{\sum xy}{\sum x^2} = \frac{60}{28} = 2.142\ 857$$

Step 5 The trend line equation by the coded method is

$$y_p = 14.286 + 2.143x.$$

FIGURE 6.A2 **Scatter Diagram with Trend Line and Trend Line Projection — Coded Method**

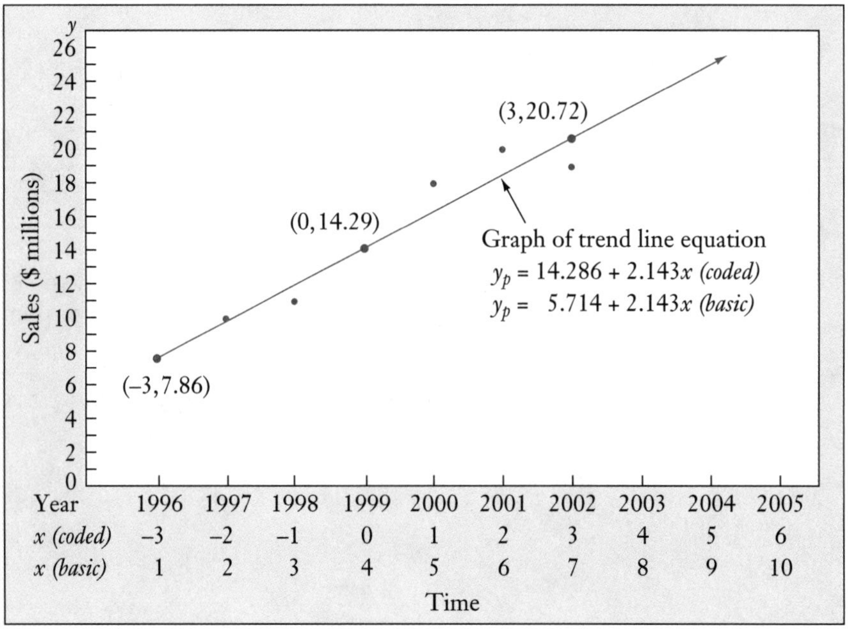

Step 6

$$\text{For } x = 0, \quad y_p = 14.286 + 2.143(0) = 14.286$$

$$\text{For } x = -3, \quad y_p = 14.286 + 2.143(-3) = 14.286 - 6.429 = 7.857$$

$$\text{For } x = 3, \quad y_p = 14.286 + 2.143(3) = 14.286 + 6.429 = 20.715$$

Step 7 Sales projection for 2004.
The x value for 2004 by the coded method is $x = 5$.

$$y_p = 14.286 + 2.143(5) = 14.286 + 10.715 = 25.001$$

C. Comparison of the Two Methods When n is an Odd Number

Plotting the points obtained by substituting in the coded trend line equation in the scatter diagram (see Figure 6.A2) and joining the points results in the same graph as shown in Figure 6.3 (basic method). While the value of $b = 2.142\ 857$ is the same in both equations, the value of a is different because the origin ($x = 0$) has been shifted from 1995 for the basic method to 1999 for the coded method.

D. Using the Coded Method When n is an Even Number

A complication in coding arises when n is an even number, since there are two middle years. The value $x = 0$ is located *between* the two middle years. The value $x = -1$ is assigned to the chronologically earlier of the two middle years and the value $x = 1$ is assigned to the following year. This means that the difference between the two middle years is two time units (see Figure 6.A3).

FIGURE 6.A3 Coding the Years When n Is an Even Number

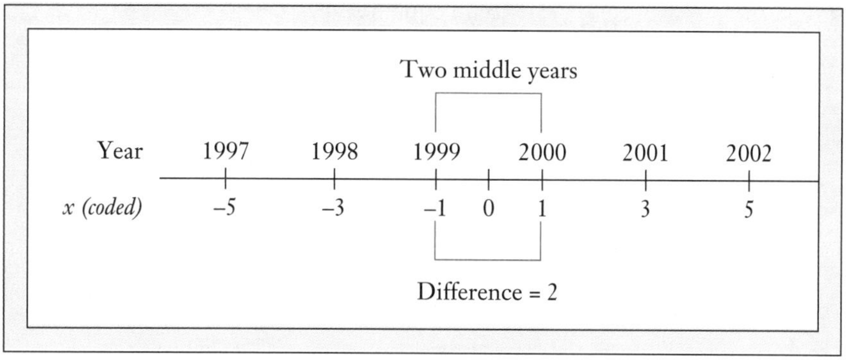

For consistency, the other years must be numbered –3, –5, –7, etc., and 3, 5, 7, etc.

○ **EXAMPLE 6.A2**

For the following time series,

a) determine the trend line equation by the coded method;

b) draw a scatter diagram and plot the trend line equation.

Year	1993	1994	1995	1996	1997	1998	1999	2000	2001	2002
Units	7	8	6	5	6	4	5	3	2	3

● **SOLUTION**

a) Determining the trend line equation by the coded method:

Year	x	y	xy	x^2
1993	–9	7	–63	81
1994	–7	8	–56	49
1995	–5	6	–30	25
1996	–3	5	–15	9
1997	–1	6	–6	1
1998	1	4	4	1
1999	3	5	15	9
2000	5	3	15	25
2001	7	2	14	49
2002	9	3	27	81
$n = 10$	$\sum x = 0$	$\sum y = 49$	$\sum xy = -95$	$\sum x^2 = 330$

$$a = \frac{\sum y}{n} = \frac{49}{10} = 4.900\,0$$

$$b = \frac{\sum xy}{\sum x^2} = \frac{-95}{330} = -0.2879$$

The trend equation is $y_p = 4.9000 - 0.2879x$.

b) Scatter diagram and plotting the trend line:

$$y_p = 4.9000 - 0.2879x$$

for 1993 when $x = -9$,

$$\begin{aligned} y_p &= 4.9000 - 0.2879(-9) \\ &= 4.9000 + 2.5911 \\ &= 7.4911 \end{aligned}$$

for 2001 when $x = 7$,

$$\begin{aligned} y_p &= 4.9000 - 0.2879(7) \\ &= 4.9000 - 2.0153 \\ &= 2.8847 \end{aligned}$$

FIGURE 6.A4 Scatter Diagram with Trend Line

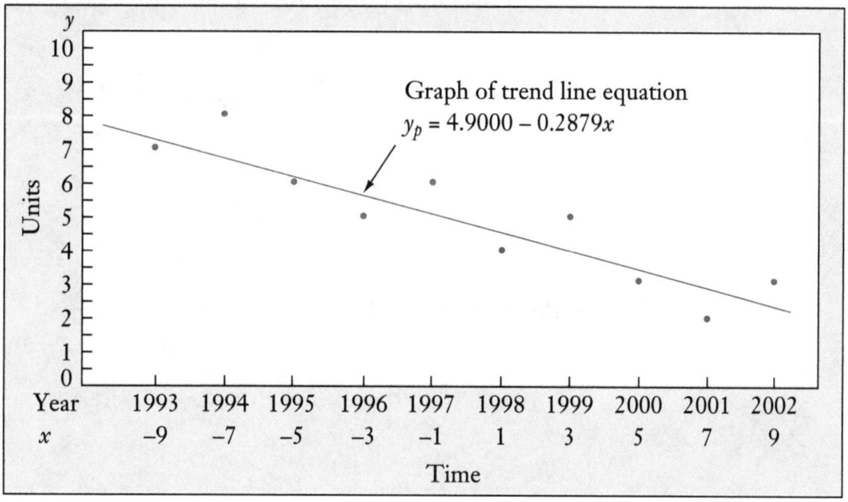

For an online glossary, go to **www.pearsoned.ca/hummelbrunner.**

Key Terms

Cyclical relative 180
Cyclical variation 173
Deseasonalized data 190
Irregular movement 174
Least squares method 174
Monthly index 194
Moving average method 182
Percent of trend 180
Quarterly index 190
Scatter diagram 175
Seasonal analysis 189
Seasonal index 189
Seasonal variation 174
Seasonally adjusted values 190
Secular trend 173

Summary of Formulas

1. General trend line equation

$$y_p = a + bx$$ ←*Formula 6.1*

2. Formulas for computing *a* and *b*:

$$b = \frac{n(\sum xy) - (\sum x)(\sum y)}{n(\sum x^2) - (\sum x)^2}$$

$$a = \frac{\sum y}{n} - b\left(\frac{\sum x}{n}\right)$$ ←*Formula 6.2*

3. Percent of trend

$$\text{PERCENT TREND (or CYCLICAL RELATIVE)} = \frac{y}{y_p}(100)$$ ←*Formula 6.3*

4. Seasonally adjusted value

$$\text{SEASONALLY ADJUSTED VALUE} = \frac{\text{ACTUAL VALUE}}{\text{SEASONAL INDEX}}(100)$$ ←*Formula 6.4*

CHAPTER 7

An Introduction to Probability

Introduction

In the first six chapters of this text we have dealt with the basic ideas of descriptive statistics. We have discussed the various ways of presenting data in tables, charts, and graphs, and of reducing large bodies of data to a few summarizing statistics such as the mean and the standard deviation.

In chapters 8 to 13 we will be concerned with inferential statistics. This is the area of statistics that concerns itself with drawing conclusions about a given set of data by analyzing a sample drawn from that data. To deal with inferential statistics we must first become familiar with the basic concepts of probability.

Learning Outcomes

Upon completion of this chapter you will be able to

1. differentiate between the classical, relative frequency, and subjective approaches to probability theory;
2. explain the terms random, experiment, outcome and event, and determine the probability of an event;
3. use tree diagrams to solve problems involving probabilities;
4. use counting rules to solve more complex problems;
5. construct and use Venn diagrams to illustrate and define the concepts of complementary, mutually exclusive, and joint events, and to deal with the union and intersection of events;
6. use Venn diagrams to solve simple problems;
7. explain and use the basic rules of probability.

SECTION 7.1

Approaches to Probability

A. The Classic View of Probability

Probability theory started with the study of games of chance such as playing cards or throwing dice. The phrase "games of chance" implies that the result of a particular roll of a pair of dice or the drawing of a particular card from an unmarked deck of cards is uncertain.

In the context of probability, the rolling of a die or the drawing of a card from a well-shuffled deck of cards, or any other activity for which the result depends on chance alone, is called a **random experiment**.

Consider the experiment of tossing a "fair" coin. The result of the experiment can go two ways — "head" or "tail." The results of an experiment are called **outcomes**.

Similarly, the experiment of rolling a die has six possible outcomes, one of which must occur, as shown in Figure 7.1.

FIGURE 7.1 The Six Outcomes of Rolling One Die

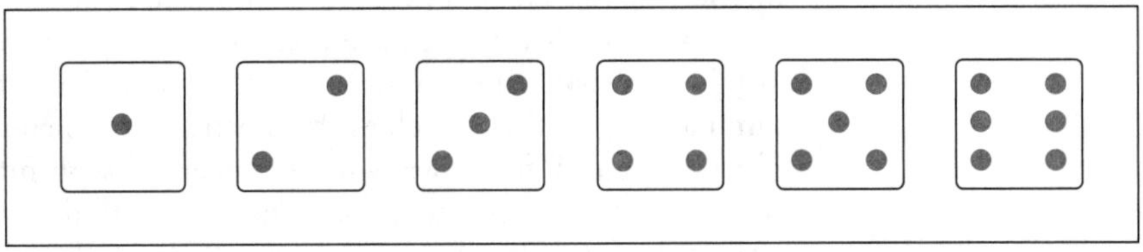

Provided the die is "fair," each of the six outcomes is equally likely to occur.

A more complex situation arises when we use a pair of dice. In the experiment of rolling a pair of dice the outcomes could be grouped by the total number of spots showing. There are 11 possible totals — 2 spots, 3 spots, 4 spots and so on to 12 spots. A group of one or more outcomes is called an **event**.

To illustrate the experiment let us use a pair of coloured dice — one red die and one black die. Now consider the Event (Four Spots). As indicated in Figure 7.2, this event is made up of the three possible arrangements (**outcomes**) of the two dice.

FIGURE 7.2 The Three Possible Outcomes of Rolling Two Dice for the Event (Four Spots)

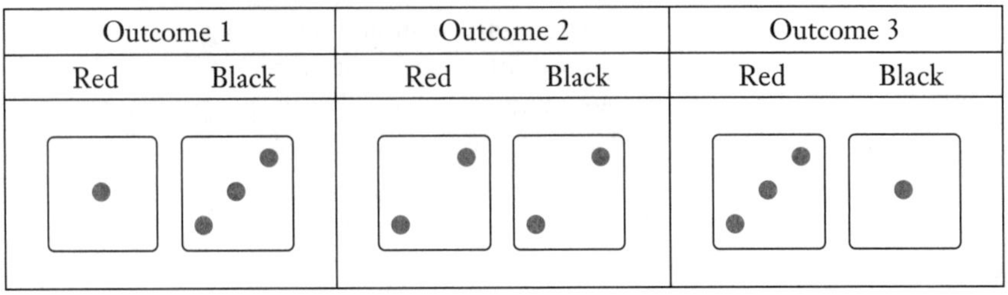

The 11 possible events (2 spots, 3 spots, 4 spots, and so on to 12 spots) are illustrated in Figure 7.3. As shown, there are 36 possible arrangements of the two dice; that is, there are 36 possible outcomes to the experiment of rolling two dice.

The number of outcomes that make up a particular event are referred to as *favourable* outcomes. For example, the three outcomes that result in the Event (Four Spots) are referred to as the favourable outcomes for this event. Similarly, there are four favourable outcomes for the Event (Nine Spots).

FIGURE 7.3 The 36 Possible Outcomes of Rolling Two Dice

Event (No. of Spots)	Possible outcomes allowing for the colour												Number of outcomes in each event
	Red	Black	Red	Black	Red	Black	Red	Black	Red	Black	Red	Black	
2	⚀	⚀											1
3	⚀	⚁	⚁	⚀									2
4	⚀	⚂	⚁	⚁	⚂	⚀							3
5	⚀	⚃	⚁	⚂	⚂	⚁	⚃	⚀					4
6	⚀	⚄	⚁	⚃	⚂	⚂	⚃	⚁	⚄	⚀			5
7	⚀	⚅	⚁	⚄	⚂	⚃	⚃	⚂	⚄	⚁	⚅	⚀	6
8	⚁	⚅	⚂	⚄	⚃	⚃	⚄	⚂	⚅	⚁			5
9	⚂	⚅	⚃	⚄	⚄	⚃	⚅	⚂					4
10	⚃	⚅	⚄	⚄	⚅	⚃							3
11	⚄	⚅	⚅	⚄									2
12	⚅	⚅											1
Number of events = 11							Number of possible outcomes = 36						

Since there is a total of 36 different outcomes, the probability of the Event (Four Spots) $= \frac{3}{36} = \frac{1}{12} = 0.0833$, while the probability of the Event (Nine Spots) $= \frac{4}{36} = 0.1111$.

In general, if the outcomes are equally likely,

$$\text{PROBABILITY OF AN EVENT, } P(\text{EVENT}) = \frac{\text{NUMBER OF FAVOURABLE OUTCOMES}}{\text{TOTAL NUMBER OF POSSIBLE OUTCOMES}}$$

←*Formu*

For the 11 events in Figure 7.3, the probabilities are

$$\frac{1}{36}, \frac{2}{36}, \frac{3}{36}, \frac{4}{36}, \frac{5}{36}, \frac{6}{36}, \frac{5}{36}, \frac{4}{36}, \frac{3}{36}, \frac{2}{36}, \frac{1}{36}.$$

○ **EXAMPLE 7.1a**

What is the probability of drawing an ace from a well-shuffled, unmarked deck of 52 cards?

● **SOLUTION**

Since the total number of cards is 52, there are 52 *equally likely outcomes* on a draw of a single card.

There are four aces in the deck. The Event (Drawing an Ace) consists of the four equally likely possible outcomes of drawing the ace of clubs, the ace of diamonds, the ace of hearts, or the ace of spades.

$$P(\text{DRAWING AN ACE}) = \frac{\text{NUMBER OF FAVOURABLE OUTCOMES}}{\text{TOTAL NUMBER OF POSSIBLE OUTCOMES}}$$
$$= \frac{4}{52} = 0.0769 = 7.69\%$$

B. *The Relative Frequency Concept of Probability*

There are many situations in which the outcomes of an experiment are not equally likely to occur. The likelihood of your car starting on any given morning is not equal to the likelihood of its stalling. Similarly, rain, snow, or sunny skies are not equally likely events on any particular day in any place in Canada. In such situations the *relative frequency* of the occurrence of the event in the past is taken as its probability of occurrence.

The relative frequency interpretation of probability is based on historical data and can be defined as the *proportion of the time that the event will occur over the long run*.

For example, if you use public transit to get to work each day, you will eventually get a "feel" for its reliability in terms of whether the system gets you to work on time "every time," "nearly every time," or "about half the time" and so on.

If you were to count the total number of trips to work over a long period of time and the number of times you were late because of delays in the transportation system, you could put a numerical value to your "feeling" about the reliability of the system. Suppose, for example, that out of 240 working days you were late 12 times due to delays in the system. Your long-run probability of being late would be

$$P(\text{LATE TO WORK}) = \frac{\text{NUMBER OF TIMES LATE}}{\text{NUMBER OF WORKING DAYS}}$$
$$= \frac{12}{240} = 0.05 = 5\%$$

C. *The Concept of Subjective Probability*

Both the classical concept of probability and the relative frequency approach to probability are objective in that they rely on counting the frequency of occurrence of outcomes. In the classical case this can be done theoretically; in the relative frequency approach it is done by an actual count of what has happened.

In the subjective approach to probability the individual assigns his or her own *personal estimate* of the chance that an event may happen. This estimate will be based on the person's previous experience with similar situations. This subjective approach is useful in situations where neither theoretical data nor actual data are available.

EXERCISE 7.1

1. How many outcomes are possible for the following experiments:
 a) rolling a single die once?
 b) rolling a single die twice?

2. How many outcomes are possible for
 a) tossing a single coin once?
 b) tossing a single coin twice?
 c) tossing a single coin three times?

3. State which of the following selection methods are random:
 a) drawing a number out of a hat;
 b) choosing the first name in the phone book under each letter of the alphabet;
 c) spinning an equally divided wheel;
 d) drawing the winning entries for a contest from a barrel.

4. Is asking a person to pick a number between 1 and 10 a random selection method? Explain.

5. Assume the event of interest is "heads." How many events are possible for
 a) a single coin tossed once?
 b) a single coin tossed twice?
 c) a single coin tossed three times?

6. How many events are possible for the experiment of rolling three dice?

7. What is the probability of drawing a face card (ace, king, queen, jack) from a deck of 52 cards?

8. Determine the probability of drawing from a deck of 52 cards
 a) a red card;
 b) a club;
 c) the queen of spades.

9. During the past semester Jenna Rak was late for classes 4 times out of 80 scheduled classes. What is the probability that Jenna will arrive for classes on time?

10. As part of the basketball team tryouts, each player was asked to get as many baskets as possible in one minute. Mike has so far scored on 18 attempts and missed 7. What is the probability that Mike will miss the next attempt?

11. A computer-controlled lathe requires periodic maintenance or it will break down. Maintenance records of similar models disclosed the following information:

Production time (days)	0 to 14	15 to 29	30 to 44	45 to 59
Probability of breakdown	2%	5%	30%	95%

a) What is the probability of the lathe working at least 29 days without breakdown?
b) After how many days of operation should periodic maintenance be performed if we are willing to accept a 5% risk of a breakdown?

12. The following data represent regional mortgage lending by a Canadian mortgage broker:

	Mortgage loans ($ 000s)	
Region	Residential	Non-residential
Eastern Canada	71 878	5224
Western Canada	28 024	2378

a) What is the probability that the next dollar granted by the mortgage broker for a mortgage will be in western Canada?
b) What is the probability that the next mortgage will be a non-residential mortgage in eastern Canada?

SECTION 7.2

Tree Diagrams

A **tree diagram** is a convenient method of graphically showing all possible outcomes of an experiment.

○ **EXAMPLE 7.2a**

Draw a tree diagram to show all possible outcomes of tossing a coin three times and determine the probabilities of the Event (Number of Heads).

● **SOLUTION**

First toss. Since one toss of a coin has two possible outcomes, the tree diagram is started by drawing two branches from a point on the left side of the diagram, as shown in Figure 7.4. The endpoints of the two branches are marked *H* (for "head") and *T* (for "tail") to represent the possible outcomes for the first toss of the coin.

Second toss. The second toss has the same two outcomes. To allow for each possible outcome, two branches are drawn from the endpoint of the branch marked *H*. The endpoints of these two new branches are marked *H* and *T* respectively to indicate the possible outcomes of the second toss, given that the outcome of the first toss was *H* (head). Similarly, two branches are drawn from the endpoint marked *T*. The endpoints of these two new branches are marked *H* and *T* respectively to indicate the possible outcomes of the second toss, given that the outcome of the first toss was *T* (tail).

Third toss. Two branches are drawn from each of the four endpoints resulting from the second toss to indicate the possible outcomes of the third toss. The eight endpoints are marked *H*, *T*, *H*, *T*, *H*, *T*, *H*, *T*, as shown in Figure 7.4.

FIGURE 7.4 Tree Diagram for Three Tosses of a Coin

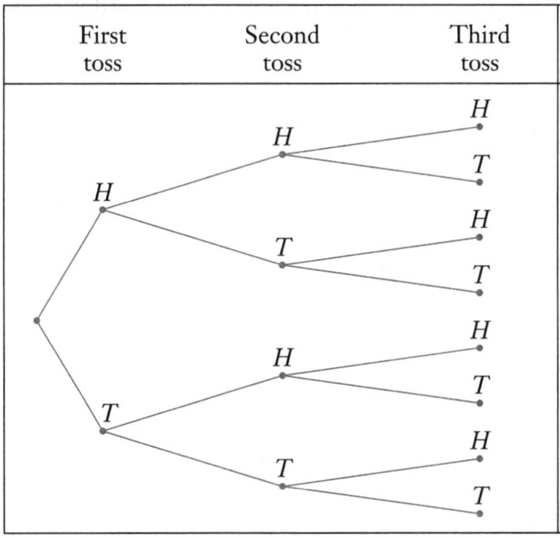

Possible outcomes	Event No. of Heads
HHH	3
HHT	2
HTH	2
HTT	1
THH	2
THT	1
TTH	1
TTT	0

The eight possible outcomes of tossing a coin three times are now listed under the heading of possible outcomes (*HHH*, *HHT*, *HTH*, etc.). The number of heads in each of the eight possible outcomes is shown in the last column of Figure 7.4.

The resulting events (Number of Heads) and their frequency and probability of occurrence can now be determined, as shown in Table 7.1 below.

TABLE 7.1 Probabilities of Tossing a Coin Three Times

Event (No. of Heads)	Frequency of occurrence	Probability of occurrence (relative frequency)
Three heads	1	$P(3 \text{ heads}) = \frac{1}{8} = 0.125$
Two heads	3	$P(2 \text{ heads}) = \frac{3}{8} = 0.375$
One head	3	$P(1 \text{ head}) = \frac{3}{8} = 0.375$
Zero heads	1	$P(0 \text{ heads}) = \frac{1}{8} = 0.125$
Total	8	1.000

EXAMPLE 7.2b

The 24-Hour Taxi Service employs three drivers and uses three cars. Determine the number of possible ways of assigning the three drivers to the three cars.

SOLUTION

Let the drivers be identified as *D1*, *D2*, *D3* and the cars as *A*, *B*, *C* respectively.

Draw three branches from the starting point to indicate that a car can be assigned to the first driver (whether it be *D1*, *D2*, or *D3* does not matter) in three ways.

Draw two branches from each of the three endpoints to indicate that a car can be assigned to the second driver in two ways.

Draw one branch from each of the six new endpoints to indicate that the remaining car can be assigned to the third driver in only one way.

The total number of ways of assigning three cars to three drivers is 6.

FIGURE 7.5 Tree Diagram

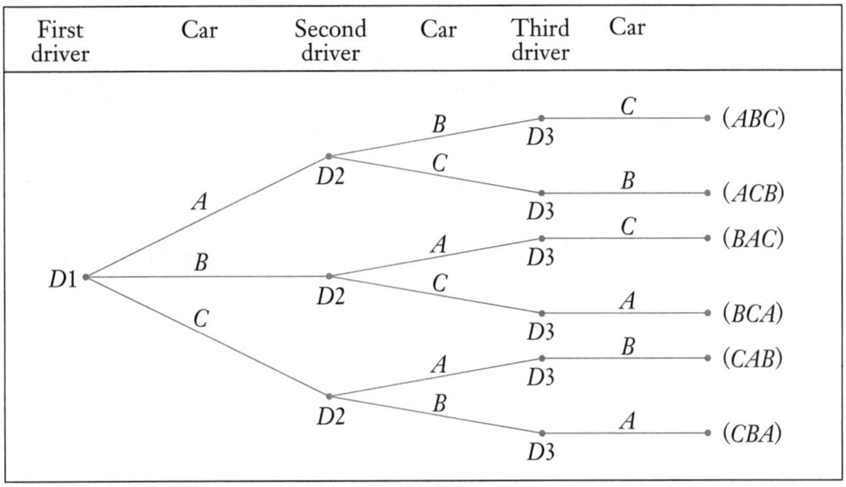

EXERCISE 7.2

1. A panel of consumers was asked to rate two products as "excellent," "average," or "poor." Determine the number of possible outcomes by drawing a tree diagram.

2. A sales representative must call four customers to find out if they will be ordering for the second quarter (yes or no). Construct a tree diagram to determine the number of ways in which the representative can be answered.

3. Third-year accounting students at a college face the task of choosing two courses, ranked by preference, from four courses offered. Use a tree diagram to determine in how many ways a student can make a choice of two courses ranked by order of preference.

4. A club has four candidates to fill the offices of president, treasurer, and secretary. Draw a tree diagram to show in how many different ways the offices can be filled.

SECTION 7.3

Counting Rules

For complex problems involving many outcomes, the listing of all possible outcomes may not be feasible. To deal with such problems, a variety of counting rules are available. The counting rule used to determine the number of outcomes depends on the type of situation represented by the problem.

A. Multiplication Rule

If there are m ways (outcomes) of doing one thing (event) and n ways (outcomes) of doing another thing (event), there are $(m)(n)$ ways (outcomes) of doing both things.

○ **EXAMPLE 7.3a**

A computer store is offering students a special price on three different computer systems (IBM, Apple, Sun) with the choice of scanner or printer included in the package deal. Determine how many different package deals the store is offering

(a) using a tree diagram;
(b) using the multiplication rule.

● **SOLUTION**

a)

FIGURE 7.6 Tree Diagram

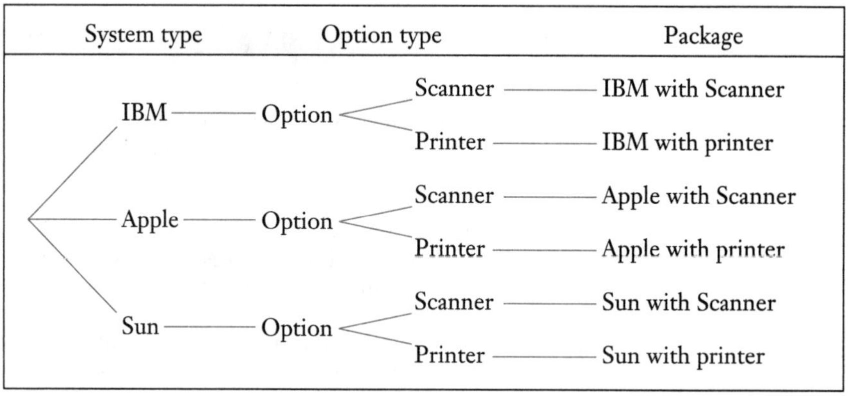

The store offers six different packages.

b) Using the multiplication rule:
the number of computer systems, $m = 3$ (IBM, Apple, Sun);
the number of options, $n = 2$ (scanner, printer);
the number of outcomes (package deals), $mn = (3)(2) = 6$.

○ **EXAMPLE 7.3b**

A purchasing agent for a large shoe store is thinking of buying a new Euro-design shoe. The shoe comes in five colours in any size. Store policy is to always carry the 14 most-popular sizes in stock. If the purchasing agent wants to order at least one pair of shoes of every one of the 14 most-popular sizes in every colour, what is the minimum number of pairs of shoes that must be ordered?

SOLUTION

Using the multiplication rule:
the number of shoe sizes, $m = 14$;
the number of shoe colours, $n = 5$;
the minimum number of pairs of shoes, $mn = (14)(5) = 70$.

B. Repeating Selection Rule

If any one of m things can be selected more than once up to n times, the number of possible outcomes is m^n.

EXAMPLE 7.3c

Jack and Jill intend to apply to the same three colleges (Algonquin, Fanshawe, Mohawk). Keeping in mind that both can select the same college, determine the number of possible ways the three colleges can be selected by Jack and Jill
a) using a tree diagram;
b) using the repeating selection rule.

SOLUTION

a)

FIGURE 7.7 Tree Diagram

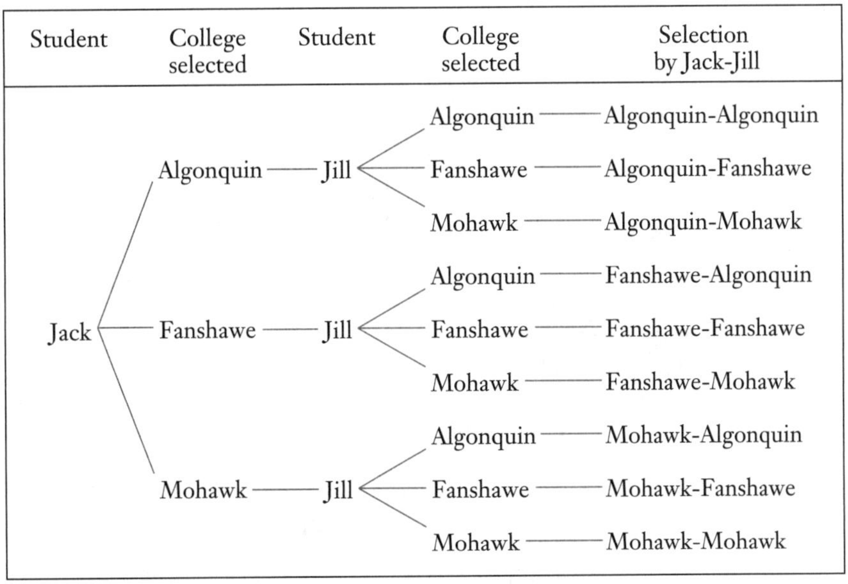

Jack and Jill can select from the three colleges in nine different ways.

b) Using the repeating selection rule:
the number of things, $m = 3$ (colleges);
the number of times each thing can be selected, $n = 2$ (students);
the number of possible ways, $m^n = 3^2 = 9$.

○ **EXAMPLE 7.3d**

The federal government issues nine-digit social insurance numbers to all eligible residents of Canada. Each of the nine digits can take a value ranging from 0 to 9. How many social insurance cards can the government issue before running out of numbers?

● **SOLUTION**

Using the repeating selection rule:
the number of things, $m = 10$ (the digits 0, 1, 2, 3, 4, 5, 6, 7, 8, 9);
the number of times a thing (digit) can be chosen, $n = 9$;
the number of possible outcomes $= m^n = 10^9 = 1\ 000\ 000\ 000$.

C. Permutation Rule

The term **permutation** refers to the number of ways in which a subset of a group of objects can be arranged in order. A change in the order of the objects is considered a new arrangement. Each possible arrangement is a permutation.

The number of permutations — that is, the number of ways in which r objects selected from an entire group of n objects can be arranged in order — is given by the formula

$$_nP_r = \frac{n!}{(n-r)!}$$ ←*Formula 7.2*

where n = the number of objects in the entire group;
r = the number of objects to be selected from the group of n objects;
$_nP_r$ = the number of permutations (ordered arrangements) in which the r selected objects can be arranged;
$n! = n(n-1)(n-2)(n-3)\ldots(3)(2)(1)$.

Notes

1. The symbol $n!$, read as "n factorial," denotes the product of the first n whole numbers.
   For example,

$$6! = (6)(5)(4)(3)(2)(1) = 720;$$
$$15! = (15)(14)(13)(12)\ldots(3)(2)(1) = 130\ 767\ 436\ 800.$$

2. The value of $0! = 1$.
3. For the special case in which all objects are included — that is, when $r = n$ — Formula 7.2 simplifies to

$$_nP_n = \frac{n!}{(n-n)!} = \frac{n!}{0!} = \frac{n!}{1} = n!.$$

○ **EXAMPLE 7.3e**

Four students (Brian, Margaret, Pierre, and Sheila) are nominated for the offices of president and vice-president in a student council election. The person getting the most votes becomes president and the runner-up becomes vice-president. Determine the number of possible selections for the offices of president and vice-president

a) using a tree diagram;
b) using the permutation rule.

● **SOLUTION**

a)

FIGURE 7.8 Tree Diagram

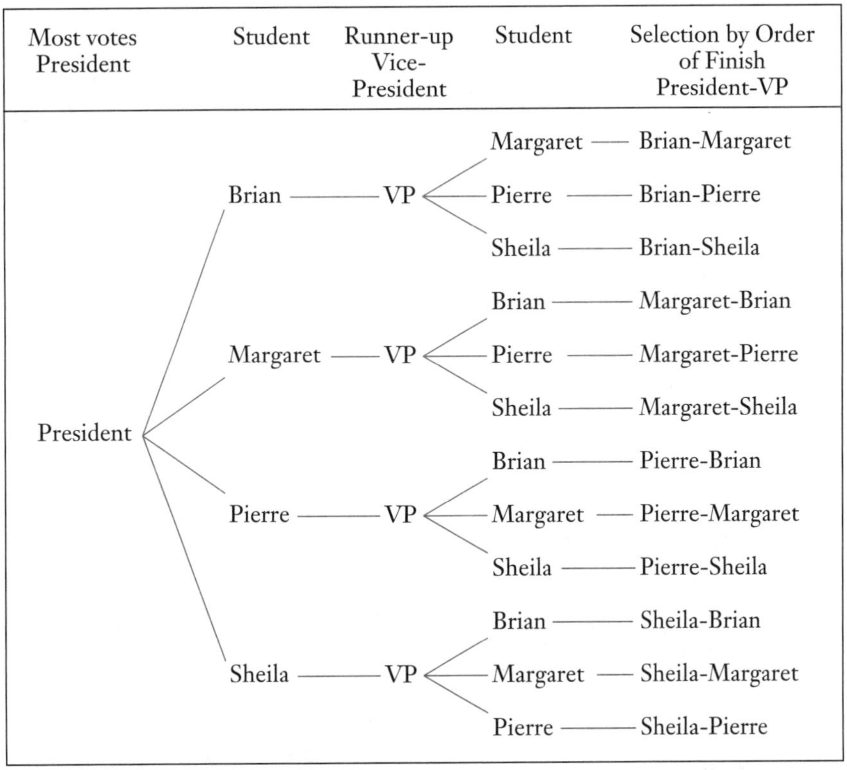

The number of possible selections (ordered arrangements) is 12.

b) Using the permutation rule:
Since the order of finish (first or second) is all-important, the permutation rule may be used to determine the number of possible selections as follows:
the entire group of objects, $n = 4$ (persons);
the number of objects to be selected, $r = 2$ (persons);
the number of ordered arrangements,

$$_nP_r = {}_4P_2 = \frac{4!}{(4-2)!} = \frac{4!}{2!} = \frac{(4)(3)(2)(1)}{(2)(1)} = 12.$$

These calculations can be completed using EXCEL, as demonstrated in USING EXCEL 7.1.

USING EXCEL 7.1

Use the permutation rule to calculate the number of ordered arrangements in Example 7.3e.

1. Type the note **The entire group of objects (persons)** into cell B1.
2. Type the note **The number of objects (persons) to be selected** into cell B2.
3. Type the note **The number of ordered arrangements** into cell B3.
4. Enter 4 into cell A1 (represents the entire number of students nominated for office).
5. Enter 2 into cell A2 (represents the number of students to be selected).
6. Select cell A3.
7. On the toolbar, click on the **Paste Function** button (or on the **Insert** menu, click **Function...**)
8. The **Paste Function** dialog box appears. From the **Function category** list, select **Statistical**; from the **Function name** list, select the **PERMUT** function; and then click the **OK** button.
9. The input dialog box appears. In the **Number** input box, type **A1** (or click on beside the **Number** input box to temporarily hide the input dialog box; select cell A1 on the worksheet; then click on or press the **Enter** key). In the **Number_chosen** input box, type **A2** (or select cell A2 and return to the input dialog box). When finished, click the **OK** button.

OUTPUT

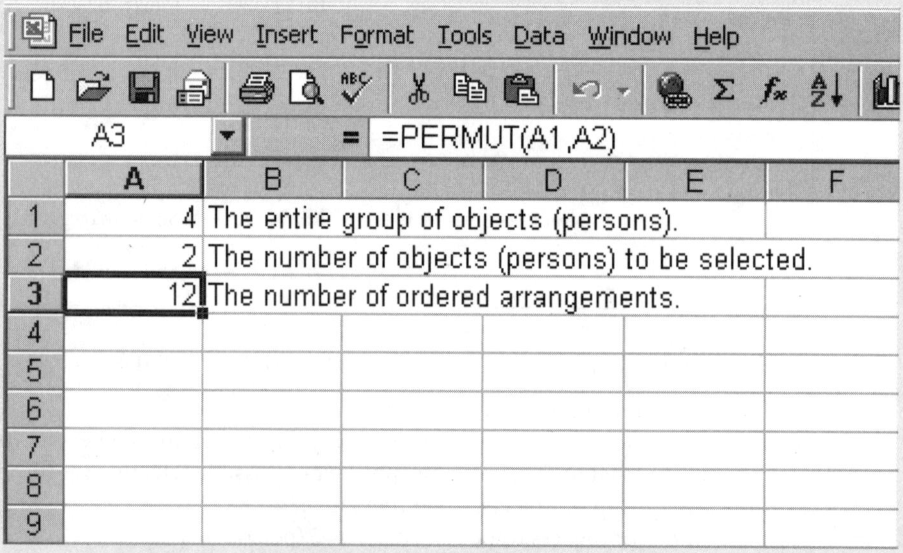

EXAMPLE 7.3f

The 24-Hour Taxi Service employs three drivers and uses three cars. Determine the number of possible ways of assigning the three drivers to the three cars (see Example 7.2b)

a) using a tree diagram;
b) using the permutation rule.

SOLUTION

a) Let the drivers be identified as *D*1, *D*2, *D*3 and the cars as *A*, *B*, *C* respectively.

FIGURE 7.9 Tree Diagram

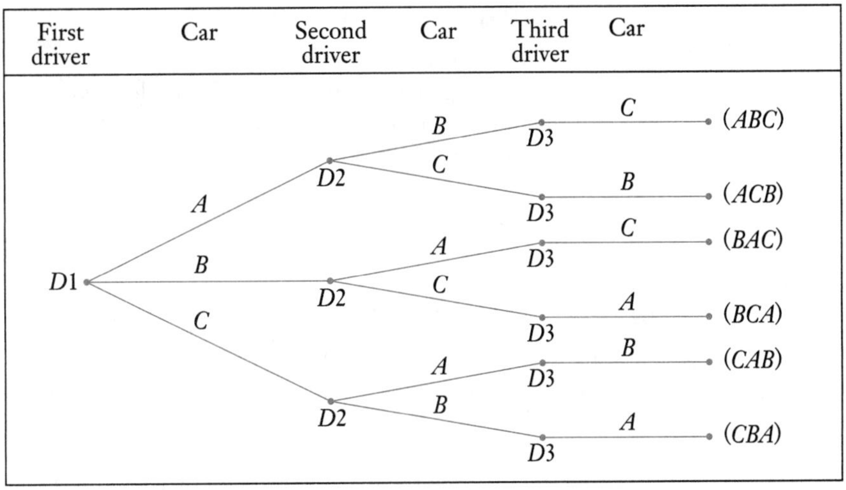

The number of possible ways of assigning the three drivers to the three cars is 6.

b) Using the permutation rule:
the entire group of objects, $n = 3$ (cars);
the number of objects selected, $r = 3$ (cars);
the number of ordered arrangements (permutations),

$$_3P_3 = \frac{3!}{(3-3)!} = \frac{3!}{0!} = \frac{(3)(2)(1)}{(1)} = 6.$$

EXAMPLE 7.3g

A supervisor must schedule five of nine part-time employees to each work one day of the next five-day work week. How many different work schedules can be made?

SOLUTION

The order in which the employees are assigned to the five work days is important. Using the permutation rule:

the entire group of objects, $n = 9$ (part-time employees);
the number of objects selected, $r = 5$ (employees);
the numbers of possible different schedules (permutations),

$$_9P_5 = \frac{9!}{(9-5)!} = \frac{9!}{4!} = \frac{(9)(8)(7)(6)(5)(4)(3)(2)(1)}{(4)(3)(2)(1)} = 15\ 120.$$

EXAMPLE 7.3h

A manager must schedule a job performance evaluation with each of seven employees. There are seven different dates available for interviews. In how many different ways can the interviews be scheduled?

SOLUTION

Using the permutation rule:
the entire group of objects, $n = 7$ (employees);
the number of objects selected, $r = 7$ (employees);
the number of different ways to schedule the interviews (permutations),

$$_7P_7 = \frac{7!}{(7-7)!} = \frac{7!}{0!} = \frac{(7)(6)(5)(4)(3)(2)(1)}{(1)} = 5040.$$

D. *Combination Rule*

In determining the number of permutations (ordered arrangements) of n objects selected r at a time, it is important to consider the order in which the objects are selected.

Arrangements in which the order is of no consequence are called **combinations** of n objects selected r at a time, and are denoted by the symbol $_nC_r$.

The number of such combinations is given by the formula

$$_nC_r = \frac{n!}{r!(n-r)!}$$ ←*Formula* 7.3

where n = the number of objects in the entire group;
r = the number of objects to be selected from the group;
$_nC_r$ = the number of combinations or ways in which r objects can be selected without regard to order.

○ EXAMPLE 7.3i

Four students (Brian, Margaret, Pierre, and Sheila) are nominated in a student council election. (See Example 7.3e)

a) Assume the election is for the positions of president and vice-president of the student council. The person getting the most votes becomes president and the runner-up becomes vice-president. Determine the number of possible selections for the offices of president and vice-president.

b) Assume the election is for two student representatives on the board of governors. The two top vote-getters will become the elected representatives. Determine the number of possible selections of two student representatives to the board of governors.

● SOLUTION

(a)

For (a) the order of finish (first or second) is important.

Permutation

The number of possible selections

Brian-Margaret
Margaret-Brian

Margaret-Pierre
Pierre-Margaret

Brian-Pierre
Pierre-Brian

Margaret-Sheila
Sheila-Margaret

Brian-Sheila
Sheila-Brian

Sheila-Pierre
Pierre-Sheila

The number of possible ordered arrangements (permutations) is 12.

The number of permutations could have been determined using the permutation formula where $n = 4$ and $r = 2$.

$$_nP_r = {}_4P_2 = \frac{4!}{(4-2)!} = \frac{4!}{2!}$$

$$= \frac{(4)(3)(2)(1)}{(2)(1)} = (4)(3) = 12$$

(b)

For (b) the order of finish (first or second) does not matter.

Combination

The number of possible selections

Brian and Margaret

Margaret and Pierre

Brian and Pierre

Margaret and Sheila

Brian and Sheila

Sheila and Pierre

The number of possible arrangements without regard to order (combinations) is 6.

The number of combinations could have been determined using the combination formula where $n = 4$ and $r = 2$.

$$_nC_r = {}_4C_2 = \frac{4!}{2!(4-2)!} = \frac{4!}{2!(2!)}$$

$$= \frac{(4)(3)(2)(1)}{(2)(1)(2)(1)} = (2)(3) = 6$$

These calculations can be completed using EXCEL, as demonstrated in USING EXCEL 7.2.

USING EXCEL 7.2

Use the combination function in EXCEL to calculate the number of arrangements in Example 7.3i regardless of order (combinations).

1. Type the note **The entire group of objects (persons)** into cell B1.
2. Type the note **The number of objects (persons) to be selected** into cell B2.
3. Type the note **The number of selections without regard to order** into cell B3.
4. Enter 4 into cell A1 (represents the entire number of students nominated for office).
5. Enter 2 into cell A2 (represents the number of students to be selected).
6. Select cell A3.
7. On the toolbar, click on the **Paste Function** button (or on the **Insert** menu, click **Function...**)
8. The **Paste Function** dialog box appears. From the **Function category** list, select **Math & Trig**; from the **Function name** list, select the **COMBIN** function; and then click the **OK** button.
9. The input dialog box appears. In the **Number** input box, type **A1** or select cell A1 and return to the input dialog box. Likewise, in the **Number_chosen** input box, type **A2** or select cell A2 and return to the input dialog box. When finished, click the **OK** button.

OUTPUT

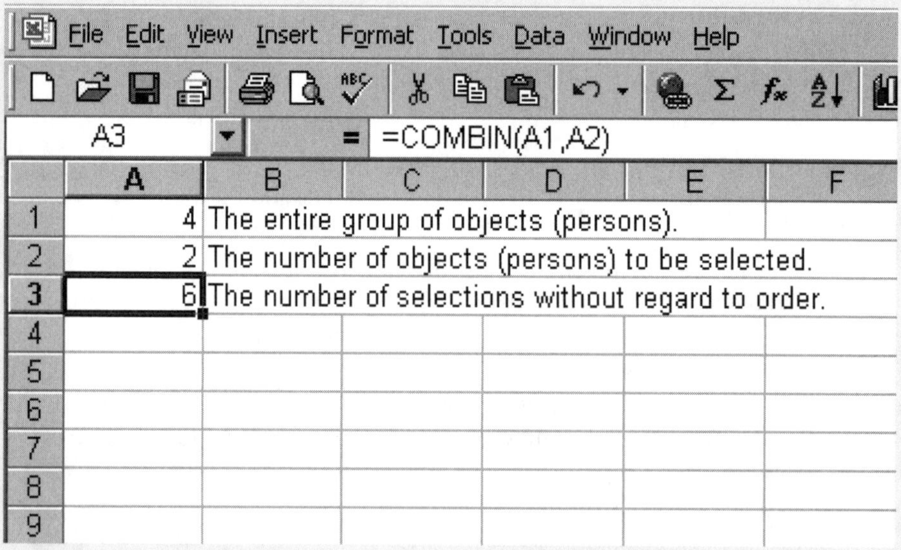

○ **EXAMPLE 7.3j**

Nortel Networks has decided to split design contracts for testing equipment between two of seven companies submitting bids. Determine the number of different ways that the two winning contracts can be selected.

● **SOLUTION**

Since the order of selecting the two winning bids does not matter, use the combination rule.

The entire group of objects, $n = 7$ (companies);
the number of objects selected, $r = 2$ (companies);
the number of different ways of selecting two winning bids (combinations),

$$_nC_r = {_7C_2} = \frac{7!}{2!(7-2)!} = \frac{7!}{2!(5!)} = \frac{(7)(6)(5)(4)(3)(2)(1)}{(2)(1)(5)(4)(3)(2)(1)} = \frac{(7)(6)}{(2)(1)} = 21.$$

○ **EXAMPLE 7.3k**

To have the winning number in Lotto 6/49 you must match six numbers between 1 and 49 drawn at random and displayed in ascending order. What is the probability of matching the winning set of numbers with one selection of six numbers?

● **SOLUTION**

First determine the total number of possible outcomes. Since the order in which the numbers are selected does not matter, use the combination rule for $n = 49$; $r = 6$.

$$_{49}C_6 = \frac{49!}{6!(49-6)!} = \frac{49!}{6!(43!)} = \frac{(49)(48)(47)(46)(45)(44)}{(6)(5)(4)(3)(2)(1)}$$

$$= \frac{10\,068\,347\,520}{720} = 13\,983\,816$$

Since there are 13 983 816 possible outcomes, the probability of having the winning combination with one set of six numbers $= \frac{1}{13\,983\,816}$, that is, about 1 chance in 14 million.

○ **EXAMPLE 7.3l**

A safety committee of 5 is to be chosen from a group of 10 employees who have indicated their willingness to stand for election to the committee. In how many ways can the committee be made up?

● **SOLUTION**

Since the order in which the candidates are elected does not matter, the number of combinations of 5 persons from a group of 10,

$$_{10}C_5 = \frac{10!}{5!(10-5)!} = \frac{10!}{5!(5!)} = \frac{(10)(9)(8)(7)(6)}{(5)(4)(3)(2)(1)} = 252.$$

EXERCISE 7.3

1. A sales representative must call on 5 customers in the same area. In how many ways can the representative arrange his itinerary?

2. Third-year students at a college must choose 3 courses, ranked in order of preference, from 8 courses offered. In how many ways can a student choose the three courses?

3. Management has offered to let all staff in a department attend courses to learn a new computer software program. Three of the 12 staff will be permitted to attend classes during business hours. In how many ways can the three employees be chosen?

4. In how many ways can 3 marketing representatives be selected from 10 applicants to serve different regions?

5. Six different desks are available for allocation to 6 distinct office areas. In how many ways can the desks be assigned?

6. A committee of 3 must be formed from 18 managers. In how many ways can the committee be formed?

7. An early-retirement package is to be offered to a group of 20 employees with the stipulation that only 12 of the employees will be able to take advantage of the offer. In how many ways can the offer be accepted by the group of employees?

8. A college's board of governors has student and faculty representation. In the first election 5 students are running for 2 seats and 15 faculty for 3 seats. In how many ways can the 5 board vacancies be filled?

9. How many four-digit passwords can be made from the numbers 0 through 9?

10. In how many ways can 4 men and 4 women make up a special committee looking into safety in the workplace if 3 persons are to be selected and at least 1 committee member must be a woman?

SECTION 7.4

Venn Diagrams

A. Basic Concepts

The basic components of probability are the outcomes associated with some process such as a game of chance, a weather forecast, the price movements of a particular stock, or the number of rejects in a manufacturing process. The possible outcomes of a process can be graphically represented by diagrams named after their developer, John Venn.

A **Venn diagram** starts with an *enclosed* area that contains all possible outcomes of the process. This area is called the **sample space**. In the case of tossing a coin, the sample space consists of two outcomes: Head or Tail. When one die is rolled, the sample space consists of the six possible outcomes: One Spot, Two Spots, and so on to Six Spots. The enclosed area can then be subdivided into parts representing the event or events under consideration.

B. Representative Diagrams

The following set of diagrams are Venn diagrams illustrating basic concepts of probability.

FIGURE 7.10 Venn Diagram 1: Complementary Events

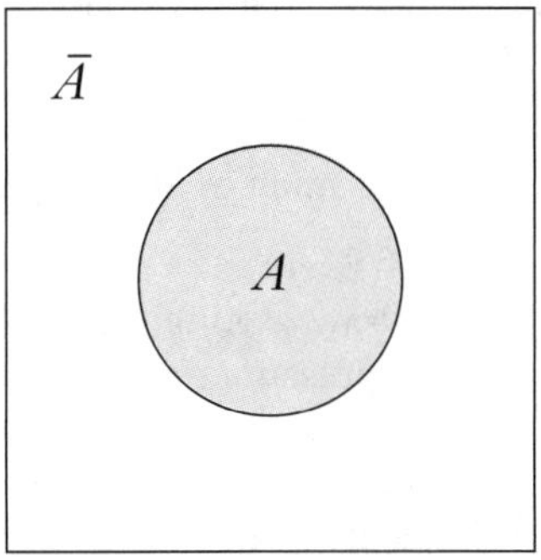

The area within the rectangle represents the sample space. The circular area within the sample space represents Event A. The remainder of the rectangular area contains all other events. These events are referred to as the **complement** of A, represented by the symbol $\bar{A}$ (read as "Not A").

For example, when a card is drawn from a deck of 52, if we define Event A as Draw an Ace, the complement of A is $\bar{A}$ = All Other Cards.

FIGURE 7.11 Venn Diagram 2: Mutually Exclusive Events

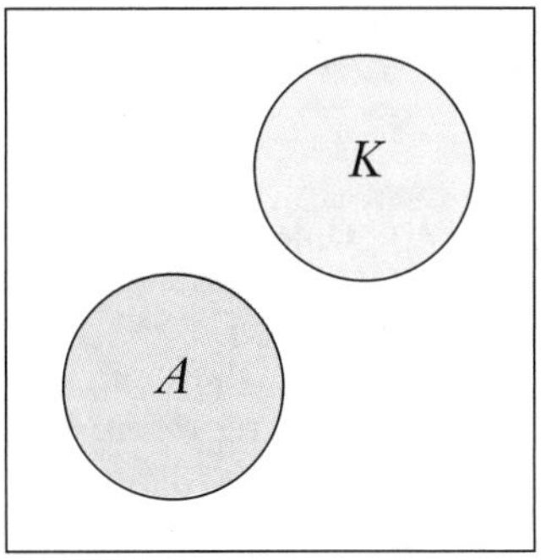

The areas within the two circles marked A and K represent two events that cannot occur at the same time — they are **mutually exclusive** events.

For example, let us define Event A as Draw an Ace and Event K as Draw a King. When one card is drawn, the events Draw an Ace and Draw a King cannot happen at the same time — they are *mutually exclusive* events.

FIGURE 7.12 Venn Diagram 3: Joint Events

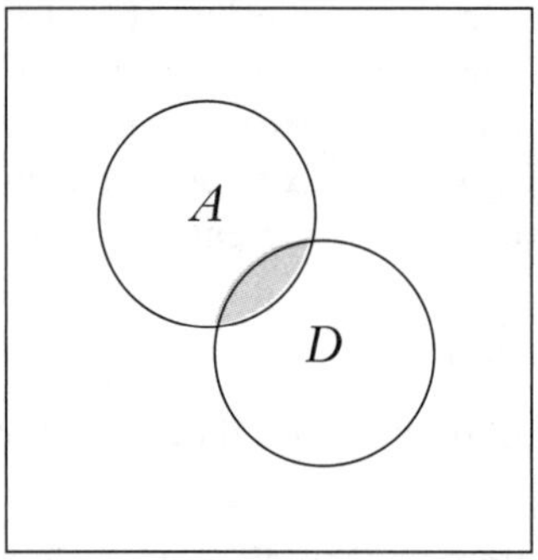

Joint events are events that have common outcomes. Joint events are represented by overlapping areas. For example, if Event A = Draw an Ace and Event D = Draw a Diamond, the events overlap when the ace drawn is the ace of diamonds.

Note that Figures 7.11 and 7.12 show that events are either mutually exclusive events or joint events.

FIGURE 7.13 Venn Diagram 4A: Union of Mutually Exclusive Events

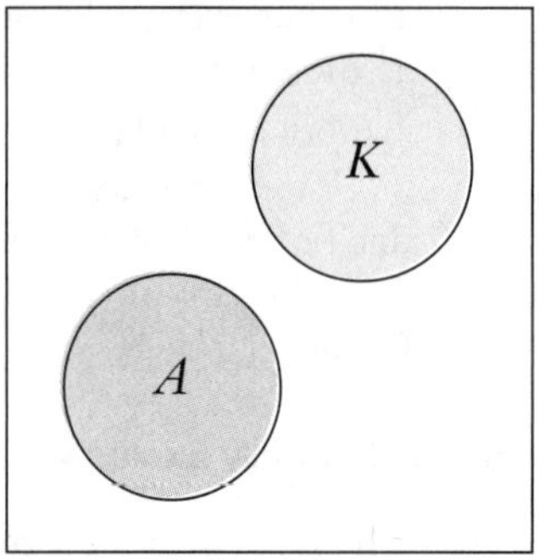

If Event A = Draw an Ace and Event K = Draw a King, the **union** of the two events represents the idea of drawing either an ace or a king with a single card. Because the two events are mutually exclusive, the areas A and K do not overlap.

The union is represented by the shaded areas. It is represented by the symbol $A \cup K$.

FIGURE 7.14 Venn Diagram 4B: Union of Joint Events

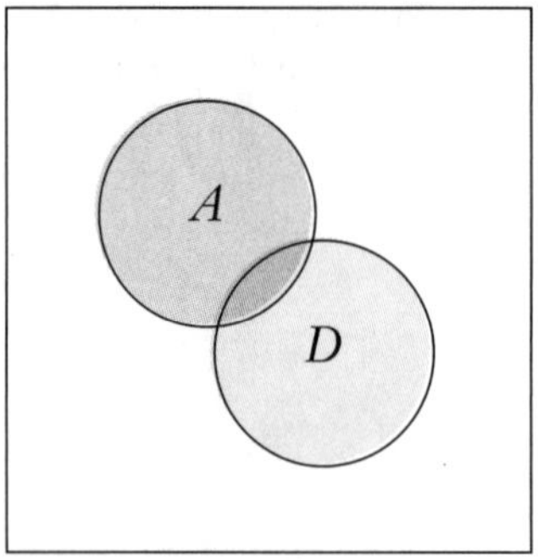

For Event A = Draw an Ace and Event D = Draw a Diamond, the union of the two events ($A \cup D$) represents the idea of drawing either an ace or a diamond. Since both events may happen when the ace of diamonds is drawn, the areas overlap.

The union ($A \cup D$) is represented by the shaded area.

FIGURE 7.15 Venn Diagram 5: Intersection of Events

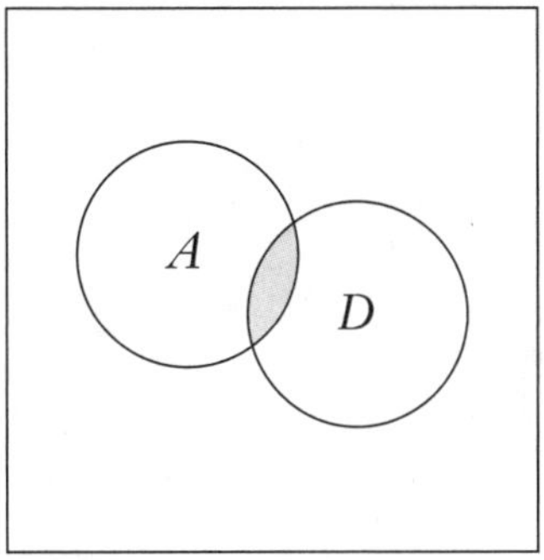

The **intersection** of two events A and D, denoted by the symbol $(A \cap D)$, is indicated by the shading in the area of overlap. It consists of all outcomes that are included in both A and D. Intersection is not possible for mutually exclusive events.

For example, the intersection of the events A (Draw an Ace) and D (Draw a Diamond) is the Event (Draw the Ace of Diamonds). It is the only outcome that belongs to both events.

C. *Examples Using Venn Diagrams*

○ **EXAMPLE 7.4a**

Consider the experiment of drawing a single card at random from a deck of 52 cards consisting of 26 red cards (diamonds, hearts) and 26 black cards (clubs, spades). The outcome is favourable if the card drawn

a) is red;
b) is a diamond;
c) is an ace.

Represent the event of drawing a card in the form of a Venn diagram, and assign the number of possible outcomes for each area.

● **SOLUTION**

First draw a rectangle representing the sample space of the 52 possible outcomes of drawing a single card.

Divide the sample space according to the three events. Draw two non-intersecting circles representing the events D(Diamond) and H(Heart) respectively. The union of the two circles $(D \cup H)$ represents all 26 red cards. The remaining sample space represents the 26 black cards.

Now draw a third circle to represent the Event A (Ace). Since there are two red aces, the ace of diamonds and the ace of hearts, this circle must overlap the two other circles, as shown in Figure 7.16. The area now outside the three circles represents the remaining black cards.

FIGURE 7.16 Venn Diagram

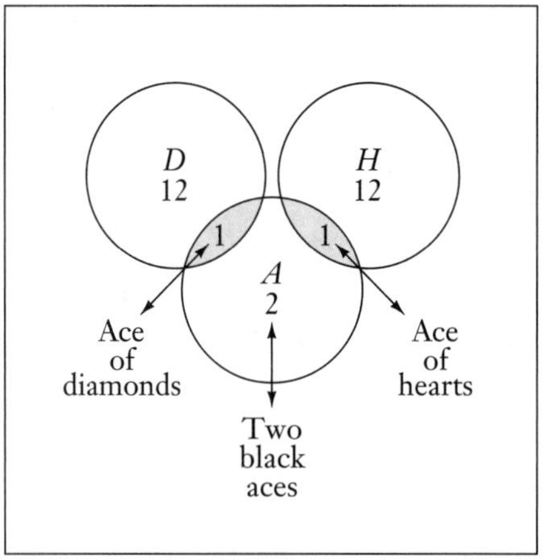

The number of possible outcomes associated with each area is as follows:

Number of outcomes	Explanation
1	(ace of diamonds) for the *intersection* of the circles A and D; $(A \cap D)$
1	(ace of hearts) for the *intersection* of the circles A and H; $(A \cap H)$
2	(the two black aces) for the remaining area of circle A
12	(the remaining diamonds) for the remaining area of circle D
12	(the remaining hearts) for the remaining area of circle H
24	(the remaining black cards) for the area of the sample space outside the three circles
52	

The total $1 + 1 + 2 + 12 + 12 + 24 = 52$ represents the sum of the possible outcomes of the experiment of drawing one card from a deck of 52.

EXAMPLE 7.4b

Of the 100 students enrolled in a business program, 52 take statistics. There are 60 female students; 45 of them take accounting, 30 take statistics, and 20 take both courses. Among male students, 32 take accounting and 18 take both accounting and statistics.

Draw a Venn diagram to represent the information and determine

a) the number of female students not taking accounting or statistics;
b) the number of male students taking statistics only;
c) the number of students taking accounting only;
d) the number of students not taking accounting or statistics.

SOLUTION

First draw a rectangle to represent the sample space for the 100 students. To divide the area inside the rectangle, draw three overlapping circles to represent three events in the problem—female, accounting, statistics. The remaining event, "male," is represented by the remaining area in the rectangle surrounding the circle representing female.

To assign numbers to the various areas, start with the area where the largest number of outcomes overlap. In this case it is the number of female students (20) taking both accounting and statistics.

a) Determine the number of female students not taking accounting or statistics.

Step 1 Locate the area of intersection of the three circles and insert the number 20.

Step 2 Since 45 of the female students take accounting and 20 of them also take statistics, the number of female students taking accounting only is $45 - 20 = 25$. Insert the number 25 in the remaining part of the intersection of circles F and A.

Step 3 Since 30 of the female students take statistics and 20 also take accounting, the number of female students taking statistics only is $30 - 20 = 10$. Insert the number 10 in the remaining part of the intersection of circles F and S.

Step 4 Since there are 60 female students and $20 + 25 + 10 = 55$ are shown in the areas of intersection with the circles representing accounting and statistics, insert the number 5 in the remaining part of the circle F. This means the number of female students not taking accounting or statistics is 5.

FIGURE 7.17 Venn Diagram

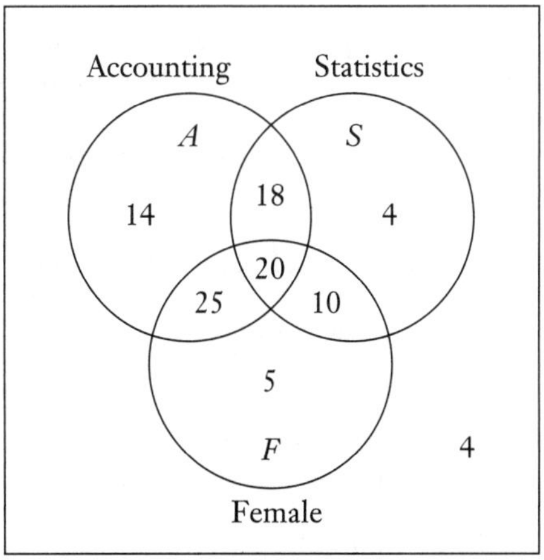

b) Determine the number of male students taking statistics only.

Step 5 Insert 18 (the number of male students taking both accounting and statistics) into the remaining area of intersection of circles A and S.

Step 6 Since 52 students take statistics, $20 + 10 = 30$ of whom are female, and 18 are male who also take accounting, insert 4 into the remaining area of circle S. The number of male students taking statistics only is 4.

c) Determine the number of students taking accounting only.

Step 7 Insert the number 14 into the remaining area of circle A since, out of 32 male students taking accounting, 18 also take statistics. Since there are also 25 female students taking accounting only, the total number of students taking accounting only is $14 + 25 = 39$.

d) Determine the number of students not taking accounting or statistics.

Step 8 We know from the Venn diagram that $14 + 18 + 4 = 36$ male students take either accounting or statistics or both courses. Since there are 40 male students enrolled, $40 - 36 = 4$ of them do not take accounting or statistics. From the diagram we also know that 5 female students do not take either course. The total number of students not taking accounting or statistics is $4 + 5 = 9$.

EXERCISE 7.4

1. What is the sample space for a single coin tossed
- **a)** once?
- **b)** twice?
- **c)** three times?

2. What is the sample space for a game of chess?

3. Which of the following pairs of events are mutually exclusive?
- **a)** A salesperson takes an order for widgets as the company's widget production line breaks down.
- **b)** The prime lending rate increases and the value of the Canadian dollar increases.
- **c)** Russell and Kerry are both hired for the same job.
- **d)** On two rolls of a die a four occurs and the sum is four.

4. Which of the following events are not mutually exclusive?
- **a)** The price of a company's stock rises while the company's net income decreases.
- **b)** A posted voters list has William Thomas listed as a male and a female.
- **c)** Cutnife Equipment sales decrease while selling expenses increase.

5. A local basketball team has 15 players, 12 of whom are right-handed. There are 5 players over six feet tall, 1 of whom is left-handed. Draw a Venn diagram and determine
- **a)** the number of right-handed players under six feet;
- **b)** the number of left-handed players under six feet.

6. The Kay Bank has 12 000 accounts of which 7000 are chequing accounts, 6000 are savings accounts, and 4000 are both. Draw a Venn diagram and determine
   a) the probability that a randomly selected account will be a savings or chequing account or both;
   b) the number of accounts that are not savings or chequing accounts.

SECTION 7.5

The Basic Rules of Probability

A. Basic Properties

The probability of an event is usually denoted by the symbol *P*(Event). In general, the probability of an Event (*A*) is given by

$$P(A) = \frac{\text{NUMBER OF FAVOURABLE OUTCOMES}}{\text{TOTAL NUMBER OF POSSIBLE OUTCOMES}}$$

Since the number of favourable outcomes cannot be smaller than zero or greater than the total number of possible outcomes, the value of the above fraction must lie between 0 and 1.

$$0 \le P(A) \le 1$$

Similarly, the probability of the complement of Event (A) is given by

$$P(\overline{A}) = \frac{\text{NUMBER OF NON-FAVOURABLE OUTCOMES}}{\text{TOTAL NUMBER OF POSSIBLE OUTCOMES}}$$

The value of this fraction also must lie between 0 and 1.

$$0 \le P(\overline{A}) \le 1$$

The combined value of the two fractions represents the sum of the probabilities in any sample space.

$$P(A) + P(\overline{A}) = 1$$

THE SUM OF THE PROBABILITIES IN ANY SAMPLE SPACE = 1.

$P(A) = 1$ means that Event (*A*) is certain to happen and implies that its complement $\overline{A}$ is not going to happen, ($P(\overline{A}) = 0$).

For example, in the toss of a two-headed coin the Event (A = Head) is certain to happen; that is, $P(A) = 1$. The complement $\overline{A}$ = Tail cannot happen; that is, $P(\overline{A}) = 0$.

In the roll of one die, which has six equally possible outcomes, the Event (A = Six Spots) has the probability $P(A) = \frac{1}{6}$. The complementary Event ($\bar{A}$ = Not Six Spots) has the probability $P(\bar{A}) = \frac{5}{6}$. $P(A) + P(\bar{A}) = \frac{1}{6} + \frac{5}{6} = 1$.

B. *The Special Rule of Addition for Mutually Exclusive Events*

If two or more events are mutually exclusive, the probability that one or any of the others will occur is the sum of their individual probabilities of occurrence. For two mutually exclusive events A and B, the addition is denoted by

$$P(A \text{ or } B) = P(A \cup B) = P(A) + P(B).$$

This special rule can be expanded for any number of mutually exclusive events. In the case of three such events, A, B, and C, the addition is denoted by

$$P(A \text{ or } B \text{ or } C) = P(A \cup B \cup C) = P(A) + P(B) + P(C).$$

EXAMPLE 7.5a

Determine the probability of drawing either a black ace or any king from a deck of 52 cards on a single draw.

SOLUTION

FIGURE 7.18 Venn Diagram

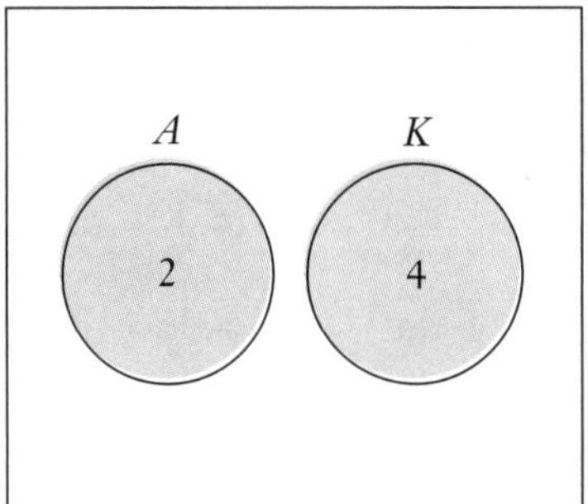

Let the Event (A) = Black Ace and the Event (K) = King. As represented in the Venn diagram, the two events are mutually exclusive.

The probability of drawing a black ace, $P(A) = \frac{2}{52}$.

The probability of drawing a king, $P(K) = \frac{4}{52}$.

The probability of drawing either a black ace or any king is

$$P(A \text{ or } K) = P(A \cup K) = P(A) + P(K)$$

$$= \frac{2}{52} + \frac{4}{52} = \frac{6}{52} = 0.1154.$$

○ **EXAMPLE 7.5b**

Determine the probability of drawing either the ace of clubs, a red king, or any queen from a deck of 52 cards.

● **SOLUTION**

FIGURE 7.19 Venn Diagram

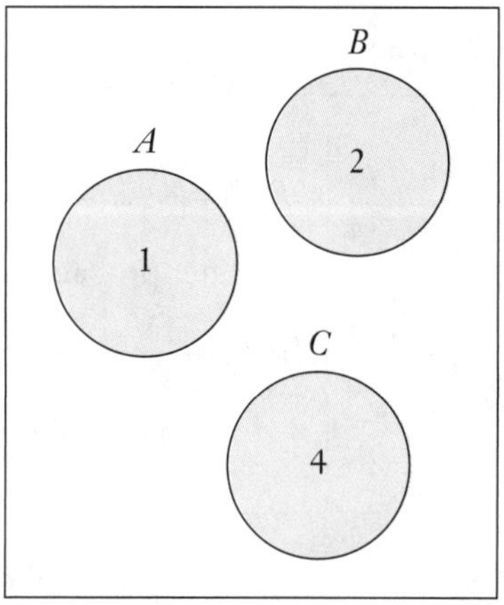

Let Event (A) = Ace of Clubs, Event (B) = Red King and Event (C) = Queen.

The probability of drawing the ace of clubs, $P(A) = \frac{1}{52}$.

The probability of drawing a red king, $P(B) = \frac{2}{52}$.

The probability of drawing a queen, $P(C) = \frac{4}{52}$.

Since the three events are mutually exclusive,

$$\begin{aligned} P(A \text{ or } B \text{ or } C) &= P(A \cup B \cup C) \\ &= P(A) + P(B) + P(C) \\ &= \frac{1}{52} + \frac{2}{52} + \frac{4}{52} \\ &= \frac{7}{52} = 0.1346 \end{aligned}$$

C. *The General Rule of Addition*

FIGURE 7.20 Venn Diagram: The Rule of Addition

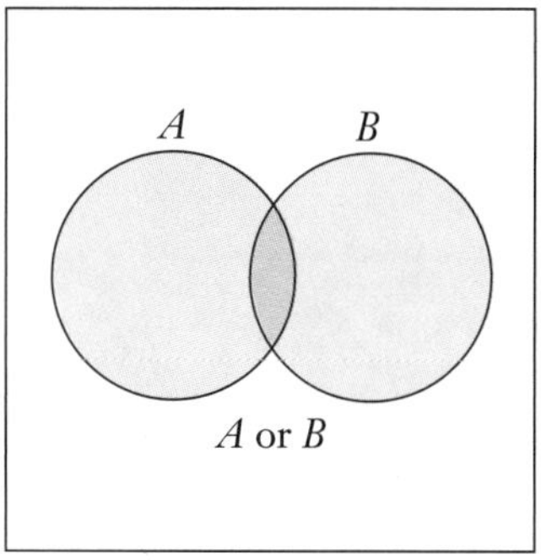

For two events that are *not* mutually exclusive (joint events), the probability that one or the other event will occur is the sum of their individual probabilities of occurrence reduced by the probability of both events occurring at the same time.

$$\begin{aligned} P(A \text{ or } B) &= P(A \cup B) \\ &= P(A) + P(B) - P(A \text{ and } B) \\ &= P(A) + P(B) - P(A \cap B) \end{aligned}$$

○ **EXAMPLE 7.5c**

Determine the probability of drawing an ace or a heart from a deck of 52.

● **SOLUTION**

Let Event (A) = Ace and Event (B) = Heart.

The two events are not mutually exclusive joint events since the ace of hearts is a common outcome to both events.

FIGURE 7.21 Venn Diagram

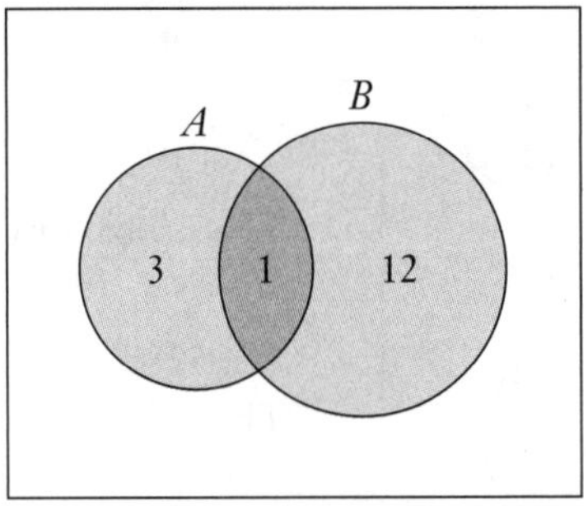

The probability of drawing an ace, $P(A) = \frac{4}{52}$.

The probability of drawing a heart, $P(B) = \frac{13}{52}$.

The probability of drawing the ace of hearts, $P(A \text{ and } B) = P(A \cap B) = \frac{1}{52}$.

$$\begin{aligned} P(A \text{ or } B) &= P(A) + P(B) - P(A \text{ and } B) \\ &= P(A) + P(B) - P(A \cap B) \\ &= \frac{4}{52} + \frac{13}{52} - \frac{1}{52} = \frac{16}{52} = 0.3077 \end{aligned}$$

Note The same result can be obtained from the Venn diagram by adding the numbers assigned to the areas and dividing by the total number of possible outcomes, $\frac{3+1+12}{52} = \frac{16}{52}$.

○ **EXAMPLE 7.5d**

The Deerfield Golf Club has 250 playing members. Fifty of them also play tennis and 75 play squash. Of the 75 squash players, 20 also play tennis. Compute the probability of finding a club member that plays either squash or tennis.

SOLUTION

FIGURE 7.22 Venn Diagram

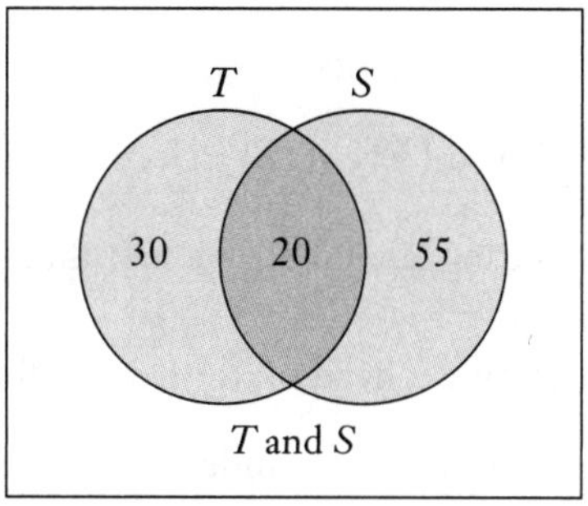

Let Event (T) = Tennis and Event (S) = Squash.

The probability of playing tennis,

$$P(T) = \frac{50}{250}.$$

The probability of playing squash,

$$P(S) = \frac{75}{250}.$$

The probability of playing tennis and squash, $P(T \text{ and } S) = \frac{20}{250}$.

$$P(T \text{ or } S) = P(T) + P(S) - P(T \text{ and } S)$$

$$= \frac{50}{250} + \frac{75}{250} - \frac{20}{250} = \frac{105}{250} = 0.42$$

Note The general rule for addition $P(A) + P(B) - P(A \text{ and } B)$ reduces to the special rule of addition for mutually exclusive events $P(A) + P(B)$, since in this case $P(A \text{ and } B) = 0$.

D. The Special Rule of Multiplication for Mutually Independent Events

Two events are mutually independent if the probability of the occurrence of one event is not affected by the occurrence of the other event. For two independent events A and B, the probability that both events will occur is found by multiplying their probabilities:

$$P(A \text{ and } B) = P(A \cap B) = P(A) \cdot P(B).$$

Note The symbol $\cdot$ is used to indicate multiplication.
This rule applies to any number of independent events.

$$P(A \text{ and } B \text{ and } C \text{ and } \ldots) = P(A \cap B \cap C \cap \ldots)$$
$$= P(A) \cdot P(B) \cdot P(C) \cdot \ \ldots$$

○ EXAMPLE 7.5e

What is the probability of getting two heads in consecutive flips of a balanced coin?

● SOLUTION

Let Event (A) = First Flip and Event (B) = Second Flip.

The probability of getting a head on the first flip, $P(A) = \frac{1}{2}$.

The probability of getting a head on the second flip, $P(B) = \frac{1}{2}$.

Since the two events are mutually independent — that is, the outcome of the first toss does not affect the outcome of the second toss — the probability of getting two heads on consecutive flips,

$$P(A \text{ and } B) = P(A \cap B) = P(A) \cdot P(B)$$
$$= \left(\frac{1}{2}\right)\left(\frac{1}{2}\right) = \frac{1}{4} = 0.25.$$

This result can be verified by listing all possible outcomes of consecutive tosses of one coin as shown below:

Toss	Possible outcomes			
First	Head	Head	Tail	Tail
Second	Head	Tail	Tail	Head

The outcome "head, head" is one of four possible outcomes. It has one chance in four to occur. Its probability of occurrence is 0.25.

○ EXAMPLE 7.5f

What is the probability of getting two aces in consecutive draws of one card from a deck of 52 if the first card is replaced and the deck is reshuffled before the second draw is made? (This process is referred to as sampling with replacement.)

● SOLUTION

Let Event (A) = First Draw and Event (B) = Second Draw.

The probability of the first card being an ace, $P(A) = \frac{4}{52}$.

The probability of the second card being an ace, $P(B) = \frac{4}{52}$.

The probability of drawing two aces in consecutive draws with replacement,

$$P(A \text{ and } B) = P(A \cap B) = P(A) \cdot P(B)$$
$$= \left(\frac{4}{52}\right)\left(\frac{4}{52}\right) = 0.005\,917\,2;$$

that is, approximately 6 chances in 1000, or once in 169 draws.

○ **EXAMPLE 7.5g**

A light bulb manufacturer guarantees its product to last 2500 h. The company knows from experience that the probability is 0.95 that its light bulb will last 2500 h. You purchase two light bulbs for a two-bulb fixture in your apartment. What is the probability that both light bulbs will last at least 2500 h?

● **SOLUTION**

Let Event ($B1$) = Length of life of light bulb #1 and Event ($B2$) = Length of life of light bulb #2.

The probability of light bulb #1 lasting 2500 h, $P(B1) = 0.95$.

The probability of light bulb #2 lasting 2500 h, $P(B2) = 0.95$.

The probability of both light bulbs lasting 2500 h, $P(B1 \cap B2) = P(B1) \cdot P(B2) = (0.95)(0.95) = 0.9025$.

E. Conditional Probability

In certain problems we are specifically interested in the probability of the occurrence of one event given that some other event has already occurred or will occur. This is referred to as **conditional probability** and is denoted by $P(A \mid B)$. The symbol $P(A \mid B)$ is read as "the probability of A given B" and means the probability that Event A will occur given that Event B has occurred.

In general,

$$P(A \mid B) = \frac{P(A \text{ and } B)}{P(B)} = \frac{P(A \cap B)}{P(B)}$$
$$= \frac{\text{PROBABILITY OF EVENTS } A \text{ AND } B \text{ OCCURRING TOGETHER}}{\text{PROBABILITY OF EVENT } B}$$

Similarly, the symbol $P(B \mid A)$ is read as "the probability of B given A" and means the probability that Event B will occur given that Event A has occurred.

$$P(B \mid A) = \frac{P(A \text{ and } B)}{P(A)} = \frac{P(A \cap B)}{P(A)}$$
$$= \frac{\text{PROBABILITY OF EVENTS } A \text{ AND } B \text{ OCCURRING TOGETHER}}{\text{PROBABILITY OF EVENT } A}$$

For example, the probability that the top card of the deck is a red king, given that the top card is known to be red, can be determined as follows:

$$P(\text{Red King} \mid \text{Red}) = \frac{P(\text{Red and King})}{P(\text{Red})} = \frac{\frac{2}{52}}{\frac{26}{52}} = \frac{2}{26} = 0.0769.$$

EXAMPLE 7.5h

The manager of Shirts Unlimited has determined that out of 100 buying customers 52 will buy a shirt, 44 will buy a tie, and 30 will buy both. Determine the probability that

a) a customer who has bought a shirt will also buy a tie;
b) a customer who has bought a tie will also buy a shirt.

SOLUTION

Let $P(S)$ be the probability that a customer buys a shirt.

$$P(S) = \frac{52}{100} = 0.52$$

Let $P(T)$ be the probability that a customer buys a tie.

$$P(T) = \frac{44}{100} = 0.44$$

The probability that a customer buys a shirt and a tie is

$$P(S \text{ and } T) = P(S \cap T) = \frac{30}{100} = 0.30.$$

a) For those customers who buy a shirt, the probability that they will also buy a tie is

$$P(T \mid S) = \frac{P(T \text{ and } S)}{P(S)} = \frac{P(T \cap S)}{P(S)} = \frac{0.30}{0.52} = 0.5769.$$

This means that approximately 58% of the customers who buy a shirt will also buy a tie.

b) For those customers who buy a tie the probability that they also buy a shirt is

$$P(S \mid T) = \frac{P(T \text{ and } S)}{P(T)} = \frac{P(T \cap S)}{P(T)} = \frac{0.30}{0.44} = 0.6818.$$

Approximately 68% of the customers who buy a tie will also buy a shirt.

F. The General Rule of Multiplication

The general rule of multiplication applies to events that are *not* independent and is derived from the formulas for conditional probability.

The two formulas

$$P(A \mid B) = \frac{P(A \text{ and } B)}{P(B)} \quad \text{and} \quad P(B \mid A) = \frac{P(A \text{ and } B)}{P(A)}$$

can be rearranged to

$$P(A \text{ and } B) = P(B) \cdot P(A \mid B) \text{ and } P(A \text{ and } B) = P(A) \cdot P(B \mid A).$$

In general, $P(A \text{ and } B) = P(B) \cdot P(A \mid B) = P(A) \cdot P(B \mid A)$. This means that for two events that are not mutually independent the probability that both will occur is given by

(Probability that one event will occur)	times	(The conditional probability that the other event will occur given that the first event has occurred or will occur)

Note It does not matter which event is called the first event or the second event, or which event is labelled Event A or Event B.

EXAMPLE 7.5i

What is the probability of getting two aces in consecutive draws of one card from a deck of 52 if the first card drawn is not replaced before the second draw is made? (This is known as sampling without replacement.)

SOLUTION

Let Event (A) = First Draw and Event (B) = Second Draw.

The probability of the first card being an ace, $P(A) = \frac{4}{52}$.

Since the first card drawn is not replaced, 51 cards are left in the deck. Also, if the first card drawn was an ace, only three aces remain.

The probability that the second card drawn will be an ace given that the first card was an ace becomes the conditional probability $P(B \mid A) = \frac{3}{51}$.

The probability that both cards drawn will be aces

$$P(A \text{ and } B) = P(A) \cdot P(B \mid A)$$

$$= \left(\frac{4}{52}\right)\left(\frac{3}{51}\right) = \frac{12}{2652} = 0.004\,524\,9.$$

This means there are about 45 chances in 10 000, or one in 221, of drawing two aces in consecutive draws.

○ EXAMPLE 7.5j

An order of 25 DVD players delivered to a store contains 5 defective DVD players. If the DVD players are selected at random, what is the probability that, of the first two selected,

a) both will be defective?
b) none will be defective?
c) one will be defective?

● SOLUTION

Let Event (A) = first player selected. Let Event (B) = second player selected.

a) The probability that the first player selected is defective,

$$P(A) = \frac{5}{25} = \frac{1}{5}.$$

The selection of the second player is from 24, and if the first player was defective, 4 defective players are left. The conditional probability of the second player also being defective given the first was defective,

$$P(B \mid A) = \frac{4}{24} = \frac{1}{6}.$$

The probability that both players are defective,

$$\begin{aligned} P(A \text{ and } B) &= P(A) \cdot P(B \mid A) \\ &= \left(\frac{1}{5}\right)\left(\frac{1}{6}\right) = \frac{1}{30} = 0.0333. \end{aligned}$$

b) The number of players that are not defective is 20. The probability that the first player selected is not defective, $P(A) = \frac{20}{25} = \frac{4}{5}.$

The selection of the second player is from 24, and if the first player was not defective, 19 non-defective players are left. The conditional probability of the second player not being defective given the first player was not defective,

$$P(B \mid A) = \frac{19}{24}.$$

The probability that both players are non-defective,

$$\begin{aligned} P(A \text{ and } B) &= P(A) \cdot P(B \mid A) \\ &= \left(\frac{4}{5}\right)\left(\frac{19}{24}\right) = \frac{76}{120} = 0.6333. \end{aligned}$$

c) The situation in which only one of the first two selected players is defective can occur in two ways:
   i) The first player selected is defective. In this case, the second player must be non-defective.
   ii) The first player selected is non-defective. In this case, the second player must be defective.

For (i), the probability that the first player is defective, $P(A) = \frac{5}{25} = \frac{1}{5}$.

The conditional probability that the second player is non-defective, given that the first player is defective,

$$P(B \mid A) = \frac{20}{24} = \frac{5}{6}.$$

The probability that the first player selected is defective while the second player is non-defective,

$$P(A \text{ and } B) = P(A) \cdot P(B \mid A)$$
$$= \left(\frac{1}{5}\right)\left(\frac{5}{6}\right) = \frac{5}{30} = \frac{1}{6} = 0.1667.$$

Similarly, for ii), the probability that the first player selected is non-defective, $P(B) = \frac{20}{25} = \frac{4}{5}$.

The probability that the second player is defective, given that the first player is non-defective,

$$P(A \mid B) = \frac{5}{24}.$$

The joint probability that the first player selected is non-defective while the second player is defective,

$$P(A \text{ and } B) = P(B) \cdot P(A \mid B)$$
$$= \left(\frac{4}{5}\right)\left(\frac{5}{24}\right) = \frac{1}{6} = 0.1667.$$

The combined probability of the two possible ways of selecting one defective player and one non-defective player $= 0.1667 + 0.1667 = 0.3334$.

Note The three conditions stated in (a), (b), and (c) cover all possible outcomes of selecting the first two players. The sum of the probabilities for the three outcomes should be 1. This is the case since $0.0333 + 0.6333 + 0.3334 = 1.0000$.

EXERCISE 7.5

1. If a student was late for 4 of the last 20 classes, what is the probability that the student will be on time for the next class?

2. A deck of cards was rescued from an angry dog who had torn 13 cards. What are the chances of being dealt a card that is not torn?

3. What is the probability of drawing the following cards from a well-shuffled deck of 52 cards?
   a) a red ace or a black queen;
   b) a black card or a red card;
   c) a black card or a red jack;
   d) a five or a face card (ace, king, queen, or jack).

4. A finance department has been equipped with 21 computers and printers. Fourteen of the printers are Canon and 3 are Lexmark. What is the probability that an employee will be given a computer with
   a) a Lexmark printer?
   b) a Canon printer?
   c) a Lexmark printer or a Canon printer?

5. Twelve student awards were given by the Faculty of Business. Seven of the recipients were women and 5 of the 12 students started their program as mature students. Four of the mature students were female. What is the probability that an award recipient chosen at random would be a mature student or female?

6. Eighteen sales representatives are being evaluated to determine which one should be promoted to manager. Four of the candidates have worked in the eastern region and 12 have post-secondary education. Two of the representatives with experience in the eastern region have post-secondary education. What is the probability that a randomly promoted individual will have worked in the eastern region or have post-secondary education?

7. A coin is tossed three times. What is the probability that a "tail" will appear all three times?

8. The probability that an office supplies sales representative following up a magazine response card will make a sale is 0.60. Given that a representative has three independent leads, what is the probability that
   a) none will buy?
   b) all three will buy?
   c) one will buy?

9. A small software developer displays and demonstrates dental and optical research software programs at trade shows. From previous shows it is known that out of 20 visitors to the booth, 8 will buy the dental program, 6 will buy the optical program, and 2 will buy both. What is the probability that a visitor buying a dental program will also buy an optical program?

10. The office manager for Bete Shoes has found in the past that 40% of internal stationery requests include pens, 74% include binders, and 18% include both pens and binders. Determine the probability that an internal order will include pens if binders are known to be on that order.

11. A box contains 15 white and 5 black marbles. What is the probability that, of the first two marbles picked,
a) both will be black?
b) both will be white?
c) the first will be black and the second will be white?
d) one will be black and one will be white?

12. A shipment of 200 steel bars is known to contain 15 defective bars. If 2 bars are randomly selected for inspection, what is the probability that 1 or 2 bars will be defective?

REVIEW EXERCISE

1. Given a shopping allowance of \$100, how many outcomes are possible for spending the total amount on the following items?

Shirt	\$25	Pants	\$50	Shoes	\$75
Tie	\$25	Sweater	\$50		

2. In a recent student election, 3 candidates ran for 2 positions. How many outcomes are possible for the election?

3. On a multiple-choice quiz, there are 5 choices each for each of 2 questions. How many possible outcomes are there for this quiz?

4. Consumers were asked to rate products A and B according to the following scale:
0 – like
1 – indifferent
2 – dislike
How many outcomes can result for rating the two products?

5. A wine tasting required participants to rate 3 characteristics of the wine as satisfactory or unsatisfactory. How many outcomes are possible for rating the 3 characteristics?

6. You have recently graduated from college and have applied for one of 3 positions at a marketing firm. Six other people have also applied for these positions. How many possible outcomes are there for these 3 positions?

7. How many events are possible for filling 2 employment positions according to the sex of the applicants?

8. Three consumers are asked whether or not they like a new cereal. They can respond either yes or no. How many events are possible?

9. Five major banks conduct a survey on customer satisfaction. Five questions with 2 possible responses (satisfied, dissatisfied) are asked. How many possible events are there?

10. If 2 coins were tossed at the same time, what is the probability that at least 1 coin would show a head?

11. You are at a magic show and asked to pick 2 cards from a standard deck of cards. What is the probability that you choose the 5 of clubs and the 3 of spades?

12. If a jar contained 8 black, 7 white, 3 blue, and 2 red marbles, what is the probability of
   a) picking a black or white marble?
   b) picking a blue, a red, or a white marble?
   c) picking a red marble?

13. A sales representative averages 35 orders for every 100 calls. What is the probability that the representative will fail to get an order on a call?

14. The probability that a telemarketer will not get a sale is 0.94. If the telemarketer makes $50/sale and calls 200 people in a day, what could he expect to make in one week?

15. Out of 1000 travellers leaving the arrival area of Airport Y, 185 took taxis. Out of 600 persons leaving the arrival area of Airport Z, 150 took taxis. What is the probability that a person will call for a taxi
   a) at Airport Y?
   b) at Airport Z?
   c) at one of the two airports?

16. The following data were gathered during a study of alcohol consumption in Canada:

Age group	At least one drink in past week	No consumption in past week
19–35	164	36
36–52	132	68

   a) What is the probability that a Canadian between the ages of 19 and 52 will not have consumed alcohol in the past week?
   b) What is the probability that a Canadian between the ages of 36 and 52 will have consumed at least 1 drink in the past week?

17. The following data represent the number of students that are taking and not taking Calculus at a community college.

Gender	Taking Calculus	Not Taking Calculus
Male	2000	1000
Female	1500	500

a) What is the probability that a male college student will be taking Calculus?
b) What is the probability that a female college student will not be taking Calculus?

18. The following table presents the major causes of death in Canada:

	Causes of Death			
Sex	Cardiovascular disease	Cancer	Other	Total
Male	395	270	335	1000
Female	434	264	302	1000

a) What is the probability that a Canadian will die from cancer?
b) What is the probability that a male will die from cardiovascular disease?
c) What is the probability that a female will die of cancer or cardiovascular disease?

19. When a statistics instructor was asked to predict class attendance on a sunny day in April if the temperature rose above 21°C, the response was as follows:

Number of students attending	Probability
0–5	5%
5–10	20%
10–15	60%
15–20	10%
Over 20	5%

a) What is the probability that 10 or more students will attend class?
b) What is the probability that fewer than 15 will attend class?

20. A recent customer satisfaction survey at a major retailer showed the following:

Satisfaction Rating	Percent
Excellent	10%
Good	40%
Fair	30%
Poor	20%

a) How many customers out of 1000 would be expected to give at least a good rating?
b) How many customers out of 40 would be expected to give a poor rating?

21. An economist for a large Canadian chartered bank has been asked to forecast the exchange rate between the U.S. dollar and the Canadian dollar for the next quarter. Using available econometric models, she feels that 1.54 is twice as likely as 1.57 and that 1.51 is three times as probable as 1.49. She also thinks that the chance of 1.49 occurring is only half of the chance of 1.57 occurring. Based on this information, what is the probability that the exchange rate will be
a) 1.51?
b) 1.54?
c) 1.49?

22. A jar has 4 red and 3 blue marbles. What is the sample space for picking
a) 1 marble?
b) 2 marbles?

23. Determine the sample space for a student who has to choose 2 options from 3 available courses.

24. As a purchasing manager for a large department store, you must choose 3 new products from a list of 5. Determine the sample space for your choice of products. Order is not important.

25. The manager of a furniture manufacturing company has determined that 20 of the company's products were not chairs, were not assembled, and were not on sale. The company makes 8 models of chairs and has 42 products on sale. Five chair models come assembled; 2 chair models are on sale; 1 chair model comes assembled and is on sale; 28 products that are not chairs come assembled and are on sale; and 2 products come assembled, are not on sale, and are not chairs. Draw a Venn diagram and determine
a) the number of products carried by the company;
b) the number of models of chairs that come unassembled or are not on sale.

26. In a college parking lot, 450 cars were counted. Registration data showed that 60 cars were made in Canada, 220 cars were red, and 280 cars belonged to students. Thirty of the cars made in Canada and 200 of the red cars belonged to students. Ten red cars were made in Canada and 5 of the red cars owned by students were made in Canada. Draw a Venn diagram and determine
a) the number of cars in the parking lot that were not red, were not made in Canada, or did not belong to students;
b) the number of red cars that did not belong to students;
c) the number of cars belonging to students but not made in Canada.

27. What is the probability of throwing a total of 3 spots or 4 spots with a roll of 2 dice?

28. What is the probability of drawing 3 aces in succession from a 52-card deck if the card is replaced each time? How does the above calculated probability differ if the cards are not replaced?

29. In American roulette there are 38 slots in which the ball may land. The slots are numbered 00, 0, and 1 through 36. The numbers 00 and 0 are green, the odd numbers are red, and the even numbers are black. If a ball rolls randomly into a slot, what is the probability of

a) a 5 or a 6?
b) red or black?
c) green or 27?
d) a number less than 20?

30. A small office is equipped with 8 computers, 5 of which run SPSS and 3 have scanners. Of the 5 computers running SPSS, 2 have scanners. What is the probability that a computer chosen at random in this office runs SPSS or has a scanner?

31. Given that $P(\overline{A}) = 0.40$, $P(B) = 0.30$ and $P(A \cap B) = 0.15$, determine the value of $P(A \cup B)$.

32. Let A be the event that a contract is awarded to your company and let B be the event that sales will increase. $P(A) = 0.6$, $P(B) = 0.3$, and $P(A \cup B) = 0.80$. What is $P(A \cap B)$?

33. Given that $P(A) = 0.20$, $P(\overline{B}) = 0.10$, $P(A \cup B) = 0.85$, determine $P(A \cap B)$.

34. Given $P(A) = 0.30$, $P(\overline{B}) = 0.50$, and $P(A \cap B) = 0.10$, determine

a) $P(A \mid B)$;
b) $P(B \mid A)$;
c) $P(A \text{ or } B)$.

35. The following data represent the reaction of men and women over the age of 18 toward a new TV commercial:

	Reaction to TV Commercial		
Gender	Like	Neutral	Dislike
Male	900	200	400
Female	1200	300	1000

a) Determine the probability that a person from this group likes the commercial, given that the person selected is a male.
b) Determine the probability that a person from this group dislikes the commercial, given that the person selected is a female.
c) What are the chances that a person from the group is neutral toward the commercial?

36. A shortlist of applicants for 2 management trainee positions is made up of 4 graduates from Kelowna College, 3 from Assiniboine College, and 2 from Fredericton College. What is the probability that, of the 2 successful applicants,

a) both will be from Kelowna College?
b) one will be from Assiniboine College and the other from Fredericton College?

37. If 2 cards are drawn from a well-shuffled deck of 52 cards and the first card drawn is not replaced, what is the probability that
a) both cards are kings?
b) the first card is a queen and the second card is a jack?
c) one card is a queen and one card is a jack?

38. The awarding of a contract for a new government office is to be announced on July 1. The timing of the announcement is conditional on 3 bids being received. If the submissions of the bids are independent events and the probabilities of the bids being late are 0.10, 0.05, and 0.02 respectively, what are the chances that the announcement will be made as scheduled?

39. Four unrelated stocks on the Toronto Stock Exchange have been judged to increase in price with the following probabilities:

Stock	J	K	L	M
Probability of price increase	0.90	0.95	0.80	0.70

a) What is the probability that all 4 stocks will increase in price?
b) What is the probability that only stocks J and L will increase in price?

40. Three unrelated parts in a car have the following failure rates:

Part	Brakes	Steering Column	Transmission
Probability of Failure	0.0001	0.000 001	0.001

a) What is the probability that all 3 will fail at the same time?
b) What is the probability that only the brakes will fail?

41. A jar contains a black, a red, and a white marble. Construct a tree diagram to show how 2 marbles can be chosen.

SELF-TEST

1. The following data represent product acceptance for a group of persons compiled by sex:

	Product Acceptance			
Sex	Excellent	Good	Fair	Poor
Male	75	225	150	25
Female	50	175	225	75

a) If a person is randomly chosen from this group what is the probability that the person
  i) is male?
  ii) considers the product to be "good"?
  iii) is female and thinks that the product is "poor"?
  iv) is male or thinks the product is "fair"?

b) Determine the probability of a person from this group rating the product as "excellent," given that the person selected is
  i) female;
  ii) male;
  iii) either male or female.

2. A pyramid-shaped, four-sided die is rolled twice. The 4 sides have 1, 2, 3, or 4 spots respectively, and the event considered is the sum of the number of spots on the face-down position of the die.
  a) Construct a tree diagram to show all possible outcomes of the experiment.
  b) Determine the possible number of outcomes.
  c) Determine the number of possible events defined above.
  d) Determine the probability of the following events.
    i) 3 spots;
    ii) 4 spots or 5 spots;
    iii) more than 6 spots.

3. Two sprinters from a region will be invited to the Canadian track-and-field championships.
  a) If 8 sprinters compete in the regional championships and the regional winner runs in the national championships while the runner-up goes as backup, in how many different ways can the 2 regional runners be selected?
  b) If a rule change allows both the regional winner and the runner-up to compete in the nationals, in how many ways can the 2 runners be chosen?

4. A local service club is selling 100 tickets at $100 each to raise money for a student exchange program. A draw of 3 prizes is offered as an incentive to the buyers of the tickets.
  a) What is the probability of winning first prize with the purchase of one ticket if the first-prize winner is the third ticket called?
  b) What is the probability of winning a prize if you purchase one ticket?
  c) What are the chances of winning at least 1 prize if you purchase 3 tickets?

For an online glossary, go to **www.pearsoned.ca/hummelbrunner**.

Key Terms

Combination 230
Complement 235
Conditional probability 247
Event 216
- **complementary** 235
- **intersection of** 237
- **joint** 236
- **mutually exclusive** 235
- **union of** 236

Outcome 216
Permutation 226
Random experiment 216
Sample space 235
Tree diagram 221
Venn diagram 235

Summary of Formulas

1. Probability of an Event

$$\text{PROBABILITY OF AN EVENT, } P(\text{EVENT}) = \frac{\text{NUMBER OF FAVOURABLE OUTCOMES}}{\text{TOTAL NUMBER OF POSSIBLE OUTCOMES}}$$ ←*Formula* 7

2. Permutations

$${}_nP_r = \frac{n!}{(n-r)!}$$ ←*Formula* 7.2

3. Combinations

$${}_nC_r = \frac{n!}{r!(n-r)!}$$ ←*Formula* 7.3

CHAPTER 8

A First Look at Probability Distributions

Introduction

A **probability distribution** is a list of all the events of an experiment together with the probability associated with each event. Many business or economic problems can be described by means of probability distributions.

Learning Outcomes

Upon completion of this chapter you will be able to

1. define the term *probability distribution*;
2. distinguish between discrete and continuous probability distributions;
3. compute the expected value (mean), variance, and standard deviation of a discrete probability distribution;
4. define the characteristics of the binomial probability distribution;
5. construct and use a binomial distribution for given values of n and p.

SECTION 8.1

Continuous versus Discrete Probability Distributions

In Example 7.2a we created a tree diagram to show all possible outcomes of tossing a coin three times. The frequencies and probabilities (relative frequencies) obtained were shown in Table 7.1 and are reproduced in Table 8.1.

A tabulation of the events together with their associated probabilities is called a probability distribution. The distribution can be represented graphically as shown in Figure 8.1.

TABLE 8.1 Probability Distribution for Tossing a Coin Three Times

Event (No. of Heads)	Frequency of occurrence		Probability of occurrence (relative frequency)
Three heads	1		0.125
Two heads	3		0.375
One head	3		0.375
Zero heads	1		0.125
		Total	1.000

FIGURE 8.1 Graphical Representation of the Probability Distribution for Three Tosses of a Coin

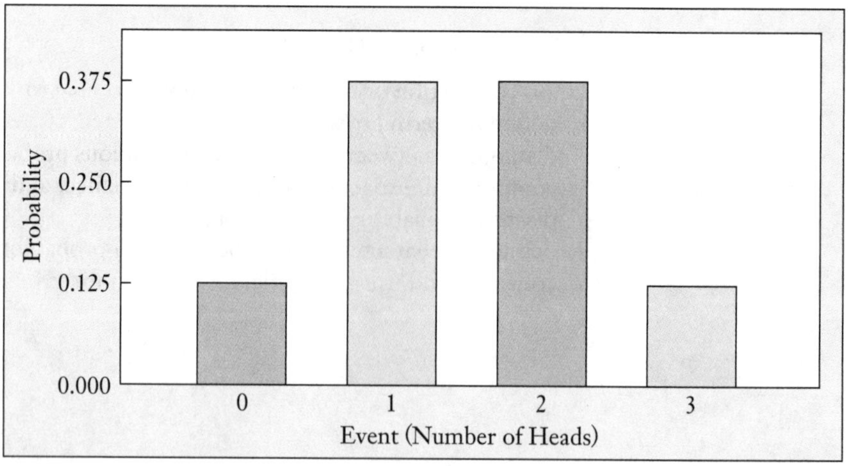

In this context the Event (Number of Heads) is referred to as a **discrete random variable**. The resulting distribution shown in Table 8.1 and Figure 8.1 is called a **discrete probability distribution**. The term *random variable* is used for quantities that result from an experiment and that take on different values by chance. In our example, the random variable Number of Heads took the values 0, 1, 2, and 3.

A *discrete* random variable is called discrete because it can only take on clearly defined, *separated* values that are obtained by counting. The distribution is referred to as a *discrete probability distribution* because it consists of a listing of the discrete values that the random variable can assume as well as their associated probabilities.

Other examples of discrete probability distributions are the number of newspapers sold per day from a corner box, the number of vehicles driving into each of the service stations located within a defined geographical area on a particular day, or the distribution of marks on a test for a group of students.

The term **continuous random variable** is usually associated with a measurement that can be made to a desired degree of precision, such as length, height, weight, or speed. For example, in downhill skiing the time it takes racers to finish the course is measured to one one-hundredth of a second. Similarly, in the long jump, distance is measured to the nearest centimetre. A tabulation of this type of variable is known as a *continuous frequency distribution* and the tabulation of the associated relative frequencies is referred to as a **continuous probability distribution.**

The following is a summary of important concepts concerning probability distributions in general:

1. A random variable is a variable whose value in a particular experiment is determined purely by chance.
2. A continuous random variable is one that can assume an infinite number of values within a specified interval.
3. A discrete random variable is one that can assume only distinct values within a specified interval.
4. Probability distributions can be either continuous or discrete, depending on the nature of the random variable described by the distribution.
5. The probability distribution of a random variable defines the probability of occurrence of every possible value that the random variable can assume.
6. The probabilities making up the probability distribution are values between 0 and 1, and their sum must equal 1.
7. A probability distribution can be presented in the form of an equation, table, or graph.

SECTION 8.2

The Expected Value (Mean), Variance, and Standard Deviation of a Discrete Probability Distribution

A. Expected Value (Mean)

Denoted by the symbol $E(x)$, the **expected value** of a random variable x is the *long-run value of* μ. This long-run value is the *mean value* that the variable x is expected to attain if an experiment is repeated an infinitely large number of times.

To compute the expected value (mean) of a random variable, use the following procedure:

Step 1 Multiply each individual value of the random variable by its corresponding probability of occurrence.

Step 2 Add the products obtained in Step 1. This procedure can be summarized in symbolic terms as

$$E(x) = \mu = \sum x \cdot P(x)$$ ←*Formula* 8.1

where x denotes the individual values that the random variable can assume;
$P(x)$ is the probability of occurrence of the individual values x;
$E(x)$ is the expected value (mean) of the random variable x.

EXAMPLE 8.2a

You are invited to join a game by paying a certain amount for each roll of a die. In return you will be paid an amount equal to the number of spots showing on the upper face of the die when it stops rolling. For example, if you pay \$2 to join the game and the six-spot turns up, you get back \$6; that is, you win \$4. Determine the expected value of the game.

SOLUTION

The random variable x (Number of Spots) can take the values $x = 1, 2, 3, 4, 5, 6$. Since each outcome for the random variable is equally likely, the probability of each outcome, $P(x) = \frac{1}{6}$.

The long-run average value $E(x)$ can now be computed as shown in Table 8.2.

TABLE 8.2 Computation of *E*(*x*)

Individual value x	Probability $P(x)$	Product $x \cdot P(x)$
1	$\frac{1}{6}$	$1\left(\frac{1}{6}\right) = \frac{1}{6} = 0.1667$
2	$\frac{1}{6}$	$2\left(\frac{1}{6}\right) = \frac{2}{6} = 0.3333$
3	$\frac{1}{6}$	$3\left(\frac{1}{6}\right) = \frac{3}{6} = 0.5000$
4	$\frac{1}{6}$	$4\left(\frac{1}{6}\right) = \frac{4}{6} = 0.6667$
5	$\frac{1}{6}$	$5\left(\frac{1}{6}\right) = \frac{5}{6} = 0.8333$
6	$\frac{1}{6}$	$6\left(\frac{1}{6}\right) = \frac{6}{6} = 1.0000$
		$E(x) = \mu = \sum x \cdot P(x) = \frac{21}{6} = 3.50$

Note For the special case in which the probability of occurrence is the same for all values of x, $P(x)$ is a common factor, and the calculation can be simplified to $E(x) = (\sum x)(P(x)) = 21\left(\frac{1}{6}\right) = 3.50$.

The result obtained indicates that a person who participates in this game for a long period of time could expect to win on the average $3.50 (even though it is not possible to receive that amount on any single roll of the die). The *expected monetary value* of the game is $3.50, and this is the *maximum* amount anyone should be willing to pay to play the game.

B. *The Variance and Standard Deviation of a Discrete Probability Distribution*

The concept of expected value is that of a long-run mean from repeated attempts or trials. More often than not, some value other than the expected value will occur for the various individual trials. In some cases, such as in Example 8.2a, the expected value ($3.50) *cannot* occur as the outcome of a single trial, since the die can only show the whole numbers 1 to 6.

A measure of the mean difference of the individual values from the expected value is the *variance* of the probability distribution. Denoted by $V(x)$, the variance of a discrete random variable can be computed by multiplying the squared deviations of the individual values from the expected value by the individual probabilities:

$$V(x) = \sigma^2 = \sum(x - \mu)^2 \cdot P(x)$$ ←*Formula* 8.2

The standard deviation may then be computed by taking the square root of the variance

$$\sigma = \sqrt{\sigma^2}$$ ←*Formula* 8.3

○ EXAMPLE 8.2b

Determine the variance and the standard deviation for the probability distribution in Example 8.2a.

SOLUTION

The individual values of the random variable are $x = 1, 2, 3, 4, 5, 6$.

The probability of occurrence for all values of x is $P(x) = \frac{1}{6}$;

the expected value $E(x) = \mu = 3.50$.

The variance can be computed as shown in Table 8.3.

TABLE 8.3 Computation of Variance

Individual value x	Deviation $(x - \mu)$	Squared deviation $(x - \mu)^2$	$P(x)$	Product $(x - \mu)^2 \cdot P(x)$
1	$1 - 3.50 = -2.50$	6.25	$\frac{1}{6}$	$6.25\left(\frac{1}{6}\right) = 1.041\,666\,7$
2	$2 - 3.50 = -1.50$	2.25	$\frac{1}{6}$	$2.25\left(\frac{1}{6}\right) = 0.375\,000\,0$
3	$3 - 3.50 = -0.50$	0.25	$\frac{1}{6}$	$0.25\left(\frac{1}{6}\right) = 0.041\,666\,7$
4	$4 - 3.50 = 0.50$	0.25	$\frac{1}{6}$	$0.25\left(\frac{1}{6}\right) = 0.041\,666\,7$
5	$5 - 3.50 = 1.50$	2.25	$\frac{1}{6}$	$2.25\left(\frac{1}{6}\right) = 0.375\,000\,0$
6	$6 - 3.50 = 2.50$	6.25	$\frac{1}{6}$	$6.25\left(\frac{1}{6}\right) = 1.041\,666\,7$
				$\sum(x - \mu)^2 \cdot P(x) = 2.916\,666\,8$

The variance $V(x) = \sigma^2 = \sum(x - \mu)^2 \cdot P(x) = 2.916\,666\,8$;

the standard deviation, $\sigma = \sqrt{2.916\,666\,8} = 1.707\,825\,2$.

The calculation can be simplified by using the alternative formula

$$V(x) = \sigma^2 = \sum x^2 \cdot P(x) - \mu^2$$

←*Formula* 8.2A

as shown in Table 8.4.

TABLE 8.4 Simplified Computation of Variance

x	x^2	$P(x)$	$x^2 \cdot P(x)$
1	1	$\frac{1}{6}$	$1\left(\frac{1}{6}\right) = \frac{1}{6}$
2	4	$\frac{1}{6}$	$4\left(\frac{1}{6}\right) = \frac{4}{6}$
3	9	$\frac{1}{6}$	$9\left(\frac{1}{6}\right) = \frac{9}{6}$
4	16	$\frac{1}{6}$	$16\left(\frac{1}{6}\right) = \frac{16}{6}$
5	25	$\frac{1}{6}$	$25\left(\frac{1}{6}\right) = \frac{25}{6}$
6	36	$\frac{1}{6}$	$36\left(\frac{1}{6}\right) = \frac{36}{6}$
	$\sum x^2 = 91$		$\sum x^2 \cdot P(x) = \frac{91}{6}$

$$\begin{aligned} V(x) = \sigma^2 &= \sum x^2 \cdot P(x) - \mu^2 \\ &= \frac{91}{6} - (3.50)^2 = 15.166\,666\,7 - 12.25 \\ &= 2.916\,666\,7 \end{aligned}$$

For the special case in which $P(x)$ is the same for all values of x, $P(x)$ is a common factor, and the calculation can be simplified to

$$\begin{aligned} V(x) = \sigma^2 &= \left(\sum x^2\right) \cdot P(x) - \mu^2 \\ &= 91\left(\frac{1}{6}\right) - (3.50)^2 = 2.916\,666\,7. \end{aligned}$$

However, in most cases the calculation of the mean and variance of a discrete probability distribution is best done by using a *tabular* format.

○ EXAMPLE 8.2c

In Chapter 7 the experiment of rolling a pair of dice was considered and the possible values of the random variable x (Total Number of Spots) were listed in Figure 7.3. The associated probabilities were listed in the accompanying discussion. Using the information from Figure 7.3, compute the mean, the variance, and the standard deviation of the probability distribution.

● SOLUTION

The random variable x (Total Number of Spots) is a discrete variable taking the values $x = 2, 3, \ldots, 10, 11, 12$. The corresponding number of outcomes of each event and the probabilities of the events are summarized in Table 8.5 and the calculated values listed.

$$E(x) = \mu = \sum x \cdot P(x) = 7.00$$

Using the Formula 8.2,

$$V(x) = \sigma^2 = \sum (x - \mu)^2 \cdot P(x) = 5.833\ 333$$

$$\sigma = \sqrt{5.833\ 333} = 2.415\ 229.$$

Using the Formula 8.2A,

$$V(x) = \sigma^2 = \sum (x^2 \cdot P(x)) - \mu^2 = 54.833\ 333 - 49.00 = 5.833\ 333$$

$$\sigma = \sqrt{5.833\ 333} = 2.415\ 229.$$

TABLE 8.5 Format for Computing the Mean and Variance of a Discrete Probability Distribution

x	No. of outcomes	Probability of event $P(x)$	$x \cdot P(x)$	$x^2 \cdot P(x)$	$x - \mu$	$(x - \mu)^2 \cdot P(x)$
2	1	$\frac{1}{36} = 0.027778$	0.055556	0.111111	−5.00	0.694445
3	2	$\frac{2}{36} = 0.055556$	0.166667	0.500000	−4.00	0.888889
4	3	$\frac{3}{36} = 0.083333$	0.333333	1.333333	−3.00	0.750000
5	4	$\frac{4}{36} = 0.111111$	0.555556	2.777778	−2.00	0.444444
6	5	$\frac{5}{36} = 0.138889$	0.833333	5.000000	−1.00	0.138889
7	6	$\frac{6}{36} = 0.166667$	1.166667	8.166667	0.00	0.000000
8	5	$\frac{5}{36} = 0.138889$	1.111111	8.888889	1.00	0.138889
9	4	$\frac{4}{36} = 0.111111$	1.000000	9.000000	2.00	0.444444
10	3	$\frac{3}{36} = 0.083333$	0.833333	8.333333	3.00	0.750000
11	2	$\frac{2}{36} = 0.055556$	0.611111	6.722222	4.00	0.888889
12	1	$\frac{1}{36} = 0.027778$	0.333333	4.000000	5.00	0.694444
Total	36	1.000000	7.000000	54.833333	0.00	5.833333

EXERCISE 8.2

1. The marketing department of B.C. Research has submitted the following information for the purpose of forecasting net income for the next year:

Sales volume	Probability
\$1 000 000	0.20
1 200 000	0.30
1 500 000	0.50

Calculate the expected sales volume.

2. The design division of Highrise Construction prepared the following scenarios to estimate the time required for a newly won contract:

Scenario	Time in days	Probability
Optimistic	100	0.15
Likely	120	0.20
Most likely	150	0.40
Pessimistic	190	0.25

Compute the expected time for the completion of the contract.

3. For the given values of a random variable and the associated probabilities, determine

a) the mean;

b) the variance and standard deviation.

x	0	1	2	3	4
$P(x)$	0.10	0.20	0.30	0.20	0.20

4. A commodities trader has assigned the following probabilities for the forward price of a bushel of wheat 3 months from now:

Price per bushel	Probability
\$2.20	0.05
2.30	0.25
2.40	0.35
2.50	0.20
2.60	0.15

a) Compute the expected value for a bushel of wheat three months from now.

b) Compute the standard deviation of the price of wheat.

SECTION 8.3

The Binomial Distribution

A. Characteristics of the Binomial Distribution

Although a probability distribution can be developed for any random variable, a number of well-known probability distributions are available as models for many business and economic situations. Of these the most widely used discrete probability distribution is the **binomial distribution**.

Many business and economic situations have the common characteristic of only two possible outcomes. The manufacture of a part has the outcome "defective" or "non-defective"; the delivery of a package is either "on time" or "late"; the impact of a sales presentation will result in a "sale" or "no sale."

The binomial distribution is based on a series of attempts (trials) in which only two outcomes are possible on a single trial. The following are the essential characteristics of a binomial distribution:

1. The trials are identical.
2. Each trial has only *two* possible outcomes classified as "success" or "failure."
3. The data collected are the result of counting; that is, the distribution is *discrete*.
4. The probability of "success" is the same for each trial. The same is true for the probability of "failure."
5. The trials are independent of each other; that is, the outcome of one trial does not affect the outcome of any other trial.

B. Formula for Constructing a Binomial Probability Distribution

For a binomial process the event of interest is "the probability of obtaining exactly x successes in n trials." This probability can be computed by using the formula

$$P(x) = ({}_nC_x)(p^x)(1-p)^{n-x}$$ ←*Formula* 8.4

where n = the number of trials;
x = the number of successes for the n trials;
p = the probability of success;
$1-p$ = the probability of failure;
$P(x)$ = the probability of x successes in n trials;
${}_nC_x$ = the number of combinations.

Since ${}_nC_x = \dfrac{n!}{x!(n-x)!}$, the formula describing the binomial probability distribution can be written as

$$P(x) = \frac{n!}{x!(n-x)!}(p^x)(1-p)^{n-x}$$ ←*Formula* 8.4A

C. Constructing and Using Binomial Distributions

EXAMPLE 8.3a

Consider the experiment of eight tosses of a coin for the Event (Number of Heads).

a) Construct the probability distribution.
b) Construct the less-than and more-than cumulative probability distributions.
c) Determine the probabilities of the following outcomes of the eight tosses of the coin:
   i) exactly four heads;
   ii) no more than five heads;
   iii) at least six heads;
   iv) between three and five heads;
   v) fewer than four heads;
   vi) fewer than three heads or more than six heads.

SOLUTION

a) The experiment of tossing a coin eight times meets the requirements of a binomial process:
   i. The number of trials is fixed, $n = 8$.
   ii. Each trial has two possible outcomes: "head" or "tail."
   iii. The data are discrete (the result of counting).
   iv. The probability of success is the same for all trials.
   v. The trials are independent of each other.

   The binomial formula for the probability of success can be used.

   $n = 8$; $p = 0.50$; $(1 - p) = (1 - 0.50) = 0.50$;
   $x = 0, 1, 2, 3, 4, 5, 6, 7$, and 8.

   In this particular case, since $p = (1 - p) = 0.50$,

$$P(x) = ({}_nC_x)(p^x)[(1-p)^{n-x}] = ({}_8C_x)(0.50^x)[(0.50)^{8-x}].$$

Since $(0.50^x)(0.50^{8-x}) = 0.50^{x+(8-x)} = 0.50^8 = 0.003\ 906\ 3$,

$$P(x) = \frac{8!}{x!(8-x)!}(0.003\ 906\ 3).$$

The binomial probability distribution for $n = 8$, $p = 0.50$ can now be constructed, as shown in Table 8.6, by evaluating $P(x)$ for the possible values of x.

TABLE 8.6 Construction of Binomial Distribution

Column 1	Column 2	Column 3	Column 4
x	Value of ${}_8C_x = \frac{8!}{x!(8-x)!}$	Value of $\frac{(p^x)[(1-p)^{n-x}]}{(0.50^x)(0.50^{8-x})} = 0.50^8$	Value of $P(x)$ rounded to four decimals (Column 2 × Column 3)
0	$\frac{8!}{(0!)(8!)} = \frac{8!}{(1)(8!)} = 1$	0.003 906 3	(1)(0.003 906 3) = 0.0039
1	$\frac{8!}{(1!)(7!)} = \frac{8}{1} = 8$	0.003 906 3	(8)(0.003 906 3) = 0.0312
2	$\frac{8!}{(2!)(6!)} = \frac{(8)(7)}{(2)(1)} = 28$	0.003 906 3	(28)(0.003 906 3) = 0.1094
3	$\frac{8!}{(3!)(5!)} = \frac{(8)(7)(6)}{(3)(2)(1)} = 56$	0.003 906 3	(56)(0.003 906 3) = 0.2188
4	$\frac{8!}{(4!)(4!)} = \frac{(8)(7)(6)(5)}{(4)(3)(2)(1)} = 70$	0.003 906 3	(70)(0.003 906 3) = 0.2734
5	$\frac{8!}{(5!)(3!)} = \frac{(8)(7)(6)}{(3)(2)(1)} = 56$	0.003 906 3	(56)(0.003 906 3) = 0.2188
6	$\frac{8!}{(6!)(2!)} = \frac{(8)(7)}{(2)(1)} = 28$	0.003 906 3	(28)(0.003 906 3) = 0.1094
7	$\frac{8!}{(7!)(1!)} = \frac{8}{1} = 8$	0.003 906 3	(8)(0.003 906 3) = 0.0312
8	$\frac{8!}{(8!)(0!)} = 1$	0.003 906 3	(1)(0.003 906 3) = 0.0039

b) The two *cumulative* probability distributions for $n = 8$, $p = 0.50$, can be determined by computing running totals, as shown in Table 8.7.

TABLE 8.7 Cumulative Probability Distributions

x	Probability distribution $P(x)$	Less-than cumulative distribution $P(\leq x)$	More-than cumulative distribution $P(\geq x)$
0	0.0039	0.0039	1.0000
1	0.0312	0.0351	0.9961
2	0.1094	0.1445	0.9649
3	0.2188	0.3633	0.8555
4	0.2734	0.6367	0.6367
5	0.2188	0.8555	0.3663
6	0.1094	0.9649	0.1445
7	0.0312	0.9961	0.0351
8	0.0039	1.0000	0.0039

c) i) From Table 8.6, the probability of the Event (Exactly Four Heads), $P(4) = 0.2734$.

ii) From Table 8.6, the probability of the Event (No More Than Five Heads),

$$\begin{aligned} P(\leq 5) &= P(0) + P(1) + P(2) + P(3) + P(4) + P(5) \\ &= 0.0039 + 0.0312 + 0.1094 + 0.2188 + 0.2734 + 0.2188 \\ &= 0.8555 \end{aligned}$$

or directly from Table 8.7 in the Less-than cumulative probability distribution column, $P(\leq 5) = 0.8555$.

iii) From Table 8.6, the probability of the Event (At Least Six Heads),

$$\begin{aligned} P(\geq 6) &= P(6) + P(7) + P(8) \\ &= 0.1094 + 0.0312 + 0.0039 = 0.1445. \end{aligned}$$

or directly from Table 8.7 in the More-than cumulative probability distribution column, $P(\geq 6) = 0.1445$.

iv) The probability of the Event (Between Three and Five Heads),

$$\begin{aligned} P(3 \text{ or } 4 \text{ or } 5) &= P(3) + P(4) + P(5) \\ &= 0.2188 + 0.2734 + 0.2188 = 0.7110. \end{aligned}$$

or directly from Table 8.7 in the Less-than cumulative probability distribution column,

$$\begin{aligned} P(3 \text{ or } 4 \text{ or } 5) &= P(\leq 5) - P(\leq 2) \\ &= 0.8555 - 0.1445 = 0.7110. \end{aligned}$$

v) The probability of the Event (Fewer Than Four Heads),

$$\begin{aligned} P(< 4) &= P(\leq 3) \\ &= P(0) + P(1) + P(2) + P(3) \\ &= 0.0039 + 0.0312 + 0.1094 + 0.2188 = 0.3633 \end{aligned}$$

or directly from Table 8.7 in the Less-than cumulative probability column, $P(\leq 3) = 0.3633$.

vi) The probability of the Event (Fewer Than Three Heads or More Than Six Heads),

$$\begin{aligned} P(< 3 \text{ or } > 6) &= P(\leq 2) + P(\geq 7) \\ &= [P(0) + P(1) + P(2)] + [P(7) + P(8)] \\ &= [0.0039 + 0.0312 + 0.1094] + [0.0312 + 0.0039] \\ &= 0.1445 + 0.0351 = 0.1796 \end{aligned}$$

or directly from Table 8.7, $P(\leq 2) + P(\geq 7) = 0.1445$ (in the Less-than cumulative probability column) + 0.0351 (in the More-than cumulative probability column) = 0.1796.

○ EXAMPLE 8.3b

In a complex manufacturing process the probability of producing a satisfactory item is 0.80. If eight items are taken from the production line, determine the probability that this group contains

a) exactly three satisfactory items;
b) at most three satisfactory items;
c) at least three satisfactory items;
d) between four and seven satisfactory items;
e) more than four satisfactory items;
f) fewer than two or more than six satisfactory items.

● SOLUTION

The process meets the requirements of a binomial process. In order to answer the questions we need to first construct the probability distribution for

$n = 8;\quad p = 0.80;\quad (1-p) = (1-0.80) = 0.20;$
$x = 0, 1, 2, 3, 4, 5, 6, 7, 8.$

Substituting in the binomial formula $P(x) = ({}_nC_x)(p^x)(1-p)^{n-x}$, we obtain

$$P(x) = ({}_8C_x)(0.80^x)(0.20^{8-x})$$
$$= \frac{8!}{x!(8-x)!}(0.80^x)(0.20^{8-x}).$$

The binomial probability distribution can be constructed as shown in Table 8.8 and the associated cumulative probabilities as shown in Table 8.9.

TABLE 8.8 Construction of Binomial Distribution, $n = 8, p = 0.80$

Column 1 x	Column 2 Value of ${}_8C_x$	Column 3 Value of $(0.8^x)(0.2^{8-x})$	Column 4 (Col. 2)(Col. 3) to 4 decimals
0	1	$(0.8^0)(0.2^8) = (1)(0.000\ 002\ 56) = 0.000\ 002\ 56$	0.0000
1	8	$(0.8^1)(0.2^7) = (0.8)(0.000\ 012\ 8) = 0.000\ 010\ 24$	0.0001
2	28	$(0.8^2)(0.2^6) = (0.64)(0.000\ 064) = 0.000\ 040\ 96$	0.0011
3	56	$(0.8^3)(0.2^5) = (0.512)(0.000\ 32) = 0.000\ 163\ 84$	0.0092
4	70	$(0.8^4)(0.2^4) = (0.4096)(0.0016) = 0.000\ 655\ 36$	0.0459
5	56	$(0.8^5)(0.2^3) = (0.327\ 68)(0.008) = 0.002\ 621\ 44$	0.1468
6	28	$(0.8^6)(0.2^2) = (0.262\ 144)(0.04) = 0.010\ 485\ 76$	0.2936
7	8	$(0.8^7)(0.2^1) = (0.209\ 715\ 2)(0.2) = 0.041\ 943\ 04$	0.3355
8	1	$(0.8^8)(0.2^0) = (0.167\ 772\ 16)(1) = 0.167\ 772\ 16$	0.1678

TABLE 8.9 Cumulative Probability Distributions, $n = 8$, $p = 0.80$

x	Probability distribution $P(x)$	Less-than cumulative distribution $P(\leq x)$	More-than cumulative distribution $P(\geq x)$
0	0.0000	0.0000	1.0000
1	0.0001	0.0001	1.0000
2	0.0011	0.0012	0.9999
3	0.0092	0.0104	0.9988
4	0.0459	0.0563	0.9896
5	0.1468	0.2031	0.9437
6	0.2936	0.4967	0.7969
7	0.3355	0.8322	0.5033
8	0.1678	1.0000	0.1678

Using the tables,

a) $P(3) = 0.0092$.

b) $P(\leq 3) = P(0) + P(1) + P(2) + P(3)$
$= 0.0000 + 0.0001 + 0.0011 + 0.0092 = 0.0104$;
or directly from the Less-than cumulative column $P(\leq 3) = 0.0104$.

c) From the More-than cumulative column, $P(\geq 3) = 0.9988$.

d) $P(4 \text{ or } 5 \text{ or } 6 \text{ or } 7) = P(4) + P(5) + P(6) + P(7)$
$= 0.0459 + 0.1468 + 0.2936 + 0.3355 = 0.8218$;
or $P(4 \text{ or } 5 \text{ or } 6 \text{ or } 7) = P(\leq 7) - P(\leq 3)$
$= 0.8322 - 0.0104 = 0.8218$.

e) $P(> 4) = P(\geq 5) = 0.9437$.

f) $P(< 2 \text{ or } > 6) = P(\leq 1) + P(\geq 7) = 0.0001 + 0.5033 = 0.5034$.

These calculations can be completed using EXCEL, as demonstrated in USING EXCEL 8.1.

USING EXCEL 8.1

EXCEL and its binomial distribution function can be used to help build the binomial probability and cumulative probability distribution tables constructed in Example 8.3b.

1. Type the column headings **Probability distribution**, **Less-than cumulative distribution**, and **More-than cumulative distribution** into cells B1–D1.
2. Type the column headings **x**, **P(x)**, **P(<=x)**, and **P(>=x)** into cells A2–D2.
3. Enter the values **0** to **8** into cells A3–A11.
4. Select cell B3.
5. On the toolbar, click on the **Paste Function** button (or on the **Insert** menu, click **Function...**)
6. The **Paste Function** dialog box appears. From the **Function category** list, select **Statistical**; from the **Function name** list, select the **BINOMDIST** function; and then click the **OK** button.
7. The input dialog box appears. In the **Number_s** input box, type **A3** or select cell A3 (representing the number of satisfactory produced items) and return to the input dialog box. In the **Trials** input box, enter **8** (representing the number of items taken from the production line). In the **Probablility_s** input box, enter **0.8** (representing the probability of producing a satisfactory item). In the **Cumulative** input box, enter **0** or type **FALSE** (which tells EXCEL to calculate the probability that there is exactly **Number_s** or **x** [column A] satisfactory produced items). When finished, click the **OK** button.
8. **Copy** and **Paste** cell B3 into cells B4–B11.
9. Select cell C1.
10. Repeat step 6, however in the **Cumulative** input box, enter **1** or type **TRUE** (which tells EXCEL to calculate the cumulative distribution function, which is the probability that there is as much as **Number_s** or **x** [column A] satisfactory produced items).
11. **Copy** and **Paste** cell C3 into cells C4–C11.
12. Select cell D11, and type **=B11** in the formula bar and enter.
13. Select cell D10, and type **=D11+B10** in the formula bar and enter.
14. **Copy** and **Paste** cell D10 into cells D9–D1.

Format the table (changing column widths, altering font sizes and styles, number format [e.g. 4 decimal places], etc.) to make it clear and readable.

OUTPUT

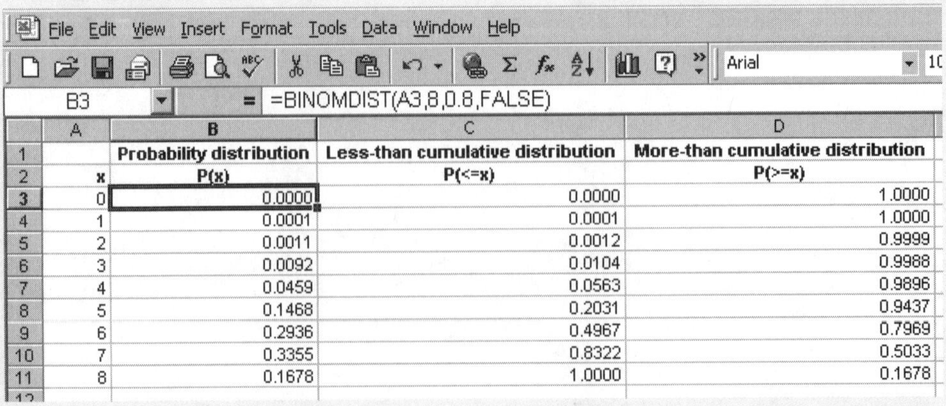

	A	B	C	D
1		Probability distribution	Less-than cumulative distribution	More-than cumulative distribution
2	x	P(x)	P(<=x)	P(>=x)
3	0	0.0000	0.0000	1.0000
4	1	0.0001	0.0001	1.0000
5	2	0.0011	0.0012	0.9999
6	3	0.0092	0.0104	0.9988
7	4	0.0459	0.0563	0.9896
8	5	0.1468	0.2031	0.9437
9	6	0.2936	0.4967	0.7969
10	7	0.3355	0.8322	0.5033
11	8	0.1678	1.0000	0.1678

D. *Binomial Tables*

In Example 8.3a we constructed a binomial probability distribution for $n = 8$, $p = 0.50$, and in Example 8.3b a similar distribution for $n = 8$, $p = 0.80$. The fact is that a different probability distribution results for every value of n and every value of p. The construction of binomial probability distributions even for small values of n is a tedious arithmetic process.

Because of the usefulness of the binomial distribution, tables have been produced for many values of n and selected values of p. One such table for $n = 8$ for selected values of p is presented in Table 8.10. A partial table for $n = 20$ and selected values of p is located at the back of the textbook.

The corresponding cumulative probability tables can be constructed without difficulty by listing the running totals for each value of p.

TABLE 8.10 Partial Binomial Probability Table for $n = 8$ and Selected Values of p

p / x	0.10	0.20	0.30	0.40	0.50	0.60	0.70	0.80	0.90
0	0.4305	0.1678	0.0576	0.0168	0.0039	0.0006	0.0001	0.0000	0.0000
1	0.3826	0.3355	0.1976	0.0896	0.0312	0.0079	0.0013	0.0001	0.0000
2	0.1488	0.2936	0.2965	0.2090	0.1094	0.0413	0.0100	0.0011	0.0000
3	0.0331	0.1468	0.2541	0.2787	0.2188	0.1239	0.0467	0.0092	0.0004
4	0.0046	0.0459	0.1361	0.2322	0.2734	0.2322	0.1361	0.0459	0.0046
5	0.0004	0.0092	0.0467	0.1239	0.2188	0.2787	0.2541	0.1468	0.0331
6	0.0000	0.0011	0.0100	0.0413	0.1094	0.2090	0.2965	0.2936	0.1488
7	0.0000	0.0001	0.0013	0.0079	0.0312	0.0896	0.1976	0.3355	0.3826
8	0.0000	0.0000	0.0001	0.0006	0.0039	0.0168	0.0576	0.1678	0.4305
Total	1.0000	1.0000	1.0000	1.0000	1.0000	1.0000	1.0000	1.0000	1.0000

To use a binomial probability table,

1. locate the table or portion of the table with the required value of n;
2. locate the column headed by the required value of p;
3. locate the row for the required value of x;
4. read off the probability $P(x)$ at the intersection of the column with the required p and the row for the required x.

EXAMPLE 8.3c

In January 1991, with the introduction of the Goods and Services Tax, Canadian supermarkets had to adjust the prices of many non-food items. In one particular store it was determined that 40% of the adjusted prices were incorrect. Use Table 8.10 to calculate the probabilities that, of eight non-food items selected, further price corrections were necessary

a) for exactly six of the items;
b) for fewer than three of the items;
c) for between five and seven of the items;
d) for more than four of the items.

SOLUTION

$n = 8; p = 0.40.$

The probabilities will be found in the column $p = 0.40$.

a) $P(6) = 0.041$

b) $P(< 3) = P(\le 2) = P(0) + P(1) + P(2)$
$= 0.0168 + 0.0896 + 0.2090 = 0.3154$

c) $P(5 \text{ or } 6 \text{ or } 7) = P(5) + P(6) + P(7)$
$= 0.1239 + 0.0413 + 0.0079 = 0.1731$

d) $P(> 4) = P(\ge 5) = P(5) + P(6) + P(7) + P(8)$
$= 0.1239 + 0.0413 + 0.0079 + 0.0006 = 0.1737$

E. *Characteristics of the Binomial Distribution*

The main characteristics of the binomial distribution are its shape, mean, and standard deviation.

1. The *shape* of the binomial distribution depends both on the number of trials n and the constant probability of success p. The graphs of three of the distributions for $n = 8$ in Figure 8.2 show what happens to the shape of a binomial distribution for different values of p.

   Note $n = 8$ is considered to be a small number of trials.

   a) When $P < 0.50$ and n is small, the distribution is *positively* skewed (see Figure 8.2, Diagram A).

FIGURE 8.2 Graphs of Binomial Distributions, $n = 8$

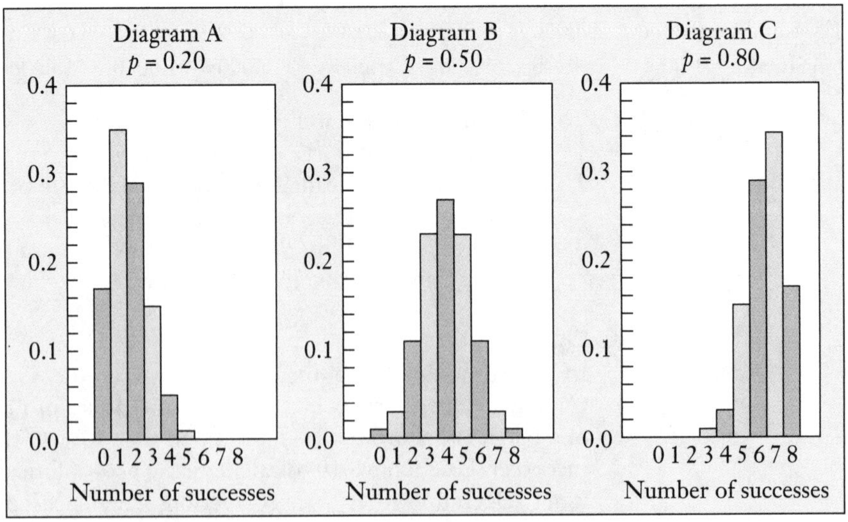

   b) When $P > 0.50$ and n is small, the distribution is *negatively* skewed (see Figure 8.2, Diagram C).

   c) When $p = 0.50$, the distribution is *symmetrical* for all values of n (see Figure 8.2, Diagram B).

2. The *mean* of the binomial distribution is shown by the formula

$$\mu = np \qquad \leftarrow \textit{Formula 8.5}$$

3. The *variance* of the binomial distribution is shown by the formula

$$\sigma^2 = np(1 - p) \qquad \leftarrow \textit{Formula 8.6}$$

and the *standard deviation* by

$$\sigma = \sqrt{\sigma^2} = \sqrt{np(1 - p)} \qquad \leftarrow \textit{Formula 8.7}$$

EXAMPLE 8.3d

Determine the mean, variance, and standard deviation for the probability distributions in Examples 8.3a, 8.3b, and 8.3c.

SOLUTION

For Example 8.3a, $n = 8$, $p = 0.50$, $(1 - p) = 0.50$.

$$\mu = np = 8(0.50) = 4.00$$
$$\sigma^2 = np(1 - p) = 8(0.50)(0.50) = 2.00$$
$$\sigma = \sqrt{np(1 - p)} = \sqrt{2.00} = 1.4142$$

For Example 8.3b, $n = 8$, $p = 0.80$, $1 - p = 0.20$.

$$\mu = np = 8(0.80) = 6.40$$
$$\sigma^2 = np(1 - p) = 8(0.80)(0.20) = 1.28$$
$$\sigma = \sqrt{np(1 - p)} = \sqrt{1.28} = 1.1314$$

For Example 8.3c, $n = 8$, $p = 0.40$, $(1 - p) = 0.60$.

$$\mu = np = 8(0.40) = 3.20$$
$$\sigma^2 = np(1 - p) = 8(0.40)(0.60) = 1.92$$
$$\sigma = \sqrt{np(1 - p)} = \sqrt{1.92} = 1.3856$$

EXERCISE 8.3

1. If we repeat 5 tosses of one coin many times, what is the probability of 4 tails and 1 head appearing?

2. A board game uses a spinning wheel with 5 equal sections (shown below) to determine *payoffs*. If we repeat 4 spins of the wheel many times, what is the probability of "Stocks" showing once and "Bust" showing 3 times?

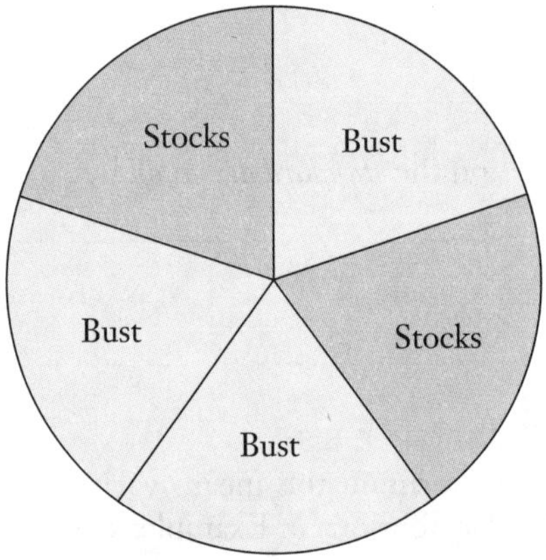

3. Auto glass companies now have a machine that can repair broken windshields with a success rate of 85%. If a random sample of six cars is taken from the customer records, determine the probability that
   a) exactly two windshields were successfully repaired;
   b) at least four windshields were successfully repaired.

4. A poll revealed that 12% of Canadians would vote for a new political party. If eight eligible voters are selected,
   a) what is the probability that exactly 3 will vote for a new party?
   b) what is the probability that no more than 5 will vote for a new political party?
   c) what is the probability that at least 2 will vote for a new political party?

5. Determine the mean and the standard deviation for Question **2**.

6. Determine the mean and the standard deviation for Question **3**.

REVIEW EXERCISE

1. An inventor is planning to go into business for himself. He uses the following estimates. Calculate the expected profits for his invention.

Event	Probability of event	Profit
Strong sales	0.04	$850 000
Fair sales	0.84	220 000
Poor sales	0.12	–75 000

2. The inventor in Question **1** uses the following estimates based on selling the rights to the product and collecting royalties. Calculate the expected profits.

Event	Probability of event	Profit
Strong sales	0.04	$500 000
Fair sales	0.84	100 000
Poor sales	0.12	5 000

3. A major league sports team is in the process of being sold. The owner uses the following estimates. Calculate the expected television revenues.

Event	Probability of event	Television revenues
Above-average season	0.10	$3 000 000
Average season	0.75	$1 000 000
Below-average season	0.15	$ 500 000

4. A potential buyer of the sports team in Question 3 uses the following estimates for television revenues. Calculate the expected television revenues.

Event	Probability of event	Television revenues
Above-average season	0.10	$2 000 000
Average season	0.75	$1 000 000
Below-average season	0.15	$ 200 000

5. In the past an automobile repair shop owner has noticed that sales increased as certain economic indicators decreased. Based on forecasts of these economic indicators and past observations, the owner has assigned probabilities to sales increases as follows:

Sales increase	Probability
5%	0.05
10%	0.15
15%	0.35
20%	0.30
25%	0.15

Calculate the expected sales increase and the standard deviation.

6. A local lottery seller has noticed that ticket sales have increased the day following the Stanley Cup based on certain conditions. The lottery seller has assigned probabilities to sales increases as follows:

Event	Sales increase	Probability
American team wins	10%	0.20
Western Canadian team wins	20%	0.30
Eastern Canadian team wins	40%	0.50

Calculate the expected sales increase and standard deviation.

7. When asked to quantify the effectiveness of a new promotional program based on their sales experience, four salespersons responded as follows:

Salesperson	A	B	C	D
Sales increase	\$3000	\$6000	\$3000	\$4000

a) If all four persons gave their best estimates, what can be said about the nature of the probability estimate in each case?
b) Compute the expected sales increase.
c) Compute the standard deviation.

8. Five math teachers have been asked to quantify the new high school curriculum based on their records as follows:

Teacher	I	II	III	IV	V
Class increase(marks)	10	5	4	12	1

a) Compute the expected mark increase.
b) Compute the standard deviation.

9. A manufacturer of photocopiers knows that the machines require regular service to avoid customer complaints. Despite this service, the failure rate of the machines is 8%. In an office that is equipped with 4 copiers, determine the probability that
a) none of the copiers will fail;
b) at least 1 copier will fail.

10. A defense contractor is awarded contracts on the basis that only 1% of the parts manufactured are defective. If 400 parts are sent out, determine the probability that
a) all the parts are good;
b) at least 1 part will fail.

11. In sensory research projects, 2 identical products are often given to participants for appraisal. If 10 persons are chosen, what is the probability that
a) only one person will show a preference for product A, while nine will show a preference for product B?
b) five persons will indicate a preference for product A, while the other five will indicate a preference for product B?

12. You are 1 of 20 people who have just won a contest and have a choice of prizes behind door I or door II. What is the probability that
a) only 2 people will pick door I and 18 will pick door II?
b) 9 people will choose door I and 11 will choose door II?

13. Canada Customs and Revenue Agency estimates that 5% of tax returns are filed after the deadline date. If a random sample of 100 tax returns is chosen for auditing,
a) what is the probability that exactly 1 tax return was filed late?
b) calculate the expected mean;
c) calculate the standard deviation.

14. An independent auditor has determined that proper accounting procedures are followed 90% of the time in a small company. If a procedure is conducted 50 times,
a) what is the probability that exactly 2 procedures were not done properly?
b) calculate the expected mean;
c) calculate the standard deviation.

15. An accounts-receivable supervisor has determined that 3% of customers default on their payments. Currently there are 1200 credit customers with outstanding balances.
a) Determine the expected mean number of bad debts.
b) Compute the standard deviation.
c) What is the probability that no more than five customers will default?

16. High-ratio mortgages account for 30% of mortgages in new housing developments.
a) Determine the expected mean number of high-ratio mortgages.
b) Compute the standard deviation.
c) What is the probability that in a sample of 100 mortgages, no more than 2 are high ratio?

17. Given that $n = 30$, $p = 0.80$, use the binomial formula to determine
a) $P(x > 28)$;
b) $P(20 < x < 22)$;
c) $P(x < 3)$.

18. A weighted coin (in favour of heads 60% of the time) is tossed 10 times. Use the binomial formula to determine
a) the probability of getting heads at least 7 times;
b) the probability of getting between 2 and 5 heads;
c) the probability of getting no heads.

19. Given that $n = 100$, $p = 0.25$, use the binomial formula to determine
a) $P(x > 98)$;
b) $P(78 < x < 80)$;
c) $P(x < 4)$.

20. A manufacturer of DVD players says that 5% of their players are defective. In a sample of 100 DVD players, use the binomial formula to determine
a) that more than 97 will be good;
b) that between 70 and 72 will be good;
c) that under 2 will be good.

21. (CGA) An investment consultant is trying to determine which of the three possible actions to recommend to a client who has \$1000 to invest: to invest 100% in a mutual fund; to invest 50% in a mutual fund and 50% in a risk-free security; or to invest 100% in a risk-free security. The rate of return of the mutual fund depends upon the strength of the stock market. The predicted rate of return under three different scenarios is given below:

Scenario	Predicted rate of return
Market is bullish	18%
Market is normal	6%
Market is bearish	–8%

Suppose an expert has assessed the probabilities of the market being "bullish," "normal," and "bearish" to be 0.60, 0.25, and 0.15 respectively. Determine the expected rate of return if the client invests 100% of the money in a mutual fund.

22. (CGA) An auomobile travel association rates motels throughout North America as 1-star to 4-star motels based on the overall quality of the service provided. Records show that 20% of the motels have a 1-star rating, 30% have a 2-star rating, 30% have a 3-star rating, and the remaining 20% have a 4-star rating. Let x represent the number of stars in a randomly chosen motel's rating.
a) Determine the probability distribution of the random variable x.
b) Determine the mean, variance, and standard deviation of x.

23. (CGA) The manager of an insurance company has determined that in a typical day an agent can sell insurance, on the average, to 10% of the customers she visits. Assume that the agent will visit 20 customers on Monday and Tuesday.
a) Determine the probability that the agent will be able to sell insurance to at most one customer on Monday.
b) Determine the probability that she will be able to sell insurance to at least four and at most six customers on Tuesday.
c) Determine the probability that she will not be able to sell any insurance on either of the two days.

24. (CGA) Suppose 90% of the account receivables of a company are free of errors. A random sample of 20 such accounts is drawn.

a) Determine the probability that 18 out of these 20 accounts will be free of errors.

b) Determine the probability that at least 18 of these accounts will be free of errors.

25. (CGA) A quality-control engineer has determined that if the manufacturing process is working properly, then, on average, only 10% of the items produced will be defective. Assume that the process is working properly.

a) Suppose you take a random sample of 4 items. What is the probability that exactly 2 of these 4 items will be defective?

b) Suppose 20 items are selected at random. Determine the probability that at most 2 items are defective.

SELF-TEST

1. Given the following weather predictions, determine

a) the mean expected rainfall;

b) the standard deviation.

Rainfall (mm)	15	12	10	8	6	4	2
Probability	5%	15%	20%	30%	15%	10%	5%

2. The personnel department has found that 59% of college students accept job offers from the company. If 12 offers have been made to recent college graduates, what is the probability that

a) three or fewer will accept?

b) nine or more will accept?

c) exactly seven will accept?

3. Compute the mean and the standard deviation for the distribution in Question 2.

For an online glossary, go to **www.pearsoned.ca/hummelbrunner**.

Key Terms

Binomial distribution 270
Continuous probability distribution 263
Continuous random variable 263
Discrete probability distribution 262
Discrete random variable 262
Expected value 263
Probability distribution 261

Summary of Formulas

1. Discrete random variable

a) Expected value (mean):

$$E(x) = \mu = \sum x \cdot P(x)$$ ←*Formula* 8.1

b) Variance:

$$V(x) = \sigma^2 = \sum (x - \mu)^2 \cdot P(x)$$ ←*Formula* 8.2

$$V(x) = \sigma^2 = \sum x^2 \cdot P(x) - \mu^2$$ ←*Formula* 8.2A

c) Standard deviation:

$$\sigma = \sqrt{\sigma^2}$$ ←*Formula* 8.3

2. Binomial probability distribution

a) Binomial formula:
Probability of x successes in n trials:

$$P(x) = ({}_nC_x)(p^x)(1 - p)^{n-x}$$ ←*Formula* 8.4

$$P(x) = \frac{n!}{x!(n-x)!}(p^x)(1-p)^{n-x}$$ ←*Formula* 8.4A

b) Mean:

$$\mu = np$$ ←*Formula* 8.5

c) Variance:

$$\sigma^2 = np(1-p)$$ ←*Formula* 8.6

d) Standard deviation:

$$\sigma = \sqrt{\sigma^2} = \sqrt{np(1-p)}$$ ←*Formula* 8.7

CHAPTER 9

The Normal Distribution

Introduction

Continuous variables are distinct from discrete variables in that they are not restricted to specific values and can assume an infinite number of values within a specified range. The computation of probabilities, expected values, and standard deviations for continuous variables requires the use of integral calculus and is beyond the scope of this text. However, this does not prevent us from using the continuous probability distribution referred to as the normal distribution.

Learning Outcomes

Upon completion of this chapter you will be able to

1. discuss the importance of the normal distribution in statistics;
2. define the characteristics of the normal curve;
3. describe the concept of the standardized normal curve;
4. compute and interpret z scores;
5. use a table of areas under the normal curve to solve problems involving the normal distribution;
6. use the normal distribution in appropriate situations as a replacement of the binomial distribution.

SECTION 9.1

Characteristics of the Normal Distribution

The **normal distribution** is the most important statistical probability distribution as far as practical applications are concerned. The three main reasons for its usefulness are as follows:

1. The distribution of much of the data collected in the physical and social sciences, and in business and industry is sufficiently close to that of the normal distribution to permit the utilization of the properties of the normal distribution in analyzing the actual distribution.
2. When the number of trials is large enough, the shape of some of the discrete probability distributions approximates a normal distribution. Specifically, even with n as small as 20, the shape of a binomial distribution becomes fairly symmetrical even when p is not very close to 0.50.
3. Because of certain properties of the sampling distribution (see Chapter 10), the normal distribution provides the basis for statistical inference.

The graphical representation of the normal distribution (see Figure 9.1) is referred to as the **normal curve**. The following are some of the important characteristics of the normal curve:

FIGURE 9.1 The Normal Curve

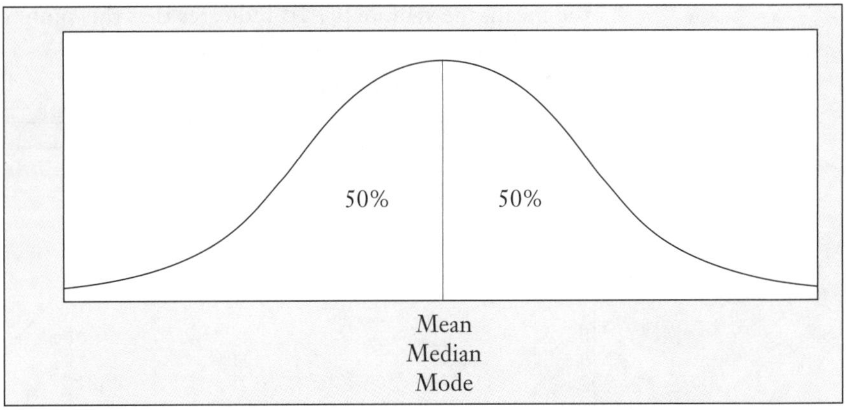

1. The curve is *bell-shaped* and has only one peak at the centre of the distribution.
2. The distribution is *symmetrical* about the vertical line drawn from the peak of the curve to the horizontal axis.
3. The measures of central tendency of the distribution — the *mean*, the *median* and the *mode* — are equal in value and are located at the peak of the normal curve.
4. The curve approaches the x axis gradually on either side of the mean but never touches the x axis. Theoretically, the tails of the distribution extend indefinitely in either direction.
5. Since the curve is completely symmetrical, the area to the left of the mean equals the area to the right of the mean, so that each side contains 50% of the total area under the curve.

6. The area under the curve represents probability. For any normal distribution, the probability is 50% that the continuous variable x will assume a value less than the mean and 50% that it will assume a value more than the mean.
7. The area between any two points under the curve represents the probability that the continuous variable x will assume some value within that interval.
8. The standard measure of central tendency of a normal distribution is its mean μ. The standard measure of variability is the standard deviation σ. Any normal distribution is completely defined by the values of its mean μ and its standard deviation σ.

SECTION 9.2

Areas under the Normal Curve

The mean μ and the standard deviation σ completely define a normal curve. The standard deviation σ measures the extent to which the data under the normal curve deviate from the mean μ and is always measured from the mean μ.

As shown in Figure 9.2, the horizontal scale (x-scale) can be divided into standard deviation units.

Because the values of the variable x to the right of the mean are *greater* than the mean, the symbol $\mu + 1\sigma$ indicates that this point on the horizontal axis is located one standard deviation *above* the mean.

FIGURE 9.2 The Normal Curve

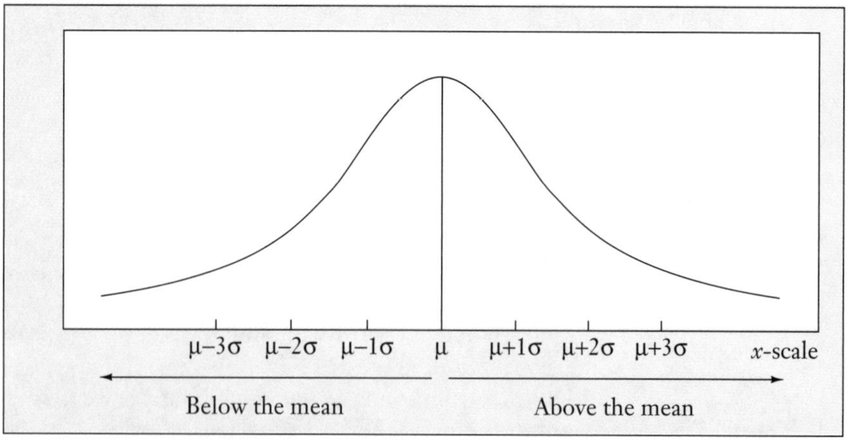

Values of the variable x to the left of the mean are *smaller* than the mean. The symbol $\mu - 1\sigma$ indicates that this point on the horizontal axis is located one standard deviation *below* the mean.

For all normal curves, the area between μ and $\mu + 1\sigma$ contains approximately 34.13% of the total area under the curve, as shown in Figure 9.3. Because of the symmetry of the normal curve, the area between μ and $\mu - 1\sigma$ also contains approximately 34.13% of the total area.

To simplify, the notations $\mu + 1\sigma$ and $\mu - 1\sigma$ can be combined by writing $\mu \pm 1\sigma$.

FIGURE 9.3 Area between μ and $\mu \pm 1\sigma$

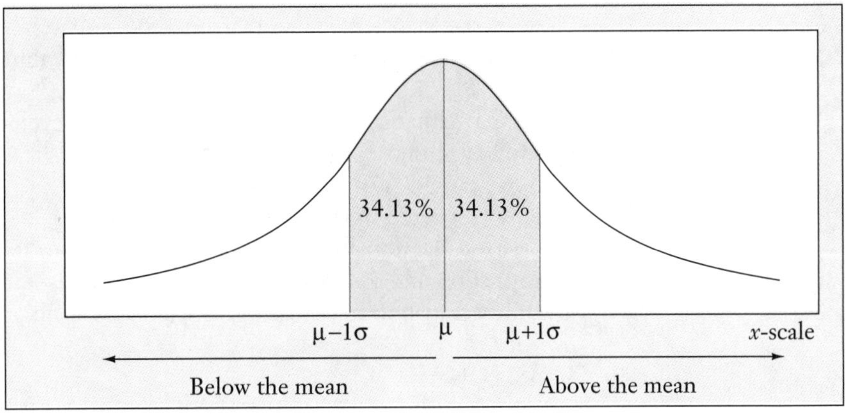

When verticals are drawn to the x axis at the points marked in standard deviation units, the total area under the normal curve is subdivided into smaller areas, each of which contains a certain proportion of the total area. The proportions are the same for all normal distributions.

The approximate proportions for each of these smaller areas are shown in Figure 9.4. As indicated, the proportion of the total area

between μ and $\mu + 1\sigma = 0.3413$;
between $\mu + 1\sigma$ and $\mu + 2\sigma = 0.1359$;
between $\mu + 2\sigma$ and $\mu + 3\sigma = 0.0215$.

FIGURE 9.4 Areas under Normal Curve

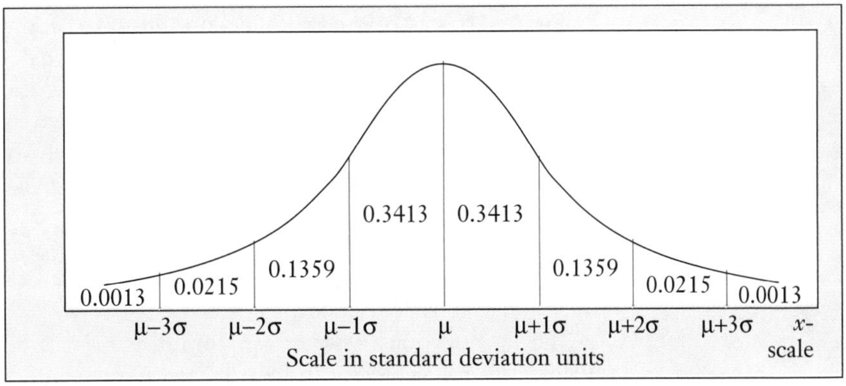

Because of the symmetry of the normal curve, the proportions are the same for the areas below the mean. From this, it follows that the proportion of the total area

a) between $\mu - 1\sigma$ and $\mu + 1\sigma = 0.3413 + 0.3413 = 0.6826 = 68.26\%$;

b) between $\mu - 2\sigma$ and $\mu + 2\sigma = 2(0.3413 + 0.1359)$
$= 2(0.4772) = 0.9544 = 95.44\%$;
c) between $\mu - 3\sigma$ and $\mu + 3\sigma = 2(0.3413 + 0.1359 + 0.0215)$
$= 2(0.4987) = 0.9974 = 99.74\%$.

The three values calculated in (a), (b), and (c) contain slight rounding errors. The more accurate and frequently used values are 68.27%, 95.45%, and 99.73%.

The mathematically derived normal curve never touches the horizontal axis. However, only 0.27% of the total area lies in the two tails below $\mu - 3\sigma$ and above $\mu + 3\sigma$. For this reason, the scale used for the normal distribution is usually restricted to the range $\mu - 3\sigma$ to $\mu + 3\sigma$.

The fixed relationship between the mean μ, the standard deviation σ, and the proportion of the area under the curve is very useful in statistics because the probability distribution of many sets of data resembles the normal distribution.

EXAMPLE 9.2a

Northern Taxi Inc. owns a fleet of 400 cars, which use an average of 12 L of fuel per 100 km with a standard deviation of 1.5 L of fuel per 100 km. Fuel consumption of the fleet of cars is normally distributed. Describe the data.

SOLUTION

The mean, $\mu = 12$; the standard deviation, $\sigma = 1.5$; the number of observations, $N = 400$.

Knowing the μ and the σ of a set of data that is normally distributed is sufficient to describe the set of data and permits us to draw certain useful conclusions.

In the graphical representation of the given normal distribution in Figure 9.5, place the value 12.0 at μ. The point marked $\mu + 1\sigma$ on the horizontal scale is one standard deviation above the μ. Since $\mu = 12.0$ and $\sigma = 1.5$, the point $\mu + 1\sigma$ is associated with a consumption of $12.0 + 1.5 = 13.5$ L.

Similarly, the point marked $\mu - 1\sigma$ is one standard deviation below the mean; that is, the point $\mu - 1\sigma$ is associated with $(12.0 - 1.5) = 10.5$ L. The remaining values can be marked in a similar manner, as shown in Figure 9.5.

The proportion of the area between μ and $\mu + 1\sigma$ is 0.3413. This means 34.13% of the fleet vehicles can be expected to consume between 12.0 and 13.5 L per 100 km.

Furthermore, since there are 400 cars in the fleet, we can expect $400(0.3413) = 136.52$, that is, approximately 137 cars, to consume between 12.0 and 13.5 L per 100 km.

The proportion between $\mu - 2\sigma$ and $\mu + 2\sigma$ is 0.9545. This means that 95.45% of the vehicles can be expected to consume between 9.0 and 15.0 L per 100 km. Approximately $400(0.9545) = 382$ cars consume between 9.0 and 15.0 L per 100 km.

The proportion of cars between $\mu - 2\sigma$ and $\mu - 3\sigma$ is 0.0215; that is, 2.15% of the cars, or approximately 9 vehicles, consume between 7.5 and 9.0 L per 100 km.

FIGURE 9.5 Normal Curve for Example 9.2a

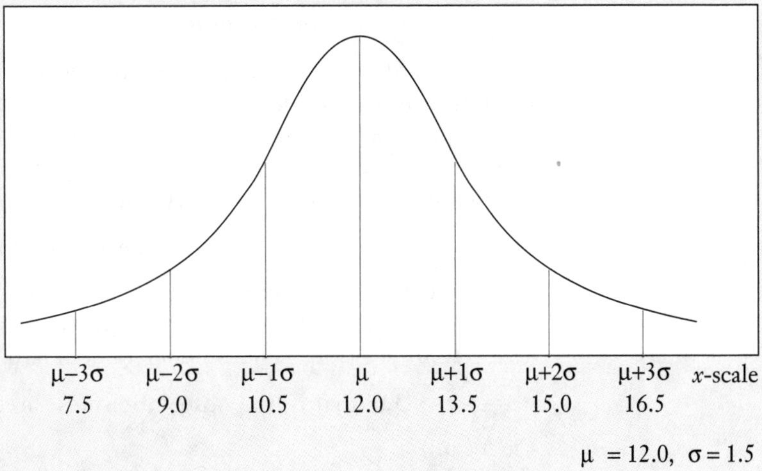

EXERCISE 9.2

1. For Example 9.2a determine the proportion of cars with a fuel consumption (per 100 km)
   - **a)** between 10.5 L and 13.5 L;
   - **b)** between 13.5 L and 16.5 L;
   - **c)** between 9.0 L and 13.5 L;
   - **d)** less than 10.5 L;
   - **e)** more than 16.5 L.

2. A normal distribution of 640 observations has a mean of 1800 cm and a standard deviation of 90 cm.
   - **a)** Draw a representative diagram for the distribution.
   - **b)** Determine the proportion of observations
     - **i)** between 1620 cm and 1980 cm;
     - **ii)** between 1710 cm and 2070 cm;
     - **iii)** above 1890 cm;
     - **iv)** below 2070 cm.
   - **c)** Determine the number of observations
     - **i)** between 1710 cm and 1890 cm;
     - **ii)** between 1530 cm and 1620 cm;
     - **iii)** below 1890 cm;
     - **iv)** above 2070 cm.

SECTION 9.3

The Standardized Normal Curve

A. Standard Normal Deviation — z Values

The standard deviation σ describes the deviation of the x values from the mean μ. Any such deviation $(x - \mu)$ can be converted into standard units by dividing the deviation by the standard deviation.

For example, if $\mu = 12.0$, $\sigma = 1.5$, and a particular observation x has a value of 15.0, the deviation of x from μ, $(x-\mu) = (15.0-12.0) = 3.0$. This deviation is equivalent to $= \frac{3.0}{1.5} = +2.0$ standard deviations; that is, the observation $x = 15$ lies two standard deviations above the mean.

Similarly, an observation $x = 7.5$ deviates from the mean by $(x - \mu) = (7.5 - 12.0) = -4.50$. The number of standard deviations in the deviation $= \frac{-4.5}{1.5} = -3.0$; that is, the observation lies three standard deviations below the mean.

The location of any value x relative to the mean μ can be described in terms of standard deviations. This is accomplished by dividing the deviation $(x - \mu)$ by the standard deviation σ. This calculation is represented by the formula

$$z = \frac{\text{ACTUAL DEVIATION}}{\text{STANDARD DEVIATION}} = \frac{x - \mu}{\sigma}$$

←*Formula* 9.1

where x is the value of an observation;
μ is the population mean;
$(x - \mu)$ is the deviation of an observation x from the mean μ;
σ is the population standard deviation;
z is referred to as the **z value** and represents the number of standard deviations between a selected value x and the mean μ.

○ EXAMPLE 9.3a

Given that $\mu = 12.00$, $\sigma = 1.50$, determine and interpret the z value when
a) $x = 15.75$;
b) $x = 11.25$;
c) $x = 8.20$.

● SOLUTION

a) For $x = 15.75$, $z = \dfrac{x-\mu}{\sigma} = \dfrac{15.75 - 12.00}{1.50} = \dfrac{3.75}{1.50} = +2.50$.
The z value +2.5 indicates that the value x = 15.75 lies 2.5 standard deviations above the mean.

b) For $x = 11.25$, $z = \dfrac{x-\mu}{\sigma} = \dfrac{11.25 - 12.00}{1.50} = \dfrac{-0.75}{1.50} = -0.50$.
The z value −0.50 indicates that the value x = 11.25 lies 0.50 standard deviations below the mean.

c) For $x = 8.20$, $z = \dfrac{x-\mu}{\sigma} = \dfrac{8.20 - 12.00}{1.50} = \dfrac{-3.80}{1.50} = -2.5333$.
The z value −2.5333 indicates that the value x = 8.20 lies 2.5333 standard deviations below the mean.

B. Table of Areas under the Normal Curve

Since a normal distribution is completely defined by the mean μ and the standard deviation σ, a *different* distribution results for each pair of values $\{\mu, \sigma\}$. However, every normal distribution can be transformed to the so-called **standard normal distribution** by changing the scale into a standard scale stated in terms of z values. In this context, z values are referred to as **standard normal deviates**.

This transformation is important because the areas under the standardized normal curve have been tabulated and can be applied to *any* normal distribution. Table 9.1 is a table of areas under the standardized normal curve, correct to four decimals, for values of z from 0.00 to 3.09.

The values listed in Table 9.1 (see also the inside front cover) are the probabilities that the random variable x will assume a value between the mean μ and a particular value of z. Entries for negative values of z are the same as for the corresponding positive values because of the symmetry of the normal curve and are not separately listed.

Table 9.1 can be used in two distinct ways:

1. to find areas to the right of, to the left of, or between z values;
2. to find z values for given areas.

TABLE 9.1 Areas under the Normal Curve

Each entry in the table indicates the proportion of the total area under the normal curve contained by a vertical line at the mean (μ) and a vertical line at z.

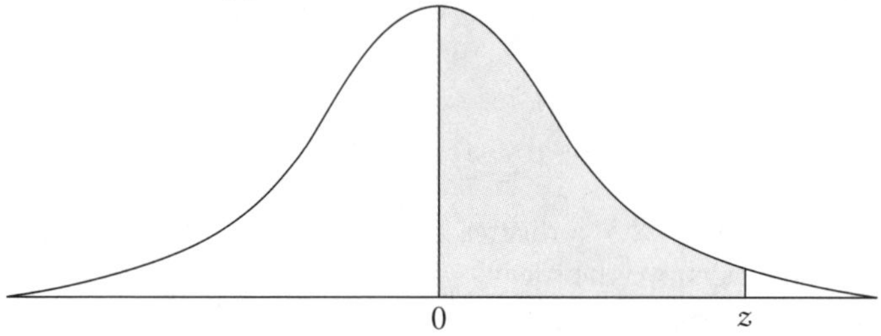

z	0.00	0.01	0.02	0.03	0.04	0.05	0.06	0.07	0.08	0.09
0.0	.0000	.0040	.0080	.0120	.0160	.0199	.0239	.0279	.0319	.0359
0.1	.0398	.0438	.0478	.0517	.0557	.0596	.0636	.0675	.0714	.0753
0.2	.0793	.0832	.0871	.0910	.0948	.0987	.1026	.1064	.1103	.1141
0.3	.1179	.1217	.1255	.1293	.1331	.1368	.1406	.1443	.1480	.1517
0.4	.1554	.1591	.1628	.1664	.1700	.1736	.1772	.1808	.1844	.1879
0.5	.1915	.1950	.1985	.2019	.2054	.2088	.2123	.2157	.2190	.2224
0.6	.2257	.2291	.2324	.2357	.2389	.2422	.2454	.2486	.2517	.2549
0.7	.2580	.2611	.2642	.2673	.2704	.2734	.2764	.2794	.2823	.2852
0.8	.2881	.2910	.2939	.2967	.2995	.3023	.3051	.3078	.3106	.3133
0.9	.3159	.3186	.3212	.3238	.3264	.3289	.3315	.3340	.3365	.3389
1.0	.3413	.3438	.3461	.3485	.3508	.3531	.3554	.3577	.3599	.3621
1.1	.3643	.3665	.3686	.3708	.3729	.3749	.3770	.3790	.3810	.3830
1.2	.3849	.3869	.3888	.3907	.3925	.3944	.3962	.3980	.3997	.4015
1.3	.4032	.4049	.4066	.4082	.4099	.4115	.4131	.4147	.4162	.4177
1.4	.4192	.4207	.4222	.4236	.4251	.4265	.4279	.4292	.4306	.4319
1.5	.4332	.4345	.4357	.4370	.4382	.4394	.4406	.4418	.4429	.4441
1.6	.4452	.4463	.4474	.4484	.4495	.4505	.4515	.4525	.4535	.4545
1.7	.4554	.4564	.4573	.4582	.4591	.4599	.4608	.4616	.4625	.4633
1.8	.4641	.4649	.4656	.4664	.4671	.4678	.4686	.4693	.4699	.4706
1.9	.4713	.4719	.4726	.4732	.4738	.4744	.4750	.4756	.4761	.4767
2.0	.4772	.4778	.4783	.4788	.4793	.4798	.4803	.4808	.4812	.4817
2.1	.4821	.4826	.4830	.4834	.4838	.4842	.4846	.4850	.4854	.4857
2.2	.4861	.4864	.4868	.4871	.4875	.4878	.4881	.4884	.4887	.4890
2.3	.4893	.4896	.4898	.4901	.4904	.4906	.4909	.4911	.4913	.4916
2.4	.4918	.4920	.4922	.4925	.4927	.4929	.4931	.4932	.4934	.4936
2.5	.4938	.4940	.4941	.4943	.4945	.4946	.4948	.4949	.4951	.4952
2.6	.4953	.4955	.4956	.4957	.4959	.4960	.4961	.4962	.4963	.4964
2.7	.4965	.4966	.4967	.4968	.4969	.4970	.4971	.4972	.4973	.4974
2.8	.4974	.4975	.4976	.4977	.4977	.4978	.4979	.4979	.4980	.4981
2.9	.4981	.4982	.4982	.4983	.4984	.4984	.4985	.4985	.4986	.4986
3.0	.4987	.4987	.4987	.4988	.4988	.4989	.4989	.4989	.4990	.4990

C. *Finding Areas for Given z Values*

For a given z value, the associated table value can be found by looking in the left-hand column headed "z" and locating the row beginning with the first two digits (0.0 to 3.0) of the given z value. The desired table value is one of the 10 numbers listed in that row.

To select the correct table value, look across the top row in the table to locate the column headed by the last digit in the z value (0.00 to 0.09). The desired table value for the given z value is the number located at the point of intersection of the selected row and the selected column.

For example, to locate the table value for $z = 2.75$, locate the row beginning with 2.7 and the column headed by 0.05. The desired table value is 0.4970.

TABLE 9.2 Finding an Area under the Normal Curve

z	0.00	0.01	0.02	0.03	0.04	0.05	0.06	0.07	0.08	0.09
0.0	.0000	.0040	.0080	.0120	.0160	.0199	.0239	.0279	.0319	.0359
0.1	.0398	.0438	.0478	.0517	.0557	.0596	.0636	.0675	.0714	.0753
0.2	.0793	.0832	.0871	.0910	.0948	.0987	.1026	.1064	.1103	.1141
0.3	.1179	.1217	.1255	.1293	.1331	.1368	.1406	.1443	.1480	.1517
⋮	⋮	⋮	⋮	⋮	⋮	⋮	⋮	⋮	⋮	⋮
2.6	.4953	.4955	.4956	.4957	.4959	.4960	.4961	.4962	.4963	.4964
2.7	.4965	.4966	.4967	.4968	.4969	.4970	.4971	.4972	.4973	.4974
2.8	.4974	.4975	.4976	.4977	.4977	.4978	.4979	.4979	.4980	.4981
2.9	.4981	.4982	.4982	.4983	.4984	.4984	.4985	.4985	.4986	.4986
3.0	.4987	.4987	.4987	.4988	.4988	.4989	.4989	.4989	.4990	.4990

Source: Extracted from Table 9.1

This number represents the proportion of the total area between the mean μ and $z = 2.75$. It corresponds to the probability that the random variable x will assume a value in the interval between the μ and $z = 2.75$.

When using Table 9.1 keep the following points in mind:

1. The *total* area under the normal curve is 1.0000.
2. The mean μ (when $z = 0$) divides the total area into halves. The area to the left of μ *equals* the area to the right of μ; that is, each part equals 0.5000.
3. The table look-up for negative values of z is the same as for the corresponding positive values of z.
4. The table values represent the areas between μ and the given values of z. In many cases it will be necessary to add or subtract table values to obtain a specific area. For this reason it is highly recommended that you draw a diagram to identify the specific area under the curve.

○ EXAMPLE 9.3b

Use Table 9.1 to determine the area under the normal curve

a) to the left of $z = 1.50$;
b) to the right of $z = -2.20$;
c) above $z = 2.50$;
d) below $z = -1.75$;
e) between $z = 1.25$ and $z = 2.96$;
f) between $z = -2.07$ and $z = -1.03$;
g) between $z = -2.33$ and $z = 1.64$;
h) below $z = -2.00$ or above $z = 2.00$.

● SOLUTION

a) The area between the mean μ and ($z = 1.50$) is 0.4332. The area below μ is 0.5000. The area to the left of ($z = 1.50$) is $0.5000 + 0.4332 = 0.9332$.

FIGURE 9.6 Normal Curve

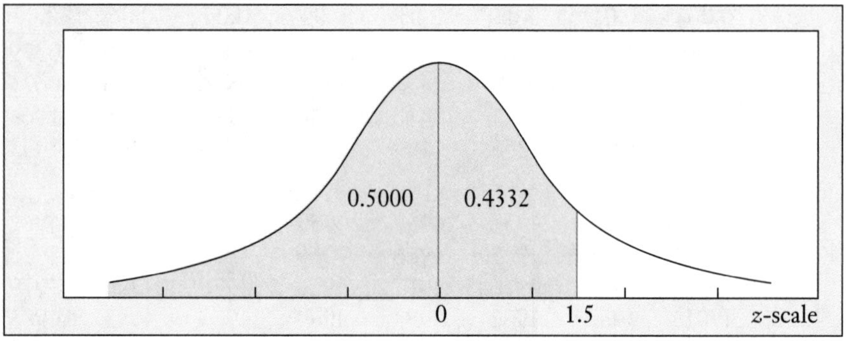

b) The area between μ and ($z = -2.20$) is 0.4861. The area to the right of $\mu = 0.5000$. The area to the right of ($z = -2.20$) is $0.5000 + 0.4861 = 0.9861$.

FIGURE 9.7 Normal Curve

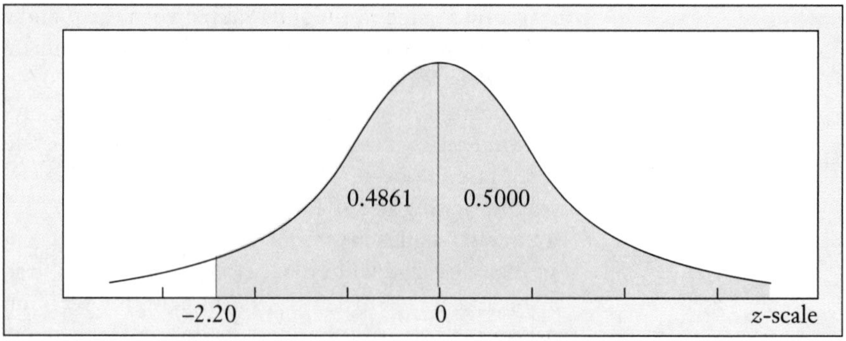

c) The area between μ and (z = 2.50) is 0.4938. The area above (z = 2.50) is 0.5000 – 0.4938 = 0.0062.

FIGURE 9.8 **Normal Curve**

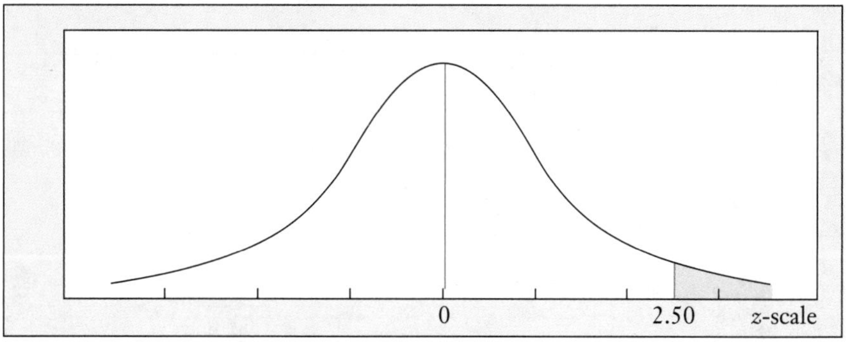

d) The area between μ and (z = –1.75) is 0.4599. The area below (z = –1.75) is 0.5000 – 0.4599 = 0.0401.

FIGURE 9.9 **Normal Curve**

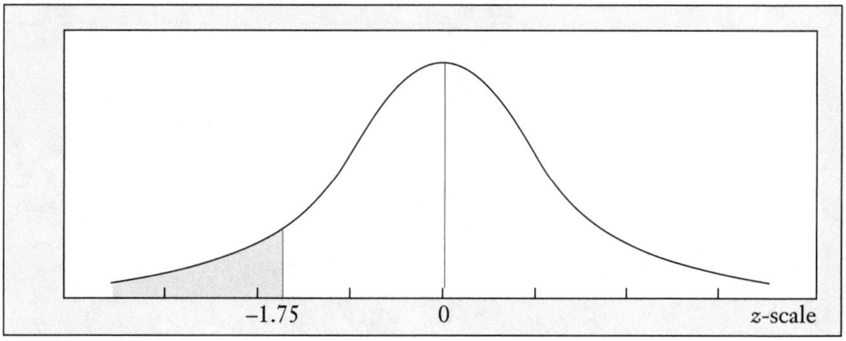

e) The area between μ and (z = 2.96) is 0.4985. The area between μ and (z = 1.25) is 0.3944. The area between (z = 1.25) and (z = 2.96) is 0.4985 – 0.3944 = 0.1041.

FIGURE 9.10 **Normal Curve**

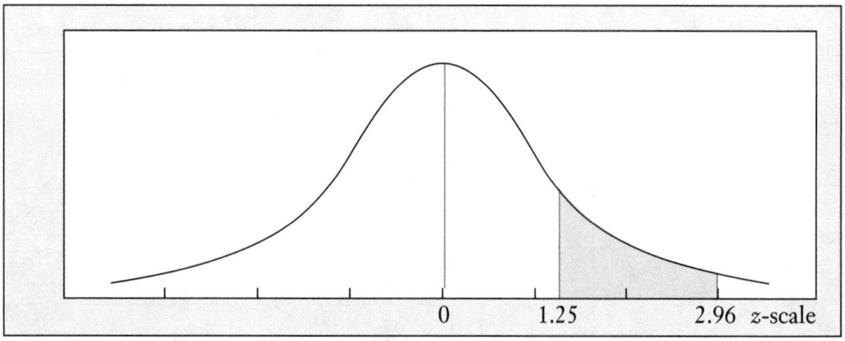

f) The area between μ and (z = −2.07) is 0.4808. The area between μ and (z = −1.03) is 0.3485. The area between (z = −2.07) and (z = −1.03) is 0.4808 − 0.3485 = 0.1323.

FIGURE 9.11 Normal Curve

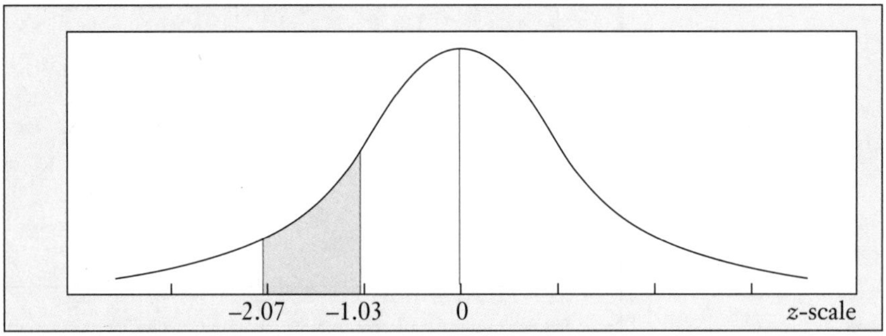

g) The area between μ and (z = −2.33) is 0.4901. The area between μ and (z = 1.64) is 0.4495. The area between (z = −2.33) and (z = 1.64) is 0.4901 + 0.4495 = 0.9396.

FIGURE 9.12 Normal Curve

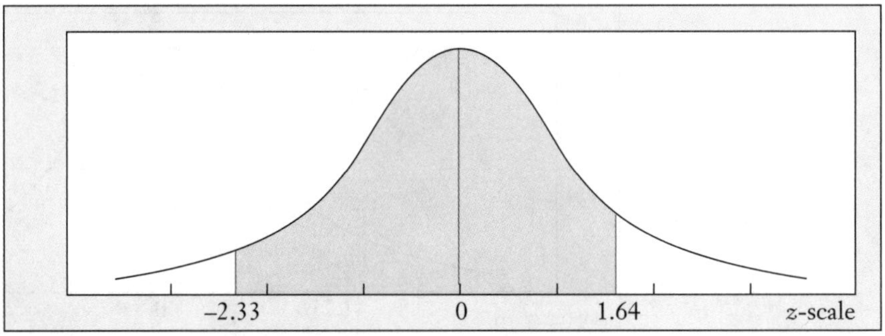

h) The area between μ and (z = −2.00) is 0.4772. The area below (z = −2.00) is 0.5000 − 0.4772 = 0.0228. The area between μ and (z = 2.00) is 0.4772. The area above (z = 2.00) is 0.5000 − 0.4772 = 0.0228. The total area below (z = −2.00) or above (z = 2.00) is 0.0228 + 0.0228 = 0.0456.

FIGURE 9.13 Normal Curve

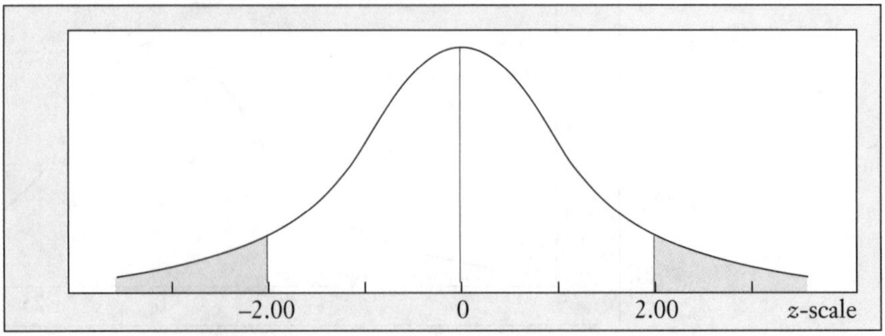

These calculations can be completed using EXCEL, as demonstrated in USING EXCEL 9.1.

USING EXCEL 9.1

EXCEL and its standard normal cumulative distribution function can be used to determine the area under the normal curve.

1. Type the column headings z and **Cumulative Distribution Function** into cells A1–B1.
2. Enter the z-values given in parts (a) to (h) of Example 9.3b into cells A2–A13.
3. Select cell B2.
4. On the toolbar, click on the **Paste Function** button (or on the **Insert** menu, click **Function...**)
5. The **Paste Function** dialog box appears. From the **Function category** list, select **Statistical**; from the **Function name** list, select the **NORMSDIST** function; and then click the **OK** button.
6. The input dialog box appears. In the **Z** input box, type **A2** or select cell A2 (representing the z-value) and return to the input dialog box. When finished, click the **OK** button.
7. **Copy** and **Paste** cell B2 into cells B3–B13.

Format the table (changing column widths, altering font sizes and styles, number format [e.g., 2 decimal places for the z-values and 6 decimal places for the Cumulative Distribution Function column], etc.) to make it clear and readable.

OUTPUT

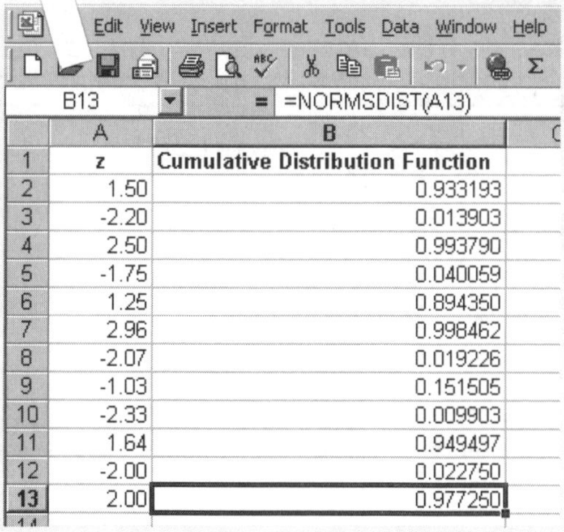

	A	B
1	z	Cumulative Distribution Function
2	1.50	0.933193
3	-2.20	0.013903
4	2.50	0.993790
5	-1.75	0.040059
6	1.25	0.894350
7	2.96	0.998462
8	-2.07	0.019226
9	-1.03	0.151505
10	-2.33	0.009903
11	1.64	0.949497
12	-2.00	0.022750
13	2.00	0.977250

The output (**Cumulative Distribution Function** column) generated by EXCEL contains the area from the left tail of the normal distribution to the given z-value. By referring to the normal curve diagrams, Example 9.3b parts (a) to (h) can be interpreted as follows:

a) Area to the left of $z = 1.50$ is 0.933193.
b) Area to the right of $z = -2.20$ is $(1 - 0.013903) = 0.986097$.
c) Area above $z = 2.50$ is $(1 - 0.993790) = 0.00621$.
d) Area below $z = -1.75$ is 0.040059.
e) Area between $z = 1.25$ and $z = 2.96$ is $(0.998462 - 0.894350) = 0.104112$.
f) Area between $z = -2.07$ and $z = -1.03$ is $(0.151505 - 0.019226) = 0.132279$.
g) Area between $z = -2.33$ and $z = 1.64$ is $(0.949497 - 0.009903) = 0.939594$.
h) Area below $z = -2.00$ or above $z = 2.00$ is $2(0.022750) = 0.0455$ or $(0.022750 + (1 - 0.977250))$.

D. *Finding the z Value for a Given Area*

To determine the z value, locate the nearest value to the given area in the body of Table 9.1. The corresponding z value is found by locating the first two digits in the left-hand column of the table and the last digit in the top row of the table.

For example, if the given area between μ and z is 0.4384, the nearest value in the table is 0.4382. This table value is associated with 1.5 in the left-hand column of the table and 0.04 in the top row. The z value corresponding to a table value of 0.4384 is approximately 1.54.

○ EXAMPLE 9.3c

Determine the z value for each of the following:

a) The area above the mean is 0.2734.
b) The area below the mean is 0.3670.
c) The area above z is 0.10.
d) The area below z is 0.05.
e) The area below z is 0.95.
f) The area above z is 0.99.

● SOLUTION

a) Since the area is above the mean μ, z is positive. The area 0.2734, located between μ and the desired z value, is listed in Table 9.1 and is associated with 0.7 in the left-hand column and 0.05 in the top row.

   Conclusion $z = +0.75$.

FIGURE 9.14 Normal Curve

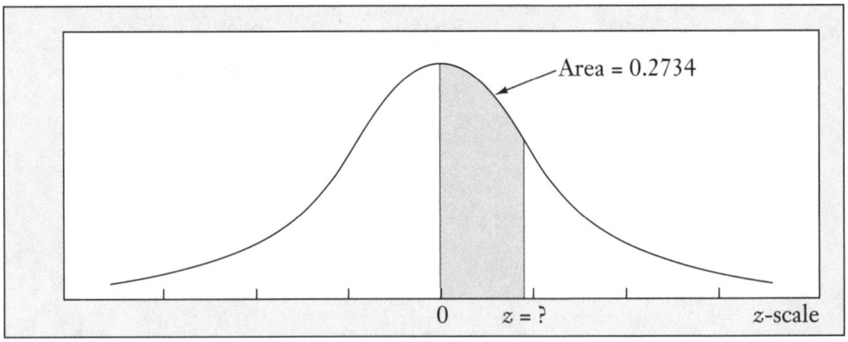

b) Since the area is below the μ, z is negative. The closest value in Table 9.1 to 0.3670 is 0.3665. This value is associated with a z value of 1.11.

Conclusion $z = -1.11$.

FIGURE 9.15 Normal Curve

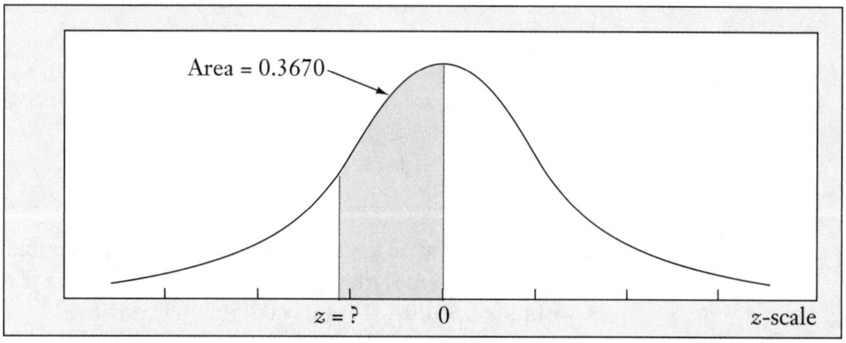

c) Since the given area is less than 0.50 and is above the desired z value, z must be positive. As the table values represent areas between μ and z, the area between μ and z is 0.5000 – 0.1000 = 0.4000. The table value closest to 0.4000 is 0.3997 and is associated with a z value of 1.28.

Conclusion $z = +1.28$.

FIGURE 9.16 Normal Curve

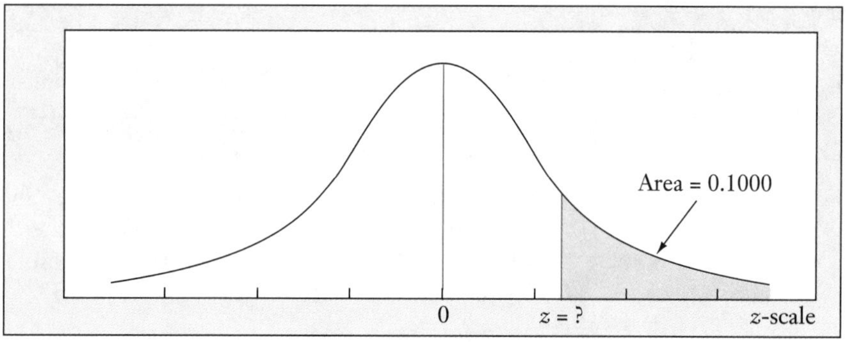

d) The given area is less than 0.5000 and below the desired z value. z is negative. The area between μ and z is 0.5000 – 0.0500 = 0.4500. The table values closest to 0.4500 are 0.4495 and 0.4505 associated with the z values of 1.64 and 1.65.

Conclusion z is approximately –1.645.

FIGURE 9.17 Normal Curve

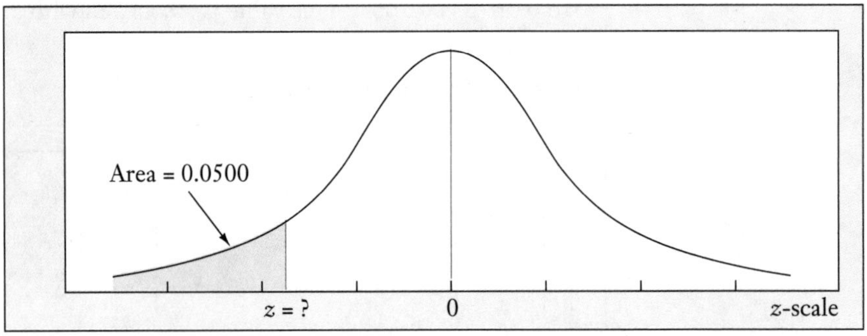

e) The given area is greater than 0.5000 and lies below the desired z value. The given area, made up of the area below the μ plus an area to the right of μ, is $0.9500 - 0.5000 = 0.4500$. z is positive.

Conclusion $z = +1.645$.

FIGURE 9.18 Normal Curve

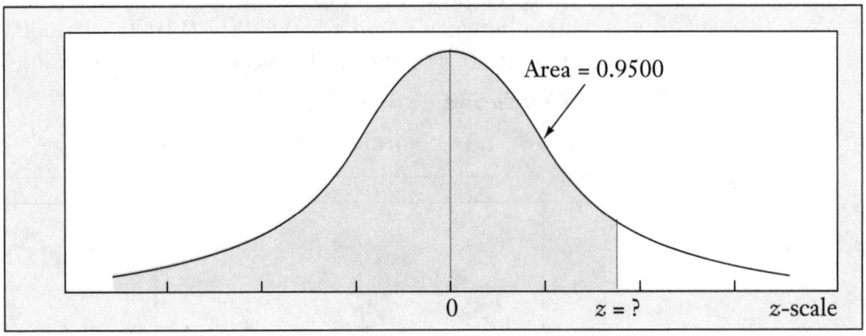

f) The given area is greater than 0.5000 and lies above the desired z value. The given area, made up of the area above μ plus an area to the left of μ, is $0.9900 - 0.5000 = 0.4900$. z is negative. The table value closest to 0.4900 is 0.4901 and is associated with a z value of 2.33.

Conclusion $z = -2.33$.

FIGURE 9.19 Normal Curve

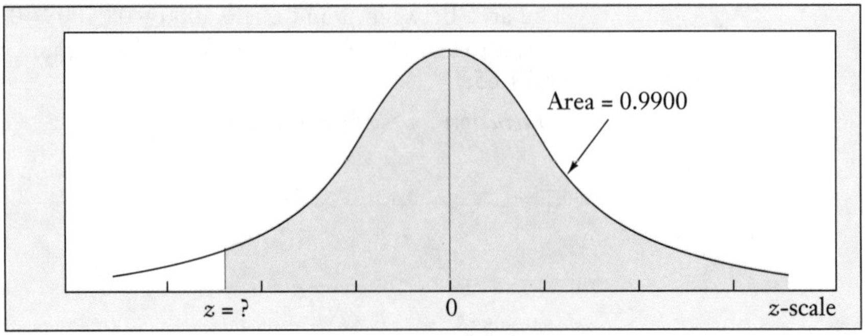

EXERCISE 9.3

1. In a normal distribution,
   a) the mean, median, and mode are __________ in value;
   b) the symbol μ represents the __________;
   c) the symbol σ represents the __________;
   d) the area under the normal curve to the left of μ is __________.

2. Using a table of areas under the normal curve, determine the area between μ and the following z values:
   a) $z = -1.30$ **b)** $z = 1.20$
   c) $z = 2.57$ **d)** $z = 1.0$
   e) $z = -0.55$ **f)** $z = -2.0$
   g) $z = -3.0$ **h)** $z = -1.0$

3. For a normal distribution with $\mu = 12.0$ and $\sigma = 3.00$, calculate z for the following values of x:
   a) $x = 9.0$ **b)** $x = 7.5$
   c) $x = 18.0$ **d)** $x = 12.3$
   e) $x = 20.5$ **f)** $x = 4.8$

4. Using a z-value table, determine the probability for each of the following:
   a) $-1.0 < z < 1.0$ **b)** $-2.0 < z < 1.0$
   c) $2.0 < z < 3.0$ **d)** $-2.0 < z < 2.0$
   e) $-3 < z < -2$ **f)** $-3 < z < 3$
   g) $-3 < z < -1$ **h)** $1 < z < 2$

5. Find the following shaded areas:

a)

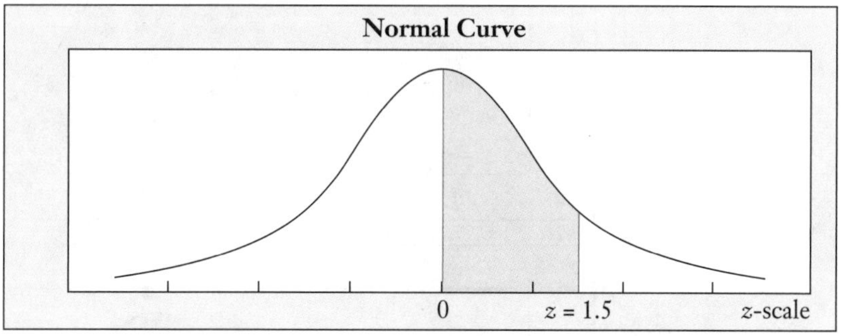

b)

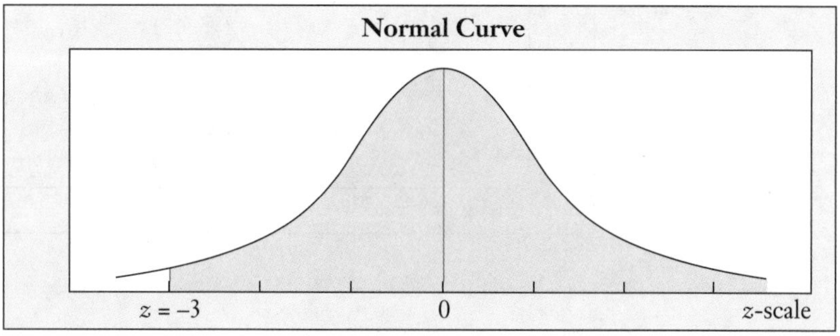

c)

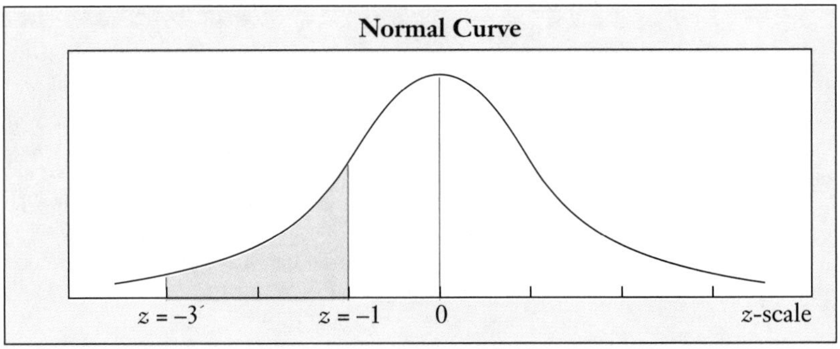
Normal Curve
z = −3
z = −1
0
z-scale

d)

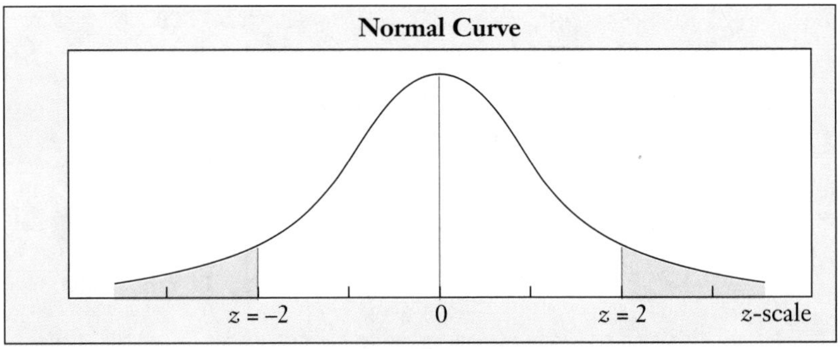
Normal Curve
z = −2
0
z = 2
z-scale

e)

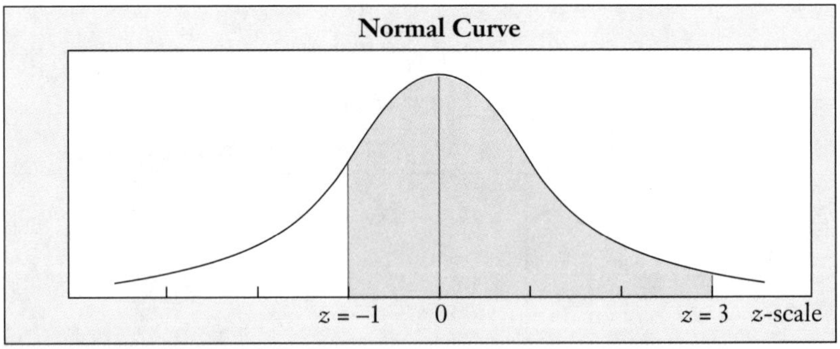
Normal Curve
z = −1
0
z = 3
z-scale

f)

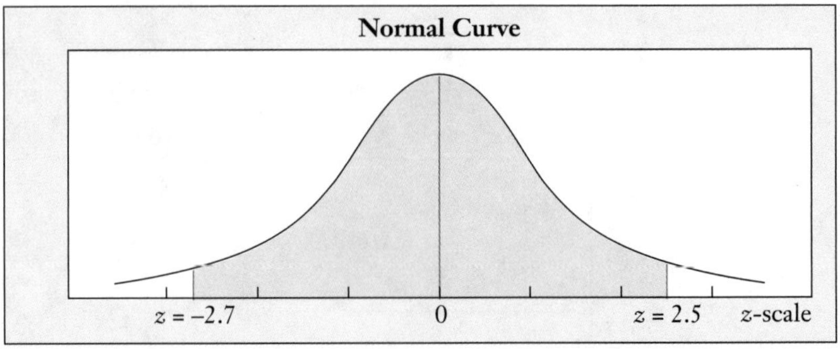
Normal Curve
z = −2.7
0
z = 2.5
z-scale

6. Find the z values associated with the following areas:

a)

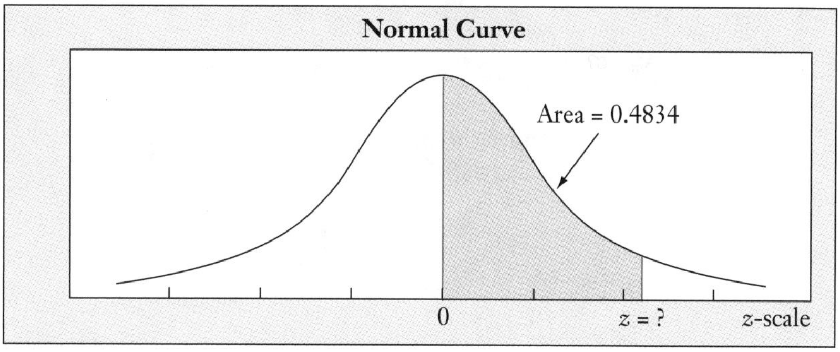

b)

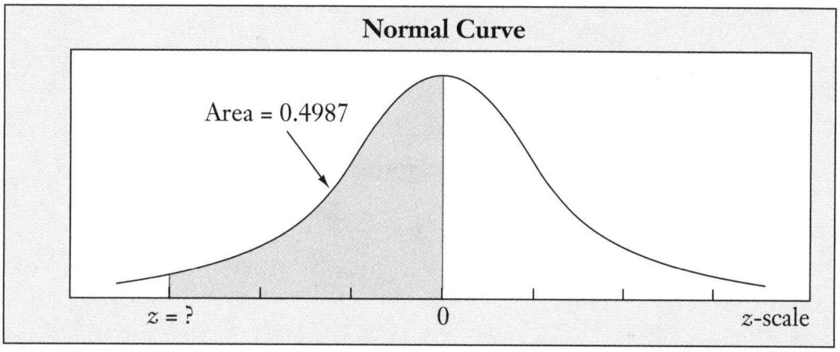

c)

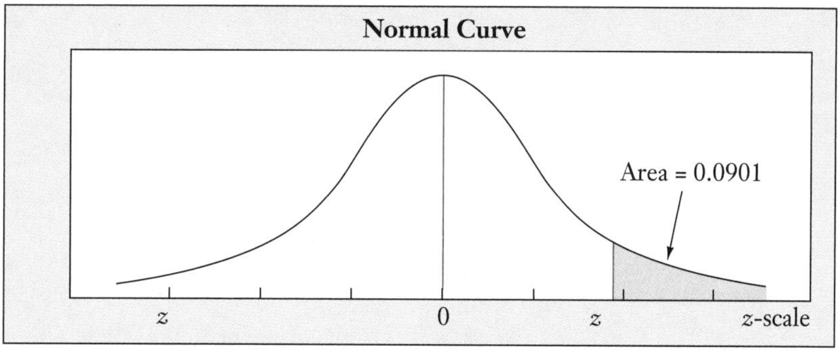

d)

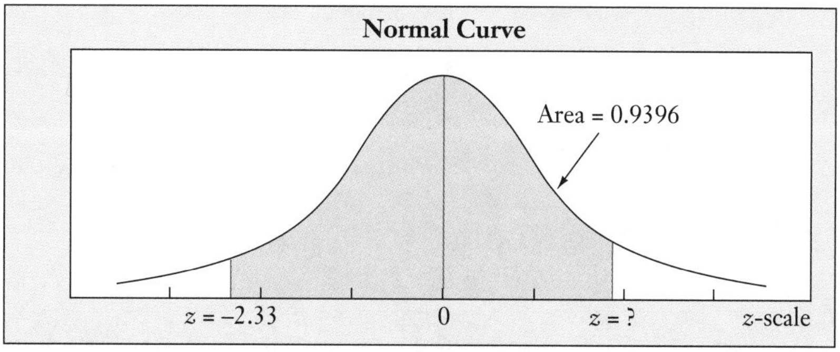

SECTION 9.4

Applications of the Normal Curve

EXAMPLE 9.4a

A distributor's accounts receivable show an average balance of \$200 with a standard deviation of \$50. Assuming that the balances are normally distributed, determine the proportion of the accounts that

a) exceed \$300;
b) are less than \$50;
c) are between \$50 and \$150;
d) are between \$125 and \$350.

SOLUTION

$\mu = 200$; $\sigma = 50$.

a) $z = \dfrac{x - \mu}{\sigma} = \dfrac{300 - 200}{50} = 2.00$. The area between μ and ($z = 2.00$) is 0.4772.
The required area = 0.5000 – 0.4772 = 0.0228.
2.28% of the accounts are expected to exceed \$300.

FIGURE 9.20 Normal Curve

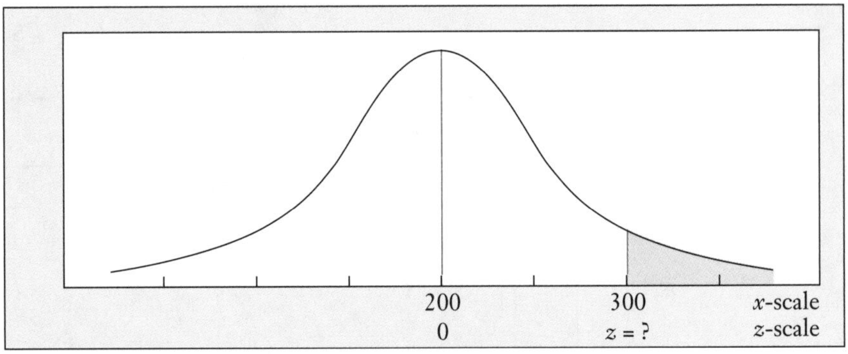

b) $z = \dfrac{50 - 200}{50} = -3.00$. The area between μ and z is 0.4987.
The required area = 0.5000 – 0.4987 = 0.0013.
0.13% of the accounts are expected to be less than \$50.

FIGURE 9.21 Normal Curve

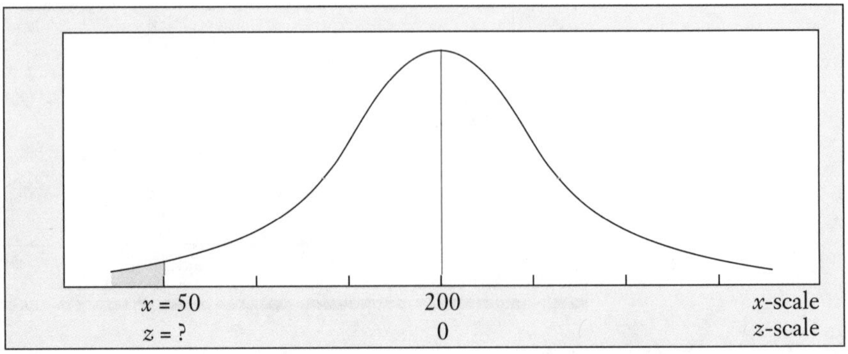

c) For $x_1 = 50$, $z_1 = \dfrac{50 - 200}{50} = -3.00$.
The area between μ and z_1 is 0.4987.
For $x_2 = 150$, $z_2 = \dfrac{150 - 200}{50} = -1.00$.
The area between μ and z_2 is 0.3413.
The required area = 0.4987 – 0.3413 = 0.1574.
15.74% of the accounts are expected to be between \$50 and \$150.

FIGURE 9.22 Normal Curve

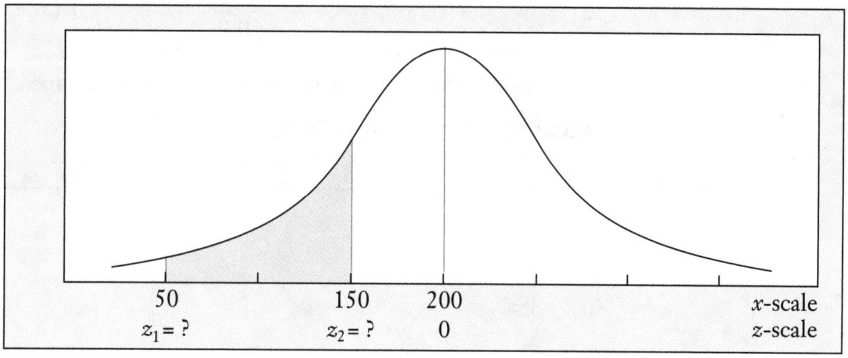

d) For $x_1 = 125$, $z_1 = \dfrac{125 - 200}{50} = -1.50$. The area between μ and z_1 is 0.4332.
For $x_2 = 350$, $z_2 = \dfrac{350 - 200}{50} = 3.00$.
The area between μ and ($z_2 = 3.00$) is 0.4987.
The required area = 0.4332 + 0.4987 = 0.9319.
93.19% of the accounts are expected to be between \$125 and \$350.

FIGURE 9.23 Normal Curve

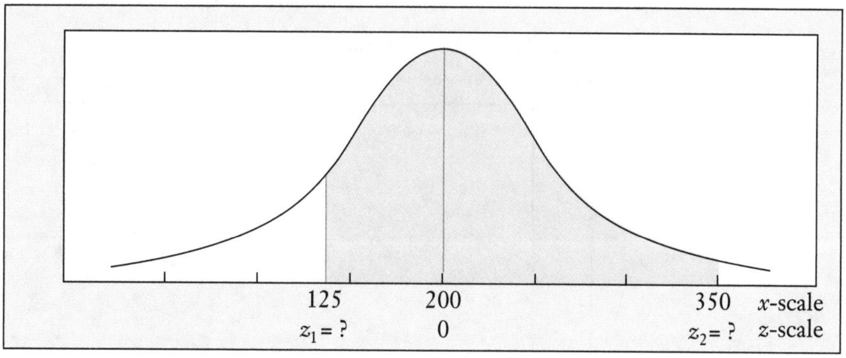

EXAMPLE 9.4b

The average price of a house in a certain area is \$500 000 with a standard deviation of \$50 000. Given that the distribution of the prices is a normal distribution,

a) determine the proportion of houses that will sell for less than \$450 000;
b) compute the limits within which the middle 50% of the house prices will be found.

SOLUTION

a) For $x = 450\ 000$, $z = \dfrac{450\ 000 - 500\ 000}{50\ 000} = -1.00$.
The required area is 0.5000 – 0.3413 = 0.1587.
15.87% of the houses in the area are expected to sell for less than \$450 000.

FIGURE 9.24 Normal Curve

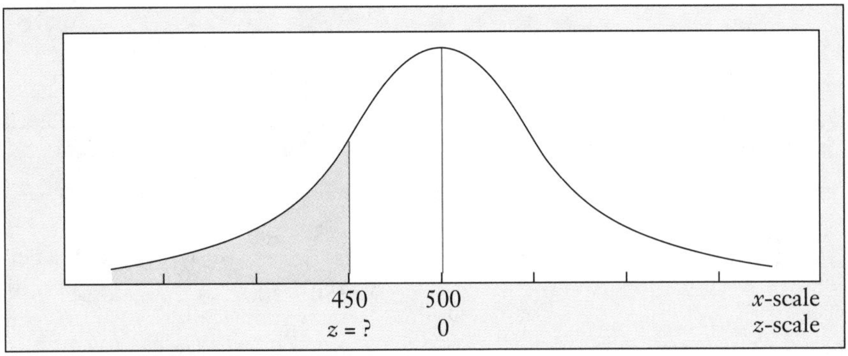

b) The middle 50% implies that 25% of the total area lies on either side of the mean μ. Let x_1 and x_2 represent the lower and upper limits respectively. The area between μ and x_2 is 0.2500. The closest value in Table 9.1 is 0.2486. The corresponding z value = 0.67.

FIGURE 9.25 Normal Curve

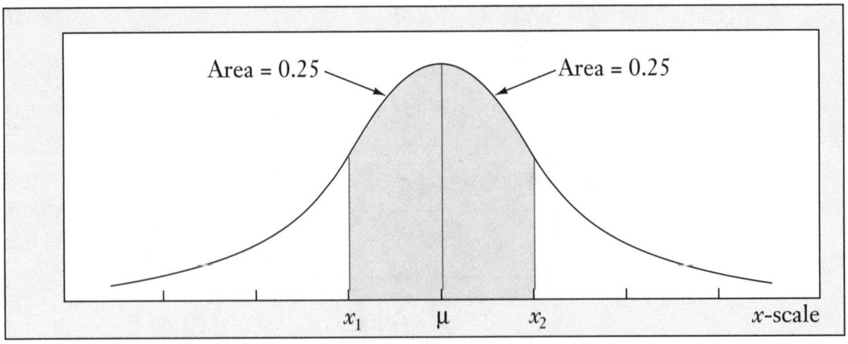

Substituting into Formula 9.1 $z = \frac{x - \mu}{\sigma}$, we obtain for the upper limit x_2

$$0.67 = \frac{x_2 - 500\,000}{50\,000}$$
$$0.67(50\,000) = x_2 - 500\,000$$
$$33\,500 = x_2 - 500\,000$$
$$x_2 = 533\,500$$

The upper limit is \$533 500.

For the lower limit, $z = -0.67$. Substituting into Formula 9.1

$$-0.67 = \frac{x_1 - 500\,000}{50\,000}$$
$$(-0.67)(50\,000) = x_1 - 500\,000$$
$$-33\,500 = x_1 - 500\,000$$
$$x_1 = 466\,500$$

The lower limit is \$466 500.
The middle 50% of the house prices are expected to lie between \$466 500 and \$533 500.

EXAMPLE 9.4c

A plastics manufacturer produces injection mouldings of a component for a complex assembly. For the assembly to work properly the minimum weight of the component must be 500 g. Thus, it is important to keep rejects (components weighing less than 500 g) to a minimum. If the weights of the components produced by the machine are normally distributed with a standard deviation of 10 g, for what weight should the machine be set so that no more than 5% of the components produced will be rejected?

SOLUTION

The desired weight is the mean weight μ.
The minimum acceptable weight $x = 500$ g.
The acceptable proportion of components with a weight less than 500 g = 0.05; the proportion of components between μ and the minimum acceptable weight = 0.45.

FIGURE 9.26 Normal Curve

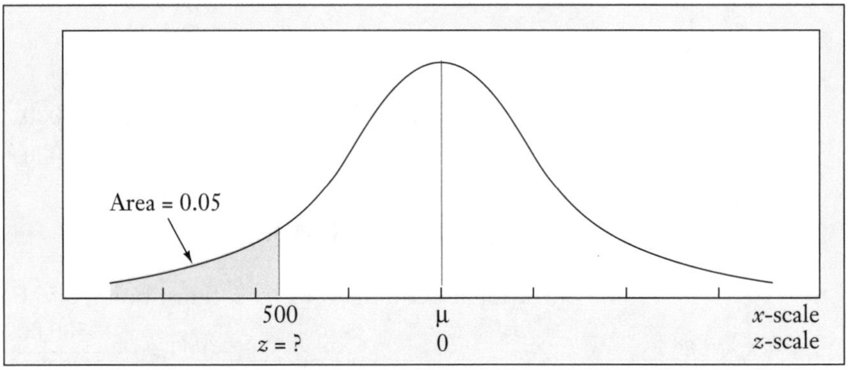

The closest values in Table 9.1 are 0.4495 and 0.4505.
The associated z values are 1.64 and 1.65. Since 0.45 is halfway between the two table values, a more precise value of $z = 1.645$.
Since $x = 500$ is located below the μ, $z = -1.645$.
The value of μ can be obtained by substituting into Formula 9.1

$$z = \frac{x - \mu}{\sigma}$$

$$-1.645 = \frac{500 - \mu}{10}$$

$$10(-1.645) = 500 - \mu$$

$$-16.45 = 500 - \mu$$

$$\mu = 516.45$$

The moulding machine should be set so that the mean weight of the components produced is 516.45 g.

EXAMPLE 9.4d

The plastics manufacturer in Example 9.4c has been told that if the machine is modified, the standard deviation can be reduced by 25% at a cost of $25 000. The cost of the plastic resin used in manufacturing the component is $2.00 per kg.

a) How many components would have to be produced to pay for the modification of the machine?
b) If the company manufactures two million components annually and requires a payback within two years, should management authorize the modification?

SOLUTION

a) The new standard deviation = 75% of 10 g = 7.5 g.
   $z = -1.645$; $x = 500$.

The new mean setting point for the machine would be

$$-1.645 = \frac{500 - \mu}{7.5}$$
$$-1.645(7.5) = 500 - \mu$$
$$-12.3375 = 500 - \mu$$
$$\mu = 512.34$$

The average amount of resin saved per component = 516.45 – 512.34 = 4.11 g.
The cost of resin per gram $\frac{\$2.00}{1000} = \$0.002$.
The average saving per component = 4.11(0.002) = \$0.008 22.
The number of components required to pay back the cost of modification $= \frac{25\ 000}{0.008\ 22} = 3\ 041\ 363$.

b) The number of years required to produce 3 041 363 components
$\frac{3\ 041\ 363}{2\ 000\ 000} = 1.52$.
Since 1.52 years is within the company guidelines for a payback period, management should authorize the modification of the machine.

EXERCISE 9.4

1. A normal distribution of 2400 observations has a mean of \$54.00 and a standard deviation of \$6.00. Complete each of the following:
   a) The value of $\mu - 3\sigma$ is \$__________.
   b) The value of $\mu + 3\sigma$ is \$__________.
   c) Since __________ % of the observations lie between $\mu + 3\sigma$ and $\mu - 3\sigma$, __________ observations lie between \$__________ and \$__________.
   d) Since the value of $\mu + 2\sigma$ is \$__________ and __________ % of all observations lie below $\mu + 2\sigma$, __________ observations have a value less than \$__________.

2. The lifespan of a particular brand of light bulb is normally distributed with a mean life of 400 h and a standard deviation of 12 h. Production for last week was 800 000 light bulbs. Use this information to answer the following questions.
   a) What is the z value of a light bulb having a life of 421 h?
   b) How many light bulbs can be expected to have a life of less than 379 h?
   c) What percent of the light bulbs should have a life less than 430 h?
   d) The life of the most short-lived 5% of the light bulbs will likely be less than how many hours?
   e) What percent of the light bulbs can be expected to have a life between 385 h and 415 h?
   f) How many of the light bulbs can be expected to have a life between 409 h and 427 h?
   g) How many of the light bulbs can be expected to have a life of more than 382 h?

3. For a normal distribution with $\mu = 3.5$ and $\sigma = 0.2$, find x if the area
   a) between μ and z is 0.4980;
   b) to the left of z is 0.9505;
   c) to the right of z is 0.0041;
   d) to the right of z is 0.6808;
   e) to the left of z is 0.0778;
   f) between $-z$ and $+z$ is 0.9544.

4. Eight hundred students applied to the popular Police Foundations program at the local college. Of the applicants, 60 were invited for an interview based on the mark obtained in an entrance examination. Of those interviewed, 32 were admitted to the program. The examination marks were normally distributed with a mean of 85 and a standard deviation of 4.6.
   a) What mark did an applicant have to achieve to receive an interview?
   b) What percent of the applicants were rejected based on the entrance examination?
   c) What percent of all applicants were admitted to the program?

SECTION 9.5

Using the Normal Distribution to Approximate the Binomial Distribution

When dealing with the binomial distribution we noted that its shape is symmetrical for all values of n if $p = 0.50$. When $p \neq 0.50$ the shape of a binomial distribution becomes more and more symmetrical as n increases and gets closer and closer to a normal distribution. In general, the normal distribution can be used as a good approximation of a binomial distribution when $np > 5$ and $np(1-p) > 5$.

A more simple approach accepts the premise that for practical purposes the binomial distribution approximates the normal distribution sufficiently closely when $n > 30$. This is the approach that this text uses.

In addition to the above conditions for using the normal distribution to approximate the binomial distribution, allowance should be made for the discrete nature of the binomial distribution. This involves the use of the so-called *continuity correction factor*. In some cases this involves adding one-half of a unit to the x values in the normal distribution. In other cases, half a unit should be subtracted.

However, since in most practical applications the increased accuracy is not significant and becomes minimal for larger values of n, this correction factor will not be considered in this text in order to avoid the increased computational complexity in solving problems.

○ EXAMPLE 9.5a

A public-opinion poll found that 54% of women in a certain group read newspapers. Calculate the probability that in a group of 100 such women,

a) at least 50 read newspapers;
b) no more than 46 read newspapers;
c) between 45 and 65 read newspapers;
d) between 30 and 50 read newspapers;
e) exactly 54 women read newspapers.

● SOLUTION

Since the poll of any one member in the group has just two possible outcomes, "read" or "not read," and the number of successes "read" is the result of counting, the corresponding probability distribution is binomial.

Since $n > 30$, the normal distribution can be used to approximate the binomial distribution.

$$\mu = np = 100(0.54) = 54$$
$$\sigma^2 = np(1-p) = 100(0.54)(0.46) = 24.84$$
$$\sigma = \sqrt{24.84} = 4.9840$$

a) The requirement of "at least 50 readers" covers the range 50 to 100. Let $x = 50$. The value $x = 50$ is less than μ. The probability $P(x \geq 50)$ is given by the area to the right of $x = 50$, as shown in the diagram.

FIGURE 9.27 Normal Curve

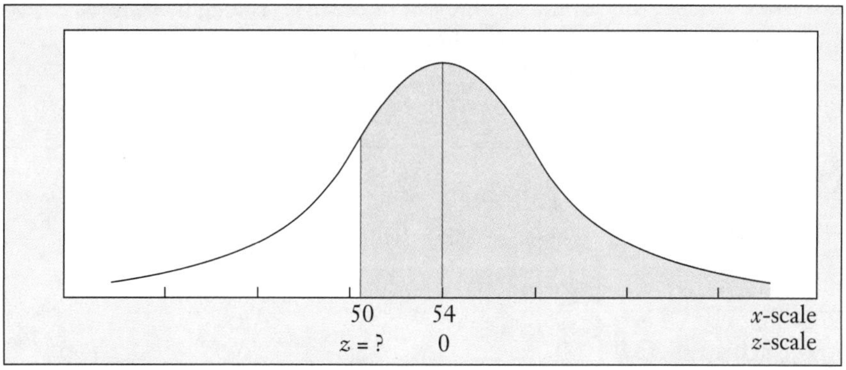

$$z = \frac{x-\mu}{\sigma} = \frac{50-54}{4.9840} = \frac{-4}{4.9840} = -0.80$$

The area between μ and ($z = -0.80$) is 0.2881. The required area is $0.2881 + 0.5000 = 0.7881$. The probability that at least 50 of the women will read newspapers is approximately 79%.

b) "No more than 46" covers the range 0 to 46. Let $x = 46$. The value $x = 46$ is smaller than μ and lies to the left of μ. The probability $P(x \leq 46)$ is given by the area to the left of $x = 46$ as shown in the diagram.

FIGURE 9.28 Normal Curve

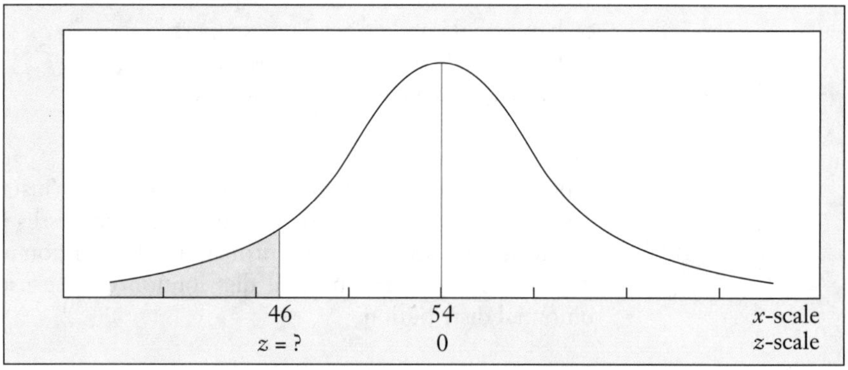

$$z = \frac{46 - 54}{4.9840} = \frac{-8}{4.9840} = -1.61$$

The area between μ and $z = -1.61$ is 0.4463. The required area is $0.5000 - 0.4463 = 0.0537$. The probability that no more than 46 of the women read newspapers is approximately 5%.

c) "Between 45 and 65" covers the range 45 to 65. Let $x_1 = 45$ and $x_2 = 65$. The value $x_1 = 45$ lies below μ, while the value $x_2 = 65$ lies above μ. The probability $P(45 \leq x \leq 65)$ is given by the area between $x_1 = 45$ and $x_2 = 65$, as shown in the diagram.

FIGURE 9.29 Normal Curve

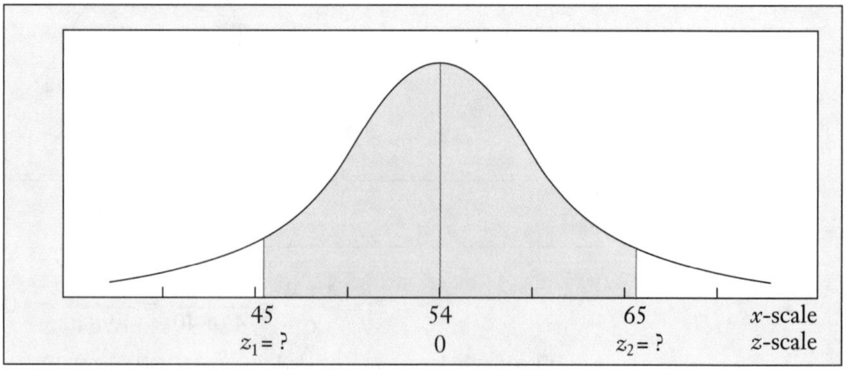

For $x_1 = 45$, $z_1 = \frac{45 - 54}{4.9840} = \frac{-9}{4.9840} = -1.81.$

For $x_2 = 65$, $z_2 = \frac{65 - 54}{4.9840} = \frac{11}{4.9880} = 2.21.$

The area between μ and x_1 is 0.4649. The area between μ and x_2 is 0.4864. The required area is 0.4649 + 0.4864 = 0.9513. The probability that between 45 and 65 of the women read newspapers is approximately 95%.

d) "Between 30 and 50" covers the range 30 to 50. Let $x_1 = 30$ and $x_2 = 50$. Both values are smaller than μ and lie below μ. The probability $P(30 \le x \le 50)$ is given by the area between z_1 and z_2, as shown in the diagram.

FIGURE 9.30 Normal Curve

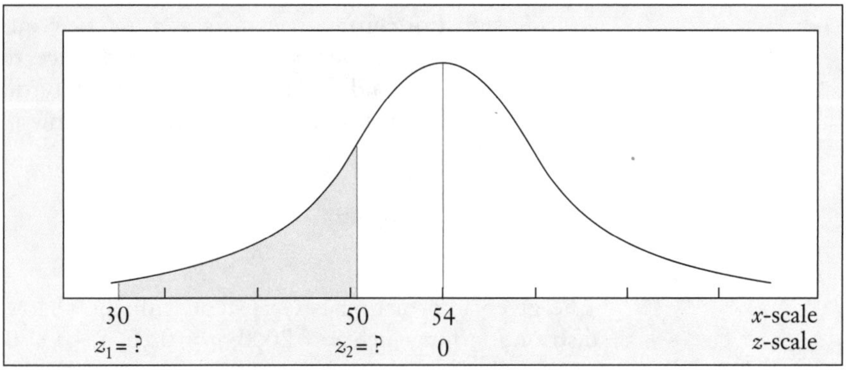

For $x_1 = 30$, $z_1 = \dfrac{30 - 54}{4.9840} = \dfrac{-24}{4.9840} = -4.82.$

For $x_2 = 50$, $z_2 = \dfrac{50 - 54}{4.9840} = \dfrac{-4}{4.9840} = -0.80.$

The z_1 value −4.82 exceeds the range covered by Table 9.1. The greatest value in the table is 0.4990 for $z = 3.09$.

The area between μ and x_1 can be assumed to be 0.4999. The area between μ and x_2 is 0.2881. The required area is 0.4999 − 0.2881 = 0.2118. The probability that between 30 and 50 women read newspapers is approximately 21%.

e) For "exactly 54" we need to create an interval. This is done by adding and subtracting 0.5 from 54. This means that $x_1 = 54.5$ and $x_2 = 53.5$.

FIGURE 9.31 Normal Curve

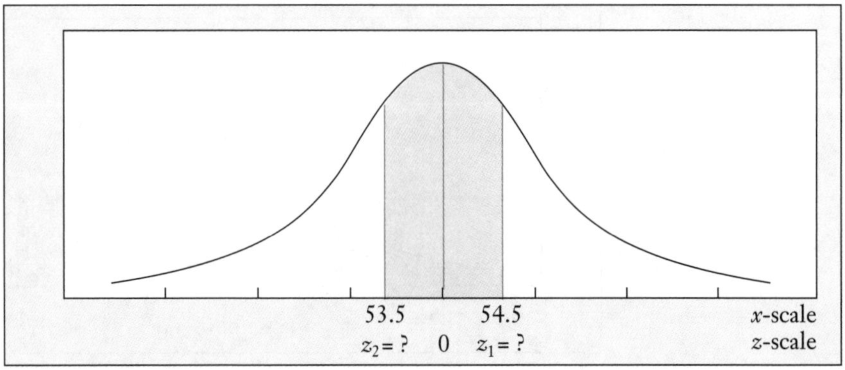

For $x_1 = 54.5$, $z_1 = \dfrac{54.5 - 54}{4.9840} = 0.10.$

For $x_2 = 53.5$, $z_2 = \dfrac{53.5 - 54}{4.9840} = -0.10.$

The area between μ and x_1 is 0.0398, as is the area between μ and x_2. The required area = 2(0.0398) = 0.0796. The probability that exactly 54 of the women read newspapers is approximately 8%.

EXAMPLE 9.5b

A professional organization mails a salary survey questionnaire to its 2000 members every year and knows from experience that about 20% of the members will respond. Determine the probability that the response by the membership to the current mailing will be as follows:

a) fewer than 375;
b) more than 440;
c) between 375 and 440.

SOLUTION

The given information is consistent with the characteristics of a binomial distribution for which $n = 2000$, $p = 0.20$, $1 - p = 0.80$. Since $n > 30$, the normal distribution can be used to approximate the binomial distribution.

$$\mu = np = 2000(0.20) = 400;$$
$$\sigma^2 = np(1 - p) = 2000(0.20)(0.80) = 320;$$
$$\sigma = \sqrt{320} = 17.89.$$

a) Let $x = 375$.

$$z = \frac{375 - 400}{17.89} = \frac{-25}{17.89} = -1.40$$

The area between μ and x is 0.4192. The required area = 0.5000 − 0.4192 = 0.0808. The probability that fewer than 375 members will respond is approximately 8.08%.

FIGURE 9.32 Normal Curve

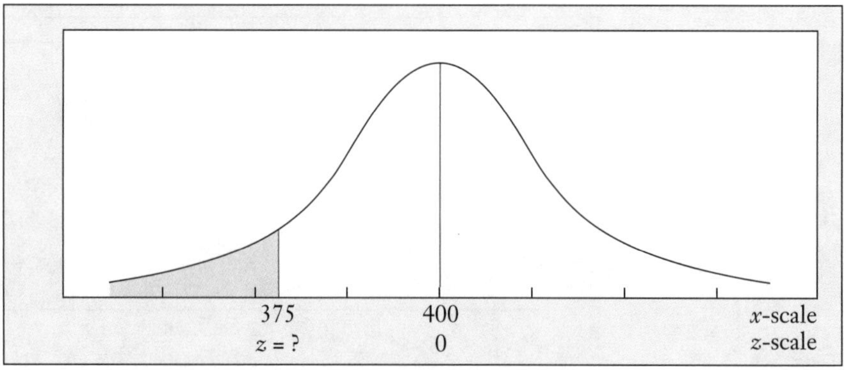

b) Let $x = 440$.

$$z = \frac{440 - 400}{17.89} = \frac{40}{17.89} = 2.24$$

The area between μ and x is 0.4875. The required area = 0.5000 − 0.4875 = 0.0125. The probability that more than 440 members will respond is approximately 1.25%.

FIGURE 9.33 Normal Curve

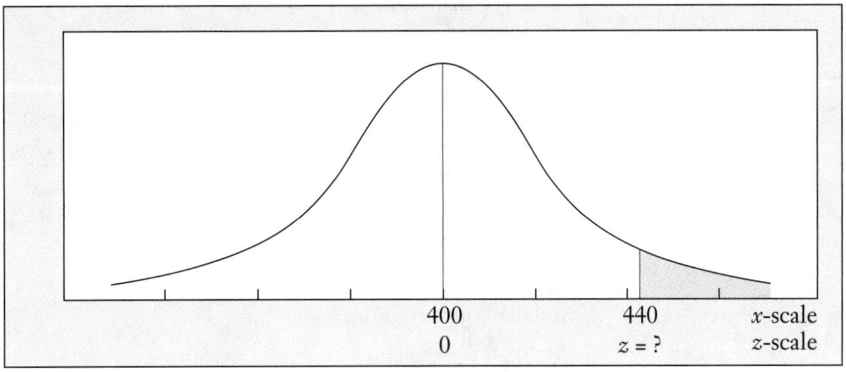

c) Let $x_1 = 375$ and $x_2 = 440$.

For x_1, $$z_1 = \frac{375 - 400}{17.89} = -1.40.$$

For x_2, $$z_2 = \frac{440 - 400}{17.89} = 2.24.$$

The area between μ and x_1 is 0.4192, and the area between μ and x_2 is 0.4875. The required area = (0.4192 + 0.4875) = 0.9067. The probability that between 375 and 440 members will respond is approximately 90.67%.

FIGURE 9.34 Normal Curve

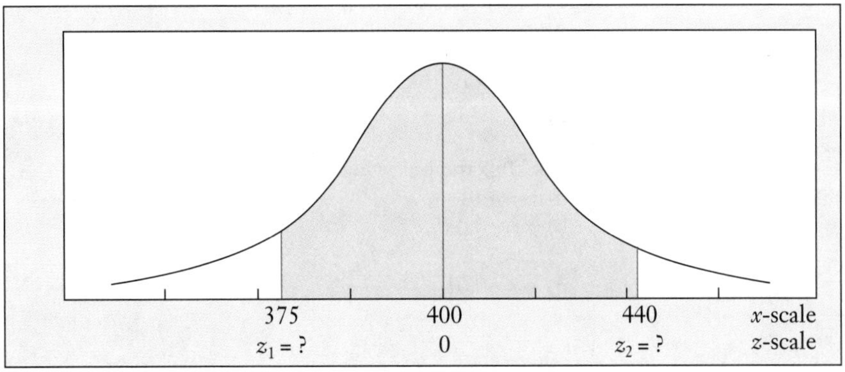

Note The three problems cover the total area. The sum of the probabilities $= (0.0808 + 0.0125 + 0.9067) = 1.0000$.

EXERCISE 9.5

1. The senior sales agent for Randy's Real Estate Company closes a deal 65% of the time. If the manager believes that the agent will see 60 buyers next month, what is the probability that the agent's sales will be
   a) fewer than 30?
   b) more than 45?
   c) between 38 and 42?

2. A computer designed to understand spoken language is 60% accurate. If an 800-word letter is dictated to the computer, what is the probability that
   a) more than 500 words will be correct?
   b) between 450 and 520 words will be correct?
   c) fewer than 400 words will be correct?

3. Given that $n = 400$, $p = 80\%$, use the normal distribution to calculate the following probabilities:
   a) $P(x \leq 300)$
   b) $P(x \geq 328)$
   c) $P(300 \leq x \leq 305)$

4. Given that $n = 3000$, $p = 10\%$, use the normal distribution to compute the following probabilities:
   a) $P(x \geq 260)$
   b) $P(320 \leq x \leq 350)$
   c) $P(x \leq 275)$

REVIEW EXERCISE

1. Look up the following values in a z table:
   a) $z = 0.65$
   b) $z = -1.82$
   c) $z = -3.04$
   d) $z = 2.33$

2. Look up the following values in the z table.
   a) $z = 1.01$
   b) $z = -0.05$
   c) $z = 3.09$
   d) $z = -0.01$

3. Tony was asked to look up the table value corresponding to $z = -2.01$. He said the value is 0.4821. Tina disagrees. If Tina is right, what z value did Tony look up?

4. You have been asked to look up the table value corresponding to $z = -0.02$. Your friend has told you it is one of the following: 0.0793, 0.4772, or 0.0080. Which is the correct answer?

5. Using a table of values under the normal curve, determine the areas for the following:
   a) $1.57 \leq z \leq 3.02$
   b) $z \leq -1.63$
   c) $-2.83 \leq z \leq -0.38$
   d) $z \geq 2.34$
   e) $-1.64 \leq z \leq 1.64$

6. Using a table of values under the normal curve, determine the areas for the following:
   a) $1.0 \leq z \leq 2.0$
   b) $z \leq -3.09$
   c) $-1.5 \leq z \leq 0.5$
   d) $z \geq 0.01$
   e) $1.1 \leq z \leq 1.1$

7. What z values when doubled will also double the area (by using the table)?

8. What z values when tripled will also triple the area (by using the table)?

9. For the following areas under the normal curve, determine the corresponding z values:
   a) the area to the right of z is 0.01;
   b) the area above z is 0.95;
   c) the area below z is 0.02;
   d) the area to the left of z is 0.90;
   e) the area between $-z$ and z is 0.95;
   f) the area between $-z$ and z is 0.98.

10. For the following areas under the normal curve, determine the corresponding z values:
    a) the area to the right of z is 0.99;
    b) the area above z is 0.0010;
    c) the area below z is 0.9890;
    d) the area to the left of z is 0.1401;
    e) the area between $-z$ and z is 0.0240;
    f) the area between $-z$ and z is 0.9616.

11. Determine the z value for the following probabilities:
a) $P(\mu \le x \le z) = 0.4505$
b) $P(-z \le x \le \mu) = 0.4901$
c) $P(x \le z) = 0.9207$
d) $P(x \ge -z) = 0.9986$
e) $P(x \le -z) = 0.0322$
f) $P(x \ge z) = 0.0401$

12. Determine the z value for the following probabilities:
a) $P(\mu \le x \le z) = 0.4989$
b) $P(-z \le x \le \mu) = 0.2123$
c) $P(x \le z) = 0.8438$
d) $P(x \ge -z) = 0.9985$
e) $P(x \le -z) = 0.0023$
f) $P(x \ge z) = 0.1492$

13. For a normal distribution, where $\mu = 70$ and $\sigma = 6$, calculate z for the following values of x:
(a)73 **(b)** 69 **(c)** 60 **(d)** 85 **(e)** 90 **(f)** 52

14. For a normal distribution, where the mean fill–value of a can (μ) is 355 mL and the standard deviation (σ) is 10, calculate z values for the following values of x:
(a) 345 **(b)** 350 **(c)** 356 **(d)** 360 **(e)** 365

15. Given $\sigma = 0.4$ and $z = -2.5$, determine the mean for $x = 6.8$.

16. Given $\mu = 200$ g and $z = -1.5$, determine σ for $x = 190$ g.

17. The average family income in the city of Tortola is \$65 000, with a standard deviation of \$9000. Assuming that family income is normally distributed, determine the income level below which 80% of the families in Tortola live.

18. The average tuition in Ontario community colleges is \$2500 with a standard deviation of \$250. Assuming that the tuition is normally distributed, determine the tuition level above which 80% of the students pay.

19. Sheridan College's Police Foundations Program received 1200 applications for 30 openings. The grades of the applicants were normally distributed with a mean of 78 and a standard deviation of 6. If applicants are chosen on the basis of grades, what will be the cutoff grade to fill the 30 openings?

20. Normally distributed observations such as a person's height or shoe size occur quite frequently in nature. Business people who are aware of this use it to their advantage. A purchasing agent for a large retailer buying 10 000 pairs of men's shoes uses the normal curve to decide on the order quantities for the various sizes. If men's average shoe size is 9 with a standard deviation of 1.5, what quantity should be ordered between sizes 7 and 11?

21. Amazed at the large choice of mutual funds, an investor used the published five-year performance reports in selecting a mutual fund. The investor determined that the return on investment for 120 funds over the five-year period was normally distributed with a mean of 32% and a standard deviation of 8.2%. Further study of the funds indicated that funds in the top decile were high-risk investments. To narrow the choice, the investor decided to consider only those funds between the 80th and 90th percentile.

a) Determine the returns on investment that correspond to the 80th and the 90th percentile.

b) What was the number of funds from which the investor had to make a choice?

22. A survey of cars in a mall parking lot found that 105 of 420 cars were imports. If a random sample of 80 of the drivers is taken, what is the probability that 26 or fewer of the drivers have imported cars?

23. A survey at a Toronto college found 40 students out of 100 were landed immigrants. If a random sample of 20 students is taken, what is the probability that 5 or fewer are landed immigrants?

24. Tabulation of a strike vote showed that 55% of those voting cast their ballot in favour of strike action. If 50 voters are randomly selected, what is the probability that at least 24 of them voted in favour of strike action?

25. (CGA) Suppose 90% of the account receivables of a company are free of errors. A random sample of 20 such accounts is drawn. Determine, using the normal approximation to the binomial distribution, the probability that at least 18 out of these accounts are free of errors.

26. (CGA) A quality-control engineer has determined that if the manufacturing process is working properly, then, on average, only 10% of the items produced will be defective. Assume that the process is working properly. The manufactured items are packed in boxes each containing 100 items. A box is considered acceptable if it contains no more than 10 defectives items. Determine the probability that a randomly chosen box is acceptable. Use the normal approximation to the binomial.

SELF-TEST

Questions **1** through **7** are based on the following sales invoice data:

	Company		
Statistical measure	AB	LM	ST
Arithmetic mean	480	525	400
Median	490	509	400
Mode	510	477	400
Standard deviation	40	50	32
Mean deviation	32	40	26
Quartile deviation	25	32	20

1. Which company's invoice amounts are most likely normally distributed?

2. Estimate the range of the invoice amounts of company ST.

3. Above what sales amount do 75% of the sales invoices of company LM fall? (Hint: Use the median.)

4. Outside what amounts do a total of 4.56% of the sales invoices of company ST fall?

5. Between what amounts do 50% of the sales invoices of company AB fall? (Hint: Use the median.)

6. If the statistical measures for company ST are based on 600 invoices, how many show amounts between \$350 and \$450?

7. Determine the probability that a sales invoice of company ST will be at least \$495.

8. The distribution of order sizes for Macrae Company is normal, with a mean of \$1500 and a standard deviation of \$225.
a) What is the z value for an order of \$1700?
b) What proportion of the orders can be expected to be less than \$1200?
c) Out of 600 orders, how many are expected to fall between \$1600 and \$2000?

9. Phone calls to the customer service department of Nichol's Equipment Company concern warranty service 60% of the time. If 200 phone calls are taken, what is the probability
a) that fewer than 100 phone calls were for warranty work?
b) that fewer than 135 phone calls were for warranty work?

For an online glossary, go to **www.pearsoned.ca/hummelbrunner**.

Key Terms

Normal curve 289
Normal distribution 289
Standard normal deviate 295
Standard normal distribution 295
***z* value** 294

Summary of Formulas

Standardized normal variable

$$z = \frac{\text{ACTUAL DEVIATION}}{\text{STANDARD DEVIATION}} = \frac{x - \mu}{\sigma}$$ ←*Formula* **9.1**

CHAPTER 10

Sampling Distributions

Introduction

In most situations it is either physically or economically impractical to examine every item in a sample space. In order to obtain information about an entire set of data a technique called sampling is used.

Learning Outcomes

Upon completion of this chapter you will be able to

1. discuss the importance of sampling and the main reasons for sampling;
2. distinguish between a population and a sample;
3. state the relationship between the characteristics of a population (parameters) and of a sample (statistics) drawn from the population;
4. discuss the symbols used to differentiate between population parameters and sample statistics;
5. describe the properties of the sampling distribution of the means and of the sampling distribution of proportions;
6. use the properties to solve problems.

SECTION 10.1

Sampling Considerations

A. The Importance of Sampling

Sampling involves selecting a portion of the population (the entire set of data) that is most representative of the population. The purpose of sampling is to provide sufficient information so that conclusions (inferences) can be drawn about the characteristics of the population.

B. Reasons for Sampling

1. *Physical constraints.* It is often physically impossible to enumerate all items in a population.
2. *Time constraints.* Even if a census is physically possible, it is usually too time-consuming to be practical.
3. *Cost constraints.* It costs money to collect information. Obtaining information from a small portion of a population is less costly than taking a complete census of the population.
4. *Test constraints.* In many cases of industrial quality control, the item tested is destroyed during the test. In such cases, sampling is the only practical means of testing.

C. Sampling Methods

A variety of sampling methods are available. The different methods can be categorized under two main headings:

1. *Probability sampling.* In these methods, items are selected at random from the population and the probability of selecting the items is known.
2. *Non-probability sampling.* In these methods, items are selected from the population according to the judgement or purpose of the researcher.

No one method of sampling is best. The appropriate method is determined by the nature of the population, the skill of the researcher, and the economics of collecting data.

A detailed examination of sampling surveys and sampling methods is beyond the scope of this text.

D. Sampling Concepts

1. *Population versus sample.* By **population** we mean the total of *all items* in the group of items in which we are interested. By **sample** we mean a *portion* of the population that has been selected for study.

   For example, if we are interested in the distribution of statistics marks for all 35 students registered in a statistics class, the population consists of the 35 statistics marks. If 10 marks are selected from the 35 marks, the 10 marks represent a sample.
2. *Finite population versus infinite population.* A **finite population** is a population that consists of a limited and specifically known number of items.

An **infinite population** is a population for which the number of items is unlimited or for which the number of items is not specifically known. For practical purposes, a population consisting of a large number of items can be considered to be an infinite population.

For example, a class known to consist of 35 students is a finite population, whereas the total number of trees in Canadian forests is considered to be an infinite population.

3. *Parameter versus statistic.* A **parameter** is a measure describing a *characteristic of a population*, such as the population mean and the population standard deviation. A **statistic** is a measure describing a *characteristic of a sample*, such as the sample mean and the sample standard deviation.

   For example, if the average statistics mark for a class of 35 students is known to be 70, the mean of 70 is a parameter. If the average mark for a sample of 10 students taken from the class is 68, the mean of 68 is a statistic.

E. Summary of Distinctions between Population and Sample

In dealing with populations and samples we must keep in mind the difference in meaning of the terms parameter and statistic and the symbols used for both.

For population parameters we use Greek letter symbols such as μ, σ, and π. For sample statistics we use Roman letters such as $\bar{x}$, s, and p.

TABLE 10.1 Population versus Sample

Area of distinction	Population	Sample
Definition	Consists of all items in a group.	Consists of a selected portion of the group.
Characteristics	Are called parameters.	Are called statistics.
Symbols used	Greek letters	Roman letters
Mean	μ	$\bar{x}$
Standard deviation	σ	s
Proportion	π	p

F. Statistical Inference

If a sample is representative of the population, the sample results will reasonably mirror the population from which the sample was taken and can be used to estimate population characteristics.

The sample mean $\bar{x}$ is used to estimate the population mean μ. The sample standard deviation s is used to estimate the population standard deviation σ. The sample proportion p is used to estimate the population proportion π.

SECTION 10.2

The Sampling Distribution of the Means

A. Sampling Variation and the Sampling Distribution of the Means

When selecting a sample from a population, we can expect that the sample mean $\bar{x}$ will differ from the population mean μ. Furthermore, when selecting samples of a given size from a population, we can expect different samples to have different means. This variation in the possible sample means is referred to as **sampling variation**.

If all possible samples of a given size n are obtained from a population and their sample means are computed, the *listing of all sample means* forms a distribution referred to as the **sampling distribution of the means.**

B. Sampling Distribution of the Means Illustrated

EXAMPLE 10.2a

A group of four students had weekly study times as shown below:

Student	A	B	C	D
Hours per week	4	6	8	10

Construct the sampling distribution of the means for samples of size $n = 2$.

SOLUTION

The sampling distribution of the means is obtained by listing all possible samples of size $n = 2$, and computing the mean of each sample as shown in Table 10.2.

The listing of the values obtained as the means of all the possible samples represents the sampling distribution of the means, illustrated in Figure 10.1.

TABLE 10.2 Sampling Distribution of the Means

Possible samples of size $n = 2$		Calculation of sample means	Sampling distribution of the means $n = 2$
Students	Hours		
A, B	4, 6	$\frac{4+6}{2}$	5
A, C	4, 8	$\frac{4+8}{2}$	6
A, D	4, 10	$\frac{4+10}{2}$	7
B, C	6, 8	$\frac{6+8}{2}$	7
B, D	6, 10	$\frac{6+10}{2}$	8
C, D	8, 10	$\frac{8+10}{2}$	9

FIGURE 10.1 Graph of the Sampling Distribution of the Means

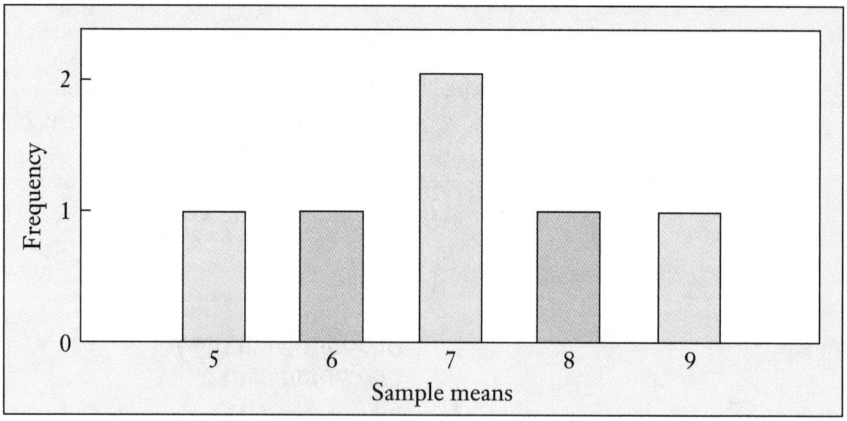

C. *The Mean of the Sampling Distribution of the Means*

The *mean of the sampling distribution of the means*, denoted by the symbol $\mu_{\bar{x}}$, is given by

$$\mu_{\bar{x}} = \frac{\text{SUM OF ALL POSSIBLE SAMPLE MEANS FOR THE GIVEN SAMPLE SIZE}}{\text{NUMBER OF POSSIBLE SAMPLES OF SIZE } n}$$

In our case the number of samples = 6 and their means are as listed in Table 10.2.

$$\mu_{\bar{x}} = \frac{5+6+7+7+8+9}{6} = \frac{42}{6} = 7$$

A useful relationship between the mean of the sampling distribution of the means $\mu_{\bar{x}}$ and the population mean μ can be obtained by comparing $\mu_{\bar{x}}$ and μ:

$$\text{The population mean, } \mu = \frac{4+6+8+10}{4} = \frac{28}{4} = 7.$$

The implication is that the mean of the sampling distribution of the means equals the population mean.

$$\mu_{\bar{x}} = \mu$$ ←*Formula* 10.1

D. *Standard Deviation of the Sampling Distribution of the Means*

While $\mu_{\bar{x}} = \mu$, the individual sample means $\bar{x}$ differ from $\mu_{\bar{x}}$ and therefore from μ. To determine the extent to which a sample mean $\bar{x}$ can be expected to differ from the population mean μ, a measure of dispersion known as the *standard deviation of the sampling distribution of the means* can be computed. This standard deviation is denoted by $\sigma_{\bar{x}}$ and is commonly referred to as the **standard error.** The computation of the standard error is shown in Table 10.3.

TABLE 10.3 Computation of the Standard Deviation of the Sampling Distribution of the Means

Sample	Sample mean $\bar{x}$	Deviation of the sample mean from the population mean, $(\bar{x}-\mu)$	Squared deviation $(\bar{x}-\mu)^2$
A, B	5	$5-7=-2$	4
A, C	6	$6-7=-1$	1
A, D	7	$7-7=\ 0$	0
B, C	7	$7-7=\ 0$	0
B, D	8	$8-7=\ 1$	1
C, D	9	$9-7=\ 2$	4
			$\sum(\bar{x}-\mu)^2 = 10$

$$\text{VARIANCE} = \frac{\sum(\bar{x}-\mu)^2}{\text{NUMBER OF SAMPLES}} = \frac{10}{6} = \frac{5}{3}$$

$$\text{The standard error, } \sigma_{\bar{x}} = \sqrt{\frac{5}{3}}$$

E. *Relationship between the Standard Error* $\sigma_{\bar{x}}$ *and the Population Standard Deviation* σ

The standard deviation of the sampling distribution of the means — that is, the standard error — can be obtained without the computations shown in Table 10.3 from the population standard deviation σ by means of the following formulas:

a) for infinite populations (N unknown),

$$\sigma_{\bar{x}} = \frac{\sigma}{\sqrt{n}} \qquad \leftarrow \textit{Formula } 10.2$$

and

b) for finite populations,

$$\sigma_{\bar{x}} = \frac{\sigma}{\sqrt{n}}\sqrt{\frac{N-n}{N-1}} \qquad \leftarrow \textit{Formula } 10.3$$

where N is the size of the population;
n is the sample size;
$\sqrt{\frac{N-n}{N-1}}$ is called the **finite correction factor**.

Note Without the finite (population) correction factor $\sqrt{\frac{N-n}{N-1}}$, Formula 10.3, the standard error for finite populations, is the same as Formula 10.2, the standard error for infinite populations. In practice, the finite correction factor is usually ignored unless the sample size n is larger than 10% of the population size N. In this book we will use the finite correction factor when N is known.

In our example, the population variance σ^2 and the standard deviation σ are readily obtainable by computing the individual squared deviations, as shown in Table 10.4.

TABLE 10.4 Computation of Population Variance

Student	Deviation $(x-\mu)$	Squared deviation $(x-\mu)^2$
A	$4-7=-3$	9
B	$6-7=-1$	1
C	$8-7=\ \ 1$	1
D	$10-7=\ \ 3$	9
		$\sum(x-\mu)^2=20$

$$\sigma^2 = \frac{\sum(x-\mu)^2}{N} = \frac{20}{4} = 5; \quad \sigma = \sqrt{5}$$

Since N is known, the population is finite. The appropriate formula is

$$\sigma_{\bar{x}} = \frac{\sigma}{\sqrt{n}}\sqrt{\frac{N-n}{N-1}}, \quad \text{where} \quad \sigma = \sqrt{5}, \quad N = 4, n = 2.$$

$$\sigma_{\bar{x}} = \frac{\sqrt{5}}{\sqrt{2}}\sqrt{\frac{4-2}{4-1}} = \frac{\sqrt{5}}{\sqrt{2}}\frac{\sqrt{2}}{\sqrt{3}} = \frac{(\sqrt{5})(\sqrt{2})}{(\sqrt{2})(\sqrt{3})} = \frac{\sqrt{5}}{\sqrt{3}} = \sqrt{\frac{5}{3}}$$

EXERCISE 10.2

1. The test scores for a group of students are given below:

Student	A	B	C	D	E
Test score	4	5	5	7	9

a) Determine the population mean and the population standard deviation.
b) Construct the sampling distribution of the means for samples of size $n = 3$.
c) Compute the mean of the sampling distribution of the means and establish that $\mu_{\bar{x}} = \mu$.
d) Compute the standard error from the basic data.
e) Use the appropriate formula to verify the result in **(d)**.

2. The number of hours of training received in the last quarter by a group of employees is listed below:

Employee	A	B	C	D	E	F
Training hours	8	9	6	8	9	5

a) Compute the population mean and the population standard deviation.
b) Construct the sampling distribution of the means for samples of size $n = 3$.
c) Determine $\mu_{\bar{x}}$ and establish that $\mu_{\bar{x}} = \mu$.
d) Compute $\sigma_{\bar{x}}$ from the basic data.
e) Use the appropriate formula to verify the result in **(d)**.

SECTION 10.3

Properties of the Sampling Distribution of the Means

The sampling distribution of the means has certain properties that are useful in drawing conclusions about populations from sample information. These properties are summarized as follows.

Property 1. The mean of the sampling distribution of the means is equal to the population mean, $\mu_{\bar{x}} = \mu$.

Property 2. The standard deviation of the sampling distribution of the means (referred to as the standard error) is given by

$$\sigma_{\bar{x}} = \frac{\sigma}{\sqrt{n}} \qquad \text{for infinite populations}$$

and

$$\sigma_{\bar{x}} = \frac{\sigma}{\sqrt{n}}\sqrt{\frac{N-n}{N-1}} \qquad \text{for finite populations.}$$

Property 3. If the sample size $n > 30$, the sampling distribution of the means will approximate the normal distribution.

Property 4. If the population is normally distributed, the sampling distribution of the means will be normal, regardless of sample size.

The following useful implications are based on properties 3 and 4:

a) There is a 68.26% chance that any sample mean will fall between $\mu \pm 1\sigma_{\bar{x}}$.
b) There is a 95.45% chance that any sample mean will fall between $\mu \pm 2\sigma_{\bar{x}}$.
c) There is a 99.73% chance that any sample mean will fall between $\mu \pm 3\sigma_{\bar{x}}$.

○ EXAMPLE 10.3a

Anne's Catering Service has selected a random sample of 100 orders. If it is known that the mean for all orders is \$120 and the standard deviation is \$25,

a) what is the mean of the sampling distribution of the means for sample size 100?
b) what is the standard deviation of the sampling distribution of the means?
c) what is the likelihood that the sample mean will fall between $\mu \pm 1\sigma_{\bar{x}}$?
d) what are the chances that the sample mean will fall between 115 and 125?
e) within what range of values does the sample mean have a 98% chance of falling?
f) what is the probability that the sample mean will fall within \$4 of the true mean?

● SOLUTION

$n = 100$; $\mu = 120$; $\sigma = 25$.

a) The mean of the sampling distribution of the means

$$\mu_{\bar{x}} = \mu = 120 \qquad \text{(Property 1).}$$

b) Since N is not known, the population is considered to be infinite. The standard deviation of the sampling distribution of the means (standard error)

$$\sigma_{\bar{x}} = \frac{\sigma}{\sqrt{n}} = \frac{25}{\sqrt{100}} = \frac{25}{10} = 2.5 \qquad \text{(Property 2).}$$

c) Since $n > 30$, the sampling distribution of the means will approximate the normal distribution. The likelihood that the sample mean will fall between $\mu \pm 1\sigma_{\bar{x}} = 68.26\%$ (Property 3).

d) For $\bar{x} = 115$,

$$z = \frac{115 - 120}{2.5} = \frac{-5}{2.5} = -2.0.$$

For $\bar{x} = 125$,

$$z = \frac{125 - 120}{2.5} = \frac{5}{2.5} = +2.0.$$

FIGURE 10.2 Sampling Distribution of the Means

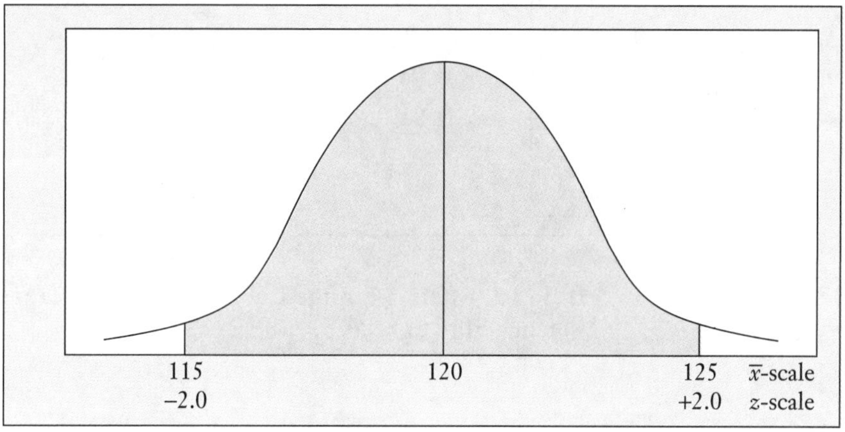

The range 115 to 125 represents the interval $\mu \pm 2\sigma_{\bar{x}}$. The likelihood that the sample mean will fall within this interval is 95.45%.

e) Let x_1 and x_2 represent the lower limit and the upper limit of the range respectively. For a normal distribution, the area between x_1 and x_2 is symmetrical about μ. The proportion of the area between μ and x_1 is 0.4900, as is the area between μ and x_2.

From Table 9.1, the z value associated with an area of 0.4900 is 2.33.

Substituting in the formula $z = \dfrac{\bar{x} - \mu}{\sigma_{\bar{x}}}$, we can compute the values for x_1 and x_2.

For x_1, $-2.33 = \dfrac{x_1 - 120}{2.50}$

$$-5.825 = x_1 - 120$$
$$x_1 = 114.175$$

For x_2, $2.33 = \dfrac{x_2 - 120}{2.50}$

$$5.825 = x_2 - 120$$
$$x_2 = 125.825$$

For a 98% chance, the range will be \$114.175 to \$125.825.

FIGURE 10.3 Sampling Distribution of the Means

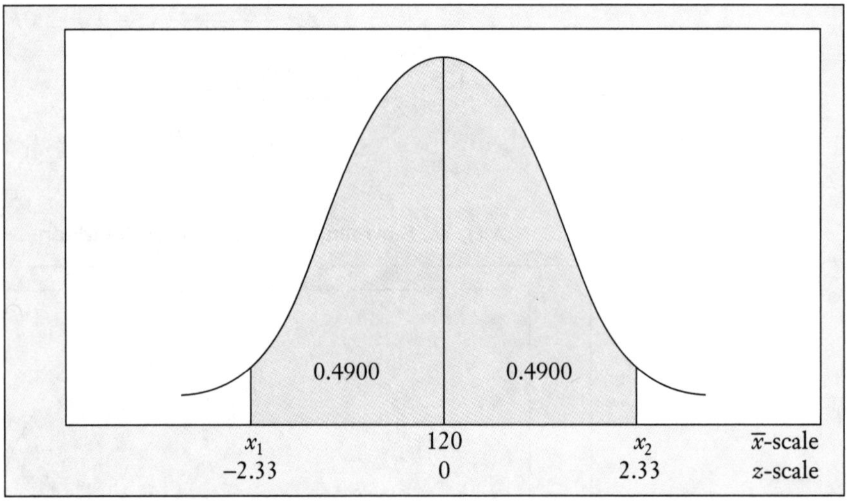

f) To fall within \$4 of the true mean, the sample mean should fall into the range \$116 to \$124.
For $\bar{x} = 116$,

$$z = \frac{116 - 120}{2.5} = \frac{-4}{2.5} = -1.6.$$

For $\bar{x} = 124$,

$$z = \frac{124 - 120}{2.5} = \frac{4}{2.5} = 1.6.$$

The area associated with a z value of 1.6 is 0.4452.
The area between 116 and 124 is 2(0.4452) = 0.8904.
The sample mean has an 89.04% chance of falling within \$4 of the true mean of \$120.

FIGURE 10.4 Sampling Distribution of the Means

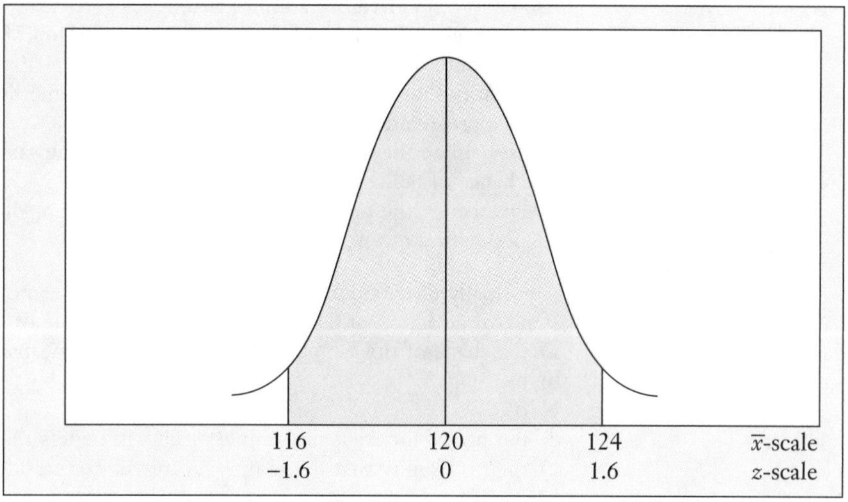

EXERCISE 10.3

1. Given that $\mu = 800$, $\sigma = 54$, and $n = 64$, determine
   (a) $\sigma_{\bar{x}}$ **(b)** $\mu + 3\sigma_{\bar{x}}$ **(c)** $\mu - 3\sigma_{\bar{x}}$

2. Given that $\mu = 250$, $\sigma = 24$, $n = 36$, and $N = 600$, determine
   (a) $\sigma_{\bar{x}}$ **(b)** $\mu \pm \sigma_{\bar{x}}$ **(c)** $\mu \pm 2\sigma_{\bar{x}}$

3. A normal population of 1500 has a mean of 400 and a standard deviation of 35. If all possible samples of size 25 are drawn from this population, and the sample means are computed and arranged in the form of a frequency distribution,
   a) determine the mean of the frequency distribution;
   b) compute the standard deviation of the frequency distribution;
   c) comment on the shape of the frequency distribution.

4. A large population is known to have a mean of \$11 500 and a standard deviation of \$2750. If all possible samples of size 225 are drawn from this population, and the sample means are computed and arranged in the form of a frequency distribution,
   a) what is the mean of the frequency distribution?
   b) what is the standard deviation of the frequency distribution?
   c) what is the shape of the frequency distribution?

5. Given that $\mu = 7.5$, $\sigma_{\bar{x}} = 0.4$, and $n = 49$, determine
   (a) $\mu_{\bar{x}}$ **(b)** σ

6. Given that $\mu_{\bar{x}} = 1.000$, $\sigma_{\bar{x}} = 0.004$, and $\sigma = 0.06$, determine
   (a) μ **(b)** n

7. A sample of 64 is taken from a large population. The population has a mean of \$200 and a standard deviation of \$20.
a) Determine the mean of the sampling distribution of the sample means.
b) Compute the standard error.
c) Identify the value that indicates that the sampling distribution of the means is approximately normal.
d) Determine the range of values within which the sample mean has a 95.44% chance of falling.
e) Determine the probability that the sample mean will fall within \$5 of the population mean.

8. A normally distributed population of 900 has a mean of 0.25 mm and a standard deviation of 0.06 mm. If a random sample of 16 is chosen, determine
a) the shape of the sampling distribution of the means;
b) $\mu_{\bar{x}}$;
c) $\sigma_{\bar{x}}$;
d) the probability that the sample mean will be less than 0.22 mm;
e) the probability that the sample mean will exceed 0.27 mm.

SECTION 10.4

The Sampling Distribution of Proportions

A. Introduction

There are many situations in business and industry in which we are interested in the proportion of items in a population that have a particular characteristic. Consider the following examples:

1. The registrar's office of a college needs to know the proportion of female students. The characteristic of interest is "female."
2. A candidate for a political office wants to know the proportion of votes she or he is likely to get in an election. The characteristic of interest is "yes votes."
3. A manufacturer of computer chips wants to know the proportion of nondefective chips in a production run. The characteristic of interest is "nondefective chips."

In such situations the variable to be analyzed is the proportion of responses that have a particular characteristic. This proportion is determined by

$$\frac{\text{NUMBER OF ITEMS THAT HAVE THE CHARACTERISTIC}}{\text{TOTAL NUMBER OF ITEMS}}$$

If all possible samples of a given size n are obtained from a population and their sample proportions are computed, the *listing of all sample proportions* forms a distribution referred to as the **sampling distribution of proportions**.

The sampling distribution of proportions is a binomial distribution since it deals with situations in which there are only two possible outcomes for a single trial and the distribution is a result of counting. Provided the sample size is sufficiently large ($n > 30$), we can use the properties of the normal distribution.

The sampling distribution of proportions can be used to consider the relationship between the population proportion and the possible values that a sample proportion may assume.

For purposes of analysis, the symbol π (read "pie") is used to denote the population proportion. The sample proportion is denoted by p

where $p = \frac{x}{n}$

x = the number of items in a sample having a specific characteristic;

n = the total number of items in the sample.

For a sample of 30 students, consisting of 18 females and 12 males, the sample proportion having the characteristic "female,"

$$p(\text{female}) = \frac{18}{30} = 0.60 = 60\%.$$

The sample proportion having the characteristic "male,"

$$p(\text{male}) = \frac{12}{30} = 0.40 = 40\%.$$

B. *Properties of the Sampling Distribution of Proportions*

Property 1. The mean of the sampling distribution of proportions, denoted by μ_p, is equal to the population proportion:

$$\mu_p = \pi$$ ←*Formula* 10.4

Property 2. The standard deviation of the sampling distribution of proportions, referred to as the **standard error of proportions** and denoted by σ_p, is given by

a) for infinite populations (N unknown),

$$\sigma_p = \sqrt{\frac{\pi(1-\pi)}{n}}$$ ←*Formula* 10.5

and

b) for finite populations,

$$\sigma_p = \sqrt{\frac{\pi(1-\pi)}{n}}\sqrt{\frac{N-n}{N-1}}$$ ←*Formula* 10.6

Property 3. For $n > 30$, the sampling distribution of proportions approximates the normal distribution.

On the basis of Property 3, chances are
a) 68.26% that a sample proportion p lies between $\pi \pm 1\sigma_p$;
b) 95.45% that a sample proportion p lies between $\pi \pm 2\sigma_p$;
c) 99.73% that a sample proportion p lies between $\pi \pm 3\sigma_p$.

Note The use of the normal distribution as an approximation to the binomial distribution is not appropriate for small values of n.

EXAMPLE 10.4a

A sample of 100 items is taken randomly from a production run of 2500 items. Normally, 90% of a production run meets quality standards and is acceptable. Determine

a) the mean of the sampling distribution of proportions;
b) the standard error of proportions;
c) the range of values within which the sample proportion has a 99.73% chance of falling;
d) the chances that the sample proportion will fall within five percentage points of the population proportion.

SOLUTION

The characteristic considered is "acceptable."
π (acceptable items) = 0.90; $n = 100$; $N = 2500$.

a) The mean of the sampling distribution of proportions, $\mu_p = \pi = 0.90$.

b) Since N is known, the population is a finite population. The standard error of proportions σ_p is given by

$$\sigma_p = \sqrt{\frac{\pi(1-\pi)}{n}}\sqrt{\frac{N-n}{N-1}}$$

$$= \sqrt{\frac{0.90(0.10)}{100}}\sqrt{\frac{2500-100}{2500-1}}$$

$$= \sqrt{\frac{0.09}{100}}\sqrt{\frac{2400}{2499}}$$

$$= \sqrt{0.0009}\sqrt{0.960\ 384\ 2}$$

$$= (0.03)(0.979\ 991\ 9)$$

$$= 0.0294$$

c) The proportion 0.9973 defines the interval $\pi \pm 3\sigma_p$; that is, $0.90 \pm 3(0.0294) = 0.90 \pm 0.0882$.
The upper limit of the range = 0.90 + 0.0882 = 0.9882;
the lower limit of the range = 0.90 − 0.0882 = 0.8118.
The sample proportion of acceptable production has a 99.73% chance of falling into the range 0.8118 to 0.9882, that is, 81.18% to 98.82%.

d) The interval to be considered is 0.90 ± 0.05, that is, 0.85 to 0.95.

FIGURE 10.5 Sampling Distribution of Proportions

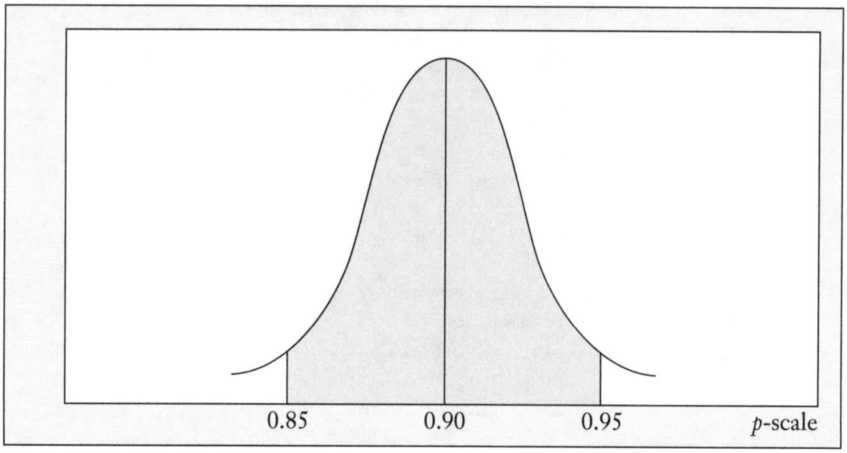

Since $n > 30$, the properties of the normal curve can be used.

$$\text{For } p = 0.85,\ z = \frac{0.85-0.90}{0.0294} = \frac{-0.05}{0.0294} = -1.70;$$

$$\text{for } p = 0.95,\ z = \frac{0.95-0.90}{0.0294} = \frac{0.05}{0.0294} = 1.70.$$

The area between π and $p = 0.85$ is 0.4554;
the area between π and $p = 0.95$ is 0.4554;

the combined area is $2(0.4554) = 0.9108$.

There is a 91.08% chance that the sample proportion will fall within five percentage points of the population proportion.

EXERCISE 10.4

1. Ward One contains 12 000 constituents. In a recent plebiscite 9600 constituents voted in favour of a "Green Plan" for the city. If 1000 voters were randomly chosen, what is the probability that the sample proportion in favour of the plan would be between 0.78 and 0.82?

2. The Lead Pipe Company has made a shipment of 400 lengths of pipe. Ten lengths were returned as they did not meet specifications. Historically, the rejection rate has been 2%. Determine the chances of selecting a sample of 400 pipes containing 10 or more rejects.

3. Given that $\sigma_p = \sqrt{\frac{0.85(0.15)}{40}}\sqrt{\frac{350-40}{350-1}}$, determine
   a) the size of the population;
   b) the sample size;
   c) the population proportion.

4. What is the maximum value that $\pi(1 - \pi)$ can take?

5. Compute the standard error for each of the following:
   a) $\pi = 0.60$, $n = 36$;
   b) $\pi = 0.75$, $n = 40$, $N = 500$;
   c) $\pi = 0.35$, $n = 100$, $N = 1000$;
   d) $\pi = 0.05$, $n = 81$, $N = 250$.

6. Determine the interval
   a) $\pi \pm 1.65\sigma_p$ given $\pi = 0.42$, $n = 48$, $N = 360$;
   b) $\pi \pm 2.50\sigma_p$ given $\pi = 0.92$, $n = 144$.

7. The college division of Pearson Education wants to determine the proportion of unsaleable books for a large production run. In the past the proportion of unsaleable books has been 7%. Compute the chances that the sample proportion for a sample of size 225 will fall within three percentage points of the population proportion.

8. A sample of 144 students is taken from a population of 2000 high-school students to estimate the proportion of students who can be expected to register at a college. Assuming that the true population proportion is 35%, determine the probability that the sample proportion will be no less than 30%.

REVIEW EXERCISE

1. Compute the upper and lower limits for the following intervals:
   a) $\mu \pm 2\sigma_{\bar{x}}$, given $\sigma = 0.22$, $n = 121$, $\mu = 0.75$;
   b) $\mu \pm 3\sigma_p$, given $\sigma = 1.8$, $n = 50$, $N = 800$, $\mu = 28$.

2. Compute the upper and lower limits for the following intervals:
   a) $\mu = \pm 3\sigma_{\bar{x}}$, given $\sigma = 0.2$, $n = 144$, $\mu = 1.5$;
   b) $\mu = \pm 4\sigma_p$, given $\sigma = 10$, $n = 200$, $N = 1000$, $\mu = 75$.

3. Compute the interval limits such that the given percent of the means of samples of the given size fall between the limits.
   a) 95% of all samples of size 100 for $\mu = 35$, $\sigma = 4$;
   b) 90% of all samples of size 225 for $\mu = 1200$, $\sigma = 36$.

4. a) For a distribution with $\mu = 31.2$, $\sigma = 3.7$, $N = 800$, compute the upper limit so that 1% of the means of samples of size 50 fall above the upper limit.
   b) For a population having a mean of 356 and a standard deviation of 33, determine the lower interval limit so that 98% of all samples of size 121 have a mean greater than the lower limit.

5. Compute the limits for the following intervals:
   a) $\mu \pm 2.5\sigma_{\bar{x}}$, given that $\mu = 16\ 000$, $\sigma = 4200$, $N = 500$, and $n = 40$;
   b) $\mu \pm 1.8\sigma_{\bar{x}}$, given that $\mu = 4500$, $\sigma = 375$, $n = 64$.

6. Compute the limits for the following intervals:
   a) $\mu = \pm 2\sigma_{\bar{x}}$, given that $\mu = 10000$, $\sigma = 500$, $N = 1000$, and $n = 49$.
   b) $\mu = \pm 1.5\sigma_{\bar{x}}$, given that $\mu = 355$, $\sigma = 5$, and $n = 81$.

7. In a normal distribution with a mean of 71.2 and a standard deviation of 6.8, a sample of 38 items is drawn. Determine the probability that the mean of the sample will be less than 68.

8. A normal distribution has $\mu = 1.69$ and $\sigma = 0.18$. From this distribution a sample of 16 observations is randomly selected.
   a) Comment on the shape of the sampling distribution.
   b) What are the chances that the sample mean falls between 1.56 and 1.78?

9. A normal distribution has $\mu = \$30\ 000$ and $\sigma = \$5000$. From a sample of 20 objects,
   a) comment on the shape of the sampling distribution.
   b) What are the chances that the sample mean falls between \$29 900 and \$32 000?

10. The Canada goose population has an average weight of 2.4 kg with a standard deviation of 0.61 kg. For a flock of 36 Canada geese flying overhead,
    a) determine the probability that some of the geese weigh more than 4 kg;
    b) compute the probability that the mean weight of the flock falls between 2.1 and 2.7 kg.

11. A gas-station owner is planning to add more gas pumps. The owner is certain that gasoline sales are normally distributed with a mean of 43.8 L and a standard deviation of 3.5 L.
    a) Will the owner add gas pumps if the criteria for adding pumps require that 10% of gas sales are more than 48.7 L?
    b) If a random sample of 16 customers is taken, what is the probability that the average gas sale is less than 41.5 L?

12. A bank is planning to add more tellers to service its customers. The manager has determined that the wait time is normally distributed with a mean wait time of 5 min and a standard deviation of 2 min.
    a) Will the manager add tellers if the criteria for adding tellers is that 20% of those waiting, wait 6 min or longer?
    b) If a random sample of 10 customers is taken, what is the probability that the average wait time is less than 3 min?

13. It was determined that 160 graduating high-school students had each watched an average of 15 000 h of television in their lives with a standard deviation of 4650 h. For a random sample of 40 graduates,
    a) compute the standard error;
    b) determine the interval in which 90% of the sample means can be expected to fall;
    c) calculate the probability that the sample selected will have a mean of less than 13 700 h.

14. From a normally distributed large population with a mean of 0.25 mm and a standard deviation of 0.03 mm, a random sample of 9 observations is chosen.
    a) Comment on the shape of the sampling distribution of the means.
    b) Compute $\sigma_{\bar{x}}$.
    c) What proportion of the population is expected to measure less than 0.24 mm?
    d) What proportion of the population is expected to measure between 0.28 mm and 0.31 mm?
    e) What is the probability that the sample mean falls between 0.23 mm and 0.27 mm?
    f) What are the chances that the sample mean will be less than 0.26 mm?

15. At D.F.R. Investments, average sales for the 124 sales representatives are \$3 200 000 with a standard deviation of \$150 000. For a random sample of 36 sales representatives,
    a) what is the standard deviation of the sampling distribution of the means?
    b) how many sales reps have sales of less than \$2 840 000?
    c) what proportion of the sales staff have sales between \$2 750 000 and \$2 960 000?
    d) what is the probability that the sample has a mean of more than \$3 250 000?
    e) what are the chances that the sample mean falls between \$3 160 000 and \$3 180 000?

16. The average price of houses sold in a city in April was \$215 000 with a standard deviation of \$28 770. If a sample of 36 of the 128 houses sold had a mean of \$206 000, will a 95% interval estimate include this sample?

17. The average test score in all math classes was 70% with a standard deviation of 10. If a sample of 49 out of 200 students tested had a mean of 68%, will a 95% interval estimate include the sample?

18. The average balance in a local bank's chequing accounts was \$4700 with a standard deviation of \$820. A random sample of 70 chequing accounts showed a mean balance of \$4810. If the bank has 1100 chequing accounts, what is the chance of selecting a sample of 70 accounts with a mean greater than \$4810?

19. A distributor of VCRs believes that the average age of videocassette recorders in his target market is 4.8 years with a standard deviation of 1.1 years. Determine the probability that the mean age of a sample of 75 is less than 5 years.

20. A car dealership has noticed that car owners in his area keep their vehicles for an average of 6 years with a standard deviation of 2 years. Determine the probability that the mean age of the sample size 100 is less than 7 years.

21. At Algonquin College, 47.3% of the faculty have a graduate degree or professional designation, while 41.2% have an undergraduate degree. In a random sample of 200 faculty, 88 had a graduate degree or professional designation, and 86 had an undergraduate degree. What is the probability of selecting a sample of 200 faculty
a) with fewer than 86 holders of an undergraduate degree?
b) with fewer than 86 holders of a graduate degree or professional designation?

22. A robot that sorts glass from containers holding recycled items is 96% correct. If a sample of 500 recycled items is selected, what is the probability that more than 6% of the items will be sorted incorrectly?

23. A auditor has determined that a certain procedure is done correctly 90% of the time. If the auditor samples 100 items, what is the probability that more than 15% of the procedures where done incorrectly?

24. Over a 365-day period a weather forecast is correct 68% of the time. If you are planning a 21-day holiday during a forecasted sunny period, what is the probability that you will have at least 15 days of sunshine?

25. An internal audit showed that 3% of the company's 820 accounts payable were processed incorrectly. If 150 accounts are reviewed at random, what is the probability that fewer than 6 accounts payable were processed incorrectly?

26. A postal station incorrectly sorted 8% of 1000 packages during a midnight shift. If 100 packages were checked at random, what is the probability that fewer than 10 were sorted incorrectly?

27. Of 1070 students registered in a business program, 78% came directly from high school. For a sample of 82 students, determine the interval that contains the sample proportion 98% of the time.

28. Given that the population proportion is 0.32 and the sample size is 48, determine the upper and the lower limits of the interval into which the sample proportion will fall with a probability of 90%.

29. Given that the population proportion is 0.60 and the sample size is 36, determine the upper and lower limits of the interval into which the sample proportion will fall with a probability of 95%.

30. In the investment industry, 4% of cold calls (selling to individuals by telephone) result in a transaction. A minimum of 30 transactions a month is required for an advisor to maintain employment with the investment firm. If a new employee averages 25 cold calls a day for the 20 working days in the first month of employment, what is the probability of continued employment?

31. Match the correct definition to the symbol shown in the first column.

a) N	**i)** population proportion
b) $\bar{x}$	**ii)** value of an observation
c) μ_p	**iii)** sample size
d) σ	**iv)** sample mean
e) $\sigma_{\bar{x}}$	**v)** sample proportion
f) π	**vi)** population mean
g) n	**vii)** mean of the sampling distribution of the means
h) $\mu_{\bar{x}}$	**viii)** mean of the sampling distribution of proportions
i) x	**ix)** population size
j) p	**x)** population standard deviation
k) μ	**xi)** standard error of proportions
l) σ_p	**xii)** standard error of the mean

32. (CGA) A survey finds that the annual income of a third-year CGA student follows a normal distribution with μ = \$30 000 and σ = \$5000. Suppose one such CGA student is chosen at random. What is the probability that her annual income is between \$25 000 and \$35 000?

33. (CGA) The Canada Customs and Revenue Agency spends, on average, 30 min per income tax return it decides to audit. The standard deviation of these audit times is known to be 10 min.

a) Suppose a tax return is selected at random for audit. What is the probability that it will take at least 24 min?

b) Suppose two tax returns are selected at random. What is the probability that both of these will take at least 24 min each to audit?

34. A local garage spends on average, 20 min per oil change. The standard deviation is 5 min.

a) What is the probability that your next oil change will take under 17 min?

a) If the garage promises oil changes in 30 min or less or it is free, what is the likelihood your oil change will be free?

35. (CGA) Assume that 1297 students took a final examination. The analysis of the data indicated that the students' scores follow a normal distribution with $\mu = 54$ and $\sigma = 10$.

a) When the pass mark was set at 51, what percentage of students passed the examination?

b) What percentage of students would have passed if the pass mark was set at 63?

c) At what pass mark would 67% of the students pass the examination?

d) Assume that the pass mark was set at 51 and that a random sample of two students' scores was taken. What is the probability that at least one of these two students pass the examination?

36. (CGA) A random sample of 100 purchases was taken from the records of a department store. The population standard deviation is known to be $25.

a) Suppose the population mean is unknown. Determine the probability that the sample mean will overstate the population mean by $4.

b) Suppose the population mean is known to be $200. Determine the probability that the sample mean will be less than $190.

SELF-TEST

1. Write the symbol that represents each of the following:

a) the mean of the sampling distribution of the means;

b) the standard error of proportions;

c) the mean of the sampling distribution of proportions;

d) the standard deviation of the sampling distribution of the means.

2. The accountant at Saw-Me Lumber Company knows that the company's suppliers are paid on the average within 34.2 days with a standard deviation of 3.1 days. If a random sample of 60 paid invoices is pulled, what is the probability that the sample average will be between 33 and 34 days?

3. A normally distributed population representing the heart rate of resting persons has a mean of 62.5 beats per minute and a standard deviation of 7.6 beats per minute.

a) Determine the standard error for a sample of 24.

b) Calculate the interval within which the sample mean has an 88% chance of falling.

4. The salaries of the employees of an auto-parts manufacturer averaged $45 280 with a standard deviation of $5790. Revenue Canada selected 45 out of the 389 employees to audit their pension plan contributions.

a) What was the salary of an employee in the top 5% of the firm's payroll?

b) What is the upper limit of the interval above which the sample mean has a 5% chance of falling?

5. The 2001 census showed that an urban community in New Brunswick consisted of 5129 households. The distribution of children per household was normal, with an average of 2.6 and a standard deviation of 0.69.
   a) How many households had between two and three children?
   b) What is the probability that a household chosen will have between two and three children?
   c) If a sample of 9 households is drawn, what is the probability that the sample mean will fall between 2 and 3?
   d) Comment on the difference between questions **(b)** and **(c)**.

6. During the last five summers, Josie sold yogurt on the main street of Grand Bend, and every summer 29% of sales were strawberry-flavoured products. For a random sample of 110 customers, what is the probability that between 25 and 35 selected a strawberry-flavoured product?

7. Peter runs a food concession at the carnival every Labour Day weekend. This year 68% of 2127 customers ordered a cola drink. A random selection of 250 customers were given free hats courtesy of Peter. What is the probability that more than 150 people wearing a free hat purchased a cola?

8. What sample size is required to maintain a standard error of no more than 1.26 for a large population having a standard deviation of 10.5?

WWW For an online glossary, go to **www.pearsoned.ca/hummelbrunner**.

Key Terms

Finite correction factor 332
Finite population 327
Infinite population 328
Parameter 328
Population 327
Sample 327
Sampling distribution of proportions 338
Sampling distribution of the means 329
Sampling variation 329
Standard error 331
Standard error of proportions 339
Statistic 328

Summary of Formulas

1. Sampling distribution of the means

a) Mean:

$$\mu_{\bar{x}} = \mu$$ ←*Formula* 10.1

b) Standard error:

i) for infinite populations (*N* is unknown),

$$\sigma_{\bar{x}} = \frac{\sigma}{\sqrt{n}}$$ ←*Formula* 10.2

ii) for finite populations (*N* is known),

$$\sigma_{\bar{x}} = \frac{\sigma}{\sqrt{n}}\sqrt{\frac{N-n}{N-1}}$$ ←*Formula* 10.3

2. Sampling distribution of proportions

a) Mean:

$$\mu_p = \pi$$ ←*Formula* 10.4

b) Standard error:

i) for infinite populations (*N* is unknown),

$$\sigma_p = \sqrt{\frac{\pi(1-\pi)}{n}}$$ ←*Formula* 10.5

ii) for finite populations (*N* is known),

$$\sigma_p = \sqrt{\frac{\pi(1-\pi)}{n}}\sqrt{\frac{N-n}{N-1}}$$ ←*Formula* 10.6

CHAPTER 11

Interval Estimation

Introduction

The value of a sample mean or sample proportion is used to develop an interval within which we can expect the population mean or population proportion to lie. The width of this interval depends on how variable the data is and how sure we want to be about the estimate of the population parameter. The more confident we want to be, the wider the interval becomes.

Learning Outcomes

Upon completion of this chapter you will be able to

1. define the terms *point estimate*, *interval estimate*, *confidence level (confidence coefficient, degree of confidence)*, *confidence limits*, and *confidence interval*;
2. construct confidence intervals about a sample mean at specified confidence levels for a large sample ($n > 30$) when
   a) the standard deviation of the population is known, and
   b) the standard deviation of the population is not known;
3. construct confidence intervals about a sample proportion for specified confidence levels for large samples ($n > 30$);
4. determine the sample size required for a specified level of confidence and a specified maximum allowable error when estimating a population mean or a population proportion;
5. construct confidence intervals about a sample mean at specified confidence levels for small samples ($n < 30$).

SECTION 11.1

Estimating Concepts

A. Estimators

The characteristics of a sample, referred to as *statistics*, are used to estimate the characteristics of a population, referred to as *parameters*. The statistics $\bar{x}$, p, and s are used to estimate the corresponding *parameters* μ, π, and σ. A statistic used in this way is called an **estimator**.

To be accepted as a good estimator, a statistic must have three properties: it must be *unbiased*, *efficient*, and *consistent*.

An **unbiased estimator** is one whose expected value (long-run average) is equal to the parameter being estimated. On this basis, the sample mean $\bar{x}$ is an unbiased estimator of the population mean μ, and the sample proportion p is an unbiased estimator of the population proportion π.

To calculate the population mean μ, we use Formula 3.1, $\mu = \frac{\sum x}{N}$. The corresponding formula for the sample mean is

$$\bar{x} = \frac{\sum x}{n}$$

←*Formula* 11.1

The sample standard deviation s is obtained as the square root of the sample variance. When calculating the population variance, we used Formula 4.5 $\sigma^2 = \frac{\sum (x-\mu)^2}{N}$. The corresponding formula for the sample variance is

$$s^2 = \frac{\sum (x-\bar{x})^2}{n-1}$$

←*Formula* 11.2

Note The denominator is $(n-1)$ in order to use the sample standard deviation as an unbiased estimator of the population standard deviation.

This means that, provided we use the formula $s^2 = \frac{\sum (x-\bar{x})^2}{n-1}$, the sample variance s^2 is an unbiased estimator of σ^2 and the sample standard deviation

$$s = \sqrt{s^2}$$

←*Formula* 11.3

is an unbiased estimator of the population standard deviation σ.

Note To avoid confusion, all references to sample variance and sample standard deviation in the remaining sections of this chapter and the remaining chapters of this text are in terms of the unbiased estimators s^2 and s.

An *efficient* estimator is one that has a relatively small variance. This implies that if a large number of samples are drawn from a population the computed values of the estimator are close to one another.

A *consistent* estimator is one in which the difference between the estimator and the parameter becomes smaller as the sample size increases.

B. *Point Estimation*

When a sample statistic is used to estimate the corresponding population parameter, the result is called a **point estimate**, and the process of estimating with a single number is referred to as **point estimation**.

EXAMPLE 11.1a

The production department of a beverage factory fills bottles with various fruit juices and soft drinks on a contract basis. One of the production lines is scheduled to fill 280-mL cans with soda pop. A random sample taken from the run provided the following data regarding the number of millilitres in the sampled cans:

284	278	285	294	277
270	265	282	276	279

Based on the information gathered from the sample,

a) obtain the best estimate of the average fill for the production run;

b) compute the associated standard deviation.

SOLUTION

Computation details for finding the mean $\bar{x}$ and the standard deviation s are shown in Table 11.1.

TABLE 11.1 Computational Details for Finding $\bar{x}$ and s

Observed sample value x	Deviation from sample mean $(x - \bar{x})$	Squared deviation $(x - \bar{x})^2$	Squared sample value x^2
284	$284 - 279 = 5$	25	80 656
278	$278 - 279 = -1$	1	77 284
285	$285 - 279 = 6$	36	81 225
294	$294 - 279 = 15$	225	86 436
277	$277 - 279 = -2$	4	76 729
270	$270 - 279 = -9$	81	72 900
265	$265 - 279 = -14$	196	70 225
282	$282 - 279 = 3$	9	79 524
276	$276 - 279 = -3$	9	76 176
279	$279 - 279 = 0$	0	77 841
$\sum x = 2790$	$\sum(x - \bar{x}) = 0$	$\sum(x - \bar{x})^2 = 586$	$\sum x^2 = 778\ 996$

a) The sample mean,

$$\bar{x} = \frac{\sum x}{n} = \frac{2790}{10} = 279.$$

Based on the sample result, the best estimate of the population mean μ is 279. This estimate of μ is a point estimate.

b) The unbiased sample variance,

$$s^2 = \frac{\sum(x-\bar{x})^2}{n-1} = \frac{586}{9} = 65.11.$$

The unbiased sample standard deviation,

$$s = \sqrt{s^2} = \sqrt{65.11} = 8.069.$$

Alternatively, the sample variance can be determined by means of the short-cut formula:

$$s^2 = \frac{n\sum x^2 - (\sum x)^2}{n(n-1)}$$ ←*Formula* 11.2A

where n = the number of observations in the sample;
x = the value of an individual observation in the sample.

$$s^2 = \frac{10(778\,996) - (2790)^2}{(10)(9)} = \frac{7\,789\,960 - 7\,784\,100}{90} = \frac{5860}{90} = 65.11$$

$$s = \sqrt{65.11} = 8.069.$$

○ **EXAMPLE 11.1b**

In a sample of 40 business administration students, 22 were female. What is the estimated proportion of female students in the business administration program?

● **SOLUTION**

The characteristic considered is "female." The sample proportion of females is

$$p(\text{female}) = \frac{x}{n} = \frac{\text{Number of females in the sample}}{\text{Total number of students in the sample}}$$

$$= \frac{22}{40} = 0.55 = 55\%.$$

Since p is an unbiased estimator of π, an unbiased point estimate of the proportion of females in the entire business administration program is 55%.

C. *Interval Estimation*

Because of *sampling variation* we know that different samples will have different sample means or sample proportions. We also know that the mean or proportion of any one sample is unlikely to have the same value as the population mean or population proportion. Thus, a point estimate of the population mean or population proportion can be expected to differ from the true population mean or true population proportion, but we have no knowledge of how large the difference may be and we have no way of assessing its size.

To overcome this weakness of point estimates, we construct an interval around the sample mean $\bar{x}$ or the sample proportion p in such a way that we can be "confident" that the "true" population mean μ or the "true" population proportion π lies somewhere within this interval. This process of estimating the value of a population parameter within a range of values is called **interval estimation**.

SECTION 11.2 Interval Estimation around the Mean When σ Is Known

A. *Construction of Confidence Intervals*

Estimation problems in which the population standard deviation is considered to be known are usually associated with situations for which a considerable amount of historical data are available, such as repetitive manufacturing processes. In the manufacturing industry the practice is to assume that output from any production process will be a normally distributed population.

EXAMPLE 11.2a

(Refer to Example 11.1a.) Assume it is known that when the filling machine is working properly, the quantity of soda pop in the cans is normally distributed with a mean of 280 mL and a standard deviation of 5 mL. In addition to the first sample with a mean of 279, four more samples of size 10 drawn during the production run had means of 282, 274, 277, and 284 respectively.

a) Construct the interval $\mu \pm 1.96\sigma_{\bar{x}}$.
b) Construct the interval $\bar{x} \pm 1.96\sigma_{\bar{x}}$ around each of the five sample means.
c) Draw a graph of the sampling distribution of the means, and show graphically the relationship among μ, the five sample means, and the intervals.

SOLUTION

a) $\mu = 280; \sigma = 5.$

$$\sigma_{\bar{x}} = \frac{\sigma}{\sqrt{n}} = \frac{5}{\sqrt{10}} = \frac{5}{3.162\ 28} = 1.58$$

The interval

$$\mu \pm 1.96\sigma_{\bar{x}} = 280 \pm 1.96(1.58) = 280 \pm 3.10$$
$$= 276.90 \text{ to } 283.10.$$

b) The desired interval $\bar{x} \pm 1.96\sigma_{\bar{x}} = \bar{x} \pm (1.96)(1.58) = \bar{x} \pm 3.10$.
For the sample with $\bar{x} = 279$, the interval is 279 ± 3.10,
that is, from 275.90 to 282.10.
For the sample with $\bar{x} = 282$, the interval is 278.90 to 285.10.
For the sample with $\bar{x} = 274$, the interval is 270.90 to 277.10.
For the sample with $\bar{x} = 277$, the interval is 273.90 to 280.10.
For the sample with $\bar{x} = 284$, the interval is 280.90 to 287.10.

c) The relationship among μ, the five sample means and the intervals is shown in Figure 11.1.

FIGURE 11.1 Relationship among the Intervals Containing μ and $\bar{x}$

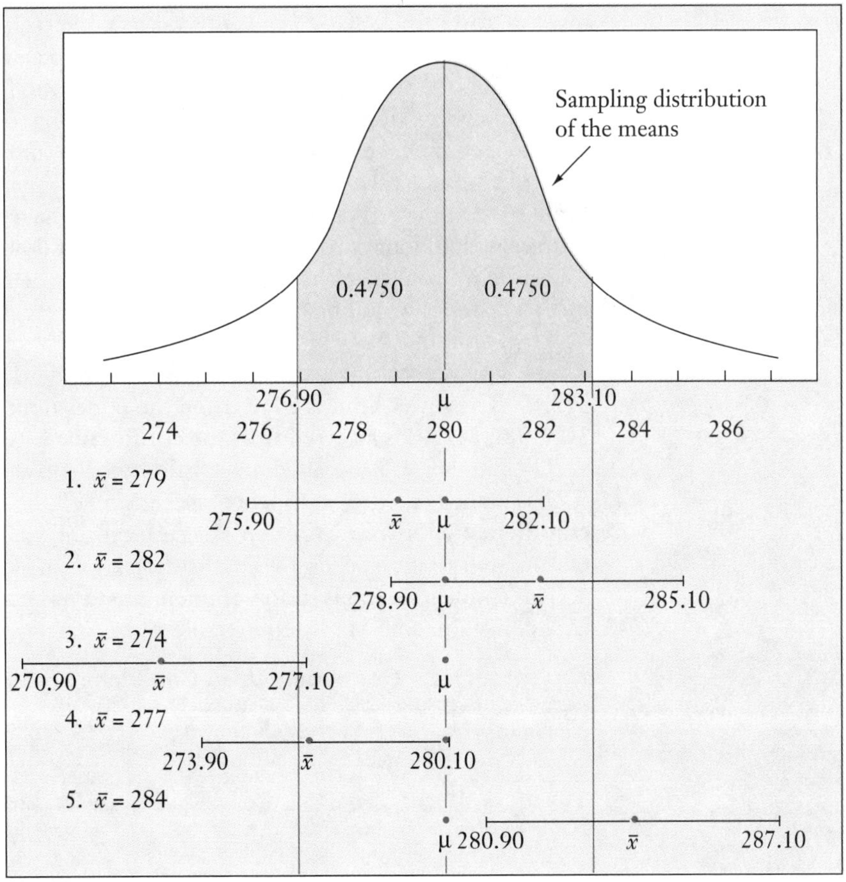

Note For Sample 1 the mean $\bar{x} = 279$ falls into the range 276.90 to 283.10; the population mean μ falls into the interval $279 \pm 1.96\sigma_{\bar{x}}$.

For samples 2 and 4 the means $\bar{x} = 282$ and $\bar{x} = 277$ also fall into the range 276.90 to 283.10; the population mean μ falls into the intervals $282 \pm 1.96\sigma_{\bar{x}}$ and $277 \pm 1.96\sigma_{\bar{x}}$.

For samples 3 and 5 the means $\bar{x} = 275$ and $\bar{x} = 284$ fall outside the range 276.90 and 283.10; the population mean μ is not included in the intervals $275 \pm 1.96\sigma_{\bar{x}}$ and $284 \pm 1.96\sigma_{\bar{x}}$.

B. Confidence Intervals and Confidence Levels

Since the area under the normal curve between μ and $z = 1.96$ is 0.4750, the area included in the inverval $\mu \pm 1.96\sigma_{\bar{x}}$ is 0.9500, that is, 95% of the total area. This means that we can expect that for $\mu = 280$ mL the means of 95% of all samples of size 10 fall between 276.90 mL and 283.10 mL.

Conversely, as indicated by Figure 11.1, the interval $\bar{x} \pm 1.96\sigma_{\bar{x}}$ includes the population mean, provided that $\bar{x}$ falls between 276.90 mL and 283.10 mL. It follows that for 95% of all possible samples we can expect the population mean μ to be included in the interval $\bar{x} \pm 1.96\sigma_{\bar{x}}$. For the remaining 5% of samples μ will not fall into this interval. We can say that we have "95% confidence" that the interval $\bar{x} \pm 1.96\sigma_{\bar{x}}$ includes the population mean μ.

Applying this to Example 11.2a, we see that only three of the five samples produced confidence intervals that included the population mean; that is, only 60% of the intervals included μ. This is so far removed from the expected result of 95% that, in practice, the production manager would suspect that the process was no longer in control and would shut down the line immediately. Adjustments would then be made to the machinery before starting up again and further samples would be taken to ensure the correct fill was being obtained.

The *upper* and *lower* limits of such intervals are referred to as **confidence limits**. For the sample with $\bar{x} = 279$, the confidence limits are 275.90 and 282.10. The lower limit is 275.90 and the upper limit is 282.10. The interval 275.90 to 282.10 is referred to as the **confidence interval**.

The number 95% is called the **confidence level** and its decimal equivalent 0.95 is known as the confidence coefficient of the interval estimate. The **confidence coefficient** (or confidence level) indicates the *degree of certainty* that an interval built around a sample mean $\bar{x}$ will include the population mean μ. The confidence levels most commonly used in business and the associated confidence intervals are listed in Table 11.2.

TABLE 11.2 Commonly Used Confidence Intervals

Confidence level	z value	Confidence interval	Confidence intervals for Example 11.2a, $\sigma_{\bar{x}} = 1.58$
90%	1.64	$\bar{x} \pm 1.64\sigma_{\bar{x}}$	$\bar{x} \pm 1.64(1.58) = \bar{x} \pm 2.59$
95%	1.96	$\bar{x} \pm 1.96\sigma_{\bar{x}}$	$\bar{x} \pm 1.96(1.58) = \bar{x} \pm 3.10$
98%	2.33	$\bar{x} \pm 2.33\sigma_{\bar{x}}$	$\bar{x} \pm 2.33(1.58) = \bar{x} \pm 3.68$
99%	2.58	$\bar{x} \pm 2.58\sigma_{\bar{x}}$	$\bar{x} \pm 2.58(1.58) = \bar{x} \pm 4.08$

Note The higher the confidence level, the wider the confidence interval. As the interval widens, the precision of the estimate decreases. If the interval becomes too wide, the estimate may have no practical value.

Confidence levels also indicate the chance of being wrong. Being 90% confident means that there is a 10% chance of error. A 95% confidence level implies a 5% chance of error. Conversely, a 2% chance of error suggests a 98% degree of confidence. *The confidence coefficient plus the chance of error always add up to 1.*

The width of the confidence interval and the precision of the interval estimate depend on the standard deviation and the choice of confidence level. In general, when σ is known, the confidence interval is given by

$$\bar{x} \pm z\sigma_{\bar{x}}$$ ←*Formula* 11.4

where $\bar{x}$ = the sample mean (point estimate);
z = the value associated with a given level of confidence;
$\sigma_{\bar{x}}$ = the standard error of the mean found by

$$\sigma_{\bar{x}} = \frac{\sigma}{\sqrt{n}} \text{ for infinite populations, or}$$

$$\sigma_{\bar{x}} = \frac{\sigma}{\sqrt{n}}\sqrt{\frac{N-n}{N-1}} \text{ for finite populations.}$$

○ **EXAMPLE 11.2b**

Assuming that the mean fill of a sample of 25 cans taken from the bottling line in Example 11.2a was 278, determine the confidence intervals for confidence levels of
a) 90% b) 95% c) 98%.

● **SOLUTION**

$\bar{x} = 278$; $n = 25$; $\sigma = 5$; N is unknown.

$$\sigma_{\bar{x}} = \frac{\sigma}{\sqrt{n}} = \frac{5}{\sqrt{25}} = \frac{5}{5} = 1$$

a) For 90% confidence, $z = 1.64$;
the confidence interval $\bar{x} \pm z\sigma_{\bar{x}} = 278 \pm 1.64(1)$.
The upper limit of the interval = 278 + 1.64 = 279.64;
the lower limit of the interval = 278 – 1.64 = 276.36.
The 90% confidence interval covers the range 276.36 to 279.64.

b) For 95% confidence, $z = 1.96$;
the confidence interval = 278 ± 1.96(1).
The 95% confidence interval covers the range 276.04 to 279.96.

c) For 98% confidence, $z = 2.33$.
The confidence interval = 278 ± 2.33(1).
The 98% confidence interval covers the range 275.67 to 280.33.

Note If, as stated, the true population mean $\mu = 280$, the 90% confidence interval does not contain μ. With regard to the 95% confidence interval, μ is very close to the upper limit but still outside the interval. μ falls within the 98% confidence interval.

○ **EXAMPLE 11.2c**

Compute the 90% confidence interval for a sample of 36 items with a mean of 1.20 taken from a population of 600 items. It is known that the population standard deviation is 0.24.

● **SOLUTION**

$N = 600$; $n = 36$; $\bar{x} = 1.20$; $\sigma = 0.24$; for 90% confidence, $z = 1.64$.
Since σ is known, the confidence interval is given by $\bar{x} \pm z\sigma_{\bar{x}}$.
Since N is known, the population is finite and the standard error is given by

$$\sigma_{\bar{x}} = \frac{\sigma}{\sqrt{n}}\sqrt{\frac{N-n}{N-1}} = \frac{0.24}{\sqrt{36}}\sqrt{\frac{600-36}{600-1}}$$

$$= \frac{0.24}{6}\sqrt{\frac{564}{599}} = 0.04\sqrt{0.941\,569\,3}$$

$$= 0.04(0.970\,344\,9) = 0.0388.$$

The 90% confidence interval is $1.20 \pm 1.64(0.0388) = 1.20 \pm 0.064$. The interval in which the true population mean is located with 90% certainty is the range 1.136 to 1.264.

EXERCISE 11.2

1. A single number used to estimate a population parameter is referred to as __________.
   A range of values used to estimate a population parameter is referred to as __________.
   A statistic used to estimate a parameter is referred to as __________, while a specific value of a statistic is referred to as __________.

2. As the confidence level increases, the interval estimate becomes __________, while the precision of the estimate __________.
   The confidence interval when σ is known is given by the expression __________.

3. The following information is available for a normally distributed infinite population:
   $\bar{x} = \$150$; $\sigma = \$35$; $n = 25$; confidence coefficient $= 0.95$.
   a) Compute the upper limit of the interval estimate.
   b) Comment on the shape of the sampling distribution of the means.

4. Given $\sigma = 1000$, $\bar{x} = 870\ 000$, $N = 900$, and $n = 100$,
   a) determine the confidence interval for a degree of confidence of
      i) 0.80, ii) 0.90, iii) 0.98;
   b) state what happens to the size of the confidence interval as the degree of confidence increases.

5. From a sample of 40 patients, a medical doctor would like to estimate the average amount charged per visit per patient. Assuming μ = \$35 and σ = \$9, what are the chances that the sample mean will have a value within \$1 of the true mean?

6. Last month John sent 850 packages by courier. He would like to know the average cost of sending a package. A random selection of 35 charges averaged \$10.50. Assuming σ = \$1.22,
   a) compute the standard error;
   b) construct the 95% confidence interval around the sample mean.

7. A sample of 200 is selected from a population whose mean is known to be 50 with a standard deviation of 9.9. Determine the probability that the sample mean falls within two units of the population mean.

8. The Steel Pipe Company has received a shipment of 900 lengths of pipe. The company's quality-control engineer wants to estimate the average diameter of the pipes to see if the shipment meets minimum standards. Historically, the standard deviation of the diameters of pipes shipped has been 5 mm. A sample of 45 pipes had a mean diameter of 150 mm. Compute the confidence interval with the chance of a 1% error.

SECTION 11.3

Interval Estimation around the Mean for Large Samples ($n > 30$) when σ Is Unknown

As stated earlier, estimation problems in which the population standard deviation is considered to be known are usually associated with situations for which a considerable amount of historical data are available. In most situations, however, σ is not known. In addition, we likely know little or nothing about the shape of the population distribution from which the sample is drawn.

This situation requires the use of the central limit theorem, which states that the sampling distribution of the means approaches a normal distribution for samples of size $n > 30$. This permits the use of z values to construct confidence intervals when σ is unknown in the same way as when σ is known, provided the sample size n is greater than 30.

The complication of not being able to determine the standard error $\sigma_{\bar{x}}$ because the population standard deviation σ is not known is overcome by using the sample standard deviation s as an unbiased estimator of σ. The estimated standard error, denoted by $s_{\bar{x}}$, is determined using the formula

$$s_{\bar{x}} = \frac{s}{\sqrt{n}}$$ ←*Formula* 11.5

for infinite populations or when N is not known. When N is known, multiply by the finite correction factor.

When σ is unknown and $n > 30$, the confidence interval in which μ can be found with a given degree of confidence is given by

$$\bar{x} \pm z s_{\bar{x}}$$ ←*Formula* 11.6

where $\bar{x}$ = the sample mean;
z = the value associated with a given confidence level;
$s_{\bar{x}}$ = the standard error found by
$s_{\bar{x}} = \frac{s}{\sqrt{n}}$ for infinite populations, or
$s_{\bar{x}} = \frac{s}{\sqrt{n}}\sqrt{\frac{N-n}{N-1}}$ for finite populations;
s = the sample standard deviation;
n = the sample size;
N = the population size.

EXAMPLE 11.3a

The Stagger Inn Tavern wants to estimate the average dollar purchase per customer. A sample of 81 customers spent an average of \$20.00 with a standard deviation of \$3.15. Estimate the true average expenditure per customer with 95% confidence.

SOLUTION

$n = 81$; $\bar{x} = 20.00$; $s = 3.15$;
the z value associated with a 95% confidence level is 1.96;
since N is unknown, the population is considered infinite;

$$s_{\bar{x}} = \frac{s}{\sqrt{n}} = \frac{3.15}{\sqrt{81}} = \frac{3.15}{9} = 0.35;$$

since σ is unknown, the interval estimate is given by

$$\bar{x} \pm z s_{\bar{x}} = 20.00 \pm 1.96(0.35) = 20.00 \pm 0.686.$$

The upper limit of the interval = 20.00 + 0.686 = 20.686;
the lower limit of the interval = 20.00 − 0.686 = 19.314.

The confidence interval in which the true average expenditure per customer can be found with 95% certainty is \$19.31 to \$20.69 .

○ **EXAMPLE 11.3b**

The average height of a sample of 36 students out of 1600 students registered in a high school is 170 cm with a standard deviation of 10 cm. Construct a confidence interval with a 1% chance of error.

● **SOLUTION**

$N = 1600$; $n = 36$; $\bar{x} = 170$; $s = 10$;
for a 1% chance of error, the confidence level is 99%;
the z value for the 99% confidence level = 2.58;
since N is known, the population is finite;

$$s_{\bar{x}} = \frac{s}{\sqrt{n}}\sqrt{\frac{N-n}{N-1}} = \frac{10}{\sqrt{36}}\sqrt{\frac{1600-36}{1600-1}} = \frac{10}{6}\sqrt{\frac{1564}{1599}}$$

$$= 1.6667\sqrt{0.978\ 111\ 32} = 1.6667(0.9890) = 1.6484.$$

Since σ is unknown and $n > 30$, the confidence interval around the mean is given by

$$\bar{x} \pm zs_{\bar{x}} = 170 \pm 2.58(1.6484) = 170 \pm 4.25.$$

The upper limit of the interval = $170 + 4.25 = 174.25$;
the lower limit = $170 - 4.25 = 165.75$.

The confidence interval in which the true average height of the group of students can be found with 99% confidence is 165.75 cm to 174.25 cm.

○ **EXAMPLE 11.3c**

The scores of 32 students on a diagnostic test drawn from 1200 students registered in the first year of a college program were as follows:

14	9	12	23	11	15	7	14
6	13	18	19	21	17	9	10
16	18	15	20	8	13	17	24
11	16	14	13	18	15	12	16

Construct the 80% confidence interval in which the true average test score for the 1200 students is located.

SOLUTION

$N = 1200; n = 32$

TABLE 11.3 Calculation of the Mean and Standard Deviation of the Sample

x	x^2	x	x^2	x	x^2	x	x^2
14	196	6	36	16	256	11	121
9	81	13	169	18	324	16	256
12	144	18	324	15	225	14	196
23	529	19	361	20	400	13	169
11	121	21	441	8	64	18	324
15	225	17	289	13	169	15	225
7	49	9	81	17	289	12	144
14	196	10	100	24	576	16	256
105	1541	113	1801	131	2303	115	1691

$$\sum x = 105 + 113 + 131 + 115 = 464$$

$$\sum x^2 = 1541 + 1801 + 2303 + 1691 = 7336;$$

$$\bar{x} = \frac{\sum x}{n} = \frac{464}{32} = 14.50;$$

$$s^2 = \frac{n\sum x^2 - (\sum x)^2}{n(n-1)} = \frac{32(7336) - (464)^2}{32(31)} = \frac{234\,752 - 215\,296}{992}$$

$$= \frac{19\,456}{992} = 19.612\,903.$$

$$s = \sqrt{s^2} = \sqrt{19.612\,903} = 4.428\,646;$$

$$s_{\bar{x}} = \frac{s}{\sqrt{n}}\sqrt{\frac{N-n}{N-1}} = \frac{4.428\,646}{\sqrt{32}}\sqrt{\frac{1200-32}{1200-1}}$$

$$= \frac{4.428\,646}{5.656\,854}\sqrt{\frac{1168}{1199}} = 0.782\,881\sqrt{0.974\,145}$$

$$= 0.782\,881(0.986\,988) = 0.7727.$$

For an 80% confidence level, the areas between μ and $\pm z$ must each equal 40% or 0.4000. The corresponding z values = ±1.28. Since σ is unknown and $n > 30$, the 80% confidence interval = 14.50 ± 1.28(0.7727) = 14.50 ± 0.989, that is, from 13.51 to 15.49.

These calculations can be completed by using EXCEL, as demonstrated in USING EXCEL 11.1.

USING EXCEL 11.1

EXCEL can be used to help construct the 80% confidence interval in Example 11.3c for which the true average test score of the 1200 students is located.

1. Type the column heading **Student Scores** into cell A1.
2. Enter the scores of the 32 students into cells A2:A33.
3. Type the notes **is the population size (N) – the number of registered students, is the sample size (n) – the number of students drawn from the population, is the sample mean, is the unbiased sample deviation, is the confidence interval for the population mean (infinite population), is the finite correction factor (because the population (N = 1200) is known), and is the confidence interval for the population mean (finite population)** into cells D3–D9.
4. Type the column heading **80% Confidence Interval:** into cell C11.
5. Select cell C3, and enter the value **1200**.
6. Select cell C4, and type **=COUNT(A2:A33)** in the formula bar and enter.
7. Select cell C5, and type **=AVERAGE(A2:A33)** in the formula bar and enter.
8. Select cell C6, and type **=STDEV(A2:A33)** in the formula bar and enter.
9. Select cell C7, and type **=CONFIDENCE (1–0.80,C6,C4)** in the formula bar and enter. The **1–0.80** represents the significance level (alpha) used by EXCEL to compute the confidence level. The alpha is equal to [100 – Confidence Level (%)]/100, and in this case, an 80% confidence level indicates an alpha of 0.20. This calculation is based upon an infinite population size, which in this case, will need to be corrected by the finite correction factor because the student population (N = 1200) is known.
10. Select cell C8, and type **=SQRT((C3–C4)/(C3–1))** in the formula bar and enter. This represents the finite correction factor.
11. Select cell C9, and type **=C7*C8** in the formula bar and enter. This is done to adjust the previously calculated confidence interval (for an infinite population) to be representative of a finite population.
12. Select cell C12, and type **=C5–C9** in the formula bar and enter.
13. Select cell D12, and type **=C5+C9** in the formula bar and enter.

The **Paste Function** button found on the toolbar (or on the **Insert** menu and clicking **Function...**) can be used to complete steps 6–10, and is recommended, so as to learn more about EXCEL's built-in statistical functions.

As manually calculated, we obtain the same results using EXCEL, where the 80% confidence interval is from 13.51 to 15.49.

OUTPUT

File Edit View Insert Format Tools Data Window Help

M2 =

	A	B	C	D	E	F	G	H	I	J
1	**Student Scores**									
2	14									
3	9		1200	is the population size (N) -- the number of registered students.						
4	12		32	is the sample size (n) -- the number of students drawn from the population.						
5	23		14.5	is the sample mean.						
6	11		4.428646	is the unbiased sample deviation.						
7	15		1.003302	is the confidence interval for the population mean (infinite population).						
8	7		0.986988	is the finite correction factor (because the population (N = 1200) is known).						
9	14		**0.990247**	**is the confidence interval for the population mean (finite population).**						
10	6									
11	13		**80% Confidence Interval:**							
12	18		13.50975	15.49025						
13	19									
14	21									
15	17									
16	9									
17	10									
18	16									
19	18									
20	15									
21	20									
22	8									
23	13									
24	17									
25	24									
26	11									
27	16									
28	14									
29	13									
30	18									
31	15									
32	12									
33	16									

EXERCISE 11.3

1. A sample of the billings of 361 doctors revealed that their mean annual income was \$210 000 with a standard deviation of \$34 000. Compute the 90% confidence limits.

2. A credit manager has chosen 225 accounts out of 16 000 and found that the average payment period was 45 days with a standard deviation of 4 days. Determine the confidence interval within which the average payment period for all accounts can be expected to be found with a 2% chance of error.

3. For the confidence interval $41 \pm 2.33\left(\frac{2}{\sqrt{36}}\right)\sqrt{\frac{2000-36}{2000-1}}$, determine

   (a) N (b) n (c) $\bar{x}$ (d) s (e) $s_{\bar{x}}$ (f) the confidence level.

4. For the confidence interval $120 \pm 1.65\left(\frac{13}{\sqrt{49}}\right)$, determine

   a) the sample size;
   b) the sample standard deviation;
   c) the sample mean;
   d) the confidence level;
   e) the standard error;
   f) the upper confidence limit.

5. The Dew Drop Pub wants to estimate the average number of litres of beer sold per day. A sampling of 48 business days produced a daily average of 125 L with a standard deviation of 16 L. Compute the confidence limits at the 90% confidence level.

6. Dr. Ayad, dentist, would like to know the average number of fillings of each of his 2160 patients. A random sample of the files of 90 patients showed an average of 5 fillings per patient with a standard deviation of 1.2 fillings. Determine the confidence interval for the 95% confidence level.

7. The Cheer Up Answering Service has collected the following data about the number of calls handled per day:

355	410	416	423	435	396	409
372	473	442	427	419	438	453
466	412	415	433	442	387	403
438	342	383	404	373	449	398
408	427	437	453	422	417	435
409	430	444	433	428	437	416
410	429	442	397	412	423	425

   Construct the 85% confidence interval.

8. Construct the 80% confidence interval for the following sample results taken from a normal distribution:

1985	636	2422	1103
3888	3962	2939	3106
2291	4909	4982	3621
1179	3665	3643	4319

SECTION 11.4

Interval Estimation of Proportions for Large Samples ($n > 30$) when π Is Unknown

Since the sample proportion p is an unbiased estimator of π, it can be used as a point estimate of π. For interval estimation problems, the sampling distribution of proportions approaches a normal distribution for samples of size $n > 30$. This permits the use of z values to construct confidence intervals.

The complication of not being able to determine the standard error of proportion σ_p because the population proportion π is not known is overcome by using the sample proportion p as an unbiased estimator of π. The estimated standard error, denoted by s_p, is determined using the formula

$$s_p = \sqrt{\frac{p(1-p)}{n}}$$ ←*Formula* 11.7

for infinite populations or when N is not known. When N is known, multiply by the finite correction factor.

The confidence interval in which π is then expected to lie is given by

$$p \pm z s_p$$ ←*Formula* 11.8

where $s_p = \sqrt{\frac{p(1-p)}{n}}$ for infinite populations or when N is unknown, or

$s_p = \sqrt{\frac{p(1-p)}{n}}\sqrt{\frac{N-n}{N-1}}$ for finite populations.

EXAMPLE 11.4a

The manager of a credit union wants to estimate the proportion of members whose biweekly salaries are deposited by electronic transfer. A random sample of 250 depositors indicated that 95 were on direct deposit. Compute the 95% confidence interval of the true proportion of direct deposit accounts.

SOLUTION

The characteristic considered is "on direct deposit."

The sample proportion, $p = \frac{x}{n} = \frac{95}{250} = 0.38 = 38\%$.

$$s_p = \sqrt{\frac{p(1-p)}{n}} = \sqrt{\frac{(0.38)(0.62)}{250}} = \sqrt{0.000\,942} = 0.0307$$

Since $n > 30$, we can use the normal distribution.

For 95% confidence, $z = 1.96$.

The confidence interval $= p \pm zs_p = 0.38 \pm 1.96(0.0307) = 0.38 \pm 0.060$, that is, 0.32 to 0.44.

The manager can be 95% confident that between 32% and 44% of the members are on direct deposit.

EXAMPLE 11.4b

The quality-control engineer of a parts manufacturer has taken a random sample of 60 from a production run of 900 parts and found 9 defective parts.

a) Determine a point estimate of the proportion of defective parts.

b) What is the interval estimate of the proportion of non-defective parts with a 2% chance of error?

SOLUTION

a) The characteristic considered is "defective."

The proportion of defective parts $= \frac{9}{60} = 0.15 = 15\%$.

A point estimate of the proportion of defective parts is 15%.

b) The characteristic considered is "non-defective." The number of non-defective parts in the sample $= 60 - 9 = 51$.

The proportion of non-defective parts, $p = \frac{51}{60} = 0.85 = 85\%$.

$N = 900$; $n = 60$.

$$s_p = \sqrt{\frac{p(1-p)}{n}}\sqrt{\frac{N-n}{N-1}} = \sqrt{\frac{(0.85)(0.15)}{60}}\sqrt{\frac{900-60}{900-1}}$$

$$= \sqrt{0.002\,125}\sqrt{0.934\,371\,5} = (0.0461)(0.9666) = 0.0446$$

Since $n > 30$, we can use the normal distribution.

For a 2% chance of error, $z = 2.33$.

The confidence interval $= p \pm zs_p = 0.85 \pm 2.33(0.0446)$

$= 0.85 \pm 0.104$, that is, 0.746 to 0.954.

The interval in which the true proportion of non-defective parts can be found with a 2% chance of error is between 74.6% and 95.4%.

EXERCISE 11.4

1. Given that $p = 0.32$, $n = 40$, and $N = 210$, compute the 90% confidence interval.

2. In a sample, 9 out of 52 observations are successes. Construct the confidence interval for the true proportion of successes in the population from which the sample was drawn with a 1% chance of error.

3. Only card-carrying college instructors can vote on union issues. Of the 320 instructors at a college in Saskatchewan a sample of 90 showed that 54 were card-carrying union members. Determine the interval estimate of the proportion of instructors at the college who can vote on union issues with a 5% chance of error.

4. A pollster working for an incumbent member of Parliament obtained the following information on an issue:
   For, 16; Against, 18; Undecided, 6.

   Using the poll, calculate the 98% confidence limits for the true proportion of voters in favour of the issue.

5. A production department experiences difficulties in the manufacture of part number 910512. A random sample of 400 parts revealed that 112 parts were defective.
   a) Determine a point estimate of the proportion of non-defective parts.
   b) Regarding the defective parts, what is the standard error of proportion?
   c) What is the interval estimate for the population proportion of defective parts using a confidence coefficient of 0.90?

6. A survey of 240 college students indicated that 96 preferred coffee to tea.
   a) Determine a point estimate of the proportion of students who prefer coffee.
   b) Compute the standard error of proportion.
   c) What is the interval estimate of the population proportion of students who prefer tea, with a 20% chance of error?

SECTION 11.5

Determination of Sample Size

A. The Maximum Error of an Interval Estimate

For the confidence intervals $\bar{x} \pm z\sigma_{\bar{x}}$, $\bar{x} \pm zs_{\bar{x}}$, and $p \pm zs_p$, the terms $z\sigma_{\bar{x}}$, $zs_{\bar{x}}$, and zs_p establish the maximum distance from the sample mean $\bar{x}$ or the sample proportion p in which the population parameters μ or π can be found with a given degree of certainty. These three terms describe the **maximum error** of an interval estimate on either side of μ or π. (See the diagram below.)

For example, in the interval $\bar{x} \pm 4$ the maximum distance from $\bar{x}$ to the upper and lower limits of the class interval is 4. This means that for the given chance of error, 4 is the maximum error that can be made when using the sample mean $\bar{x}$ to estimate the population mean μ.

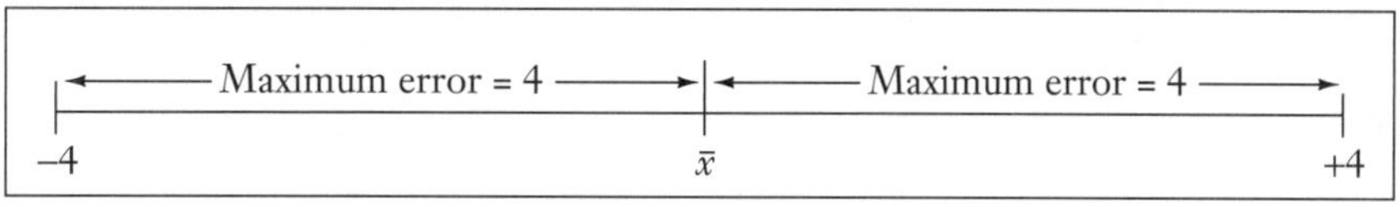

B. Finding the Sample Size for Estimating a Population Mean

The process of interval estimation requires the use of samples. In most practical business situations it is first necessary to determine the size of sample that will generate the data from which an estimate of the population mean μ will be obtained.

To determine the proper sample size, three factors must be considered:

1. the confidence level for the interval estimate;
2. the size of the maximum allowable error;
3. the standard deviation of the population from which the sample is taken.

The first two factors are influenced by the nature of the research and must be specified by the researcher.

The third factor that must be considered in determining the sample size is the population standard deviation. In some situations it is possible to use the standard deviation obtained for existing data as an estimate of σ. If no such data are available, a preliminary sample must be taken to compute s as an estimate of σ.

The two formulas

$$\text{MAXIMUM ERROR} = zs_{\bar{x}} \quad \text{and} \quad s_{\bar{x}} = \frac{s}{\sqrt{n}}$$

can then be used to calculate the sample size n.

For example, if the specified maximum error is 4, the confidence level is set at 95% (in which case $z = 1.96$), and the sample standard deviation is 15.00, the required sample size can be found by first substituting in the formula

$$\text{MAXIMUM ERROR} = zs_{\bar{x}}$$
$$4.00 = 1.96s_{\bar{x}}$$
$$s_{\bar{x}} = \frac{4.00}{1.96} = 2.0408.$$

Now substituting in the second formula

$$s_{\bar{x}} = \frac{s}{\sqrt{n}}$$

we obtain

$$2.0408 = \frac{15.00}{\sqrt{n}}$$

$$\sqrt{n} = \frac{15.00}{2.0408} = 7.35$$

$$n = 7.35^2 = 54.0225 \approx 55.$$

The two formulas can be combined into one to yield the formula

$$\text{MAXIMUM ERROR} = z\left(\frac{s}{\sqrt{n}}\right)$$

from which we obtain

$$\sqrt{n} = \frac{zs}{\text{MAXIMUM ERROR}}$$

by squaring

$$n = \left(\frac{zs}{\text{MAXIMUM ERROR}}\right)^2$$

←*Formula* 11.9

In our example,

$$n = \left(\frac{1.96(15.00)}{4.00}\right)^2 = (7.35)^2 = 54.0225 \approx 55.$$

○ EXAMPLE 11.5a

The loans manager of a credit union wants to estimate the average outstanding loan balance with 99% confidence and a maximum error of $200. To obtain information about the standard deviation a sample of 20 loans was randomly selected. This sample showed an average loan balance of $8000 with a standard deviation of $1200. What sample size is required to estimate the true average balance with 99% confidence and a maximum error of $200?

● SOLUTION

For 99% confidence, $z = 2.58$; the specified maximum error = 200; the standard deviation $s = 1200$.

$$n = \left(\frac{zs}{\text{MAXIMUM ERROR}}\right)^2 = \left(\frac{2.58(1200)}{200}\right)^2 = (15.48)^2 = 239.6304$$

The required sample size is 240 loans.

C. *Finding the Sample Size for Estimating a Population Proportion*

To determine the sample size required to estimate a population proportion we again need information about three factors:
1. the desired level of confidence;
2. the maximum allowable error (in this case stated as a percent);
3. the population proportion π.

Again, the values for the first two of these factors must be specified by the researcher. The third factor, the population proportion π, is the value that we wish to estimate at the specified level of confidence and the specified maximum error. For determining the sample size we can again resort to historical data available for situations closely resembling that being studied, or we can take a small sample to get a rough estimate of π.

However, when determining the sample size for estimating proportions we can determine the maximum sample size that will satisfy the specifications for the confidence level and the maximum error by utilizing the *maximum error term* in the confidence interval.

When p is known, the two applicable formulas

$$\text{MAXIMUM ERROR} = zs_p \quad \text{and} \quad s_p = \sqrt{\frac{p(1-p)}{n}}$$

can be combined into one formula to calculate n directly:

$$n = \frac{z^2(p)(1-p)}{(\text{MAXIMUM ERROR})^2} \quad \longleftarrow \textit{Formula } 11.10$$

When p is unknown, the value $p(1-p)$ becomes a *maximum* when $p = 0.5$, that is, $p(1-p) = (0.5)(0.5) = 0.25$,

$$n = \frac{z^2(0.25)}{(\text{MAXIMUM ERROR})^2} \quad \longleftarrow \textit{Formula } 11.11$$

This approach to computing the sample size ensures that the sample size is not too small, and can be used when it is not possible to obtain an estimate of the true population proportion. However, if the actual population proportion is either much larger or much smaller than 50%, the sample size may be much larger than needed. This, in turn, may lead to unnecessary costs.

○ EXAMPLE 11.5b

Suppose the manager of the credit union in Example 11.4a wanted to estimate the proportion of members whose biweekly salaries are deposited by electronic transfer within five percentage points of the true population proportion with

95% confidence.

a) Determine the sample size, assuming that the manager uses as an estimate of π the sample proportion of 38% obtained from the random sample of 250 depositors.

b) Determine the sample size, assuming that the manager has no idea what the proportion might be and does not want to spend time taking a sample.

SOLUTION

For 95% confidence, $z = 1.96$; the maximum error = 5% = 0.05.

(a) $p = 0.38$.

$$n = \frac{z^2(p)(1-p)}{(\text{MAXIMUM ERROR})^2} = \frac{(1.96)^2(0.38)(0.62)}{(0.05)^2}$$
$$= \frac{3.8416(0.2356)}{0.0025} = 362.03$$

The manager should sample 363 accounts.

(b) assume $p = 0.5$,

$$n = \frac{z^2(0.25)}{(\text{MAXIMUM ERROR})^2} = \frac{(1.96)^2(0.25)}{(0.05)^2}$$
$$= \frac{3.8416(0.25)}{0.0025} = 384.16$$

The manager would sample 385 accounts.

Note When dealing with calculations of sample size, always round up to the next whole number.

EXERCISE 11.5

1. Compute the sample size, given the following information:
   a) $\sigma_{\bar{x}} = 8.2$; $\sigma = 319.8$
   b) $s_{\bar{x}} = 0.13$; $s = 2.08$
   c) $\sigma_{\bar{x}} = 29.5$; $\sigma = 383.5$; $N = 1000$
   d) allowable error = 12; $z = 1.96$; $\sigma = 144$
   e) allowable error = 0.05; $z = 2.58$; $p = 0.70$

2. A population has a mean of \$680 and a standard deviation of \$25. Determine the sample size so that the sample mean will be in the interval \$670 to \$690 at a confidence level of
   a) 98%; **b)** 90%.

3. A local car dealer believes sales are in part determined by the relationship between the retail price of the automobiles and current average family income. The dealership has hired a market research firm to determine average family income in the area. Existing data indicate that the standard deviation is \$3600.

How large a sample should be taken to determine current average family income with 90% confidence and a maximum allowable error of \$200?

4. Users of a large computer system have been complaining about the slow response time to their database inquiries. Management has decided to study the problem by randomly sampling the terminals. Project guidelines require 95% confidence in the results and a maximum allowable error of 0.5 s. A small pilot study found a mean response time of 6.8 s, with a standard deviation of 1.5 s. How large a sample should be taken?

5. All new employees of Hard Sell Inc. are subject to a performance review to determine whether they should be offered a permanent job. An important consideration in assessing performance for sales staff is their success rate for closing deals. Management wants to be 98% confident with a maximum error of 2% in estimating an employee's true ability to close deals.
   a) Compute the sample size required without any estimate of an employee's success rate.
   b) Compute the sample size knowing that during a particular time period deals were closed 30% of the time.

6. A cable company wants to know the proportion of homes in a suburban area using satellite television services. In other similar areas 20% of the homes use satellite television services. Determine the sample size if the company wants to know the true proportion with a maximum error of 0.025 at the 90% confidence level.

SECTION 11.6 Interval Estimation around the Mean for Small Samples ($n \leq 30$) when σ Is Unknown

A. *The t Distribution*

When the size of the sample is small ($n \leq 30$), the use of the normal distribution for the construction of confidence intervals is no longer appropriate. In this case we use Student's ***t* distribution**.

The shape of the t distribution is similar to that of the normal distribution in that it is bell-shaped, symmetrical, and continuous. However, the t distribution is more widely dispersed and flatter, and its shape depends on the sample size.

The areas under the standardized t distribution curve depend on a factor known as **degrees of freedom**. For the t distribution, the degrees of freedom are defined to be one less than the sample size; that is, the degrees of freedom, d.f. = $(n - 1)$.

As the number of degrees of freedom increases with increasing sample size, the shape of the t distribution approaches the normal distribution more and more closely, and when $n > 30$ the normal distribution can be used.

B. The Concept of "Degrees of Freedom"

To understand the concept of degrees of freedom, consider the following example.

To estimate μ we need to know $\bar{x}$. The sample mean $\bar{x}$ is computed using the formula $\bar{x} = \dfrac{\sum x}{n}$.

For a given value of $\bar{x}$, $(n - 1)$ of the observations making up $\sum x$ can have any value, but the last observation must have a value that, when added to the other $(n - 1)$ values, equals n times the mean.

For example, if $n = 6$ and $\bar{x} = 7$, $\sum x = 6(7) = 42$. The first five values can be chosen in any way, such as 6, 4, 9, 10, and 8. The last value must equal $42 - (6 + 4 + 9 + 10 + 8) = 42 - 37 = 5$. If the first five observations have the values 3, 7, 8, 9, and 11, the last value $= 42 - (3 + 7 + 8 + 9 + 11) = 42 - 38 = 4$.

This means that for a given mean $\bar{x}$ and $n = 6$, the first five values are free to vary, but the last value has no such freedom. The computation of $\bar{x}$ is subject to $(6 - 1) = 5 = (n - 1)$ degrees of freedom.

C. Determination of the Confidence Interval

When σ is unknown and $n \leq 30$, the confidence interval is given by

$$\bar{x} \pm t_{n-1} s_{\bar{x}}$$ ←*Formula* 11.1

where $\bar{x}$ = the sample mean;

n = the sample size;

N = the population size;

$(n - 1)$ = degrees of freedom;

t_{n-1} is found in a table of t values;

$s_{\bar{x}} = \dfrac{s}{\sqrt{n}}$ for infinite populations, or when N is unknown, or

$s_{\bar{x}} = \dfrac{s}{\sqrt{n}}\sqrt{\dfrac{N - n}{N - 1}}$ for finite populations.

D. Using the t Table

A table of values of the t distribution for degrees of freedom from 1 to 30 is provided in Table 11.4 (see also the table on the inside back cover). The figures in the body of the table are the t values associated with a specified number of degrees of freedom for the areas in the tails of the curve representing a t distribution. Depending on the design of a t table, the table look-up can be based either on the area in one tail or the combined area in both tails (see Figure 11.2).

TABLE 11.4 Critical *t* Values

Degrees of freedom	Area in both tails combined: $\alpha = 0.20$ / Area in one tail: $\alpha = 0.10$	0.10 / 0.05	0.05 / 0.025	0.02 / 0.01	0.01 / 0.005
1	3.078	6.314	12.706	31.821	63.657
2	1.886	2.920	4.303	6.965	9.925
3	1.638	2.353	3.182	4.541	5.841
4	1.533	2.132	2.776	3.747	4.604
5	1.476	2.015	2.571	3.365	4.032
6	1.440	1.943	2.447	3.143	3.707
7	1.415	1.895	2.365	2.998	3.499
8	1.397	1.860	2.306	2.896	3.355
9	1.383	1.833	2.262	2.821	3.250
10	1.372	1.812	2.228	2.764	3.169
11	1.363	1.796	2.201	2.718	3.106
12	1.356	1.782	2.179	2.681	3.055
13	1.350	1.771	2.160	2.650	3.012
14	1.345	1.761	2.145	2.624	2.977
15	1.341	1.753	2.131	2.602	2.947
16	1.337	1.746	2.120	2.583	2.921
17	1.333	1.740	2.110	2.567	2.898
18	1.330	1.734	2.101	2.552	2.878
19	1.328	1.729	2.093	2.539	2.861
20	1.325	1.725	2.086	2.528	2.845
21	1.323	1.721	2.080	2.518	2.831
22	1.321	1.717	2.074	2.508	2.819
23	1.319	1.714	2.069	2.500	2.807
24	1.318	1.711	2.064	2.492	2.797
25	1.316	1.708	2.060	2.485	2.787
26	1.315	1.706	2.056	2.479	2.779
27	1.314	1.703	2.052	2.473	2.771
28	1.313	1.701	2.048	2.467	2.763
29	1.311	1.699	2.045	2.462	2.756
30	1.310	1.697	2.042	2.457	2.750
z value	1.28	1.64	1.96	2.33	2.58

Note When $n > 30$ the t values become close enough to the corresponding z values so that the normal distribution can be used.

FIGURE 11.2 ***t* Values**

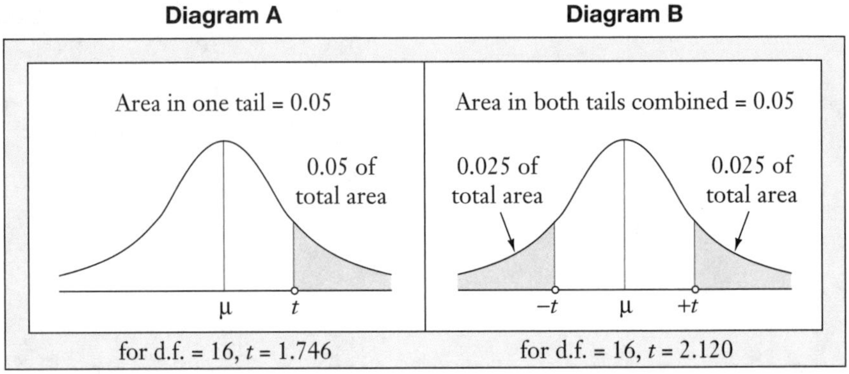

The columns in a t table are headed by selected proportions of the area in one tail or both tails combined. The most common proportions selected for one-tail tables are 0.10, 0.05, 0.025, 0.01, and 0.005 (see Diagram A).

The corresponding proportions for the combined area are 0.20, 0.10, 0.05, 0.02, and 0.01 (see Diagram B). The proportions for the combined area represent the chance of error when constructing confidence intervals and correspond to the confidence coefficients 0.80, 0.90, 0.95, 0.98, and 0.99 respectively.

Table 11.4 may be used for looking up t values for the *combined* area in the two tails (see Diagram B), or for the total area in one tail (see Diagram A).

EXAMPLE 11.6a

Find the t values for the following:

a) Sample size $n = 10$ at a confidence level of 90%.
b) Sample size $n = 20$, area in both tails combined is 0.10.
c) Sample size $n = 6$, area in one tail is 0.005.
d) Sample size $n = 24$ with a 20% chance of error.
e) Sample size $n = 13$, area in right tail is 0.01.

SOLUTION

a) The number of degrees of freedom,

$$\text{d.f.} = (n - 1) = (10 - 1) = 9.$$

For a confidence level of 90% the chance of error is 10%. The combined area in the two tails is 0.10 (0.05 in each tail). In Table 11.5 locate the row headed by 9 and the column headed by 0.10 (area in both tails combined). The desired t value = 1.833.

TABLE 11.5 Obtaining a *t* Value

Degrees of freedom			Area in both tails combined		
	α = 0.20	0.10	0.05	0.02	0.01
			Area in one tail		
	α = 0.10	0.05	0.025	0.01	0.005
1	3.078	6.314	12.706	31.821	63.657
2	1.886	2.920	4.303	6.965	9.925
3	1.638	2.353	3.182	4.541	5.841
⋮	⋮		⋮	⋮	⋮
8	1.397	1.860	2.306	2.896	3.355
9	1.383	1.833	2.262	2.821	3.250
10	1.372	1.812	2.228	2.764	3.169
11	1.363	1.796	2.201	2.718	3.106
12	1.356	1.782	2.179	2.681	3.055

Source: Extracted from Table 11.4.

FIGURE 11.3 *t* Distribution

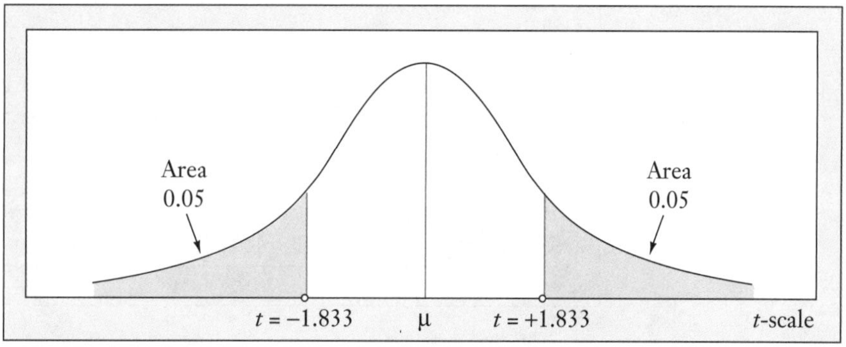

b) d.f. = $(n - 1) = (20 - 1) = 19$.
To find the value of t that corresponds to an area of 0.10 in both tails of the distribution combined, when there are 19 degrees of freedom, look under the 0.10 column (area in both tails combined), and proceed down to the 19 degrees of freedom row; the appropriate t value there is 1.729.

FIGURE 11.4 ***t* Distribution**

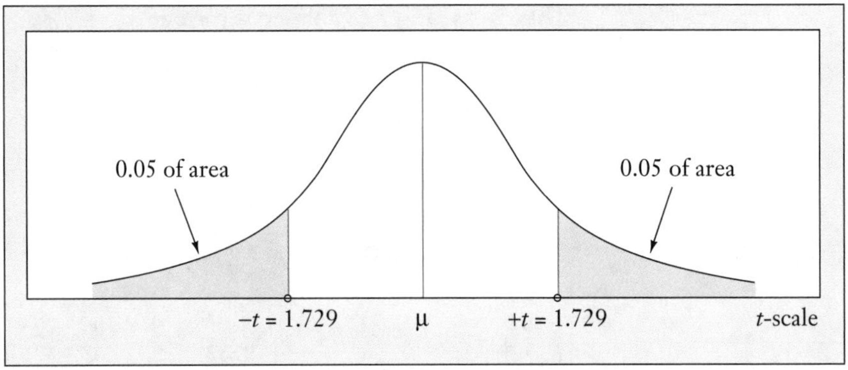

c) For $n = 6$, d.f. = 5. For the area in one tail = 0.005, and d.f. = 5, locate the row headed by 5 and the column headed by 0.005 (area in one tail). The t value = 4.032.

FIGURE 11.5 ***t* Distribution**

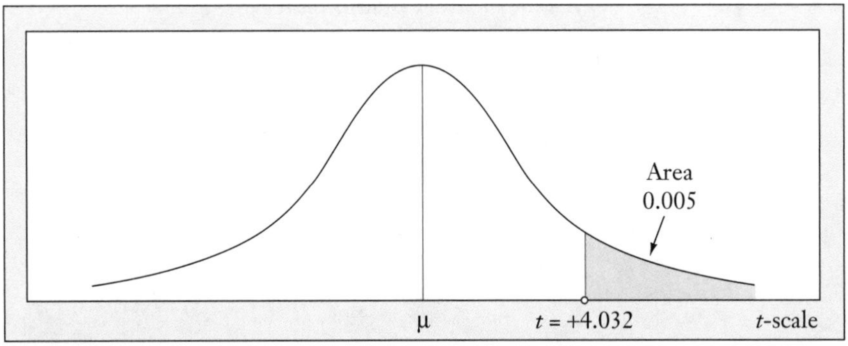

d) For a 20% chance of error the combined area in the tails is 0.20 (0.10 in each tail). For $n = 24$, d.f. = 23. The t value = 1.319.

FIGURE 11.6 ***t* Distribution**

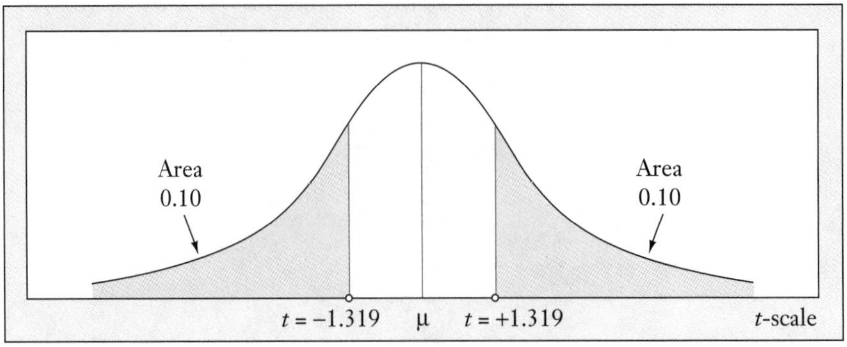

e) For $n = 13$, d.f. = 12. For area in right tail = 0.01. The t value = 2.681.

FIGURE 11.7 *t* Distribution

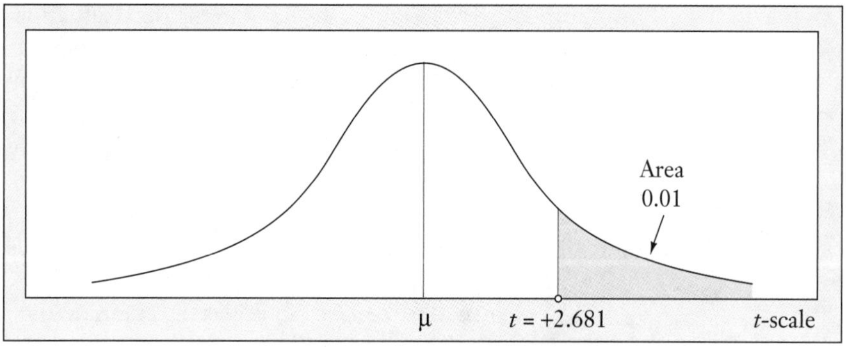

E. Constructing Confidence Intervals Using t *Values*

When σ is unknown, the confidence interval in which the mean can be found for small samples ($n \leq 30$) with a given degree of confidence is given by

$$\bar{x} \pm t_{n-1} s_{\bar{x}}$$

where $\bar{x}$ = the mean of the sample;
t_{n-1} = the value found in a t table for $(n - 1)$ degrees of freedom for a specified chance of error = (1− the confidence coefficient);
$s_{\bar{x}}$ = the standard error.

EXAMPLE 11.6b

A sample of size 25 has a mean of 150 and a standard deviation of 35. Construct a 99% confidence interval.

SOLUTION

$n = 25$; $\bar{x} = 150$; $s = 35$; N is unknown; the population is infinite.
The standard error for an infinite population

$$s_{\bar{x}} = \frac{s}{\sqrt{n}} = \frac{35}{\sqrt{25}} = \frac{35}{5} = 7$$

Since $n < 30$, the use of the t table is appropriate.
For 99% confidence the chance of error is 1%.
For combined area in both tails = 0.01, $n = 25$, d.f. = 24.
From Table 11.4 the t value for 24 degrees of freedom and a combined area in both tails of 0.01 is 2.797.
The confidence interval is given by
$\bar{x} \pm t_{n-1} s_{\bar{x}} = 150 \pm 2.797(7) = 150 \pm 19.579$, that is, 130.421 to 169.579.

EXAMPLE 11.6c

To reduce costs, the management of a delivery service is considering the use of propane or natural gas for the company's fleet of 256 panel trucks as an alternative to gasoline. To assist in the determination of cost savings, the fleet manager took a random sample of five trucks and measured their current gasoline consumption in kilometres per litre as follows:

9.0 10.8 8.4 10.3 11.7

Estimate the true gasoline consumption at the 95% confidence level.

SOLUTION

Since σ is unknown and $n < 30$, the interval in which μ will be found is $\bar{x} \pm t_{n-1} s_{\bar{x}}$.

The chance of error (area in both tails combined) = 0.05 and d.f. = $(n - 1)$ = $(5 - 1) = 4$.

The t value for d.f. = 4 and a chance of error of 0.05 = 2.776.

The sample mean $\bar{x}$ and the unbiased sample standard deviation s can be computed from the sample data.

x	9.0	10.8	8.4	10.3	11.7	$\sum x = 50.2$
x^2	81.00	116.64	70.56	106.09	136.89	$\sum x^2 = 511.18$

$$\bar{x} = \frac{\sum x}{n} = \frac{50.2}{5} = 10.04$$

$$s^2 = \frac{n\sum x^2 - (\sum x)^2}{n(n-1)} = \frac{5(511.18) - (50.2)^2}{5(4)}$$

$$= \frac{2555.90 - 2520.04}{20} = \frac{35.86}{20} = 1.793$$

$$s = \sqrt{1.793} = 1.3390.$$

Since $N = 256$, the population is finite.

$$s_{\bar{x}} = \frac{s}{\sqrt{n}}\sqrt{\frac{N-n}{N-1}} = \frac{1.3390}{\sqrt{5}}\sqrt{\frac{256-5}{256-1}} = \frac{1.3390}{2.2361}\sqrt{\frac{251}{255}}$$

$$= 0.5988\sqrt{0.984\,314} = 0.5988(0.9921) = 0.5941$$

The confidence interval = $10.04 \pm 2.776(0.5941) = 10.04 \pm 1.65$.

The interval in which μ is expected to be found is 8.39 to 11.69.

The management of the delivery service can be 95% confident that the true average gasoline consumption by its fleet of trucks is somewhere between 8.39 and 11.69 km/L.

○ **EXAMPLE 11.6d**

Assume that the manager of the delivery service took another sample of size 30. This sample yielded a mean of 9.95 km/L with a standard deviation of 1.35 km/L. Construct a 95% confidence interval using

a) the t tables; b) the z tables.

● **SOLUTION**

$N = 256$; $n = 30$; $\bar{x} = 9.95$; $s = 1.35$.

$$s_{\bar{x}} = \frac{1.35}{\sqrt{30}}\sqrt{\frac{256-30}{256-1}} = \frac{1.35}{5.4772}\sqrt{\frac{226}{255}} = 0.2465\sqrt{0.8863}$$

$$= 0.2465(0.9414) = 0.2321$$

a) For 95% confidence the chance of error = 0.05; d.f. = 29; the corresponding t value = 2.045.
The confidence interval $= \bar{x} \pm t_{n-1}s_{\bar{x}} = 9.95 \pm 2.045(0.2321)$
$= 9.95 \pm 0.475$.
The range of values in which μ is expected to be found is 9.475 to 10.425 km/L.

b) For 95% confidence, $z = 1.96$.
The confidence interval $= \bar{x} \pm zs_{\bar{x}} = 9.95 \pm 1.96(0.2321) = 9.95 \pm 0.455$.
The range of values in which μ is expected to be found is 9.495 to 10.405 km/L.

Note Since the t value is larger than the z value, the t value gives a wider confidence interval.

EXERCISE 11.6

1. Determine the t value for each of the following:
a) $n = 25$; the chance of error is 1%.
b) $n = 20$; the confidence coefficient is 0.80.
c) $n = 5$; the area in the two tails combined is 0.10.
d) $n = 11$; the area in the right tail is 0.01.
e) $n = 30$; the area in each tail is 0.025.

2. A sample of 12 items has a mean of 7.3 and a standard deviation of 2.4. Compute the 98% confidence limits for the population mean.

3. Steelco's fastener division uses statistical process control in the production of head bolts for the Big Three automakers. This requires the operators to take a random sample of eight bolts at randomly chosen intervals. One such sample had a mean diameter of 8.00 mm and a standard deviation of 0.02 mm. Determine the confidence interval using a confidence coefficient of 0.95.

4. In an effort to improve cash flow, the supervisor of an accounts receivable department decided to randomly check 20 of the company's 500 accounts on a daily basis. Yesterday's sample mean was \$10 800 with a standard deviation of \$1350. Estimate the true mean with a 10% chance of error.

5. The owner of a restaurant wants to estimate the daily average consumption of beef. A sample of seven days revealed the following daily usage in kilograms:

17.5	14.3	20.8	16.5	18.0	16.8	21.4

Construct the confidence interval for a 20% chance of error.

6. A survey of employees in comparable positions in different companies yielded the following hourly wages:

\$12.60	\$9.60	\$10.40	\$11.00	\$9.20
\$10.90	\$11.00	\$9.80	\$12.00	\$10.50

Estimate the average hourly wage with 90% confidence if the total number of employees having comparable positions is 800.

REVIEW EXERCISE

1. Calculate the confidence interval for each of the following:
   a) $\sigma = 25$, $\bar{x} = 300$, $n = 49$, confidence coefficient = 0.90;
   b) $\sigma = 9$, $\bar{x} = 36$, $n = 16$, $N = 330$, chance of error = 0.01;
   c) $s = 2$, $\bar{x} = 1300$, $n = 144$, $N = 4800$, confidence level = 98%;
   d) $s = 0.80$, $\bar{x} = 16.00$, $n = 16$, chance of error = 0.05.

2. Determine the confidence interval for each of the following:
   a) $\sigma = 3$, $\bar{x} = 20$, $n = 81$, $N = 1090$, chance of error = 0.20;
   b) $s = 0.40$, $\bar{x} = 4.60$, $n = 24$, $N = 730$, confidence level = 99%;
   c) $\sigma = 11$, $\bar{x} = 640$, $n = 25$, confidence coefficient = 0.95;
   d) $s = 40$, $\bar{x} = 1600$, $n = 36$, chance of error = 0.10.

3. From the equation $z\sigma_{\bar{x}} = 2.33\left(\frac{67.20}{\sqrt{64}}\right)$, determine
   a) the sample size;
   b) the confidence level;
   c) the standard deviation;
   d) the standard error;
   e) the maximum allowable error.

4. From the equation, $z\sigma_{\bar{x}} = 1.96\left(\frac{64}{\sqrt{49}}\right)$, determine
   a) the sample size;
   b) the confidence level;
   c) the standard deviation;
   d) the standard error;
   e) the maximum allowable error.

5. From the equation $t_{n-1}s_{\bar{x}} = 2.120\left(\frac{14.00}{\sqrt{17}}\right)\sqrt{\frac{583}{599}}$, determine

a) the population size;
b) the confidence level;
c) the standard deviation;
d) the standard error;
e) the maximum error.

6. From the equation $t_{n-1}s_{\bar{x}} = 1.706\left(\frac{27.00}{\sqrt{27}}\right)\sqrt{\frac{473}{499}}$, determine

a) the population size;
b) the confidence level;
c) the standard deviation;
d) the standard error;
e) the maximum error.

7. A sample of 56 is drawn from a population that has a standard deviation of 3.4 g. If the sample mean is 375 g, construct the confidence interval that contains the true mean with 90% certainty.

8. Fifty water samples are drawn from Lake Louise. The sample standard deviation is 0.5 mL with a sample mean of 30 mL. Construct the confidence interval that contains the true mean with 95% certainty.

9. Given a population of 4400 with a standard deviation of \$3280, compute the upper and lower limits of an 85% confidence interval for a sample of 150 with a sample mean of \$21 850.

10. J.L. Condie Publishers wants to know the time it takes from finding an author to write a textbook to publishing it. A random sample of 64 textbooks had a mean time of 20.8 months with a standard deviation of 3.6 months. Using a confidence coefficient of 0.90, determine the time interval in which the true mean can be expected to be found.

11. The administration at a college in Edmonton wants to know the time it takes for a student to register for a continuing education course. A random sample of 49 students had a mean wait time of 8.0 min with a standard deviation of 2.1 min. Using a confidence coefficient of 0.95, determine the time interval in which the true mean can be expected to be found.

12. The owner of a Tom Norton Donut Shop is reviewing staffing needs for the morning shift based on the length of lineup. If the lineup is 6 or more customers, another employee will be added to the morning shift. A record of the number of customers in the line taken at 45 different occasions over a period of one week showed an average lineup of 4.2 customers with a standard deviation of 0.8. Construct the 90% confidence interval to help the owner in making the staffing decision.

13. A truckload of fresh lobsters from the east coast awaits unloading at the food terminal. The buyer wants only market-size lobsters (0.50 kg or over). To check on the weight specification, the buyer takes a random sample of 32 lobsters. The total weight of the sample was 20 kg and the standard deviation was 0.21 kg. The buyer wants only a 2% chance of error.
a) Compute the upper and lower limits of the confidence interval.
b) Based on the confidence interval, should the buyer accept or reject the shipment?
c) Recalculate the confidence interval if the shipment consists of 200 lobsters.

14. Aglobulin's chamber of commerce has 793 members. In a confidential survey of 60 members it was learned that the members had an average income of $83 427 with a standard deviation of $5382. Compute the confidence interval at the 99% level.

15. Friday's trading volume on the TSE was 233 412 083 shares. A random sample of 50 stocks had a mean trading price of $16.42 and a standard deviation of $4.89. Calculate the interval limits for the average trading price at a confidence coefficient of 0.95.

16. A random sample of 75 cars had a mean fill-up of 37.0 L and a standard deviation of 10 L. Calculate the interval limits for the average fill-up at a confidence coefficient of 0.90.

17. ABC Distributors owns a fleet of 180 cars. A random sample of 36 cars showed their average mileage for the year to be 22 580 km with a standard deviation of 2915 km. Determine the true average mileage with 98% certainty.

18. Look up the t value for each of the following:
a) $n = 20$, the combined area = 0.10;
b) $n = 15$, the area in one tail = 0.10;
c) $n = 9$, the chance of error = 0.05;
d) $n = 26$, the confidence coefficient = 0.99.

19. Look up the t values for each of the following:
a) $n = 2$, the combined area = 0.02;
b) $n = 21$, the area in one tail = 0.01;
c) $n = 6$, the chance of error = 0.005;
d) $n = 30$, the confidence coefficient = 0.90.

20. The t values for each of the following are not listed in the t tables included in the text. Look up the two closest values in the t table that are on either side of the required value.
a) $n = 18$, the area in the right tail = 0.04;
b) $n = 28$, the combined area = 0.15;
c) $n = 7$, the confidence level = 96%;
d) $n = 14$, the chance of error = 0.08.

21. A psychologist doing research into dreams has determined that the 1380 cases reviewed showed a standard deviation of 1.8 for the number of dreams per night. If a sample of 12 from the cases reviewed had a mean of 4.6 dreams per night, construct a confidence interval around the sample mean with a 2% chance of error.

22. A financial planner reviewed the files of 1000 clients and determined the standard deviation of \$15 000 for their yearly salaries. If a sample of 20 cases reviewed had a mean salary of \$40 000, construct a confidence interval around the sample mean with a 10% chance of error.

23. For a population with a standard deviation of 13, construct an 80% confidence interval around the sample mean of 110 for a sample of size 9.

24. A pizzeria offers its product free if it is not served within 12 min after the order has been placed. Before starting this promotion, the owner had taken a small sample to obtain an estimate of the true average time elapsed between placing the order and serving the customer. Elapsed time, in minutes, for the sample was as follows:

9.3	10.0	9.8	10.1	9.5	10.3
9.1	10.5	9.9	10.5	10.1	9.7

a) Calculate the sample mean and the unbiased standard deviation.
b) Construct a 99% confidence interval.

25. Quick Clean Window Services currently charges residential customers according to the number and size of windows being cleaned. The problem with this approach is that it requires the owner to visit the customer and prepare a quote. To determine if the need for a quote could be eliminated by charging a flat fee regardless of the number of windows to be cleaned, the owner decided to research the average time spent by a work crew in cleaning the windows of a number of residences. The study showed the following times (in hours):

3.2 3.8 3.5 3.9 4.0 3.1 3.4 3.5

a) Determine the sample mean and the standard error.
b) Determine the upper and lower limits for a 0.98 confidence coefficient.
c) Should the owner go with the flat-fee approach?

26. During a 60-lap Formula One race in Mont Tremblant, Faster Foster's pit crew randomly sampled 10 laps and found the mean speed per lap to be 158 km/h with a standard deviation of 12.6 km/h. Assuming that the lap speed is normally distributed, compute the confidence interval in which the true average lap speed can be expected to be found with a 5% chance of error.

27. A consulting firm hired by a construction company (90 employees) found the mean productive time spent by 25 workers was 6.0 h with a standard deviation of 30 min. Assuming that the work time is normally distributed, compute the confidence interval in which the true mean time can be expected to be found with a 10% chance of error.

28. Robin's Bar and Grill uses an ice-cream dispensing machine that is precalibrated and can be set to dispense small, medium, or large ice-cream cones. A random sample of 24 small ice-cream cones weighed an average of 86 g with a standard deviation of 6.1 g. Compute the 98% confidence interval for the mean weight of a small cone filled by the machine.

29. The province of Alberta wants to estimate the proportion of women employed in the public sector. A random sample of 150 public-service employees contained 51 women. Construct a 90% confidence interval for the true proportion of women in Alberta's public sector.

30. A survey of 250 customers at Clip and Cut Hair Salon found that 73% of them were repeat customers. Construct a 90% confidence interval for the true proportion of customers that were repeat customers.

31. A survey of 500 college students found that 60% cheated at least once while at college. Construct a 95% confidence interval for the true proportion of students that cheated.

32. Laura's Catering Service provides a bar and bartender for catering parties. Last year, 156 parties needed a bar. A random sample of 39 of these parties showed that rye was ordered for 58% of the parties. Compute the 95% confidence interval in which the true proportion of parties for which rye was ordered can be found.

33. Out of 40 male students selected from a high school population of 376 male students, 28 watched the TV program *Survivor*. Construct the 98% confidence interval.

34. Calculate the approximate sample size required given the following information:
maximum allowable error = 1000
confidence coefficient = 0.90
sample standard deviation = 12 195

35. Compute the approximate sample size for the following:
maximum error = 0.02
chance of error = 0.02
sample proportion = 0.80

36. The true proportion for a population is 0.55. There is 90% certainty that a sample proportion will fall between 0.53 and 0.57. What sample size was used to compute the confidence limits?

37. The true mean for a population is known to be 6350 kg. It is also known that there is a 99% chance that a sample mean will fall between 6410 kg and 6290 kg. A random sample taken from the population had a standard deviation of 421 kg. What sample size was used to determine the confidence interval?

38. The research department of Gordon Products Limited has estimated the total cost of a survey of 300 households to be $34 500. The project manager believes the total survey cost to be prohibitive and wants to know if the total cost can be reduced by using a smaller sample without changing the maximum allowable error. The research department indicated that a smaller sample could be used by reducing the proposed 95% confidence level but warned that this would result in an increase in the sampling error.

a) Calculate the sample size if the confidence level is dropped to 90%.

b) Determine the increase in the sampling error and the cost savings by reducing the confidence level to 90%.

39. A freelance writer would like to submit a business article on the salaries of software engineers in the high-tech industry, including an interval estimate for the true average software engineer's salary. The publisher is very interested in the idea, provided that the writer meets the following requirements for publication:

i) the maximum error in the estimate must not exceed $2500;

ii) the estimate must have no more than a 5% chance of error.

To determine the appropriate sample size, the writer took a small random survey of software engineers and obtained the following data ($000):

85	82	79	98	105	89	95	100

Compute the sample size that will meet the publisher's conditions.

40. Algonquin Airlines would like to know the proportion of passengers who require special assistance. The company wants to select a sample that provides 95% confidence that the proportion of special-needs passengers is estimated within two percentage points of the true proportion. How large a sample is required?

41. A large company would like to know the proportion of workers who need safety retraining. The company wants to select a sample that provides a 99% confidence that the proportion of workers is estimated within ten percentage points of the true proportion. How large a sample is required?

42. A city's urban planning department is looking into rerouting trucks around the downtown core. Joseph Lahda, the senior planner, has proposed that a traffic study be done to establish the proportion of trucks using downtown streets. The study is to provide 98% confidence in the results, with a maximum allowable error of 0.015. Previous studies on file suggest that passenger car traffic accounts for 83% of traffic volume. How large a sample should be used for the study?

43. (CGA) In examining the credit accounts of a department store, an auditor would like to estimate the true mean account error (book value – audited value). To do so, the auditor selected a random sample of 100 accounts and found the average account error to be $60 with a standard deviation of $30.

a) Construct a 95% confidence interval for the true mean account error.

b) How large a sample is actually needed to ensure with 95% confidence that the sample estimate is within ± $3 of the true mean?

c) Can you obtain a meaningful 100% confidence interval? Explain why or why not.

44. (CGA) A politician is interested in estimating the true proportion of voters in his riding (numbering over 100 000) who favour his party's stand on a very controversial clause proposed for the Canadian Constitution.

a) How large a sample is needed to ensure that the sample proportion is within plus or minus 2 percentage points of the true proportion with 95% confidence?

b) Recalculate **(a)** if the politician had the additional information that about 70% of the voters favour his party's position on this issue.

c) Suppose a random sample of 900 voters is taken and it is found that 702 favour the party's stand. Obtain a 98% confidence interval for the true proportion of voters who favour the stand.

45. (CGA) Canada Post is attempting to audit, for a major metropolitan post office, the revenues obtained through mailed packages in a given period. The records indicate that 8000 packages were mailed during this period. Rather than record the weights of all these packages, the auditor takes a random sample of 144 packages and records the weights. The sample mean is found to be 800 g and sample standard deviation of these packages is 240 g.

a) Obtain a 97% confidence interval for the true mean package weight.

b) Suppose the rate for mailing packages is $5/kg. For this post office, obtain a 95% confidence interval for the expected total revenue, obtained through mailed packages.

c) The auditor is not satisfied with the margin of error of the interval obtained in **(a)**. It is desired that the estimate of the true average weight be within 30 g with 99% confidence. How large should the sample size be to satisfy the above constraints?

46. The following seven values represent random observations from a normal parent population of daily sales of used automobiles at a particular dealership: 5, 3, 6, 5, 6, 2, and 8. Obtain a 98% confidence interval for the mean of the parent population.

SELF-TEST

1. The variation in the number of persons employed by the businesses of a small community is indicated by the standard deviation of 4 persons. A random sample of 32 businesses showed the average number of persons employed to be 10.

a) Construct a confidence interval in which the true average number of employees can be found with 95% certainty.

b) Construct the corresponding interval if the number of businesses in the community is 210.

2. An import-export company has randomly selected 35 days and determined that the average daily cost of postage is \$32.85, with a standard deviation of \$2.15. The sample also indicated that 65% of the company's mail is international.
  a) Construct a confidence interval for the mean daily cost of postage with a chance of error of no more than 2%.
  b) Construct an 85% confidence interval for the proportion of domestic mail.

3. Peter sorts mail in the local post office and was speculating about the mean number of pieces of mail he put into each post-office box. His daughter Alexandra, a business student, suggested that he randomly choose 55 boxes and provide her with the count of pieces of mail in each box. For the sample provided by her father the next day, Alexandra found the mean to be 6.8 pieces of mail per box, with a standard deviation of 2.7 pieces. Construct a 99% confidence interval for the average number of pieces of mail per post-office box.

4. Cutrate Lumber Company would like to know the proportion of boards rejected per lift. A sample of 60 lifts showed that 9.8% of the boards in each lift were non-saleable. Construct a 90% confidence interval for the true proportion of rejects.

5. A small brewery monitors the alcohol content of its beer by taking 6 samples from every vat brewed. The following are the percent alcohol content data for the samples taken from vat No. 010527-M:

5.3 5.0 5.1 5.4 5.3 5.3

  a) Calculate the mean and standard deviation for the alcohol content of the samples taken.
  b) Construct a confidence interval for the mean alcohol content with a 2% chance of error.

6. A major chain of food stores wants to determine the proportion of customers who buy on impulse. The company decided to use a sample large enough to estimate the proportion of impulse buyers within 2.5 percentage points of the true proportion with 95% certainty. How large should the sample be?

7. Wedgewood Golf Products plans to retail golf tees in a most unusual manner. For a flat price, customers put one hand into a large jar and take out as many tees as they can grab. To determine the flat price, the manager wants to estimate the average number of tees per handful with a maximum error of 1 tee and a 5% chance of error. For the small number of store employees who took part, the standard deviation was 3 tees. What is the required size for the sample?

For an online glossary, go to **www.pearsoned.ca/hummelbrunner**.

Key Terms

Confidence coefficient 356
Confidence interval 356
Confidence level 356
Confidence limits 356
Degrees of freedom 373
Estimator 351
Interval estimation 354
Maximum error 368
Point estimate 352
Point estimation 352
***t* distribution** 373
Unbiased estimator 351

Summary of Formulas

1. Sample mean

$$\bar{x} = \frac{\sum x}{n}$$ ←*Formula* 11.1

2. Sample variance

$$s^2 = \frac{\sum(x - \bar{x})^2}{n - 1}$$ ←*Formula* 11.2

$$s^2 = \frac{n\sum x^2 - (\sum x)^2}{n(n - 1)}$$ ←*Formula* 11.2*a*

3. Sample standard deviation

$$s = \sqrt{s^2}$$ ←*Formula* 11.3

4. Estimated standard error of means for infinite populations when σ is not known

$$s_{\bar{x}} = \frac{s}{\sqrt{n}}$$ ←*Formula* 11.5

5. Estimated standard error of proportion for infinite populations when π is not known

$$s_p = \sqrt{\frac{p(1-p)}{n}}$$ ←*Formula* 11.7

6. Confidence interval for the mean

a) when σ is known:

$$\bar{x} \pm z\sigma_{\bar{x}}$$ ←*Formula* 11.4

b) when σ is not known and the sample size is large ($n > 30$):

$$\bar{x} \pm z s_{\bar{x}}$$ ←*Formula* 11.6

c) when σ is not known and the sample size is small ($n \leq 30$):

$$\bar{x} \pm t_{n-1} s_{\bar{x}}$$ ←*Formula* 11.12

7. Confidence interval for a proportion when π is not known and the sample size is large ($n > 30$)

$$p \pm z s_p$$ ←*Formula* 11.8

8. Finite correction factor

When the population size N is known, the standard errors $\sigma_{\bar{x}}$, $s_{\bar{x}}$, σ_p, and s_p in formulas 11.4 to 11.8 and 11.12 should be modified by multiplying by the finite correction factor $\sqrt{\frac{N-n}{N-1}}$.

9. Sample size for mean

$$n = \left(\frac{zs}{\text{MAXIMUM ERROR}}\right)^2$$ ←*Formula* 11.9

10. Sample size for proportions

a) when the sample proportion p is known:

$$n = \frac{z^2(p)(1-p)}{(\text{MAXIMUM ERROR})^2}$$ ←*Formula* 11.10

b) when the sample proportion p is not known:

$$\text{MAXIMUM VALUE OF } n = \frac{z^2(0.25)}{(\text{MAXIMUM ERROR})^2}$$ ←*Formula* 11.11

CHAPTER 12

Hypothesis Testing of a Mean or a Proportion

Introduction

When estimating the population mean or the population proportion from sample information, our main concern was determining the interval within which μ or π could be expected to be found for a chosen confidence level. In this chapter we will deal with hypothesis testing as another way of drawing conclusions about the population mean μ or the population proportion π from the sample statistics $\bar{x}$ or p.

Learning Outcomes

Upon completion of this chapter you will be able to

1. discuss the concept of hypothesis testing;
2. set up null and alternate hypotheses for given problem situations in both descriptive and symbolic terms;
3. distinguish between one-tail and two-tail tests;
4. describe the concept of significance level and the importance of choosing the significance level for a test;
5. determine the critical value of the test statistic for a test;
6. state the decision rule for a test;
7. compute the sample test statistic and interpret the result;
8. discuss the concept of Type I and Type II error;
9. determine the actual significance level (p value) of a test.

SECTION 12.1

The Hypothesis Testing Procedure

The basic idea behind hypothesis testing is to formulate a hypothesis and then decide, on the basis of sample evidence, whether to accept the hypothesis as a reasonable description of the situation or to reject it as unreasonable.

The procedure for carrying out a statistical hypothesis test is as follows:

1. Formulate the null hypothesis and the alternate hypothesis.
2. Identify the type of test to be used.
3. Select the level of significance.
4. Identify the appropriate test statistic to be used.
5. Determine the critical region for the test statistic.
6. State the decision rule.
7. Take a sample and compute the value of the sample test statistic.
8. Apply the appropriate decision rule and interpret the result.

In this procedure, steps 1 to 6 must precede the taking of the sample and must not be changed when the value of the sample test statistic has been determined. The reason for doing this is to prevent the creation of hypotheses to fit the sample result.

SECTION 12.2

Basic Concepts

A. Null Hypothesis and Alternate Hypothesis

In many business situations we start with a belief (hunch) that the population mean μ or the population proportion π is *greater than*, *less than*, or *not equal to* some specific value.

For example, we may believe that

1. a filling machine that is supposed to fill packages with 500 g of some product is incorrectly set — that is, the contents of the packages do not weigh 500 g;
2. the concentration of some pollutant in the atmosphere is greater than 10 ppm (parts per million);
3. the yield of a new production process is greater than the yield of the current process;
4. the time required to perform a task after a training program is less than the time required to perform the task before the training program;
5. the proportion of defective items in a consignment is greater than 5%.

More often than not, we cannot test the truth of such statements directly. However, problems of this nature can be approached indirectly by assuming that the logical opposite of this belief is not reasonable.

In our five examples we set up the following statements as the logical opposites of our beliefs:

1. Our belief is that the machine is not filling the packages with 500 g. The logical opposite of this belief is that the machine is correctly set — that is, the net weight in the packages equals 500 g.

2. The concentration of the pollutant in the atmosphere is less than or equal to 10 ppm.
3. The yield of the new production process is less than or equal to the current yield.
4. The time required to perform the task after the training program is more than or equal to the time required before the training program.
5. The proportion of defective items in the consignment is less than or equal to 5%.

In the context of hypothesis testing any such logical opposite is referred to as the **null hypothesis**. Denoted by H_0, the null hypothesis is a statement about some specific value of μ or π that we hope to be able to reject at the completion of the testing procedure.

The statement that we hope to demonstrate to be true is referred to as the **alternate hypothesis**. Denoted by H_a, the alternate hypothesis is a statement about a range of values for μ or π.

For belief 1, the hypotheses, stated in *descriptive* terms, are

H_0 : The net weight of the packages equals 500 g.
H_a : The net weight of the packages is not equal to 500 g.

Stated in symbolic terms,

$$H_0 : \mu = 500 \text{ g.}$$
$$H_a : \mu \neq 500 \text{ g.}$$

Note that the focus of the test of hypothesis is on the null hypothesis. Upon taking a sample, we use the relevant sample statistic ($\bar{x}$ or p) to demonstrate whether it is reasonable to *accept* the null hypothesis as being true or to *reject* it as being false.

If the value of the sample statistic is such as to indicate that the null hypothesis H_0 is unlikely to be true, then the alternate hypothesis H_a is considered to be a more reasonable statement about the true state of affairs.

B. Types of Tests — One-Tail Tests versus Two-Tail Tests

The range of values specified by the alternate hypothesis determines the type of test. An alternate hypothesis that specifies a complete range of values *either* greater than *or* less than the specific value stated in the null hypothesis defines a one-sided, or *one-tail test*.

The direction of the symbol for "greater than" (>) or "less than" (<) can be used to identify the test as being a right-tail test or a left-tail test. Alternate hypotheses of the type $\mu > 500$ involve a right-tail test (the symbol > points to the right) while alternate hypotheses of the type $\mu < 500$ involve a left-tail test (the symbol < points to the left).

Alternate hypotheses of the type $\mu \neq 500$ imply that μ may take a complete range of values below 500 as well as above 500. This type of test is called a two-sided, or *two-tail test*.

The null hypotheses, alternate hypotheses, and types of tests for the five situations described are summarized in Table 12.1.

TABLE 12.1 Summary of Hypotheses and Types of Test

Example	Hypothesis and type of test	Meaning of test
1	$H_0 : \mu = 500$ g $H_a : \mu \neq 500$ g Two-tail test	The symbol $\neq$ in H_a implies that we expect the true population mean to be either more than or less than 500 g.
2	$H_0 : \mu \leq 10$ ppm $H_a : \mu > 10$ ppm Right-tail test	The symbol > in H_a implies that we expect the true population mean to be greater than 10 ppm.
3	$H_0 : \mu \leq y$ kg/batch $H_a : \mu > y$ kg/batch Right-tail test	The symbol > in H_a implies that we expect the true population mean to be greater than y kg per batch.
4	$H_0 : \mu \geq t$ min $H_a : \mu < t$ min Left-tail test	The symbol < in H_a implies that we expect the true population mean to be smaller than t min.
5	$H_0 : \pi \leq 0.05$ $H_a : \pi > 0.05$ Right-tail test	The symbol > in H_a implies that we expect the true population proportion to be more than 0.05.

C. *Significance Level*

The purpose of hypothesis testing is to determine what values of the sample test statistic will lead us to decide whether to reject the null hypothesis as false or to accept it as true.

To do so we need to establish the probability level at which we are prepared to reject the null hypothesis as being a very unlikely statement about the true population parameter and therefore are willing to accept the alternate hypothesis as being a more likely statement about it.

The probability chosen is called the **significance level** of the test. Denoted by the Greek letter α (read "alpha"), the significance level represents the *chance of error*, that is, the risk that the null hypothesis will be rejected when it is in fact true.

In business situations the significance levels are often set by company policy. The most frequently chosen values of α are 0.10, 0.05, 0.02 and 0.01. These selections are referred to as 10%, 5%, 2%, and 1% levels of significance.

D. *Test Statistic to Be Used*

As we are only dealing with testing a population mean or a population proportion, the test statistic of concern will involve either the normal distribution or the t distribution. This means that, depending on the testing situation, the statistic to be used will be either a z value or a t value.

The choice of distribution in a particular test depends on

1. whether or not the population distribution is known to be normal;

2. whether or not the standard deviation of the population distribution σ is known;
3. the sample size.

In the business world a z value is usually used as the test statisic because of the robustness and familiarity of the normal curve. The exception to this practice is when the population standard deviation σ is not known and a small sample ($n \leq 30$) is taken. In this case the test statistic used is a t value.

When the test statistic is a z value, Table 12.2 can be used to select the appropriate value for the chosen significance level and the type of test to be used.

TABLE 12.2 *z* Values for Hypothesis Testing

Significance level α	z value	
	One-tail test	Two-tail test
0.01	2.33	2.575
0.02	2.055	2.33
0.05	1.645	1.96
0.10	1.28	1.645

When the test statistic is a t value, use Table 11.4.

E. Critical Values and Critical Regions

Referred to as **critical values**, the test statistics divide the total area under the curve representing the specific sampling distribution into two regions: the **acceptance region** and the **rejection region** (see figures 12.1, 12.2, and 12.3).

For a two-tail test the significance level establishes the combined area in the tails of a standardized sampling distribution below the negative value of the associated test statistic z or t and above their positive values as the rejection region.

A two-tail test is appropriate for an alternate hypothesis involving a "not equal to" ($\neq$) situation (see Figure 12.1).

FIGURE 12.1 Critical Regions for Two-Tail Tests

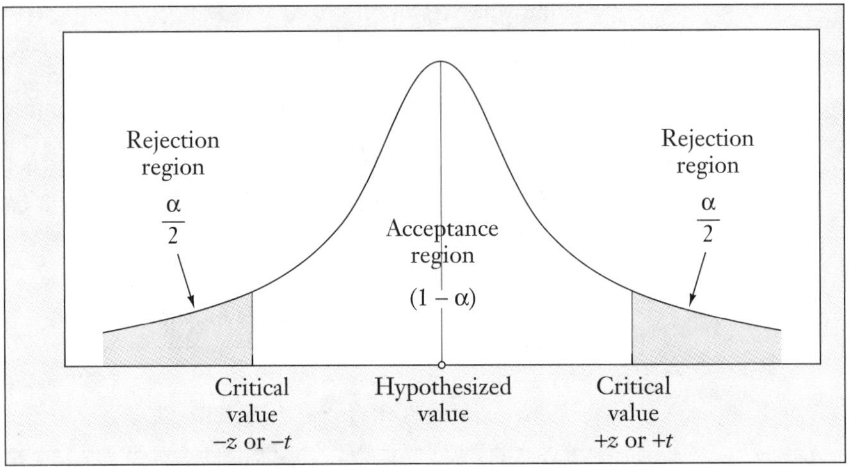

For a right-tail test the significance level (α) determines the area in the tail to the right of the positive value of the test statistic. The critical value of the test statistic divides the total area under the curve representing the sampling distribution into the acceptance region to the left and the rejection region to the right.

A right-tail test is appropriate for an alternate hypothesis involving a "greater than" (>) situation (see Figure 12.2).

FIGURE 12.2 Critical Regions for Right-Tail Tests

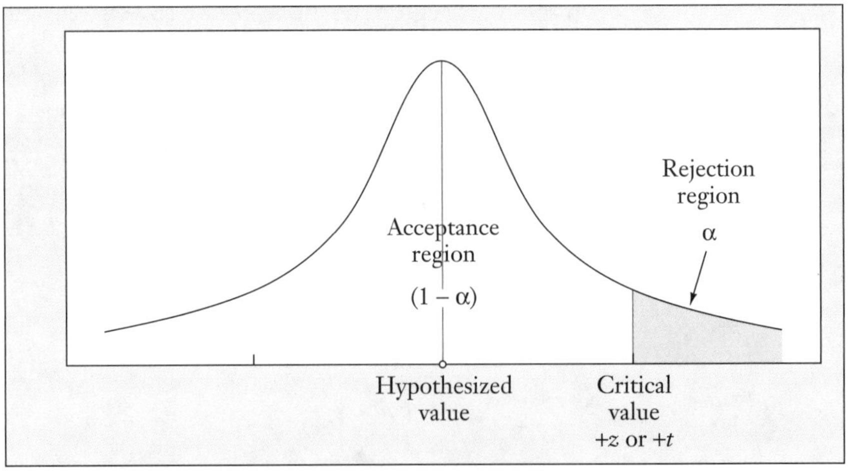

Note that in the case of a right-tail test we have acceptance if the test statistic is negative. This is an important consideration when using the combined decision rule stated in Section F.

For a left-tail test, α represents the area in the tail below the negative value of the test statistic. This critical value of the test statistic divides the total area under the curve representing the sampling distribution into the acceptance region to the right and the rejection region to the left.

FIGURE 12.3 Critical Regions for Left-Tail Tests

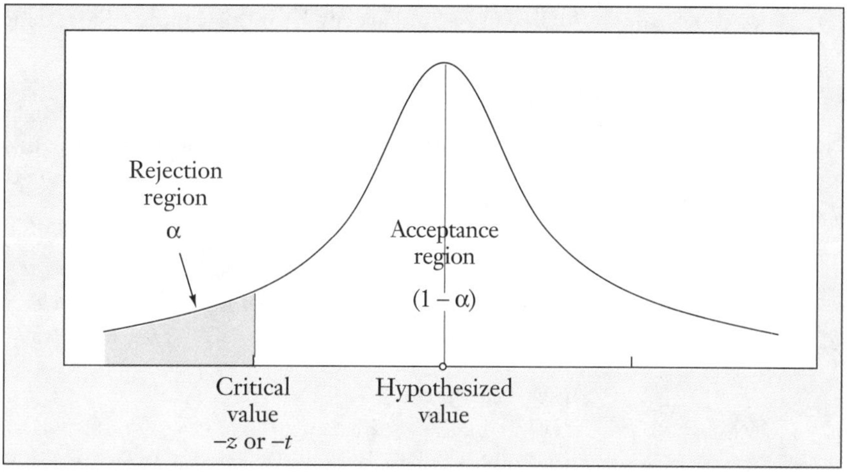

A left-tail test is appropriate for an alternate hypothesis involving a "less-than" (<) situation (see Figure 12.3).

Note that in the case of a left-tail test we have acceptance if the test statistic is positive. This is important when using the combined decision rule stated in Section F.

F. Stating the Decision Rule

The decision rule outlines the conditions under which the null hypothesis will be accepted or rejected.

1. Decision rule for a two-tail test:

   "Accept the null hypothesis if the sample test statistic falls between the positive and negative critical values of the test statistic, or reject the null hypothesis and accept the alternate hypothesis if the sample test statistic is less than the negative critical value or greater than the positive critical value of the test statistic."

   In symbolic terms:

   "Accept H_0 if ($-z$ or $-t$) < sample test statistic < ($+z$ or $+t$)"

   or

   "Reject H_0 and accept H_a if the sample test statistic < ($-z$ or $-t$) or if the sample test statistic > ($+z$ or $+t$)."

2. Decision rule for a right-tail test:

   "Accept H_0 if the sample test statistic < ($+z$ or $+t$)"

   or

   "Reject H_0 and accept H_a if the sample test statistic > ($+z$ or $+t$)."

3. Decision rule for a left-tail test:

"Accept H_0 if the sample test statistic > ($-z$ or $-t$)"

or

"Reject H_0 and accept H_a if the sample test statistic < ($-z$ or $-t$)."

Subject to immediately accepting H_0 in the case of a right-tail test if the sample test statistic is negative, and in case of a left-tail test if the sample test statistic is positive, the specific ways of stating the decision rule for each type of test can be combined in one decision rule by using the absolute values of the test statistics.

Combined decision rule *If the absolute value of the sample test statistic is greater than the critical value of the test statistic for the chosen significance level, reject* H_0*; otherwise do not.*

In symbolic terms,

If |sample test statistic| > |critical value of z or t| reject H_0; otherwise do not.

G. Computing the Value of the Sample Test Statistic

1. *When testing a mean.*
   The calculation of the sample test statistic depends on whether the population standard deviation σ is known or not known.

   a) If σ is *known*, the sample test statistic

$$z = \frac{\bar{x} - \mu}{\sigma_{\bar{x}}}$$ ←*Formula* 12.1

where $\bar{x}$ = the sample mean;
μ = the hypothesized population mean;
σ = the population standard deviation;
n = the sample size;
$\sigma_{\bar{x}}$ = the standard error of the mean.

   b) If σ is *not known* and $n > 30$, the sample test statistic

$$z = \frac{\bar{x} - \mu}{s_{\bar{x}}}$$ ←*Formula* 12.2

or, if σ is *not known* and $n \leq 30$

$$t_{n-1} = \frac{\bar{x} - \mu}{s_{\bar{x}}}$$ ←*Formula* 12.2a

where $\bar{x}$ = the sample mean;
μ = the hypothesized mean;
s = the sample standard deviation;
n = the sample size;
$s_{\bar{x}}$ = the estimated standard error of the mean.

2. *When testing a proportion.*
Provided $n > 30$, the sample test statistic for testing a proportion is found by

$$z = \frac{p - \pi}{\sigma_p}$$ ←*Formula* 12.3

where p = the sample proportion;
π = the hypothesized population proportion;
n = the sample size;
σ_p = the standard error of proportion.

EXERCISE 12.2

1. A hypothesis test is to be performed for each of the following statements:
   a) A fuel additive is said to improve performance by at least 10%.
   b) Company A's light bulbs will last two thousand hours.
   c) Vitamin XYZ reduces cholesterol levels.
   For each of the statements,
   i) write a reasonable null and alternate hypothesis in descriptive terms;
   ii) state the hypotheses in **(i)** in symbolic form;
   iii) indicate the type of test to be used.

2. A hypothesis test is to be performed for each of the following statements:
   a) The average person has an IQ of 100.
   b) 70% of cola drinkers prefer Coke to Pepsi.
   c) Washing the hulls of boats in dry dock will reduce the zebra mussel population in the Great Lakes.
   For each of the statements,
   i) write a reasonable null and alternate hypothesis in descriptive terms;
   ii) state the hypotheses in **(i)** in symbolic form;
   iii) indicate the type of test to be used.

SECTION 12.3

Hypothesis Testing of a Mean

The choice of test statistic in a particular test depends on whether

1. the population standard deviation σ is known or not;
2. the sample size is large ($n > 30$) or small ($n \leq 30$).

Based on the above factors, we will examine three cases.

Case 1 The population standard deviation σ is known.

The use of the z statistic, $z = \dfrac{\bar{x} - \mu}{\sigma_{\bar{x}}}$, is appropriate in this case.

Case 2 A large sample ($n > 30$) is taken from a population distribution whose standard deviation σ is not known.
When the sample size is greater than 30, the sampling distribution of the means will approximate the normal distribution. The use of the z statistic, $z = \dfrac{\bar{x} - \mu}{s_{\bar{x}}}$, is appropriate in this case.

Case 3 A small sample ($n \leq 30$) is taken from a population whose standard deviation σ is not known.
The appropriate sampling distribution of the means is the t distribution and the appropriate test statistic is the t value, $t = \dfrac{\bar{x} - \mu}{s_{\bar{x}}}$.

Care must be taken in using the t tables depending on whether the test is a two-tail test or a one-tail test.

The t table supplied in this text (Table 11.4) gives t values for the area in one tail or the combined area in both tails. For a *two-tail* test the table proportions 0.20, 0.10, 0.05, 0.02, and 0.01 correspond *directly* to the significance levels {20%, 10%, 5%, 2%, 1%}. For example, for a two-tail test at the 5% level of significance, the appropriate t value can be located in the column headed by 0.05. However, in the case of a *one-tail* test, the level of significance must be found in the heading labelled "Area in one tail" to locate the proper column.

EXAMPLE 12.3a

The population has an assumed mean of 500 and a standard deviation of 35. A sample of 25 items had a mean of 483. Conduct a two-tail test with a significance level of 0.01 on whether the assumed mean of 500 is reasonable.

SOLUTION

$\mu = 500; \bar{x} = 483; n = 25; \sigma = 35; \alpha = 0.01.$

Step 1 Statement of hypotheses.
Null hypothesis, $H_0 : \mu = 500.$
Alternate hypothesis, $H_a : \mu \neq 500.$

Step 2 Type of test.
Two-tail test is required since the alternate hypothesis involves a "not equal to" situation.

Step 3 Significance level, $\alpha = 0.01$.
The area in each tail, $\frac{\alpha}{2} = 0.005$.

Step 4 Since the population standard deviation σ is known, the z statistic is appropriate regardless of the sample size.

Step 5 For a significance level of 1% ($\alpha = 0.01$) and a two-tail test, the critical value of the test statistic $z = 2.58$.

FIGURE 12.4 Critical Regions for Two-Tail Test

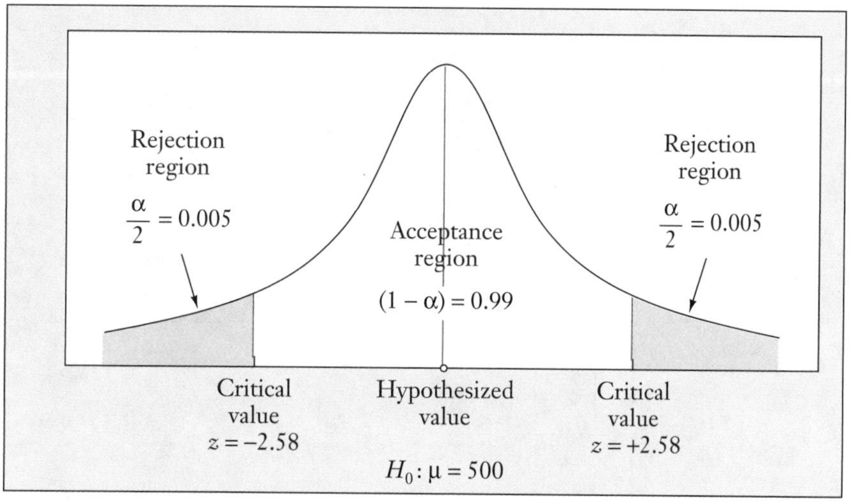

Step 6 Decision rule.
Reject H_0 and accept H_a if the absolute value of the sample test statistic is greater than 2.58.

Step 7 Compute the sample test statistic.
Since σ is known,

$$\sigma_{\bar{x}} = \frac{\sigma}{\sqrt{n}} = \frac{35}{\sqrt{25}} = \frac{35}{5} = 7.00$$

$$\text{Sample test Statistic, } z = \frac{\bar{x} - \mu}{\sigma_{\bar{x}}} = \frac{483 - 500}{7.00} = \frac{-17}{7.00} = -2.43$$

$$|z| = 2.43$$

Step 8 Apply the decision rule and interpret.
Since the absolute value of the sample test statistic is less than 2.58, accept H_0. The sample result supports the assumption that the population mean $\mu = 500$.

EXAMPLE 12.3b

The shape of the population distribution is normal with an assumed mean of 53. A sample of 100 had a sample mean of 54 and a standard deviation of 5.

Conduct a right-tail test at the 5% level of significance since you believe the population mean to be greater than 53.

SOLUTION

$\mu = 53; \bar{x} = 54; n = 100; s = 5; \alpha = 0.05.$

Step 1 $H_0 : \mu = 53;$
$H_a : \mu > 53.$

Step 2 Right-tail test is required since the alternate hypothesis involves a "greater than" situation.

Step 3 For a one-tail test, $\alpha = 0.05$ represents the area in the right tail.

Step 4 Since $n > 30$ the use of the z statistic is appropriate, even if the population standard deviation is not known.

Step 5 Using Table 12.2, for a one-tail test and $\alpha = 0.05$, the critical value of the test statistic $z = 1.64$.

FIGURE 12.5 Critical Regions for Right-Tail Test

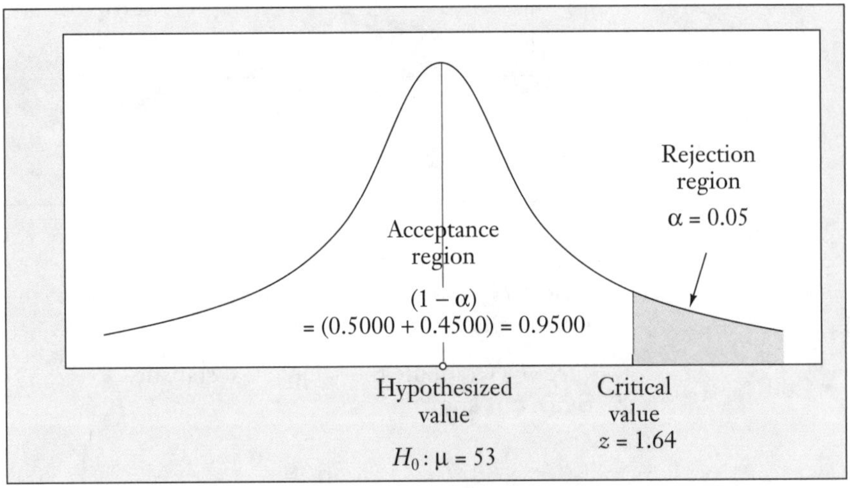

Step 6 Provided the sample test statistic z is not negative, reject H_0 and accept H_a if the absolute value of the sample test statistic > 1.64.

Step 7 Since $s = 5$ and $n = 100$,

$$s_{\bar{x}} = \frac{s}{\sqrt{n}} = \frac{5}{\sqrt{100}} = \frac{5}{10} = 0.50$$

$$\text{Sample test statistic, } z = \frac{\bar{x} - \mu}{s_{\bar{x}}} = \frac{54 - 53}{0.50} = \frac{1}{0.50} = 2.00$$

Step 8 Since z is not negative and the absolute value of the sample test statistic $z > 1.64$, reject H_0 and accept H_a. The sample result does not support the assumption that the population mean is 53.

EXAMPLE 12.3c

The population mean is assumed to be 6425. A sample of 49 items had a mean of 6320 with a standard deviation of 285. Conduct a left-tail test at the 2% level of significance since the population mean is believed to be less than 6425.

SOLUTION

$\mu = 6425; \bar{x} = 6320; s = 285; n = 49; \alpha = 0.02.$

Step 1 $H_0 : \mu = 6425;$
$H_a : \mu < 6425.$

Step 2 Left-tail test is required since the alternate hypothesis involves a "less than" situation.

Step 3 $\alpha = 0.02.$

FIGURE 12.6 Critical Regions for Left-Tail Test

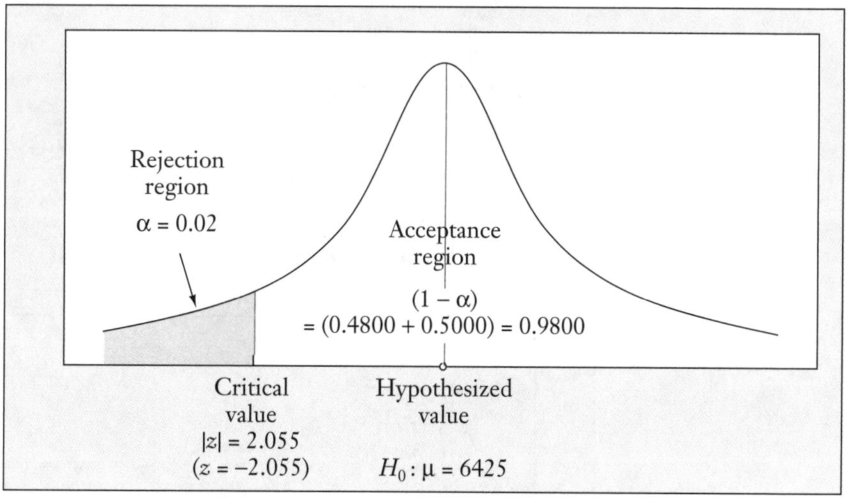

Step 4 Since σ is unknown and $n > 30$, the z statistic can be used.

Step 5 Using Table 12.2, for a one-tail test and $\alpha = 0.02$, the critical value of the test statistic $z = 2.055$.

Step 6 Provided that z is not positive, reject H_0 and accept H_a if the absolute value of the sample test statistic > 2.055.

Step 7

$$s_{\bar{x}} = \frac{s}{\sqrt{n}} = \frac{285}{\sqrt{49}} = \frac{285}{7} = 40.71$$

$$z = \frac{\bar{x} - \mu}{s_{\bar{x}}} = \frac{6320 - 6425}{40.71} = \frac{-105}{40.71} = -2.58$$

$$|z| = 2.58$$

Step 8 Since z is not positive and the absolute value of the sample test statistic $z > 2.05$, reject H_0 and accept H_a. The sample result does not support the assumption that $\mu = 6425$.

○ EXAMPLE 12.3d

The population mean is assumed to be 400. A sample of 20 had a mean of 381 with a standard deviation of 40. Test the claim that the mean is 400 using a two-tail test at the 5% level of significance.

● SOLUTION

$\mu = 400$; $\bar{x} = 381$; $s = 40$; $n = 20$; $\alpha = 0.05$.
$H_0 : \mu = 400$;
$H_a : \mu \neq 400$.
Two-tail test is required.
$\alpha = 0.05$.
Since σ is unknown and $n < 30$, the appropriate test statistic is the t value for $\alpha = 0.05$ and $(n - 1) = 19$ degrees of freedom. From the t table (Table 11.4) the critical value of the test statistic $t = 2.093$.

FIGURE 12.7 Critical Regions for Two-Tail Test

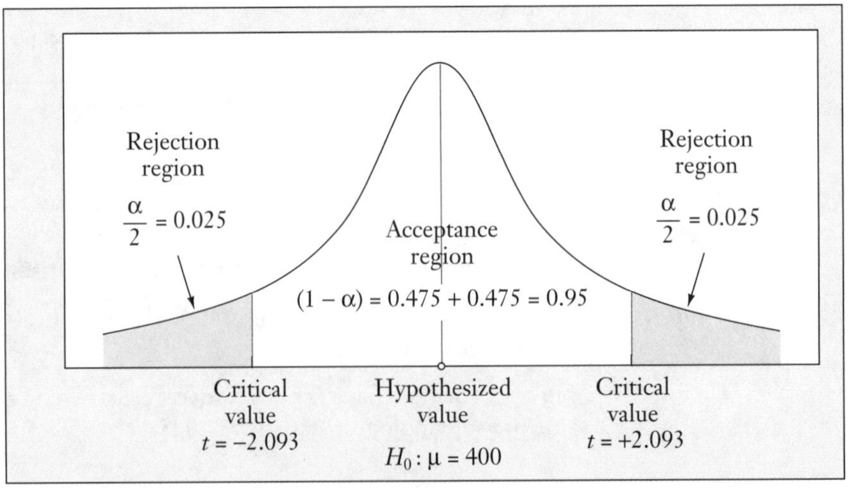

Reject H_0 and accept H_a if the absolute value of the sample test statistic $t > 2.093$.

$$s_{\bar{x}} = \frac{s}{\sqrt{n}} = \frac{40}{\sqrt{20}} = \frac{40}{4.472136} = 8.9443$$

$$\text{Sample test statistic, } t = \frac{\bar{x} - \mu}{s_{\bar{x}}} = \frac{381 - 400}{8.9443} = \frac{-19}{8.9443} = -2.124$$

$$|t| = 2.124$$

Since the absolute value of the sample test statistic $t >$ the absolute value of the critical value $t = 2.093$, reject H_0 and accept H_a. The sample result does not support the assumption that $\mu = 400$.

EXAMPLE 12.3e

The population mean is assumed to be 4500. A sample of 25 items had a mean of 4620 and a standard deviation of 250. Conduct a right-tail test at the 1% level of significance.

SOLUTION

$\mu = 4500$; $\bar{x} = 4620$; $s = 250$; $n = 25$; $\alpha = 0.01$.
$H_0 : \mu = 4500$;
$H_a : \mu > 4500$.
Right-tail test is required.
Since σ is unknown and $n < 30$, the appropriate test statistic is the t value with $(n - 1) = 24$ degrees of freedom. The significance level of 0.01 represents the area in the right tail. The critical value for the test statistic t is obtained from Table 11.4 in the section labelled one-tail values; this critical value is $t = 2.492$.

FIGURE 12.8 Critical Regions for Right-Tail Test

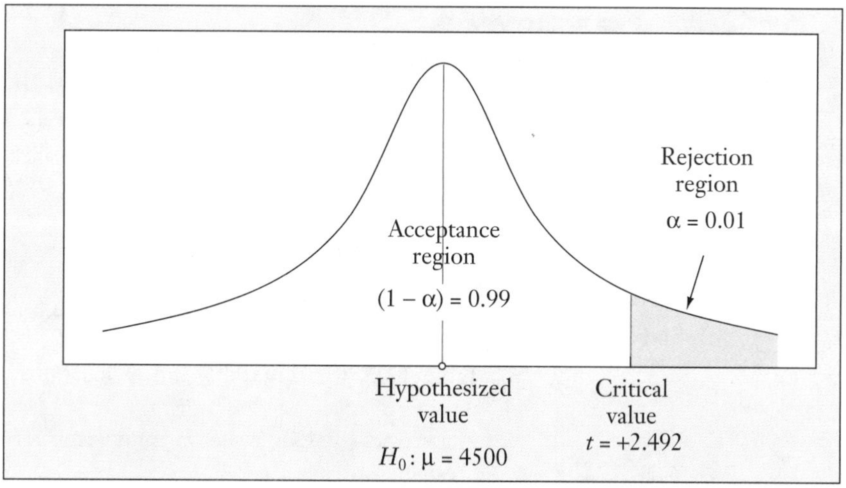

Provided t is not negative, reject H_0 and accept H_a if the absolute value of the sample test statistic $t > 2.492$.

$$s_{\bar{x}} = \frac{s}{\sqrt{n}} = \frac{250}{\sqrt{25}} = \frac{250}{5} = 50$$

$$\text{Sample test statistic, } t = \frac{\bar{x} - \mu}{s_{\bar{x}}} = \frac{4620 - 4500}{50} = \frac{120}{50} = +2.40$$

Since t is not negative and the absolute value of the sample test statistic $t <$ the absolute value of the critical value $t = 2.492$, accept H_0. The sample results support the assumption that the population mean $\mu = 4500$.

Examples 12.3a to 12.3e illustrate when to use and how to compute the value of the sample test statistic z or t.

In most practical situations the most difficult aspect of hypothesis testing is determining the appropriate alternate hypothesis and the type of test to be performed. The following examples show how to deal with this aspect of testing.

EXAMPLE 12.3f

On a university entrance examination, the students' scores are known to be normally distributed with a mean of 500 points and a standard deviation of 75 points. One high-school principal claims that her school's graduates scored higher than the stated mean. To support her claim she asked the examiners to randomly select 50 of her school's students who wrote the examination. She learned that the mean score for this sample was 520 points. Does this result support her claim at the 5% significance level?

SOLUTION

$\mu = 500$; $\bar{x} = 520$; $\sigma = 75$; $n = 50$; $\alpha = 0.05$.

Since the claim is that this school's students do better than average, our concern is that the population mean for this school may be greater than the stated mean μ.

$H_0 : \mu = 500$;

$H_a : \mu > 500$.

The test to be performed is a right-tail test.

$\alpha = 0.05$.

Since the population standard deviation σ is known, the appropriate test statistic is z.

Using Table 12.2, for $\alpha = 0.05$ and a one-tail test, the critical value of $z = 1.64$.

Provided z is not negative, reject H_0 and accept H_a if the absolute value of the sample test statistic $z > 1.64$.

$$\sigma_{\bar{x}} = \frac{\sigma}{\sqrt{n}} = \frac{75}{\sqrt{50}} = \frac{75}{7.0711} = 10.6066$$

$$\text{Sample test statistic, } z = \frac{\bar{x} - \mu}{\sigma_{\bar{x}}} = \frac{520 - 500}{10.6066} = \frac{20}{10.6066} = +1.89$$

Since z is not negative and the absolute value of the sample test statistic $z >$ the absolute value of the critical value $= 1.64$, we reject H_0 and accept H_a. The sample result supports the claim that graduates of this high school score better than the average on the university entrance examination.

EXAMPLE 12.3g

An industrial engineer determined on the basis of some rough calculations that it should take 150 h to produce a complex part for a new airplane. After production of the new part had been carried on for some time, the engineer followed the production of nine such parts and found the mean production time to be 147.5 h with a standard deviation of 2.5 h. Test at the 5% level of significance whether the original estimate of 150 h was reasonable.

SOLUTION

$\mu = 150$; $\bar{x} = 147.5$; $s = 2.5$; $n = 9$; $\alpha = 0.05$.

Since the engineer's estimate could be either high or low, our concern is that the true population mean may be either greater than 150 or less than 150.

$H_0 : \mu = 150$;

$H_a : \mu \neq 150$.

The test to be performed is a two-tail test.

$\alpha = 0.05$.

Since σ is not known and $n < 30$, the appropriate test statistic is the t statistic.

Using Table 11.4, for a two-tail test, $\alpha = 0.05$ and $(n - 1) = 8$ degrees of freedom, the critical value of the test statistic t is found in the column headed by 0.05. Therefore, $t = 2.306$.

Reject H_0 and accept H_a if the absolute value of the sample test statistic $t > 2.306$.

$$s_{\bar{x}} = \frac{s}{\sqrt{n}} = \frac{2.5}{\sqrt{9}} = \frac{2.5}{3} = 0.8333$$

$$\text{Sample test statistic, } t = \frac{\bar{x} - \mu}{s_{\bar{x}}} = \frac{147.5 - 150.0}{0.8333} = \frac{-2.5}{0.8333} = -3.00$$

$$|t| = 3.00$$

Since the absolute value of the sample test statistic t is greater than the critical value 2.306, reject H_0 and accept H_a. The sample test result suggests that the average production time is significantly different from the engineer's original estimate.

EXAMPLE 12.3h

A steel fabrication mill manufactures cotter pins with a mean length of 15 mm. The customer may accept pins that are longer than the mean length specified but not those that are shorter. The customer takes a sample of 10 pins from each batch received and measures their lengths to determine whether the batch should be accepted or rejected at the 1% level of significance.

The sample from a recently arrived batch showed the following lengths (in mm):

14.35	14.65	14.75	14.35	14.15
14.95	14.65	14.85	15.15	14.75

Should the batch be accepted?

SOLUTION

$\mu = 15.00$; $n = 10$; $\alpha = 0.01$.

Since we are willing to accept pins longer than but not shorter than 15 mm, our concern is that the population mean may be less than the specified mean of 15 mm.

$H_0 : \mu = 15.00$;

$H_a : \mu < 15.00$.

The test to be performed is a left-tail test.

$\alpha = 0.01$.

Since σ is unknown and $n < 30$, the appropriate test statistic is the t statistic.

For a one-tail test, $\alpha = 0.01$ and $(n - 1) = 9$ degrees of freedom, the critical value of the test statistic is found in Table 11.4 in the one-tail values section. Therefore, $t = 2.821$.

Provided t is not positive, reject H_0 and accept H_a if the absolute value of the sample test statistic $t > 2.821$.

To compute the sample test statistic we must first determine the sample mean and the standard error of the sample mean.

x	x^2
14.35	205.9225
14.65	214.6225
14.75	217.5625
14.35	205.9225
14.15	200.2225
14.95	223.5025
14.65	214.6225
14.85	220.5225
15.15	229.5225
14.75	217.5625
$\sum x = 146.60$	$\sum x^2 = 2149.9850$

$$\bar{x} = \frac{\sum x}{n} = \frac{146.60}{10} = 14.66$$

$$s^2 = \frac{n(\sum x^2) - (\sum x)^2}{n(n-1)} = \frac{10(2149.9850) - (146.60)^2}{10(9)}$$

$$= \frac{21\,499.850 - 21\,491.560}{90} = \frac{8.29}{90} = 0.092\,111\,11$$

$$s = \sqrt{0.092\,111\,11} = 0.303\,498\,12$$

$$s_{\bar{x}} = \frac{s}{\sqrt{n}} = \frac{0.303\,498\,12}{\sqrt{10}} = \frac{0.303\,498\,12}{3.162\,277\,66} = 0.095\,97$$

$$\text{Sample test statistic, } t = \frac{\bar{x} - \mu}{s_{\bar{x}}} = \frac{14.66 - 15.00}{0.095\,97} = \frac{-0.34}{0.095\,97} = -3.543$$

$$|t| = 3.543$$

Since t is not positive and the absolute value of the sample test statistic $t >$ the critical value 2.821, reject H_0 and accept H_a. The sample result does not support the assumption that the batch mean is 15.00 mm. The batch should not be accepted.

These calculatons can be completed using EXCEL, as demonstrated in USING EXCEL 12.1.

USING EXCEL 12.1

EXCEL can be used to help us calculate the critical t value, the sample mean, the standard error of the sample mean, and the sample test statistic (t) for the data in Example 12.3h.

1. Type the column heading **Lengths** into cell A1.
2. Enter the lengths of the 10 samples from the received batch into cells A2:A11.
3. Type the notes **Population Mean, Level of Significance, Degrees of Freedom, Critical *t* Value (one tail), Sample test statistic (*t*)**, and **Absolute value of test statistic (|*t*|)** into cells C17–C22.
4. On the **Tools** menu, click **Data Analysis...** (You may need to install the **Analysis ToolPak** add-in on your computer and then load it into EXCEL with the **Add-Ins** dialog box accessed on the **Tools** menu. If you try to load the **Analysis ToolPak** add-in and EXCEL does not install it, you can either install it with the **Add/Remove Programs** feature found in Windows' **Control Panel** or from Microsoft's Office 2000 CD-ROM).
5. The **Data Analysis** dialog box appears. From the **Analysis Tools** list, select **Descriptive Statistics** and click the **OK** button.
6. The **Descriptive Statistics** dialog box appears. In the **Input Range** input box, type **$A$2:$A$11** (or select cells A2–A11 and return to the input dialog box). From the **Grouped By** options, select **Columns**. Ensure that the **Labels in First Row** checkbox is deselected (unchecked). From the **Output options**, select the **Output Range** option and type **$C$1** in its input box (or select cell C1 and return to the input dialog box). Ensure that the **Summary Statistics** checkbox is selected (checked) and the **Confidence Level for Mean, Kth Largest**, and **Kth Smallest** checkboxes are deselected (unchecked). Click the **OK** button when finished.
7. Select cell D17, and enter the population mean of **15**.
8. Select cell D18, and enter the level of significance of **0.01**.
9. Select cell D19, and type **=D15-1** in the formula bar and enter. This is to calculate the degrees of freedom.
10. Select cell D20, and type **=TINV(2*D18, D19)** in the formula bar and enter. This is to calculate the critical t value. We multiply the level of significance by 2 to represent a one-tail test.
11. Select cell D21, and type **=(D3-D17)/D4** in the formula bar and enter. This is to calculate the sample test statistic (t).
12. Select cell D22, and type **=ABS(D21)** in the formula bar and enter. This is to calculate the absolute value of the sample test statistic.
13. Resize column C to better view the contents of the spreadsheet.

As previously calculated, we obtain the same results using EXCEL. Since the absolute value of the calculated t (3.54) is greater than the critical value (2.821), we reject H_0 and do not accept the batch.

OUTPUT

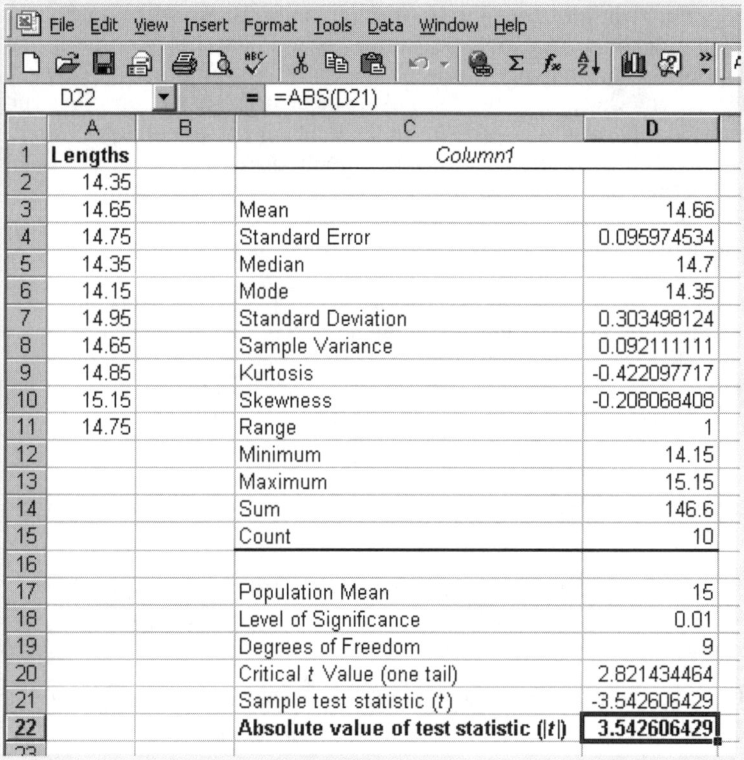
File Edit View Insert Format Tools Data Window Help

D22 = =ABS(D21)

	A	B	C	D
1	**Lengths**		*Column1*	
2	14.35			
3	14.65		Mean	14.66
4	14.75		Standard Error	0.095974534
5	14.35		Median	14.7
6	14.15		Mode	14.35
7	14.95		Standard Deviation	0.303498124
8	14.65		Sample Variance	0.092111111
9	14.85		Kurtosis	-0.422097717
10	15.15		Skewness	-0.208068408
11	14.75		Range	1
12			Minimum	14.15
13			Maximum	15.15
14			Sum	146.6
15			Count	10
16				
17			Population Mean	15
18			Level of Significance	0.01
19			Degrees of Freedom	9
20			Critical t Value (one tail)	2.821434464
21			Sample test statistic (t)	-3.542606429
22			**Absolute value of test statistic ($\|t\|$)**	**3.542606429**

EXERCISE 12.3

1. Given $H_0 : \mu = 8.0$, $H_a : \mu \neq 8.0$, $\bar{x} = 7.8$, $s = 2.1$, $n = 15$, and $\alpha = 0.05$, should H_0 be accepted or rejected?

2. $H_0 : \mu = 110$; $H_a : \mu < 110$. Given that $\bar{x} = 108$, $s = 18$, and $n = 40$, should the null hypothesis be accepted or rejected at the 98% confidence level?

3. Accept or reject the null hypothesis given the following data:

	Sample test statistic	Critical value of test statistic	Type of test
a)	2.9	3.2	two-tail
b)	−1.5	−1.6	left-tail
c)	1.8	0.8	right-tail
d)	−2.5	−2.3	left-tail

4. Last year, a retailer found that mean credit card sales were \$60.00 with a standard deviation of \$12.00. Because the cost of accepting credit cards is inversely related to the dollar amount per credit card sale (that is, as the dollar amount per credit card sale goes up, the cost per transaction goes down), it is important for the retailer to know if there has been any change in the average amount per credit card sale.
   To test for any change, the retailer took a sample of 225 credit card slips and determined the mean to be \$65.00 and the standard deviation to be \$9.00. The retailer wants the chance of error to be no more than 2%.
   a) Set up the decision rule for the test.
   b) Determine the critical value and the computed value of the test statistic.
   c) Should the null hypothesis be rejected?

5. A sample of pressurized tanks received from a supplier are destroyed to determine if the shipment meets minimum pressure requirements of 1000 kPa (kilopascals). From the shipment of 400 tanks, 8 were randomly chosen and found to have an average pressure of 980 kPa and a standard deviation of 8 kPa. The company requires a 99% confidence level for the test.
   a) Why can the shape of the distribution be assumed to be normal?
   b) Should the shipment be accepted?
   c) Why does the company not use a larger sample size to increase the precision of the test?

6. United Way contributions at a Moncton hospital last year averaged \$220 per person for 325 employees. The chairperson for this year's campaign hopes to increase the contribution per person by at least 10% through a media blitz. A sample of 40 employees taken following the advertising campaign showed an average contribution of \$260 per person with a standard deviation of \$18 per person. Test the null hypothesis at $\alpha = 0.05$ to determine if the media blitz was successful.

SECTION 12.4

Hypothesis Testing of a Population Proportion for Large Samples ($n > 30$)

Provided that the sample size is large, we can use the z statistic to perform a hypothesis test of a population proportion. The accepted rule is that the z statistic can be used if $n > 30$.

EXAMPLE 12.4a

The population proportion is assumed to be 80%. Conduct a two-tail test at the 10% level of significance for a sample of 144 items with a proportion of 83%.

SOLUTION

$\pi = 0.80$; $p = 0.83$; $n = 144$; $\alpha = 0.10$.
$H_0 : \pi = 0.80$;
$H_a : \pi \neq 0.80$.
Two-tail test is required.
$\alpha = 0.10$.

Since $n > 30$, the z statistic can be used as a test statistic.

Using Table 12.2, for a two-tail test and $\alpha = 0.10$, the critical value of the test statistic $z = 1.64$.

Reject H_0 and accept H_a if the absolute value of the sample test statistic $z > 1.64$.

$$\sigma_p = \sqrt{\frac{\pi(1-\pi)}{n}} = \sqrt{\frac{(0.80)(0.20)}{144}} = \sqrt{0.001\ 111\ 11}$$

$$= 0.033\ 333\ 33$$

$$\text{Sample test statistic, } z = \frac{p-\pi}{\sigma_p} = \frac{0.83-0.80}{0.033\ 333\ 33} = \frac{0.03}{0.033\ 333\ 33} = 0.900$$

Since the absolute value of the sample test statistic $z <$ the critical value 1.64, accept H_0. The test result supports the null hypothesis.

EXAMPLE 12.4b

A large retailer considers signing a long-term contract with a supplier of waterproof boots. Before doing so, the retailer wants to be certain that the proportion of defective boots is less than 5%. Specifying a 1% level of significance, the retailer accepted on consignment a shipment of 100 pairs of boots for test marketing and found three pairs to be defective. Should the retailer sign the contract?

SOLUTION

$\pi = 0.05$; $n = 100$; number defective = 3; $p = \frac{3}{100} = 0.03$; $\alpha = 0.01$.
Since the retailer hopes to establish that the true proportion of defective boots is less than 5%, the null hypothesis to test is that the proportion of defective pairs of boots is equal to or greater than 5%.
$H_0 : \pi \geq 0.05$;
$H_a : \pi < 0.05$.
Perform a left-tail test.
$\alpha = 0.01$.

Since $n > 30$, we can use the z statistic.

For a one-tail test and $\alpha = 0.01$, the critical value of the test statistic $z = 2.33$.

Provided that the sample test statistic is not positive, reject H_0 and accept H_a if the absolute value of the sample test statistic $z >$ the critical value 2.33.

$$\sigma_p = \sqrt{\frac{\pi(1-\pi)}{n}} = \sqrt{\frac{(0.05)(0.95)}{100}} = \sqrt{0.000\,475} = 0.021\,794$$

$$\text{Sample test statistic, } z = \frac{p-\pi}{\sigma_p} = \frac{0.03-0.05}{0.021\,794} = \frac{-0.02}{0.021\,794} = -0.92$$

$$|z| = 0.92$$

Since z is not positive and the absolute value of the sample test statistic $z <$ the critical value 2.33, accept H_0. This means that the sample does not support the alternate assumption that the true proportion is less than 5%. The retailer should not sign the long-term contract.

EXERCISE 12.4

1. A random sample of 120 financial analysts were polled on the issue of company valuation. Ninety-six favoured inclusion of third-party company valuation with any prospectus. Test the claim that more than 75% of all financial analysts are in favour of including third-party valuations with any prospectus at the 1% level of significance.

2. The Trendsetters retail chain, vendors of fashionable clothing, wish to confirm that 65% of its target market are college and university students. If the true proportion were different from the claimed 65%, a new marketing program would be required. Of 400 potential customers included in a random sample, 160 were not college or university students. Test the claim at the 2% level of significance.

3. In a blindfold taste test, buyers of Brand A coffee were asked to compare their brand with a competing Brand B coffee. Final results of the test showed that 240 preferred Brand A while 200 preferred Brand B. The product manager claims that there is a definite preference for Brand A over Brand B. Is the product manager's claim correct based on the test information? Use $\alpha = 0.05$ to support or contradict the product manager's claim.

4. Lucky Strike Bowling Alley has a Monday-night league consisting of 120 bowlers. A vote at the beginning of the season indicated 61% support for a year-end banquet. Some members of the organizing committee now feel that support for the banquet has dropped. A random sample of 40 bowlers shows support now to be 54%. Test at the 5% level of significance if there has been a drop in support.

SECTION 12.5

Type I and Type II Errors, *p* Values

A. Type I and Type II Errors

As the decision to accept or reject the null hypothesis is based on a sample, we can never be absolutely sure that the decision is correct. There are four possible outcomes to a decision made about a null hypothesis: two of them correct and two of them incorrect.

The two correct decisions are
1. to accept H_0 when it is true;
2. to reject H_0 when it is not true.

The two incorrect decisions are
1. to reject H_0 when it is true — referred to as a **Type I error**;
2. to accept H_0 when it is not true — referred to as a **Type II error**.

A Type I error occurs when we reject the null hypothesis but should accept it. The probability of making this type of error is the specified chance of error. For this reason, a Type I error is sometimes called an α error.

A Type II error occurs when we accept the null hypothesis but should reject it. The probability of making this type of error is denoted by β (read "beta") and is sometimes called a β error.

The four possible outcomes and their associated probabilities are summarized in Table 12.3.

TABLE 12.3 Summary of Type I and Type II Errors

Decision based on test	Null hypothesis is true		Null hypothesis is not true	
	Decision	Probability	Decision	Probability
Accept H_0	correct	$1 - \alpha$	incorrect	β Type II error
Reject H_0	incorrect	α Type I error	correct	$1 - \beta$

Table 12.4 summarizes Type I and Type II errors for Example 12.4b.

TABLE 12.4 Type I and Type II Errors for Example 12.4b

Action concerning the null hypothesis H_0	True state of null hypothesis	
	H_0 is true (Consignment shipment meets reject specifications)	H_0 is false (Consignment shipment does not meet reject specifications)
Accept H_0 (Reject shipment)	no error	Type II error (Reject a shipment that should be accepted)
Reject H_0 (Accept shipment)	Type I error (Accept a shipment that should be rejected)	no error

In quality control work, a Type I error is also known as the *producer's risk* since it could involve, for example, shutting down a production line on the sample evidence that a machine was incorrectly set when, in fact, it was operating correctly.

Conversely, a Type II error is known as the *consumer's risk* since it could involve, for example, a retailer accepting a consignment of goods on the basis of sample evidence that the consignment met specifications when, in fact, it did not.

Both types of errors can be very costly in terms of lost production time on one hand and customer dissatisfaction on the other hand. As a result, decisions about the levels at which α and β should be set usually involve consideration of economic costs.

The risk of making a Type I error has traditionally been considered the more serious of the two types of errors. For this reason the value of α is usually specified first. In most business situations $\alpha = 0.05$ and $\alpha = 0.01$ are the most common values used.

In very sensitive situations, such as medical research, much smaller values may be chosen. For example, in testing the effectiveness of a new drug, the null hypothesis is that the current practice is the best procedure. The alternate hypothesis is that the new drug is "better." In these situations an extremely serious Type I error could result if H_0 is rejected when, in fact, it represents the better alternative and the new drug proves to have terrible side effects.

B. An Alternative Method of Reporting the Result of a Hypothesis Test — p Values

The hypothesis procedure shown in this chapter follows the traditional approach to testing. In modern practice, however, the results of such tests are frequently given in terms of a ***p* value**.

In Example 12.3g, which involved the testing of the time estimate required to produce a new part for an airplane, we determined the critical value of the test statistic $t = 2.306$ while we found the absolute value of the sample test statistic $t = 3.00$.

Since our decision rule was to reject H_0 if the absolute value of the sample test statistic t was greater than 2.306, we rejected H_0 at the 5% level of significance and concluded that the engineer had incorrectly estimated the time required to manufacture the new part. Note what happens if we specify a 1% level of significance instead.

For a two-tail test, $\alpha = 0.01$ and $(n - 1) = 8$ degrees of freedom, the critical value of the test statistic $t = 3.355$.

Our decision rule would be to accept H_0 if the absolute value of the sample test statistic is less than 3.355. This being the case, we would accept the null hypothesis at the 1% level of significance.

The choice of significance level influences the decision to accept or reject the null hypothesis. Specification of the level of significance before the test is carried out is important since it prevents choosing after the test a level of significance that suits the particular objectives or preconceptions of the decision-maker.

Now consider the values in the t table for 8 degrees of freedom for the selected values of α.

α	0.20	0.10	0.05	0.02	0.01
d.f. = 8	1.397	1.860	2.306	2.896	3.355

In our case the absolute value of the sample test statistic ($t = 3.000$) is less than the critical value of the test statistic $t = 3.355$. This means that the actual significance level of our result lies somewhere between $\alpha = 0.02$ and $\alpha = 0.01$. However, in the absence of a complete t table, we cannot determine the precise value of the probability of the sample result.

This probability is known as the p value of the test. In our case it can be interpreted as "the probability of obtaining a sample mean as small as 147.5 h if the true population mean is 150 h lies somewhere between 2% and 1%."

Stated another way, "a sample mean as low as 147.5 h would occur by chance only about 1.5 times in 100 if it is true that the population mean is 150 h." We can therefore be reasonably sure that drawing a sample with a mean of 147.5 h is not a chance event and that the engineer's estimate was too high.

The p value is the actual value of the level of significance as distinct from a specified value such as $\alpha = 0.05$ or $\alpha = 0.01$. Accordingly, an alternative version of our decision rule is

> "Reject H_0 if the p value is less than the specified value of α; otherwise do not reject H_0."

In Example 12.3f, which involved a test of entrance examination results for a high school at the 5% level of significance, the critical value of the test statistic $z = 1.64$, while the absolute value of the sample test statistic $z = 1.89$. Following the decision rule for a right-tailed test, we rejected the null hypothesis and concluded that the entrance examination test results obtained by the graduates of the high school were above the average at the 5% level of significance.

From the z table (Table 9.1) we know that the area between μ and $z = 1.89$ is 0.4706. The area above $z = 1.89$ is $(0.5000 - 0.4706) = 0.0294$. The p value = 2.94%.

Since the p value is less than the specified significance level of 5%, we reject the null hypothesis and interpret the result to indicate that "a sample mean score as high as 520 points when the population mean score is 500 points would happen by chance only about 3 times in 100." We can therefore be quite confident that it is not a chance event and that these students, in fact, scored higher than average.

EXERCISE 12.5

1. A toothpaste manufacturer tested the following hypothesis:

$$H_0 : \mu = 350 \text{ mL}; \qquad H_a : \mu \neq 350 \text{ mL}$$

a) Explain the meaning of a Type I error in this example.
b) Explain the meaning of a Type II error in this example.

2. The credit manager of a credit union set up the following hypotheses:

$$H_0 : \pi = 0.10; \qquad H_a : \pi < 0.10$$

a) What does a Type I error mean in this case? Explain.
b) What does a Type II error mean in this case? Explain.

3. Based on return on assets, financial services stocks were among the top performers last year. This group of stocks had a return on assets of 6.3% with a standard deviation of 3.9%. A random sample of 38 stocks belonging to the financial services group taken this year showed an average return on assets of 4.8%.

a) State a hypothesis for this situation.
b) Compute the p value for the hypothesis test.

4. A retailer promotes its own brand of tires on the basis of a guaranteed life span of at least 60 000 km. A random sample of 100 tires showed a mean of 62 000 km and a standard deviation of 7800 km.

a) State the hypotheses for this test.
b) Compute the p value for the test.

5. A Canada Customs supervisor believes that at least 60% of Canadians returning from the United States are not declaring purchases made in the United States. A survey of 81 car occupants crossing the Canadian border revealed that 55 of them did not declare their purchases.
   a) Compute the p value for a hypothesis test (assume $\alpha = 0.05$).
   b) State your conclusion about the validity of the supervisor's belief.

6. A quarterly survey of 500 business executives measures their perception of the economy. In January, 80% of the executives believed that the economy was going to go down further. A sample of 42 executives taken in April indicated that 28 thought the economy was going down further.
   a) Calculate the p value.
   b) At the 10% level of significance would you conclude that there has been a change in attitude?

REVIEW EXERCISE

1. A sailboat charter company in the Virgin Islands claims that rainfall in the month of February is less than 5 mm. State the null and alternate hypotheses.

2. A fast food outlet claims that the fat content in their small order of French fries is less than 20 g. State the null and alternate hypotheses.

3. The test weight of a fishing line (e.g., 5 kg) is the minimum weight needed to break the line. State the null and alternate hypotheses.

4. The average number of sick days per month at Hab Corporation was 56. A new fitness program has been started to reduce the number of sick days.
   a) State the null and alternate hypotheses.
   b) Identify the type of test.

5. Average attendance in a college math course was 70%. A new protocol was introduced to increase attendance.
   a) State the null and alternate hypotheses.
   b) Identify the type of test.

6. Marketing research studies reveal that the average consumer adds two teaspoons of sugar to breakfast cereal.
   a) State the null and alternate hypotheses.
   b) Identify the type of test.

7. Determine what type of test is required for each of the following:
   a) $H_0 : \mu = 30$ mL; $H_a : \mu \neq 30$ mL
   b) $H_0 : \pi = 0.05$; $H_a : \pi < 0.05$

8. Determine the type of test required for the following:
a) H_0: $\mu = 355$ mL; H_a: $\mu > 355$ mL
b) H_0: $\pi = 0.01$; H_a: $\pi < 0.01$ mL

9. State the type of test required for the following:
a) $H_0 : \pi = 0.90$; $H_a : \pi > 0.90$
b) $H_0 : \mu = 75$; $H_a : \mu < 75$

10. In a certain year the mean return on foreign-equity mutual funds was 9.75% and the standard deviation was 0.20%. One year later a random sample of 100 foreign-equity mutual funds had an average return of 9.68%. Would you be willing to conclude that the average return has changed significantly? Assume a 5% risk of making a Type I error.

11. In the old math curriculum, the average grade in high-school algebra was 70% with a standard deviation of 10%. One hundred students in the new curriculum were found to have an average algebra grade of 68%. Would you be willing to conclude that the average grade has changed significantly? Assume a 5% risk of making a Type I error.

12. An audit of mortgages held by a local trust company showed the mean mortgage to be \$76 500 with a standard deviation of \$8900. Six months later the trust company was asked by the regulatory body to supply details regarding its mortgage portfolio. A random sample of 70 mortgages had a mean principal of \$80 700. Using a 2% level of significance, determine if the trust company's portfolio has changed.

13. A normal population has a mean of 92 and a standard deviation of 31. Some of the data were found to be erroneous. A random sample of 20 data points had a mean of 98. Does the population mean change significantly ($\alpha = 0.02$) if the erroneous data are removed?

14. A normal population has mean sales of \$100 with a standard deviation of \$40 for a clothing store. It was determined that the salesman had overstated his sales. A random sample of 25 sales showed the sales mean to be \$95. Does the population mean change significantly ($\alpha = 0.02$) if the false data are removed?

15. Lance Bell is a sales representative for a pharmaceutical company. He averaged 42 sales calls per week with a standard deviation of 3.8 sales calls per week before he was involved in a car accident. A random sample of 10 weeks shows Lance averaged 37 sales calls per week after the accident. Assume a normal population and 0.05 significance level to test if Lance's performance dropped after the accident.

16. Trylex's corporate objectives require an average inventory value of \$850 000 for each of its retail outlets throughout the year (312 days). A random sample of 60 days at a store identified by the code 50712 found the average daily inventory to be \$823 000 with a standard deviation of \$33 500. Does store 50712 significantly deviate from the corporate objective over a one-year period at the 1% level of significance?

17. The average weight of a box of cereal is 675 g. A random sample of 70 boxes had an average weight of 673.5 g with a standard deviation of 2 g. Does the sample significantly deviate from the stated weight of 675 g at the 1% level of significance?

18. Trans-Port-It Trucking uses special corrugated boxes so that the cartons can be piled higher than normal boxes. The special boxes are supposed to withstand 100 kg of weight. The company's records show that 35 damage claims were due to crushed cartons that carried an average weight of 95 kg and a standard deviation of 3.4 kg. Assume $\alpha = 0.02$.
a) Do the crushed cartons differ significantly from the manufacturer's claim?
b) What is suspect about the sample used?

19. Russell Cousins purchased a new rechargeable electric shaver that is supposed to last an average of 14 shaves before requiring recharging. Russell believes his shaver is not living up to the manufacturer's claim. He randomly selected 5 recharging periods and obtained a mean of 12.3 shaves between recharges with a standard deviation of 1.8 shaves. At the 1% level of significance, is Russell's shaver significantly different from the manufacturer's claim?

20. A consumer purchased a new "improved light bulb" which is advertised to last 1000 h. The consumer believes the light bulb doesn't live up to the manufacturer's claim. He tested 10 light bulbs and found the mean life was 900 h with a standard deviation of 100 h. At the 1% level of significance, are the consumer's light bulbs significantly different from the manufacturer's claim?

21. Tally Greenberg is an artist who makes jewellery. Tally has based her prices on the assumption it takes 11 h to design and make a piece of jewellery for a customer. A random sample of her work showed the following:

Customer	A	B	C	D	E	F	G
Time (h)	9.8	11.1	10.8	10.1	11.0	10.6	10.0

At the significance level $\alpha = 0.05$, determine if the sample times are significantly different from what Tally expected.

22. R.T. Kolly Advertising was awarded an advertising contract by the government to communicate the need for electricity conservation. To prove the effectiveness of its work the agency surveyed 220 people and found 80 believed in electricity conservation. After the survey, the same 220 people were shown the advertisement. Fifty of them were selected randomly for a follow-up survey. The agency found that 24 of the 50 believed in electricity conservation.
a) State the null and alternate hypotheses.
b) Is there evidence of a change in attitude at the 1% level of significance?
c) Does this measurement of attitude seem valid? Comment.

23. It is believed that 47% of Canadians drink coffee. A consumer study asked 1500 Canadians about their drinking habits and found 41% said they drink coffee. At $\alpha = 0.02$ determine if the study results are significantly different from the assumed proportion.

24. Last year 39% of a high school's graduating class went on to university. A sample of 40 graduates from this year's graduating class showed 18 will be going to university. The high school graduates 500 students yearly. Has there been a significant change in the proportion of students going to university ($\alpha = 0.01$)?

25. One of Toronto's institutional investment companies has a special mailing list of 185 clients who buy their research. Twenty percent of the customers normally act on the research recommendations. A survey of 36 clients after the latest mailing indicated 9 had made a transaction as a result of the information received in the mailing. Allowing for a 5% chance of a Type I error, determine if the latest mailing significantly increased business.

26. Last year Aquamarine Ltd. reported 85% of all sales orders were shipped on or before the required date. A new computerized tracking system was installed to increase the company's compliance rate. A random sample of 120 sales orders shipped after the installation of the new system showed a 93% compliance rate. At the 2% level of significance, has the new system made a positive difference?

27. A marketing research company pays people $25 to come to their office, taste new products, and answer a questionnaire. Historically, 28% of consumers who said they would participate were no-shows. Because of the time and money lost due to missed bookings, the company decided to increase the payment to $50 per visit. A random sample of 100 bookings taken after the increase in payment showed 15 people did not show up as scheduled. Would you conclude, at the 1% level of significance, that there has been a change in the proportion of missed bookings?

28. A train running between City A and City B averaged 26 min per trip with a standard deviation of 7.8 min per trip last year. A random sample of 25 trips made this year showed a mean of 30 min per trip. The sample seems to indicate that the train takes longer to complete the trip this year.

a) Compute the p value.

b) If the significance level were 0.02, what would you conclude about the time taken to make the trip?

29. Last year Jack's Orchards harvested a mean of 0.65 bushels of apples per tree with a standard deviation of 0.04 bushels. A sample of 200 trees for this year's crop averaged 0.61 bushels per tree. It seems that this year's drier growing season has affected the crop.

a) Compute the p value.

b) What would you conclude about this year's apple harvest at the 1% level of significance?

30. Ellen assembled 240 components per shift when she was paid an hourly rate. Now she is paid a piecework rate. A random sample of 64 of her shifts shows output to average 261 components per shift with a standard deviation of 70 components.

a) Compute the p value.

b) Comment on the effect of changing Ellen's basis of remuneration.

31. Management has installed new equipment which will allow the production of 1000 parts per hour. A random sample of 49 one-hour shifts was conducted, and it was found that that an average of 1002 parts per hour was produced with a standard deviation of 5 parts.

a) Compute the p value.

b) Does the new equipment live up to its claim?

32. A restaurant manager claims that the mean bill for the customers for dinner is \$85. A random sample of 8 such bills showed the following amounts:

\$79 \$98 \$73 \$83 \$121 \$57 \$68 \$61

a) Determine the p value.

b) Do the sample data support the manager's claim?

33. A dentist claims she treats an average of 90 patients per week. A random sample of 5 weeks during the last year showed the following number of patients treated:

80 75 84 86 90

a) Determine the p value.

b) Do the data support the dentist's claim at the 5% level of significance?

34. A courier service requires its employees to sort 40 parcels a minute. The night supervisor conducted a survey and found that in a 10-min period, the following number of parcels were sorted:

35 42 38 38 37 50 35 36 36 39

a) Determine the p value.

b) Is the employee working to the prescribed standard?

35. Paul's Diner advertises lunch will be served in 10 min or less. A random sample of 50 lunch orders showed a mean serving time of 12.3 min per order with a standard deviation of 4.7 min. Assume $\alpha = 0.05$.

a) Determine the p value.

b) Does the sample substantiate Paul's advertised claim?

36. Suppose you work for a toy company that specializes in making toys for small children. Recently your company has received complaints of small pieces breaking off certain toys, which could be hazardous if swallowed. Before the company accepts a shipment of 8000 kadidles used in the production of the toys, a quality control program is implemented allowing a maximum rejection rate of 2% of the incoming parts. The new program is willing to run a 1% chance of rejecting the shipment when it actually meets the specified rejection rate. In a random sample of 250 kadidles from the shipment, 9 were rejected.

a) Determine the p value.

b) Should the shipment be accepted?

37. The director of a city's harbour commission believes that 65% of the sailboats mooring overnight are under 8 m in length. In a sample of 150 moored boats, 45 were over 8 m. Allowing for 5% error, determine the p value to assess the director's estimate.

38. The manager of a grocery store believes that 35% of his customers wait no longer than 5 min in the checkout line. In a sample of 100 customers, 60 waited more than 5 min. Allowing for 5% error, determine the p value to assess the manager's claim.

39. (CGA) Canada Post is attempting to audit, for a major metropolitan post office, the revenues obtained through mailed packages in a given period. Suppose the weights of the packages are normally distributed with $\sigma = 240$ g. We would like to test the following hypotheses:

$$H_0 : \mu = 780;$$

$$H_a : \mu > 780$$

We want to test this with a 5% level of significance. A random sample of 144 packages is planned for this purpose.

a) State the decision rule in terms of the sample mean values that would lead us to reject the null hypothesis.

b) What is the probability of making a Type I error based on the decision rule in **(a)**?

c) Assume a sample of 144 packages yielded a sample mean of 800 g. Does the sample mean provide sufficient evidence to reject the null hypothesis? Explain.

40. (CGA) An advertisement by a fast-food chain claims that people prefer broiling to frying by at least a 3:1 ratio. That is, the probability π that a randomly chosen person prefers broiling to frying is at least three-quarters. A consumer advocate believes that the advertisement is faulty and that the probability π is no more than 0.5. A random sample of 50 persons has revealed that 32 preferred broiling to frying.

a) Is there sufficient evidence in the sample to refute the claim made by the advertisement? Set up the null and alternate hypotheses and justify your reasoning. State your decision rule clearly. Finally, draw your conclusion. Use a 1% level of significance for the test.

b) Is there sufficient evidence to refute the consumer advocate's claim? State the H_0 and H_a, the decision rule, and your conclusion. Use a 1% level of significance for the test.

c) Calculate the p values for the test in **(b)**.

41. (CGA) Love Burger, a fast-food chain in Paris, France, is considering opening a new restaurant at a certain location. From previous studies, the company has determined that for a site to be acceptable, the number of vehicles passing that side of the road must be at least 500/h. The company wants sufficient statistical evidence to determine if this site is acceptable before it invests in the venture. To collect data, the number of vehicles passing the proposed site was recorded for 100 different randomly chosen hourly periods. From these 100 x values, it has been found that $\bar{x} = 520$ and $s = 50$.

a) Set up the null and alternate hypotheses. Justify your setup.

b) Describe the Type I error and the Type II error in the context of your setup for **(a)**. What are the consequences of making each of these two errors?

c) Do the sample data provide sufficient statistical evidence to claim that the proposed site is acceptable? Use $\alpha = 0.01$.

42. (CGA) Consider the following null and alternate hypotheses:

$$H_0 : \mu = 500; \quad H_a : \mu \neq 500$$

Assume that the population is normal and its variance $\sigma^2 = 400$. You are planning to take a random sample of 25 observations. The following decision rule is being used to determine if the null hypothesis should be rejected or not: Reject H_0 if the sample mean exceeds 505 or is less than 495; do not reject H_0 otherwise.

a) Determine the probability of making a Type I error.

b) What should the sample size be if you follow the same decision rule but require that the probability of making a Type I error be 0.05?

43. (CGA) Consider the following parts of this question to be independent of each other.

a) In a test of hypothesis, the p value was found to be 0.04. Should the null hypothesis be rejected at the 1% level of significance? Explain.

b) In a two-sided test for μ, the test statistic z was calculated to be 2.03. Calculate the p value for the test.

c) In a study, a 95% confidence interval for μ was found to be 18 ± 4. Does this mean, then, that in repeated sampling on the average 95% of the time μ would be in the range 18 ± 4? Explain.

d) In a test of hypothesis, based on the available data, the null hypothesis was rejected. Choose the appropriate alternative from those given below and justify your choice.

i) Type I error was made.
ii) Type II error was made.
iii) Possibly both type of errors were made.
iv) No error was made.
v) None of the above statements is correct.

e) In a test of hypothesis, based on the available data, the null hypothesis was rejected using a 5% level of confidence. Would the conclusion change if the level of significance were lowered from 5% to 1%? Explain.

SELF-TEST

1. The owner of a small shopping mall surveyed the households within a five-block radius and found household income was normally distributed with a mean of \$47 000 and a standard deviation of \$4800. A potential tenant thinks the income numbers are inflated and undertakes his own survey. The random sample of 25 households shows a mean income of \$45 800.

a) Set up reasonable hypotheses.

b) Indicate the type of test to be used.

c) At the 1% level of significance would you accept or reject the null hypothesis?

2. A window manufacturer claims its special tinting will decrease heating costs an average of 10%.
a) State the null and alternate hypotheses to test this claim.
b) Identify the type of test to be used.

3. Balline Corporation's sales department claims that its sales staff make an average of 80 sales per week with a standard deviation of 4 sales per week. The corporation's claim is to be tested at the 2% level of significance using a large sample.
a) State the 2 hypotheses for the test.
b) Identify the test to be used.
c) State the value of α.
d) Identify the test statistic to be used.
e) Determine the critical value of the test statistic.
f) State the decision rule.

4. Given the following data, show all detail to determine whether the null hypothesis should be accepted or rejected.
$H_0 : \mu = 61$; $H_a : \mu < 61$.
$\bar{x} = 60$; $s = 20$; $n = 400$; $\alpha = 0.01$.

5. After the introduction of a new brand of cigarettes, 600 consumers of the new brand were surveyed to determine, among other things, the frequency of purchase. The study found the mean to be 2.7 packs per week. Six months later, a sample of 60 people selected at random from the original group surveyed found the mean frequency of purchase to be 2.5 packs per week with a standard deviation of 0.7 packs per week. The company wonders if the "novelty" has worn off and the frequency of purchase is dropping. At the 5% level of significance, can you conclude that the frequency of purchase has changed?

6. Lauren Thomson, dentist, has determined that her patients wait an average of 28 min before seeing her. Instead of booking a person every 10 min, the office manager has been instructed to find out the purpose of each patient visit and to make bookings based on the estimate of how long each visit should take. A random sample of 70 patients taken after the change in procedure showed an average waiting time of 18 min and a standard deviation of 5 min. Assume a 1% chance of a Type I error.
a) State the hypotheses.
b) Has the new procedure significantly decreased the patients' waiting time?

7. The Robotics Industrial Association estimates that 56% of all industrial robots in Canada are used for welding. A random sample of companies with a total of 200 robots showed that 61% of the robots are used for welding. At the 0.05 significance level, would you conclude the sample results support the Association's estimate?

8. Soni Metals just installed a new piece of equipment to form a special fastener. The engineering department supplied the cost accountant with a production standard of 3.8 min per fastener. After the first month of operation, the cost accountant identified cost overruns associated with the operation of the new equipment. A random selection of production times (in minutes) was recorded as follows:

3.9 4.0 3.8 3.9 4.0 3.7 3.7 3.9 4.0 4.1

a) Calculate the mean and standard deviation of the sample.
b) Explain your choice of test statistic for a hypothesis test.
c) If $\alpha = 0.05$, can you conclude that the new machine does not meet the established time standard?

9. Employee satisfaction at Signet Inc. averaged 7.2 points on a 9-point scale. The survey was given to all 2850 employees last spring. Recently a random sample of 49 employees showed an average score of 7.0 points with a standard deviation of 1.19 points. The company is concerned that the employees' level of satisfaction has changed.
a) State the hypothesis test.
b) Compute the p value.
c) At the 98% confidence level, would you conclude there was a significant change in the level of employee satisfaction?

10. A major credit card company knows from past experience that 38% of its cardholders pay their account balance in full to avoid interest charges. The company also knows that if the proportion of cardholders who pay their account in full drops significantly the number of accounts in arrears increases. A random sample of 121 account statements showed 79 accounts past due. Assuming a 5% level of significance, determine if the company should be concerned about an increase in the number of past-due accounts.

WWW For an online glossary, go to **www.pearsoned.ca/hummelbrunner**.

Key Terms

Acceptance region 397
Alternate hypothesis 395
Critical value 397
Null hypothesis 395
***p* value** 418
Rejection region 397
Significance level 396
Type I error 417
Type II error 417

Summary of Formulas

1. Sample test statistic for hypothesis testing of a mean

a) When σ is known:

$$z = \frac{\bar{x} - \mu}{\sigma_{\bar{x}}} \quad \text{where } \sigma_{\bar{x}} = \frac{\sigma}{\sqrt{n}}$$ ←*Formula* 12.1

b) When σ is not known and $n > 30$:

$$z = \frac{\bar{x} - \mu}{s_{\bar{x}}} \quad \text{where } s_{\bar{x}} = \frac{s}{\sqrt{n}}$$ ←*Formula* 12.2

c) When σ is not known and $n \leq 30$:

$$t_{n-1} = \frac{\bar{x} - \mu}{s_{\bar{x}}} \quad \text{where } s_{\bar{x}} = \frac{s}{\sqrt{n}}$$ ←*Formula* 12.2a

2. Sample test statistic for hypothesis testing of a proportion

Large sample ($n > 30$):

$$z = \frac{p - \pi}{\sigma_p} \quad \text{where } \sigma_p = \sqrt{\frac{\pi(1 - \pi)}{n}}$$ ←*Formula* 12.3

3. Finite correction factor

The values of $\sigma_{\bar{x}}$, $s_{\bar{x}}$, and σ_p in the above formulas should be modified by multiplying by the finite correction factor $\sqrt{\frac{N - n}{N - 1}}$ whenever the value of N is known.

CHAPTER 13

Simple Linear Regression and Correlation Analyses

Introduction

Simple linear regression and correlation analyses examine a possible relationship between two variables. Simple regression describes the relationship between the variables, while correlation measures the closeness of that relationship. These methods are widely used in business, economic, and scientific applications.

Learning Outcomes

Upon completion of this chapter you will be able to

1. distinguish between dependent and independent variables;
2. determine the regression equation by the least squares method;
3. plot the regression line on a scatter diagram;
4. interpret the meaning of the regression coefficients;
5. use the regression equation to predict values of the dependent variable for selected values of the independent variable;
6. compute the standard error of estimate;
7. construct forecast intervals;
8. compute the coefficients of determination r^2 and correlation r;
9. interpret the meaning of the coefficients r^2 and r.

SECTION 13.1

Simple Linear Regression Analysis

Many situations arise in which two things appear to be related. For example, it is reasonable to speculate that there is a relationship between

a) the number of litres of gasoline sold at service stations and the volume of traffic passing their locations;
b) the number of meals sold in a company cafeteria and the number of company employees;
c) advertising expenditures and sales revenue.

In the analysis of the relationship, the two things (*variables*) are identified by the symbols x and y. The variable denoted by y is called the **dependent variable**. The variable denoted by x is referred to as the **independent variable**. The use of these two labels implies that the value of the variable y depends on the value of the variable x.

Simple regression analysis is the process of constructing a mathematical model that can be used to predict one variable by another variable. Regression analysis with two or more independent variables is called multiple regression analysis.

The crucial first step in the analysis involves determining which variable is the dependent variable y and which is the independent variable x. A good approach is to ask the following two questions and select the more reasonable one.

1. Does the first variable depend on the second variable?

   or

2. Does the second variable depend on the first variable?

○ EXAMPLE 13.1a

For statements (a), (b), and (c) above, select the dependent and the independent variables.

● SOLUTION

For statement (a), the two questions are

1. Does the number of litres of gasoline sold depend on the volume of traffic?
2. Does the volume of traffic depend on the number of litres of gasoline sold?

Question 1 is more reasonable. The number of litres of gasoline sold is the dependent variable and is assigned as variable y. The volume of traffic is the independent variable and assigned as variable x.

For statement (b), the two questions are

1. Does the number of meals sold in a cafeteria depend on the number of employees?
2. Does the number of employees depend on the number of meals served?

Question 1 is more reasonable. The number of meals served is the dependent variable y. The number of employees is the independent variable x.

For statement (c), the two questions are

1. Does advertising expenditure depend on sales revenue?
2. Does sales revenue depend on advertising expenditure?

Question 2 appears to be more reasonable. Sales revenue is the dependent variable y. Advertising expenditure is the independent variable x.

Once it has been established which variable is the dependent variable y and which is the independent variable x, the data can be portrayed graphically in the form of a *scatter diagram*. The diagram may indicate that the relationship can be represented by a straight line. In this case a simple linear regression model is appropriate for the analysis. If the data graph as a curve, more complex curvilinear models should be used.

The following four scatter diagrams are typical results of plotting data sets involving two variables.

FIGURE 13.1 Scatter Diagrams for Plotting Two Variables

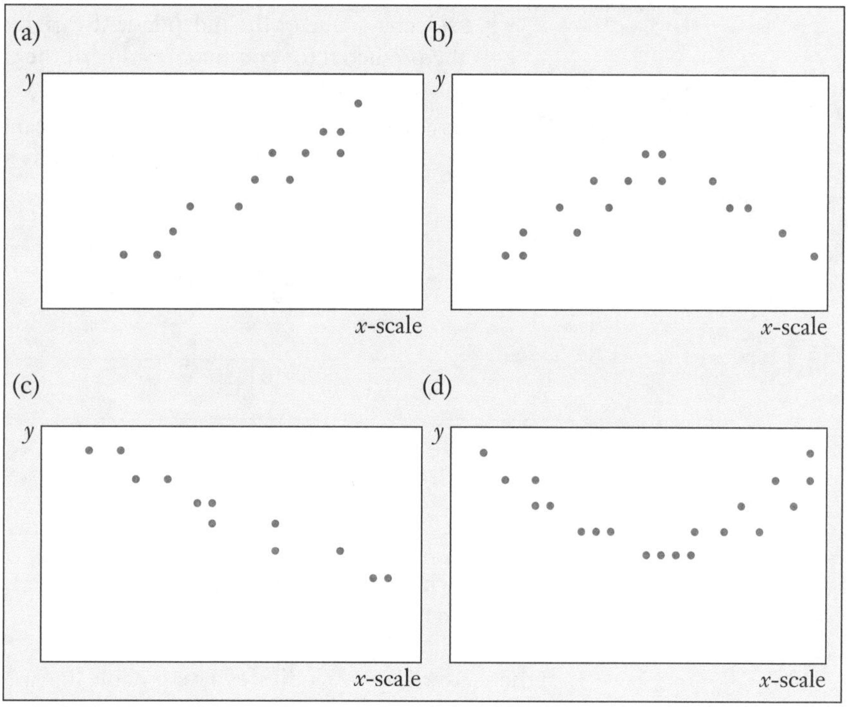

Diagrams (a) and (c) are appropriate for linear analysis, while the data represented by diagrams (b) and (d) require the use of curvilinear models. In this text only the most common straight-line model, referred to as the least squares model, is considered.

SECTION 13.2

The Least Squares Method

The **least squares method** provides a mathematical procedure for determining the equation of a straight line that best fits the data. The equation is referred to as the **regression equation**. The graphical representation of the equation is known as the **regression line**. This line is called the *line of best fit* since the procedure *minimizes* the sum of the vertical deviations of the data points about the line.

The general form of the least squares equation is given by

$$y_p = a + bx$$ ←*Formula* 13.1

where a is the value of y when $x = 0$; that is, a is the y intercept;
b is the slope of the regression line and indicates the change in the dependent variable y for a change of one unit in the independent variable x;
x is a selected value of the independent variable;
y_p is the predicted (or computed) value of the dependent variable for a given value of x.

The regression equation for a specific set of data can be uniquely determined by computing the values of the **regression coefficients** a and b from the following formulas:

$$b = \frac{n(\sum xy) - (\sum x)(\sum y)}{n(\sum x^2) - (\sum x)^2}$$ ←*Formula* 13.2

$$a = \frac{\sum y}{n} - b\frac{\sum x}{n}$$ ←*Formula* 13.2

The following procedure is suggested when using the least squares method:

1. Determine the dependent variable.
2. Construct the scatter diagram.
3. If the scatter diagram indicates a reasonable linear relationship between the two variables, use the two formulas to determine a and b.
4. Determine the regression equation.
5. Plot the regression line on the scatter diagram.

○ EXAMPLE 13.2a

Many companies involved in assembly operations use aptitude tests on potential employees before hiring them and on current employees before promoting them to more demanding tasks. To obtain a reading on the usefulness of a particular test, the personnel department of Mega Tech, Inc., has administered the aptitute test to a group of employees. The resulting test scores matched to output data are listed in Table 13.1.

TABLE 13.1 Test Scores and Output Data

Employee	Output	Test score
A	31	5
B	40	11
C	30	4
D	34	5
E	25	3
F	20	2

a) Determine the dependent variable.
b) Construct the scatter diagram.
c) Determine the regression equation.
d) Plot the regression line.
e) Compute the predicted output for aptitude test scores of 6 and of 10.

SOLUTION

a) To determine the dependent variable, pose the two questions
   1. Does aptitude depend on output?
   2. Does output depend on aptitude?

   Question 2 is the more reasonable question. Output becomes the dependent variable y; the aptitude test scores become the independent variable x.

b) The scatter diagram is now constructed as shown in Figure 13.2.

FIGURE 13.2 Scatter Diagram of Output versus Aptitude Test Score

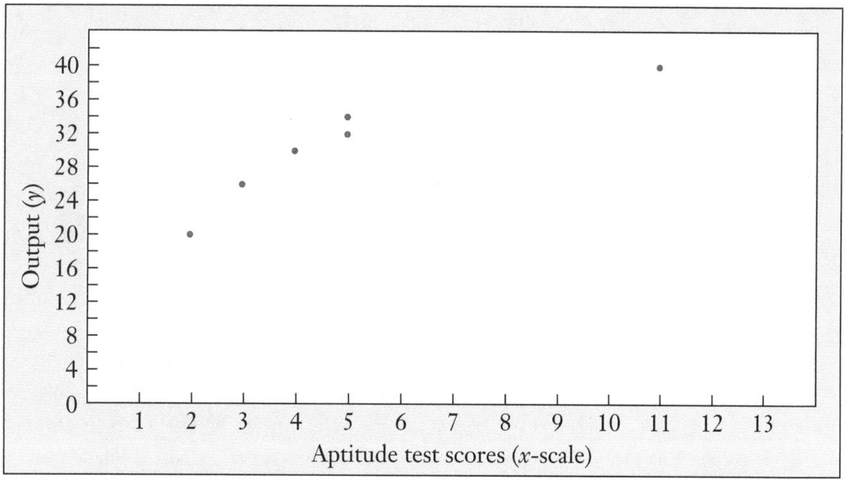

c) The scatter diagram indicates that there is a reasonable linear relationship between the two variables. Use of the least squares method is appropriate.

   To determine the specific regression equation we must compute the values of the regression coefficients a and b. To do so we first need to determine $\sum x$, $\sum y$, $\sum xy$, and $\sum x^2$.

In addition, $\sum y^2$ is also computed at the same time since this value is needed in sections 13.3 and 13.5. Details of the calculation of these values are shown in Table 13.2

TABLE 13.2 Calculations for Finding *a* and *b*

Employee	Output y	Test scores x	xy	x^2	y^2
A	31	5	155	25	961
B	40	11	440	121	1600
C	30	4	120	16	900
D	34	5	170	25	1156
E	25	3	75	9	625
F	20	2	40	4	400
$n = 6$	$\sum y = 180$	$\sum x = 30$	$\sum xy = 1000$	$\sum x^2 = 200$	$\sum y^2 = 5642$

The values of the regression coefficients can now be found by substituting the appropriate values listed in Table 13.2 into Formulas 13.2 and 13.2a.

$$b = \frac{n(\sum xy) - (\sum x)(\sum y)}{n(\sum x^2) - (\sum x)^2} = \frac{6(1000) - (30)(180)}{6(200) - (30)^2}$$

$$= \frac{6000 - 5400}{1200 - 900}$$

$$= \frac{600}{300} = 2$$

$$a = \frac{\sum y}{n} - b\frac{\sum x}{n} = \frac{180}{6} - 2(\frac{30}{6}) = 30 - 10 = 20$$

The regression equation is $y_p = 20 + 2x$.

d) To graph the regression line on the scatter diagram we need a minimum of two points on the line. A third point is recommended as a check.

The coordinates of three such points can be obtained by selecting three values of x. These three values are substituted into the regression equation and the corresponding values of y computed.

Any three values of x can be selected but it is preferable to select *convenient* values of x that are as far apart as the scatter diagram allows.

In our case two convenient extreme values are $x = 0$ and $x = 10$. The third value of x should be between the extreme values. In our case $x = 5$ is an appropriate selection.

For $x = 0, y_p = 20 + 2(0) = 20$; point (0, 20) is on the line.
For $x = 10, y_p = 20 + 2(10) = 40$; point (10, 40) is on the line.
For $x = 5, y_p = 20 + 2(5) = 30$; point (5, 30) is on the line.

The three points can now be plotted on the scatter diagram reproduced from part (b) and the **regression line** drawn by joining the three points (0, 20), (5, 30), and (10, 40).

Note The three points must lie on a straight line.

FIGURE 13.3 Scatter Diagram with Regression Line

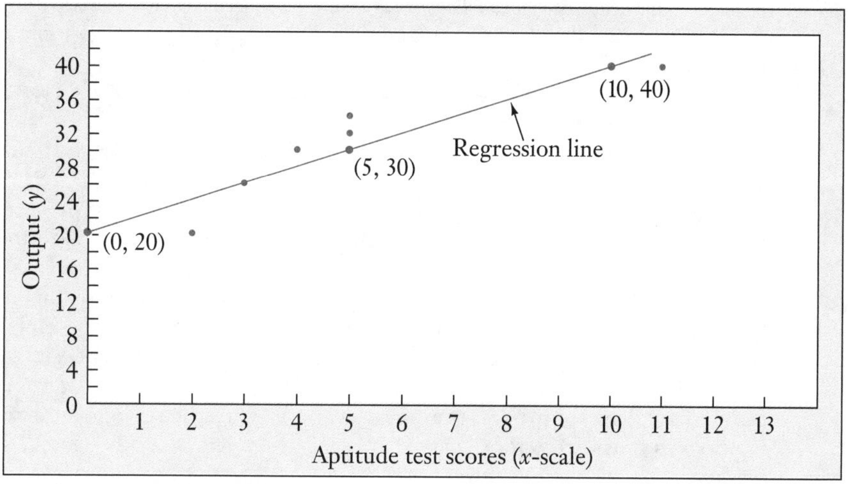

Note that $a = 20$ gives us the y intercept. The value $b = 2$ determines the *slope* of the line and indicates that, for an increase of one unit in x, the value y_p increases by two units.

e) To predict y_p, substitute the chosen values of x in the regression equation and compute y_p.
For $x = 6$, $y_p = 20 + 2(6) = 20 + 12 = 32$.
For $x = 10$, $y_p = 20 + 2(10) = 20 + 20 = 40$.

These calculations can be completed using EXCEL, as demonstrated in USING EXCEL 13.1.

USING EXCEL 13.1

Using EXCEL, we can also determine the dependent variable, construct the scatter diagram, determine the regression equation, plot the regression line, and compute the predicted output for the aptitude test scores given in Example 13.2a.

1. Type the column headings **Employee**, **Output**, and **Test Score** into cells A1–C1.
2. Enter the information found in Table 13.1 into cells A2:C7.
3. On the toolbar, click on the **Chart Wizard** button (or on the **Insert** menu, click **Chart...**).
4. The **Chart Wizard** dialog box appears. Click on the **Standard Types** tab and from the **Chart type** list, select **XY (Scatter)**; and in the **Chart sub-type** section select the chart that corresponds to the **Scatter: Compares pairs of values** image. When finished, click the **Next >** button.
5. Click on the **Data Range** tab and click on beside the **Data range** input box and select cells B2–C7 on the worksheet. Return to the input dialog box and select **Columns** from the **Series in** options.
6. Click on the **Series** tab. From the **Series** list, select **Series1**; click in the **X Values** input box and ensure that cells C2–C7 are selected (these represent the independent variables); click in the **Y Values** input box and ensure that cells B2–B7 are selected (these represent the dependent variables). When finished, click the **Next >** button.
7. Click on the **Titles** tab. In the **Chart title** input box, type **Scatter Diagram of Output versus Aptitude Test Score**. In the **Value (X) axis** input box, type **Aptitude test scores (x-scale)**. In the **Value (Y) axis** input box, type **Output (y)**. Click on any of the other remaining tabs found in the dialog box to select or deselect options to customize the display of your graph. When you are finished with your selections, click on the **Next >** button.
8. From the **Place chart** options, select the **As object in** option and then click on the **Finish** button.
9. Select the newly created chart and from the **Chart** menu, click on **Add Trendline...**
10. The **Add Trendline** dialog box appears. Click on the **Type** tab, and in the **Trend/Regression type** section, select the image that corresponds to the **Linear** type. In the **Based on series** list, select **Series1**. Click on the **Options** tab, and in the **Trendline name** section, select **Automatic**. In the **Forecast section**, ensure that **Forward** and **Backward** options are set to 0 and 2 respectively. Ensure that the **Set intercept =** checkbox is deselected (unchecked); the **Display equation on chart** checkbox is selected (checked); and the **Display R-squared value on chart** checkbox is selected (checked). When finished, click the **OK** button.
11. Select the chart and move it to line up underneath your data table. Also, you can alter the look of your chart by selecting the various components of your chart and then clicking on the **Format** menu to change the format of the selected chart item.
12. Type the column headings **Predicted Output** and **Test Score** into cells B28 and C28.
13. Enter the test scores of **6** and **10** into cells C29 and C30.
14. Select cell B29, and type **=FORECAST (C29,$B$2:$B$7,$C$2:$C$7)** in the formula bar and enter.
15. **Copy** and **Paste** cell B29 into cell B30.

OUTPUT

B30 = =FORECAST(C30,$B$2:$B$7,$C$2:$C$7)

	A	B	C
1	**Employee**	**Output**	**Test Score**
2	A	31	5
3	B	40	11
4	C	30	4
5	D	34	5
6	E	25	3
7	F	20	2

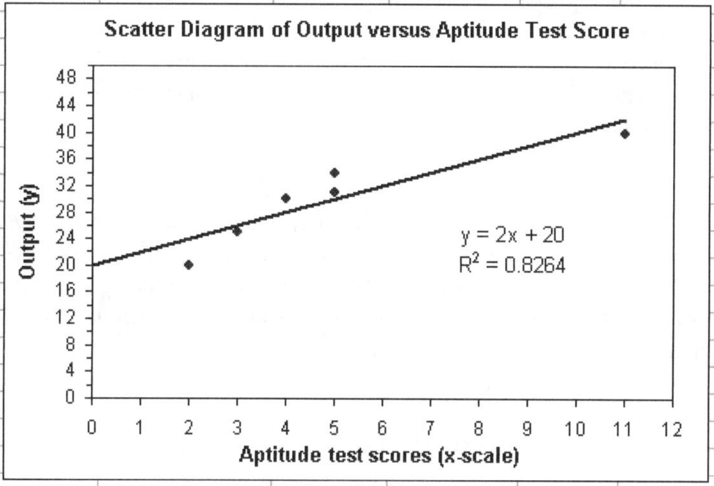

	A	B	C
28		**Predicted Ouput**	**Test Score**
29		32	6
30		40	10

○ EXAMPLE 13.2b

A statistics instructor claims that he knows there is a distinct relationship between a student's statistics mark and the student's class attendance. To prove the point, the instructor has taken a random sample from last year's class and obtained the following information:

Student	A	B	C	D	E	F	G	H
Statistics mark	90	75	55	73	70	85	63	45
Number of classes missed (out of 32)	2	7	13	9	7	4	13	16

a) Determine the dependent variable.
b) Draw the scatter diagram.
c) Obtain the regression equation.
d) Plot the regression line.
e) Interpret the meaning of the regression coefficients *a* and *b*.
f) Predict the statistics marks for two students who miss 3 classes and 10 classes respectively.

● SOLUTION

a) To identify the dependent variable, pose the two questions
   1. Does class attendance depend on the statistics mark?
   2. Does the statistics mark depend on class attendance?

   Question 2 is more reasonable. The statistics mark data become the dependent variable y.

b) Scatter diagram. See Figure 13.4.

FIGURE 13.4 Scatter Diagram with Regression Line

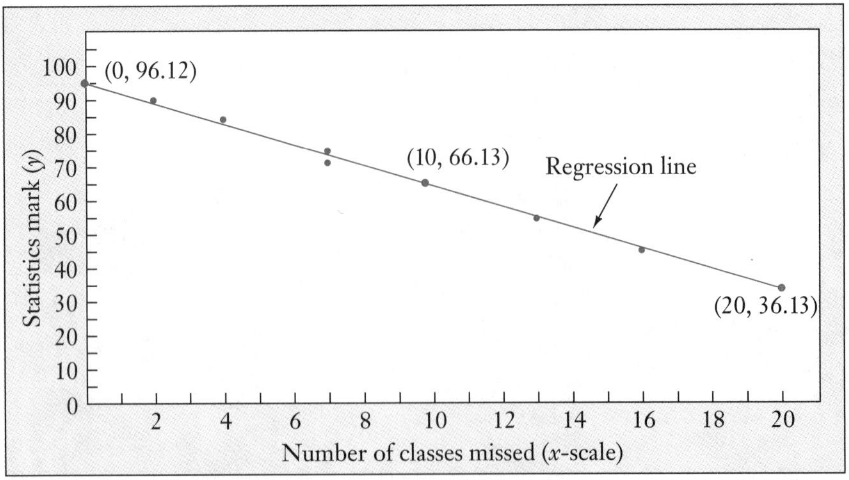

c) The distribution of the points in the scatter diagram indicates that there is a reasonable linear relationship between the statistics mark and the number of classes missed. The use of the least squares method is appropriate.

The values required to obtain the values of the regression coefficients a and b are listed in Table 13.3.

TABLE 13.3 Calculations for Finding *a* and *b*

Student	Statistics mark y	Number of classes missed x	xy	x^2	y^2
A	90	2	180	4	8100
B	75	7	525	49	5625
C	55	13	715	169	3025
D	73	9	657	81	5329
E	70	7	490	49	4900
F	85	4	340	16	7225
G	63	13	819	169	3969
H	45	16	720	256	2025
$n = 8$	$\sum y = 556$	$\sum x = 71$	$\sum xy = 4446$	$\sum x^2 = 793$	$\sum y^2 = 40\,198$

Substituting into Formulas 13.2 and 13.2a, we obtain

$$b = \frac{n(\sum xy) - (\sum x)(\sum y)}{n(\sum x^2) - (\sum x)^2} = \frac{8(4446) - (71)(556)}{8(793) - (71)^2}$$

$$= \frac{35\,568 - 39\,476}{6344 - 5041}$$

$$= \frac{-3908}{1303} = -2.9992$$

$$a = \frac{\sum y}{n} - b\frac{\sum x}{n} = \frac{556}{8} - (-2.9992)(\frac{71}{8}) = 69.5 + 26.6179 = 96.1179$$

The regression equation is $y_p = 96.1179 - 2.9992x$.

d) Graph of the regression line.

Three convenient values of x for plotting the regression line are $x = 0$, $x = 10$, and $x = 20$.

For $x = 0$, $y_p = 96.1179 - 2.9992(0) = 96.1179$.

For $x = 10$, $y_p = 96.1179 - 2.9992(10) = 96.1179 - 29.992 = 66.1259$.

For $x = 20$, $y_p = 96.1179 - 2.9992(20) = 96.1179 - 59.984 = 36.1339$.

The regression line passes through points (0, 96.1), (10, 66.1) and (20, 36.1).

e) The regression coefficient $a = 96.1179$ indicates that a student who misses no classes ($x = 0$) can expect to achieve a statistics mark of 96.

The coefficient $b = -2.9992$ indicates a negative slope of approximately 3; that is, for every class missed the statistics mark can be expected to drop by three marks.

f) The expected statistics mark for a student missing three classes is

$$y_p = 96.1179 - 2.9992(3) = 96.1179 - 8.9976 = 87.1203,$$

that is, 87. The expected mark for a student missing 10 classes is

$$y_p = 96.1179 - 2.9992(10) = 96.1179 - 29.992 = 66.1259,$$

that is, 66.

Note When a regression equation is used for prediction purposes we should theoretically confine our prediction to within the range of the x values of the original data. For Example 13.2a, we should not calculate expected y values for x values below 2 and above 11. Similarly, for Example 13.2b we should restrict our calculation of expected y values to the range of x values 2 to 16. The reason for this restriction is that there is no guarantee that the regression equation is valid beyond these limits. In practice, this restriction is often ignored and predictions are made beyond the limits of the sample data.

EXERCISE 13.2

1. Select the dependent variable that seems most appropriate for each of the following pairs of variables:

a) The age of manufacturing equipment and the number of rejects produced by the equipment.

b) Interest rates and the level of foreign investment in Canada.

c) Sales volume and the number of marketing representatives.

2. Select the independent variable that seems most likely for each of the following pairs of variables:

a) Number of bankruptcies and gross domestic product.

b) Sales commissions and sales volume.

c) Number of sales transactions and the amount of accounts receivable.

3. State whether the following scatter diagrams look like linear relationships or curvilinear relationships. In the case of a linear relationship, indicate whether the slope of the line is positive or negative.

(a) **(b)** **(c)**

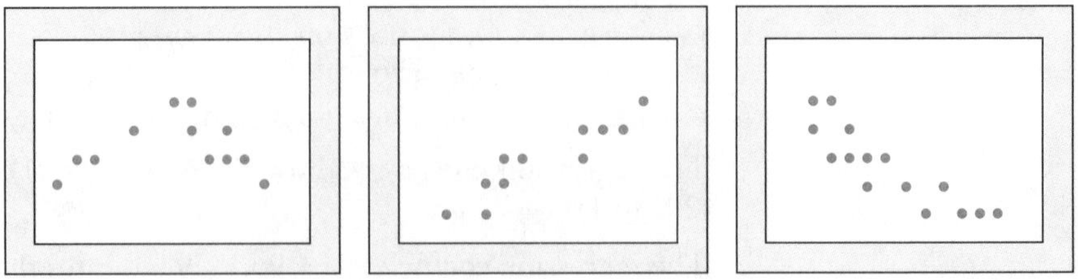

4. State whether the following scatter diagrams indicate linear relationships or curvilinear relationships. For linear relationships state whether the slope of the line is positive or negative.

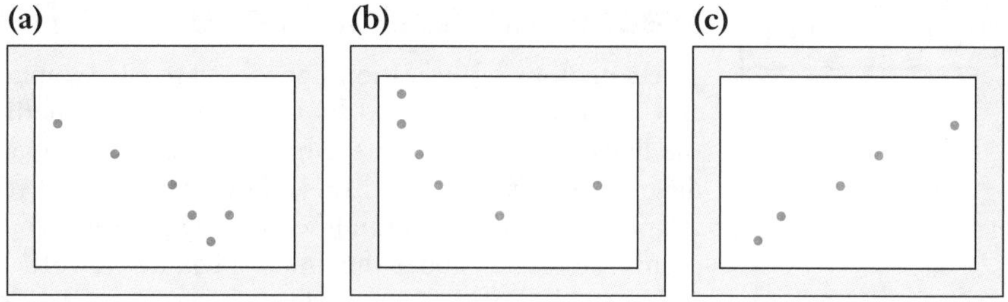

5. The following statistics were calculated from 45 pairs of data points: $\sum x = 60$; $\sum y = 180$; $\sum xy = 1159$; $\sum x^2 = 406$.
   a) Determine the least squares equation.
   b) Estimate y_p for $x = 2.5$.

6. Consider the following statistics:
   $n = 4$; $\sum x = 13.5$; $\sum y = 47.5$; $\sum xy = 2600$; $\sum x^2 = 734$.
   a) Determine the regression equation.
   b) When $x = 10$, what is the estimated value of y?

7. The guidance counsellor of a high school believes a linear relationship exists between students' high-school averages and college averages. The counsellor has collected the following data about a group of students:

Student	A	B	C	D	E	F	G	H
College average	45	82	30	80	71	95	67	56
High-school average	50	74	57	73	70	91	69	63

   a) Determine the dependent variable.
   b) Draw a scatter diagram.
   c) Determine the regression equation.
   d) Interpret the meaning of the regression coefficients.
   e) Plot the regression line.
   f) Predict the values of y for **(i)** $x = 60$; **(ii)** $x = 90$.

8. The sales manager of a company wants to gain insight into the relationship between the unit sales price and the number of units sold for a particular product. Using past sales data, the sales department supplied the following information:

Price per unit	\$20	\$24	\$30	\$33	\$42	\$45	\$51
Number of units sold (000s)	20	18	16	14	12	10	8

   a) Determine the regression equation and interpret the meaning of the regression coefficients.
   b) Construct a scatter diagram and plot the regression line.
   c) Predict the value of y for $x = 9$ and $x = 17$.

SECTION 13.3

Measuring Variability about the Regression Line

The equations of regression lines fitted to the sample data in examples 13.2a and 13.2b were calculated by the least squares method, which ensures that the lines fit the data with the minimum amount of variation. The associated diagrams (figures 13.3 and 13.4) show that the observed values are unlikely to fall on the fitted regression line but are scattered around it. Some of the data points are located above the line and some below it.

When dealing with a single variable x, we developed a measure of the variability of the observed values around the mean value $\bar{x}$, called the sample standard deviation. We computed it by using the formula

$$s = \sqrt{\frac{\sum(x - \bar{x})^2}{n - 1}}$$

Similarly, when dealing with two variables x and y, a measure of the variability of the observed y values from the predicted y values (y_p), known as the **standard error of the estimate**, is given by

$$s_e = \sqrt{\frac{\sum(y - y_p)^2}{n - 2}}$$

where s_e = standard error of the estimate;
y = an observed value of y for a given value of x;
y_p = predicted (expected) value of y for the given value of x;
n = the number of paired observations (x, y).

The computation of the standard error of the estimate is facilitated by use of the alternative formula:

$$s_e = \sqrt{\frac{\sum y^2 - a(\sum y) - b(\sum xy)}{n - 2}}$$ ←*Formula* 13.3

Except for $\sum y^2$, all values in the formula are available from the regression line computations. As done in Table 13.2, $\sum y^2$ is frequently computed at the same time.

EXAMPLE 13.3a

Compute the standard error of the estimate of y based on x for Examples 13.2a and 13.2b.

SOLUTION

For Example 13.2a the following values are needed from Table 13.2:
$n = 6$; $\sum y = 180$; $\sum xy = 1000$; $\sum y^2 = 5642$.
Substituting in Formula 13.3 we obtain

$$s_e = \sqrt{\frac{5642 - 20(180) - 2(1000)}{6-2}}$$

$$= \sqrt{\frac{5642 - 3600 - 2000}{4}} = \sqrt{\frac{42}{4}}$$

$$= \sqrt{10.5} = 3.2404$$

For Example 13.2b the values obtained from Table 13.3 are
$n = 8$; $\sum y = 556$; $\sum xy = 4446$; $\sum y^2 = 40\ 198$.
Substituting into Formula 13.3 we obtain

$$s_e = \sqrt{\frac{40\ 198 - 96.1179(556) - (-2.9992)(4446)}{8-2}}$$

$$= \sqrt{\frac{40\ 198 - 53\ 441.552 + 13\ 334.443}{6}} = \sqrt{\frac{90.891}{6}}$$

$$= \sqrt{15.1485} = 3.8921$$

The values obtained for s_e in the above calculations indicate the variation of the data points around the fitted regression lines.

For the fitted regression line $y_p = 20 + 2x$ in Example 13.2a, $s_e = 3.2404$.

For the fitted regression line $y_p = 96.1179 - 2.9992x$ in Example 13.2b, $s_e = 3.8921$.

The interpretation of the standard error of the estimate is similar to that of the sample standard deviation. The sample standard deviation for a single variable x measures the variability of the data about the arithmetic mean $\bar{x}$. The standard error of the estimate for two variables (x, y) measures the variability of the data about the *fitted least squares regression line* $y_p = a + bx$.

EXERCISE 13.3

1. Determine the standard error of the estimate for Question **7** in Exercise 13.2.

2. Determine the standard error of the estimate for Question **8** in Exercise 13.2.

SECTION 13.4

Constructing Confidence Intervals

An important use of the regression line is to forecast (predict) values or point estimates of the dependent variable y given some *specific* value of the independent variable x.

Just as we used the sample standard deviation in developing an interval estimate around the mean $\bar{x}$, we can use the standard error of the estimate in developing interval estimates around the expected values y_p.

Two types of confidence intervals can be developed:

1. a confidence interval to estimate the *mean value* of y for a given (specified) value of x;
2. a confidence interval to estimate a single *value* of y for a given value of x.

Both types of confidence intervals are obtained by first determining the point estimate by substituting the given value of x in the regression equation $y_p = a + bx$.

In Example 13.2a the best point estimate of y_p when $x = 5$ is $y_p = 20 + 2(5) = 30$. This means that the best point estimate of the *average output* of all employees who score 5 on the dexterity test is 30 units. Similarly, the best point estimate of the *single output* of an individual employee who scores 5 on the dexterity test is also 30 units.

While both point estimates equal 30 units, there is a difference when we construct the two types of interval estimates. An interval estimate is *centred* on a point estimate and the calculation of the upper and lower limits of the interval involves the standard error of the estimate.

The *standard error of the estimate for the mean value* of y is adjusted for accuracy using

$$(S_{y \cdot x})\sqrt{\frac{1}{n} + \frac{n(x-\overline{x})^2}{n(\sum x^2) - (\sum x)^2}}$$

The *standard error of the estimate for a single value* of y is adjusted for accuracy using

$$\sqrt{1 + \frac{1}{n} + \frac{n(x-\overline{x})^2}{n(\sum x^2) - (\sum x)^2}}$$

The confidence interval estimate for predicting an *average* value of y is

$$y_p \pm t_{n-2}(s_e)\sqrt{\frac{1}{n} + \frac{n(x-\overline{x})^2}{n(\sum x^2) - (\sum x)^2}}$$ ←*Formula* 13.4

and the confidence interval estimate for predicting a *single* value of y is

$$y_p \pm t_{n-2}(s_e)\sqrt{1 + \frac{1}{n} + \frac{n(x-\overline{x})^2}{n(\sum x^2) - (\sum x)^2}}$$ ←*Formula* 13.5

where y_p = the point estimate for a specified value of x;
x = a specified value of the independent variable x;
$\overline{x}$ = the mean of the observed values of x;
s_e = the standard error of the estimate of y based on x;
t_{n-2} = the t table value for $(n-2)$ degrees of freedom at a specified level of confidence;
n = the number of paired observations.

EXAMPLE 13.4a

With reference to Example 13.2a, determine at the 95% level of confidence

a) the confidence interval for the output of a group of employees with aptitude test scores of 8;
b) the confidence interval for the output of an individual employee with an aptitude test score of 8.

SOLUTION

From Table 13.2, $n = 6$; $\sum x = 30$; $\sum x^2 = 200$.
The regression equation is $y_p = 20 + 2x$;
for $x = 8$, $y_p = 20 + 2(8) = 20 + 16 = 36$;
$s_e = 3.2404$ (see solution to Example 13.3a).

$$\overline{x} = \frac{\sum x}{n} = \frac{30}{6} = 5.$$

The number of degrees of freedom $(n-2) = (6-2) = 4$.
t_{n-2} at the 95% level of confidence = 2.776.

a) First calculate

$$\begin{aligned}
&\sqrt{\frac{1}{n} + \frac{n(x-\overline{x})^2}{n(\sum x^2) - (\sum x)^2}} \\
&= \sqrt{\frac{1}{6} + \frac{6(8-5)^2}{6(200) - (30)^2}} \\
&= \sqrt{0.1667 + \frac{6(9)}{1200 - 900}} \\
&= \sqrt{0.1667 + 0.18} \\
&= \sqrt{0.3467} \\
&= 0.5888.
\end{aligned}$$

The confidence interval for the mean value of y is

$$\begin{aligned}
y_p \pm t_{n-2}(s_e)\sqrt{\frac{1}{n} + \frac{n(x-\overline{x})^2}{n(\sum x^2) - (\sum x)^2}} &= 36 \pm 2.776(3.2404)(0.5888) \\
&= 36 \pm 5.2965.
\end{aligned}$$

The confidence limits are 30.7035 and 41.2965.

This means we can be 95% certain that the average output of a group of employees, each of whom scored 8 on the aptitude test, will lie between 31 and 41 units.

b) First calculate $\sqrt{1+\frac{1}{n}+\frac{n(x-\overline{x})^2}{n(\sum x^2)-(\sum x)^2}}$

$$= \sqrt{1+\frac{1}{6}+\frac{6(8-5)^2}{6(200)-(30)^2}}$$

$$= \sqrt{1+0.1667+0.18} = \sqrt{1+0.3467} = \sqrt{1.3467}$$

$$= 1.1605.$$

The confidence interval for a single value of y is

$$y_p \pm t_{n-2}(s_e)\sqrt{1+\frac{1}{n}+\frac{n(x-\overline{x})^2}{n(\sum x^2)-(\sum x)^2}} = 36 \pm 2.776(3.2404)(1.1605)$$

$$= 36 \pm 10.4391.$$

The confidence limits are 25.5609 and 46.4391.

This means we can be 95% certain that the output of an individual employee in the group who scored 8 on the aptitude test will lie between 26 and 46 units.

○ EXAMPLE 13.4b

For Example 13.2b determine the 90% confidence interval for

a) a group of students who miss 16 classes;

b) an individual student who misses 16 classes.

● SOLUTION

From Table 13.3, $n = 8$; $\sum x = 71$; $\sum x^2 = 793$.

The regression equation is $y_p = 96.1179 - 2.9992x$;

substituting $x = 16$, $y_p = 96.1179 - 2.9992(16) = 48.1307$;

$s_e = 3.8921$ (see solution to Example 13.3a).

$$\overline{x} = \frac{71}{8} = 8.875.$$

The number of degrees of freedom, $(n-2) = (8-2) = 6$;

t_{n-2} at the 90% level of confidence = 1.943.

a) First calculate $\sqrt{\frac{1}{8}+\frac{8(16-8.875)^2}{8(793)-(71)^2}}$

$$= \sqrt{\frac{1}{8}+\frac{8(50.7656)}{6344-5041}}$$

$$= \sqrt{0.125+\frac{406.1248}{1303}}$$

$$= \sqrt{0.125+0.3117} = \sqrt{0.4367}$$

$$= 0.6608.$$

The confidence interval for the mean value of y is

$$y_p \pm t_{n-2}(s_e)\sqrt{\frac{1}{n}+\frac{n(x-\bar{x})^2}{n(\sum x^2)-(\sum x)^2}}$$

$= 48.1307 \pm (1.943)(3.8921)(0.6608) = 48.1307 \pm 4.9972.$
The confidence limits are 43.1335 and 53.1279.

This indicates that we can be 90% certain that the average mark obtained by a group of students in this class who miss 16 classes can be expected to lie between 43 and 53.

b) First calculate $\sqrt{1+\frac{1}{8}+\frac{8(16-8.875)^2}{8(793)-(71)^2}} = \sqrt{1+0.125+\frac{406.125}{1303}}$

$= \sqrt{1+0.125+0.3117} = \sqrt{1.4367} = 1.1986.$

The confidence interval for a single value of y is

$$y_p \pm t_{n-2}(s_e)\sqrt{1+\frac{1}{n}+\frac{n(x-\bar{x})^2}{n(\sum x^2)-(\sum x)^2}}$$

$= 48.1307 \pm (1.943)(3.8921)(1.1986) = 48.1307 \pm 9.0642.$
The confidence limits are 39.0665 and 57.1949.

This means that we can have 90% confidence that an individual who misses 16 classes can be expected to obtain a mark between 39 and 57.

Shape of the Confidence Intervals

Note that the intervals for the two types of confidence intervals are different because their adjusted standard errors are different. Since the standard error for an individual value of y is always larger than the standard error for the mean value of y, the forecast intervals for an individual value of y_p will always be wider than those for the average value of y_p.

For both types of confidence intervals the size of the adjustment to the standard error of the estimate depends on the specified value of x. As the given value moves farther away from the mean $\bar{x}$, the numerical value of the expression under the square-root sign increases. As a result, the confidence interval becomes wider and the forecast becomes less accurate.

Table 13.4 and Figure 13.5 show the 95% confidence intervals for Example 13.4a for values of x ranging from 0 to 10. Note that the minimum width of both intervals, 7.34 and 19.43, occurs at $x = \overline{x} = 5$. The largest width, 14.69 and 23.23, occurs at $x = 10$, the given value of x that differs most from the mean value $\overline{x} = 5$.

TABLE 13.4 Confidence Intervals for Example 13.4a

		Interval forecast for average value of y			Interval forecast for individual value of y		
x	y_p	Upper limit	Lower limit	Width of interval	Upper limit	Lower limit	Width of interval
0	20	27.3447	12.6553	14.6893	31.6129	8.3871	23.2259
1	22	28.2753	15.7247	12.5506	32.9679	11.0321	21.9359
2	24	29.2963	18.7037	10.5926	34.4387	13.5613	20.8775
3	26	30.4676	21.5324	8.9352	36.0437	15.9563	20.0874
4	28	31.8864	24.1136	7.7729	37.7990	18.2010	19.5980
5	30	33.6723	26.3277	7.3447	39.7161	20.2839	19.4322
6	32	35.8864	28.1136	7.7729	41.7990	22.2010	19.5980
7	34	38.4676	29.5324	8.9352	44.0437	23.9563	20.0874
8	36	41.2963	30.7037	10.5926	46.4387	25.5613	20.8775
9	38	44.2753	31.7247	12.5506	48.9679	27.0321	21.9359
10	40	47.3447	32.6553	14.6893	51.6129	28.3871	23.2259

FIGURE 13.5 Confidence Intervals around Regression Line

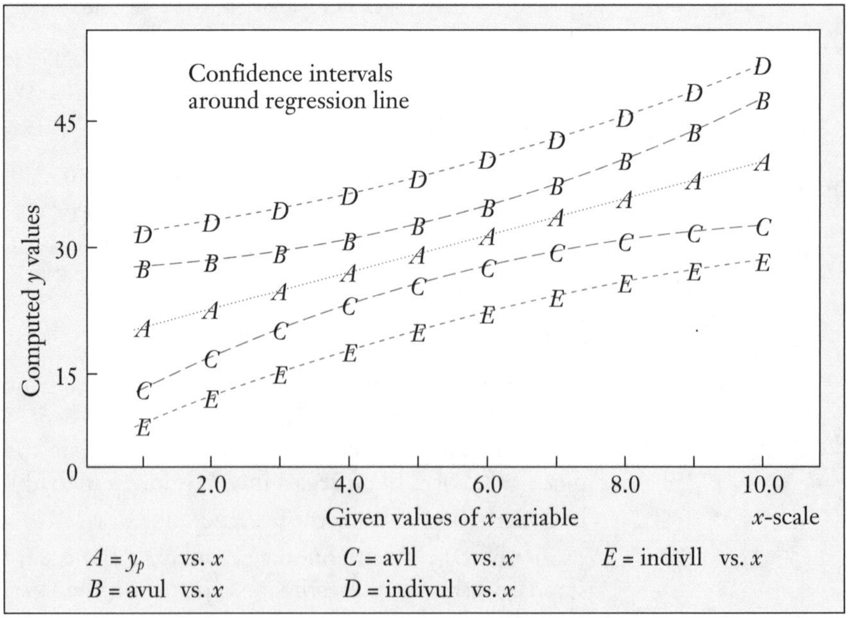

EXERCISE 13.4

1. For Question **7** in Exercise 13.2, determine the 99% confidence interval in which the college average will fall
   a) for a group of students who have a high-school average of 65;
   b) for Cynthia if her high-school average is 65.

2. For Question **8** in Exercise 13.2, determine the 98% confidence interval in which
   a) the average number of units sold can be expected to be found if the unit price is \$15;
   b) the specific number of units that will be sold at a special sale if the price is set at \$15.

3. An engineering department has compiled unit cost data for a series of production runs of different quantities as shown below.

Quantity (000s)	20	13	14	18	13	17	10
Cost per unit (\$)	2.10	2.39	2.34	2.19	2.43	2.18	2.50

   a) Obtain the least squares regression equation.
   b) Construct a scatter diagram and plot the regression line.
   c) Compute the standard error of the estimate of y based on x.
   d) Calculate the cost per unit associated with a production run of 15 000 units.
   e) Construct the 90% confidence interval for the expected unit cost of all production runs of 15 000 units.
   f) Determine the 90% confidence interval for the next run of 15 000 units.

4. A random sample from a class of mathematics students comparing student marks with student class attendance yielded the following data:

Number of classes attended	30	28	16	25	32	32	20	25
Mathematics mark	86	81	41	63	97	90	47	72

   a) Obtain the least squares regression equation.
   b) Construct a scatter diagram and plot the regression line.
   c) Calculate the standard error of the estimate.
   d) Compute a point estimate of the mathematics mark for a student attending 18 classes.
   e) Construct the 99% confidence interval for Stephanie, who will be able to attend just 22 classes.

SECTION 13.5

Correlation Analysis

A. Introduction

The procedures used in the previous sections of this chapter provide the least squares equation, which describes the relationship between two variables. To measure the closeness of association between variables we use **correlation analysis**. The closer the actual data points are to the fitted regression line, the closer is the relationship between the variables.

The two main measures of the strength of the relationship are

1. the coefficient of determination, r^2;
2. the coefficient of correlation, r.

B. Total Deviation, Explained Deviation, and Unexplained Deviation

The two coefficients take into account three related vertical deviations for each value of y.

1. The *total vertical deviation* is the difference between an observed value y and the mean value y.

$$\text{TOTAL DEVIATION} = (y - \bar{y})$$

2. The *explained deviation* is part of the total deviation. It is the difference between y_p, the value of the dependent variable obtained when a particular value of x is substituted into the regression equation, and the average value $\bar{y}$.

$$\text{EXPLAINED DEVIATION} = (y_p - \bar{y})$$

3. The *unexplained deviation* is the remaining part of the total deviation.

$$\text{UNEXPLAINED DEVIATION} = (y - y_p)$$

It follows that

$$\text{TOTAL DEVIATION} = \text{EXPLAINED DEVIATION} + \text{UNEXPLAINED DEVIATION}$$

$$(y - \bar{y}) = (y_p - \bar{y}) + (y - y_p)$$

The concept of the three deviations is illustrated in Figure 13.6, which is based on data from Example 13.2a.

The regression equation for Example 13.2a was $y_p = 20 + 2x$.

Since $n = 6$ and $\sum y = 180$, $\bar{y} = \dfrac{\sum y}{n} = \dfrac{180}{6} = 30$.

FIGURE 13.6 Illustrations of Vertical Deviations

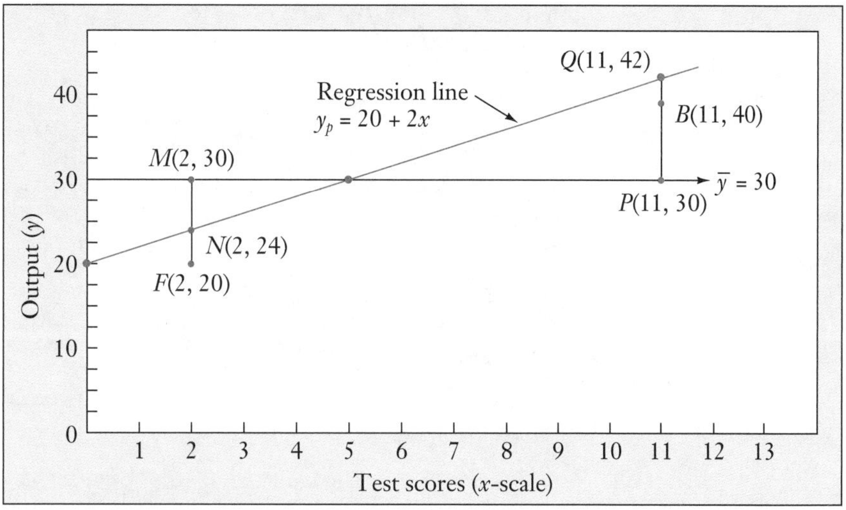

Let us consider the data for Employee F from Example 13.2a.
Output, $y = 20$.
Test score, $x = 2$.
Computed output, $y_p = 20 + 2(2) = 24$.

The data for Employee F are reflected in the excerpt from Figure 13.6 shown as Figure 13.7.

FIGURE 13.7 Vertical Deviations for Employee F

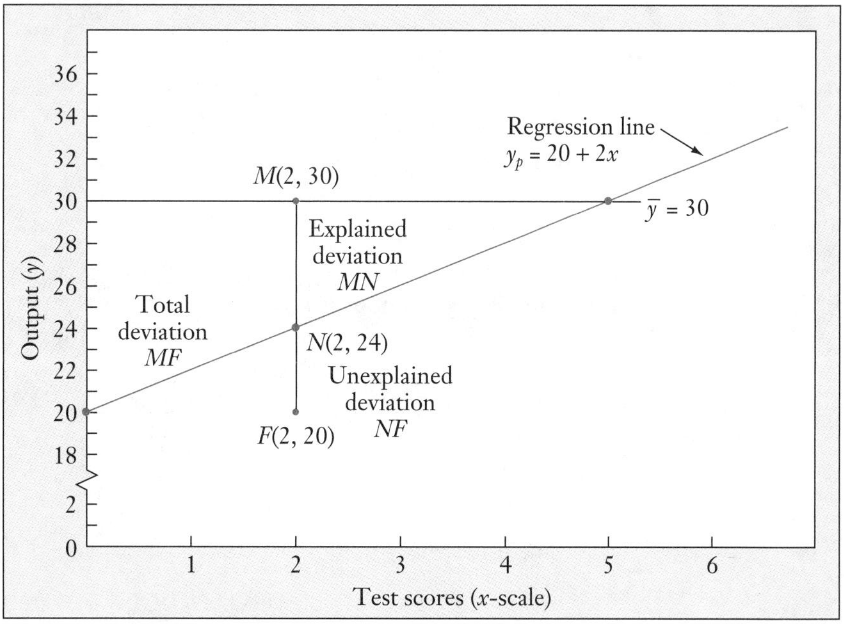

The vertical line segment FM joining point $F(2, 20)$ to point $M(2, 30)$ on the $\bar{y}$ line represents the total deviation of the output of Employee F from the average output for the group of employees.

$$\text{TOTAL DEVIATION, } (y - \bar{y}) = (20 - 30) = -10$$

The line segment FM intersects the regression line at N. This point represents the output that is expected for a test score of 2.

$$y_p = 20 + 2(2) = 24$$

The coordinates of N are (2, 24).
The line segment MN represents the difference between expected output $y_p = 24$ for a test score of 2 and the average output $\bar{y}$. Because this deviation is determined by the dependency of y on x, it is referred to as the explained deviation.

$$\text{EXPLAINED DEVIATION, } (y_p - \bar{y}) = (24 - 30) = -6$$

The line segment FN is the remaining part of the total deviation and represents the deviation that cannot be explained by the dependency of y on x. It is referred to as the unexplained deviation.

$$\text{UNEXPLAINED DEVIATION, } (y - y_p) = (20 - 24) = -4$$

From this we obtain

$$\begin{aligned} &\text{EXPLAINED DEVIATION + UNEXPLAINED DEVIATION} \\ &\quad = (-6) + (-4) \\ &\quad = -10 \\ &\quad = \text{TOTAL DEVIATION} \end{aligned}$$

Now consider the data for Employee B.
Output, $y = 40$.
Test score, $x = 11$.
Computed output, $y_p = 20 + 2(11) = 42$.

As shown in Figure 13.6, the line segment BP represents the total deviation of employee B's output from the average output.

$$\text{TOTAL DEVIATION, } (y - \bar{y}) = (40 - 30) = 10$$

Point $Q(11, 42)$ represents the expected output for a test score of 11. The line segment QP represents the explained deviation for y when $x = 11$.

$$\text{EXPLAINED DEVIATION, } (y_p - \bar{y}) = (42 - 30) = 12$$

The line segment QB represents the unexplained deviation.

$$\text{UNEXPLAINED DEVIATION, } (y - y_p) = (40 - 42) = -2$$

From this we obtain

$$\begin{aligned} \text{EXPLAINED DEVIATION} + \text{UNEXPLAINED DEVIATION} \\ &= (12) + (-2) \\ &= 10 \\ &= \text{TOTAL DEVIATION} \end{aligned}$$

C. *Total Variation, Explained Variation, and Unexplained Variation*

The closeness of the association between y and x can be measured by considering the relationship between the explained variation and the total variation for the group of observations.

EXAMPLE 13.5a

For the data used in Example 13.2a, compute the total variation, explained variation, and unexplained variation.

SOLUTION

Step 1 Compute the deviations for the individual observations and then total the deviations as shown in Table 13.5.

TABLE 13.5 Computations of Deviations

Employee	Test score x	Out-put y	Predicted output y_p	Total deviation $y - \bar{y}$	Explained deviation $y_p - \bar{y}$	Unexplained deviation $y - y_p$	Check: EXPLAINED + UNEXPLAINED = TOTAL DEVIATION
A	5	31	30	31 − 30 = 1	30 − 30 = 0	31 − 30 = 1	0 + 1 = 1
B	11	40	42	40 − 30 = 10	42 − 30 = 12	40 − 42 = −2	12 − 2 = 10
C	4	30	28	30 − 30 = 0	28 − 30 = −2	30 − 28 = 2	−2 + 2 = 0
D	5	34	30	34 − 30 = 4	30 − 30 = 0	34 − 30 = 4	0 + 4 = 4
E	3	25	26	25 − 30 = −5	26 − 30 = −4	25 − 26 = −1	−4 − 1 = −5
F	2	20	24	20 − 30 = −10	24 − 30 = −6	20 − 24 = −4	−6 − 4 = −10

Step 2 Use the deviations computed in Table 13.5 to determine the squared deviations as shown in Table 13.6.

TABLE 13.6 Computations of Squared Deviations

Employee	Total squared deviation $(y - \bar{y})^2$	Explained squared deviation $(y_p - \bar{y})^2$	Unexplained squared deviation $(y - y_p)^2$
A	$(1)(1) = 1$	$(0)(0) = 0$	$(1)(1) = 1$
B	$(10)(10) = 100$	$(12)(12) = 144$	$(-2)(-2) = 4$
C	$(0)(0) = 0$	$(-2)(-2) = 4$	$(2)(2) = 4$
D	$(4)(4) = 16$	$(0)(0) = 0$	$(4)(4) = 16$
E	$(-5)(-5) = 25$	$(-4)(-4) = 16$	$(-1)(-1) = 1$
F	$(-10)(-10) = 100$	$(-6)(-6) = 36$	$(-4)(-4) = 16$
	$\sum(y - \bar{y})^2 = 242$	$\sum(y_p - \bar{y})^2 = 200$	$\sum(y - y_p)^2 = 42$

The three resulting variations are defined as follows:

1. The sum of the total squared deviations is called the

$$\text{TOTAL VARIATION} = \sum(y - \bar{y})^2 = 242$$

2. The sum of the explained squared deviations is called the

$$\text{EXPLAINED VARIATION} = \sum(y_p - \bar{y})^2 = 200$$

3. The sum of the unexplained squared deviations is called the

$$\text{UNEXPLAINED VARIATION} = \sum(y - y_p)^2 = 42$$

For the three variations,

$$\begin{aligned}\text{TOTAL VARIATION} &= \text{EXPLAINED VARIATION} + \text{UNEXPLAINED VARIATION} \\ &= 200 + 42 = 242\end{aligned}$$

D. The Coefficients of Determination and Correlation

The **coefficient of determination** is the ratio of the explained variation to the total variation.

The **coefficient of correlation** is the square root of the coefficient of determination.

The two coefficients can be determined for Example 13.3a as follows:

$$\begin{aligned}\text{COEFFICIENT OF DETERMINATION, } r^2 &= \frac{\text{EXPLAINED VARIATION}}{\text{TOTAL VARIATION}} \\ &= \frac{200}{242} = 0.826\,446 \\ &= 82.6\%\end{aligned}$$

The coefficient r^2 indicates that 82.6% of the total variation is explained by the dependency of output on the test scores.

COEFFICIENT OF CORRELATION, r

$$= \sqrt{\text{COEFFICIENT OF DETERMINATION}}$$

$$= \sqrt{r^2} = \sqrt{0.826\,446} = 0.909\,091$$

E. *Computation of the Coefficient of Determination r^2 and the Coefficient of Correlation r by Formula*

Computation of the individual deviations and squared deviations is usually avoided because it is tedious. The value of the coefficient of determination r^2 can be more readily calculated from the values required for determining the regression equation.

$$r^2 = \frac{[n(\sum xy) - (\sum x)(\sum y)]^2}{[n(\sum x^2) - (\sum x)^2][n(\sum y^2) - (\sum y)^2]}$$ ←*Formula* 13.6

$$r = \sqrt{r^2}$$ ←*Formula* 13.7

○ **EXAMPLE 13.5b**

Compute the coefficients of determination and correlation for Example 13.2a.

● **SOLUTION**

From Table 13.2 we know that $n = 6$; $\sum x = 30$; $\sum y = 180$; $\sum xy = 1000$; $\sum x^2 = 200$; $\sum y^2 = 5642$.

Substituting into Formula 13.6 the coefficient of determination

$$r^2 = \frac{[6(1000) - 30(180)]^2}{[6(200) - (30)^2][6(5642) - (180)^2]}$$

$$= \frac{(6000 - 5400)^2}{(1200 - 900)(33\,852 - 32\,400)}$$

$$= \frac{(600)^2}{(300)(1452)} = \frac{360\,000}{435\,600} = 0.826\,446 = 82.6\%$$

COEFFICIENT OF CORRELATION, $r = \sqrt{0.826\,446} = 0.909\,091$

For some obvious and some not-so-obvious reasons the coefficient of correlation r is used much more than the coefficient of determination r^2.

One significant advantage the coefficient of correlation has over the coefficient of determination is that it indicates whether the relationship between the variables is *direct* or *inverse*.

The not-so-obvious reasons for preferring the use of the coefficient of correlation deal with more complex issues related to its arithmetic relationship with the regression equation.

The user of statistical information should be critical of research that suggests a correlation coefficient as low as 0.40 indicates a substantial relationship between two variables. Since $(0.40)^2 = 0.16$, a correlation of this size indicates that only 16% of the variance in one variable is predictable from the other. It takes a coefficient of correlation of 0.707 before 50% of the variance of y is explained by x.

A rule of thumb says that a coefficient of correlation is significant if the absolute value of the sample correlation exceeds $\frac{2}{\sqrt{n}}$.

These calculations can be completed using EXCEL, as demonstrated in USING EXCEL 13.2.

USING EXCEL 13.2

Compute the coefficients of determination and correlation for Example 13.2a. Note that other statistics such as the explained variation, the unexplained variation, and the total variation can also be computed using EXCEL's **Data Analysis ToolPak**.

1. Type the column headings **Employee**, **Output**, and **Test Score** into cells A1–C1.
2. Enter the information found in Table 13.1 into cells A2:C7.
3. On the **Tools** menu, click **Data Analysis...** (You may need to install the **Analysis ToolPak** add-in on your computer and then load it into EXCEL with the **Add-Ins** dialog box accessed on the **Tools** menu. If you try to load the **Analysis ToolPak** add-in and EXCEL does not install it, you can either install it with the **Add/Remove Programs** feature found in Windows' **Control Panel** or from Microsoft's Office 2000 CD-ROM).
4. The **Data Analysis** dialog box appears. From the **Analysis Tools** list, select **Regression** and click the **OK** button.
5. The **Regression** dialog box appears. In the **Input Y Range** input box, type **$B$1:$B$7** (or select cells B1–B7 and return to the input dialog box) – these cells represent the dependent variables. In the **Input X Range** input box, type **$C$1:$C$7** (or select cells C1–C7 and return to the input dialog box) – these cells represent the independent variables. Ensure that: the **Labels** checkbox is selected (checked); the **Constant is Zero** checkbox is deselected (unchecked); and the **Confidence Level** checkbox is deselected (unchecked). From the **Output options**, select the **Output Range** option and type **$A$9** in its input box (or select cell A9 and return to the input dialog box). Ensure that all the **Residuals** and **Normal Probability** options are deselected (unchecked). Click the **OK** button when finished.
6. Select cell C12, and type the note **is the Coefficient of Correlation.**
7. Select cell C13, and type the note **is the Coefficient of Determination.**
8. Resize the columns to make the contents of the spreadsheet clear and readable.

OUTPUT

File Edit View Insert Format Tools Data Window Help

Arial 10 B

I30 =

	A	B	C	D	E	F	G
1	**Employee**	**Output**	**Test Score**				
2	A	31	5				
3	B	40	11				
4	C	30	4				
5	D	34	5				
6	E	25	3				
7	F	20	2				
8							
9	SUMMARY OUTPUT						
10							
11	*Regression Statistics*						
12	Multiple R	0.909090909	is the Coefficient of Correlation.				
13	R Square	0.826446281	is the Coefficient of Determination.				
14	Adjusted R Square	0.783057851					
15	Standard Error	3.240370349					
16	Observations	6					
17							
18	ANOVA						
19		*df*	*SS*	*MS*	*F*	*Significance F*	
20	Regression	1	200	200	19.04762	0.012021037	
21	Residual	4	42	10.5			
22	Total	5	242				
23							
24		Coefficients	Standard Error	t Stat	P-value	Lower 95%	Upper 95%
25	Intercept	20	2.645751311	7.55928946	0.001641	12.65420151	27.34579849
26	Test Score	2	0.458257569	4.364357805	0.012021	0.727670379	3.272329621

○ **EXAMPLE 13.5c**

Compute the coefficients r^2 and r for Example 13.2b.

● **SOLUTION**

From Table 13.3 we know that $n = 8$; $\sum x = 71$; $\sum y = 556$; $\sum xy = 4446$; $\sum x^2 = 793$; $\sum y^2 = 40\ 198$.

Substituting into Formula 13.6 the coefficient of determination

$$r^2 = \frac{[8(4446) - 71(556)]^2}{[8(793) - (71)^2][8(40\ 198) - (556)^2]}$$

$$= \frac{(35\ 568 - 39\ 476)^2}{(6344 - 5041)(321\ 584 - 309\ 136)}$$

$$= \frac{(-3908)^2}{(1303)(12\ 448)} = \frac{15\ 272\ 464}{16\ 219\ 744} = 0.9416 = 94.16\%$$

The coefficient of correlation

$$r = \sqrt{0.9416} = 0.9704$$

F. *Interpretation of the Coefficients*

The coefficient of determination relates the explained variation for a set of data to the total variation. *At most*, the explained variation can *equal* the total variation.

If the explained variation equals the total variation, all the variation in y is explained by the dependency of y on x and $r^2 = 1$.

The smallest value for the explained variation is zero, in which case $r^2 = 0$.

In most cases, r^2 has a value somewhere between 0 and 1, that is,

$$0 \leq r^2 \leq 1.$$

The coefficient of correlation, as the square root of r^2, can take positive or negative values between +1 and −1, that is,

$$-1 \leq r \leq 1.$$

The coefficient of correlation is used as a common index to measure the degree of association between two variables.

Positive values of r indicate a *direct* relationship between the two variables; that is, as x increases y increases. This case is referred to as **positive correlation** and is associated with a regression line that slopes upward to the right. This means that when the value of the regression coefficient b is *positive*, the variables are *positively correlated.*

The closer r is to +1, the stronger the relationship. If $r = 1$, the relationship between x and y is *direct and perfect.* This situation is referred to as *perfect positive correlation.* Representative scatter diagrams indicating positive correlation between two variables are shown in Figure 13.8.

FIGURE 13.8 Scatter Diagrams Showing Positive Correlation

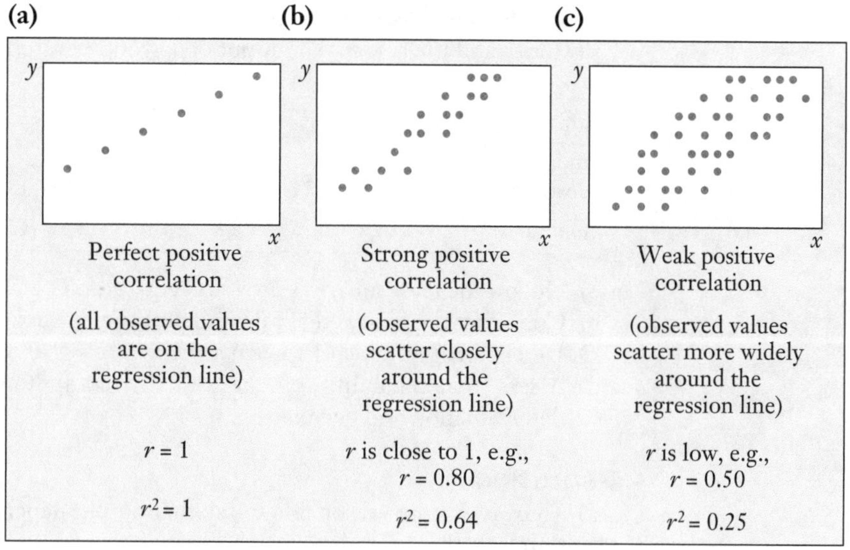

Negative values of r indicate an *inverse* relationship between the two variables; that is, as x increases y decreases. This case is referred to as **negative correlation** and is associated with a regression line that slopes downward to the right. This means that when the regression coefficient b is negative, the variables are negatively correlated.

If $r = -1$ the relationship between x and y is *inverse* and *perfect*. This situation is referred to as *perfect negative correlation*. Representative scatter diagrams indicating negative correlation are shown in Figure 13.9.

FIGURE 13.9 Scatter Diagrams Showing Negative Correlation

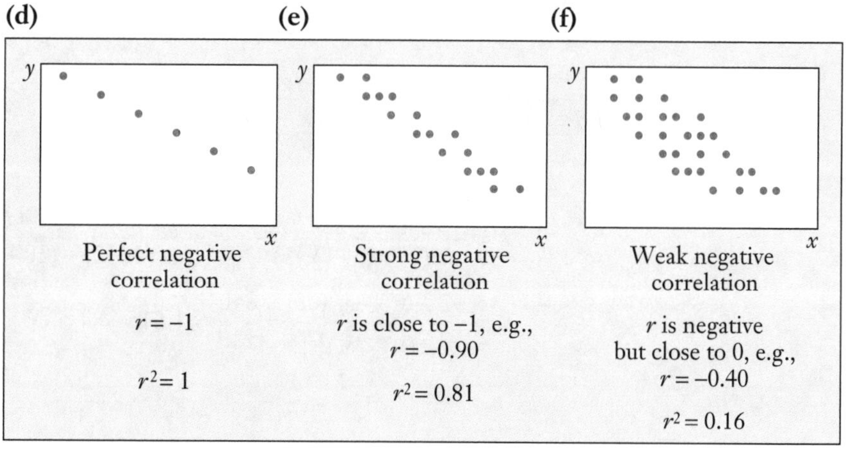

○ EXAMPLE 13.5d

The following data relate to the results of a test producing an index of digital dexterity and the associated output of a group of assembly-line operators.

Operator	A	B	C	D	E	F	G	H	I	J
Index of dexterity	21	20	22	23	21	22	15	18	18	20
Output	23	19	25	24	25	22	12	16	19	22

a) Obtain the least squares regression equation.
b) Construct the scatter diagram and plot the regression line.
c) Determine the value of y when $x = 16$.
d) Assess the reliability of the test by computing the coefficients of determination and correlation.

● SOLUTION

a) Since it is more reasonable to say that output depends on digital dexterity, output is the dependent variable y.

TABLE 13.7 Computations Required

Employee	x	y	xy	x^2	y^2
A	21	23	483	441	529
B	20	19	380	400	361
C	22	25	550	484	625
D	23	24	552	529	576
E	21	25	525	441	625
F	22	22	484	484	484
G	15	12	180	225	144
H	18	16	288	324	256
I	18	19	342	324	361
J	20	22	440	400	484
$n = 10$	200	207	4224	4052	4445

$$b = \frac{n(\sum xy) - (\sum x)(\sum y)}{n(\sum x^2) - (\sum x)^2} = \frac{10(4224) - (200)(207)}{10(4052) - (200)^2}$$

$$= \frac{42\,240 - 41\,400}{40\,520 - 40\,000} = \frac{840}{520} = 1.615\,384\,6$$

$$a = \frac{\sum y}{n} - b\frac{\sum x}{n} = \frac{207}{10} - 1.615\,384\,6(\frac{200}{10})$$

$$= 20.7 - 1.615\,384\,6(20) = 20.7 - 32.307\,692 = -11.607\,692$$

The regression equation is $y_p = -11.6077 + 1.6154x$.

FIGURE 13.10 Scatter Diagram with Regression Line

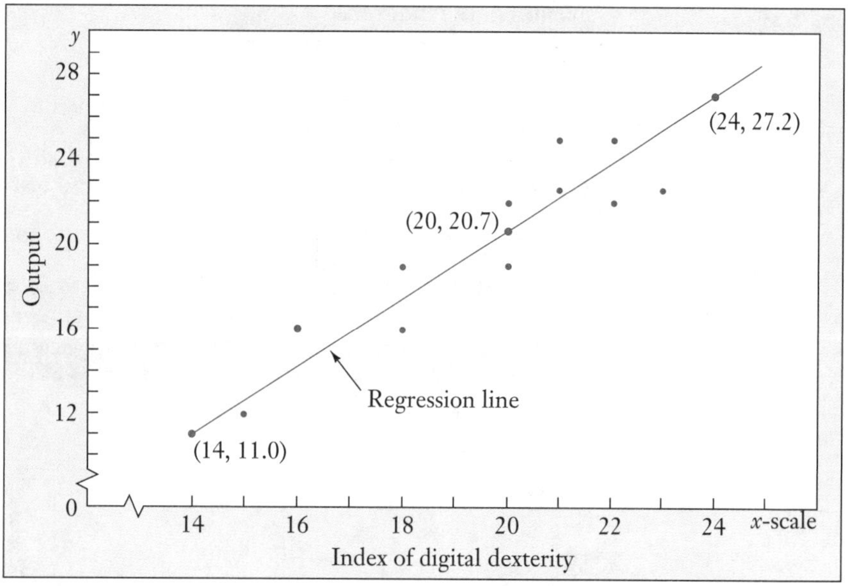

b) For $x = 14$, $y_p = -11.6077 + 1.6154(14)$
$= -11.6077 + 22.6156 = 11.0079.$
For $x = 20$, $y_p = -11.6077 + 1.6154(20)$
$= -11.6077 + 32.3080 = 20.7003.$
For $x = 24$, $y_p = -11.6077 + 1.6154(24)$
$= -11.6077 + 38.7696 = 27.1619.$

To draw the regression line, plot points (14, 11.0), (20, 20.7), and (24, 27.2) and join the three points.

c) The predicted output level for $x = 16$ is

$$\begin{aligned} y_p &= -11.6077 + 1.6154x \\ &= -11.6077 + 1.6154(16) \\ &= -11.6077 + 25.8464 = 14.2387 \end{aligned}$$

d) The coefficient of determination is given by

$$\begin{aligned} r^2 &= \frac{[n(\sum xy) - (\sum x)(\sum y)]^2}{[n(\sum x^2) - (\sum x)^2][n(\sum y^2) - (\sum y)^2]} \\ &= \frac{[10(4224) - (200)(207)]^2}{[10(4052) - (200)^2][10(4445) - (207)^2]} \\ &= \frac{(42\,240 - 41\,400)^2}{(40\,520 - 40\,000)(44\,450 - 42\,849)} \\ &= \frac{840^2}{(520)(1601)} = \frac{705\,600}{832\,520} = 0.847\,547\,2 = 84.75\% \end{aligned}$$

This means that 84.75% of the total variation in output y is determined by changes in the index x.

The coefficient of correlation

$$r = \sqrt{0.847\,547\,2} = 0.9206$$

The coefficient of correlation is positive and high. This indicates that there is a strong direct relationship between output and test results. Rule of thumb: Since $|r = 0.9206| > \frac{2}{\sqrt{10}} = 0.6325$, the correlation is significant. The index of digital dexterity appears to be a good predictor of output.

EXERCISE 13.5

Refer to graphs A, B, and C to answer questions **1** to **6**.

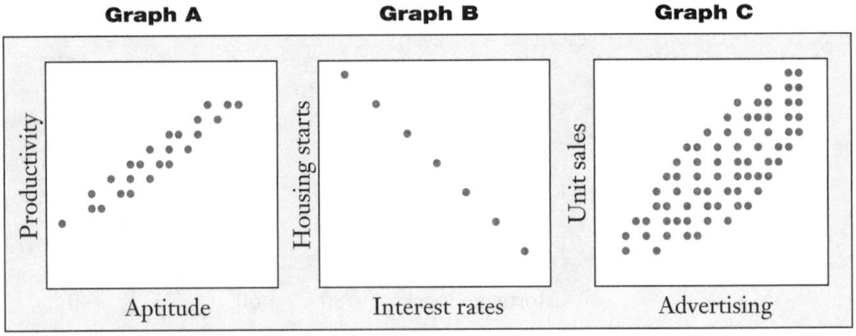

1. **a)** Name the predicted variable in Graph B.
b) Name the independent variable in Graph C.

2. **a)** What is the dependent variable in Graph A?
b) What is the independent variable in Graph B?

3. For which graph is the relationship between the two variables weakest?

4. For which graph is the relationship between the two variables strongest?

5. What is the approximate coefficient of correlation for Graph B?

6. Select the most reasonable value as coefficient of correlation for Graph A from the following four values:
(a) 0.50 **(b)** –0.50 **(c)** 0.80 **(d)** –0.80

7. If the coefficient of determination is 0.81, what is the coefficient of correlation?

8. If the coefficient of correlation is 0.64, what is the coefficient of determination?

9. If the regression coefficient $b = -2.25$ and the coefficient of determination is 0.16, what is the coefficient of correlation?

10. If the regression coefficient $a = -4.00$ and $b = 3.50$ and the coefficient of determination is 0.36, what is the coefficient of correlation?

11. A sales manager thinks the annual sales in a territory depend on the number of retail outlets located within the territory. The sales manager is responsible for 10 sales territories and has the following information:

Sales territory	Annual sales	Retail outlets
1	$177 950	1536
2	$211 290	675
3	$189 680	569
4	$158 900	632
5	$262 470	982
6	$203 680	863
7	$140 820	874
8	$200 570	724
9	$289 940	1760
10	$101 350	546

a) Compute the regression equation.
b) Construct a scatter diagram and plot the regression line.
c) Compute the coefficient of determination.
d) Comment on the results.

12. The following are data on mortgage loans and prime rates:

Mortgage loans	80	60	75	40	54	66	47
Prime rate	9%	12%	10%	15%	13%	11%	14%

a) Compute the regression equation.
b) Construct a scatter diagram and plot the regression line.
c) Compute the coefficient of correlation.
d) Comment on the results.

REVIEW EXERCISE

1. For each of the following sets of data,
a) determine the regression equation;
b) construct a scatter diagram and plot the regression line;
c) compute the coefficient of correlation.

Data set **(i)**

x	10.0	8.0	13.0	9.0	11.0	14.0	6.0	4.0	12.0	7.0	5.0
y	8.04	6.95	7.58	8.81	8.33	9.96	7.24	4.26	10.86	4.82	5.68

Data set **(ii)**

x	10.0	8.0	13.0	9.0	11.0	14.0	6.0	4.0	12.0	7.0	5.0
y	9.14	8.14	8.74	8.77	9.26	8.10	6.13	3.10	9.13	7.26	4.74

Data set **(iii)**

x	10.0	8.0	13.0	9.0	11.0	14.0	6.0	4.0	12.0	7.0	5.0
y	7.46	6.77	12.74	7.11	7.81	8.84	6.08	5.39	8.15	6.42	5.73

Data set **(iv)**

x	8.0	8.0	8.0	8.0	8.0	8.0	8.0	19.0	8.0	8.0	8.0
y	6.58	5.76	7.71	8.84	8.47	7.04	5.25	12.50	5.56	7.91	6.89

2. Comment on the results for Question **1**.

3. For each of the following sets of data,
a) determine the regression equation;
b) construct the scatter diagram and plot the regression line;
c) compute the coefficient of correlation.

Data set **(i)**

x	90	90	90	90	89
y	30	40	25	35	40

Data set **(ii)**

x	1	2	3	4	5
y	30	40	50	40	30

Data set **(iii)**

x	2	4	7	9	11
y	5	11	22	23	25

Data set **(iv)**

x	10	30	50	70	90
y	40	20	24	30	34

4. Comments on the results for Question **3**.

5. Consider the following data:

Student	A	B	C	D	E	F	G	H
Hours of study	5.5	8.2	4.0	8.0	7.1	9.5	6.7	6.6
History mark	50	90	37	73	70	91	73	63

a) Determine the regression equation.
b) Compute the coefficient of correlation.
c) Obtain a point estimate of the history mark for students who studied 7.0 h.
d) Determine the 90% confidence interval for the students in part **(c)**.
e) Predict the history mark for Kelly, who studied 7.0 h.

6. Consider the following data:

Employee	I	II	III	IV	V
Grade level	10	13	9	17	15
Hourly wage	$7.00	$11.00	$6.50	$15.00	$13.00

a) Determine the regression equation.
b) Compute the coefficient of correlation.
c) Obtain a point estimate of the hourly wage for employees with 11 years of school.
d) Determine the 90% confidence interval for the employees in part **(c)**.
e) Predict the hourly wage for someone with 11 years of school.

7. The local Chamber of Commerce conducted a study on the profitability of newly established, home-based businesses in the community. The revenue and net income data for a random sample of 7 such firms are listed below.

Company	Revenue	Net income
Tech Computer Associates	$11 256	$ 132
Russell's Lawn Care	$10 000	$ 127
Tiny Tots Day Care	$ 8 831	$1 016
Stitch-it Tailoring	$ 4 003	$ 45
Honest Bookeepng Inc.	$ 8 449	$ 155
Jane's Catering Ltd.	$ 3 290	$ 166
PixGraphic Design	$ 2 321	$ 15

a) Determine the regression equation.
b) Compute the coefficient of correlation.
c) Compute the standard error of the estimate.
d) Calculate the net income point estimate when revenue is $2000.
e) Determine the 95% confidence interval for businesses reporting revenue of $1500.

8. A management consultant has been hired to determine the relationship between sales volume and the number of salespersons. The data for a random sample of five companies are listed below.

Company	Number of Salespersons	Volume of Sales (000s)
A	1000	120
B	800	101
C	600	75
D	50	5
E	30	2

a) Determine the regression equation.
b) Compute the coefficient of correlation.
c) Compute the standard error of estimate.
d) Calculate the sales volume if the number of salespersons is 300.
e) Determine the 95% confidence interval for a company that has 500 salespersons.

9. The human-resources manager of a real estate company is faced with determining the firm's staffing needs. As a first step the manager considered the overall activity in the housing market and compiled the following information:

Five-year mortgage rate	8%	9%	10%	11%	12%	13%	14%
Number of homes sold	1480	1235	890	670	445	250	120

a) Determine the regression equation.
b) Compute the coefficients of determination and correlation.
c) Compute the 98% confidence interval when the five-year mortgage rate is 9.5%.

10. The rate for Guaranteed Investments Certificates (GIC) and the number of investors investing at these rates are listed below:

GIC Rates	1.75%	2.30%	2.75%	2.95%	3.35%
Number of investors	400	300	200	75	25

a) Determine the regression equation.
b) Compute the coefficients of determination and correlation.
c) Compute the 98% confidence interval if the GIC rate is 2.00%.
d) Comment on the usefulness of the information obtained in parts (a), (b), and (c).

11. The owner of a small auto body shop has compiled quarterly sales data for the last 2 years and asked his accountant to determine if the data might be useful in operational planning.

Quarter	I	II	III	IV	V	VI	VII	VIII
Economic indicator	13.2	11.6	12.1	15.3	12.2	11.6	9.9	12.5
Sales ($000)	265	290	275	224	285	280	338	265

a) Determine the regression equation.
b) Compute the coefficients of determination and correlation.
c) If the forecast economic indicator for the next quarter was 14.4, what sales level should be expected?
d) Compute the 99% confidence interval for an economic activity level of 13.8.
e) Interpret the interval obtained in part **(d)**.

12. A downtown college has compiled enrollment data for the last five years and the registrar has been asked to determine if the data might be useful for facilities planning.

Year	I	II	III	IV	V
Percent of immigrants in city	40	42	45	46	47
Enrollment (number of students)	4000	4100	4300	4400	5000

a) Determine the regression equation.
b) Compute the coefficients of determination and correlation.
c) If the percent of immigrants is 50% , what enrollment level would be expected?
d) Compute the 99% confidence interval for 43% level of immigrants.
e) Interpret the interval obtained in part (d).

13. The following data have been collected by a company's controller:

Year	1997	1998	1999	2000	2001	2002
Bad debts ($000)	3	12	10	5	4	16
Index of business activity	210	100	110	140	160	80

a) Explain your choice of dependent variable.
b) Determine the least squares regression equation.
c) Construct a scatter diagram and plot the regression line.
d) Calculate r for the data.
e) Compute s_e.
f) Comment on the usefulness of the information with regard to the company's credit-granting policies.

14. The following data have been collected by a credit card company:

Year	1998	1999	2000	2001	2002
Average monthly bill	$1000	$1500	$1200	$1100	$2000
Index of business activity	100	170	120	180	200

a) Explain your choice of dependent variable.
b) Determine the least squares regression equation.
c) Construct a scatter diagram and plot the regression line.
d) Calculate r for the data.
e) Compute s_e.

15. An advertising account representative is hoping to use information gained from the following data to increase business:

Advertising ($000)	2000	200	1000	800	1500	500
Sales ($ millions)	9.0	6.8	7.8	8.0	8.4	7.4

a) Determine the regression equation.
b) Construct a scatter diagram and plot the regression line.
c) Compute r^2 and s_e.
d) What are the predicted sales for an advertising campaign costing $1 800 000?
e) Could the account representative use this information to increase the advertising company's business?

16. A local radio station has collected the following data from its sales department:

Number of commercials in a 24-h period	48	100	150	200	250
Number of listeners in a 24-h period (000s)	410	400	380	350	300

a) Determine the regression equation.
b) Construct a scatter diagram and plot the regression line.
c) Compute r^2 and s_e.
d) What are the predicted number of listeners if the number of commercials is 125?
e) Could the sales department use the information to increase the number of listeners?

17. The manager of a bakery shop wishes to determine the relationship between the number of loaves of bread per order and the direct labour cost per order. Six orders were randomly selected and the following data were obtained:

Order number	Number of loaves	Direct labour cost per order
5	6	$4.75
8	3	2.45
12	7	5.30
13	10	7.90
18	5	4.25
25	6	4.95

a) Obtain the regression equation.
b) Calculate r^2 and r and comment on the type and closeness of the relationship between the two variables.
c) If the manager receives an order for eight loaves, determine the associated direct labour cost for that order.

18. The supervisor of a telemarketing firm would like to determine the relationship between the number of calls made and the resulting sales. Data were collected from 5 salespeople during an 8-h shift.

Salesperson Employee #	Number of calls	Number of sales
13	200	7
7	400	15
3	300	9
6	420	11
28	250	8

a) Obtain the regression equation.
b) Calculate r^2 and r and comment on the type and closeness of the relationship between the two variables.
c) If the supervisor has a salesperson call 500 people, determine the expected number of sales.

19. A labour efficiency consultant compiled the following data for the employees of a production department:

Productivity (parts per hour)	43	52	60	66	59	73	68	65	49	40
Employees' stress (scale 0–10)	8	7	5	3	7	0	2	3	9	10

a) Determine the regression equation.
b) Calculate r and comment on the type and the closeness of the relationship between the two variables.
c) Predict with 90% confidence the stress scale score for John who was off work on the day of testing. His production is known to be 62 parts per hour.

20. A professor in the school of education compiled the following data for community college students:

Test grade	90%	80%	70%	60%	50%
Hours studied	7	5	3	2	1

a) Determine the regression equation.
b) Calculate r and comment on the type and the closeness of the relationship between the two variables.
c) Predict the test score of a student who studies 4 h.

21. (CGA) Any manufacturing operation essentially incurs three kinds of expenses: raw material expenses, direct labour expenses, and overhead expenses. A manufacturer of certain auto parts is interested in knowing if there exists a linear relationship between its monthly overhead (in thousands of dollars) and total number of parts produced per month. The data have been collected for 12 consecutive months. Number of parts (in thousands) is stored in a file called NPARTS, and the corresponding overhead costs are in the file OVRHD. Following is the output from a spreadsheet program:

FILE NAMES FOR REGRESSION	
Which file is the dependent variable?	OVRHD
File name for independent variable #1?	NPARTS

REGRESSION OUTPUT	
Constant	12.86967
Std Err of *Y* Est	1.316093
R squared	0.9720
No. of observations	12
Degrees of freedom	10
X coefficient(s)	1.495209
Std err of coef.	0.080138

a) State and interpret the regression equation.
b) Predict the overhead costs for manufacturing 18 000 parts. Is it reasonable to make such a prediction? Explain.
c) What is the proportion of variability explained by regression?

22. (CGA) A realtor is interested in determining if there is any statistical linear relationship between the initial list price and the final selling price of a residential dwelling in a certain area. A random sample of 16 houses was chosen from a list of houses sold in that area during the last six months. The sample data were stored in the following files:

INITIAL: Initial list price (in $1000 units)
FINAL: Final selling price (in $1000 units)

These data were analyzed using a spredsheet program with the following edited computer output:

FILE NAMES FOR REGRESSION	
Which file is the dependent variable?	FINAL
File name for independent variable #1?	INITIAL

REGRESSION OUTPUT	
Constant	–35.7064
Std Err of *Y* Est	5.7321
R squared	0.7727
No. of observations	16
Degrees of freedom	12
X coefficient(s)	1.237465

a) State and interpret the regression equation.
b) A house in the area under consideration is listed for $ 130 000. Forecast its selling price.
c) What is the proportion of variability explained by regression?

23. (CGA) A prestigious credit card company is interested in identifying the characteristics of card holders who spend close to or exceed their spending limits. The company feels that the composite index obtained by the CED (Credit Evaluations Department) for each card holder, prepared at the time of evaluation of the membership application, might be a useful independent variable in studying this relationship. This index, a number between 70 and 100, is calculated from the applicant's income, nature of employment, family size, age, and other data. Any applicant with a score of less than 70 is politely denied the card membership. A random sample of 150 card holders is taken, and the data are stored in the following two files:

RATING: Composite index for the card holder
DOLLARS: Average monthly amount spent over the last year

The following computer output was obtained using a spreadsheet program:

FILE NAMES FOR REGRESSION

Which file is the dependent variable?	DOLLARS
File name for independent variable #1?	RATING

REGRESSION OUTPUT

Constant	–1752.7
Std Err of Y Est	286.723
R squared	0.7056
No. of observations	150
Degrees of freedom	148
X coefficient(s)	52.65

a) State and interpret the regression equation.

b) Determine the percentage of total variability explained by this regression model.

c) Forecast the monthly credit card bill of a member with a composite rating index of 85.4. (Round your calculations to 2 decimal places.)

SELF-TEST

1. The regression equation $y_p = 19\ 665 + 0.000\ 002\ 7x$ shows the relationship between a company's total assets and the number of employees it has.

   a) Is the linear relationship direct or inverse?

   b) How many employees would you estimate to find in a company with assets of approximately \$20 223 500 000?

2. Consider the following data:

Dependent variable	16	10	26	32
Independent variable	4	3	5	6

a) Construct a scatter diagram.
b) Determine the least squares equation.
c) Draw the regression line in the scatter diagram.

3. Consider the following:

x	5	2	6	3
y	11	31	9	24

a) What type of linear relationship appears to exist between the two variables?
b) State whether the value of b in the least squares equation is positive or negative.
c) Compute the coefficients of determination and correlation.

4. A research group is interested in predicting the gasoline consumption in a geographic area based on the number of automobiles registered. The sample of randomly selected geographic areas showed the following gas consumption and automobile registrations:

Geographic area	Gasoline consumption (millions of litres)	Automobile registration (000s)
A	16	17
B	8	10
C	3	6
D	9	13
E	18	22
F	6	8
G	15	16
H	4	5
I	9	15
J	10	16

a) Determine the least squares equation.
b) Compute the coefficient of correlation.
c) Estimate gasoline consumption in an area with an automobile registration of 14 000.
d) Determine the 90% confidence interval for a mean value of 14 000.
e) Determine the 90% confidence interval for an individual value of 14 000.

For an online glossary, go to **www.pearsoned.ca/hummelbrunner**.

Key Terms

Coefficient of correlation 456
Coefficient of determination 456
Correlation analysis 452
Dependent variable 432
Independent variable 432
Least squares method 433
Negative correlation 461
Positive correlation 460
Regression analysis 432
Regression coefficients 434
Regression equation 433
Regression line 433
Simple regression analysis 432
Standard error of the estimate 444

Summary of Formulas

1. Regression line equation

$$y_p = a + bx$$ ←*Formula* 13.1

2. Regression coefficients

$$b = \frac{n(\sum xy) - (\sum x)(\sum y)}{n(\sum x^2) - (\sum x)^2}$$ ←*Formula* 13.2

$$a = \frac{\sum y}{n} - b\frac{\sum x}{n}$$ ←*Formula* 13.2a

3. Standard error of the estimate

$$s_e = \sqrt{\frac{\sum y^2 - a(\sum y) - b(\sum xy)}{n - 2}}$$ ←*Formula* 13.3

4. Confidence interval to estimate an average value of y_p

$$y_p \pm t_{n-2}(s_e)\sqrt{\frac{1}{n} + \frac{n(x-\bar{x})^2}{n(\sum x^2) - (\sum x)^2}}$$

←*Formula* 13.4

5. Confidence interval to estimate a single value of y_p

$$y_p \pm t_{n-2}(s_e)\sqrt{1 + \frac{1}{n} + \frac{n(x-\bar{x})^2}{n(\sum x^2) - (\sum x)^2}}$$

←*Formula* 13.5

6. Coefficient of determination

$$r^2 = \frac{[n(\sum xy) - (\sum x)(\sum y)]^2}{[n(\sum x^2) - (\sum x)^2][n(\sum y^2) - (\sum y)^2]}$$

←*Formula* 13.6

7. Coefficient of correlation

$$r = \sqrt{r^2}$$

←*Formula* 13.7

Answers to Selected Problems, Review Exercises, and Self-Tests

CHAPTER 2

EXERCISE 2.1

1. **(b)** **(i)** 68 **(ii)** 245 **(iii)** 245 **(d)** less-than cumulative frequencies: 1, 3, 5, 8, 16, 20, 23, 24; less-than cumulative percents: 4.2, 12.5, 20.8, 33.3, 66.7, 83.3, 95.8, 100.0 **(e)** more-than cumulative frequencies: 24, 23, 21, 19, 16, 8, 4, 1; more-than cumulative percents: 100.0, 95.8, 87.5, 79.2, 66.7, 33.3, 16.7, 4.2

3. **(b)** **(i)** 28 **(ii)** 30 **(c)** **(i)** 85% **(ii)** 30%

EXERCISE 2.3

3. $P_{65} = 37.5$, $D_4 = 26.0$, $Q_1 = 20.0$, $P_{50} = 30.0$, $x = 17.5\%$

5. **(b)** $Q_1 = 157.3$, $Q_3 = 188.15$, $P_{50} = 171.74$, $x = 77.1\%$

7. **(a)** 14.28 years **(b)** 17.61 years **(c)** 22.44 years **(d)** 92.19%

REVIEW EXERCISE

1. **(b)** **(i)** 61% **(ii)** 35%

3. **(b)** 708 **(c)(i)** 23% **(ii)**10% **(iii)** 85% **(iv)** 63% **(d)(i)** \$9.32 **(ii)** \$3.05 **(e)** 68.6%

5. **(b)** **(i)** P.E.I. **(ii)** Ont. **(c)** **(i)** \$4.47 **(ii)** None **(iii)** \$17.69

7. **(b)** **(i)** 64 **(ii)** 130 **(c)(i)** 1.4% **(ii)** 54.3%

9. **(b)** **(i)** 55 **(ii)** 63 **(iii)** 68 **(d)** less-than cumulative frequencies: 3, 9, 26, 40, 46, 48; less-than cumulative percents: 6.3, 18.8, 54.2, 83.3, 95.8, 100.0 **(e)** more-than cumulative frequencies: 48, 45, 39, 22, 8, 2; more-than cumulative percents: 100.0, 93.8, 81.3, 45.8, 16.7, 4.2 **(f)** **(i)** 66 **(ii)** 77.1 **(g)** 84.6%

11. **(a)** \$15 023 **(b)** \$28 749 **(c)** social work, legal assistant, chemistry, marketing, accounting, business administration

15. **(c)** **(i)** 14.69 **(ii)** 24.86 **(iii)** 8.95

17. **(b)** median **(c)** \$756.68 **(d)** \$899.46 **(e)** **(i)** 81.45% **(ii)** 67.45% **(f)** **(i)** 94.2% **(ii)** 32 **(g)** 143

19. **(b)** **(i)** 76% **(ii)** 52% **(iii)** 69% **(iv)** 13% **(c)** **(i)** 32.6 **(ii)** 42.04 **(iii)** 60.29 **(iv)** 36.4%

SELF-TEST

1. **(b)** **(i)** 65 **(ii)** 55

2. **(c)** 91.2% **(d)**17.13%

3. **(a)** \$16.36 **(b)** \$19.77 **(c)** \$18.41 **(d)** \$26.50 **(e)** 85% **(f)** 6%

CHAPTER 3

EXERCISE 3.2

1. 69.15

3. 40.5

5. 34.51

EXERCISE 3.3

1. 71 units, 41 hours, 31.48

EXERCISE 3.4

1. 63

3. 27.69

EXERCISE 3.5

1. **(a)** median = 11.5, mode = 8 **(b)** 11.75 **(c)** 13.25 **(d)** positively skewed

3. positively skewed

REVIEW EXERCISE

1. **(a)** \$20.417 million **(b)** \$19.5 million

3. **(a)** mean = 16 083, median = 16 626

5. \$6.36

7. 43 seconds

9. 70 kg

11. 27

13. \$129.95

15. **(a)** 250 000 **(b)** 31 500

17. **(a)** \$8.425 **(b)** \$9.268

19. **(a)** median = 20, mode = 19 **(b)** 20.5 **(c)** 23.5 **(d)** positively skewed

21. **(a)** mean = \$24.25, median = \$12.50 **(b)** 5, 10

23. **(b)** positively skewed **(c)** mean = 56.8, median = 55.8, mode = 53.8

25. mean = \$0.65, negatively skewed

27. \$93 333

29. **(a)** negatively skewed **(b)** positively skewed **(c)** negatively skewed **(d)** symmetrical

SELF-TEST

A. 1. median = 24.5, mode = 24.0

2. 24.75

3. 27.61

4. positively skewed

B. 5. $Q_1 = 5.32$, $Q_3 = 18.94$

6. mean = 12.60, median = 10.09, mode = 6.07

7. positively skewed

C. 9. 1134.25 km/h

CHAPTER 4

EXERCISE 4.1

1. **(a)** \$15 023 **(b)** business admin., accounting, marketing, chemistry, legal assistant, social work **(c)** Q_3 =\$35 099.75 **(d)** Q_1 =\$25 747.75

3. **(a)** \$7.00 **(b)** \$1.75 **(c)** \$3.27

EXERCISE 4.2

1. 45.33

3. 4.29

EXERCISE 4.3

1. **(a)** 70.92 **(b)** 49.08 **(c)** 7.005

3. **(a)** 5.46 **(b)** 2.55 **(c)** 1.60

5. **(a)** 29.35 **(b)** 346.51 **(c)** 18.615

7. Class A: 0.437, Class B: 0.174; marks for Class A are much more variable than Class B's.

REVIEW EXERCISE

1. **(a)** 77 **(b)** 82.5 **(c)** 39 **(d)** 25.75 **(e)** 11.25 **(f)** 163.125 **(g)** 12.772

3. **(a)** 13.0 **(b)** 13 **(c)** 14 **(d)** 6 **(e)** 3.2 **(f)** 15.50 **(g)** 3.937

5. **(a)** 17 160.70 **(b)** 16 825 **(c)** \$40 000 **(d)** 11 385.42 **(e)** 7882.64 **(f)** 24 260 **(g)** 77 500 331 **(h)** \$8803.43

7. **(a)** 128 **(b)** **(i)** 72.5 **(ii)** 45.25 **(iii)** 23.94

9. **(a)(i)** 74 **(ii)** 28.0

11. 13.7

13. **(a)** 2.38 **(b)** variance = 10.259, standard deviation = 3.203

15. **(a)** 1.01 **(b)** 1.205

17. **(a)** 883.0 **(b)** 1555.143 **(c)** 39.39

19. **(a)** 13 323 **(b)** 6116 **(c)** 90 732 536 **(d)** 9525.36

21. **(a)** 10.86 **(b)** 9.16 **(c)** 103.59 **(d)** 10.2

23. **(a)** 2.62 **(b)** 5.12 **(c)** 2.26

25. mean = 2.08, standard deviation = 1.29

27. **(a)** 62 **(b)** 25.21

29. **(b)** 4.06 kg

31. 62

33. **(a)** Company A = 0.01, Company B = 0.015, Company C = 0.05 **(b)** Choose Company A because its sales are less variable year to year compared with its average sales.

35. **(a)** Ashley = 12 000, Riley = 32 000
(b) Ashley = 2273.03, Riley = 4536.89
(c) Ashley = 18.9%, Riley = 14.2% **(d)** 33%

SELF-TEST

A. 1. 40

2. $9.94

3. $18.38

4. $18.00

5. variance = $45.946, standard deviation = $6.778

B. 6. $175 000

7. $121.25 thousand

8. $Mean_{2001}$ = $321 875.00, $mean_{2002}$ = $265 625, $median_{2001}$ = $332 500, $median_{2002}$ = $282 500

9. $54 375.00

10. 2001 = $60 670.09, 2002 = $42 752.01

11. 2001 = 18.9%, 2002 = 16.1%

CHAPTER 5

EXERCISE 5.3

1. **(a)** price: bread = 175.0, milk = 133.3, butter = 133.3; quantity: bread = 180.0, milk = 133.3, butter = 75.0; value: bread = 315.0, milk = 177.8, butter = 100.0 **(b)** 139.6 **(c)** price = 152.0, quantity = 130.7, value = 207.8

EXERCISE 5.4

1. 124.3

EXERCISE 5.5

1. **(a)** $0.94 **(b)** $47 713.66

EXERCISE 5.6

1. Company A 100 108.8 119.7 130.2 132.4 126.6
Company B 100 104.1 112.0 129.8 138.9 142.5

3. 2.3 7.2 37.4 72.3 100.0 121.0 164.1 249.3 372.3

REVIEW EXERCISE

1. **(a)** price = 120.7, quantity = 150.0, value = 181.0

3. **(a)** price = 67.6, quantity = 92.1, value = 62.3

5. **(a)**

	Price	Quantity	Value
Gas	160	80	128
Train pass	114	125	143
Subway token	113	125	141

(b) 120 **(c)** price = 129.5, quantity = 109.6, value = 137.2

7. **(a)**

	Price	Quantity	Value
Gas	108.3	111.1	120.3
Electricity	107.5	104.3	112.2
Water	102.6	120	123.1

(b) 104.6 **(c)** price = 107.4, quantity = 111.5, value = 119.6

9. **(a)** 107.75 **(b)** 102.7 **(c)** 110.0

11. **(a)** price = 84.5, quantity = 94.2, value = 85.4

13. 100.0 200.0 450.0 650.0 750.0

15. **(a)** Women's: 2001 = 1248, 2002 = 1268; Men's: 2001 = 936, 2002 = 906; Children's: 2001 = 624, 2002 = 664
(b) price = 112.6, quantity = 100.6, value = 113.3

17. **(a)** Hammers: 1999 = $8.50, 2002 = $7.95; Screwdrivers: 1999 = $2.25, 2002 = $1.95; Wrenches: 1999 = $4.65, 2002 = $4.55
(b) price = 96.1, quantity = 98.5, value = 95.2

19. 81.9

21. 380.0

23. 131.07

25. 122.21

27. 1998 = $0.92, 1999 = $0.90

29. 2000 = $156 666, 2001 = $168 516

31. **(a)** 5672.1 6099.1 6927.3 6927.6 6929.7

33. 104.6 119.8 89.9

35. **(a)** 100.0 103.4 97.4 99.2 108.2 112.5 **(b)** 102.6 106.1 100.0 101.8 111.1 115.4

37. Canada: 100.0 111.8 114.3 117.7 123.6; USA: 100.0 104.0 105.5 105.5 105.8

39. A: 76.4 85.7 95.2 100.0 105.1 110.0
B: 60.7 70.4 82.2 100.0 105.2 108.4

41. 95.2 97.1 97.6 100 110 115 119.3

43. 77.3 82.4 87.2 93.4 100.0 104.4 109.2 114.6 118.5

45. **(a)** 141.4 **(b)** 1992

SELF-TEST

1. **(a)** 95.2 100.0 105.2 110.2 120.0 125.3 **(b)** 25.3% **(c)** 13.6%

2. 151.7

3. $37 662.98

4. more

5. $0.86

6. CPI = 116.4, Locker rental = 151.7

7. Country A

8. **(a)** price = 135.2, quantity = 121.2, value 164.1

9. **(a)** 92.0

10. **(a)** 83.8 92.3 100.0 108.8 110.6 105.7 **(b)** Company A: 100.0 110.1 119.3 129.8 131.9 126.1; Company B: 100.0 104.4 110.1 116.4 125.3 126.8

CHAPTER 6

EXERCISE 6.2

1. **(b)** $y_p = 9.71 + 0.68x$ **(c)** **(i)** 15.15 **(ii)** 16.51

3. **(b)** $y_p = 22.29 - 1.62x$ **(d)** **(i)** 6.09 **(ii)** 2.85

EXERCISE 6.3

1. 101.6 99.7 91.8 107.5 105.7 87.5 109.6 96.5

EXERCISE 6.4

1. 10.2 10.6 11.4 12.2 13.4 14.4 13.8 13.2

3. 8.5 9.3 10.3 11.3 12.0 13.0 13.5 14.8 15.3 14.5

EXERCISE 6.5

1. 1998: 5.4 5.0
1999: 5.2 5.6 6.7 6.2
2000: 7.0 7.4 8.1 8.1
2001: 10.4 9.3 9.4 10.0
2002: 8.7 8.3 5.4 7.5
2003: 7.0 8.3

3. 1998: 13.9 13.1 13.8 15.3 13.9 13.7 13.7 13.4 14.0 14.2 14.1 14.3
1999: 13.9 14.4 17.3 14.2 14.9 14.8 14.9 12.3 12.8 15.2 16.6 17.0
2000: 16.2 15.8 16.1 16.4 16.0 15.8 16.2 16.7 16.3 15.2 15.8 16.4
2001: 17.4 17.1 17.3 17.5 18.1 19.0 19.9 21.2 19.8 19.0 19.1 19.1
2002: 18.5 18.4 18.4 19.7 19.2 20.0 21.1 23.4 21.0 19.9 21.6 21.2

REVIEW EXERCISE

1. **(b)** $y_p = 3543.2 + 146.95x$
(c) **(i)** 4865.76 **(ii)** 5159.66

3. **(b)** $y_p = 9.33 - 0.99x$ **(c)** $1.41 per share

5. **(b)** $y_p = 461.9 + 4.27x$
(c) **(i)** 496.1 million **(ii)** 504.6 million

7. **(b)** $y_p = 1440 - 180x$ **(c)** 0

9. **(b)** $y_p = 130 - 22x$ **(c)** –24

11. **(a)** $3080 **(b)** $500 **(c)** $6080

13. **(a)** 75 000 **(b)** 2019

15. **(c)** 8.4 7.0 5.6 4.2 2.8
(d) 107.1 100.0 71.4 119.0 107.1

17. **(a)** $y_p = 311.27 + 7.49x$
(c) $371.19 thousand
(d) 99.8 98.7 103.8 97.4 100.5

19. **(b)** $y_p = 0.9 + 2.5x$ **(c)** 23 400
(d) 117.6 84.7 95.2 110.1 97.0

21. **(a)** 189.2 195.8 204.2 210.8 212.5

23. **(a)** 150 146 138 135 132.5

25. **(a)** 73.1 81.9 83.9 85.5 89.5 94.5 103.0 101.5 95.0 85.5 70.7 63.5 60.2 56.3 54.0 53.4

27. 833.33 825.0 833.33 841.67 850.00 850.00 866.67 875.00 866.67 858.33 858.33 866.67 883.33 900.00 883.33 875.00 866.67 866.67 858.33 866.67 866.67 883.33 891.67 891.67 883.33

29. (a) 661.50 645.00 597.25 547.75 553.25 544.50 543.25 522.25 517.50 502.00 497.00 527.25 549.75
(c) Year 1: 630.6 758.2 766.6 521.1
Year 2: 572.6 549.2 547.6 542.2
Year 3: 541.8 543.8 454.6 524.0
Year 4: 487.2 521.9 588.5 610.4

31. 3.45052 3.34029 2.79146 2.67559 3.64583 3.9660 4.76190 5.57414 6.11979 6.88935 7.38916 6.68896 6.05469 5.94989 6.07553 6.13155

SELF-TEST

1. (a) $y_p = 10.31 + 1.07x$ **(c) (i)** \$22.08 **(ii)** \$24.22

2. (a) $y_p = 574.60 - 12.46x$
(b) –\$12 460 per year **(c)** \$462 460
(d) 99.6 100.4 100.1 99.5 100.9 99.4

3. (a) \$110 000 per year **(b)** \$2 150 000
(c) \$2 590 000

4. (a) 33 875.3 31 828.0 30 312.3 28 989.8 28 100.0 30 585.0 32 929.5 36 673.5 38 968.0

5. 1998: 8786.2 8628.0 8809.6 9083.7
1999: 9272.5 9504.0 9743.5 9998.0
2000: 10204.7 10632.0 10969.9 11046.3
2001: 11631.2 11792.0 12240.5 12173.4

CHAPTER 7

EXERCISE 7.1

1. (a) 6 **(b)** 36

3. a, c, d

5. (a) 2 **(b)** 3 **(c)** 4

7. 30.8%

9. 95%

11. (a) 95% **(b)** 29 days

EXERCISE 7.2

1. 9

3. 12

EXERCISE 7.3

1. 120

3. 220

5. 720

7. 125 970

9. 5 040

EXERCISE 7.4

1. (a) 2 **(b)** 4 **(c)** 8

3. c, d

5. (a) 8 **(b)** 2

EXERCISE 7.5

1. 0.80

3. (a) 0.077 **(b)** 1 **(c)** 0.539 **(d)** 0.385

5. 0.667

7. 0.125

9. 0.25

11. (a) 0.053 **(b)** 0.553 **(c)** 0.197 **(d)** 0.395

REVIEW EXERCISE

1. 5

3. 25

5. 6

7. 3

9. 6

11. 0.00074

13. 0.65

15. (a) 0.1156 **(b)** 0.0938 **(c)** 0.209

17. (a) 0.40 **(b)** 0.10

19. (a) 0.75 **(b)** 0.85

21. (a) 0.30 **(b)** 0.40 **(c)** 0.10

23. 3

25. (a) 69 **(b)** 7

27. 0.139

29. (a) 0.053 **(b)** 0.947 **(c)** 0.079 **(d)** 0.553

31. 0.75

33. 0.25

35. **(a)** 0.60 **(b)** 0.40 **(c)** 0.125

37. **(a)** 0.0045 **(b)** 0.006 **(c)** 0.012

39. **(a)** 0.479 **(b)** 0.011

SELF-TEST

1. **(a)** **(i)** 0.475 **(ii)** 0.400 **(iii)** 0.075 **(iv)** 0.70 **(b)** **(i)** 0.095 **(ii)** 0.158 **(iii)** 0.125

2. **(b)** 16 **(c)** 7 **(d)** **(i)** 0.125 **(ii)** 0.438 **(iii)** 0.188

3. **(a)** 56 **(b)** 28

4. **(a)** 0.01 **(b)** 0.03 **(c)** 0.088

CHAPTER 8

EXERCISE 8.2

1. $1,310,000

3. **(a)** 2.2 **(b)** variance = 1.56, standard deviation = 1.249

EXERCISE 8.3

1. 0.1563

3. **(a)** 0.0055 **(b)** 0.9527

5. mean = 1.6, standard deviation = 0.9798

REVIEW EXERCISE

1. $209 800

3. $1 125 000

5. expected average sales increase = 16.75%, standard deviation = 5.31%

7. **(b)** $4000 **(c)** $1224.74

9. **(a)** 0.7164 **(b)** 0.2836

11. **(a)** 0.0098 **(b)** 0.2461

13. **(a)** 0.0312 **(b)** 5 **(c)** 2.1794

15. **(a)** 36 **(b)** 5.909 314 7 **(c)** 0

17. **(a)** 0.0105 **(b)** 0.0676 **(c)** 0.0

19. **(a)** 0 **(b)** 0 **(c)** 0

21. 11.1%

23. **(a)** 0.3918 **(b)** 0.1306 **(c)** 0.0148

25. **(a)** 0.0486 **(b)** 0.6770

SELF-TEST

1. **(a)** 8.35 mm **(b)** 3.087 mm

2. **(a)** 0.0183 **(b)** 0.2047 **(c)** 0.2284

3. mean = 7.08, standard deviation = 1.7038

CHAPTER 9

EXERCISE 9.2

1. **(a)** 0.6826 **(b)** 0.1574 **(c)** 0.8185 **(d)** 0.1587 **(e)** 0.0014

EXERCISE 9.3

1. **(a)** equal **(b)** mean **(c)** standard deviation **(d)** 0.500

3. **(a)** −1.0 **(b)** −1.5 **(c)** 2.0 **(d)** 0.1 **(e)** 2.83 **(f)** −2.40

5. **(a)** 0.4332 **(b)** 0.9987 **(c)** 0.1574 **(d)** 0.0456 **(e)** 0.8400 **(f)** 0.9903

EXERCISE 9.4

1. **(a)** $36 **(b)** $72 **(c)** 99.74%, 2394, $36, $72 **(d)** $66, 97.72%, 2345, $66

3. **(a)** 4.076 **(b)** 3.830 **(c)** 4.028 **(d)** 3.406 **(e)** 3.216 **(f)** 3.1 and 3.9

EXERCISE 9.5

1. **(a)** 0.73% **(b)** 5.16% **(c)** 39.74%

3. **(a)** 0.62% **(b)** 15.87% **(c)** 2.42%

REVIEW EXERCISE

1. **(a)** 0.2422 **(b)** 0.4656 **(c)** 0.4988 **(d)** 0.4901

3. −2.10

5. **(a)** 0.0569 **(b)** 0.0516 **(c)** 0.3497 **(d)** 0.0096 **(e)** 0.8990

7. 0.01, 0.02, or 0.04

9. **(a)** 2.33 **(b)** −1.645 **(c)** −2.05 **(d)** 1.28 **(e)** ±1.96 **(f)** ±2.33

11. **(a)** 1.65 **(b)** −2.33 **(c)** 1.41 **(d)** −2.98 **(e)** −1.85 **(f)** 1.75

13. **(a)** 0.50 **(b)** −0.17 **(c)** −1.67 **(d)** 2.50 **(e)** 3.33 **(f)** −3.00

15. 7.8

17. \$72 560

19. 89.76%

21. **(a)** 80th percentile: 38.888%, 90th percentile: 42.496% **(b)** 12

23. 0.0853

25. 0.50

SELF-TEST

1. Company ST

2. \$192

3. \$477

4. \$311.36 and \$488.64

5. \$465 and \$515

6. 529 invoices

7. 0.15%

8. **(a)** 0.89 **(b)** 9.18% **(c)** 190 orders

9. **(a)** 0.19% **(b)** 98.50%

CHAPTER 10

EXERCISE 10.2

1. **(a)** mean = 6, standard deviation = 1.7889
(b) $\overline{ABC}$ = 4.6667 $\overline{ABD}$ = 5.3333 $\overline{ABE}$ = 6.0000
$\overline{BCD}$ = 5.6667 $\overline{BCE}$ = 6.3333 $\overline{CDE}$ = 7.0000
$\overline{ACD}$ = 5.3333 $\overline{ACE}$ = 6.0000 $\overline{ADE}$ = 6.6667
$\overline{BDE}$ = 7.0000
(c) $\mu_{\bar{x}} = 6$ **(d)** $\sigma_{\bar{x}} = 0.7303$ **(e)** 0.7303

EXERCISE 10.3

1. **(a)** 6.75 **(b)** 820.25 **(c)** 779.75

3. **(a)** 400 **(b)** 6.944 **(c)** normal, population normal

5. **(a)** 7.5 **(b)** 2.8

7. **(a)** \$200 **(b)** \$2.5 **(c)** $n = 64$ **(d)** \$195 and \$205 **(e)** 95.44%

EXERCISE 10.4

1. 90.1%

3. **(a)** 350 **(b)** 40 **(c)** 0.85

5. **(a)** 0.0816 **(b)** 0.0657 **(c)** 0.0453 **(d)** 0.02

7. 92.16%

REVIEW EXERCISE

1. **(a)** 0.71 and 0.79 **(b)** 27.26 and 28.74

3. **(a)** 34.216 and 35.784
(b) 1196.052 and 1203.948

5. **(a)** 14 406 and 17 594
(b) 4415.625 and 4584.375

7. 0.19%

9. **(a)** normal **(b)** 49.92%

11. **(a)** no **(b)** 0.0043

13. **(a)** 638.73 hours **(b)** 13 949.29 and 16 050.71 hours **(c)** 2.07%

15. **(a)** \$21 146.03 **(b)** 2 **(c)** 0.0535 **(d)** 0.91% **(e)** 14.17%

17. yes

19. 94.18%

21. **(a)** 69.85% **(b)** 11.12%

23. 4.75%

25. 78.52%

27. 0.68 and 0.88

29. 0.44 and 0.76

31. **(a)** ix **(b)** iv **(c)** viii **(d)** x **(e)** xii **(f)** i **(g)** iii **(h)** vii **(i)** ii **(j)** v **(k)** vi **(l)** xi

33. **(a)** 72.57% **(b)** 52.66%

35. **(a)** 61.79% **(b)** 18.41% **(c)** 49.6 **(d)** 0.8543

SELF-TEST

1. **(a)** $\mu_{\bar{x}}$ **(b)** σ_p **(c)** μ_p **(d)** $\sigma_{\bar{x}}$

2. 30.72%

3. **(a)** 1.5513
(b) 60.1 and 64.9 bpm

4. **(a)** \$54 804.55 and higher **(b)** \$46 616.91

5. **(a)** 2702 **(b)** 52.68% **(c)** 95.46% **(d)** Part b references households whereas part c references sample means.

6. 66.87%

7. 99.81%

8. 70

CHAPTER 11

EXERCISE 11.2

1. point estimate, interval estimation, estimator, estimate

3. **(a)** \$163.72 **(b)** normal, population is normal

5. 51.60%

7. 99.58%

EXERCISE 11.3

1. \$207 056.32 and \$212 943.68

3. **(a)** 2000 **(b)** 36 **(c)** 41 **(d)** 2 **(e)** 0.3304 **(f)** 98%

5. 121.2 and 128.8 L

7. 414.0 and 424.7 calls per day

EXERCISE 11.4

1. 0.211 and 0.429

3. 0.514 and 0.686

5. **(a)** 0.72 **(b)** 0.02245 **(c)** 0.243 and 0.317

EXERCISE 11.5

1. **(a)** 1521 **(b)** 256 **(c)** 145 **(d)** 554 **(e)** 560

3. 877

5. **(a)** 3394 **(b)** 2851

EXERCISE 11.6

1. **(a)** 2.797 **(b)** 1.328 **(c)** 2.132 **(d)** 2.764 **(e)** 2.045

3. 7.98 and 8.02 mm

5. 16.5 and 19.3 kg

REVIEW EXERCISE

1. **(a)** 294.1 and 305.9 **(b)** 30.34 and 41.66 **(c)** 1299.6 and 1300.4 **(d)** 15.57 and 16.43

3. **(a)** 64 **(b)** 98% **(c)** 67.20 **(d)** 8.4 **(e)** 19.57

5. **(a)** 600 **(b)** 95% **(c)** 14.00 **(d)** 3.349 843 **(e)** 7.102

7. 374.3 and 375.7 g

9. \$21 470.94 and \$22 229.06

11. 7.412 and 8.588

13. **(a)** 0.546 and 0.704 kg **(b)** accept shipment **(c)** 0.55 and 0.70 kg

15. \$15.06 and \$17.78

17. 21 564.7 and 23 595.3 km

19. **(a)** combined area = 0.02, d.f. = 1, t = 31.821 **(b)** one-tail area = 0.01, d.f. = 20, t = 2.528 **(c)** combined area = 0.005, d.f. = 5, t = 4.773 **(d)** combined area = 0.10, d.f. = 29, t = 1.699

21. 3.19 and 6.01

23. 104.45 and 115.55

25. **(a)** mean = 3.5 hours, error = 0.1150 hours **(b)** 3.21 and 3.89 hours **(c)** yes

27. 5.855 and 6.1459 hours

29. 0.2764 and 0.4036

31. 0.557 and 0.643

33. 0.5402 and 0.8598

35. 2172

37. 327

39. 54

41. 165

43. **(a)** \$54.12 and \$65.88 **(b)** 385 accounts

45. **(a)** 756.99 and 843.01 grams **(b)** \$30 279.60 and \$33 720.40 **(c)** 427 packages

SELF-TEST

1. **(a)** 8.6 and 11.4 **(b)** 8.7 and 11.3

2. **(a)** \$32.00 and \$33.70 **(b)** 0.2339 and 0.4661

3. 5.9 and 7.7 pieces

4. 0.0349 and 0.1611

5. **(a)** $\bar{x} = 5.2333$, $s = 0.1506$ **(b)** 5.03 and 5.44

6. 1537

7. 35

CHAPTER 12

EXERCISE 12.2

1. **(a)** **(ii)** H_0: $\mu \leq 10\%$, H_a: $\mu > 10\%$ **(iii)** one-tail **(b)** **(ii)** H_0: $\mu = 2\ 000$, H_a: $\mu < 2\ 000$ **(iii)** one-tail **(c)** **(ii)** H_0: μ = current level, H_a: μ < current level **(iii)** one-tail

EXERCISE 12.3

1. $(|t_{\bar{x}}| = 0.3689) < (t_c = 2.145)$, accept H_0

3. **(a)** accept H_0 **(b)** accept H_0 **(c)** reject H_0 **(d)** reject H_0

5. $(|t_{\bar{x}}| = 7.134) > (t_c = 2.998)$, reject H_0

EXERCISE 12.4

1. $(|z_p| = 1.265) < (z_c = 2.33)$, accept H_0

3. $(|z_p| = 2.098) > (z_c = 1.645)$, reject H_0

EXERCISE 12.5

3. **(a)** H_0: $\mu = 6.3\%$, H_a: $\mu \neq 6.3\%$ **(b)** p value = 1.8%

5. **(a)** p value = 14.7% **(b)** p value > α, accept H_0

REVIEW EXERCISE

1. H_0: $\mu \geq 5$ mm, H_a: $\mu < 5$ mm

3. H_0: $\mu = 5$ kg, H_a: $\mu < 5$ kg

5. **(a)** H_0: $\mu = 70\%$, H_a: $\mu > 70\%$ **(b)** one-tail

7. **(a)** two-tail **(b)** one-tail

9. **(a)** one-tail **(b)** one-tail

11. $(|z_{\bar{x}}| = 2.0) > (z_c = 1.96)$, reject H_0

13. $(|z_{\bar{x}}| = 0.866) < (z_c = 2.33)$, accept H_0

15. $(|z_{\bar{x}}| = 4.16) > (z_c = 1.645)$, reject H_0

17. $(|z_{\bar{x}}| = 6.275) > (z_c = 2.58)$, reject H_0

19. $(|t_{\bar{x}}| = 2.112) < (t_c = 3.747)$, accept H_0

21. $(|t_{\bar{x}}| = 2.628) > (t_c = 2.447)$, reject H_0

23. $(|z_{\bar{p}}| = 4.66) > (z_c = 2.33)$, reject H_0

25. $(|z_{\bar{p}}| = 0.83) < (z_c = 1.645)$, accept H_0

27. $(|z_{\bar{p}}| = 2.90) > (z_c = 2.33)$, reject H_0

29. **(a)** p value = 0 **(b)** p value < 1%, reject H_0

31. **(a)** p value = .26%, one-tail

33. **(a)** 5% < p value < 10%, (two-tail) **(b)** yes

35. **(a)** p value < 0.1% **(b)** p value < α, reject H_0

37. p value = 10.03%, accept H_0

39. **(a)** reject H_0 if $\bar{x} > 812.9$ grams **(b)** 5% **(c)** $(|\overline{X}_{\text{sample}}| = 800) < (\overline{X}_{\text{critical}} = 812.9)$, accept H_0

41. **(a)** H_0: $\mu \geq 500$, H_a: $\mu < 500$ **(c)** $(|Z_{\bar{x}}| = 4) > (|Z_c = 2.33)$, reject H_0

43. **(a)** $(p$ value $= 0.04) > (\alpha = 0.01)$, accept H_0 **(b)** 0.0424 **(c)** yes **(d)** (iv)

SELF-TEST

1. H_0: $\mu = \$47\ 000$, H_a: $\mu < \$47\ 000$ **(b)** one-tail **(c)** $(|z_{\bar{x}}| = 1.25) < (z_c = 2.33)$, accept H_0

2. **(a)** H_0: $\mu = 10\%$, $Ha = \mu < 10\%$; **(b)** one-tail

3. **(a)** H_0: $\mu = 80$, H_a: $\mu < 80$ **(b)** one-tail **(c)** $\alpha = 0.02$ **(d)** normal distribution **(e)** $z_c = 2.05$ **(f)** accept H_0 if $|z_{\bar{x}}| < 2.05$

4. $(|z_{\bar{x}}| = 1) < (z_c = 2.33)$, accept H_0

5. $(|z_{\bar{x}}| = 2.33) > (z_c = 1.645)$, reject H_0

6. **(a)** H_0: $\mu = 28$, H_a: $\mu < 28$ **(b)** $(|z_{\bar{x}}| = 16.73) > (z_c = 2.33)$, reject H_0

7. $(z_p = 1.425) < (z_c = 1.645)$, accept H_0

8. **(a)** mean = 3.9, standard deviation = 0.1333 **(b)** t distribution, small sample **(c)** $(|t_{\bar{x}}| = 2.372) > (t_c = 1.833)$, reject H_0

9. **(a)** H_0: $\mu = 7.2$, H_a: $\mu < 7.2$ **(b)** p value = 11.7% **(c)** p value > α, accept H_0

10. $(|z_p| = 0.746) < (z_c = 1.645)$, accept H_0

CHAPTER 13

EXERCISE 13.2

5. **(a)** $y_p = 0.2413 + 2.819x$ **(b)** 7.29

7. **(c)** $y_p = -41.5002 + 1.5685x$ **(f)** **(i)** 53 **(ii)** 99.7

EXERCISE 13.3

1. 9.4702

EXERCISE 13.4

1. (a) 47.5 to 73.4 **(b)** 23.0 to 97.9

3. (a) $y_p = 2.940 - 0.042x$ **(c)** 0.02746 **(d)** \$2.30 **(e)** \$2.28 and \$2.32 **(f)** \$2.24 and \$2.36

EXERCISE 13.5

1. (a) Housing starts **(b)** Advertising

3. Graph C

5. –1

7. 0.9 or –0.9

9. –0.4

11. (a) $y_p = 123\ 654.29 + 76.42x$ **(c)** 0.330

REVIEW EXERCISE

1. (a) (i) $y_p = 2.997 + 0.5006x$ **(ii)** $y_p = 3.001 + 0.500x$ **(iii)** $y_p = 3.0024 + 0.4997x$ **(iv)** $y_p = 3.0017 + 0.4999x$ **(c) (i)** 0.816 **(ii)** 0.816 **(iii)** 0.816 **(iv)** 0.816

3. (a) (i) $y_p = 707.5 - 7.5x$ **(ii)** $y_p = 38.0 + 0x$ **(iii)** $y_p = 2.3008 + 2.0150x$ **(iv)** $y_p = 30.1 - 0.01x$ **(c) (i)** 0.5145 **(ii)** 0 **(iii)** 0.9612 **(iv)** 0.0399

5. (a) $y_p = -3.863 + 10.394x$ **(b)** 0.9579 **(c)** 69 **(d)** 65 to 73 **(e)** 57 to 81

7. (a) $y_p = 21.7559 + 0.0312x$ **(b)** 0.3214 **(c)** 361.298 **(d)** \$84.22 **(e)** \$599.98 and \$737.18

9. (a) $y_p = 3278.75 - 231.96x$ **(b)** $r^2 = 0.985$, $r = -0.9922$ **(c)** 966 to 1185; 819 to 1332

11. (a) $y_p = 521.828 - 19.844x$ **(b)** –0.9634 **(c)** 236.07 **(d)** 209.73 and 286.24

13. (b) $y_p = 21.7066 - 0.1003x$ **(d)** –0.9165 **(e)** 2.3092

15. (a) $y_p = 6.7716 + 0.0011x$ **(c)** $r^2 = 0.9442$, $s_e = 0.2025$ **(d)** \$8.7516 million **(e)** yes

17. (a) $y_p = 0.2527 + 0.7590x$ **(b)** $r^2 = 0.9907$, $r = 0.9953$ **(c)** \$6.32

19. (a) $y_p = 74.7317 - 3.1911x$ **(b)** –0.9516

21. (a) $y_p = 12.86967 + 1.495209x$ **(b)** \$ 39 783 **(c)** 97.2%

23. (a) $y_p = -1752.7 + 52.65x$ **(b)** 70.56% **(c)** \$2743.61

SELF-TEST

1. (a) direct **(b)** 74 269 employees

2. (b) $y_p = -13.2 + 7.6x$

3. (a) inverse **(b)** negative **(c)** $r^2 = 0.9764$, $r = -0.9881$

4. (a) $y_p = -1.3615 + 0.8720x$ **(b)** 0.9338 **(c)** 10.8465 million litres **(d)** 9.684 and 12.009 **(e)** 7.082 and 14.611

Index

Acceptance region, 397
Aggregate index number, 142
Alternate hypothesis, 395
Array, 40
Average deviation from the mean, 117
Base period, 142
Bi-directional bar chart, 25
Binomial distribution, 270
Class frequency, 42
Class interval, 41
Class width, 41
Clustered bar chart, 16
Coefficient of correlation, 456
Coefficient of determination, 456
Coefficient of variation, 126
Combination, 230
Complement, 235
Composite index, 151
Conditional probability, 247
Confidence coefficient, 356
Confidence interval, 356
Confidence level, 356
Confidence limits, 356
Consumer price index, 152
Continuous probability distribution, 263
Continuous random variable, 263
Correlation analysis, 452
Critical value, 397
Cumulative frequency diagram, 54
Cumulative frequency distribution, 43
Cumulative relative frequency distribution, 43
Cyclical relative, 180
Cyclical variation, 173
Data, 2
Deciles, 62
Degrees of freedom, 373
Dependent variable, 432
Descriptive statistics, 1
Deseasonalized data, 190
Deviation, 116
Discrete probability distribution, 262
Discrete random variable, 262
Estimator, 351
Event, 216
  Complementary, 235
  Intersection of, 237
  Joint, 236
  Mutually exclusive, 235
  Union of, 236
Expected value, 263
Finite correction factor, 332
Finite population, 327
Frequency distribution, 41
Frequency polygon, 53
Hanging bar chart, 25
High-low-close chart, 27
Histogram, 52
HLCO chart, 27
Independent variable, 432
Index number, 142
Inferential statistics, 1
Infinite population, 328
Interpercentile range, 111
Interquartile range, 113
Interval estimation, 354
Irregular movement, 174
Least squares method, 174, 433
Line graph, 11
Lower limit, 42, 48
Maximum error, 368
Mean, 83
Measures of central tendency, 83
Measures of variability, 109
Median, 41, 62, 83
Mode, 41, 83
Monthly index, 194
Moving average method, 182
Multiple line graph, 11
Negative correlation, 461
Normal curve, 289
Normal distribution, 289
Null hypothesis, 395
Outcome, 216
p-value, 418
Parameter, 328
Percent of trend, 180
Percentile, 60
Permutation, 226
Pie chart, 21
Point estimate, 352
Point estimation, 352
Population, 1, 327
Positive correlation, 460
Probability distribution, 261
Purchasing power of the dollar, 152
Quarterly index, 190
Quartile, 62
Random experiment, 216
Range, 40, 110
Real income, 154
Regression analysis, 432
Regression coefficients, 434
Regression equation, 433
Regression line, 433, 437
Rejection region, 397
Relative frequency distribution, 42
Sample, 1, 327
Sample space, 235
Sampling distribution of proportions, 338
Sampling distribution of the means, 329
Sampling variation, 329
Scatter diagram, 9, 175
Seasonal analysis, 189
Seasonal index, 189
Seasonal variation, 174
Seasonally adjusted values, 190
Secular trend, 173
Shifting the base, 155
Significance level, 396
Simple area chart, 15
Simple bar chart, 14
Simple index number, 142
Simple price index, 143
Simple quantity index, 144
Simple regression analysis, 432
Simple value index, 145
Single line graph, 11
Skewed distribution, 96
Special-purpose index, 151
Splicing, 156
Stacked area chart, 19
Stacked bar chart, 18
Standard deviation, 119
Standard error, 331
Standard error of proportions, 339
Standard error of the estimate, 444
Standard normal deviate, 295
Standard normal distribution, 295
Statistic, 328
t-distribution, 373
Tree diagram, 221
Type I error, 417
Type II error, 417
Unbiased estimator, 351
Unweighted aggregate index, 146
Upper limit, 48
Variance, 119
Venn diagram, 235
Weighted aggregate index, 146
Weighted mean, 84
XY graph, 9
z-value, 294

Partial Binomial Probability Table for $n = 20$ and Selected Values of p

p / x	0.10	0.20	0.30	0.40	0.50	0.60	0.70	0.80	0.90
0	0.1216	0.0115	0.0008	0.0000	0.0000	0.0000	0.0000	0.0000	0.0000
1	0.2702	0.0576	0.0068	0.0005	0.0000	0.0000	0.0000	0.0000	0.0000
2	0.2852	0.1369	0.0278	0.0031	0.0002	0.0000	0.0000	0.0000	0.0000
3	0.1901	0.2054	0.0716	0.0123	0.0011	0.0000	0.0000	0.0000	0.0000
4	0.0898	0.2182	0.1304	0.0350	0.0046	0.0003	0.0000	0.0000	0.0000
5	0.0319	0.1746	0.1789	0.0746	0.0148	0.0013	0.0000	0.0000	0.0000
6	0.0089	0.1091	0.1916	0.1244	0.0370	0.0049	0.0002	0.0000	0.0000
7	0.0020	0.0545	0.1643	0.1659	0.0739	0.0146	0.0010	0.0000	0.0000
8	0.0004	0.0222	0.1144	0.1797	0.1201	0.0355	0.0039	0.0001	0.0000
9	0.0001	0.0074	0.0654	0.1597	0.1602	0.0710	0.0120	0.0005	0.0000
10	0.0000	0.0020	0.0308	0.1171	0.1762	0.1171	0.0308	0.0020	0.0000
11	0.0000	0.0005	0.0120	0.0710	0.1602	0.1597	0.0654	0.0074	0.0001
12	0.0000	0.0001	0.0039	0.0355	0.1201	0.1797	0.1144	0.0222	0.0004
13	0.0000	0.0000	0.0010	0.0146	0.0739	0.1659	0.1643	0.0545	0.0020
14	0.0000	0.0000	0.0002	0.0049	0.0370	0.1244	0.1916	0.1091	0.0089
15	0.0000	0.0000	0.0000	0.0013	0.0148	0.0746	0.1789	0.1746	0.0319
16	0.0000	0.0000	0.0000	0.0003	0.0046	0.0350	0.1304	0.2182	0.0898
17	0.0000	0.0000	0.0000	0.0000	0.0011	0.0123	0.0716	0.2054	0.1901
18	0.0000	0.0000	0.0000	0.0000	0.0002	0.0031	0.0278	0.1369	0.2852
19	0.0000	0.0000	0.0000	0.0000	0.0000	0.0005	0.0068	0.0576	0.2702
20	0.0000	0.0000	0.0000	0.0000	0.0000	0.0000	0.0008	0.0115	0.1216